POINTING OUT THE GREAT WAY

POINTING OUT THE GREAT WAY

THE STAGES OF MEDITATION IN THE MAHĀMUDRĀ TRADITION

Daniel P. Brown, Ph.D.

Foreword by Robert A.F. Thurman

WISDOM PUBLICATIONS • BOSTON

Wisdom Publications, Inc.
199 Elm Street
Somerville MA 02144 USA
www.wisdompubs.org

Library of Congress Cataloging-in-Publication Data

Brown, Daniel P., 1948–
   Pointing out the great way : the stages of meditation in the mahāmudrā tradition / Daniel Brown.
      p. cm.
   Includes bibliographical references and index.
   ISBN 0-86171-304-4 (pbk. : alk. paper)
   1. Mahāmudrā (Tantric rite) 2. Meditation—Tantric Buddhism.
3. Buddhism—China—Tibet. I. Title.
BQ7699.M34B76 2006
294.3'4435—dc22

                                                     2006020146

ISBN 0–86171–304-4

First Printing
10   09 08 07 06
5   4   3   2   1

Cover and interior design by Gopa & Ted2, Inc.
Set in DiacriticalGaramond 10.9pt/13.6pt.
Cover photograph: Yoshio Sawaragi/Dex Image/Getty Images

Wisdom Publications' books are printed on acid-free paper and meet the guidelines for permanence and durability of the Production Guidelines for Book Longevity set by the Council on Library Resources.

Printed in the United States of America.

This book was produced with environmental mindfulness. We have elected to print this title on 50% PCW recycled paper. As a result, we have saved the following resources: 36 trees, 35 million BTUs of energy, 3,178 lbs. of greenhouse gases, 13,191 gallons of water, and 1,694 lbs. of solid waste. For more information, please visit our website, www.wisdompubs.org

CONTENTS

LIST OF TABLES

FOREWORD

I am pleased and honored to write a brief foreword to Dan Brown's marvelous *Pointing Out the Great Way,* a spiritual manual, meditation instruction, psychological study, and cross-cultural bridge. I am sure all his gurus and teachers are delighted that his many years of study and practice of Tibetan and Indian Buddhist meditation, and his almost as many years of psychotherapeutic practice and research, have come to this extraordinary sharing of his garnered wisdom in a true "pointing-out" spiritual instruction for our times.

The Sanskrit *mahāmudrā* (Tibetan, *phyag rgya chen po*) literally means "great seal" or "great gesture" or, somewhat esoterically, "great consort," or, most esoterically, "great embrace." Mahāmudrā is a description of the most profound, ultimate, absolute reality that is otherwise called *nirvāṇa, emptiness-compassion-womb, bliss-void-indivisible, clear-light relativity, buddhahood, truth realm, reality body, nonduality.* Mahāmudrā conveys in its own context the Buddha's foundational discovery that reality, when it is mentally and viscerally, intellectually and experientially known as it truly is, is perfect freedom, infinite life, omnicompetent love and compassion, bliss. All paths of study, reasoning, ethics, and meditative practice taught by Buddha intend to provide us—beings who unrealistically take this bliss-freedom-indivisible reality as a realm of conflict, isolation, and fear—with appropriate paths to become more realistic and thereby discover the all-pervasive freedom and happiness that is really ours. The path of mahāmudrā, as this pointing-out book abundantly and lucidly explains, is the most immediate and unexcelled of all such paths. It is given the name of the ultimate goal, *great embrace,* because it proceeds directly to the tender reality of blessed release; in all aspects of space and time, it perceives our existence as nondually and blissfully embraced in absolute freedom. Our extraordinary happiness automatically overflows as glorious love and compassion for all other beings, who are seen swimming with us in the ocean of luminosity.

Even though this supreme path is unexcelled, the teachers in the tradition have voluminous experience in dealing with all different kinds of human beings in various societies and levels of societies. They are fully aware that very few will be helped by such quintessential teaching alone, beyond perhaps a brief moment of hopeful ease upon first hearing about such a nature of reality and such a potential fulfillment in enlightenment of their own love and wisdom. Thus, those great teachers have developed a systematic path of preliminaries, clearly described developmental stages, potential pitfalls and troublesome detours, and various points of entry. These are drawn from chronicles of actual practitioners, from their failures and successes. So there is a way of entry and a plan of evolution to suit almost any kind of person, and in addition most of the writings are meant to be tailored for transmission within unique teacher-student relationships.

Dan Brown has thoroughly investigated and experimented with the enormous literature and tradition derived from these thousands of years of codified experience, collected in the Indian and Tibetan scientific and psychological literature. To this he has added comprehensive research and insightful understanding of contemporary depth, behavioral, cognitive, and the newly nascent meditational, psychologies, which enable him to transmit the tradition in language accessible to any practitioner without linguistic access to the primary sources. Finally, he speaks not only as a scholar and an external scientist, but also as an inner scientist, a yogin of knowledge and experience, as he has practiced these paths in his own mind, with his own body, and so can make clear the discoveries that texts of observation can only describe, while manuals of practice must evoke, to help us to embody them in realization ourselves.

It is a dream realized to see this part of his life work emerge at last. I can remember him in the old days in Massachusetts and New Jersey; he always seemed somehow like a siddha, an adept from somewhere else, wandering through the corridors of the elite institutions or in the humble but more colorful structures of the Dharma Centers. I rejoice and congratulate him for this grand achievement, and I rejoice and congratulate the readers, who will find by working through and living with this monumental book a real pointing out of the gentle, great embrace that this beautiful reality holds them in right now, whatever else they think might be going on.

Robert A. F. Thurman
Jey Tsong Khapa Professor of Indo-Tibetan Buddhist Studies,
Columbia University

PREFACE

THROUGHOUT HISTORY those genuinely motivated to embark on a path of spiritual development encountered many obstacles. Often they did not live at a time or in an area where quality spiritual teachings were available. If valuable spiritual teachings existed, political unrest or war may have prevented them from engaging in practice. If the spiritual teachings were available during a time of peace, students typically had to seek far and wide for a qualified teacher. Finding such a teacher did not guarantee that the teacher would consent to take on the student. Finally, even when the teacher agreed to teach, students often had to endure many hardships, such as harsh climate, sickness, and scarce or poor-quality food.

Today, in contrast, we live in a remarkable time wherein a good deal of the wisdom from many heretofore esoteric spiritual traditions has become readily available to just about anyone. The speed of information delivery through books, self-development seminars, audio and video recordings, and the Internet on the one hand, and a world now intricately interconnected through air travel, telecommunications, and email on the other has fundamentally changed the path of spiritual development. You need only surf the Internet in your own home to discover the listings of seminars and retreats with many of the now world-traveling contemporary teachers. If it is too inconvenient to attend a particular teaching in person, audio and videotapes of teachings are available for download, and you can practice on your own meditation pillow in front of your sound system or television. It is no longer necessary to memorize the meditation instructions, because if you forget, you can replay the recording.

In the Tibetan Buddhist tradition, while many texts were destroyed during the Chinese Cultural Revolution, thousands yet have been preserved, many through the efforts of one man, E. Gene Smith. While working for Library of Congress in India during the 1960s, 70s, and 80s, Gene had rare texts reproduced and shipped to various U.S. libraries for preservation while also amassing an extensive personal library. More recently, through his

Tibetan Buddhist Resource Center (tbrc.org), Gene has continued to acquire texts from India, Tibet, and China, and has been scanning his entire library into digital files, so that the great majority of the indigenous Tibetan Buddhist literature on spiritual development will be available with a simple click of a mouse. When I first started working with the mahāmudrā tradition over thirty years ago, Gene was a precious source of primary texts. Some thirty years later I am now able to download most of these same texts directly into my laptop from the Internet, again owing to his kind efforts.

As Westerners it is easy to take for granted how comfortable the conditions of our lives are, as compared to all the masters who ever walked the spiritual path throughout history. We enjoy relative peace along with more political and economic security than those living in most other countries. We can practice meditation very comfortably, in a temperature-controlled environment, and we don't have to worry unduly about eating healthily, getting sick, or getting distracted from our practice by invasions, robbers, animals, or insects. As the Tibetans would say, we as modern Westerners have a rare and precious opportunity.

The migration of Eastern spiritual traditions to the West is a kind of experiment. How will our culture be transformed? How will our culture transform the character of the Buddhism that takes hold here? What meditations are best suited to Westerners? My own opinion as a psychologist is that, while the Zen Buddhist and the Burmese mindfulness traditions have established an extensive network of Western practitioners, the approach to teaching Buddhist meditation in these schools is not ideally matched to how many Westerners think. Similarly, I have taught meditation retreats with a number of Tibetan lamas who are often remarkably accomplished as meditation masters, yet I have observed they often do not present their knowledge in a form best utilized by Western students.

There are at least three areas where Buddhist meditation teachings in their indigenous form are not ideally matched to Western students. First, traditional meditation development includes a set of preparatory practices, which are designed to make the body and mind fit for meditation, and make progress with meditation more likely. In the East, it is not unusual to spend five to ten years doing these preparatory practices prior to formal meditation training. Many Westerners balk at these preparatory practices because the form of presentation is quite foreign to us. Such practitioners are more likely to begin immediately with formal meditation. They are likely to recreate many of the bad habits of everyday living on the meditation pillow and never progress as a result. Other practitioners readily embrace these preparatory practices in a mindless way and spend years making prostrations, reciting prayers without knowing their meaning, offering various acts of devotion, and blindly imitating or idealizing a teacher in such a way that not only fails to make the body and mind fit for meditation, but also undermines self-confidence, further hindering their development.

Second, we need to see what methods have been most effective for Westerners in bringing about real inner change. The various schools of psychotherapy currently exist as the West's great tradition of growth and development (cf. Reiff 1959). A fundamental feature of most psychotherapy is the primacy of the therapeutic relationship. In fact, whereas only 15 percent of the improvement due to psychotherapy comes from specific therapeutic techniques, just about double the variance, 30 percent, comes from relationship factors like empathy, acceptance, encouragement (Lambert 1992). Some schools of therapy view the main vehicle of change in psychotherapy to be the therapist providing an emotionally corrective relationship for the patient (Alexander and French 1946; Luborsky and Crits-Christoph 1998). Understanding that our great tradition of psychological development is strongly relationship-based means that a relationship-based method of teaching meditation is best matched to this culture. Western psychotherapy may be a culturally congruent way to accomplish at least some of the same objectives as the preparatory practices. Psychotherapy is indeed a good preparation for genuine meditation practice, as I have argued elsewhere (Wilbur, Engler, and Brown, 1987), although psychotherapy alone fails to accomplish the broad range of skills cultivated by the preparatory practices of the great contemplative traditions.

We need to appreciate the extent to which Western culture will transform Buddhist meditation practice. What will be the unique character of American Buddhism? In my opinion American Buddhism is likely to become much more relationship-based, and therefore will represent a transformation of the monastic forms of Buddhism that have found their way to this country. While Tibetan Buddhism certainly professes the centrality of the teacher-student relationship, the reality is that access to a spiritual teacher is the exception rather than the norm, particularly in a relationship that allows for authentic interchange. Typically, the Western student offers devotion and service in support of a teacher's organization while a teacher gives group discourses in return, with occasional private meetings that are often fraught by cultural barriers to understanding. My particular interest in the mahāmudrā tradition stems from the fact that its original form was very much relationship-based, with what was called a pointing-out style of teaching. The teacher closely followed the student's practice as part of an ongoing relationship in order to ensure that the student's meditation progress stayed on the right track and to help the student learn to identify and self-correct problems that might otherwise arrest progress. I firmly believe that relationship-based forms of meditation, with this kind of dynamic feedback, are ideal for contemporary Western practitioners.

We can address the third area where indigenous meditation practices are not ideally suited for Westerners by looking at the impact on psychotherapy practice in particular, and on popular culture in general, of the cognitive-behavioral revolution in psychotherapy over the past three decades. A unique contribution of the cognitive-behavioral literature is the targeting of specific behaviors, detailed step-by-step instructions for change, and clear benchmarks of progress. Based on the psychotherapy outcome literature that has evolved over these decades, step-by-step treatment manuals are now widely available for addressing anxiety disorders, obsessive-compulsive disorder, depression, bipolar disorder, chronic pain, and many other clinical syndromes. Contemporary Westerners have learned to think in terms of step-by-step manuals. For Western practitioners, Eastern meditation traditions that present clearly defined meditation stages are perhaps most helpful, especially those that describe the main techniques, intended results, and benchmarks of progress, and carefully delineate common problems and how to remedy them. Therefore, I firmly believe that the Indo-Tibetan Buddhist gradual "meditation-stages" approach to teaching meditation is well matched to Western thinking. I have tried to write a book that both preserves the step-by-step approach to meditation instruction characteristic of the original Tibetan meditation-stages literature, and yet adopts the step-by-step approach that Westerners are now quite familiar with.

♦ ♦ ♦ ♦

My own journey into the Eastern meditative traditions began thirty-six years ago. As part of an undergraduate course on Eastern religious traditions, I read Evans-Wentz's *Tibetan Yoga and Secret Doctrines* (1935). The translation of Pema Karpo's mahāmudrā meditation manual in that volume spoke to me, and I knew I wanted to learn more about meditation. In a Religion and Psychological Studies graduate program at the University of Chicago, I had the opportunity to study with some of the great historians of religion of that time, such as J. Z. Smith and Mircea Eliade, both of whom served as dissertation advisors and helped me to learn interpretive methods for historical texts. I learned a very modest amount of Sanskrit at the University of Chicago, and supplemented my language study with classes on Buddhist Sanskrit and Tibetan language at the University of Wisconsin at Madison. My first exposure to the Tibetan language, and a Buddhist way of living in the world, came from my root lama, the Ven. Geshe Wangyal, with whom I had a ten-year relationship, living with him summers in New Jersey until he died in 1983. E. Gene Smith visited Chicago around 1973 and provided me with a good number of the important blockprint versions of the Tibetan mahāmudrā texts on which this book is based. Now armed with mahāmudrā's "greatest hits," I spent the next ten years translating most of this material. In the early days at Wisconsin, Stephen Beyer helped me to learn enough of the technical language of Tibetan texts to produce my own rough retranslation of Pema Karpo's mahāmudrā manual and Jampel Pawo's commentary on it. George Hart helped me work on a translation of Kamalaśīla's *Stages of Meditation* from Sanskrit. Geshe Sopa helped me with my own translation of Śāntideva's *Guide to the Bodhisattva Way of Life* from a Tibetan translation of the original Sanskrit. Frances Cook helped me with translating some of Saraha's early mahāmudrā songs from a vernacular dialect of Pali.

At the University of Chicago, J. A. B. van Buitenen assisted my translation of some of the tantric mahāmudrā texts from Sanskrit. The training in anthropology and history of religions I received at Chicago gave me linguistic tools to tackle the rich technical language of meditation texts. The training that I had in psychology of religion, primarily from my main advisors, Don Browning and Peter Homans of the Psychology and Religion Program at Chicago helped me to understand the Indo-Tibetan tradition of meditation-stages using our own Western tradition of psychological methods. I owe a special debt to my primary mentor, Erika Fromm, who guided not only my professional training as a clinical psychologist but also the development of character. In addition, she encouraged me to use psychological research tools to study meditative states and outcomes. This approximately decade of work led to my dissertation, which described both the gradual development of the stages of meditation in the mahāmudrā tradition and interpreted these meditative states of consciousness in terms of social and cognitive psychology.

After leaving Chicago to continue clinical training in Boston, I did a two-year postdoctoral program in clinical research at the Cambridge Hospital of Harvard Medical School under the supervision of Charles Ducey. For my research I used the Rorschach to measure changes in perception among practitioners who developed some proficiency in deep concentration. We used participants on a three-month intensive retreat in Burmese mindfulness meditation at the Insight Meditation Society in Barre, Massachusetts. As a research psychologist over the next decade, I and my colleagues (especially Michael Forte, whose dedication to this research was tireless) conducted a wide variety of pre-post outcome studies and/or clinical interviews of intensive meditators both at the Barre site and also in South Asia (with Jack Engler). My colleagues and I studied changes in phenomenological experience, personality, pain perception, and tachistoscopic high-speed information-processing as a result of various meditative practices. We also studied the changes in consciousness due to deep concentration, special insight practices, and extraordinary meditation practices using a self-report methodology I learned from Erika Fromm and Father Andrew Greeley of the National Opinion Research Center at the University of Chicago. We also conducted detailed field interviews of the descriptions practitioners gave of enlightenment experiences and the impact these experiences had on everyday life. As clinicians, Jack Engler and I, along with others, began to research the kind of clinical problems that Western students encountered during intensive retreats, specifically how unresolved psychopathology interfered with progress in meditation. Over that decade I got to see firsthand the problems that enthusiastic Western meditators were commonly having in their meditation practice, and how either psychological problems or progressively learned bad habits of meditation typically arrested progress.

My own meditation practice began when I first encountered Patañjali's *Yogasūtras* in Mircea Eliade's book, *Yoga: Immortality and Freedom* (1969) along with his own personal commentary on these works. He helped orient me to the stages of practice in the Indian Saṃkhya-Yoga system. I am also thankful for Dr. Arwind Vasavada's generous and inspiring teaching on Patañjali's yoga and meditation during my stay in Chicago.

In the mid 1970s I started attending meditation retreats derived from the Burmese mindfulness tradition. I am thankful to a number of the

Western meditation teachers of that tradition, like Jack Kornfield, Joseph Goldstein, Sharon Salzberg, and Christopher Titmuss, and also to some of the South Asian teachers who occasionally visited this country, namely Mahasi Sayadaw, his successor U Pandita Sayadaw, the forest dweller Tungpulo Sayadaw, and the Thai master Ajahn Chah. At one point I went to Burma to study directly with Mahasi Sayadaw and U Javanah Sayadaw. I am grateful for Mahasi Sayadaw's invitation and personal teaching, and also for the many friends and staff at his retreat center, Thathana Yeiktha in Rangoon, who provided all of the comforts so that I could focus on meditation full time while there.

For over three decades I have had the fortune of many Tibetan meditation teachers. The Ven. Geshe Wangyal holds a dear place in my heart as my root lama. He provided the model for what it means to awaken the mind and to live that every moment of daily life. I learned the Asaṅga-Maitreya tradition of concentration meditation and Madhyamaka special insight meditations from Geshe Denma Lochö Rinpoche, Geshe Yeshe Tapkay, Geshe Gedün Lodrö, and H.H. The Dalai Lama. Joshua Cutler, a fellow student of Geshe Wangyal and the chief translator of Tsongkhapa's *The Great Treatise on the Stages of the Path to Enlightenment* has been a collaborator, teacher, and friend. I learned a great deal about Tsongkhapa's approach to concentration from the times Joshua and I have taught together. I learned mahāmudrā from a number of Kagyü lamas who came to this country offering mahāmudrā empowerments, meditation courses, and personal instruction, namely, Kalu Rinpoche, the Sixteenth Karmapa Rangjung Rigpé Dorjé, Chetsang Rinpoche, the Third Jamgön Kongtrül, Khenpo Könchog Gyaltsen, and Ven. Drubwang Konchok Norbu Rinpoche.

Over the past decade I have co-taught meditation courses with my friend and colleague Andrea Lindsay, LICSW. She helped show me that meditation is not an activity conducted while sitting on the pillow but a way of being, a way of living with complete awareness. As much an artist as a clinician, she also helped bring a fresh approach to teaching meditation, a contrast to my predilection for precise technical language; she helped me to see that art, poetry, and cooking are wonderful media to express meditation experience. Over the last few years a former meditation student of mine, George Protos, has assisted me in teaching meditation retreats. His immovable presence as a meditator, and clear-minded, fresh descriptions of meditative states and the nature of the mind have really enhanced the quality of the courses. I have learned the most about meditation from trying to teach it, so I am very grateful to my many students who have been forthcoming with clear descriptions of their states, their discoveries, and their struggles. I am also very appreciative of the assistance in teaching given by other advanced students, such as Susan Mickel, Julie Yau, JoAnn Lux, and Robin Woo, especially for their ability to bring to teaching a depth of compassion and kindness.

In the past fifteen years I have learned a great deal about the needs of Western meditation students as I have tried to teach one-day and two-day workshops on meditation for psychologists, and week-long or longer retreats for Western practitioners of meditation. At the Buddhist Learning Center in Washington, New Jersey, team teaching concentration and special insight meditations over a ten-year period with Joshua and Diana Cutler, with the former lamas in residence, namely Geshe Lobzang Tsetan, Geshe Nawang Lhundup, and Geshe Thupten Gyatso, and with the visiting senior lamas, namely Geshe Denma Lochö Rinpoche and Geshe Yeshe Tapkay, helped me to better understand how to adapt the traditional Tibetan form of meditation instruction to the needs of Westerners. I have greatly appreciated the openness, flexibility, and patience of the senior lamas, Denma Lochö Rinpoche and Yeshe Tapkay, to my experiments with modifying the concentration meditation techniques in fundamental ways. For example, I assigned Western students the breath as the object of concentration rather than the traditional Tibetan method of using an image of the Buddha. The senior lamas remained remarkably open to my belief that the *nine states of the mind staying* could be accomplished more quickly using the breath than a visual object.

While teaching meditation I have had ample opportunity to discover the common problems that Western students developed during protracted meditation practice. I was amazed to discover a significant corpus of indigenous Tibetan meditation texts that mapped out similar problems and their remedies in great detail. By comparing the descriptions of our Western students' problems to those found in the indigenous Tibetan meditation texts, I began to appreciate the wide range of very specific methods that the masters had developed hundreds of years earlier in India and Tibet to correct and even to prevent such problems. For example, I began to see how skillful practice of "intensifying" and "easing-up" enabled the meditator to stay more continuously and completely on the intended meditation object. I also began to appreciate a range of methods that had been developed to prevent subtle laxity or dullness of mind, such as the use of intelligence to self-monitor the quality of the meditation and the use of shorter meditation sessions to insure depth of concentration and brightness of mind during meditation.

As I studied these Indo-Tibetan texts I began to discover that the Burmese tradition regarding concentration meditation, within which I had clocked so many hours over several decades on the meditation pillow, did not have clearly delineated meditation instructions regarding intensifying and self-monitoring. Nor did it have detailed instructions regarding switching from the event- to the mind-perspective during insight meditation. From a historical perspective, the Burmese mindfulness tradition is rather young, a tradition revitalized by the teachings of Mahasi Sayadaw and others over a half a century ago. The Indo-Tibetan Asaṅga-Maitreya tradition of concentration and special insight meditation has existed at least since the fourth century, and considering this much longer time span, it is not at all surprising that a sophisticated set of meditation methods evolved to handle most of the problems and common points meditators get stuck. When I began to compare the insights about the nature of the mind in the Burmese tradition and the Indo-Tibetan Mahayana tradition directly during meditation practice, I again discovered some important differences in the direct experience of insight regarding the nature of the self.

From the essence traditions, like mahāmudrā and dzogchen, I began to appreciate that the depth of realization possible during ordinary concentration and special insight meditation was enhanced remarkably by shifting to the very subtle or extraordinary level of mind. In other words, the issue became less about concentration on the intended meditation object and much more about the level of mind brought to the concentration, and that, from the mind-perspective, shifting from the ordinary self-representation to the extraordinary essence of the mind's real nature as the vantage point during meditation quickly brought the meditation practice within the range wherein awakening the mind was a definite possibility.

Finally, my over three decades as a therapist conducting both individual and small-group psychotherapy taught me that it is quite possible to teach meditation in a relationship-based way—both as part of an ongoing relationship and also in the context of the small-group format of a meditation retreat.

The outcome of these various influences and experiences have led me to become quite skeptical of what some have called the "odometer" approach to meditation in the West, namely the assumption that the more hours the meditator clocks on the pillow, the deeper the meditation. Both as a Western psychologist conducting outcomes research on meditators and as a meditation teacher, I have come to see that the great majority of Western meditation students, while they may become relaxed during meditation, rarely attain the deepest levels of concentration as described in the classical literature on the nine states, rarely have more than a rudimentary understanding of emptiness, and very rarely fully awaken or even partially awaken to the mind's real nature. Some people might argue that I am advocating for an achievement-oriented approach to meditation that is anti-meditative. It is fair to say, however, that within the traditions themselves, very clear goals of meditation have been marked. The goal of concentration is to stabilize the mind so that the mind stays continuously and completely on the intended meditation object; the goal of ordinary special insight is the direct experience of emptiness; and the goal of the extraordinary or essence practices is full awakening, or enlightenment.

As a therapist who has some training in cognitive-behavioral therapy, I have also come to see how many Western meditation students harbor stable, self-defeating beliefs and schemas regarding their sense of self, perception of relationships, and the world in general. These same negative schemas also influence meditation practice in particular, in such a way that many students make limiting assumptions either about their own self-efficacy in deepening the meditation or about the outcome. Few take their meditation practice seriously enough that during every meditation session they approach each and every moment of meditation with a deliberate carefulness based on the assumption that any single moment of flawless practice could establish the conditions to awaken the mind fully. I am not saying this out of criticism. It is simply an honest statement of what I have observed across many Western meditation students.

My hope is that Western students of meditation find available to them the very best meditation tools that evolved over the centuries, and are given very detailed descriptions of: the ways to practice, the type of intended states of meditation they should try to cultivate with these methods; clear specification of the signs of progress to look for; and a clear delineation of the problems that typically occur and how to correct them. However, instead of re-inventing a step-by-step meditation manual for this time and this culture, I have come to appreciate that the original pointing-out style of instruction in the gradual meditation-stages approach to mahāmudrā comes very close to this ideal. In some small way I hope that my approach to this book is helpful to Western meditators along the path.

◆ ◆ ◆ ◆

This book has enjoyed a rather long evolution. The first drafts of my translations of the gradual meditation-stages traditions of Indo-Tibetan mahāmudrā were written in the mid to late 1970s as part of my doctoral dissertation. During that time I compared all of the Tibetan mahāmudrā texts I had available for every stage of the meditation practice. I tried to discover what the majority of texts had in common with respect to the main techniques, key terms, and delineation of stages. The outcome was a comprehensive description of the stages of meditation from beginning to completion.

Around four years ago a mutual friend informed me that E. Gene Smith, who originally gave me the Tibetan mahāmudrā texts, was ironically now living in the same city that I was living. We met shortly thereafter over lunch, and he expressed some curiosity about what I had done with the mahāmudrā material. He asked to see a copy of the dissertation, which I sent him. At that time Gene was the acquisitions editor at Wisdom Publications. Some time thereafter at another lunch meeting he told me that he had sent the manuscript to several Western and Tibetan scholars on Buddhism who reviewed it favorably and that he wanted to publish it through Wisdom. To make the job easier, he also told me that he had scanned the entire text onto a Word file, and then handed me a disc ready to edit. He suggested that I "update" the book with the now-existing literature on mahāmudrā. I am very grateful to Gene Smith, without whose persistence I probably would have never published this material.

After the meeting with Gene, I discovered that a significant number of English books had appeared on mahāmudrā over the past thirty years, and that interest in and demand for mahāmudrā material had grown over the decades. Ironically, a work I had written around thirty years ago now seemed timely. While I originally wrote my dissertation largely as an academic treatise at a time that I had at best only very modest actual meditation experience, I could now revisit the manuscript after over thirty years of meditation experience and around fifteen years of teaching meditation. Instead of simply editing and updating the manuscript, I decided to rewrite a good deal of the manuscript for a third time. I had hoped to give many sections the "fresh" perspective of direct experience of some of these meditative states along the path, while yet preserving the technical precision of the original Tibetan texts.

In addition to Gene's efforts, this book would not have been possible without the patient and skilled assistance of staff at Wisdom Publications. Mari Jyvasjarvi spent many hours scanning the original dissertation into the computer so that it could be edited without retyping. David Kittelstrom, as the primary editor, patiently tried to convince me that there was a way to preserve the technical precision of the language of meditative states and still produce a manuscript that is reader-friendly. I was also fortunate to have as copyeditor Daia Gerson, who is both a seasoned copyeditor as well as a devoted practitioner of mahāmudrā. If this book is at all useful to your understanding of meditation the credit goes to the staff at Wisdom Publication for making the work available.

My hope is that these next chapters will enable you to enter the remarkably rich inner world of meditation experience, and for your meditation practice to be carefully guided along this path toward awakened wisdom and contentment in everyday life.

Daniel Brown, Ph.D.
Newton, Massachusetts
November 2005

INTRODUCTION

．．．．

THIS BOOK IS INTENDED as a spiritual manual. It describes the Tibetan Buddhist meditation known as *mahāmudrā* from the perspective of the gradual path. The gradual path is a progressive process of training that is often contrasted to sudden realization. As such, this book contains a step-by-step description of the ways to practice, precise descriptions of the various stages and their intended realizations, and the typical problems that arise along with their remedies.

Though it is found in several schools of Tibetan Buddhism, mahāmudrā meditation is the heart practice of the Kagyü school, where it is considered the pinnacle of all the various practices. Simply put, mahāmudrā meditation involves penetrative focus, free of conceptual elaboration, upon the very nature of conscious awareness.

A unique feature of this book is its integrative approach to the stages of mahāmudrā meditation. A number of works on Buddhist meditation stages in general and mahāmudrā meditation in particular are already available in English. Yet no single text or commentary on the stages of mahāmudrā meditation captures the inner experience of these stages in sufficient detail to convey its richness. Many of these texts, particularly the root texts and practical manuals, are written in a highly condensed style that was never meant to describe the meditation practice in detail. They act as crib sheets for practitioners already conversant with the training. Likewise, the commentaries on these texts often do not elaborate on these meditation experiences either, because their primary purpose is to relate these practices to the wider Buddhist tradition by citing passages from well-known texts. Thus none of these texts describes the stages in sufficient detail for the reader to adequately understand the actual practice. This book offers an alternative. By integrating material from a variety of root texts, practical manuals, and commentaries, I have created a comprehensive step-by-step guide to the path of mahāmudrā meditation.

PUTTING MEDITATIVE EXPERIENCE INTO WORDS

A good deal of Western scholarship on religion assumes that mystical experience is ineffable. Mystical states are said to be so profound that they are indescribable. This view is wrong. Rechungpa, a contemporary of the great Tibetan saint Milarepa, wrote an extremely detailed work on all the changes that occur in the body and mind at the moment of enlightenment. The most striking feature of his *Clear Wisdom Mahāmudrā* is the extreme technical precision used to describe internal states. As a tradition, Tibetan Buddhism is perhaps unique in the level of technical precision used to describe meditation experience; there is nothing comparable in Western mystical literature. Western mysticism largely has been restricted to individual practitioners, small groups, or time-limited movements, wherein the mystics either didn't express their spiritual attainments in much detail, or expressed these attainments in idiosyncratic ways according to their unique realizations and cultural context.

Tibetan Buddhism, in contrast, is a highly organized lineage tradition that has been around since the seventh century, with Indian roots that go back much further. The early oral tradition spawned a loose but extensive network of itinerate practitioners who shared or traded teachings and specific spiritual exercises. The monastic tradition beginning in the eleventh century was characterized by tightly organized, stable communities of large groups of meditators who engaged in continuous dialogues about meditative attainments. They developed an elaborate inner science of spiritual development. During this period the technical language for spiritual development became more consensual, technically sophisticated, and refined as standards for discussing attainments developed. This body of technical knowledge was transmitted from generation to generation until the present day.

The central problem then for the Western reader in understanding spiritual development in the Tibetan Buddhist tradition is not its alleged ineffability but the opposite: namely, understanding the vast and sophisticated technical language of internal meditative experience. This book is designed to give the reader a precise map of internal meditative states.

Another unique feature of this book is its relational approach. In the West we have the stereotype of an isolated practitioner who rarely talks about meditation experience. Meditation in the early mahāmudrā tradition was grounded in an intense relationship between teacher and student. The teacher typically "pointed out" the real nature of the mind and gave personalized instructions about the practice, the desired outcomes, and the problems that arise at each stage. The teacher then observed the student's progress and helped the student make corrections whenever meditation practice strayed from the desired outcome. It was only with the development of the monastic tradition that a formalized retreat structure evolved. An inevitable consequence of monastic meditation was that direct observation and intervention by the teacher became less frequent.

This book is intended as a return to the original relational style of teaching meditation, which may be better suited to Western culture than the monastic or retreat style of practice. The presumption is that meditation development can advance more quickly when the teacher gives detailed instructions at each step. In the spirit of this original pointing-out style of teaching, the aim of this book, as exemplified in the title, *Pointing Out the Great Way,* is to provide the reader with richly detailed descriptions of meditation practices from the very beginning to the end of the gradual path. While instructions given in a book certainly cannot be personalized for each reader, nevertheless, the very richness of these descriptions of internal states of mind follows the spirit of the early pointing-out teachings.

INTELLECTUAL UNDERSTANDING VERSUS ACTUAL EXPERIENCE

Successful spiritual development entails finding a balance between intellectual understanding of each stage of meditation and actual meditative experience. Placing too much emphasis on either alone significantly decreases the likelihood of genuine progress.

Popular Buddhist literature illustrates these extremes with characterizations of the pandit and the kusali. The pandit stereotype is the scholar who devotes considerable energy to understanding the philosophy associated with a particular form of spiritual practice but who never practices. The pandit may rationalize this avoidance by saying that meditation is anti-intellectual. The term *kusali* is derived from the name of the grass commonly used to make meditation cushions. The kusali stereotype is the fervent meditator who clocks long hours on the cushion trying to deepen meditation experience. The kusali rarely reflects on the quality of the meditation experience, rarely shares the experience with other meditators, and rarely reads the authoritative literature on meditation or compares his or her experiences against classical descriptions. Without any perspective and without systematic reflection, the kusali risks developing subtle and not so subtle bad habits that eventually arrest his or her progress.

Skillful practitioners find the right balance between direct meditation experience and intellectual understanding of the texts by earlier masters. In this way, they are able to make the necessary adjustments and ensure that their unfolding meditation experiences and realizations aren't flawed.

The Technical Language of Spiritual Development

The problem of understanding practical Buddhist meditation texts is like trying to understand the journals of a modern Western scientific discipline without having any familiarity with that area of science. According to Toulmin in *Human Understanding*,[1] science is a rational yet practical enterprise. Any subdiscipline within science, like chemistry or psychology, is made up of a community of scientists who share certain "disciplinary ideals" and "basic questions." Each subdiscipline develops a set of "application procedures" used to solve these basic questions. As an ongoing knowledge base develops, a growing body of progressively sophisticated technical terms evolves. According to Toulmin introduction into any subdiscipline of science entails learning its technical language.

Toulmin categorizes scientific disciplines along a continuum, from "would-be," to "diffuse," to "compact," depending on the degree of explicitness and consensualness of the basic ideals, commitment to use standard procedures without undue dispute, and the degree of precision of its technical language. Chemistry, for example, is considered to be a compact discipline, while psychology, with its methodological pluralism and division into numerous schools of thought, is considered a would-be discipline.

Comparing spiritual traditions according to Toulmin's criteria, Western mysticism meets the criteria of a would-be discipline while Tibetan Buddhism meets the criteria of a compact discipline, not because the spiritual realizations in these respective traditions are more or less compelling, but because of the differences between the technical precision by which these realizations are expressed and transmitted. This book distills and codifies the experiences of many great masters who have traversed the path of meditation to the point of perfect mastery.

Like the apprentice of a scientific discipline the reader must enter at the beginning stage and learn the basic concepts and technical language. It would be presumptuous for a layman to expect to comprehend a journal article on electron transfer or polymer science. Should we really be surprised, then, when early Western Buddhist scholars concluded that very advanced tantric Buddhist texts like the *Hevajra Tantra,* with its specialized technical language, contained an "absence of rationality"?[2] This book is meant to help the reader develop a working knowledge of Buddhist spiritual development from the simplest to the more advanced, and particularly by learning the concepts, terms, and methods characteristic of each stage of practice.

How This Book Is Structured

The rest of this introduction sets mahāmudrā meditation within its wider Buddhist context and includes a basic overview of the key concepts in the mahāmudrā tradition as well as a brief history of mahāmudrā. The remainder of the book walks the reader through the actual practices. Chapter 1 describes the practices that turn the beginner toward sincere interest in spiritual practice. Chapter 2 describes preliminary practices that make the body and mind fit for meditation and ensure that the practitioner does not simply recreate all the problems of everyday life on the meditation pillow. Chapters 3 to 5 describe concentration meditation designed to stabilize the mind. Chapter 6 describes the ordinary form of emptiness meditation. Chapter 7 describes the extraordinary mahāmudrā practices—*one taste yoga* and *nonmeditation yoga.* These set the foundation for enlightenment. This chapter contains a detailed description of enlightenment experience along with the subtle flaws in practice that, unless identified, will prevent full awakening. Chapter 8 describes the post-enlightenment practices known as *path-walking practices,* by which the practitioner learns to manifest profound realization within the coarsest levels of everyday reality.

See the end of this introduction for a more detailed description of the sources and approach used in this book.

Mahāmudrā in Context

The Aim of Spiritual Development in Buddhism

We in the West are accustomed to treating everyday unhappiness with psychotherapy. However, as Freud notes in *Civilization and Its Discontents,* successful psychoanalysis merely alleviates neurotic suffering but does not address everyday unhappiness. Buddhism picks up where successful therapy leaves off, addressing ordinary unhappiness and how to overcome it.

Buddhism from the beginning has emphasized the importance of liberation from suffering. This emphasis is exemplified by the doctrine of the four noble truths, according to which every aspect of life is characterized by some form of suffering. The goal of spiritual development through Buddhist meditation is to eradicate suffering by attacking its root cause.

The Pali word typically translated as "suffering" is *dukkha*, which could also be rendered as "reactivity." For, as we experience events unfolding in our stream of consciousness moment-by-moment, the ordinary mind reacts based on ingrained habits. If the event is experienced as pleasant, the mind habitually gravitates toward the event. If it is experienced as unpleasant, the mind pushes it away. In Buddhism these automatic reactive tendencies are referred to as *clinging* and *aversion,* and lapses in the continuity of awareness are called *nonawareness,* or *ignorance.* Together these "three poisons" mark every moment of ordinary experience. They are habitual. They obscure the mind's natural condition from us and in so doing become the fundamental cause of everyday unhappiness. In other words, Buddhism defines everyday unhappiness in terms of a habitual dysfunction in the way we process our experience. Seen in this way, it can be identified and corrected, and the root of everyday unhappiness can be eradicated.

Disciplined meditation practice leads to a series of changes in consciousness that result in a transformation known as *enlightenment.* In early Buddhism, enlightenment meant the eradication of the mind's reactive tendency and its lapses in awareness. Such enlightenment does not change the content of our experience. Instead, whatever event we experience is experienced with full awareness and without any reactivity whatsoever. All life experiences—positive and negative—are embraced equally, with complete and continuous awareness, so that the quality of everyday experience is greatly enriched, moment-by-moment.[3]

The later *Mahāyāna* Buddhism developed a new perspective on enlightenment. Early Buddhism is cast primarily from the perspective of the individual practitioner, and enlightenment means freedom from suffering for the individual. In the Mahāyāna perspective, the practitioner strives to awaken the minds of every sentient being. In this lofty perspective, individual meditative experience can access a fundamental level of consciousness common to all minds, a consciousness, at the very subtle level, that is the very mind of the realized Buddha. Mahāyāna meditative practice toward enlightenment is, in essence, enlightenment for all sentient beings. For when the individual attains enlightenment, the experience, through dependent origination, subtly affects all beings. Thus, for the Mahāyāna, enlightenment is both liberation and also a manifestation of omniscience— the awakened wisdom of the Buddha. The awakened mind of the Buddha manifests as infinite wisdom and inexhaustible compassion. Thus while early Buddhism emphasizes the eradication of negative qualities, Mahāyāna enlightenment entails the full manifestation of all positive qualities of mind, the quintessence of our human potential.

INDIAN ANTECEDENTS TO MAHĀMUDRĀ

The writings on buddha-nature *(tathagatagarbha)* first appeared in the fourth and fifth centuries. These texts, which include the *Saṃdhinirmo-cana Sūtra* and the *Uttāratantra Śāstra,* go beyond the basic cataloging of mental states in Buddhist Abhidharma texts and describe the deeper layers of the mind. According to Jamgön Kongtrül, the nineteenth-century Tibetan master, the teachings on buddha-nature in the *Uttāratantra Śāstra* paved the way for the later mahāmudrā view.[4]

The basic idea of this buddha-nature literature is that awakened wisdom (Skt., *jñāna;* Tib., *yes shes*), which manifests in the three buddha bodies (the truth body, enjoyment body, and emanation body), is the mind's natural condition. However, our karmically created mistaken conceptions and negative emotions defile the mind's inherent purity and obscure us from our buddha-nature. Enlightenment is in fact already inherent in our experience, if we can only recognize it. Concentration (Skt., *śamatha;* Tib., *zhi nas*) and special insight (Skt., *vipaśyanā;* Tib., *lhag mthong*) meditation lay the foundation for recognizing this awakened wisdom.

The teachings on buddha-nature were characteristic of the Yogācāra school in India, and its view of the mind's essence was debated for centuries with the other dominant Indian school, the Madhyamaka, which emphasized the mind's essential emptiness. Both of these traditions made their way to Tibet, but the Madhyamaka school came to predominate, at least nominally, through the popularity of such teachers as Śāntideva, author of the famous *Guide to the Bodhisattva Way of Life.* Yogācāra ideas have never disappeared from Tibetan Buddhism, however, and their influence is particularly distinct within the teachings on mahāmudrā.

These early debates in Buddhism's history continue to resonate, and they find their way into the gradual path of mahāmudrā discussed in this book. The preliminary stage of mahāmudrā meditation traces its roots to Atiśa and the Tibetan Kadampa tradition. The core meditation stages—concentration and special insight meditation—trace their roots to the Indian Yogācāra masters Asaṅga and Kamalaśīla, though the mahāmudrā tradition eventually recast its special insight practices from Asaṅga's Yogācāra emphasis into a Madhyamaka interpretation. The extraordinary mahāmudrā practices rely on a theory of the natural mind whose roots can be traced to the early works on buddha-nature and later commentators on the early mahāmudrā source tradition. The mahāmudrā meditation stages in this book are syncretic in that they incorporate keys elements from many levels of Indo-Tibetan Buddhist history.

SŪTRA, TANTRA, AND ESSENCE

One of the unique features of Buddhism is the concept of skillful means (Skt., *upāya*). Depending on their time in history, their cultural context, and their temperament, different individuals require very different methods of spiritual instruction. Finding just the right match for each person is the heart of skillful means. The implication is that methods of spiritual development, if they are to be vital and effective, do and must vary greatly. What follows is an explanation of some distinct approaches within the Buddhist tradition.

In Buddhism a popular distinction is made between the *sūtra* and *tantra* methods for spiritual development. The sūtra methods generally are drawn from the practices of early Buddhism and are typically threefold: (1) preliminary practices to make the body and mind fit for formal meditation, (2) concentration training to stabilize the mind, and (3) special insight practice to realize the mind's essential nature. The tantric practices are twofold: (1) generation stage practice, which entails complex visualizations to stabilize the mind and manifest its essential nature, and (2) completion stage practice, which enhances these realizations at the subtle and very subtle levels of mind. Completion stage practices may involve manipulating the body's energy currents in order to make the very subtle mind more readily accessible.

Some authors add a third category: sūtra vs. tantra vs. essence.[5] *Essence* traditions are exemplified by the mahāmudrā and the *dzogchen* ("great perfection") systems of meditation. The essence viewpoint asserts three levels of mind: coarse, subtle, and very subtle. The coarse level pertains to mental content, such as thoughts, sense perceptions, and emotions. The subtle level is the fleeting mental activity surrounding sensory experience before that activity becomes full-blown mental content. The very subtle, or extraordinary, level is the level where impressions due to past actions are accumulated before these ripen in fresh experience. This very subtle mind is sometimes called the *storehouse consciousness*. The point of observation of this storehouse consciousness transcends our ordinary sense of self and individual consciousness. Like a vast ocean of awareness, this vantage point for the extraordinary meditation is typically referred to as the *always-here mind* or as *awareness in and of itself.* When the mind operates primarily at this very subtle level, the individual is significantly more prepared to realize the mind's primordial nature, which is always there, unaffected by all the mental activity at the coarse and subtle levels. Thus, the essence perspective cuts right to the heart of the mind's natural state, and invites the practitioner to awaken to it in direct experience, the result of which is enlightenment.

The early essence tradition did not include extensive descriptions of spiritual practice. The extraordinary view of the mind was directly transmitted from master to student:

> In the past, for transmission, it was sufficient for the master and disciple to simply rest their minds together in the composure of innate wakefulness.[6]

The skillful means in the essence tradition is this pointing-out instruction. In this context, the master's job is (1) to assess accurately the state of the student's mind, (2) to directly influence the student's very subtle mind, so as to remove hindrances that might otherwise obscure realization, (3) provide a precise description of the mind's real nature, and (4) awaken the student to direct realization of the mind's natural condition.

The extraordinary practitioner gains this realization once the master directly points out the real nature of the mind. Ordinary practitioners generally do not understand the pointing-out instructions because their minds are too clouded by coarse-level thoughts, mistaken ideas, negative emotions, and dualistic perception of the external world. Therefore, ordinary practitioners must refine their minds through standard practices before the essence view can be introduced. The difference between ordinary and extraordinary meditation practice is the difference between working on the conventional and the deeper layers of the mind.[7]

In the original mahāmudrā tradition, the earliest masters literally sang the disciples into enlightenment with poems called *dohās*. The mind's natural condition was directly pointed out by the master, who then gave instructions to negate any artificial activity during meditation. Realization of the mind's awakened wisdom was a consequence of these pointing-out and nonmeditation instructions. This is *essence mahāmudrā*. Later in the tradition, mahāmudrā practitioners first learned to refine the ordinary mind through mastering traditional generation-stage and completion-stage tantric practices, and then they took up mahāmudrā either concurrent with or following completion-stage practice. This is *tantric mahāmudrā*. Still later in the tradition, practitioners first refined the ordinary mind through mastering standard concentration and special insight meditation, and after some degree of mastery had been achieved, mahāmudrā was then introduced. This is *sūtra mahāmudrā*. Thus, mahāmudrā can be a sūtra, tantra, or essence practice, depending on which practices are used to refine the coarse and subtle levels of the mind before essence instructions are given to address the very subtle mind.

GRADUAL OR INSTANTANEOUS

It is customary to speak of two paths to enlightenment—an instantaneous path, in which enlightenment seems to occur all at once, and a gradual path, in which progress toward enlightenment occurs in systematic, predictable stages. Only the rare student becomes instantaneously enlightened when the mind's true nature is pointed out by the master. Most students can spend years in practice without achieving the end-state. How do we account for these remarkable differences in progress?

The most frequent answer to this question is that practitioners have different capacities—ordinary, exceptional, or extraordinary. Those of extraordinary ability are likely to realize enlightenment immediately after the true nature of the mind has been pointed out by the master. Sometimes they even come to the realization on their own. Those of exceptional ability realize the deepest levels of mind and reach enlightenment after systematic meditation using the skillful means specific to their culture and historical moment. For those of ordinary ability, negative states of mind obscure genuine realization. Such individuals require extensive preliminary practice to make the mind fit for spiritual development.[8]

In reality, type of practitioner is only a partial explanation for the differences in spiritual realization, which is a function of several variables, including: (1) practitioner traits (such as intelligence, the capacity to recognize and correct problems, the relative distribution of negative and positive states of mind, the level and range of meditative experience, and the state of mind at the time of pointing out); (2) teacher characteristics (quality of the teacher's realization, capacity to teach or otherwise transmit realization); (3) nature of the teachings (clarity, depth, sophistication); and (4) context, which means the extent to which teachings are generally available. Various skillful means are simply different ways to access the awareness capable of realizing the mind's intrinsic nature.

THE VIRTUES OF THE GRADUAL PATH

For ordinary individuals the gradual path of spiritual development is generally recommended, a path traversing definable stages with distinct objectives and methods for each stage. This gradual path to spiritual development is generally called the stages of the path *(lam rim)*, or more specifically with respect to meditation practice, the stages of meditation *(sgom rim)*.

The gradual path is a process of discovery and learning. In the West we have learning theory, a model well known within psychotherapeutic circles. According to learning theory, the more we repeat a behavior or establish associations with it, the better learned a behavior becomes. Having established a learned pathway through practice, we generalize that knowledge to other situations. Access to that learned behavior becomes more immediate and automatic.

Buddhism has its own version of learning theory. We could call it *karma theory*. Just as learning theory emphasizes behaviors, karma theory addresses actions—both observable and mental. But whereas learning theory stresses that strengthening associations reinforces learning, karma theory simply asserts that: (1) actions have predictable consequences, (2) repeated actions increase the force or weight of any action, and (3) discontinuing the action diminishes the consequences. The main emphasis of karma theory is that all actions have consequences. The consequences of any given action are said to ripen *(smin ba)* over time, first as mental events and later as behaviors. A cumulative consequence of habitual negative actions is obscuration of the ordinary mind. Conversely, an accumulation of positive actions over time decreases negative mindstates, and increases positive states that make the mind fit for higher spiritual realizations and enlightenment.

The gradual path involves progressive learning. According to karma theory the skillful practitioner gradually refines the ordinary mind and its dysfunction so that the subtle and very subtle minds become manifest. Sometimes this process is likened to refining crude ore into a precious metal.

There are many models for the stages of meditation. The older Theravada Buddhism developed standard manuals for meditation practice like the *Path of Purification (Visuddhimagga)*[9] Around the same time, one of the first major stage models for meditation in the Indian Mahāyāna tradition appeared in the work of Asaṅga and Maitreya. In *Ornament for the Mahāyāna Sūtras (Mahāyānasūtrālaṃkāra)* and other works, Asaṅga describes two main stages of meditation—concentration and special insight.[10] He further subdivides concentration practice into nine substages called the *nine stages of the mind staying.* Concentration practice entails placing and holding the mind on the intended meditation object for longer and longer periods without distraction, learning to make the mind "stay" continuously and completely on the intended object. Reports by meditators over time led to the articulation of these nine discrete gradations or refinements in this capacity. This model eventually found its way into Tibet through the efforts of Atiśa and Kamalaśīla and was eventually adopted there as a standard presentation.[11]

In the twelfth century the Tibetan master Gampopa (1079–1153) developed a stage model for meditation called the *four-yoga* model, which integrated both the ordinary concentration and special insight practices with the extraordinary mahāmudrā practices. It consists of two ordinary stages—concentration followed by special insight meditation—and two extraordinary stages—one-taste yoga followed by nonmeditation yoga. Earlier mahāmudrā masters rarely delineated clear-cut stages because they were primarily concerned with the essence tradition and its emphasis on instantaneous realization within direct oral transmission. Gampopa's contribution was to give detailed instructions on the stages of ordinary concentration and special insight practice to establish a foundation for such realizations. Using the four-yoga approach, Gampopa integrated the sūtra and essence approaches into a single system.

TIBETAN DEVELOPMENTS

Buddhism was first introduced into Tibet in the seventh century through the efforts of itinerate Indian yogis who were invited there by Tibet's rulers. Over the centuries Tibetan Buddhism came to be organized into distinct sects or lineages. The earliest of these, the Nyingma school, venerates Padmasambhava and the dzogchen system of meditative practice. The Sakya school arose from the efforts of the Tibetan Drogmi (992–1072), who traveled to India and Nepal to study the *Hevajra Tantra* with Śāntipa. Gampopa's mahāmudrā teachings came through the lineage stemming from the Indian mahāsiddha Nāropa and his Tibetan student Marpa (1012–96). This sect became the Kagyü school, which produced the lineage of the Karmapas. The eleventh century also brought Atiśa to Tibet, and his ethical reforms, graduated teachings, and early mind-training practices permeated all the Tibetan Buddhist schools. The teachings of Atiśa and his heirs were particularly instrumental for Tsongkhapa, the great scholar of the fourteenth and fifteenth centuries. Tsongkhapa's legacy evolved into the Gelug school, which consolidated political power in Tibet in the seventeenth century under the leadership of the Dalai Lama.

The nineteenth century saw the rise of the *rimé,* or ecumenical movement, whose central figures included Dza Patrül, Mipham Rinpoche, and Jamgön Kongtrül (1813–99).[12] Kongtrül valued the contributions of all the Tibetan sects and compiled and presented the best works in a nonpartisan manner. His *Treasury of Instructions and Techniques for Spiritual Realization (Gdams ngag mdzod)* contains most of the important Kagyü meditation texts, including the primary mahāmudrā texts.

KEY TERMS IN MAHĀMUDRĀ

As a manual of meditation based on sophisticated inner technologies and traditions, this book relies on the use of precisely defined technical terms for states of mind and levels of practice. An understanding of a few key terms will help the reader navigate the book more easily.

The fundamental view of the mind in mahāmudrā is that the mind in its original state reflects its inherently awakened condition, what in earlier Buddhism was called *buddha-nature.* In the mahāmudrā tradition it is called *the way the realized mind stays (gnas lugs).* The ordinary individual, however, is blocked from realizing the mind's real nature by negative habits and erroneous ideas.

Understanding the nature of the mind in mahāmudrā is conveyed by the term *simultaneous mind (lhan cig skye sbyor)*. The term signifies that the mind's awareness and its manifest events literally "arise together" in each moment of experience. Another way to say this is that the mind's awareness and the events of ordinary consciousness form an inseparable pair, and that the perception of a duality is erroneous. Direct realization of the mind's nonduality is an essential prerequisite to awakening the mind.

The observational perspective during mahāmudrā meditation is not the ordinary sense of self. Ordinary special insight meditation on emptiness helps determine that there is no substantial, self-existing self that can serve as the point of observation during meditation. In mahāmudrā, *awareness-itself (rang rig)*, instead of ordinary self-representation, serves as the vantage point of observation during meditation, as captured by the metaphor "awareness like space." The moment-by-moment events that seem to arise in the mind during meditation are also determined to be empty. Such events are called *mere appearance* or *clarity*, and are captured by the metaphor of clear-light. Awareness-itself and mere appearance; emptiness and clarity; or space and clear-light—these are simultaneous yet nondual perspectives intrinsic to every moment of experience.

Awareness-itself, as an intrinsic property of the mind, is reflexively aware of its own nature all the time. It is described as "always staying *(gnas ba)* on the mind's real nature." The term *the way the realized mind stays (gnas lugs;* literally "the way it stays") signifies that from a certain perspective, or level of realization, awareness-itself continuously abides in realization of the mind's real nature. From that extraordinary perspective, the real nature of the mind reflects itself and remains intrinsically pure from the beginning.[13]

Another key concept in the mahāmudrā tradition is *artificial activity*. In everyday perception, dualistic perception comes from artificially constructing coarse perceptions based on the subtle mental activity associated with sense experience. This occurs habitually because of the filter of dualistic perception, and the result is the perception of self as independent and self-existing. According to the mahāmudrā tradition, the practitioner who refrains from such artificial constructions will be less obscured and therefore more likely to correctly realize the mind's real nature. When all artificial activity is eradicated, the practitioner will recognize the mind's real nature correctly. The initial realization is called *certain knowledge (nges shes)*, which happens when the ordinary mind realizes the natural condition of the extraordinary mind. The extraordinary mind sees that this realization was always there, and viewed from this extraordinary perspective, the realization is called the *recognition of awakened wisdom.*[14]

Adopting the view that the mind's real nature is nondual and already awakened has profound implications for meditation practice. From the perspective of the extraordinary mind, *any* ordinary meditation practice necessarily entails artificial activity, which risks obscuring the mind's real nature. If the intrinsic nondual condition of the simultaneous mind were properly understood, there would be no need to interfere with the mind's moment-by-moment manifestations. During meditation there would be no need to prevent or induce any particular experience *('dag sgrub).* There would be no need to release or hold on to anything. The early mahāmudrā source tradition introduced the important term *amanisakara* (Tib., *yid la ma byed pa*), or *not taking to mind.* It is sometimes translated as "no mental engagement." The term signifies that the mahāmudrā practitioner does not engage any object of awareness with any artificial mental activity whatsoever.

The companion term to *not taking to mind* is *mindfulness without [artificial activity]* (Skt., *asmṛti;* Tib., *dran med*). The term signifies that the mahāmudrā practitioner takes the mind's real nature as the object of continuous and uninterrupted mindfulness in such a way that no artificial activity whatsoever is necessary to set up or sustain mindfulness of the mind's real nature. Since the mind's real nature is awareness-itself, this kind of mindfulness essentially implies uninterrupted awareness of awareness-itself, free of any artificial activity that might otherwise obscure such awareness. Thus, mahāmudrā meditation is sometimes called *nonmeditation yoga* to distinguish between ordinary meditation, which presumes some artificial activity and a conventional object of concentration, and extraordinary meditation, which goes beyond all artificial activity and takes awareness-itself as both the vantage point and the object. These nonmeditation instructions only make sense, however, to a practitioner who has directly realized the simultaneous mind through either pointing out by the teacher or conventional meditation practices.

THE EARLY MAHĀMUDRĀ SOURCE TRADITION

The mahāmudrā tradition began as part of a spiritual folk movement in northeastern India during the Pāla dynasty (760–1142). The Pāla dynasty encompassed what is today Bengal, Bihar, Orissa, and Assam, and came into power around the time the rest of India was being conquered by Muslim invaders. Many important Pāla kings converted to Buddhism and used their power to spread Buddhism. Buddhist monastic centers like Nālandā were revitalized, and a number of other new important institutions, like Vikramaśila and Somapurī, were built.[15] Debate among Buddhist scholars was encouraged, Buddhism was translated into vernacular languages, and the royal court hired bards to sing Buddhist teachings to the populace.[16] It was during this period that Buddhism spread to Tibet.

Parallel to these advances within institutionalized Buddhism there arose a remarkable spiritual folk movement cutting across all castes. This movement consisted of a loose network of wandering *siddhas,* or adepts, who developed a variety of genuinely innovative spiritual practices, including tantric *sādhanas* and the mahāmudrā and dzogchen practices. Particularly during the eighth and ninth centuries, a virtual renaissance in spiritual innovations arose in that area of India. The key figures of this movement became known as the eighty-four siddhas. These wandering siddhas shared many practices and realizations with each other, and some also migrated northward into Tibet.

The origin of mahāmudrā is attributed to the Bengali Brahmin, Rāhula, who later became known as Saraha. While the exact dates of Saraha's life are unknown, he probably lived during the late eighth and early ninth centuries.[17] According to the oral tradition, Saraha received the direct transmission of mahāmudrā from a celestial ḍākinī. The name Saraha literally means "the one who shot the arrow," symbolizing the penetrating realization of mahāmudrā. After his realization Saraha reportedly stopped performing his Brahmin rites, gave up celibacy, and took up with a consort, a low-caste woman.[18]

Saraha is said to be the source of the first song-poems on mahāmudrā. These early songs were written in the vernacular languages of Bengal. Two very early forms of this literature survive. The *cāryapādas* are written in old Bengali, and the *dohās* are written in Western Apabhraṃsa. Both collections are in verse, and probably were sung from teacher to student for generations before they were written down. About fifty cāryapādas survived and a number of major and lesser dohās, comprising what has been called the *source tradition.* Three dohās attributed to Saraha—the *People's Songs,* the *King's Songs,* and the *Queen's Songs*—together are known as the *Heart of Siddhi.*[19] A collection of lesser works attributed to Saraha is called the *Ten Teachings of Mahāmudrā.*[20]

These works introduce some of mahāmudrā's main features. These teachings claim that direct pointing-out instructions from teacher to student are necessary to establish the correct view of the very subtle mind.[21] The correct view of mind is the mind in its natural condition, described by the concept of the simultaneous mind that couples absolute truth with the bliss of relative truth,[22] and by the fundamental nonduality of mind. The texts stress the importance of not obstructing the spontaneous relative activity of the mind. This extraordinary view of the mind is achieved through appreciating the inseparability of wisdom and skillful means, and through negation of all conventional means to achieve this realization, because these are based on artificial activity. Saraha negates conventional practices such as Brahmanic rites, asceticism, meditation, doctrinal study, and tantric sādhana practice. The innovative skillful means Saraha advocates are based on "nonaction" (las med) or "nonmeditation," because any conventional meditation practice is based on artificial activity. The practitioner must set up the exact conditions for realizing the mind's natural condition without resorting to artificial meditative activity. The practitioner simply lets the mind "stay"—connected with the correct view continuously—learns to recognize awakened wisdom as an intrinsic property of the mind in its natural state, and then protects the realization.[23] Saraha also introduced the two innovative methods of *mindfulness without activity* and *not taking to mind.*

According to the *Blue Annals,* the Indian masters transmitted the mahāmudrā teachings to Tibet over roughly three hundred years.[24] Saraha taught mahāmudrā to his main disciple, Śabari, an untouchable from a hunting and gathering tribe from Vindhya. The lineage continued with Lūipa, Ḍeṅgipa, Vajraghaṇṭa, Kambala, Jālandhara, Kṛṣnācārya, Vijayapāda, Tilopa, Nāropa, and then Marpa, who brought it to Tibet and taught it to Milarepa.[25] Tibetan sources give the lineage as Śabari, Maitripa, and then Vajrapāṇi, with the latter two figures playing crucial roles in transmitting the mahāmudrā teachings to Tibet, as we will see below.[26]

TANTRIC MAHĀMUDRĀ

Tantric practice involves complex visualizations and practices working with subtle energy currents. *Tantric mahāmudrā* is a synthesis of mahāmudrā and tantric practices. Many of the eighty-four siddhas, including Saraha, learned and transmitted both mahāmudrā as well as a number of tantric practices, especially the Guhyasamāja, Cakrasaṃvara, and Hevajra tantras.

There is some reason to believe that the tantric version of mahāmudrā was the innovation of Padmavajra, a Brahmin from Bengal, much as the original source mahāmudrā was the innovation of Saraha. Padmavajra is also credited with originating the *Hevajra Tantra*.[27]

In tantric mahāmudrā the practitioner masters tantric generation-stage and completion-stage practices. Generation-stage practice involves complex visualizations of deities within celestial *maṇḍalas* or mansions, and the practitioner supplicates the deities with offerings, prayers, mantra recitations. During the completion stage, the practitioner directs the energy currents into the central channel, activating the indestructible subtle consciousness in the heart. The resultant very subtle clear-light mind is then used to realize emptiness.[28] In tantric mahāmudrā, mahāmudrā is introduced as an advanced practice concurrent with or after mastery of the completion stage.[29]

While sūtra mahāmudrā addresses the simultaneous mind's thought and appearance, tantric mahāmudrā addresses the simultaneous mind's great bliss.[30] Texts from the early tantric mahāmudrā tradition depart from the source tradition texts that negate all forms of practice, including tantric sādhana practice, as forms of artificial activity. Instead, tantric mahāmudrā advocates the mastery of tantric meditation as a prerequisite for receiving the pointing out of the mahāmudrā view.

THE SOURCE TRANSLATION LINEAGE

Some Tibetan sources describe transmissions of mahāmudrā to Tibet other than the transmission through Marpa. These other transmissions are known as the *source translation lineage*. According to the *Blue Annals,* the source translation lineage had three waves, the early, intermediate, and later transmissions. All three waves have Maitripa as their common root and occurred in the eleventh and early twelfth centuries.

Maitripa is said to have taught the mahāmudrā directly to Atiśa, who in turn taught it to the Tibetan layman Dromtön. However, Dromtön did not sanction the practice for Tibetans. Maitripa also taught the mahāmudrā to Karopa, who then taught it to Dempa Korba, who in turn taught it to Nirūpa. Nirūpa is said to have taken the mahāmudrā teachings directly to Lhasa at the end of the eleventh century. Maitripa also taught the mahāmudrā to Vairocanarakṣita, who traveled to many countries spreading the mahāmudrā teachings, particularly Saraha's *Heart of Siddhi* teachings and Śabari's *Oral Advice on Mahāmudrā*. These transmissions constitute the early phase of the source translation lineage in Tibet.

Maitripa is said to have had twenty-one disciples, of which there were "four great ones." Of these the most important is Vajrapāṇi. Vajrapāṇi and his companion disciple Dharmaśrī had thirty important Tibetan disciples who spread the teachings throughout Tibet. This is known as the upper school of the intermediate phase of the source translation lineage in Tibet. Maitripa also had a Nepalese disciple named Asu who developed a special way of teaching mahāmudrā among the Tibetans called the *Cycle of Pebbles (Rde'u skor)*. This tradition became known as the lower school of the intermediate phase of the source translation lineage in Tibet.

Of Vajrapāṇi's numerous disciples who spread mahāmudrā teachings in Tibet, one, Rechungpa, transmitted the oral teachings in the form of the ear-whispering tradition. Another, Nagpo Serdad, transmitted the mahāmudrā to Lama So. This wave of teachings became known as the later phase of the source translation lineage in Tibet.

All three waves of the source translation lineage are said to have degenerated, and it died out as a distinct lineage after the twelfth century.[31]

THE SUBSIDIARY LINEAGE

The subsidiary *(zhur 'gyur)* transmission of mahāmudrā from Nāropa in India to Marpa in Tibet, also in the eleventh century, survived largely because it was popularized by the great saint Milarepa and then codified by Gampopa and integrated into the emerging monastic system. The subsidiary lineage originated with Tilopa (988–1069), who lived in what is now Bangladesh. He is said to have come from a lineage of *kusulipas*, practitioners with extensive experience in meditation.[32] This is important because Tilopa may have been the first to integrate ordinary meditation practice with mahāmudrā. He supposedly learned mahāmudrā first from a ḍākinī and then from the cosmic Buddha Vajradhāra.[33] Tilopa wrote two important works on mahāmudrā—the *Treasury of Songs* and the *Ganges Mahāmudrā*.[34] Tilopa used the same kind of direct pointing out as did Saraha and Śabari. However his writings introduce the requirement that the student "enter into samādhi" in order to receive the instructions about the mind's real nature. In order words, Tilopa departs from the source tradition texts that negate all forms of practice, including traditional concentration and insight meditation, as forms of artificial activity. Instead, Tilopa advocates mastery of traditional meditation as a prerequisite for pointing-out instructions. After receiving the pointing-out instructions during a special, extraordinary samādhi, the practitioner then uses nonmeditation instructions to develop awakened wisdom. For example, the *Treasury of Songs* states:

> Make an offering to the Buddha while in a nonconceptual still state.
> Do not stay in saṃsāra or nirvāṇa.
> Enter into the samādhi of skillful means on awakened wisdom.
> Once immovable and firm in that,
> You'll have the realization [of awakened wisdom].[35]

Tilopa taught mahāmudrā to Nāropa (1016–1100), who was born in Bengal and attended the famous Buddhist university at Nālandā. There he presumably studied ordinary concentration and special insight meditation, and he eventually became one of the principal abbots. He left in search of Tilopa, studied with him for twelve years, and eventually taught mahāmudrā at a hermitage in Phummahari.[36] Nāropa wrote the *Aphorisms of Mahāmudrā,* wherein the entire body of mahāmudrā teachings is condensed into thirteen stanzas. Nāropa explains that the special samādhi approach to mahāmudrā involves setting up continuous, uninterrupted awareness of the mind's intrinsic nature. This awareness is free of ordinary, artificial meditative activity, such as visualizing a meditation object in concentration or reviewing the field of experience in special insight meditation. Apparently, these nonmeditation instructions were developed for less advanced students who do not immediately realize the real nature of the mind upon hearing the pointing-out instructions.[37] Nāropa makes a clear distinction between ordinary concentration and special insight meditation, which involve artificial mental activity, and extraordinary mahāmudrā meditation, which does not. This distinction between levels of meditation paves the way for the eventual development of a meditation-stages version of sūtra mahāmudrā.

Nāropa taught mahāmudrā to the Tibetan Marpa. Born in Lhodrak in southern Tibet (1012–96), Marpa learned Sanskrit and became a translator for Drogmi Lotsāwa, who originated the Sakya lineage of Tibetan Buddhism. Marpa received mahāmudrā instructions from Maitripa as well as Nāropa,[38] and therefore he was able to synthesize the source translation and subsidiary transmissions of mahāmudrā at the end of the eleventh century and pass on an integrated version that was destined to have a lasting influence.[39] Marpa used a number of metaphors to describe how to set up the extraordinary samādhi—the small child, the outcast, the elephant, and the bee. He also expanded the instructions for protecting the realization of the mind's natural state and gave a detailed description of the basis, path, and fruition moments of enlightenment in the mahāmudrā tradition.[40]

One of Marpa's main disciples was Milarepa (1052–1135). Milarepa was famous for preserving the oral tradition of teaching mahāmudrā through songs, for example, *The Hundred Thousand Songs of Milarepa.*[41] He was also famous for passing the teachings to his main disciple Gampopa, who codified the sūtra mahāmudrā tradition.

In the nineteenth century, Jamgön Kongtrül classified the surviving mahāmudrā texts into the *Cycle of Source Texts and Their Commentaries* and the *Oral Advice and Practice Texts for Stages of Mahāmudrā Meditation.*[42] The former texts trace a lineage from Saraha in India to Marpa in Tibet, and then to his students Turtönpa, Rechungpa, and Milarepa, and then from Milarepa to Gampopa. Turtönpa and Rechungpa continued the original oral transmission of mahāmudrā teachings as part of the cycle of oral transmission, also known as the ear-whispering lineage. They continued to use the old style of direct pointing-out instructions. Rechungpa's *Clear Wisdom Mahāmudrā*[43] describes the stages of practice and the ripening of enlightenment retrospectively. The first two sections of his text describe the body and the actual meditation practices from the perspective of the enlightened mind. The third, expanded section describes in detail the exact conditions for setting up enlightenment, the stages in recognizing awakened wisdom, the changes in the subtle energy currents that accompany the dawning of awakened wisdom, and the stages of enlightenment. Rechungpa's text gives one of the richest accounts ever recorded of all the subtle changes prior to, during, and following mahāmudrā enlightenment. The last section also gives a detailed description of post-enlightenment path-walking instructions. This text illustrates that by the beginning of the twelfth century, an extremely sophisticated technical language had evolved for extraordinary-level mahāmudrā practices and experiences.

GAMPOPA AND MONASTIC MAHĀMUDRĀ

Gampopa codified the emerging subsidiary lineage integration of ordinary meditation practice and the extraordinary mahāmudrā practices into a standardized monastic practice at the beginning of the twelfth century.

He institutionalized mahāmudrā practice by forming Dagpo Monastery. This monastic practice was built on a foundation of ethical precepts, followed by mastery of traditional meditation-stages practice—concentration training followed by special insight practice. Dagpo became the "seat" of the new Kagyü order.

That Gampopa is responsible for a new form of mahāmudrā is exemplified by his *Explanation of the Sole Path of Mahāmudrā* and also to some extent his *Jewel Ornament of Liberation*. According to Jamgön Kongtrül the *Explanation* is Gampopa's primary source text on his version of mahāmudrā practice. The *Explanation* is divided into three parts: Resolving the Way the Realized Mind Stays, Pointing Out the Way of Existence, and Purifying the Path [Based on the View of] Thatness. The first two parts point out the correct view of the simultaneous mind, its absolute and relative dimensions, respectively. The last section presents the actual meditation-stages instructions in the following sequence: (1) preliminary practices, including guru yoga, (2) essential practices of concentration and ordinary special insight to develop an undistracted view of the mind's real nature, (3) concluding, extraordinary practices, in which awareness-itself, undistracted, tracks the simultaneous mind and its manifestations until the realization of awakened wisdom dawns.

The structure of this text illustrates Gampopa's innovative synthesis. Until the third and last section, none of the practices are specific to mahāmudrā. Following that, the practitioner learns a set of extraordinary practices based on the mahāmudrā view of the simultaneous mind and on nonmeditation, the mahāmudrā skillful means. This four-yoga model, although very different from that of the source tradition, became the standard mahāmudrā instruction for monastic Buddhism from the twelfth century to the present.

Mahāmudrā Schools and Lineages of the Kagyü Tradition

Gampopa had twelve important disciples, and these spawned the Four Primary Lineages and the Eight Secondary Lineages that comprise the Dagpo Kagyü tradition. The Four Primary Dagpo lineages derived from Gampopa's four principal disciples: Düsum Khyenpa, Barom, Pagmodrupa, and Tselpa.

Düsum Khyenpa (1110–93) received and mastered the six yogas of

Nāropa and the mahāmudrā teachings directly from Gampopa, and studied mahāmudrā with Vairocanarakṣita as well. Following that he established many monasteries, the most important being Tsurpu, which became the seat of the Karma Kamtsang lineage, the lineage of the Karmapa. Düsum Khyenpa was the first Karmapa. There has been an unbroken lineage of Karmapas until the present Seventeeth Karmapa, Orgyen Trinlé Dorjé.[44] Within the Karmapa lineage, the Third Karmapa, Rangjung Dorjé (1284–1339) came from a family of masters of concentration meditation. He wrote several important works on mahāmudrā, including a very popular *Devotional Prayer* that has been translated in this book as well as elsewhere.[45] The Ninth Karmapa, Wangchug Dorjé (1555–1603) is well known for several mahāmudrā texts, including *The Mahāmudrā: Eliminating the Darkness of Ignorance.*[46] The Karmapa lineage developed a particular approach to mahāmudrā known as the *simultaneously arisen as merged* school of mahāmudrā. This tradition emphasizes that the simultaneous mind is the dharmakāya and that all thought and appearances are manifestations of the dharmakāya and that therefore these are inseparable, like water and waves.[47]

One of the other four primary disciples, Pagmodrupa (1110–70),[48] had eight disciples, who in turn formed the Eight Secondary Lineages of mahāmudrā. Of these eight, two—Lingrepa and Jigten Sumgön—originated lineages that have had lasting historical importance, the Drugpa Kagyü and Drigung Kagyü, respectively.

The Drugpa Kagyü lineage is especially important. They developed a school of mahāmudrā known as the *six aspects of one taste rolled into a ball.* This tradition is said to have originated from Rechungpa, who wrote and buried an original one-taste text. Later unearthed by Lingrepa's disciple, Tsangpa Gyaré, the text became the backbone of the Drugpa mahāmudrā tradition. This school developed a method for taking difficult life situations—thoughts, emotional states, illnesses, spiritual influences, everyday suffering, and dying—as a way of enhancing the realization of awakened wisdom at the extraordinary level of mahāmudrā practice. The Drugpa lineage produced some of the main authorities on mahāmudrā, namely Pema Karpo, who wrote important root texts, and Tashi Namgyel, who wrote the extensive authoritative commentary known as the *Moonlight.*

The Drigung Kagyü lineage, founded by Pagmodrupa's chief disciple, Jigten Sumgön (1143–1217),[49] developed the *five parts* school of mahāmudrā. This school places considerable emphasis on guru yoga and the necessity of pointing-out instructions and also the development of mental stabilization and insight into emptiness via traditional concentration and special insight practices as preparation for advanced mahāmudrā realizations.[50] One of his successors, Künga Rinchen (1475–1527) wrote *The Garland of Mahāmudrā Practices.*[51]

Independent of all the Dagpo lineages is the Shangpa Kagyü lineage, which originated with Khyungpo Neljor (910–1139). The Shangpa lineage developed a particular approach to mahāmudrā called the *amulet box* tradition. The amulet box tradition emphasizes how the three attainments of deep concentration—nonconceptual stillness, clarity, and bliss—become the flaws of advanced practice due to attachment to these attainments. The corresponding aspects of the real nature of the mind are emptiness, clear appearance, and clear light. The practitioner with the correct realization purifies these three flaws, and the corresponding aspects of the intrinsic mind give rise to the three buddha bodies, the truth body *(dharmakāya),* enjoyment body *(saṃbhogakāya),* and emanation body *(nirmāṇakāya),* respectively. These three attainments of stillness, clarity, and bliss are either sources of attachment or awakening depending on your perspective, like two sides of an amulet box. Realizing the very subtle clear-light mind is a central focus in the amulet box tradition.[52]

The *four syllables* school of mahāmudrā originated with Maitripa and survived in some Dagpo Kagyü lineages.[53] The "four syllables" name is taken from the Sanskrit technical term, *amanasi,* derived from the compound *amanasikara (a/ma/na/si/kara;* Tib., *yid la ma byed pa).* The four points to this teaching on mahāmudrā include: (1) cutting off the root of ignorance by realizing emptiness, (2) settling the mind in samādhi on the correct view of the natural mind, (3) protecting against errors, and (4) taking the natural mind and its manifestations as the path.[54]

Padampa Sangyé, an Indian disciple of Maitripa who taught in Tibet, developed the Pacifier (Tib,. *zhi byed*) school,[55] which no longer exists but which historically had close ties to the Shangpa Kagyü. The Pacifier tradition emphasized how realization of awakened wisdom in mahāmudrā practice pacifies all impurities and false cognitions.

These various schools of mahāmudra all share a similar view of the mind's natural condition, namely the simultaneous mind with its absolute and relative dimensions being nondual and inseparable. They differ primarily in their emphasis on which manifestations of mind serves as the vehicle for the realization and in the method prescribed. For example, some emphasize clear light as the foundation for realization, others emphasize thought, appearance, adversity, or the dharmakāya. As for method, some emphasize the pointing-out instruction, for example, while others emphasize nonmeditation. These differences do not represent doctrinal differences as much as they represent different ways of organizing and presenting the teachings to practitioners.

Mahāmudrā in the Nyingma and Gelug Traditions

As the mahāmudrā tradition evolved over the centuries, attempts to forge an integration of mahāmudrā with the main practices of the other Tibetan sects was inevitable. The main integrative works appeared around the seventeenth century.

Karma Chagmé (1613–78) is known for his important synthesis of Nyingma dzogchen practice with Kagyü mahāmudrā. His primary work is *Meaningful to Behold,* and a related more condensed work is *Buddhahood in the Palm of Your Hand.*[56] Karma Chagmé was an accomplished dzogchen master who also received teachings from the Karmapa. After a thirteen-year meditation retreat, he wrote these two works based on his direct experiential synthesis of the two traditions. Karma Chagmé states that mahāmudrā and dzogchen share a fundamental concern with the essential nature of the mind, particularly the mind's intrinsic nature at the extraordinary or very subtle level. At this level of mind, emptiness (the absolute perspective) and clarity (the relative perspective) are nondual, and being inseparable there is no need to obstruct the mind's manifestations. The main difference between mahāmudrā and dzogchen according to Karma Chagmé is that:

> Unlike the view that the mind is at first contaminated and then gradually, through practice, becomes pure, in this context the essential nature of the mind is originally pure, and it corresponds to the *dharmakāya.*[57]

In this sense Karma Chagmé advocates for a view of mahāmudrā that is closer to the original source tradition than the meditation-stages model of the Dagpo lineage. While Karma Chagmé concedes that ordinary concentration and special insight meditation lay the foundation for mahāmudrā/dzogchen practice, his work mainly addresses the extraordinary level of practice. As previously explained, in the mahāmudrā, the extraordinary level of practice is defined as one-taste yoga followed by nonmeditation yoga, which leads to enlightenment. Karma Chagmé recasts meditation of the relative aspects of thought and appearance characteristic of one-taste yoga in terms of the dzogchen concept of *spontaneous presence (lhun gyis grub)*. Consistent with the mahāmudrā, however, he sees all relative events as "creative expressions of the nature of awareness."[58]

A unique feature of his synthesis is that he greatly expands the description of nonmeditation practice. His version of nonmeditation yoga contains the traditional mahāmudrā instructions regarding (1) continuous mindfulness of the real nature of the mind without any artificial activity (recast as an aspect of spontaneous presence), and (2) not taking to mind anything. However, Karma Chagmé gives considerably greater detail than most mahāmudrā texts (except Rechungpa's) about how to set up the exact conditions for the initial recognition of awakened wisdom and its ripening as full enlightenment in the form of the three buddha bodies. He draws upon the dzogchen concepts of *breaking through* and *leaping over* to give a highly elaborate description of the visions occurring when awakened wisdom dawns, as well as of how to shift awareness from seeming individual consciousness to the ground of awareness-itself, the dharmakāya. The instructions on crossing over to enlightenment in the mahāmudrā tradition are rarely as detailed as the breaking through and leaping over instructions in Karma Chagmé's integrated work.

In the Gelug school, the First Panchen Lama, Lobsang Chökyi Gyeltsen (1567–1662), illuminated an important synthesis of the Gelug emphasis on a refined understanding of emptiness with the extraordinary level of mind described in the mahāmudrā tradition. The Kagyü-Gelug integration originated with Tsongkhapa, but the First Panchen Lama wrote the primary text of that integrated lineage, *A Root Text for the Precious Gelug/Kagyü Tradition of Mahāmudrā*.[59] The concept of the simultaneous mind in the mahāmudrā tradition implies the fundamental inseparability of absolute truth (emptiness) and relative truth (clarity). According to the First Panchen Lama, the Kagyü mahāmudrā tradition emphasizes the relative dimension—namely the clear-light mind and its manifestations as thought and appearance—while the Gelug tradition emphasizes the absolute dimension—namely the realization of emptiness. In this sense, both traditions are quite compatible and reinforce each other's main realization. Gelug works on the relationship between emptiness and dependent arising, paralleling the Kagyü emphasis on the inseparability of the mind and its appearances. The First Panchen Lama offers a stage-model for integrating Kagyü and Gelug mahāmudrā practice that uses the Gelug meditations on emptiness as a foundation for the Kagyü mahāmudrā extraordinary practice, namely mindfulness of the real nature of the mind and its clear-light dimension. In this synthesis, clear-light mind is used ultimately as the level of mind meditating on emptiness.[60]

Navigating this Book

Types of Texts

In Buddhism the stages of spiritual development are commonly divided into motivational practices, preliminary practices, concentration training, ordinary special insight practice, followed by extraordinary practice. Some texts pertain to only a certain stage, while others cut across several stages. Some texts cover the overall path of spiritual development, like *stages of the path (lam rim)* texts.

Root texts (rtsa ba) are highly condensed instructions. Such texts are very difficult for the scholar to unpack because of the density of technical terms. Root texts are designed as concise distillations of key instructions to be used in meditation. It is understood that the reader already has a deep knowledge of the terms referenced in the root text, and the root text thus serves as an aid to memory. Sometimes these brief root texts are expanded into *practical manuals (khrid)*. Practical manuals give the basic meditation instructions with sparse explanation.

To get a more detailed explanation the practitioner turns to the commentaries. There are several types of commentaries. *Expansion commentaries (khrid yig)* describe a particular practice in greater detail than found in the root texts or manuals. *Explanatory commentaries ('grel ba)* generally place the practices within the wider Buddhist context. *Oral advice (man ngag)* are instructions given in a form tailored to the recipient. Sometimes path-stages *(lam rim)* and meditation-stages *(sgom rim)* texts intentionally leave out critical instructions to prevent the uninitiated from trying to practice without the help of a teacher. The teacher generally gives the missing instructions in the form of oral advice. Most oral advice is never written down, but some has been written down and has passed from generation to generation.

This book uses root texts, practice manuals, oral advice, and expanded commentaries. Root texts were used because they present the practice exactly as presented to practitioners on retreat. These instructions are amplified using important practical manuals, commentaries, and oral teachings.

An Integrated Synthetic Text

A number of the most widely cited texts spanning six hundred years of the sūtra mahāmudrā meditation-stages tradition were selected as source material for this study. Each of these primary texts was compared to all the other texts in an effort to construct a complete picture of spiritual development stage by stage, from the very beginning of practice to the post-enlightenment practices.

One problem encountered in comparing texts was that not all of the texts describe the stages of meditation in the same way. Some texts adopt an outline method of presentation *(sa bcad)*, but these outlines do not necessarily follow the progression in actual experience as meditation unfolds. Other texts utilize a stages method of presentation *(rim pa)*, wherein each stage represents a discrete set of practice instructions along with a description of resultant meditation experience. Still other texts divide meditation into practice modules *(thun)*, in which the set of instructions is given with the expectation that it be mastered before going on to the next practice module. Practice modules may be given for part of a single meditation stage or may span several meditation stages.

Despite these different forms of presentation, a careful comparison of texts nevertheless reveals a deep structure to the mahāmudrā meditation-stages that cuts across all these styles. Based on this comparative approach, this book maps the deep structure for the sūtra mahāmudrā tradition with the following progression.

I. Motivational practices
    A. Generating interest
    B. Causing faith to arise
II. Preparatory practices
    A. Preliminary practices
        1. Ordinary preliminaries
        2. Extraordinary preliminaries
        3. Advanced preliminaries

Gampopa's four-yoga model includes the main ordinary and extraordinary insight practices—concentration, nonelaboration, one taste, and nonmeditation—but fails to elaborate on the beginning motivational and preliminary practices and also on the enlightenment and post-enlightenment practices. The complete map includes seven main stages, each of which has three substages (three substages to the preliminaries, three substages to the isolations, three substages to concentration with support, three to concentration without support, three to special insight, three to one-taste yoga, and three substages to nonmeditation yoga), making a total of twenty-one stages. In addition, these twenty-one stages are prefaced and concluded with two practices—two preparatory motivational practices, and two enlightenment/post-enlightenment practices—bringing the total number of stages to twenty-five. This book will describe the practices and resultant experiences for each of the twenty-five stages in step-by-step detail.

Using this comparative method it was also possible to identify the essential elements for each stage of sūtra mahāmudrā meditation practice. The traditional Indo-Tibetan Buddhist way to present meditation-stage practice is in terms of four dimensions: (1) the view of the mind adopted *(lta ba),* (2) the way to practice *(tshul),* i.e., the specific meditation instructions given, (3) the resultant meditation experience or desired outcome *(yon tan; dngos ba)* described with often very precise technical terms, and (4) the technical description of the mistakes, errors, and other problems that prevent the outcome. This book will follow the traditional Indo-Tibetan method in that each of the twenty-five stages include a description of the underlying assumptions about or view of the mind, the most commonly used meditation methods, a detailed technical description of the resultant meditation experience, and a review of the problems and mistakes that typically occur and how to correct them. Comparing a number of widely cited texts allowed me to extract the specific meditation methods at each stage of practice and reconstruct the resultant state in technically precise detail. The creation of a synthetic text, rather than translating an existing text, was intended to open up the entire world of meditation experience and give the reader the opportunity to enter that world with all its richness and complexity.

One problem encountered in working with these texts is that some texts present meditation experience in a stage-by-stage model *(rim gyis)*. Some even elaborate or expand upon *(chug zad spros ba)* the description of experience for each stage of meditation. Other texts, especially root texts and practical manuals, present the practice in a highly condensed form *(bsdu ba)*, wherein a number of stages or substages of meditation are covered by the strategic juxtaposition of a small number of technical terms. Yet other texts take a series of meditation-stages practices and mix them *('dres ba)* into a single practice. To effectively handle this common style of presentation in this book, the reader is first introduced to an expanded version of each stage of meditation through a detailed account of the meditation instructions and technical terms describing the resultant experience. Along with an elaborate description of this internal landscape for each stage, condensed passages are cited from the root texts, practical manuals, or commentaries to illustrate how this material is actually used by the practitioner. After the reader has become familiar with a detailed description of a particular stage, a mixed practice is presented to give the reader an appreciation of the condensed and rapid way that skilled practitioners review stages of meditation.

SEMANTIC FIELD ANALYSIS

The primary approach used to analyze these meditation texts is the *ethno-semantic* or *semiotic* approach in cognitive anthropology, specifically a method called *semantic field analysis*.[61] This method developed as a way to understand how indigenous groups conceptualize culture-specific experiences and express them in technical language. Every technical term used in each of the selected mahāmudrā meditation texts was recorded along with its specific contexts of usage. After seeing how a given technical term was used many times at different points within a given text and across a number of texts, it was possible to construct a semantic field for that term. A semantic field defines the primary meaning and cluster of associated meanings for any given term and also defines or delimits its specific context or contexts of usage. Studying patterns of usage leads to mapping the interrelationship or degree of association between different technical terms.

One result of this approach for this book is that each major meditation stage has its own unique fabric of technical terms. The terms used to describe the motivational practices are distinct from those used to describe the preliminary practices, as are those to describe concentration meditation, ordinary special insight meditation, and the extraordinary one-taste and nonmeditation practices. The semantic field approach thus yields the reader a linguistic cartography or map for the entire landscape of each stage of meditation practice, with a richness and precision of technical detail not generally found in the available Western literature.

The semantic field method assists the reader in understanding the inner experiences of meditation for all twenty-five stages of the sūtra mahāmudrā meditation-stages according to how they are understood by practitioners within Tibetan Buddhism. As this book is strictly about how mahāmudrā meditation is conceived by indigenous Tibetan practitioners, no attempt has been made to use Sanskrit terms to control for translation. Nor has any attempt been made to make the translations fluid or poetic; such translations, while easily readable, discard a good deal of the technical precision necessary to describe inner meditation experiences accurately. The translations in this book are highly technical, and at times may seem awkward in English, yet they preserve the original technical terms and their structure of presentation in a manner that challenges the reader to enter the world of mahāmudrā meditation as it is actually practiced.

THE SELECTION OF TEXTS

The primary texts used in this book come from the Dagpo lineage of sūtra mahāmudrā. Jamgön Kongtrül's *Treasury of Instructions* served as the source for many of the primary root texts, oral advice, and practical manuals consulted.[62] The texts are drawn from both the Karma Kagyü and Drugpa Kagyü lineages.

According to Jamgön Kongtrül the most important Kagyü mahāmudrā root text was written by Dagpo Tashi Namgyel (1513–87), the fourth Drugchen, who wrote his famous work nearly four centuries after Gampopa at a time when the meditation-stages approach was highly developed. The text is called *The Natural Condition of Thatness and Clarity: A Practical Manual on Mahāmudrā and Its Explanation.*[63] Tashi Namgyel's own massive commentary to his root text is called *The Moon's Clear Light: A Detailed Explanation that Makes Clear the Mahāmudrā Meditation-Stages and Certain Truth.*[64] The *Moonlight* is by far the most influential single text in the mahāmudrā tradition.

I've also used several important mahāmudrā texts written by the Karmapas. The Third Karmapa, Rangjung Dorjé (1284–1339), wrote *A Practical Manual for the Simultaneous School of Mahāmudrā*[65] as well the *Devotional Prayer* mentioned earlier. Rangjung Dorjé is said to have originated the intensive practice instruction lineage, which plays an important role in the three-year meditation retreat later popularized by Jamgön Kongtrül.[66] From the Ninth Karmapa, Wangchug Dorjé (1556–1603), I use two related root texts, the first a brief practical manual and the second an expanded version of that manual. Wangchug Dorjé also composed a liturgical text related to these two[67] and a larger text for meditation retreat masters.[68]

The famous reformist of the Drugpa Kagyü sect, Pema Karpo (1597–92), composed a short but significant root text called *Practice Guidelines of the Simultaneous School of Mahāmudrā of the Drugpa Kagyü Sect.*[69] Jampel Pawo (1720–80) wrote an expanded commentary on Pema Karpo's root text called *The Certainty of the Diamond Mind.*[70]

Many of the above texts greatly condense their coverage of the beginning, preliminary practices and the ending, post-enlightenment path-walking practices because these have been described elsewhere. Therefore, this book draws upon several important works devoted to the mahāmudrā preliminary practices, such as Jamgön Kongtrül's *Torch of Certainty.*[71] The most encyclopedic commentary on the preliminary practices is Künga Tendzin's (1680–1728) *Jewel of Essential Wisdom.*[72] Together, these two works provide the basis for the detailed explanations of the preliminary practices described in this book. This book also uses two popular post-enlightenment path-walking texts, *The Oral Transmission of the Six Cycles of Same Taste* by Pema Karpo and *The Oral Advice on Path-Walking in Five-Parts Mahāmudrā* by the Eighth Situ.[73]

The primary texts used as source material for this book are summarized in the table at the end of this introduction. Abbreviations will be used throughout the book when citing passages from these texts.

TECHNICAL NOTES

To help the reader identify and appreciate the technical terms for meditation experience used throughout the book, I have adopted certain conventions for marking technical terms. Transliteration of the Tibetan terms follows the Wylie system of transliteration.[74] Whenever a technical term is first introduced, I give the English rendering followed by the Tibetan term in parentheses. Whenever a technical term appears subsequently, it is not highlighted. Since the root texts and practical meditation manuals are characterized by a profuse juxtaposition of technical terms, their complexity is often missed in English translations. The astute reader will discern that juxtaposition of terms in the original Tibetan is meant to convey the structure of the meditation experience.

Because of their highly condensed syntax, many root texts are unintelligible without supplemental words. I have added such clarifying words in brackets after consulting other sources so that the reader may have a more complete understanding of the meaning in its full context.

The location of terms and cited passages are marked by an abbreviation of the author's frequently cited works, followed by the blockprint folio where it is found. For example "JP, f. 32a" means that the passage cited is found on folio 32, side a, of Jampel Pawo's commentary on Pema Karpo's root text.

Source Text Abbreviations

BCA   *Bodhicaryāvatāra* of Śāntideva (my own translation from the Sanskrit). The classical guide to the path of the bodhisattva.

JK   Jamgön Kongtrül. *The Torch of Certainty (Phyag chen sngon 'dro bzhi sbyor dang dngos gzhi'i khrid rim mdor bsdus nges don sgron me).* An important work on the preliminary practices.

JP   Jampel Pawo. *The Certainty of the Diamond Mind (Phyag rgya chen po lhan cig skyes sbyor dngos gzhi'i khrid yig cung zad spros pa sems kyi rdo rje'i nges gnas gsal bar byed pa).* A detailed commentary on Pema Karpo's root text.

KT   Künga Tendzin. *The Jewel of Essential Wisdom (Phyag rgya chen po lhan cig skyes sbyor gyi sngon 'gro'i khrid yig zab rgyas chos kyi rgya mtsho chen po nas snying po ye shes kyi nor bu 'dren par byed pa'i gru chen).* An extensive commentary on the preliminary stages of mahāmudrā practice.

PK   Pema Karpo. *Practice Guidelines of the Simultaneous School of Mahāmudrā. (Phyag chen gyi zin bris bzhyes).* A popular root text from the Drugpa Kagyü lineage.

PK-S   Pema Karpo. *The Oral Transmission of the Six Cycles of Same Taste: Rolled into a Ball [Path-Walking] Instructions (Ro snyoms skor drug gi nyams len sgong du dril ba).* Instructions on post-enlightenment practices.

RD   Rangjung Dorjé, the Third Karmapa. *A Practical Manual for the Simultaneous School of Mahāmudrā (Phyag rgya chen po lhan cig skyes sbyor gyi khrid yig).* A popular root text.

TN   Tashi Namgyel. *The Moonlight Mahāmudrā (Nges don phyag rgya chen po'i sgom rim sgal bar byed pa'i legs bsad zla ba'i od zer)*. The main commentary on the sūtra mahāmudrā meditation-stages.

TN (root)   Tashi Namgyel. *The Natural Condition of Thatness and Clarity (Phyag rgya chen po'i khrid yig chen mo gnyug ma'i de nyid gsal ba)*. The root text that serves as the basis of the commentary.

Si   Eighth Situpa, Chökyi Jungné. *The Oral Advice on Path-Walking in Five-Parts Mahāmudrā (Phyag chen lnga ldan gyi khrid yig)*. Instructions on post-enlightenment practices.

WD   Wangchug Dorjé, the Ninth Karmapa. *An Introductory Practical Manual on Simultaneous Mahāmudrā (Phyag rgya chen po lhan cig skyes sbyor gyi khrid kyi spyi sdom rtsa tshig)* and *An Expanded Practical Manual on Simultaneous Mahāmudrā (Phyag rgya chen po lhan cig skye sbyor gyi khrid yig zin bris snying po gsal ba'i sgron me sdud rtsi nying khu chos sku mdzub tshugs su ngo sprod pa)*. A short root text followed by an expanded set of practical instructions.

1. Cultivating the Motivation ....

I. Generating Interest
75

A. Interest

ORDINARY LIFE IS FILLED with suffering, and this suffering is the result of attachments and passions. Such attachments obscure *(sgrib pa)* understanding. Our belief systems and view of reality are inevitably limited, so ordinary beings are not capable of judging which beliefs are false and which hold certain truth *(nges don)*. The Buddha's teachings, the Dharma *(chos)*, are said to be valuable precisely because they directly *(mngon du)* pertain to the condition of everyday life. Yet, blinded by ignorance, sentient beings fail to realize even the first noble truth about their lives and the world around them; namely, that the condition of everyday life and of the entire phenomenal realm—saṃsāra *('khor ba)*—is one of misery. Sentient beings are often so blind that they fail to grasp even the "smallest particle" of the world's misery, let alone the extent of their own suffering.

How, then, are we to recognize the value of Buddhist teachings? How do we make the decision to begin a spiritual practice? Though all practice is, in part, motivated by an awareness of our own and others' misery, what makes us aware of the extent of it? Though the hardships of a spiritual discipline are but a trifling compared to the endless suffering—past, present, and future—of sentient beings, how do we come to see this? Some profound reorientation in attitude and motivation is called for. The very critical question of how a person becomes reoriented toward spiritual practice is the fundamental one addressed by Künga Tendzin in his authoritative commentary on the mahāmudrā entitled *The Jewel of Essential Wisdom.*76 He begins his discussion of the preliminaries *(sngon 'gro)* with a section entitled "How to Generate Interest by Explaining the Benefit and Advising One to Listen" *('dor ba sgro bskyed;* KT, pp. 8–11).

Künga Tendzin believes that most sentient beings, due to their ignorance *(mi shes)* and past karma *(las)*, are not likely to believe in the Dharma

· 37 ·

teachings enough to undertake spiritual practice of their own accord. Whatever their individual reasons, very few people become genuinely interested in spiritual practice. Others who begin the hardships of monastic or meditative discipline eventually succumb to the cumulative effect of bad habits and laziness over many lifetimes; thus even such well-intentioned actions are not likely to get the novice practitioner very far. Except in very rare cases, Künga Tendzin says, most will lose interest in the discipline and revert to previous bad habits.[77] Therefore in the Mahāyāna Buddhist tradition, where the role of a teacher as spiritual friend *(dge bshes)* is central,[78] a sentient being is said to take up the Dharma in a lasting way mainly through direct intervention by a teacher. Such intervention is purely an act of kindness *(drin)* by a perfected teacher, or lama *(bla ma),* who is the embodiment of the Buddha's realization:[79]

> Each one of us, right now, must find the truth of the Dharma as transmitted through the compassion of the Conqueror [the Buddha]. Consider the many hardships of former [practitioners] when the Dharma was once [practiced and readily available] in India. Consider that the Dharma is now on the decline [here] in Tibet. Then seek the Dharma. Such secret Tantrayāna as this, and such profound advice, is [indeed] very difficult to find! (KT, p. 9)

A lama is said to have attained the perfection of giving *(sbyin pa),*[80] which ripens *(smin ba)* into full compassion. As a manifestation of compassion, the lama sets up an occasion for sentient beings to hear *(thos pa)* and listen *(nyan pa)* to the Dharma. Except under very extraordinary circumstances, a sentient being does not actively seek the Dharma—the Dharma comes to him or her. Künga Tendzin calls such a preordained auspicious occasion "meeting with the holy Dharma" *(dam pa'i chos dang 'phrad pa).*

On such a meeting, advice *(gdams pa)* is given by the spiritual teacher. It is the same kind of advice that one might give a close friend when concerned about that friend's welfare. The friend might be asked, for example, to reflect upon what he has done or is doing with his life, and whether that lifestyle enhances or diminishes the preciousness *(dal 'byor)* of human life (KT, p. 8).

The entire interest-generating event has three components: (1) meeting, (2) giving advice, and (3) hearing the advice. The advice is given by an extraordinarily realized, yet friendly being. It is heard by someone typically so blinded by ignorance as to fail even to realize the extent to which his or her own ordinary lifestyle serves to perpetuate everyday unhappiness. Just as someone is likely to listen to another's friendly concern, likewise the practitioner-to-be is at least able to sense that the lama seems to be concerned for his or her welfare.

The entire event, though seemingly mundane, is in fact an extraordinary event *(thun mong ma yin pa)*. Simple advice about the preciousness of life seems straightforward enough. It is always personally relevant. Why, then, is meeting a lama and hearing his advice so profoundly transformative? The answer resides in the person who gives the advice. He is a holy being *(skyes bu dam pa; KT, p. 24)*. He is the embodiment of realized truth and is capable of directly transmitting this truth to others.

According to the Buddhist psychology exemplified in the Abhidharma literature, the continuum *(rgyun)* of conscious experience derives from a complex interrelationship between a number of mental factors *(sems 'byung)*.[81] The second noble truth states that one's own mental continuum is the source of perpetual suffering. Suffering is caused by conflictual emotions *(nyon mong; Skt., kleśa)*, erroneous conceptualization *(rtog pa)*, and bad actions *(las; Skt., karma)*. The ongoing continuum of negative emotional states, conceptualizations, and bad actions, in turn, is contingent upon the configuration of mental factors at any given moment.[82]

It is not possible to follow Künga Tendzin's reasoning or, for that matter, to understand spiritual practice at all without reference to the doctrine of cause and effect, for it provides the rationale for why meditative practice works as a solution to suffering. According to this doctrine, all actions are believed to ripen *(smin ba)* into effects *(byas)* over time, and the repetition of certain actions further multiplies the effects. These effects become manifest in our experience in the form of signs *(brtags)* that appear first as mental events that arise in our stream of consciousness and then later in our observable behavior. The continuum of mental experience, once defiled by cumulative bad karmic actions, tends to perpetuate itself and deepen its defiled condition over time, and over many lifetimes. As a result, the ordinary mind at any given moment is characterized primarily by the unfolding of habitually negative mind-states.

According to Künga Tendzin, it is very difficult to reverse the negative momentum of the ordinary mind without very effective counteraction. Over and against the enormous weight *(mthu)* of negative past actions, current corrective actions have little likelihood of making any significant impact. Some external intervention is needed. This intervention is none other than the auspicious meeting with a spiritual being.

The entire aggregate of mental factors that constitutes the continuum of unfolding mental experience, and their link through the entire chain of being throughout time, is slightly but significantly altered upon hearing the advice of a spiritual person. Since all actions have an effect, the kind advice of a spiritual person also has its effect on the student's mental continuum. Because the spiritual being has perfected his own mental continuum, his ability to affect another individual is said to carry very great weight. The lama is able to alter the mental continuum of the other person just enough to clear away some of the ignorance, momentarily, and thereby open a window of opportunity to hear *(thos pa)*.[83] As with any action, the effect of hearing advice is not immediately apparent, but it will ripen over time. Künga Tendzin emphasizes the profundity of this seemingly mundane meeting when he says, "[to hear] even one word of the Dharma properly is to set about the pursuit of truth" (KT, p. 16).

The importance of obtaining advice to counteract the great weight of negative mental forces that prevent an ordinary being from hearing the Dharma cannot be overemphasized. Tashi Namgyel, another authoritative commentator on the mahāmudrā preliminary practices, also stresses its importance. The comparable section of his commentary is entitled "Generating Belief [First by] Advising One About the Profundity of the Dharma That Will Be Experienced." He says:

> If you want to understand the real truth and don't have the advice on mahāmudrā, it is said to be difficult to understand the way the realized mind stays *(gnas lugs)*, which is absolute truth, the clear light, mahāmudrā. Simply [understanding] the sūtras or tantras alone isn't enough. All the realizations of the various sūtras won't help you see the clear light, mahāmudrā. But if you depend on the advice of mahāmudrā, you will subsequently understand the way the realized mind stays, which is absolute truth.[84]

Without advice, genuine practice is unlikely; with advice, it has, in one sense, already begun. Therefore, as Künga Tendzin says, "one should take advice accordingly, because it generates a mind that links itself to the inspiration *[kun slong]* of the master."[85]

What kind of advice can have such potentially pervasive effects on the ordinary mind? The following is an example of one type of advice given at the beginning of Tashi Namgyel's famous, but brief root text:

> I bow to the lineage of siddhas, beginning with Gampopa, who composed the doctrine on this pervasive secret of certain [truth], [a truth] that is difficult to understand by any other path. He composed it as an open gesture for direct understanding of the [real nature of the] mind. The practice of this path, called mahāmudrā, is said to be like the sun or moon that melts the glacier snows [of ignorance]. [This doctrine] is adorned with the oral advice *(man ngag)* for [direct] experience,[86] therefore give up trying to reason about it and speak in the clarity [of direct experience]. These instructions are for those whose minds have become very tired of saṃsāra's misery; for those who have the willingness to renounce [ordinary activities] so that perfection of buddhahood can quickly come; for those who become purified on the path, empowered by an understanding lama; and for those intent upon the way the realized mind stays; that is, it is for those who are content because they have had occasion to believe.[87]

Tashi Namgyel is raising the problem of certain truth *(nges don),* and also the problem of its acquisition. One purpose of the lama's advice is to confront the listener's ignorance and ordinary ways of thinking. The beginner is told to give up thinking in favor of direct experience. Jampel Pawo, another important commentator on the mahāmudrā says, "This discourse is difficult to understand for those who [only] have ears for reason."[88] The earliest mahāmudrā songs state that people actually run away in fear when they hear such advice.[89]

The advice also serves as a promise. Tashi Namgyel alludes to some profound, secret truth awaiting the listener who is astute enough to listen. He devotes an entire section of his large commentary, the *Moonlight,* to an exposition of his root instructions on giving advice. The section is entitled "Above All, the Certainty of Generating Belief." This is divided into two subsections: "The Greatness of the Phenomenon to Be Experienced" and "The Greatness of the Person Who Experiences It." As the titles make clear, Tashi Namgyel's advice is intentionally promissory. He hopes to capture the interest of the listener by speaking of a profound secret *(gsang ba)* and then saying that it will be difficult for any listener to comprehend it. He says that the true characteristics *(mtshan don)* of mahāmudrā are such that they encompass the entire scope of saṃsāra and nirvāṇa. Mahāmudrā is a symbol for, or literally a gesture *(phyag rgya;* Skt., *mudrā)* of, the enlightened mind:[90]

> The world of the gods and goddesses is pervaded by that symbol. Being the symbol of the Tathāgata, it is also the symbol of the unborn. (TN, p. 165)

Mahāmudrā is great *(chen po;* Skt., *mahā);* it is the "highest of all meditations" (TN, p. 165), and is common to each of the three vehicles of Buddhism. Whatever is renowned *(rnam grangs)* in Buddhist teaching is equated with mahāmudrā.[91]

After promising an all-encompassing doctrine, Tashi Namgyel reminds his listener that such truth is difficult to understand.[92]

> The real nature [of the enlightened mind], mahāmudrā, does not stay anywhere [in particular] and is completely empty of any and all attributes. It is said to be all-pervasive like space. (TN, p. 168)[93]

It is beyond notions *(blo 'das),* clear *(gsal),* and nonconceptual *(mi rtog).* The truth is not a [self-existent] entity *(ngo bo)* that can be grasped by the intellect or located in any part of the phenomenal world. The truth has special distinction *(rab dbye).* Though it pervades itself *(khyab bdag)* through all saṃsāra and nirvāṇa, it also transcends any object of reflection or speaking (TN, p. 169). Tashi Namgyel carefully induces a conflict in his listener: He tells his listeners how great his secret is, and then tells them that they probably won't come to know this secret. What listener would fail to become more interested?

To intensify the internal dissonance in his listeners, Tashi Namgyel then systematically refutes all other spiritual practice. He tells them that whatever practices they may be engaged in are faulty *(skyon)* because they are based upon ignorance instead of on certain truth.[94] Such accusations are designed to instill doubt *(the tshoms)* in the listener. When someone experiences a healthy doubt about his or her life condition, he or she is likely to become more receptive to genuinely hearing the advice of a holy being:

> If you do not know the way the enlightened mind stays, then you will not attain the fruit of liberation, even if you were to know one hundred thousand other practitioners' practices. But if you understand this, you will become [the Buddha], Dorjé Sempa [himself].[95]

So that his listener not confuse mahāmudrā with other Buddhist practices, Tashi Namgyel compares it with the two common divisions of Mahāyāna Buddhism. The sūtra path of the Mahāyāna sets forth the doctrine of emptiness as the absolute truth in Buddhism (TN, pp. 172–74). The tantra path accepts the relative activity of the ordinary mind and the everyday world as conventional truth *(drang don)* and as the embodiment of compassion *(snying rje)* (TN, p. 174). Mahāmudrā is said to be "the way of the profound truth in all the sūtras and tantras,"[96] and is said to be inclusive of these other practices. It transcends the limitations inherent in other practices and sets forth the ultimate perspective on attainable knowledge. If the listener were to understand this secret path *(gsang lam),* he would "turn away from [the sūtras and tantras, or from any other practice for that matter, and] be guided by these words" (TN, p. 201). Tashi Namgyel urges his listeners to recognize *(ngo shes pa)* what is profound about this teaching and to distinguish its impact from that of lesser teachings (TN, pp. 197–201). After having all other practices refuted, the listener's only recourse is to hear.

In contrast to Künga Tendzin, who addresses his comments largely to nonpractitioners, Tashi Namgyel's root text is clearly written for practitioners.[97] The root text says that it is "for those who...have had occasion to believe."[98] He speaks to an audience of Buddhist practitioners who, as of yet, do not have the ultimate perspective on truth, here known as certainty *(nges don).* This type of advice, written in traditional Tibetan debate style, is not particularly relevant to non-Buddhists because his remarks fail to answer the question of what generates belief *(yid ches pa)* in the first place. He assumes his audience believes, at least to some extent.

Künga Tendzin, on the other hand, does not make such an assumption. He analyzes a whole set of psychological operations that precede the development of belief. These psychological operations begin with interest *('dun pa)*. Interest is generated by meeting with the holy being who imparts advice. However, the advice given to noninitiates is of a different sort than that given to practitioners. Künga Tendzin's comments are meant for beginners, those who do not show any spiritual interest whatsoever. Thus he uses an existential appeal, urging reflection upon life and its course.[99] He asks his listener to reflect upon what a remarkable fact it is to be born human instead of in some other form. Humans are the only beings capable of pursuing truth and grasping it. It is even more remarkable if the listener has had an opportunity to meet with a holy being. Such an occasion is a rare chance *(skal ba)*. One could well have lived in an uninhabited land, a land of barbarians, a land where Buddhism is not taught, or a land where Buddhism has degenerated. Instead the listener sits before a realized being who is the very embodiment of the teaching. As the text says, "Such profound advice is difficult to find" (KT, p. 9).

The holy being urges his listener not to be afraid, only to listen. Moreover he urges his listener to reflect upon the great importance that pervades all meetings in one's life. Nothing lasts, and the opportunity of one moment may never return again:

> Now that you have obtained a precious human body and have met with the holy Dharma, you should follow the lama, your virtuous friend. If you feel unable to sit and wait long enough to ask for several teachings on the Dharma, ask yourself at what other time you think you will do so. When do you think this chance will come [again]? Where there is cause to be born in the form of a demon, a ghost, or an animal such as a horse or cow [in future lives], what other time do you think there can be but now? You *must* give up each and every thought that prevents you from going from a lower to a higher state [of being]. When [in the future] each opportunity to receive the teachings is cut short and you ask yourself when there will be a chance to be shown the teachings again, you will become furious! (KT, p. 10)

What makes the meeting convincing is the actual presence of the spiritual being. Many Buddhist texts give accounts of unusual qualities and deeds of perfected masters—the Buddha, the arhat, the bodhisattva, and the tantric saddhu.[100] The spiritual friend is an exemplar. His living presence inspires the listener even more than any tactical advice he may give.

The spiritual being is considered to be an example of perfected existence, the embodiment of the promised truth. Such a teacher is capable of directly pointing out the truth according to the listener's capacity and level of experience.

The result of such a meeting is called *the certainty that generates belief (yid ches bskyed pa'i rnam nges)* by Tashi Namgyel, and *generating an open, interested mind through listening (nyan du yod par 'dun sems spros bskyed pa)* by Künga Tendzin. The meeting produces a definitive effect; something is generated within the mental continuum of the listener. For a beginner, interest *('dun pa)* is generated; for a more clever listener, interest develops into belief *(yid ches pa)*. Interest is a very important mental factor among the approximately fifty mental factors that comprise ordinary consciousness.[101] The term *interest* is taken from perceptual psychology. It is first in a series of five mental factors that make an object certain *(yul nges lnga)*. These five factors are seen along a continuum of intensity, where interest is the first in the continuum. Interest is defined as a mental factor that gets involved with an object so as to highlight its particular qualities. It sets the foundation for further exploration of the object. Advice that generates interest enables the listener to get involved with the Dharma just enough to lay the foundation for eventually taking up spiritual practice. Being fascinated by the particular qualities of the spiritual being during this meeting may further cause the listener to ask about *(zhu ba)* the Dharma, or even to develop his or her own reflections *(bsam pa)* upon the advice. At any rate, something has happened. The spiritual being and the listener have made a connection *('brel 'jog tsam gyis;* KT, p. 11). Their respective actions *(las)* have become linked, if only for a rare moment. Künga Tendzin summarizes the effect of this auspicious meeting as follows:

> Each time you have a chance [to hear] the Dharma, the conditions that block its secrets from you subside. The conditions that bring harmony, the richness of perfection, grow. You are certain to attain fruition, blissful enlightenment hereafter. Anyone who simply makes a connection to the Dharma will [subsequently] put an end to saṃsāra. (KT, p. 11)

The entire path toward enlightenment begins to ripen from this moment of interest generated during the auspicious meeting.

B. ADMIRATION

The doctrine of cause and effect posits that any action ripens in its effects over time. The generation of interest, therefore, has an important effect on other mental factors. Künga Tendzin continues his consideration of ripening interest *(smin ba'i 'dun pa)*[102] with a discussion of admiration *(mos pa)*. Just as Buddhist psychology lists five mental factors, along a continuum, toward making a perceptual object certain, these same five mental factors become important in the realization of certain knowledge, mahāmudrā.[103] Just as interest can lead to greater and greater involvement with a perceptual object, until one discerns its real qualities, interest can also lead to greater and greater involvement with the Dharma, eventually evoking wisdom.

To carry this perceptual analogy one step farther, interest is said to ripen into admiration *(mos pa)*.[104] The term *mos pa* is difficult to translate with a single word. It could be translated as "intensified interest,"[105] or better, as "admiration." Admiration implies something beyond mere interest, which only picks out a particular object for inspection. Admiration requires sufficient attention to examine the perceptual object in greater detail, that is, to fix the object as a mental representation *(dmigs pa)*. It also requires sufficient concentration so as "not to be taken away from the object easily."[106] The object has become so interesting that the perceiver is able to sustain attention on it. Furthermore, admiration implies that the perceptual object has had sufficient impact on the observer to require further involvement with it. For example, a particular object in the environment may stand out and capture one's attention, compelling one to examine it more closely and from many angles. As a result, the perceiver is able more carefully to distinguish the specific features of that object from other objects. With further involvement, all of the features of the object should become clear. Therefore admiration is one of the five factors that make an object certain *(yul nges)*. Suppose, for example, when scanning the environment, one's attention were to fall upon a blue crystal. Not only might one pick this object out and focus upon it, but one might further admire its particular qualities, such as its form *(gzhugs)* and color *(kha dog)*. These qualities would become even clearer with greater involvement.

Another feature of admiration is that the object is taken as precious *(gnyes)*,[107] as if the blue glass were a precious jewel. Although the translation of *mos pa* as "admiration" is not exact, it is meant to capture the entire fabric of meaning: intensified interest; making an impact; distinguishing the features of the object; having all the features become clear; and finally, taking the object as precious. The term may mean any of these, depending on the extent to which interest has ripened.

This same semantic field for the term *mos pa* applies whether it pertains to an encounter with a mundane object of perception *(ma dag pa)* or to an encounter with a sacred holy being *(dag pa)*.[108] To recapitulate, the stages of admiration with respect to a sacred object are as follows: Greater involvement with the teacher during the meeting leads to an appreciation of the true impact of the teacher's qualities and teachings. The listener is more carefully able to distinguish the unique qualities of the teacher and his teachings from other things that might have captured the listener's interest. The importance of this extraordinary meeting and the depth of the teachings become clear. As a result, the listener comes to recognize the precious qualities of the teacher and the unique message of the teachings. As the listener's interest in this spiritual being ripens during their interchange, he or she gradually comes to admire the spiritual being and his message. Recognition of preciousness is said to become self-evident *(mngon du)* over time.

By generating admiration, the beginner goes beyond the simple passive hearing of advice. Künga Tendzin carefully distinguishes between the terms *hearing (thos pa)* and *listening (nyan pa)*, just as he makes a technical distinction between interest and admiration, respectively. Listening requires more active participation than hearing. Admiration is something "generated deep in the heart" *(snying thag pa nas mos pa bskyed do; KT, p. 21)*.[109]

By this point in the developing process, the teacher has made some impact. Künga Tendzin describes "the benefit of listening,"[110] by which he means that the listener grasps the full impact of the teaching and thereby becomes amazed at its potential benefit *(phan yon)*. Just as a mundane perceptual object may compel its observer to pay closer attention, the teacher, as an object of interest, invites the beginner to listen closely so as to perceive the benefit directly.

Even the most rudimentary interest in the teachings is said to be sufficient to generate admiration:

> Any bhagavan who takes even a single step toward the cause [of spiritual development], by listening to the Dharma or its explanation, or even takes in or gives out a single breath [of its message], will [eventually] completely grasp the holy Dharma, because this is the proper thing to do. So it is said. (KT, p. 18)

Künga Tendzin warns against trying to intellectually understand *(go ba)* the Dharmic message at this premature point (KT, p. 17). Admiration is a perceptual factor, and likewise the type of listening in question is a perceptual, not an intellectual, event. The listener merely takes it in. Mere hearing *(thos tsam)* with open ears is required if one is to get beyond the muddle of ordinary thinking just enough to be fascinated by the spiritual being's message.

Just as a perceptual object may seize one's attention, so also the beginner may be struck by the spiritual friend's advice. Künga Tendzin describes the value the beginner sees in the spiritual friend. He discovers a person freely offering *(mchod pa),* offering not material wealth but something far more valuable and practically applicable, namely a profound understanding of the beginner's existential condition. The spiritual friend is someone who is giving *(sbyin pa),* not out of pride but out of compassion. He is someone with a right hold *(gzhung rigs),* who seems to directly know the way to end conflict and ignorance, and who does not appear to manifest either conflict or ignorance by his presence. He is said to be someone who manifests in his being and lifestyle all the benefits *(yon tan)* spoken of in the scriptures, for example the six perfections.[111] To the extent that a teacher manifests these four qualities while giving advice, he is said to generate admiration in the beginner. He amazes the listener with his virtuosity.

Künga Tendzin continues with a discussion of the effect upon the listener:

> So, although very little intellectual understanding occurs, nevertheless when you merely hear the words of the Dharma in your ears, you will set up the propensities for the Dharma [to ripen] thereafter, and subsequently put an end to confusion. Moreover, to hear *[thos pa],* then to reflect *[bsam pa],* and then to make earnest application *[nan tan]* to what is not completely intellectually understood at first will bring intellectual understanding in time. From that you will come to the great wisdom [over time]. (KT, p. 17)

Considered negatively, the impact of listening removes confusion. Considered positively, the impact "sets up propensities." The act of admiration establishes karmic seeds that will come to fruition at a later time. Without these propensities, practice would have no effect.

When one carefully observes any object of perception, its features become more vivid. Other objects in the perceptual field become less important. The blue crystal, for example, stands out from other objects in the perceptual field. Likewise the beginner comes to distinguish the values of the Dharmic message from his usual way of seeing himself. Künga Tendzin introduces something beyond listening. He calls it seeing the benefit.[112] The beginner is better able to distinguish the Dharma from the mundane activities of everyday life. As the beginner "sees the benefit," he or she is able to take up the Dharma and abandon *(blang dor)* unvirtuous and untrue activities. This encounter with the holy man begins to show its effect in the way a person sees his everyday world, and in his actions and preferences.

The qualities of the teacher and the nature of the Dharma become certain.[113] The process of admiration unfolds such that the beginner, for the first time, is clearly able to discern the preciousness of the holy being, as well as that of the "profound teaching" he encountered in the momentous meeting. He does not yet "grasp [the value] in thought," but rather admires (KT, p. 26). Genuine special insight will come later.

The lama alone is the embodiment of the Three Jewels. That is, he is a fully perfected buddha, an exemplar of the teaching, and holder of the entire assembly of practitioners in his all-encompassing mind (KT, p. 22). To come in contact with the lama is synonymous with contacting the entirety of the Dharma. At his present stage of development, the admiring beginner is in a position to appreciate the lama's qualities as being truly unique. The Buddhist texts are filled with many lists of the lama's perfected qualities of body, speech, and mind. The admiring beginner is compelled to look more closely at the perfect bodily form of a living buddha, which manifests the thirty-two major and eighty minor marks of bodily perfection.[114] His speech is said to carry conviction and to bring penetrating special insight in a way that cuts through others' confusion. He is able to speak to different practitioners on various levels simultaneously, according to their respective needs. The qualities of the lama's mind are of prime importance. He embodies perfect wisdom and compassion. His sole purpose is to manifest absolute truth *(don dam)* in its conventional forms *(kun zlob)*. Yet the lama is not a supracosmic being. He is "an ordinary being who has realized the highest truth in himself" (KT, p. 24), thus embodying what is ultimately possible for any ordinary being. In seeing the benefit for the first time, it begins to occur to the beginner that he has encountered an enlightened being.

There are numerous traditional lists of a lama's unique qualities (*mtshan nyid;* KT, p. 21), such as the eight precious qualities, four buddha bodies, ten powers of understanding, four types of fearlessness, four types of word comprehension, and eighteen types of buddha knowledge.[115] These lists are not important in themselves. What is important is the extent to which the beginner has increased his awareness of certain qualities in the presence of the lama and becomes increasingly certain *(nges)* about their preciousness. In Künga Tendzin's words, the beginner perceives someone "who can only be called a holy being" (*skyes bu dam pa;* KT, p. 24). There are nevertheless different kinds of lamas, with "better, intermediate, and lesser qualities" (KT, p. 22). Here is Künga Tendzin's description of the lama with "better qualities":

First, the better: Generally, he is a good practitioner. Specifically, his mind is well disposed toward the Dharma, due to the greatness of his previous accumulation of merit. He is able to intellectually understand the nature of saṃsāra's miseries, due to his great renunciation *[nges 'byung]*. He doesn't allow himself even the slightest thought toward the world and its appearance due to the great extent to which he has severed attachment. As he lives his life, he protects all the gross and subtle vows and restraints, due to his great reflection *[bsam pa]*. His thoughts never go beyond the lama and the Three Jewels, and he is able to effect great service due to his great faith *[dad pa]*. He is able to offer and give whatever he has, due to his great renunciation. He is able to distinguish taking up the highest truth from [ordinary] causes and effects; give advice; explain the Dharma; and also distinguish intellectual understanding from [genuine] self-awareness due to his great wisdom. He never becomes lazy for even a moment when walking the path. He walks it all the time and is never dull or tired, due to his great diligence. He never doubts, for example, that he could place one hundred thousand people under the folds of the Dharma, due to his great compassion and kindness. He has kindness toward all sentient beings and enjoyment for teaching, so that he may generate the greatness of an enlightened attitude [in others] with his compassion. He never views anyone with malice, due to his great purity. In sum, his mind is fixed to bring about nothing less than the elaboration of truth to [all] sentient beings because he has become a buddha in this very body, in this very lifetime. (KT, pp. 24–25)

The lama is considered to be the embodiment of truth. He is not a teacher yet carries the qualities of the teaching, the Dharma *(chos)*. As the Dharma is the cause *(rgyu)* of realization (KT, p. 45), the beginner must directly experience *(mngon du)* its impact by listening to it. Going beyond mere admiration of the lama's qualities, the listener begins to wonder more about what kind of teaching brought about this transformation in the lama. Having established admiration in the listener, the lama now gives him or her a brief synopsis of the teachings and conveys the specific benefits of the practice. Propensities *(bag chags)* have been established that will eventually ripen into full understanding of the Dharma. Although the beginner is able to "listen and see the benefit" for the first time, such actions still constitute a perceptual event. Künga Tendzin reminds us that the essential teachings are not penetrated by reflection *(bsam gyis mi khyab)* and that they pass beyond ideas *(blo yi yul las das pa;* KT, p. 26). The listener should stop trying to think and simply admire the profundity of what is to be listened to *(nyan bya)*. In response, the lama is ready to speak more specifically about the Dharma.

What does the Dharma offer that other teachings do not? After citing a series of famous passages from the sūtras and tantras, Künga Tendzin summarizes what he feels to be the essence of the Dharma, namely, an understanding of emptiness *(stong ba):*

> So, what is taught according to the various vehicles [Hīnayāna, Mahāyāna, Tantrayāna] that is to be mastered in order to realize truth is a penetration of emptiness. (KT, p. 27)

Following a tradition of other mahāmudrā authors, Künga Tendzin makes a distinction between the rougher and finer levels of understanding emptiness. The rougher understanding is penetration of the two truths—emptiness of the person and emptiness of phenomena.[116] The finer understanding of emptiness is penetration of simultaneous *(lhan skyes)* and eventually of awakened wisdom, the central teachings of the mahāmudrā tradition. This is called *the highest emptiness (mchog ldan gyi stong)*. This more refined view of emptiness is introduced to the listener as the promised goal. The lama speaks to the beginner about highest emptiness and thereby establishes the propensities that will eventually ripen in his or her realization. Yet Künga Tendzin warns that unlike the rougher emptiness, which can be taught, the finer emptiness can only be "directly experienced" (KT, p. 31). One can, however, prepare for the eventual direct realization of awakened wisdom by grasping the rougher levels of emptiness through the respective stages of hearing *(thos),* listening *(nyam),* reflecting *(bsam),* and meditating *(bsgom;* KT, p. 27).[117]

Jampel Pawo also begins his mahāmudrā commentary by explaining the rougher levels of emptiness:

> Let me protect the gates so as to increase these aspects of the Dharma…. This path quickly yields the nectar in one's heart that causes the perfect enlightenment of mahāmudrā, the entirety of the Dharma, the preciousness of the profound seed *[snying po'i thig le].* This great discourse is difficult to take for those with ears for logic. One who [genuinely] listens reaches the goal of mahāmudrā as did the victorious Dorjé Chang [Skt., *Vajradhara].* Even so, bhagavans speak few words of instruction…. Now, even though there appear to be particular categories of things that seem other than mind, for example, substances *[dngos po]* such as an external form, a sound, and so on, this is because of failing to know the way the realized mind stays in its original state. The [ordinary mind] appears as both a subject and an object. By accumulating the propensities of grasping [duality] as such, there can only be the illusory [though seemingly real] appearance of external objects. (JP, f. 3a)

Essentially, Jampel Pawo is drawing a contrast between ordinary subject-object consciousness, or mistaken view *(sems 'khrul),* and right view, offered in the Dharma teachings. This is similar to the way in which a reader unfamiliar with Buddhism may not fully grasp the meaning of the above passage, but he or she may still perceive *(snang ba)* enough value in the distinction being made to be able to admire what is offered. Listening to and seeing the benefit does not require that the listener understand. As the passage indicates, the essential function of listening is to act at the level of the propensities *(bag chags).* According to the doctrine of cause and effect, propensities, good or bad, eventually ripen into actions. The virtuous actions *(las)* of listening and seeing the benefit, even when not fully comprehended, may ripen into the resultant action *(byes)* of becoming a buddha. The groundwork has now been laid for the eventual realization of buddhahood.

C. RESPECT

Even though the beginner may admire the precious qualities of the lama and the uniqueness of his teachings, he has not yet, in a strict sense, been taught anything.[118] He is far from being ready to participate in a teacher-student relationship. First, the beginner must learn the manner of orienting himself toward the lama while in his presence. According to Künga Tendzin, there is a specific "way to listen to what is taught" (*bshad pa de nyan pa'i tshul;* KT, p. 43). The beginner must give up disrespect *(ma gus pa)* and build respect *(gus pa)* with the actions of his body, speech, and mind *(lus ngag yid gsum ma gus pa)*. Genuine respect is free from the extremes of overdependence and rebellion.[119] Genuine respect is reflected in subtle ways. For example, beginners seldom concern themselves with their posture, dress, and behavior while in the presence of a lama. They may "stand up, stretch out their legs, lazily lie on their side, and so forth" (KT, p. 43). They may dress disrespectfully. They may appear to be restless, distracted, or bored (KT, p. 44). These outward actions do not exemplify the inner qualities of a good listener. They do not present the picture of someone who is eager and ready to learn. By way of contrast, someone who sits quietly composed and "listens undistractedly as if he were in a deep meditative state" is said to manifest bodily respect (*lus gus;* KT, p. 43).

Likewise, a beginner who disputes the Dharma, forgets it, or ignores it has not taken it seriously or listened carefully (KT, p. 44). In contrast, "repeating the teachings over and over to oneself as if continuously singing a song" is an example of speech-respect (*ngag gus;* KT, p. 44).

Künga Tendzin says that mental respect (*yid gus*)[120] requires that a beginner orient his mind toward the lama's presence and teachings "as if looking into a mirror" (*me long la bltas nas shes pa;* KT, p. 45).[121] The beginner monitors the ongoing events exactly as they occur in his own mental continuum *(rgyun)* while simultaneously observing the behavior of and listening to the lama. This special mode of attention is called *putting in order one's own mental continuum* (*rang gi rgyun gtan la dbab pa;* KT, p. 45). The verb *to put in order (gtan la dbab)* is a technical term with a very specific usage. It refers to the act of looking at seemingly external appearances introspectively, such that one's perspective is transformed or rearranged:

> For the sake of putting in order one's own mental continuum it is necessary to listen. If you desire *['dod pa]* to know how to eradicate [mental] defilements, which are like the evil deeds of a criminal, then when you have looked into the mirror, you'll know how. When you listen to the Dharma, the arising conditions *[rkyen chags]* of your own undefined practice will appear to you in the mirror of the Dharma. At that moment, you will generate a longing in your mind *[yid la gdung bskyed]*. This is known as your own mental continuum going according to the Dharma. Hereafter, because you are now capable [both] of removing faults and bringing about the benefit, you must follow the teachings. (KT, p. 45)

An inner transformation takes place by which one's own mental continuum begins to "mirror" the virtuous qualities of the lama. The teachings are the cause *(rgyu),* while the beginner's own efforts to listen with respect are the conditions *(ryken)* of putting in order the unfolding mental continuum, much the way a seed is the cause of a tree, while water and sunlight are the conditions of its development.[122]

Künga Tendzin introduces another important technical term associated with respect. The term is *bsam pa,* a secondary form of the verb *to think.* Here the term means "to reflect." The reference to a mirror is intentional. According to the great master of the early mahāmudrā tradition Tilopa, *bsam pa* refers only to those thinking operations that pertain to immediately present perceptual objects, not to past memories or future anticipations.[123] Up to now the beginner has engaged only perceptual processes in his meeting with the lama. Now he utilizes cognitive operations *(rtog pa).* Respect *(gus pa)* goes one step beyond admiration *(mos pa).* It is a more internalized state. To admire a lama's qualities is to witness an external event. The transition to greater internalization begins with shifting one's perceptions from the lama's external qualities to internal reflection on the teaching.

The teacher gets the beginner thinking. The beginner continues to "reflect again and again" so as to become progressively more capable of recalling the lama's qualities and teachings within himself, independent of

the lama's actual presence. Repetitive reflection has important consequences, namely, effects that ripen over time and eventually manifest in
behaviors that support spiritual practice.[124] The respectful and reflective
beginner generates service (*rim gro;* KT, p. 43) and develops the ability to
pray (*bsrgo ba;* KT, p. 54).

Respect also requires more conscious participation and volitional control than admiration. The beginner must decide to give up certain actions
and replace them with others. Any active choice to change one's behavior
toward the lama, no matter how subtle—from a slight shift in posture to
paying a little more attention—already reveals a desire (*'dod pa;* KT, p. 45)
to learn. On some level, the beginner must want to emulate the qualities
of the teacher and the nature of the teachings enough to alter his actions
even in small ways. As spiritual development ripens, respect becomes fervent (KT, p. 45). The beginner has generated a longing in the mind (*yid la
gdung ba skyes;* KT, p. 45).

Only when the beginner realizes that the final aim of the teaching is to
eradicate all suffering will desire grow into a deep longing. The beginner
reflects upon the teachings "as if hearing words that could cure a disease"
(KT, p. 43). The more the benefits of spiritual practice are realized, the less
likely the resistance to the process. Now the beginner is said to be "very
joyful to drink the nectarous words" (*dge dang ldan pa;* KT, p. 43). Künga
Tendzin likens this emerging respect to an attitude of mind that is undefiled
(*dri med*) and compliant (*dang la yid*). The cultivation of respect is referred
to as *taming the mind (dul byi sems).*

It is not enough for a beginner to long for the teachings, nor even to
reflect them. These reflections must be purified (*dag pa;* KT, p. 52). Purified
reflections are those that are capable of grasping preciousness (*gces pa
bzhung;* KT, p. 53):

> First, when listening in order to completely grasp [the teachings]
> in yourself, you should have given up the six defilements, the
> three faults of the vessel, and those [faults] of not grasping. You
> must [instead] listen with purified reflections for knowledge. In
> general, it is most important to have admiration-respect toward
> the lama and the teachings. Further, in general [consider that]
> there will never be a better chance to bring bliss to all the sen-
> tient beings who dwell in saṃsāra, but there will be more
> bondage for this artifice [i e., the human body] of misery. Then,

when you find no use for saṃsāra, you will be consumed by the flightiness and desire for liberation.... Nothing will turn you back once you consider the benefit that is offered by the lama and the teachings. It is necessary to act with admiration-respect, in which you look to the lama who teaches the Dharma as being Buddha himself. (KT, pp. 52–53)

Just as a respectful attitude potentiates spiritual development, certain other attitudes or behaviors can interfere with this development. Künga Tendzin first discusses the six defilements *(dri ma drug):* (1) pride *(nga rgyal),* that is, looking without really listening, or listening disrespectfully; (2) lack of faith *(ma dad pa);* (3) lack of effort toward the truth *(don du mi gyer ba nyid);* (4) distraction toward external things *(phyi rol gyi man pa la yengs),* so as not to mirror the teaching in thought; (5) shutting down the mind *(yid bsdus),* that is, falling asleep; and (6) fatigue *(skyo ba),* that is, listening with a wandering mind and failing to intellectually understand *(go ba)* the meaning of the teachings (KT, pp. 45–50). Such defilements must be abandoned *(spang ba;* KT, p. 49), and the beginner must "listen without defilements day and night" (KT, p. 50). Otherwise, Künga Tendzin says, "You will not desire to listen to the teachings," or will engage in activities that will cause you to "cast aside the teachings" (KT, p. 46). The effort it takes to abandon the six defilements is the first significant step toward virtuous action. The greater the effort, the more one has given up, the greater the virtuous effect that ripens over time.

Although there is some overlap,[125] the six defilements are mainly concerned with the beginner's active approach to the teaching, whereas the three faults focus upon the student as receptacle for the teaching. Künga Tendzin likens the process of purification to building a vessel *(snod kyi dag pa;* KT, p. 43), and he presents each of the three faults using the metaphor of a vessel. First, precious nectar cannot be poured into a vessel filled with poison without its becoming contaminated. The five poisons in the mental continuum are attachment, anger, ignorance, pride, and doubt. These must be abandoned (KT, p. 50). Second, nectar cannot be poured into an upside-down vessel. The beginner may act decisively toward the teachings but not be able to control attention. Such a student looks about with "wandering eyes" and does not listen fully. The mind is said to have become diffuse with too many of its own opinions *(rgya 'byams).* Unable to intellectually understand the meaning of the teachings, such a student thereby "fails to establish virtuous propensities" (KT, p. 51). In this kind of vessel "the water spills around the vessel but does not find its proper opening" (KT, p. 51). Third, nectar cannot be successfully poured into a vessel that has a leak in it. Such a vessel is analogous to the mind that forgets what it has learned.

Reflection is a cognitive process *(rtog pa),* [126] and therefore subject to possible error *(nor ba).* Künga Tendzin concludes his comments on building the vessel with a discussion of the "five faults of not grasping the basis" (KT, pp. 51–60). The potential errors are as follows: not grasping the words, not grasping their meaning, not grasping their subsequent explanation, grasping the meaning incorrectly, and grasping only part of the meaning. These errors must be guarded against, and abandoned when discovered.

The beginner desires to "listen more and more" and "reflect again and again" (KT, p. 54). Admiration-respect[127] requires a constant reflection on virtue, through which the beginner discovers that his own unfolding mental continuum gradually mirrors the teachings more and more. The term *purified reflection* means none other than an ongoing self-corrective process arising from repeated reflection (KT, p. 52). The beginner is yet very far from purifying defilements in the mental continuum. These are said to have accumulated from beginningless time. The beginner's modest but definitive efforts succeed only in purifying those specific moments of reflection upon the teachings. Throughout the remainder of waking and sleeping, the mental continuum remains as defiled and confused as ever.

The beginner has, however, successfully completed the very first stage of spiritual development. By opening to the possibility that something "precious" has transpired, the novice has succeeded in cultivating the seeds of trust *(yid ches pa).* These seeds eventually ripen into observable signs, for example, the discovery that spontaneous reflections and behaviors sometimes "tend toward the teachings." A positive momentum begins to develop as more of the beginner's mental factors are enlisted in the process of spiritual transformation. Table 1 summarizes the progress of the beginner in this ripening transformation.[128]

TABLE 1: THE PROCESS OF SPIRITUAL DEVELOPMENT ACCORDING TO THE DOCTRINE OF CAUSE AND EFFECT

Action, Attitude	Resultant Quality
Completed	
Hearing *(thos pa)*	Interest *('dun pa)*
Listening *(nyan pa)*	Admiration *(mos pa)*
Reflection *(bsam pa)*	Respect *(gus pa)*
Reflection again and again *(yang du yang bsam pa)*	Admiration-respect *(mos gus pa)*
Forthcoming	
Knowledge/intellectual understanding *(go ba)*	Faith *(dad pa)*

II. CAUSING FAITH TO ARISE: THE DECISION TO TRY SPIRITUAL PRACTICE

A. GENERATING FAITH

It is impossible to pour liquid into a vessel without some belief that, first, you are capable of pouring it, and second, the vessel can contain the liquid. An action as mundane as pouring liquid requires at least some degree of faith. Likewise, a beginner cannot pour the nectar of the teachings into the vessel of the mental continuum without faith *(dad pa)*. One dimension of faith is a decision to try. Faith always involves an element of the unknown. In an act of faith, one goes beyond one's present capacity. A beginner who acts in faith no longer requires the presence of the spiritual being but acts independently.

Without the presence of the mental factor of faith, a beginner may question the new experience. Being riddled with doubt *(the tshoms)* during the interaction with the holy being interferes with independent action and spiritual development. The doubtful beginner is lacking in faith. In Buddhist psychology faith and doubt are opposites.[129]

Most commentators concur that faith is the cornerstone of spiritual development. As the next mental factor to ripen in the process of spiritual transformation, faith is an outgrowth of admiration and respect. Künga

Tendzin says, "Faith is born from having grasped preciousness" (KT, p. 53).
By awakening faith, the beginner makes a major stride in spiritual development. Beyond passive admiration, or even acting respectfully toward a
lama, faith requires a most decisive act. The beginner starts to entertain the
possibility that he or she, too, might become such a perfected spiritual
being, and even thinks that such a thing might be accomplished in this
lifetime. Entertaining this proposition at first may seem unlikely, if not pre-
posterous, in light of the beginner's entrenched worldview and lifestyle.
Ordinary resistance to change attests to the difficulty of cultivating faith.
Nevertheless to even consider the possibility of spiritual development at all
is the first sign *(rtags pa)* of faith.[130]

Künga Tendzin defines faith as follows:

> It says in the *Abhidhānatantra* that…the best practitioners depend
> on the absolute truth, mahāmudrā. These practitioners are in har-
> mony with the cause. They link [their awareness] to the immov-
> able [ground of enlightenment] and meditate in the samādhi of
> bliss-emptiness. In three years or so they, too, have attained the
> great siddhi [of enlightenment]. So it is said! Now, when you
> believe this again and again, recognition develops, so it is neces-
> sary to generate a faithful mind *(dad pa'i sems)*. Thereafter you
> should reflect on it. Then, having gathered together each and
> every one of your notions *(blo)* about it, you then let go of [all]
> reflections *(bsam)*, notions *(blo)*, and reasoning *(gzhig)*. Gener-
> ally you need only examine and analyze the immediacy of the six
> sense-systems, through which [directly] comes [the truth], That-
> ness, whose nature is incapable of being obscured by any bad
> karma. If merely a single moment of these teachings were to
> become clear, they would appear to each of us like a flash of light-
> ning in the midst of the darkness—[the same] darkness by which
> we wander endlessly in saṃsāra and by which we end up in lower
> reincarnations over and over again because of our having only an
> unvirtuous and miserable nature. If ordinary people try to ana-
> lyze that [rather than just taking the teaching in through the
> senses], they will become distracted from the teachings. Ordinary
> people hear only their own ideas of the teachings. Ordinary peo-
> ple become attached to the words. [On the other hand,] great
> practitioners pursue the truth to understand it through leaving[131]

this [ordinary] state of affairs, and also through the precious wish-granting gem *[yid bzhin nor bu]*. They seek only what is rare. (KT, pp. 87–88)

In order to fully appreciate the passage, it is important to note that Künga Tendzin has relied upon Abhidharma Buddhist psychology sources for his definition of faith. According to Abhidharma literature, there are three types of faith: (1) faith that is belief *(yid ches gyi dad pa)*, (2) faith that purifies *(dang ba'i dad pa)*, and (3) faith that desires direct experience *(mngon 'dod gyi dad pa)*.[132] The preceding passage briefly summarizes each of these three types of faith.

First, the line "believe this again and again" is a reference to faith. Faith is not blind. Künga Tendzin uses the verb *to depend on (bsten pa)* because faith necessarily takes something as its support *(bstan)*. In Buddhism the typical supports of faith are the Three Jewels, the doctrine of cause and effect, the four noble truths, the certain truth of mahāmudrā, and also the lineage who embodies this truth. The supporting dimension of faith is sometimes described as being like a hand reaching out to accept something valuable.[133] Essentially, to believe is to decide that the teachings are an appropriate object of faith.

Furthermore, to reach out in faith is also to reach beyond one's limitations. Künga Tendzin describes faith as a way of letting go *(gtong lugs;* KT, p. 88). The beginner is told to abandon higher cognitive operations, such as reflection, having notions, reasoning, and so on and is advised simply to take in what has been listened to without thinking about it. The beginner must go beyond the habitual security of ordinary thinking in a leap of faith. Faith requires the beginner to trust, even though present intellectual knowledge may not provide an adequate basis for trust.

This kind of faith demands decisiveness toward the object of faith and, moreover, determination to persist over and against episodes of intense doubt. For example:

> Adhimoksa [faith] is defined...as "having the nature of determination,...the function of not dawdling along, the actuality of decidedness, and the basis on which it functions is the object that has been decided upon. Owing to the unshakableness in relation to this object it should be regarded as a stone pillar."[134]

Second, the line in Künga Tendzin's passage that reads "whose nature is incapable of being obscured by any bad karma" is a reference to the faith that purifies. The Abhidharma literature uses the example of a water-purifying gem, which when placed in murky water makes it instantly calm and clear.[135] Verbs such as "to obscure" *(mun pa)* and "to purify" *(dag pa)* are most often used in connection with conflictual emotions *(nyon mong)*. Just as doubt pertains to an intellectual aspect of faith, namely, belief, so emotions pertain to the affective aspect of faith, namely, purification. In order to take up the teachings, the beginner must overcome fear *(dogs pa),* the emotional counterpart to doubt. A person who acts decisively to try put the teachings into practice acts like a fearless warrior, one who enters a battle without the slightest doubt about being victorious. A warrior who becomes afraid during a battle fights much less effectively. Being hesitant makes the warrior quite vulnerable. Likewise, a single moment of decisive action cuts through all the unvirtuous mental factors that might otherwise inhibit spontaneous, proper action, much like a flash of lightning or a water-purifying gem. Such a warrior acts swiftly at the opportune moment. Seeing victory unfold, the fruits of decisive action become self-evident. Likewise, the beginner who acts decisively toward the teachings quickly sees the value of such acts: His or her entire attitude becomes "bright and clear."[136]

Third, the more a warrior fights, the greater the desire for victory. Similarly, the more decisive the act of faith toward the teachings, the more the beginner exhibits faith that desires direct experience. To have this kind of faith is to yearn for something. The image of the wish-granting gem exemplifies this dimension of faith. Künga Tendzin defines the wish-granting gem in terms of a desire:

> By finding this precious secret, from which the desire *('dod 'byung)* for the precious wish-granting gem arises, you purify the path in which you want only one thing, buddhahood. You [begin to] improve by virtue of its greatness. (KT, p. 89)

The beginner now wishes to "seek only what is rare" and wants only that which will bring enlightenment, the Dharma teachings. Furthermore, the beginner yearns more and more for direct experience of the truth, so much so that all else loses importance. He or she is "not satisfied with" ordinary unvirtuous mental states and behaviors (KT, pp. 89–91).

Faith is said to be the "basis of all positive qualities," and also the "basis of sustained interest." Faith has direct impact upon the intricately balanced system of positive and negative mental factors that constitute the mental continuum. According to Abhidharma psychology, the enumeration of mental factors is as follows: ten neutral factors, which determine perception (five ever-present and five that make the object certain); eleven positive factors; six primary negative factors; twenty subsidiary negative factors; and four factors that can be either positive or negative depending on the context.[137] The higher number of negative than positive factors on this list (twenty-six versus eleven) depicts how ordinary unfolding experience in the mental continuum is generally biased toward negative states.

A goal of spiritual practice is to progressively increase the proportion of positive states that spontaneously manifest in the mental continuum. However, due to the weight *(mthu)* of past karma, it is extraordinarily difficult to tip the balance toward greater manifestation of positive mental factors. The momentous meeting with the spiritual being only served to generate interest and other neutral factors. The meeting, as such, has had no lasting impact on the balance of positive and negative mental factors. The beginner must awaken faith through his or her own effort. The balance of mental factors is tipped only when faith comes forth. Faith, then, is the cornerstone of practice. It establishes a foundation from which all other positive mental factors subsequently ripen, such as patience, diligence, and so on.[138] Awakening faith also insures that interest will continue. As more positive mental factors become manifest, the beginner directly experiences the beneficial effects in his or her life, which greatly intensifies interest in what else the teachings may have to offer.

Faith has been called "the mother of all that is positive."[139] Through awakening faith, the beginner experiences profound changes. This is called "knowing the benefit of faith" (*phan yon du shes pa;* KT, p. 94):

> You must have the support of unwavering faith in the root lineage
> and in the complete teachings....
> Without that, you come to amass all the evils and harms of saṃsāra.
> Without faith, there is no chance of finding bliss, like being thrown
> naked into a deep well.
> Without faith, practice fails to come forth. You grieve, as if you
> were clinging to the edge of a deep abyss.
> Without faith, you fail to see the gods' blissful faces....
> Without faith, emotions become your enemy....

Without faith...you are vulnerable to Māra's evils....

In short, you will come to know and experience all the miseries of saṃsāra's realms from the harm of having no faith.

Now, faith is like a wish-granting gem; the numerous desired benefits come from it.

If you have faith, you eradicate the five poisons, like curing a sickness.

If you have faith, you walk the narrow path of deliverance from saṃsāra, like a mountain goat.

If you have faith, you amass the root of all virtues, like the newborn's first grasp.

If you have faith, you increase the benefit that comes from letting go of defects, like a fatherly benefactor.

If you have faith, you remove the blocks to self-awareness, like the sun and moon after an eclipse.

If you have faith, you are guided on the path of liberation, like a ship.

If you have faith, you are born and live as a virtuous being, [whose mind is] like a great ocean.

If you have faith, you sow [the seeds of] advice like plants in a burying-ground.

If you have faith, awareness-itself reveals the sense objects as virtuous, and the five sense gates manifest the enjoyment body.

If you have faith, whatever arises becomes bliss, like a newborn's wonder of the truth.

In short, you will come to know the benefit of faith, the perfection of [direct] experience, the bliss of attainment, which transforms you from an [ordinary] sentient being into a buddha. (KT, pp. 94–95)

Faith is assigned a special role in the configuration of mental factors, because it has influence *(dbang po)* and power *(stobs)*.[140] Not all mental factors have influence or power. A mental factor that lacks influence is unable to affect the balance of other mental factors. Faith has strong influence over other mental factors. As faith gains in strength, it has greater influence over more and more mental factors. It is the only mental factor capable of countering the great inertia of negative mental factors, as well as stimulating the cultivation of all other positive factors.

A powerful mental factor such as faith, once developed, gives way to other factors only with great difficulty. Negative mental factors also have great weight. In order to compete with the negative mental factors, a positive factor must have power. Künga Tendzin expects beginners to develop unwavering faith *(dad pa 'gyur med)*, because only unwavering faith has this kind of power. Less than that, faith can diminish. Unwavering faith does not lose ground and therefore is capable of effecting a substantial alteration in the entire balance of the positive and negative mental factors. In this sense, faith is the "basis of all positive qualities."

The commentators begin a new chapter on spiritual development when they discuss faith. Künga Tendzin entitles his chapter "Explaining the History of the Lineage of the Siddhas" *(grub thos brgyud pa'i lo gyus bshad la;* KT, p. 87). Tashi Namgyel calls his chapter "The Greatness of the Person Who Experiences [the Teaching]" *(nyam su blang pa'i gang zag gi che ba;* TN, p. 207). These titles indicate that the subject of faith is approached by enumerating the lineage and giving brief accounts of the more famous saints in the tradition. After learning the history of transmission, the beginner is expected to read about the lives of the great saints. These accounts may include *The Biography of the Eighty-Four Siddhas,* a collection of brief accounts of the lives of the great Indian masters of the early mahāmudrā tradition. There are also the accounts of favorite Tibetan masters of the mahāmudrā tradition, for example *The Life and Teachings of Naropa, The Hundred Thousand Songs of Milarepa,*[141] and the like. There are many such works that are similar in structure and content. The characters are usually ordinary—dancers, fishermen, oil pressers, scholars, shepherds.[142] At the outset of the scenarios, these people are either totally ignorant of spiritual teachings or are very proud of superficial attainments in spiritual matters. They encounter a genuine teacher, often with difficulty. More important, their spiritual development proceeds very slowly at first. They make many mistakes or appear incapable of being taught. They sometimes rebel and leave their practice, often indulging heavily in worldly matters. Still, they grow, receive the complete teachings, become fully enlightened, and live out the remainder of their lives as great saints or teachers.

In each of these stories the stereotyped plot is roughly the same. It is designed that way for a purpose. These are exactly the types of stories beginners can relate to because they are about men and women much like the beginner, whose personality and life situation pose enormous difficulties for spiritual development but who somehow manage to develop into great saints. In being given heroes with whom the beginner can identify, such spiritual development becomes seen as an attainable reality. The reader senses that although such profound realization is beyond his or her immediate reach, it *must* be possible since so many seemingly normal, fallible individuals in the past have become great saints. "Faith comes from knowing the benefit [embodied by] the lamas of the lineage" (KT, p. 93). Instructing a beginner to read these stories is a skillful means *(thabs)* of cultivating faith. As Künga Tendzin summarizes the purpose of the stories, "it is necessary to generate a faithful mind" *(dad pa'i sems bskyed;* KT, p. 87).

B. Faithful Recognition

At the stage of generating faith, the beginner is told to abandon higher cognitive operations such as reasoning and reflection. During the next stage, called *faithful recognition (dad pa la ngo shes pa),* however, cognitive processes play an important role. A beginner who has faith is said to be capable of intellectually understanding *(go ba)* the truth *(don).* Künga Tendzin introduces several new technical terms when discussing the faithful beginner. These are "to intellectually understand" *(go ba)* and "to know" *(shes ba).* Other intellectual operations, in addition to reflection *(bsam pa),* are harnessed in the service of spiritual transformation. By constantly reflecting on the lives of the saints—regardless of one's own unfavorable life circumstances or the unavailability of the lama's teaching presence—the beginner is able to slowly awaken faith and build its power as a positive mental factor. Gradually the entire balance of mental factors shifts. Though still essentially defiled, the mental continuum—now under the influence of faith—is considered a suitable vessel for direct reception of the teachings.

The beginner is now ready to receive advice as to the basis *(gzhi)* of practice. The word *basis* refers to a condensed version of the right view *(blta ba)* expressed by the perfectly enlightened mind. Direct transmission of this view, the basis of enlightenment, constitutes a fundamental shift in the beginner's perspective, though it is a shift that manifests only over time as it ripens *(smin ba)* in the beginner's mental continuum. The beginner is now capable of gaining some rudimentary special insight into the fundamental view of the mind espoused in this meditative tradition. Intellectual understanding—an event that occurs directly within the mental continuum—is considered to be the first type of direct *(mngon du)* experience of the truth.

The commentators make a distinction between interpreted truth *(drang don)* and certain truth *(nges don).*[143] Reading about the saints or the teachings secondhand is considered to be interpreted truth because it is merely knowledge of others' experiences. A beginner cannot commence the practice without some special insight into the fundamental belief system and ultimate goals of the practice of mahāmudrā. Special insight must come from direct experience. Reading about mahāmudrā meditation is not enough. Some change must occur directly within the beginner's mental continuum. The resultant change of view is called *certainty (nges).* Certain truth is direct experience of the way things really are.[144]

The lama initiates this change through an advice-giving encounter, but the advice is given in a special way. It is given first in the form of an oral reading *(lung)* and later as oral advice *(man ngag).*[145] The beginner's receptivity to the oral reading requires the actual presence of the lama,[146] who rapidly reads the basic instructions in a condensed form, from a root text. This quick reading is a kind of ceremonial permission to practice. The beginner must generate faith and then listen in a special way. He must "give up all mental activity when learning and let himself be guided" (TN, p. 201). As a result of this ceremony, the propensities to understand the basis are established in the beginner's mental continuum. Listening to an oral reading is like listening to a poetry reading. One may listen to a poem for its total impact even though individual lines of the poem may not be clear.

The beginner follows up the oral reading by reflecting on its message. The effort expended in the process gives weight to the ripening seeds of understanding in the beginner's mental continuum. Gradually the beginner will be ready to receive the more detailed oral advice.

According to Künga Tendzin, the benefit of experiencing an oral reading is threefold: (a) direct experience, (b) empowerment, and (c) the onset of ethical training. Consider the following passage:

> Direct experience is the essence of what the lineage lamas mean as the basis that [eventually] directly grasps the fruition [of enlightenment]. Without direct experience through empowerment by the lamas of the Kagyü lineage there is no promise of attaining the prescribed practices of the saddhus. (KT, p. 86)[147]

The oral reading "puts in order" direct experience of the basis. The following example explains how this happens: Two friends stand on a road and scan the horizon. One sees a stranger far off in the distance. The other does not yet see him. The former has direct experience of the stranger. The latter does not. The latter can only be given an oral description until he himself directly sees the stranger. Eventually the latter sees the stranger. He is surprised at his new discovery. When looking a second and a third time, he no longer makes the same mistake because now his vision has been corrected. Likewise, gaining intellectual understanding of the lama's oral reading transforms the beginner's own vision so that from that moment on he or she correctly views the nature of the mind and the practice. This transformation of view is directly experienced. Furthermore, both the beginner and the lama now share the same right view, though the lama's understanding of it is considerably more mature. Just as both friends along a road come to share the same view of the distant stranger, empowerment *(byin gyis brlabs)* means that the lama and the beginner now, on some level, share exactly the same mind.[148] Just as the more aware friend, who sees clearly, demonstrated the stranger to the other, the lama "empowers" his student to see correctly. This is called *settling the view.*[149] Once both see the stranger, they may proceed to prepare a greeting for him or her. Likewise, following direct experience, the beginner takes up the practice according to the tradition. He or she is ready to begin formal training.

It is not always necessary to have a lama present once the oral reading has been received. Any new cycle of meditation that has a specific goal must be initiated by an oral reading, and each specific meditation practice requires its own oral reading. More experienced practitioners follow up an oral reading with a visualization meditation *(dmigs pa)* in which they simply imagine the lama giving oral advice. Tashi Namgyel writes for this more advanced audience. He advises his listeners to practice a type of tantric visualization known as *the generation stage (bskyed rim):*[150]

> The meditation is said to be done without any [specific] nature [to meditate on], and without any [specific] activity toward liberation. First comes the path empowerment. It purifies the energy currents and their channels.[151] This comes through the support of the generation stage, in which the body of a deity [is visualized]. Second comes direct experience of the path; namely, of the natural mind, mahāmudrā. Third comes the basis for abandonment *[gzhi sprang];* namely, the [six] perfections. Then, by practicing the usual antidotes [i.e., the ethical training characterized by the six perfections] and by considering what is to

be abandoned [i.e., all emotional states], both of these are given up. The path that transforms this basis is tantra. The [entire] cause-and-effect world is generated as if yours were the deity's body. [Visualize] the worldly sense faculties as a diamond and a lotus [of the deity's body]; [visualize] changing phenomena, such as emotions, as the path; [visualize] thought as wisdom. [Then] defilements will wash away other defilements. Thought will cut through other thought. The path of knowing, the basis, is mahāmudrā. It is beyond letting anything go and also beyond any remedy. It is beyond anything changing and beyond anything bringing about the change. Everything becomes the magic show of the mind. By recognizing the mind as the Dharma body,[152] the truth of the awakened mind, always there, yet that still manifests [various] self-appearances, you will become a buddha. There are three paths: (1) those walking along the lesser path of the assembly, who come to the [six] perfections [of the sūtras]; (2) those walking along the path of skillful means, an intermediate path, who use emotions and conceptualization as in the tantras; and (3) those walking along the very path in question, who use their clever faculties and awakened wisdom, and come to mahāmudrā. So according to such sayings, [the latter] is called a secret path *(gsang lam)* because it turns you from both the sūtras and the tantras. It is called a path of empowerment. He who has the best kind of understanding will give up all [ordinary] mental activity when learning it, and be guided. (TN, pp. 200–201)

The basis of mahāmudrā practice is the simultaneous mind,[153] by which the absolute *(don dam)* and conventional *(kun rdzob)* levels of truth are realized as nondual—and in that way awakened wisdom about the true nature of the mind arises. The mind is at once empty *(stong)* and always there *(ma skyes),* and yet it seems to appear *(snang)* in various ways and be active *(las).* This extraordinary view is said to subsume both sūtra and tantra philosophy and practice.

When Tashi Namgyel says, "The meditation is said to be done without any [specific] nature [to meditate on], and without any [specific] activity toward liberation," he presents the beginner with an enormous dilemma. The paradox of the "secret path" is that mahāmudrā, unlike many other systems of practice, has no final goal that can be grasped through ideas, nor any specific means of attaining it. Therefore faith is especially essential in the mahāmudrā tradition. The lama is asking his listener to grasp what cannot be grasped and practice what cannot be attained by practice. The listener must "give up all [ordinary] mental activity…and be guided." This is another way of saying he or she must have "unwavering faith."

No practice is likely to be fruitful without the oral reading that transmits the basis. The power of ignorance is not easily overcome without such a reading. The very clever need not engage in the intervening stages of practice *(rim gyis)* or meditation *(sgom ba)*. The rare individual can reach full enlightenment immediately upon hearing the oral reading. Most others, however, will need considerable practice for the view to ripen over and against the cumulative power of ignorance. In either case, direct transmission of the basis is important. It lays the foundation for the practice as well as giving it formal direction.

What follows is a classic example of the oral reading. It is the reading that Vairocanarsksita heard from the great Śabarapāda, who was in turn the first practitioner to receive mahāmudrā oral advice from its originator, Saraha. Vairocanarakṣita wrote it down so that it might lead others to direct experience:

> Substance and nonsubstance; appearance and emptiness;
> Caused and uncaused; moving and nonmoving—
> All, nothing more, whose nature is like space—
> Never going anywhere over time.
> Space is called "space," but
> No substance to space can be found anywhere.
> Without existing, not existing, neither existing nor not existing,
> what's more, passing beyond any sense object and its [specific]
>   attributes;
> The events of the mind, and the mind like space also,
> Do not have the slightest difference;
> Without difference [they] are merely momentary ideas;
> without [real] meaning, wherein [they] become false words.
> All phenomena everywhere are mind only.
> Without even a [single independent] atom, phenomena are none
>   other than mind.
> Whosoever understands no mind, from-the-beginning,

is endowed with the holy contemplation of the Conqueror of the
    three times.
This is known as the "basket of the Dharma"
Through which there can be no other wrong phenomena again.
From the beginning, the nature of the simultaneous [mind]
shall not exist in any explanation of this and that.
As [it is] beyond words, [it] is also beyond intellectual
    understanding.
If it had a self, it should have [specific] attributes;
altogether without self, what does it have?
Through the mind, you know all phenomena;
without mind, you merely cognize[154] phenomena.
All appearances as mind and phenomena:
if sought, are not found; [they are] without a "searcher."
If you don't interfere with the nonexistent, always-here mind,
    the three times do not become [something] other;
its nature is the way the realized mind stays, great bliss.
Henceforth, all appearance is the Dharma body.
All sentient beings are the very Buddha.
All activity of the [sense] aggregates are the dharmadhātu.
All conceptual phenomena are [imaginary] like the horns of a
    rabbit.[155]

This is not the proper place to examine the many technical terms that
appear in the oral reading. Such texts are always very condensed. They are
seldom immediately understood in anything but a general sense. Understanding will ripen only through practice. Reception of the oral reading
concludes the process of spiritual transformation, since the beginner now
has both of the necessary prerequisites—faith and the foundation for practice, the basis. Having "changed his mind," he is ready to begin.[156]

2. PRELIMINARY PRACTICE

I. THE ORDINARY PRELIMINARIES

GENUINE CHANGE TAKES PLACE at the point when the beginner sees his or her life and world differently and begins to take a new course of action. Oral advice imparts an intellectual understanding of a radically new view of the nature of the mind and of the practice that supports its realization. Subsequently the beginner will be better able to distinguish between the mental factors that potentiate and those that hinder spiritual development. Over time there will be a relative increase in the frequency of positive mental factors and a decrease in the number of negative mental factors unfolding in the mental continuum. However, this fundamental rearrangement in the unfolding stream of experience is not easily accomplished. The sheer power *(stobs)* of the negative mental factors and the habitual bad actions that arise from them is difficult to overcome. The ordinary preliminaries *(thun mong yin pa'i sngon 'gro)* are the primary means for helping the beginner to overcome these accumulated negative tendencies.

In the mahāmudrā tradition, the common way of practicing the ordinary preliminaries is with a set of exercises known as *the four notions (blo bzhi)*. These are skillful means *(thabs)* to help overcome the negative momentum of unfolding mental factors in the mental continuum so as to insure further spiritual transformation. Künga Tendzin says that the four notions work "well in service of the teachings" (KT, p. 7). Jamgön Kongtrül defines them as "four thoughts which turn the mind to religion" (Jamgon Kongtrul [1977], p. 29).

Künga Tendzin introduces two technical terms to depict these mental states and actions. The first of these, *yid 'byung*, means "restless mind." *'Byung* is the verb "to be." *Yid* is a technical term for "mind"—more specifically, the mind that is constantly active in its interpretation of sensory events. As long as such ordinary mental activity *(yid)* occurs,[157] the mental continuum is restless *('khor ba)*. Various thoughts, emotional states, and sense perceptions arise. This restlessness defines the condition of the ordinary mental continuum. This largely useless mental activity continuously ripens, perpetuating the experience of suffering and the world of saṃsāra.[158] The restless mind also leads to greater attachment *(zhen ba)*. The second term that Künga Tendzin introduces, *nges 'byung*, means the opposite, namely "renunciation" of attachment, which comes as a consequence of developing certainty about the teachings. *Nges 'byung* literally means "the occurrence of certainty," and this is what makes the everyday world and its attachments less interesting.

The focus of the ordinary preliminaries is clearly on the individual practitioner, not on an encounter with an extraordinary being. Before presenting the four notions in his classic work, *The Torch of Certainty*, Jamgön Kongtrül confronts beginners with stern advice. He demands that they thoroughly examine the quality of their everyday experience:

> The root of the entire Dharma is mental rejection of the concerns of this life. But all your religious practice up to now has not destroyed your attachment for this life. Your mind has not turned away from desire. You have not given up your longing for relatives, friends, attendants and servants. You have not even slightly curtailed your desire for food, clothing and conversation. You have missed the whole point of applying wholesome action: the stream of your existence is on the wrong course! You do not consider the extent to which your practice has weakened the conflicting emotions, but only the number of months and years you have been working at it. You examine others' faults but not your own. You are proud of every good quality you possess. Your thoughts are lost in trivialities such as your reputation and amusements. You indulge in meaningless chatter. You imagine that you have integrated religious and worldly achievements when in fact not even one of these goals has been met. You have failed from the start to think about impermanence and so are in the clutches of your own brutish mentality.
>
> The Excellent One of Drikung has said: "The [Four Ordinary] Foundations are more profound than the actual practice [of Mahamudra]." It follows that it is better to instill these Four Foundations in the stream of your existence, even to a limited extent, than to practice all the recitations and meditations of the four tantras currently in use.

An individual who practices Dharma in a half-hearted manner is cheating both himself and others and wasting his human life.

In short, if you lack the determination to leave samsara, all the meditation [you may practice in your mountain retreat] will accumulate nothing but a pile of feces on the mountainside! So, consider the miseries of samsara and the uncertainty of the time of death. Then, no matter how varied your concerns, narrow them down! (Jamgon Kongtrul [1977], pp. 47–48)

The beginner is called to greater responsibility, yet Jamgön Kongtrül knows it is unnatural to expect any beginner to arbitrarily take up the hardships of spiritual discipline, especially when such practices call into question his or her entire ordinary existence. Therefore skillful means are used to assist the beginner in making this spiritual transformation. Each of the four notions is a specific prescription for changing one's attitude about everyday life and actions while continuing to go about one's daily affairs. By letting each of the four notions guide daily experience, the beginner is gradually brought to deeper and deeper resolve *(brtan po)* and renunciation. The change occurs in two areas: (1) the beginner resolves to engage in spiritual practice, and (2) he or she slowly but progressively renounces everyday concerns.

Tashi Namgyel uses the phrase *blo brtan po,* which literally means "firmness of notions," or better, "conviction." Elsewhere he explains it as a "notion to strive for truth" *(don du gnyer gyi blo;* TN, p. 22). These terms suggest a fixed goal orientation, the goal being certain truth. Since, as already stated, the companion term, *nges 'byung* (often translated as "renunciation"), literally means "the occurrence of certainty," it is actually due to increasing certainty that the beginner loses interest in everyday affairs and becomes bent upon spiritual practice. The Third Jamgön Kongtrül says, "What renunciation really means is developing the certainty that the conditioned world of samsara is devoid of true value."[159] Resolve and renunciation are two aspects of the same process.

Certain verbs are also used to describe this. The compound *blang dor* means "to take up and to abandon." These verbs refer to karmic action *(las)* that has great weight *(mthu, lci).* The beginner is required to make an active, weighty decision, which is expressed in such phrases as "to take up" *(blang ba),* "to strive for" *(gnyer ba),* and "to earnestly apply oneself" *(nan tan).*

The beginner is required to abandon *(spang ba)* ordinary behavior and habits of mind. Rangjung Dorjé's root text clearly expresses both aspects of this process when he says, "Having abandoned the activities of this [ordinary] life, you should practice earnestly for the truth of perfect enlightenment" (RD, p. 2).

Though the overall purpose of the four notions, in general, is to sow and cultivate the seeds of resolve and renunciation, these attitudes are said to ripen slowly over time. Each of the four notions, respectively, is designed to bring the beginner closer and closer to complete resolve/renunciation through a specific exercise of attitude training. Each one depicts both a particular exercise and a distinct stage *(rim pa)* in the ripening process. The four notions are called respectively (1) precious opportunity, (2) impermanence, (3) the cause and effect of karma, and (4) the sufferings of saṃsāra.

A. THE FOUR NOTIONS

1. Opportunity

Wangchug Dorjé's root instructions for the first notion say, "Act to have the truth now, for it is easy to lose that which is difficult to attain" (WD, p. 63). He is referring to human life, which is said to be "difficult to attain." Essentially the *opportunity* exercise is designed to instill awareness about the extraordinary preciousness of human life. The beginner is first told to recognize the opportunity *(dal 'byor ngo bzung ba)*[160] this human life affords. The practice entails reflecting upon how difficult it is to attain a human birth by contrasting one's current life to a variety of other possible lives, each of which is systematically imagined as a counterpoint to this one.

The practice begins with the eight obstacles, the first four of which are called *the four obstacles of being nonhuman.* The beginner systematically imagines being born in a variety of nonhuman forms in order to appreciate why nonhumans are unable to engage in spiritual practice. For example, the practitioner vividly imagines existing as a hell being, suffering from perpetual extreme heat or cold and so constantly preoccupied with this that he never thinks of spiritual practice. Similarly the beginner vividly imagines himself as a hungry ghost, so obsessed with obtaining food that nothing else matters. Then the practitioner vividly imagines being some kind of animal, who while perhaps more comfortable nevertheless lacks the intelligence to engage in spiritual practice. Finally the beginner vividly imagines being born in the god realm. As a god, all of one's desires are met, yet the attachment to pleasure becomes so great that one never thinks about spiritual practice. The systematic visualization ends by contrasting these four obstacles with a reflection on human existence in general and on the practitioner's own life circumstances in particular. As a human, the beginner is not unduly concerned with survival needs, has sufficient intelligence to see the value of spiritual practice, and is not so comfortable or secure as to be completely disinterested in the teachings (Jamgon Kongtrul [1977], p. 31).

The latter four obstacles are *the four obstacles pertaining to humans (mi yi mi khom pa bzhi)*. Being born as a human does not guarantee the occasion to understand the Dharma teachings. For example, the beginner systematically imagines being born in various barbaric lands where no one has ever heard of spiritual teachings, and then imagines being born at various dark ages in history when no spiritual teachings were available or taught. Next the beginner imagines being born at various times throughout history when spiritual practices were available but when so much controversy and so many conflicting views existed about them that it was virtually impossible to gain a clear understanding. Finally the beginner systematically imagines being born with various disabilities such as a congenital physical illness, deafness, or mental retardation, and then imagines developing a life-threatening illness such as cancer, or a mental illness such as depression or dementia. Life conditions like these become so preoccupying or limiting that they make it difficult to adequately take in spiritual teachings even when such teachings are available. According to Jamgön Kongtrül, such humans "do not turn their thoughts to the Dharma" (Jamgon Kongtrul [1977], p. 31). In contrast, the beginner in whom the seeds of faith have been planted has already gained an intellectual understanding of the preciousness of Dharma teachings. Systematically imagining living other, less fortunate lives and contrasting each of them to the current, more fortunate one progressively develops a receptive attitude. The beginner genuinely comes to appreciate what a rare and precious opportunity it is to be relatively healthy of body and mind, to live at a time when great spiritual teachings are readily and easily available, and to have the intelligence to understand them.

The next set of "opportunity" exercises are *the sixteen obstacles to the conditions [of being influenced by spiritual teachings] (rkyen gyi mi khom)*. The first set of eight conditions pertains to ways someone might fail to build an appropriate vessel. The beginner systematically imagines that his mental continuum is too corrupted by the five poisons to take in spiritual teachings. Then he imagines various situations, such as being surrounded by friends who are bad influences and who encourage him to stray from spiritual practice. Next he imagines the various possibilities of a disempowered life, such as being a slave, servant, or victim of oppression, each of which denies the basic freedom of life required to choose spiritual practice. Then the practitioner imagines leading various lives rigidly holding various ideologies and belief systems that prevent him from ever being open to spiritual practice. Next he imagines having the opportunity to listen to genuine spiritual teachings yet being too lazy to actually practice them. The next exercise is to imagine actually trying to practice but becoming completely overwhelmed by obstacles due to the ripening of previous bad karmic actions. Next the beginner imagines becoming somewhat successful in spiritual practice but then using the gains in various selfish ways or to support spiritual materialism. Finally the practitioner imagines making modest gains in spiritual practice but using them narrowly, only as a means of escaping unfortunate life circumstances, not as a way of helping others.

The latter eight conditions are for those who have properly built the vessel. They pertain to ways a practitioner might lose sight of spiritual teachings once he or she has made genuine gains. The beginner imagines various ways of straying from diligent spiritual practice. These include strong attachments, ripening of bad karmic actions, lack of concern for the consequences of one's behavior, lack of faith, behaving in unvirtuous ways, being ill inclined to practice, being unable to restrain oneself from negative karmic behaviors, and/or failing to live up to spiritual commitments.

The eight obstacles and sixteen conditions are not merely lists. They are instructions for systematic imagination exercises. In the context of everyday life the beginner is instructed to systematically reflect *(bsam pa)* upon the current condition of his or her life in light of these categories. Such systematic reflection is a skillful means of identifying those elements in one's present lifestyle or behavior most likely to facilitate or obstruct the ripening of resolve to practice and the renunciation of useless mundane concerns.

Once the beginner is able to identify those elements in everyday life that cause him or her to lose sight of the task, he or she is more capable of grasping the genuine value of spiritual practice. *The ten treasures ('byor bcu)* are designed to strengthen the growing conviction that spiritual practice is valuable. There are *five personal treasures* to imagine: (1) being born as a human, (2) being born in a land where the Dharma is taught, (3) having a sound

mind and body, (4) having met with a holy being, and (5) having generated faith in the teachings. There are also *five treasures given by others*. Imagine that (1) a buddha has appeared in this age, (2) a buddha has appeared
who is inclined to teach, (3) the teaching has not deteriorated but flourishes,
(4) there are many spiritual friends to support practice, and (5) there are bene-
factors to support the practice. In short the beginner is more likely to continue his pursuit after careful reflection upon how lucky he is. Each of these
notions is a skillful means of increasing overall motivation.

Even with his newly found enthusiasm, the beginner should not become
overly confident. Next come the reflections on the difficulty of attaining
realization *(gnyer dka'i ba bsam pa)*. Just as a tree is a result of certain causes
(seed) and conditions (water, sun), so also a precious human life, one that
correctly turns toward Dharma teachings, is also a result of the ripening of
past karmic action. Such favorable causes and conditions rarely occur, and
the opportunity is easily lost by changing life conditions, such as illness,
famine, war, economic decline, and so forth.[161] The beginner reflects on
how infrequently individuals ever come to practice spiritual teachings seriously, let alone reach enlightenment. Just as few seeds ever find the appropriate soil and climatic conditions to ripen into a fruiting tree, likewise
individuals rarely encounter favorable conditions for Dharma practice.

Once the beginner has systematically imagined each of these conditions
a number of times over, a change in attitude develops. The first notion concludes when the beginner thinks the following:

> From this day onward I must earnestly apply myself to practic-
> ing the Dharma. I must act to have the truth now, for it is easy
> to lose that which is difficult to attain. (WD, p. 53)

The beginner thus develops firm resolve. Tashi Namgyel says, "Generate
a fervent desire to strive for the truth that liberates you" (TN, p. 229).[162] The
resolve to find this truth becomes an ongoing process of transformation:

> A precious human body like this one will never be found
> again. Do not let it go to waste! [it is]…the means to achieve
> enlightenment.[163]

2. Impermanence

Opportunity is likened to the act of rolling a rock up a hill. If effort slackens, the rock rolls down the hill again. Similarly, failure in earnest application *(nan tan)* results in a fall to a lower state of existence in future lifetimes *(ngan de song)*. The weight of ripening past karmic seeds is so influential that it becomes very easy to neglect spiritual practice, despite having made the decision to follow the spiritual path. It is also difficult to endure the hardships of practice, especially at the earliest states, when the force of positive mental factors is still weak. Therefore the second of the four notions, *impermanence* (*mi rtag*), is designed to generate diligence (*brtson 'grus;* WD, p. 63). Wangchug Dorjé's root instructions continue:

> All the nectar in the vessel [of the mind] is impermanent. Life is like a stream that flows as it must. When death shall come cannot be known. Once dead, you're but a corpse! So, with diligence bring about the teachings' benefit henceforth. (WD, p. 63)

There is no greater motivating force (*kun slong;* KT, p. 8) for earnest spiritual practice than the raw awareness of the certainty of one's own death.[164] According to Jamgön Kongtrül, there are five ways to reflect upon impermanence and death. First, the beginner should "reflect that nothing lasts," that is, reflect on the changes occurring in the external world as perceived over time, such as the passing of days, months, and years, or how much of his or her own life has already been used up. Seeing that time passes so very quickly, the beginner becomes frightened and worries more about what to do with his or her life (Jamgon Kongtrul [1977], pp. 36–37).

Second, the practitioner should "think that many other people have died" (Jamgon Kongtrul [1977], p. 36). He or she should think about the people of all ages, rich or poor, and also about friends and relatives, who have already died. Knowing that the same end will come to him or her, the beginner decides that the only real preparation for death is to be found in spiritual practice.

Third, the beginner should "reflect upon the nine causes of sudden death"—improper nutrition, eating too much, eating too frequently, irregularity of bowels, untreated illness, demonic possession, ingesting poison, violence, and heedless sex (Jamgon Kongtrul [1977], p. 36). The beginner systematically reflects upon each of these causes of death so as not to become deluded into believing that the same end might not happen to him or her. Each of these three notions strengthens the decision to follow Dharma teachings as a proper course of action.

Fourth, the practitioner visualizes *(dmigs pa)* the actual time of his or her own death (Jamgon Kongtrul [1977], p. 37),[165] when it is too late to alter the course of life. This visualization leads to great regret *(rnam par sun pa)*.[166] This visualization, when practiced over time, brings greater conviction, and as a result the beginner is unlikely to delay earnestly applying himself to spiritual practice. Fifth, the beginner should "meditate on what will happen at the hour of death" (Jamgon Kongtrul [1977], p. 37) and on how specific after-death experiences follow the ripening course of the good and bad karmic actions of one's lifetime. The cumulative result of these five reflections *(bsam lnga)* is summarized as follows:

> In brief, there is nothing for you to do but practice Dharma from now on. You cannot simply "let it be!" You must make it part of your very existence. You must meditate on making it part of your existence. Once you have achieved stability, you must become the type of person who will be happy at death, and whom others will venerate, saying, "He was a true religious man!"...
>
> Think: "Right now, since death is at my door, I must forget about things like food, money, clothing and fame. There is no time to spare!" and fit yourself, body, speech and mind into the path of the Dharma. (Jamgon Kongtrul [1977], pp. 37–38)

Reflecting on death without having established a connection to Dharma teachings is said to lead to intense fear *(gzhigs pa;* TN, p. 230).[167] Yet, in the context of Dharma practice, the same reflection upon death does much to deepen motivation for practice. These particular reflections are powerful in reversing one's previous harmful course *(nyes pa las slar ldog pa'i slobs)* and, in this respect, are second only to an understanding of emptiness.[168] This initial special insight into the fleeting nature of all phenomena is the first genuine realization in Buddhism, a realization that is directly available to any beginner who practices the second notion, impermanence. The overall benefit of this set of reflections is described as a decision to constantly practice *(kun spyod)* or earnestly apply oneself to the practice in order to escape from saṃsāra.[169]

3. The Cause and Effect of Karmic Action

Making a decision to practice says nothing about the course of action to follow. The third of the four notions is designed to develop greater sensitivity to everyday actions and their effects. The exercise is called *the cause and effect of karmic actions (las 'bras)*. The beginner self-monitors ongoing behavior, reflects on which actions are virtuous *(dge ba)* and which are nonvirtuous *(dge med)*, and then takes steps to modify his or her behavior accordingly. Here are Wangchug Dorjé's root instructions, directly following the reflection on impermanence:

> After you're dead, your actions will come to you when you once again take another human form. So abandon bad actions henceforth; continually go beyond them by acting virtuously. (WD, p. 63)

The essential teaching of the doctrine of cause and effect is quite simple. Wangchug Dorjé's commentator, Jamgön Kongtrül, summarizes:

> In brief: the result of wholesome action is happiness; the result of unwholesome action is suffering, and nothing else. These results are not interchangeable; when you plant buckwheat, you get buckwheat; when you plant barley, you get barley. (Jamgon Kongtrul [1977], p. 42)

Nothing could be more "black and white,"[170] to use a Tibetan colloquialism.

There is no more direct way to realize the essential principle of the doctrine of cause and effect than to reflect upon one's own actions—past, present, and future. Tashi Namgyel instructs the beginner to reflect upon "the way you are influenced by karmic action" *(dbang du song nas;* TN, p. 229). The task is to reflect upon the significant events, as well as the momentary acts, of one's life and their respective consequences.

There are *four general aspects (spyi)* to the doctrine of cause and effect: (1) the result *(byes ba)* of an action *(las)* becomes certain over time *(las nges pa)*, that is, it ripens *(smin)*;[171] (2) actions, however small, proliferate in their results *(las 'phel che ba)*, just like a seed that grows into a fruit tree and then produces many potential seeds; (3) an action that is not taken up will not manifest any result over time *(las ma byas pa dang mi 'phrad pa)*, so it is possible to restrain *(sdom pa)* oneself from certain actions and thereby cut off *(gcod pa)* any resultant effect; and (4) the results of any given action, though not immediately manifest, never diminish *(byas pa chud mi za ba)*.[172]

Every action has a relative weight (*lci'i khyad par;* TN, p. 229), and a number of factors influence this. First, there is the type *(gshis)* of action: For example, killing is a more serious kind of nonvirtuous action than idle talk, so it will have a more substantial result. Second is the power *(stobs)* of that action: For example, criticism does not carry the same power as trying to kill a person. Third is the quality *(rnam)* of the action: Torturing a person to death carries more weight than impulsively killing them. Fourth is the object *(don)* toward which the action is directed: Nonvirtuous actions directed toward one's mother, father, a bodhisattva, a buddha, or a member of the Buddhist community are said to carry the greatest weight.

There are *opponent powers (ldog pa'i stob)* for any form of bad action. Opponent powers are often called antidotes *(gnyen po)* because they remedy nonvirtuous deeds. Just as a disease develops in the body when there are no antidotes to reverse the course of its action, nonvirtuous actions ripen with greater weight when there are no opponent powers. Practicing virtue, then, counteracts the weight of previous bad karma by establishing a force antagonistic to it.[173]

There are *three effects of karma (las 'bras gsum myong tshul;* TN, p. 229). According to oral commentary,[174] the three effects are (1) the [main] effect, (2) its secondary ripening over time *(rgyu mthun pa'i 'bras bu),* and (3) the environmental effect *(dbang gi 'bras bu).* For example, an act such as killing would manifest three effects over time. The main effect is rebirth in one of the lower realms. The secondary effect would be premature death due to illness or violence during the next or subsequent lifetimes. The environmental effect would be difficulty in finding sufficient food, shelter, or medicine in subsequent lifetimes.[175]

There are also *specific aspects (khyad pa)* to the doctrine of cause and effect. These specific aspects bring the doctrine out of the realm of philosophical speculation and into the immediacy of one's own experience. A beginner is instructed to reflect upon his or her own current actions and to consider the potential consequences of each, according to the general laws of karma. The commentators speak of *ten nonvirtuous actions (mi dge ba bcu),* that is, "actions which lead to samsara" (Jamgon Kongtrul [1977], p. 38). They are killing, stealing, harmful sex, lying, slander, criticism, idle talk, greed, ill-will, and erroneous views.[176] There are "ten [corresponding] virtuous actions." These ten are the standard Buddhist precepts *(tshul khrims),* that is, actions that "lead to liberation" (Jamgon Kongtrul [1977], p. 41).

The way *(tshul)* to practice (TN, p. 229) is to recognize *(ngo shes pa)* non-virtuous and virtuous actions for what they are in one's immediate experience. Upon recognition, the beginner should reflect on *(sems pa)* their possible results over time.[177] Then the practitioner should use willpower to refrain *(sdom pa)* from nonvirtuous actions and take up *(blang ba)* corresponding virtuous actions. As soon as any nonvirtuous act is recognized in one's immediate experience, one should not only restrain oneself from indulging in it but should make an extra effort to cultivate its opposite. There are *four remedial powers:* (1) remorse for the misdeed, (2) reliance on spiritual teachings, (3) resolve to turn away from misdeeds, and (4) purification of misdeeds by applying the remedies to neutralize their effects.[178] Wangchug Dorjé instructs, "Abandon bad actions henceforth, continually go beyond them by acting virtuously" (WD, p. 63).

The cause/effect exercise is said to bring great benefit *(phan yon)*. Although its overall result will not become apparent until much later, certain signs *(rtags)* manifest quite soon after starting the practice. First, the beginner experiences great regret *(rnam par sun 'byin pa)* for past actions. The use of an intensifier, *rnam par,* suggests that the regret is profound and deep. In consequence, the beginner "generates firm notions" (TN, p. 229). If only self-restraint has been practiced, the beginner will merely experience painful remorse. If, however, he or she has simultaneously practiced taking up the practice of virtue, remorse changes into "strong determination regarding the course of actions" (TN, p. 229). Becoming assured of the proper course of action, the beginner now sets about the practice with greater conviction.

4. The Sufferings of Saṃsāra

At this juncture the course of action becomes clearer. The beginner has had some success in restraining himself or herself from the ten nonvirtuous actions—for example, ill-will or stealing.

However, the beginner's everyday life is still filled with a host of more subtle nonvirtuous actions that are difficult to recognize and restrain. Though subtle, the cumulative effect on the mental continuum is not innocuous. The only way to emphasize the necessity *(dgos ba)* of eradicating these more subtle forms of nonvirtuous action is with an exercise designed specifically "to cut off the roots of attachment" (WD, p. 63). The fourth of the four notions, *the sufferings of saṃsāra ('khor ba'i nyes dmigs pa),* is a skillful means for driving home the full impact of the miseries of the everyday world. This meditation is designed to persuade us "to become disillusioned with all the mundane pursuits we value."[179] Wangchug Dorjé's root instructions say:

> Because you will be forever tormented by the obvious happiness and miseries of the saṃsāric realms, you should cut off the roots of attachment and accomplish the realization [of truth], as if you were an executioner enjoying a fresh kill. (WD, p. 63)

The actual practice requires a systematic visualization of the typical sufferings (sdug bsngal) of each type of sentient being in the six realms of saṃsāra. For example, each of the hell worlds (dmyal ba)—the eight hot hells, the eight cold hells, and the other hells—has a specific suffering to be visualized:

> For those born in the eight hot hells, all the mountains and valleys are blazing red-hot iron. The rivers and lakes are molten copper and bronze. The trees send a rain of swords and other sharp weapons. The inhabitants enjoy not a moment's rest, but are incessantly slaughtered by wild beasts and horrible demons. (Jamgon Kongtrul [1977], p. 43)

Likewise, the beginner visualizes the realm of hungry ghosts (yi dwags):

> The spirits cannot find any food or drink. Increasingly tormented by hunger and thirst but finding only mucus and feces, they are wearied by their hopeless search. Naked, they burn in summer and freeze in winter. (Jamgon Kongtrul [1977], p. 43)

The animal realm (dud'gro) has its own form of suffering:

> Animals in the sea are as crowded as grains of malting barley. They survive by eating each other. Constantly tormented by fear, they wander about, carried by waves.
>
> Even animals who live in more spacious mountain habitats are unhappy, always fearing some enemy's approach. They kill each other. Even domesticated ones are hitched to ploughs or killed for meat and hides. They are stupid. In addition to the

misery of stupidity, they suffer as much from heat and cold as do the hell-beings and spirits. (Jamgon Kongtrul [1977], p. 44)

The sufferings of the three lower realms are easiest to visualize due to their vividness and intensity. The three higher realms are harder, but successful visualization of these leads to greater conviction about spiritual practice. After visualizing the numerous pleasures of the god realms, the beginner imagines their downfall, and the tremendous suffering that comes with the loss of great pleasure. Giants inhabit another of the higher realms. The beginner visualizes what it is like to be one of these giants, who are deeply envious of the pleasures the gods enjoy but never manage to have for themselves.

The misery of the human realm is the most difficult of the six visualizations. The beginner systematically visualizes each of the eight kinds of human misery: birth, aging, illness, death, not achieving one's goals, loss, insecurity, and experiencing unpleasure. There are many life situations that can be used for the visualization across each of these categories. In the words of Jamgön Kongtrül:

The Five Miseries of Aging
The miseries of aging include: (1) fading of complexion, (2) deterioriation of the form, (3) dissipation of energy, (4) impairment of the senses, and (5) decline of wealth.

The Five Miseries of Illness
The miseries of illness include: (1) sufferings in the increase of frustration and anxiety, (2) the body's natural changes, (3) the inability to enjoy pleasant things, (4) the need to rely on what is unpleasant and (5) the approaching separation from life.

The Five Miseries of Death
The miseries of death include: (1) separation from wealth, (2) from influence, (3) from attendants and friends, (4) and even from your own body, and (5) violent anguish.

The Misery of Not Finding What You Seek
Although you strive so hard for it that you lose all regard for the injury, suffering or malicious talk you inflict on others, you do

not obtain the food, money or fame you desire. This is the misery of not finding what you seek.

The Misery of Not Retaining What You Have
Dreading the approach of an enemy, thief or a violent robber; being left with only the stars for a hat and the frost for boots; being exhausted from too much work; worrying about your ability to protect [your dependents]; and worrying that your enemies will not [be punished]: this is the misery of not retaining what you have.

The Misery of Separation from What Is Dear
Loss of essential persons such as parents, siblings, servants, students and so on; decline of wealth and power; loss of a large sum of money; anxiety about slander you have incurred through bad deeds or another's jealousy: this is the misery of separation from what is dear.

The Misery of Encountering the Undesirable
Encountering illness, dangerous enemies, the arm of the law, a murderer, a bad reputation, evil rumors; incurring punishment in return for help; having lazy servants, and so on: this is the misery of encountering the undesirable. (Jamgon Kongtrul [1977], pp. 44–46)

To conclude the exercise, the beginner reflects on the miseries common to all sentient beings across the six realms. These three miseries include: the misery of misery, the misery of impermanence, and the misery of dependent origination. After gaining some experience with each of the visualizations of the six realms, the beginner imagines that all the potential sufferings of saṃsāra can be found within his or her own mental continuum. The various sufferings imagined become vivid emanations *(spros ba)* of the mind,[180] and help the beginner to grasp how misery is built into the very structure of existence. The beginner has come full circle. Starting with reflection on human life as a precious opportunity, the exercise now concludes with the special insight that this same human life contains the seeds of all the potential types of human misery leading to future rebirth in any of the six saṃsāric realms.

Just as faith is the cause *(rgyu)* of spiritual development, the four notions are its preliminary conditions *(rkyen)*, much in the same way that water and sunlight are conditions by which a seed ripens.[181] Apart from practicing the four notions and restraint of harmful actions, the beginner has done little else to alter his or her everyday activities. Nevertheless, he or she has established the necessary conditions for spiritual development, as if watering an unsprouted seed. The first signs of ripening are said to be great regret *(rnam par sun pa)* and an urge to renounce *(nges 'byung)* everyday activity. These signs are directly experienced within the mental continuum as if a sprout were breaking through fresh soil.

Tashi Namgyel summarizes the benefit of mastering the four notions:[182]

> Constantly generating a strong interest in striving for the truth that liberates is so very important because it is the root of the teachings. So it is called the feet [upon which you walk when] meditating to turn back attachment. It is also called the "master who meditates to turn back attachments." (TN, p. 229)

5. Concluding the Four Notions

The inward dimension of this process of gradual spiritual transformation is signified by an important shift in terminology. Table 2 summarizes these changes.

TABLE 2: THE RIPENING OF MENTAL AND BEHAVIORAL ACTIONS PERTAINING TO SPIRITUAL TRANSFORMATION

Mental Factor	Behavior
Intellectual understanding *(go ba)*	Unwavering faith *(dad pa mi 'gyur ba)*
Reflecting upon notions *(blo bsam)*	Earnest application *(nan tan)*
Representing *(dmigs pa)*	Striving *(gnyer)*

Intellectual understanding *(go ba)* ripens into reflection upon notions *(blo bsam)* and finally into representing. Unwavering faith ripens into earnest application *(nan tan)*. Everyday intellectual operations and motivational patterns are now drawn into the arena of spiritual transformation. The verb "to reflect" *(bsam pa)* is used for practicing the first several notions. The verb "to represent" *(dmigs pa)* is used for the fourth notion, and sometimes for the third. The verb "to meditate" *(sgom ba)* is sometimes used for the fourth notion.[183] Such verb usage suggests a deepening process of internalization of the teachings, concomitant with their outward expression in behavior. With greater internalization, awareness shifts more and more away from its usual worldly preoccupations. All the commentators concur that the overall effect of practicing the four notions is to "cause nonattachment."

The reason for the shift in terminology is made clear in the oral accounts: Renunciation is not an outward but an inward action; it means primarily that one uses the object of the five senses but does not depend on them or become attached to them. The opposite of this is what is called in Tibetan "hairy renunciation," referring to the sudden outward abandoning of the pleasures of this life. Owing to a sudden passion to renounce what he thinks to be saṃsāra, someone might abandon all belongings and escape to a mountain retreat, only to return a week or two later feeling very discouraged and weak. Such "renunciation" is generally insincere and rarely lasts for more than a short time.

Attachment is the inability to separate oneself from something or someone and is also giving all of one's energy to satisfying a desire, taking it as an ultimate goal. This is what is to be abandoned. In relations with people, detachment means realizing the truth of impermanence and the non-ultimate character of human relationships. Having developed such detachment, one should be happy to be with others but at the same time be able to adapt to changing circumstances.[184]

Genuine renunciation is never an impulsive act, but rather a slow transformation in the configuration of mental factors comprising the mental continuum and the karmic actions based on these. Renunciation is the outcome of a natural process—the accumulation of many moment-to-moment decisions to "abandon and take up nonvirtue and virtue," respectively. Renouncing nonvirtue is like emptying a water bucket drop by drop rather than pouring its contents out.[185]

According to Tashi Namgyel, the moment-by-moment earnest application of the antidote—acting virtuously—makes one the master of one's own karmic unfolding. He succinctly illustrates how spiritual development must be seen as a slowly ripening process, according to the doctrine of cause and effect:

Each time the truth is heard, it comes more and more. It is grasped more and more in what is reflected and remembered. Then, from a deep desire to know *[zhen chags gting]* more about this, you generate the extraordinary mind, which turns about and strives [only] for certain truth. This is because you have thoroughly examined and analyzed the advantages of Dharmic activity. Whoever knows the uselessness and harmfulness of former [activities]…will thereby establish the foundation for meditation experience according to the way of the Dharma teaching, and will also increase it. (TN, pp. 221–22)

A growing desire to meditate arises naturally from the cultivation of the attitude of renunciation over time. The sincere beginner does not make any arbitrary decision to become a meditator. He or she does not impulsively leave everyday life, find a cave, and meditate. Meditation begins as an attitude, not as formal sitting practice. It is an attitude that is generated *(skye ba)* as an outcome of practicing the four notions as an approach to everyday living. As the beginner becomes less interested in the everyday world and its suffering, the natural recourse is meditation. Nāgārjuna says that at a certain point in this gradual process of spiritual transformation while remaining immersed in everyday life, "one becomes more disposed to meditate" *(de las sgom pa la ni rab tu sbyor).*[186]

Incorporated into the four notions are the first two noble truths, namely the truth of suffering and the causes of suffering (karmic actions and afflictive emotions). The beginner has gone beyond mere intellectual understanding *(go ba)* of these truths to direct experience *(nyams len)* of them in the unfolding mental continuum. At this stage the beginner is now ready to take up the practice more formally by taking refuge in the Three Jewels.

II. THE EXTRAORDINARY PRELIMINARIES

The ordinary preliminaries require the beginner to reflect upon everyday actions in the world and also on the condition of that world. The more one contrasts these affairs with the preciousness of the Dharma teachings, the greater the desire to let go of them. With this shift in focus away from the world and toward the teachings, the beginner is now ready for a new set of practices, the extraordinary preliminaries *(sngon 'gro thun mong ma yin ba).*[187]

The term *extraordinary* has at least two meanings. In a general sense, it means that the practices are not open to everyone. Through practicing the extraordinary preliminaries, the beginner becomes a practitioner of Buddhism. Künga Tendzin says, "Good training comes by way of the extraordinaries" (KT, p. 7). These practices specifically mark the beginner as a true practitioner of Buddhism. The verbal noun *sbyong ba* means "to clean," as well as "to get training." Technically, it means that one's body and mind become "pliable" *(shin sbyangs)* in carrying out a particular action, which in this case is practice of the Dharma.[188] Künga Tendzin adds the intensifier *rnam par.*[189] He describes the extraordinary preliminaries as systematic, intense training until the beginner's bodily and mental states are sufficiently pliable to undertake more advanced meditation practice.

The actual practice of the extraordinary preliminaries requires a particular type of visualization meditation *(sgom dmigs)* in combination with ritual practice *(sbyor ba)*. When not meditating, the practitioner is expected to study *(slob pa)* the scriptures and follow the ethical precepts *(tshul khrims)* of Buddhism. In contrast to the ordinary preliminaries, the focus is now on the Dharma teachings themselves, not on everyday life. The verb *sgom ba* means "to meditate," in contrast to hearing *(thos pa)* and reflecting *(bsam pa)*. The beginner must now direct his or her attention in a prescribed way, in contrast to ordinary discursive thinking. Literally, *sgom ba* means "to become, to bring about"—in this context, to bring about or directly manifest the Dharma teachings within the practitioner's own mental continuum. As already stated, the verb *dmigs pa* means "to make a representation" of sense data from any of the six sense systems, for example, to visualize or to construct an auditory representation and so on. The compound *sgom dmigs* implies that whatever one visualizes in a systematic way leads to directly manifesting that experience more and more in the unfolding mental continuum. The mind identifies completely with whatever is visualized. In a more technical sense, the practitioner takes it to mind *(yid la byed pa)* or grasps it *('dzin pa)*. To practice visualization meditation on some aspect of Dharma teaching, or even to study it, is to build up *(bcos pa)* the mental continuum into a living example of the teaching, and eventually to bring about enlightenment in one's own mind.

The practitioner is now more disposed to meditate *(sgom ba)* as well as to practice *(sbyor ba)* in other ways apart from these visualizations. According to the doctrine of cause and effect, certain mental actions *(sems las)*, such as visualization meditation, manifest results *(byes ba)* in subsequent behavior *(spyod lam)*. The practitioner spontaneously acts more and more like a buddha-to-be, both in virtuous deeds (as defined by the six perfections) and in the visualization meditations. The extraordinary practices incorporate both mental actions (in the form of visualization meditations) and prescribed behaviors into a set of practices, all of which are designed to progressively "build the vessel" in such a way that the practitioner's mental continuum eventually becomes "indistinguishable from all the objects of refuge, the enlightened beings, in body, speech, and mind" (WD, p. 64).

The essence of the extraordinary practices is found in the term *ngo sprod pa,* which means "to point out." Jampel Pawo says that the extraordinary practices provide:

> ...guidance in which one's ordinary mind and the wisdom [of the enlightened ones] are pointed out as being one and the same, namely the simultaneous mahāmudrā. (PK, f. 1b; JP, f. 3a)

The extraordinary practices are the means by which the practitioner adopts the attitude that his or her mind is already enlightened.

According to Tashi Namgyel, there are two very different types of extraordinary practices. Gampopa is the primary source of the nontantric method (TN, p. 226). The four nontantric exercises are: (1) taking refuge in the lama and the Three Jewels, (2) meditating upon the enlightened attitude with compassion, (3) removing sins [by confession] and offering the maṇḍala, and (4) fervent prayer (TN, p. 226).

The tantric method is said to be a much faster means toward the goal of identifying with the perfected buddhas, and is the more common practice in the mahāmudrā commentarial tradition. The tantric method, however, requires the influence *(dbang)* of an extraordinary being, who affects the ripening of the practitioner's mental continuum in a prescribed way.[190] Influence must be received directly from one's root lama in a special initiation ceremony (TN, p. 227). The four tantric exercises are: (1) taking refuge and generating the enlightened attitude, (2) the Vajrasattva meditation and recitation, (3) the maṇḍala offering, and (4) guru yoga.

Both the nontantric and the tantric exercises are built upon the same foundational practices, namely taking refuge and generating the enlightened attitude. Both contain practices for the removal of obstacles to practice, namely confession and the Vajrasattva meditation, respectively. Both contain practices for the cultivation of virtuous mental factors that potentiate the practice, namely the maṇḍala offerings. Though the outcome is the same, the respective practices used to remove obstacles and cultivate virtue differ in whether or not they require influence. The major difference, however, is between the nontantric use of prayer and the tantric use of guru yoga, in that the latter, tantric practice requires a special initiation ceremony in which one's root lama confers influence. Such influence clears away obstacles in the mental continuum of the practitioner long enough to get a glimpse of the natural, untainted condition. Following the initiation ceremony, the tantric practitioner adopts a radically different perspective on practicing the extraordinary preliminaries. Instead of using the ordinary mind, the tantric practitioner takes the extraordinary perspective, with the practice being conducted as if the mind were of someone already enlightened, who moment by moment already knows exactly how to proceed with just the right state of mind.[191] Guru yoga establishes a link between the practitioner's mind and the mind of the enlightened masters.[192]

Table 3 summarizes each of the four nontantric and tantric extraordinary preliminaries and the outcome of each, respectively. The cumulative effect is the ripening wisdom of emptiness in the mental continuum.

TABLE 3: THE STRUCTURE OF THE EXTRAORDINARY
PRELIMINARIES AND THEIR OUTCOME

Nontantric	Tantric	Outcome
Refuge	Refuge	Becoming a Buddhist
Enlightened attitude	Enlightened attitude	Compassion
Confession	Vajrasattva meditation	Removal of obstacles
Maṇḍala offering	Maṇḍala offering	Cultivating virtue
Prayer for enlightenment	Guru yoga	Wisdom (Emptiness)

A. TAKING REFUGE

Tashi Namgyel's opening comments on refuge illustrate the smooth transition from the last ordinary preliminary—imaging the sufferings of saṃsāra—to the first extraordinary preliminary—taking refuge:

> Anyone who strives for true liberation from the terrors and fears
> of saṃsāra's misery has already taken refuge in the precious Three
> Jewels. Taking refuge is very important because it is the root of
> the holy Dharma. (TN, p. 230)

According to this commentary, fear of misery[193] is the prerequisite to taking refuge.

There are both appropriate and inappropriate (*chog;* TN, p. 231) objects
of refuge *(skyabs yul).* For example, Wangchug Dorjé begins his expanded
root instructions this way:

> [Here are] the guiding instructions for generating a refuge mind,
> for entering upon the path of liberation. Take what is proper,
> namely the lineage, into the vessel [of the mental continuum].
> (WD, p. 789)

According to Gampopa, ordinary desires such as wealth and fame constitute improper objects of refuge because, being impermanent, they eventually lead to suffering. Putting faith in relatives or friends, even in gods, are
improper objects because these beings have not entirely eradicated suffering themselves.[194] Only the Buddha, who has completely eradicated suffering; the Dharma teachings, which are the means to becoming such a
buddha; and the saṅgha, the community that supports this spiritual transformation, constitute proper objects *(skyabs yul).* These objects are called
the Three Jewels *(dkon mchog gsum),*[195] all three of which are embodied in
the person of the lama. Taking refuge in the lama is the same thing as taking refuge in the Three Jewels.

Gampopa distinguishes between three special *(khyad par)* perspectives by
which to view the object of refuge, the lama: (1) The beginner visualizes the
lama as an object in front *(mngon du),* that is, as a projected image; (2) the
beginner becomes self-aware *(rang rig pa)* that this image of the lama is also
the very manifestation of the three bodies of wisdom *(sku 'sum)*—an emanation body *(sprul sku),* which transforms ordinary appearances; an enjoyment body *(longs spyod sku),* which acts in the extraordinary realms to
protect practitioners and inspire them toward enlightenment; and a
Dharma body *(chos sku),* the ultimate enlightened awareness of the Buddha; (3) the practitioner adopts the perspective of absolute truth *(dom dam),*
in which the lama is viewed as merely an emanation of his or her own mind,

which, like the rest of the world, is empty.[196] The more advanced practitioner knows there is no self-existing *(yod pa)* external object of refuge, proper or improper. Jamgön Kongtrül says:

> When you reach the goal, your awareness will be the same as the enlightened awareness of all the Buddhas. You will no longer need the Dharma and Sangha. (Jamgon Kongtrul [1977], p. 57)

To the extent that a practitioner understands that "one's ordinary mind and truth, Wisdom, are one and the same, the simultaneous mind," then the ultimate source of refuge is one's very own mind (PK, f. 2a). However, this realization depends upon taking a very particular perspective on one's own mind in order to see its truly extraordinary nature in its primordial, undefiled condition. Exceptional practitioners who adopt that perspective transcend the need for the Three Jewels as objects of refuge. For such practitioners Gampopa says:

> The Dharma that is taught is only a collection of words and letters and has to be discarded like a raft when we have reached the other shore.[197]

The level at which one understands the lama as an object of refuge depends upon the capacity of the practitioner. Very few beginners are able to understand that the ultimate object of refuge is the ground of enlightenment, the Dharma body itself. Therefore an external object of refuge is typically used as a focus toward which the practitioner develops a devotional mind *(smon pa'i sems)*.[198]

Whereas the ordinary preliminaries inculcate personal experience of the first two noble truths (suffering and its cause), the extraordinary preliminaries require an act of faith directed toward the last two noble truths— the cessation of suffering and the path leading to it.[199] The act of taking refuge is considered to be a passageway *('jug sgo;* TN, p. 231) that generates an entering mind *('jug pa sems;* TN, p. 231). Taking refuge is the onset of the path *(lam)* to enlightenment. The practitioner has gone through a door. The beginner *(las dang po pa)* becomes transformed into a Buddhist, an insider *(nang pa;* TN, p. 231):

If you practice taking refuge continuously and it never leaves your thoughts, you become a Buddhist. (Jamgon Kongtrul [1977], p. 59)

You also become part of a spiritual community, the saṅgha. The Tibetan word for saṅgha, *dge 'dun,* literally means "those interested in virtue." The act of taking refuge is like becoming a member of a spiritual family. The holy beings who make up the family protect the practitioner. They serve as role models with whom he or she can identify. They strengthen the practitioner's faith.

At this stage of the practice, however, the emphasis is more on the practitioner himself than on the community. Wangchug Dorjé instructs, "Take what is proper, the lineage, into your vessel and generate a refuge mind to walk along the path of liberation" (WD, p. 78).[200] Though still defiled in so many ways, the beginner's mental continuum is now considered an adequate support *(brten)* for subsequent realizations.[201]

Tashi Namgyel discusses the benefit *(phan yon)* of taking refuge:

> In particular, the benefits of going for refuge are the following: becoming a Buddhist, becoming the support for all the [ethical] restraints, finding an end to harmful deeds resulting from previous actions, accumulating precious merit, never again falling to a lower state [of existence], remaining unharmed by the obstacle of [the extreme views of] eternalism and nihilism, bringing to fruition whatever has been reflected upon, the eight [virtuous dharmas] that quickly increase purification, and taking refuge in the Mahāyāna. These are the most important benefits. (TN, pp. 231–32)[202]

The way *(tshul)* to take refuge is by a formal acknowledgment that the lama and the Three Jewels are the appropriate support *(brten)* for practice. Such acknowledgment may take the form of either a simple mental prayer or a more elaborate ceremony. There are many variations on this ceremony in which the practitioner visualizes the root lama in front of oneself, surrounded by the many other lamas of the lineage, the buddhas, and the great bodhisattvas, all of whom stand to witness the formal acknowledgment of refuge.[203] Wangchug Dorjé reduces the complicated ritual to its basic structure in his root text:

> Bring forth the object of refuge, the five assemblies, so that they all stay in front of you. In order to take refuge, visualize these as such and recite the refuge [prayer]. (WD, p. 64)

After repeating the refuge vow *(dam tshig)*, the beginner affirms that he is a Buddhist practitioner. This entitles him not only to "enter the door" of the Dharma but also to "walk along the path" *(lam bgrod)*. Wangchug Dorjé elaborates:

> Now, if there is any skillful means for liberation and capacity for refuge from the miseries of saṃsāra, it is taking the support of the object of refuge, the Three Jewels. Having grasped the Buddha as the teacher, the Dharma as the path, and the Saṅgha as friends on the path, it is [then] necessary to walk along that path. (WD, p. 78)[204]

To "walk along that path" means to behave according to Buddhist teachings, as exemplified in the perfected lamas and the community of practitioners. Both Tashi Namgyel and Gampopa emphasize the rigorous ethical training that the new practitioner adopts. Extraordinary practice begins with the precepts or ethical rules *(sdom pa'i tshul khrim;* Skt., *pratimokṣa).*[205] According to the commentator:

> Taking refuge without ethical training is merely to have entered a door. Doing little to remain [a Buddhist] henceforth, the practitioner doesn't go on with his learning and becomes lax in the restraints that have been learned. These difficulties show he isn't very wise, even if he is a Buddhist. (TN, p. 231)

Therefore the best way of practicing after taking refuge is to learn the ethical training through gradual stages *(rim ba;* TN, p. 231). The mental action—taking refuge—followed by the adoption of a set of prescribed behaviors—the precepts—together constitute the training *(spyod pa)* of the practitioner, whereby one's own mental continuum tends toward greater conformity with the minds of the perfected masters. In so doing, the practitioner establishes himself or herself as a support *(rten)* for the enlightened attitude.

B. The Enlightened Attitude

If the act of taking refuge opens a door to a path that leads to the end of individual suffering, the enlightened attitude *(byang chub sems pa)* opens the same door, but it leads to end of suffering for all sentient beings. Taking refuge and the enlightened attitude are interrelated means for taking up *(blang ba)* the path. Though differing greatly in emphasis, they are usually combined into a single exercise.[206]

Taking refuge gives the practitioner a way of having his or her own mental continuum approximate the mind of the perfected beings of the lineage. In Hīnayāna Buddhism, whose ideal is the arhat, the perfected being has conquered only his own suffering. In the Mahāyāna, whose ideal is the bodhisattva, the perfected being has the intention of eradicating the suffering of all beings. The enlightened attitude is the "passageway" into the Mahāyāna (TN, p. 232). Here, taking refuge is linked to generating an enlightened attitude, by which the practitioner strives to become, and then does become, a bodhisattva. Wangchug Dorjé says in his root text:

> Generating the most excellent enlightened attitude for the sake of [all] sentient beings must in itself bring about the lofty state of perfect buddhahood [for all]. (WD, p. 79)

Gampopa defines the enlightened attitude as follows:

> The essence of the formation of an enlightened attitude is the desire for perfect enlightenment in order to be able to work for the benefit of others.[207]

The enlightened attitude is, first of all, a "desire for perfect enlightenment." The Tibetan phrase *byang chub sems pa* contains the verbal noun *sems pa*. This word often refers to the future and may therefore be translated as "to anticipate." The entire phrase means "to anticipate enlightenment." Gampopa discusses the importance of cultivating this frame of mind:

> A man who does not even begin to wish for enlightenment cannot, however excellent and perfect his behavior may be, enter the fold of the Mahāyāna and so cannot attain perfect Buddhahood.

But he will do so once he has started to desire supreme enlightenment and has entered the Mahāyānic fold.[208]

The practitioner who lacks an enlightened attitude cannot practice the specific ethical training of the bodhisattva, for example the six perfections. On the other hand, one who has generated an enlightened attitude has already set in motion a process that is likely to ripen into perfect enlightenment, if it does not go astray *('gol sa)*.

Secondly, the enlightened attitude is "for the benefit of others." This makes it a uniquely Mahāyāna attitude. According to Gampopa, a bodhisattva does not wish enlightenment for one or several others. A true bodhisattva will not be satisfied until all sentient beings, as limitless as the atoms of space, have ended their suffering through enlightenment.[209] This is why Wangchug Dorjé calls it a lofty state *(bla na med pa)*. Only a superior practitioner *(rab tu)* can generate such a noble attitude.[210]

In general *(spyi)* most commentators agree that the enlightened attitude is the primary support of the entire body of Mahāyāna teachings. For example:

> Generally speaking, once an individual's thoughts have turned to the Dharma, he will travel the Dharma-path only if he develops the enlightened attitude. If he does not develop it, he will not travel the Dharma-path. Whether his wholesome acts have been many or few, once he has acquired the means of attaining Buddhahood, he is said to have started on the Dharma-path. (Jamgon Kongtrul [1977], p. 60)[211]

In particular *(khyad par)*, the enlightened attitude is the "support" for the specific ethical training of a bodhisattva. Gampopa draws upon a number of similes to emphasize the significance of the enlightened attitude. It is "like the earth" because it is the ground of all virtues. It is "like gold" because it never changes until enlightenment is attained.[212] The oral tradition likens it to the foundation of a house, upon which the entire framework of practice is built. Even a small amount of this attitude is said to be "precious."[213]

A practitioner who fails to generate an enlightened attitude is said to experience bad results *(nyes dmigs)*. These include failure to realize enlightenment in this lifetime, failure to work for the benefit of others in this lifetime, and falling to lower states of existence in future lifetimes.[214] An enlightened attitude must be generated *(skye ba)*. Once it is generated, and continues to be generated again and again, it eventually stays *(gnas)* in the unfolding mental continuum and deepens *('phel ba)* at every stage of the path, on up through enlightenment. Gampopa makes this analogy:

> When an enlightened attitude which is like a seed has been planted in the life of a sentient being, which is like a field watered with benevolence and compassion, the thirty-seven branches conducive to enlightenment spread and by having ripened into the fruit of perfect Buddhahood bring about the happiness and welfare of sentient beings. Therefore, by the formation of this enlightened attitude the seed of Buddhahood is planted.[215]

Just as a seed contains the potential of a tree within itself, the enlightened attitude contains the potential of perfect buddhahood within it. Just as someone who sees a new moon knows it will become a full moon, a practitioner who generates the enlightened attitude also knows it will eventuate in buddhahood. These metaphors illustrate the doctrine of cause and effect and its importance in understanding the effect of generating an enlightened attitude.

The greater the force associated with an action, the more likely it will ripen in obvious ways. Therefore development of an enlightened attitude is typically accompanied by the taking of a vow *(dam tshig)*. Being difficult to break, a vow carries greater weight *(mthu)* relative to other actions and, as such, is more likely to insure that enlightenment for self and others will come to fruition. On the other hand, breaking the vow through lax practice cuts off *(bcod pa)* the effect, namely maturation toward enlightenment.

There are two types of enlightened attitudes, relative and ultimate, which correspond to the relative *(kun rdzob)* and absolute *(don dam)* levels of truth, respectively. The initiate cultivates the relative enlightened attitude by practicing the four immeasurables *(tshad med bzhi)*. For example, Wangchug Dorjé instructs in his root text, "Bring forth in your heart a mind meditating on the four immeasurables" (WD, p. 64). The four immeasurables are (1) kindness, or wishing only the best for others, (2) compassion for others' sufferings, (3) joy for others' gains, and (4) equanimity toward all beings. The ultimate enlightened attitude is the fruition of realization that comes only after some direct experience of emptiness. Nevertheless the potential for realizing the ultimate enlightened attitude is available to any initiate who sets the proper foundation by cultivating the relative enlightened attitude.[216]

There are two kinds of relative enlightened attitudes, namely *an enlightened-attitude-that-desires ('dod pa'i…)*; and *an enlightened-attitude-that-perseveres (gnyer ba'i…)*, and there is a different way *(tshul)* of cultivating each.

In his commentary on Wangchug Dorjé's root text, Jamgön Kongtrül explains that the enlightened-attitude-that-desires develops by "constantly think[ing], 'I will attain omniscient Buddhahood for the sake of all sentient beings'" (Jamgon Kongtrul [1977], p. 61). Thus the practitioner vows to strive for enlightenment for all sentient beings and then repeats the vow many times, day and night, so that it gathers force.[217] In addition to simple repetition of the vow, sometimes more elaborate ceremonies are used to generate such an attitude. These practices originated with Atiśa, whose way of conducting the ceremony *(sbyor tshul)* contained the following six steps:

1. Generating equanimity *(btang snyoms):* The practitioner starts by visualizing people who bring forth in him or her a strong feeling of love, then people who bring out a strong feeling of hatred, and finally people who bring out only a neutral feeling. This is repeated until the practitioner is able to generate equanimity toward these respective people, and ultimately toward all sentient beings. It is said to be impossible to generate an enlightened attitude without first developing equanimity.

2. Next the initiate imagines that over countless lifetimes all sentient beings were at one time his or her own mother *(mar shes)*. This practice is said to generate love *(byams)* toward all.

3. Next the practitioner recalls specific instances of kindness *(drin)* given by his or her own mother, and then visualizes the kindness of every sentient being, each of whom was also once the practitioner's mother in a former life.

4. Next comes a more systematic mindfulness of kindness *(drin dran)*, through which the practitioner specifically imagines the kindness given by close friends and also by his or her spiritual teacher(s), who were also the practitioner's mother in former lives.

5. Practicing these visualizations eventually leads to grasping the preciousness *(gces 'dzin pa)* of human life and also to the development of a desire *('dod pa)* to bring love *(byams)*, compassion *('snying rje)*, and joy *(dga' ba)* to all sentient beings. The signs that an enlightened-attitude-that-desires is developing typically include the spontaneous emergence of this feeling of preciousness in everyday life, a greater likelihood of restraining oneself

(sdom pa) from harmful behavior, and a greater willingness to serve *(bkol ba)* others.

6. Finally, these signs ripen into the enlightened-attitude-that-desires. At that point a powerful sense of kindness toward others manifests itself in nothing less than a desire for enlightenment for all others, even above that of the practitioner himself.[218]

Having generated the enlightened-attitude-that-desires, the initiate must act in accordance with his or her vow. The force of this developing attitude is strengthened through repeated practice. In short, the practitioner must train *(spyod pa)*. Training is necessary because of the risk of breaking the vow, or of letting it deteriorate *(nyams pa)*. For example, Jamgön Kongtrül explains:

> Regardless of the number of sentient beings involved, harboring malicious thoughts, such as, "Even if I have a chance to help you, I won't," or being filled with hate, envy or anger toward others is the transgression called "mentally abandoning sentient beings."
>
> Likewise, thinking, "I can't do anything to help myself or others! I may as well become a common worldly man! Complete Buddhahood is so hard to attain that it doesn't matter if I engender bodhicitta or not! I can't possibly help anyone!" adopting the attitude of a Shravaka or Pratyekabuddha, who is merely concerned with his own welfare; thinking "The benefits of bodhicitta are not that great"; or relaxing the vow—all these are attitudes contrary to bodhicitta.
>
> If you do not correct these attitudes within three hours, the vow is broken. (Jamgon Kongtrul [1977], p. 62)

If a broken vow is not immediately followed by acknowledgment of harm through confession, then the ceremony must be repeated to regenerate the enlightened-attitude-that-desires.

Gampopa describes five stages *(rim pa)* in the ripening of the enlightened-attitude-that-desires. First is nonabandonment *(sbang med)* of the attitude by thinking about the welfare of sentient beings at all times, in all situations. Second is protecting *(skyong ba)* one's newly awakened bodhicitta. A practitioner who does not abandon the enlightened attitude begins to manifest virtuous qualities much like those first encountered in the holy being, though to a lesser degree. Once these virtuous qualities are recognized within oneself, the practitioner begins to see their benefit *(phan yon)*. Not wishing to lose these precious qualities, the practitioner tries to protect them by striving more diligently in his or her training. Third, the practitioner tries to accumulate *('tshogs pa)* such qualities by more rigorously following the Buddhist ethical code. Fourth, by living in greater accordance with these ethical rules in all one's activities, the enlightened attitude is said to increase *('phel ba)*. Fifth is never forgetting *(brjed med)*. Forgetting the enlightened attitude is the result of the four black deeds *(nyes bzhi)*, which ripen from actions of previous lifetimes. These are lying, regret, slander, and deceit. The corresponding four white deeds serve as antidotes. The practitioner makes an active effort to refrain from committing the four black deeds and to counter them by intentionally doing the opposite of each—being truthful, acting in ways that cause no regrets, speaking favorably about others, and acting honestly.

Through continuous training of the enlightened-attitude-that-desires, the attitude is said to stay *(gnas)* more and more. It does not degenerate *(nyams pa)*. Rather, the practitioner is able "to keep bodhicitta continually in mind" (Jamgon Kongtrul [1977], p. 64). This positive attitude accompanies the practitioner as if it were his or her own shadow.[219] Over time the practitioner begins to notice how the enlightened-attitude-that-desires brings about subtle changes in behavior.

The enlightened-attitude-that-desires naturally evolves into the enlightened-attitude-that-perseveres. By itself, wishing is not enough. At some point the practitioner comes to realize that the entire course of everyday behavior must change and that it must approximate that of a bodhisattva. This realization is a natural outgrowth of understanding the doctrine of cause and effect. A mere vow to strive for the enlightenment of all beings is insufficient to overcome the great weight of accumulated negative karmic actions that constitute everyday behavior. The practitioner senses the enormous disparity between the intention of the vow being made and his or her everyday behavior. According to the doctrine of cause and effect, the vow made has only two possible outcomes: Either it can degenerate in the face of the practitioner's current behavior, or else he or she must change the entire course of everyday behavior and strive *(gnyer ba)* to act differently, moment by moment. The practitioner now strives to act like a bodhisattva.

At this point the practitioner enters a second phase of attitude training. Practice moves beyond the mere mental repetition of a wish into the arena of behavior. The attitude-that-desires is like opening a door. The attitude-that-perseveres is like walking through that door. Jamgön Kongtrül defines this latter attitude as follows:

> ...to perform wholesome acts which will actualize that promise, while thinking, "To that end, I will apply the instructions for...[simultaneous] Mahamudra meditation." Perseverance is like actually starting out on a path. (Jamgon Kongtrul [1977], p. 61)

The commentator likens the attitude-that-perseveres to the work it takes to cultivate crops once seeds have been planted:

> Carry out these tasks assiduously! As for the training in perseverance: just as a farmer who wants a good harvest must not simply seed his crops but cultivate them as well, you who want to attain Buddhahood need more than aspiration [desire]. You must also perform all types of Bodhisattva-activity to the best of your ability. (Jamgon Kongtrul [1977], p. 64)

Though there are many ways to act like a bodhisattva, it is especially important to try to act genuinely like a bodhisattva in some way, and to persevere regardless of the particular type of practice.

Even though an initiate may set out to act like a bodhisattva, his or her initial attempts are often subject to various errors *(gol ba)*. Those just beginning to act like bodhisattvas are often very pretentious. The two most common "'roots of degeneracy' are: 1. To pretend to be a Bodhisattva while hoping to be seen as a 'good Buddhist,' hoping to obtain food, clothing or fame, or hoping to appear better than others. 2. To act hypocritically, and call yourself a 'realized being' or siddha" (Jamgon Kongtrul [1977], p. 65).

The root cause of these errors is self-cherishing *(bdag gces 'dzin)*:[220]

> All humans make a great mistake in that they are very concerned about external enemies, which can only harm them in this life, yet they cherish their internal enemies—primarily self-grasping and self-cherishing—which harm them for countless lives. One should be less concerned with one's environment and more concerned with the motivation to deliver all beings from suffering.

> To attempt to develop bodhicitta [enlightened attitude] for the
> sake of one's own progress is still very selfish.[221]

These errors are due to a defective vow, which must be corrected before
proceeding. A practitioner who has recognized self-cherishing and over-
comes it is prepared to undergo the hardships entailed in acting like a bodhisattva (Jamgon Kongtrul [1977], p. 66).

There are numerous skillful means for training the enlightened-attitude-
that-perseveres. Ordered by degree of difficulty, these include: the ten deeds,
four immeasurables, six perfections, and giving and taking. In a general
sense, every practitioner is expected to manifest the ten deeds of a bodhisattva, which include staying faithful, studying the Dharma teachings, acting virtuously, avoiding harmful actions, helping sentient beings along the
path, adhering to the teachings, never being satisfied with the amount of
merit accumulated, striving for wisdom, remembering the overall goal of
the practice, and adopting skillful means.[222]

Most commentators concur that beginners use the four immeasurables
to train the attitude-that-perseveres. The practitioner is expected to
earnestly apply *(nan tan)* himself or herself in these practices, to repeat them
again and again. Rather than setting aside some arbitrary period, for example, in which to cultivate the four immeasurables, the practitioner now lets
them guide all behavior and interactions in the world—while sitting, walking, conversing, and so forth (Jamgon Kongtrul [1977], p. 66).

The six perfections *(phar phyin drug)* describe standard bodhisattva
behavior. These are more difficult to perform, and are usually taken up only
after gaining some proficiency with the four immeasurables. The six perfections include (1) giving *(sbyin pa)*, (2) ethical training *(tshul khrims)*, (3)
patience *(bzod pa)*, (4) diligence *(brtson 'grus)*, (5) contemplation *(bsam
stan)*, and (6) special insight *(shes rab)*. Many detailed descriptions of these
are available in English.[223] According to Gampopa, from whom these practices originated, the six perfections are practiced in a "fixed order,"[224] starting from the coarse and proceeding to the more subtle levels of bodhisattva
activity.

After gaining experience with these various types of bodhisattva activities,
the initiate may take up still other forms of training. For example, Wangchug
Dorjé describes the more advanced practice of giving and taking *(gtong len)*
this way. He says, "Give all profit and victory to others; accept all loss and
defeat for yourself" (Jamgon Kongtrul [1977], p. 63). The practitioner now

fully realizes the harm of self-importance, and therefore gives away whatever merit has accumulated through practice; he then imagines taking on the suffering of others as if it were his own pain. More detailed instructions on the way to practice giving and taking are as follows:

> First visualize a black spot in the centre of your body, representing selfishness, and when inhaling, imagine taking in all the sufferings of the world—all of them converging upon and destroying this black spot. When exhaling, send out your virtue and merit to all sentient beings for the sake of their happiness. This is a great method for increasing your own merit. If one is very competent in this practice, it is possible to transfer another's suffering to oneself, providing there is a close karmic relationship between the two beings.... Once while the Yogi known as the "Compassionate One" was giving a discourse, someone nearby hit a dog with a stone. The Yogi cried out in pain, and a bruise appeared on his body. The dog had been relieved of its suffering. The main object of *"tong len"* however is not to relieve another individual of his suffering immediately, but rather to attain Bodhicitta. Likewise, the greatest blessing of the Buddhas is not their power to relieve individual suffering, but the deliverance of the Dharma.[225]

The practitioner converts all the misfortunes and sufferings of life into skillful means to generate an enlightened-attitude-of-perseverance. When some unfortunate life circumstance occurs, the practitioner views it as none other than the ripening of past negative karma. Deep awareness of the suffering that has resulted from these past deeds leads to a greater motivation to persevere with spiritual practice. The practitioner becomes open to discovering the positive qualities inherent in all suffering. Illness and afflictive emotions, for example, are seen as potential teachers of the first noble truth of suffering. This realization further strengthens training the enlightened-attitude-of-perseverance. The initiate also goes beyond mere acceptance of his or her own misfortunes to take on the sufferings of others:

> When you are beset by illness or demons, tormented by gossip or by an upsurge of conflicting emotions, take on the misfortunes of all other sentient beings. (Jamgon Kongtrul [1977], p. 66)

The skillful practitioner more and more welcomes misfortune and rejects gain until he or she can keep the enlightened-attitude-of-perseverance synchronized with the very rhythm of the breath.[226]

The practitioner has made definitive progress along the path. His or her mental continuum and outward actions reflect greater alignment with those perfected bodhisattvas of the lineage. Jamgön Kongtrül sums up this progress as an attitude "continually in mind" (Jamgon Kongtrul [1977], p. 64), summarized in a single phrase, "great compassion" (*snying rje chen po;* Jamgon Kongtrul [1977], p. 68). Tashi Namgyel devotes an entire section of his commentary to a discussion of the immense benefits *(phan yon)* of generating the relative enlightened attitude. As with Jamgön Kongtrül, he stresses the centrality of compassion:

> To have just that one teaching is the same as having all the teachings in the palm of your hand. What is the one? It is great compassion. (TN, p. 233)[227]

Tashi Namgyel goes on to list the eight benefits of the enlightened attitude:

> Moreover, of the many benefits of [cultivating] the mind-that-enters [spiritual practice], there are the following: (1) entering into the Mahāyāna, (2) laying a foundation for all the teachings on the enlightened attitude, (3) eradicating the root of all harms, (4) penetrating the root of the enlightened attitude, (5) attaining immeasurable merit, (6) winning the delight of all the buddhas, (7) coming to the aid of all sentient beings, and (8) coming to buddhahood quickly. These are the eight benefits of the devotional mind *[smon sems].* Foremost of these [benefits] of the mind-that-enters is that the truth arises in your own mental continuum and also arises in the multitude of others [that you imagine as reaching enlightenment]. Therefore beginners who practice visualization meditation on love, compassion, and the enlightened attitude must also earnestly apply themselves as if discovering certainty in these. Without that, practicing the meditation on the enlightened attitude, in general, as the root of all virtue for those who do not yet have it, and in particular on emptiness, will not lead to the Mahāyāna

nor become the cause of perfect enlightenment. (TN, pp. 234–35)

The enlightened attitude lays the foundation for the remainder of the extraordinary practices. As the seed of compassion, it leads to abandoning harmful actions and the taking up of virtuous actions in the subsequent Vajrasattva recitation and maṇḍala offering, respectively. As the seed of emptiness, it sets the stage for the eventual realization of emptiness in the guru yoga exercise.

C. Eradicating Harmful Factors and Cultivating Factors That Potentiate Spiritual Development

Making a commitment to act according to the ideal of the bodhisattva is typically followed by painful awareness of how utterly impossible it seems to attain this lofty ideal, especially in comparison to one's present condition. Those with little faith quickly give up their vow. Those with stronger faith persist, yet with a deep-felt awareness of the distance from their ideal. Taking the vow heightens awareness of the ordinary mind's dysfunctional condition. From his knowledge of the doctrine of cause and effect, the practitioner knows that previous bad karmic actions have tremendous power. As these ripen in the present, they manifest as obstacles *(bar chod)* to spiritual development.

How does the practitioner overcome the weight of past obstacles that seriously interfere with his making real progress in spiritual development? There are two types of skillful means for accomplishing this. First, there are the means of cleansing *(sbyang thabs)* the harmful effects of past karma and obstacles through the mental act of confession *(gshags pa)* and of restraining oneself *(sdom pa)* from engaging in additional harmful behaviors. Second, there are the means of cultivating *(bsags thabs)* virtuous mental factors that serve to potentiate spiritual development. According to Buddhist psychology the means used to eradicate obstacles to spiritual development lead only to a reduction or eradication of obstacles but do not lead to potentiating states. Conversely, the means used to cultivate virtuous states that potentiate spiritual development only serve to develop virtuous states but do not eliminate obstacles. Therefore both sets of methods are necessary, and each method complements the other. Practicing both methods concurrently leads to the eradication of factors that hinder as well as to the cultivation of factors that potentiate spiritual development.

There are both nontantric and tantric practices to accomplish each of these ends. The nontantric, or sūtric, means for removing obstacles are confession, self-restraint, prayer, the four opponent powers, and the six antidotes. A common tantric method is the Vajrasattva meditation and recitation. The sūtric means of cultivating virtuous or potentiating states are the six perfections, the seven-limbed worship, also known as the seven branches, and various offerings. The traditional tantric means for cultivating these states is the maṇḍala offering. The great majority of commentaries in the mahāmudrā tradition follow the tantric methods, but sometimes incorporate various sūtric methods along with them.

Both sūtric and tantric means are visualization *(dmigs pa)* methods, although the object *(yul)* of the visualization differs in each. In the sūtric method, the practitioner takes the mental continuum and all its obstacles as the object of visualization. In the tantric method, an extraordinary being initially serves as the object, who through kindness *(drin pa)* bestows influence *(dbang)* upon the practitioner's mental continuum so that it is transformed in the process. The practitioner visualizes an extraordinary being, Vajrasattva, blessing the practitioner in such a way that all obstacles are cleared from the defiled mental continuum. Then the practitioner imagines shifting perspective and proceeding with spiritual practice as if Vajrasattva's extraordinary mind, not his or her own ordinary defiled mind, were conducting the practice. The practitioner imagines the mind becoming transformed into the purified model, Vajrasattva himself. The prerequisite for this practice is a special ceremony in which a holy being bestows influence to "cause the ripening" *(smin byed)*. Despite important differences between the sūtric and tantric methods, both outcomes—removing obstacles and cultivating virtuous or potentiating factors—result from either.

1. Removing Obstacles: Sin and Obscuration
a. The Nontantric Background

The mahāmudrā commentators Tashi Namgyel and Jamgön Kongtrül make a point of setting forth the sūtric practice upon which the tantric Vajrasattva meditation builds. The practice emphasizes the necessity of cleansing *(spyang ba)* the mental continuum of obstacles to spiritual development. There are two main types of obstacles—sin *(sdig pa)* and obscuration *(sgrib pa)*. Following the bodhisattva vow, the practitioner becomes more acutely aware of past harmful or sinful actions and their inevitable continuation into future mental states in a way that will obscure realization of the mind's true nature. Tashi Namgyel tells the practitioner:

> You will come to experience the ripening of these sinful actions, which result from [previous] sinful actions done out of weakness. (TN, p. 288)

Likewise, Jamgön Kongtrül says:

> Because of the similarity between cause and result, you will be naturally inclined to do harm, and your suffering will continually and uninterruptedly increase. (Jamgon Kongtrul [1977], p. 83)

In short, the practitioner is required to reflect on the bad result (*nyes byas;* TN, p. 238) of past and present conditions, especially the great weight of previous bad karmic actions to be overcome. Without an appreciation of the persistent negative influence of these states upon all attempts at spiritual development, it is very difficult to make any progress:

> It is difficult to directly come to realization, understanding the path of omniscience and its fruit, when obscured by the ripening of sins accumulated from the very beginning of each [negative] action up to now. These [negative states] have very great power. If they are not cleansed, you will experience only the misery of endless wandering in saṃsāra hereafter. What misery of saṃsāra is really necessary [when you can handle it], like water spilling from its container? So you must make the effort to cleanse these sins and obscurations. (TN, p. 238)[228]

The terms *sin* and *obscuration* have very particular meanings. The former pertains to transgressions of the Buddhist code of ethics. The latter pertains to the generally defiled and obscured condition of one's mental continuum that interferes with realizing the mind's true nature; however, obscurations are generally not associated with ethical infractions. Both types are classified as obstacles in that they hinder progress in spiritual development.

The fundamental sūtric means of cleansing obstacles are confession (*gshags pa*), self-restraint (*sdom pa*), and prayer (*gsol ba 'debs pa*). Confession is a mental act that directly follows reflection upon one of the four notions, namely the cause and effect of actions. For example, Tashi Namgyel says:

> Confession is done from the perspective of regretting [*'gyod pa*] previous sinful actions. (TN, p. 239)

Genuine confession involves more than going through the motions:

> To say "I committed this misdeed" is to admit wrongdoing. To say so with strong regret and mental anguish is to confess. To confess is to regard with reverence and wonder those who have not committed such misdeeds, to feel remorse and shame for your own misdeeds and to directly and sincerely pray: "Regard me with compassion, and purify this deed of mine." (Jamgon Kongtrul [1977], p. 84)

While confession reduces the potentially ripening effects of previous harmful actions, it does not prevent one from repeating a similar action in the future. When the occasion arises to repeat the same harmful action, the practitioner must make an active effort to restrain himself from the action. The mental act of confession is more corrective of the effects of past actions, while the behavioral act of self-restraint is more preventative.

The effects of confession and self-restraint are based upon the doctrine of cause and effect. The four powers of any karmic action comprise the following facts: (1) that the effects of the action are certain to ripen over time, (2) that the effects always proliferate, (3) that effects will not be incurred if one restrains oneself from performing the action, and (4) that the effect of any karmic action never diminishes.[229]

The four opponent powers (*stobs bzhi;* TN, pp. 239–40) are the means of counteracting each, respectively. The four opponent powers constitute a more systematic way of practicing confession and self-restraint. The first opponent power is "constant practice to bring about weakening" (TN, p. 239). Weakening *(rnam par sun pa)* is the opposite of ripening *(rnam par smin ba);* it occurs when confession and self-restraint are practiced "from the perspective of regretting previous sinful actions" (TN, p. 239).

The second opponent power is "to constantly practice the antidote" (TN, p. 239) in order to cut off the proliferation of negative karmic propensities over time. Preoccupation with practicing virtuous actions leaves little opportunity for previous negative karmic actions to increase in weight over time.

The third opponent power is to "turn back the resultant negative action" by means of resisting *(sdom pa)* the same action in the future (TN, p. 239). The practitioner makes the promise, "Even if my life is at stake, I will never do it again" (Jamgon Kongtrul [1977], p. 84). This is self-restraint. Because karmic effects never diminish, the only way to achieve the complete cessation of suffering is to achieve enlightenment.

The fourth opponent power uses taking refuge and the enlightened attitude as a support *(rten)* for spiritual development, which eventually comes to fruition with enlightenment.

Another common way of removing obstacles to spiritual development is by means of the the six antidotes *(gnyen drug)*. These are telling others about the precious qualities of buddhas and bodhisattvas, making offering altars and offerings, reading the sūtras and other Buddhist scriptures, reciting mantras, and appreciating important Buddhist ideas, such as the doctrine of emptiness (Jamgon Kongtrul [1977], p. 85).

Prayer *(gsol ba 'deb pa)* is another method used to cleanse sin. Confession and restraint are self-initiated and self-fulfilling positive actions. Prayer, on the other hand, though self-initiated, is directed toward someone else, namely a holy being, who is imagined to bring about the cleansing of obstacles from one's mental continuum. Wangchug Dorjé, in his mahāmudrā root text, illustrates how prayer becomes a vehicle for confession:

> I take refuge in the highest of beings.
> I make a confession about any of my vows that may have deteriorated, as these are the roots and branches of my [eventually realizing] the body, speech, and mind [of the Buddha].
> I pray to cleanse the entire mass of obstacles, which [otherwise would] bring about my fall [into a lower existence due to] the negative effect of [previous] sins and obscurations.
>
> After praying, [visualize your mental continuum being cleansed of obstacles as if] nectar from the big toe of Vajrasattva were pouring down like a stream and entering through the crown of your head. (WD, p. 81)

Although it is essentially a sūtra-type method for cleansing the mental continuum of obstacles, prayer bridges the gap between common sūtric methods such as confession and self-restraint and the tantric Vajrasattva method. The difference between them is that the latter is said to utilize direct influence *(dbang)* by an extraordinary being, in this case Vajrasattva, to transform the practitioner's mental continuum:

> When Śakyamuni Buddha attained Enlightenment, he showed the Dorje Sempa form to his Vajrayāna practitioners. He showed this extraordinary form because to have emanated an ordinary vision would have only generated ordinary mind. He showed the extraordinary Dorje Sempa form, the Buddha's Body of Bliss, Saṃbhogakaya, in order to generate in his practitioners the extraordinary mind.[230]

Through his kindness, Vajrasattva is imagined to have direct influence *(dbang)* on the ordinary mind of the practitioner in such a way as to clear away the potential ripening of all previous negative karmic influences.

The tantric Vajrasattva meditation yields the same result as sūtric methods such as the four opponent powers, only it does so more quickly due to the imagined direct intervention by an extraordinary being. Tashi Namgyel likens the meditation to a forest fire, which, once ignited by the winds of ethical training, quickly consumes all obstacles to spiritual development (TN, p. 240). This simple, brief meditation is said to have profound effects. Tashi Namgyel likens it to a tiny lamp lit in a dark room that is capable of quickly illuminating the entire room (TN, p. 240):

> Sins and obscurations accumulated from former lives are quickly eradicated by the tiny lamp of the Vajrasattva meditation and recitation.[231]

b. The Tantric Vajrasattva Meditation

The Vajrasattva meditation and recitation incorporates the sūtric practices of confession, self-restraint, and the four opponent powers. Wangchug Dorjé's root instructions give the essential outline of the practice, which has two parts, meditation *(sgom ba)* followed by recitation *(bzlas ba):*

1. Reflect, [then visualize] Vajrasattva on the crown of your head. He has the [hundred-syllable] mantra [in his heart]. After having

confessed and restrained, [imagine that] a stream of nectar pours [from him] and settles in your own body, wherein it cleanses all the sins and obscurations.

2. By reciting the hundred syllables, the signs of purification of obscurations arise [in your body and mind]. (WD, p. 84)

The procedure begins with reflection *(bsam pa)* on one of the four notions, the cause and effect of karma. Then the practitioner adopts a meditative posture and visualizes *(dmigs pa)* Vajrasattva on the crown of his or her head. He or she then prays to Vajrasattva directly to eradicate sins and obscurations and then imagines Vajrasattva's response. Nectar streams down from Vajrasattva and enters the practitioner's body, where it immediately purifies all sins and obscurations. The practitioner's body fills with pure light, just like the body of Vajrasattva. With the meditation now complete, the practitioner next recites the hundred-syllable mantra.[232] Vajrasattva is imagined as bestowing his direct influence *(dbang),* and says, "O son or daughter! All your sins and obscurations and degenerated vows are purified from this moment on."[233] The practitioner then visualizes that Vajrasattva dissolves into light, which is then absorbed into him "so that the body and mind of Vajrasattva and his own body, speech, and mind are indistinguishable" (WD, p. 81). The practitioner ends the meditation and recitation by dedicating the merit gained from the practice.[234]

The benefit of the Vajrasattva meditation and recitation is complete purification *(rnam par dag pa)* and also prevention from falling *(ltung ba)* into a lower state of existence in a future life as past negative karmic actions ripen (TN, p. 241).[235] The practitioner's mental continuum becomes purified before previous negative karmic actions can fully ripen:

> Actions which are wholly motivated by attachment, aversion and stupidity but have not assumed a concrete physical or verbal form are mental actions. Those which have assumed concrete form are physical or verbal actions. All actions begin as mental actions. Therefore it is said: "The mind is the source of the poison which leads the world into darkness." (Jamgon Kongtrul [1977], p. 82)

The practitioner is now more capable of making progress in spiritual practice without serious obstacles within the mental continuum.

Tashi Namgyel summarizes the benefit by saying "a completely purified sense of self will follow" (TN, p. 241). During the meditation the practitioner considers his or her ordinary self *(bdag nyid)* to be identical to that of the extraordinary being, Vajrasattva. After the meditation the practitioner becomes alert to certain signs *(rtags)* of the resultant purification, namely lightness of the body, less need for sleep, better health, clear-mindedness, and fleeting moments of special insight (Jamgon Kongtrul [1977], p. 82). Nevertheless the results of the meditation are short-lived. Without continual repetition of the meditation, along with daily ethical behavior, the practitioner is unable to sustain the momentary purification.[236]

2. Cultivating Virtue:
Factors That Potentiate Spiritual Development

Removing weeds and rocks doesn't guarantee that a seed will grow into a tree. It is far more important to supply the right positive conditions for the seed's development, such as water, sunlight, and nutrition. Likewise, eradication of obstacles to spiritual development does not automatically lead to progress in spiritual development, but simply to the removal of conditions that prevent progress. Genuine progress is a function of active cultivation of positive mental factors that have the ability to potentiate spiritual development. In the earlier Theravada Buddhist tradition these factors are known as the factors of enlightenment.[237] In the later Mahāyāna tradition such potentiating factors are found in the sūtra tradition of the six perfections[238] and in the tantric maṇḍala offering. Active cultivation of these virtuous *(dge ba)* mental factors over time gradually shifts the balance within the unfolding mental continuum in the direction of predominately positive states, which in turn lays the foundation for genuine spiritual progress and potentiates the likelihood of achieving the desired goal of enlightenment. The mahāmudrā refers to these positive changes in the mental continuum as "building a suitable vessel" *(snod kyi dag pa;* KT, p. 43).

a. The Sūtric Background

Like the Vajrasattva meditation, the tantric instructions for the maṇḍala offering are not readily intelligible apart from their sūtric background. As was the case for cleansing obstacles through the Vajrasattva meditation, the cultivation of virtue through the maṇḍala offering arises from the practitioner's understanding of the doctrine of cause and effect. Following some attempt to live up to the bodhisattva vow, the practitioner becomes acutely aware of his lack of virtuous thoughts and deeds, past and present, and anticipates the inevitable continuation of negative states into the future. Practitioners who have established a good foundation with the enlightened attitude now reflect upon the bodhisattva's virtuous qualities and strive to manifest them as the vessel of spiritual progress.

Yet, thinking and acting virtuously like a bodhisattva does not come readily. According to the doctrine of cause and effect, the practitioner must sow the seeds, or propensities *(bag chags)*, of virtue in current everyday practice. In time, these will ripen, first into an accumulation *(tshogs)* of positive propensities in the mental continuum and then into virtuous behaviors *(dge ba'i las)*. The greater the cultivation of virtuous propensities, the greater the power they carry to potentiate spiritual progress over time. Therefore it is advisable to make every effort to cultivate these virtuous states in thought and deed because, as Jamgön Kongtrül says, they lay the foundation for subsequent spiritual realization:

> Each individual who has begun to practice Dharma and acquired a degree of faith certainly has propensities toward wholesome conduct. However, just as a spark cannot become a flame [if you do not take the time to prepare the fuel], such propensities cannot be awakened in an instant. Until they have been awakened [or transformed into] wholesome conduct, you will experience no realization. The little you do experience will not grow. But if you perform the wholesome deeds [described below], this will create the proper conditions for the awakening of your propensities. As soon as they have been awakened, you will experience a powerful wave of realization. (Jamgon Kongtrul [1977], p. 105)

The "powerful wave of realization" refers to the initial signs *(rtags)* of positive propensities ripening in the mental continuum that serve to potentiate further spiritual growth. Later these positive signs, first arising spontaneously in the mental continuum, eventually manifest as virtuous behavior in everyday life. The means of cultivating *(bsags thabs)* virtuous propensities in the mahāmudrā tradition are the six perfections and the seven-limbed worship, in general, and the maṇḍala offering, in particular. The former two are the sūtric foundation upon which the latter, tantric maṇḍala offering rests.

The fundamental means of cultivating virtue is through the two accumulations *(tshogs gnyis)*. The verb *sog pa* (derivative, *tshogs*) means "to heap up, collect, or gather." The verb is translated here as "to cultivate," in order to capture the meaning of ripening over time, according to the doctrine of cause and effect. The verb *to cultivate* also captures the sense of active effort on the part of the practitioner since, as Tashi Namgyel says, one must be diligent when cultivating accumulations so that they hold sufficient power. The noun *tshogs* refers to that which is gathered—an "assembly, heap, or accumulation."

There are two types of accumulations, the accumulation of merit *(bsod nams)* and the accumulation of awakened wisdom *(ye shes)*. The former pertains to virtuous propensities accumulated by one's own skillful effort, which ripen in the form of positive mental states and virtuous behavior in the future, but which do not ripen in the form of realization. The latter are virtuous propensities resulting from one's skillful effort, which eventually ripen in the form of direct realization of spiritual truth:

> In general, if you have not accumulated the assembly of merit, the cause, then you will not attain good opportunities or the blissful realms [of the gods in future lives]. In particular, if you have not accumulated the assembly of wisdom—the effect—along with the assembly of merit, then you will not understand the view of emptiness. (TN, p. 235)

Commentators concur that the primary means for developing the two accumulations is practicing the six perfections. The first five perfections—giving, ethical training, patience, diligence, and contemplation—correspond to the accumulation of merit, whereas the last perfection, special insightfulness, corresponds to the accumulation of wisdom (TN, p. 236).[239] The six perfections are virtuous actions, epitomized in the behavior of a bodhisattva or buddha. The practitioner's initial cultivation of the six perfections typically falls far short of this lofty ideal, but nevertheless serves to awaken virtuous propensities. Such actions, however insignificant they may seem at first, necessarily proliferate, according to the third principle of the doctrine of cause and effect. A process is initiated that slowly builds a positive karmic force and eventually ripens into perfection.

As the ordinary mind is so defiled and lacking in virtuous thought, it is very difficult for a beginner to start with meditations designed to cultivate virtue. According to the usual sequence of instructions, the practitioner first establishes a foundation of external, virtuous behaviors according to the six perfections and then proceeds to establish internal virtuous states through reflective visualization. The very popular seven-limbed worship (*yan lag bdun*)[240] combines external ritual action with internally oriented reflection (*bsams pa;* TN, p. 237). The maṇḍala offering combines ritual action with more elaborate visualization. Here is a brief summary of the seven-limbed worship:

OBEISANCE

I bow down with pure body, speech, and mind
To all without exception of all
The lions of men, the Tathāgatas of the three times
In the worlds of the ten directions.
Through the power of my aspirations for good deeds
I bow down to all the Conquerors with extreme respect,
Myself adopting forms as numerous as the particles of the worlds,
And with all the Conquerors vivid before my mind.
I consider that in one particle are Buddhas as numerous
As the particles of the worlds, sitting in the middle
Of Buddha Sons, and that the Conquerors fill all
Without exception of the entities of phenomena.
I praise all the Sugatas and express
The qualities of all the Conquerors with all
The oceans of sounds of the melodious intoner [the tongue],
Inexhaustible oceans praising them.

OFFERING

I offer to all the Conquerors
Excellent flowers, excellent garlands,
Pleasant sounds, fragrant ointments,
Superior umbrellas, superior lamps, and excellent incense.
I offer to all the Conquerors
Excellent clothing, superior fragrances,
Fragrant powders, and mounds of incense equal to Mount Meru,
And all specially arrayed marvels.
I also consider all extensive, unequalled acts
Of offering to be for all the Conquerors.

By the powers of faith in good deeds
I bow down and revere all the Conquerors.
[Visualization of the Assembly]

CONFESSION

I confess individually all sins
Done by me with body, speech,
Or mind through the power of
Desire, hatred, ignorance.

ADMIRATION

I admire and will emulate the meritorious actions
Of all the Conqueror Buddhas of the ten directions,
The Buddha Sons, the Solitary Realizers, those still learning,
Those with no more learning, all the migrators.

ENTREATY

I entreat all the protectors, who have found non-attachment
And have progressively awakened into enlightenment
And are the lights of the world systems of the ten directions,
To turn the unsurpassed wheel [of doctrine].

SUPPLICATION

I supplicate with pressed palms those planning
To show *nirvāṇa* to the world to dwell here
Even as many aeons as the particles in the realms
To help bring happiness to all migrators.

DEDICATION

I dedicate all the little virtue
I have accumulated through obeisance,
Offering, confession, admiration, entreaty,
And supplication toward perfect enlightenment.[241]

b. The Tantric Maṇḍala Offering

The tantric maṇḍala offering yields the same outcome as the sūtric seven-limbed worship, but the result comes much more quickly due to the direct influence of extraordinary beings. Jamgön Kongtrül likens the sūtric practice to firewood that slowly smolders, and the tantric practice to a spark that suddenly ignites all virtuous propensities (Jamgon Kongtrul [1977], p. 105). He says:

> In brief, the profound Mandala-Offering is included in these instructions in the Foundations because it is so useful for the rapid perfection of the Accumulations. (Jamgon Kongtrul [1977], p. 111)

Wangchug Dorjé's root instructions give the essential outline of the practice:

1. The preparation maṇḍala: on five heaps [of rice].
2. The offering maṇḍala: Generating these [as] five jewels through offering the various prepared substances.
The signs of developing the two accumulations are generated in these [two] stages. (WD, p. 64)

The maṇḍala offering incorporates the seven-limbed worship within its structure. The practice begins with the construction of a preparation maṇḍala *(sgrub pa'i mandala)*, in which five accumulations *(tshom ba'i lnga)*, which are symbolized by using external substances such as gold, shells, or grain, are set out and imagined to represent the five objects of refuge *(yul)*. The five objects are the tutelary deities *(yidams);* the buddhas and bodhisattvas; the Dharma teachings; the saṅgha community; and the Dharma protectors. Sometimes the practitioner's root lama is considered to be a sixth object of refuge.[242]

The second stage is the construction of the offering maṇḍala *(mchod pa'i mandala)*, in which the practitioner visualizes an ideal universe according to thirty-seven standard iconographical features, among which are oceans, continents, mountains, lakes, cities, palaces, sun, moon, sky, special wealth, offering goddesses, precious objects, and so forth. These components of the symbolized universe are then offered, in a standardized sequence, to the refuge objects. Though the visualization is sometimes very elaborate, the essence of the practice is as follows:

> In brief, imagine that you are offering all the possessions of gods and men that can possibly be accumulated, as well as all the

wonderful things in the ten directions which are not owned by anyone. (Jamgon Kongtrul [1977], p. 104)

The practitioner then prays for the essential realizations of the mahāmudrā tradition and does the seven-limbed worship and a final prayer. Then he or she imagines light radiating from the objects of refuge in the preparation mandala and striking all sentient beings, thereby activating the two accumulations in them (Jamgon Kongtrul [1977], p. 105). The objects of refuge then dissolve into light and are absorbed into the practitioner's heart. The meditation ends with a dedication of merit.[243]

The ripening effects of the maṇḍala offering first become manifest as certain signs *(rtags)* in the form of auspicious dreams, fleeting moments of special insight, and ease in visualizing the maṇḍala offering. As a practice, the maṇḍala offering is inclusive of both the accumulation of merit (by offering up the entire universe in symbolic form) and the accumulation of wisdom (by understanding what is offered to be empty of any self-existent reality). *The ten benefits of accumulating merit* pertain to future human rebirths. They are as follows: having a handsome face, good complexion, influential speech, influence over associates, the affection of gods and men, the companionship of holy men, robust health, wealth, higher rebirth, and enlightenment. Additional benefits are sometimes described, such as being reborn in the blissful god realms (Jamgon Kongtrul [1977], p. 110; TN, p. 235). The benefit of accumulating wisdom is complete purification of all negative emotional states as an outgrowth of understanding the view of emptiness (TN, pp. 235–36), and also potential attainment of mahāmudrā enlightenment in this lifetime (Jamgon Kongtrul [1977], p. 104).

The most important benefit, however, is the acquisition of a solid foundation of virtuous propensities within the practitioner's mental continuum. Over time the practitioner will become a spreader of virtuous action *(las 'phro)* in the form of a greater tendency to do good deeds and to emulate the bodhisattva ideal. As the power of the virtuous states increases, the practitioner more spontaneously and naturally acts like a bodhisattva.

Cleansing obstacles from the mental continuum empties this vessel of negative states. Offering the maṇḍala fills the vessel of the mind with positive, potentiating states, namely the two accumulations. The very act of such profound offering—symbolically offering the entire universe—is a step toward emptiness of self. The practitioner has now sown the seeds for understanding emptiness. Such understanding becomes the topic of the last of the extraordinary preliminaries, namely guru yoga.

c. Guru Yoga

Having mastered the ordinary and extraordinary practices and built the mental continuum as a suitable vessel for spiritual realization, the practitioner is now in a position to deepen his or her spiritual knowledge. The developing knowledge goes beyond mere intellectual understanding *(go ba)*, and ripens first into direct experience *(nyams ba)* and eventually into understanding *(rtogs ba)*.[244] Both stages are attained through the practice of guru yoga, the goal of which is to lay the foundation for direct experience of the natural state of the mind, which in turn becomes the basic understanding, and eventually perfect realization, of mahāmudrā. Since, ultimately, wisdom and compassion are manifestations of the same nondual condition of the fully realized mind, guru yoga becomes the skillful means by which the seed of awakened wisdom is planted, which then complements the seed of compassion previously planted through the development of an enlightened attitude. Guru yoga forges the link between the previously established relative enlightened attitude and the ultimate enlightened attitude wherein wisdom and compassion become the same nondual aspect of the enlightened mind.

Tantric guru yoga works much more quickly than the sūtric method of prayer, because in the tantric method the lama directly transmits influence *(dbang)*. This helps the initiate to become capable of understanding the fundamental view *(lta ba)* of the realized mind espoused in the mahāmudrā tradition, an understanding that has the potential to eventually ripen into the awakened wisdom of enlightenment. The key element of tantric guru yoga is empowerment *(byin gyis brlabs)*. Tashi Namgyel says, "For the sake of empowerment, [practice] guru yoga" (TN, p. 654). The term *empowerment* literally means "bestowing a gift or blessing" ("gift-waves"). The type of blessing given, however, has a very specific field of meaning.

First, the lama formally authorizes the initiate to practice according to the mahāmudrā tradition. He extends to the initiate the gift of direct influence by an extraordinary, enlightened mind, through which the practitioner becomes relatively free of those obstacles *(bar cad)* continuously blocking direct realization of the natural condition of the enlightened mind according to its view depicted in the mahāmudrā tradition. Kyabje Kalu Rinpoche says, "The root lama is the one who causes us to recognize the nature of our mind; he is the source of the blessings that introduce us to mahāmudrā, the ultimate nature of mind; he shows us how to recognize our mind as the dharmakaya."[245] Jamgön Kongtrül stresses the necessity *(dgos ba)* of such direct influence by an extraordinary being. He also says, "In general, in order to follow the [tantric] Mantrayana or Vajrayana, especially to receive instructions in the meditation of the Perfection or Fulfillment Stage,[246] you must first receive the guru's blessing. Until you have received it, you will not be on the true path" (Jamgon Kongtrul [1977], p. 123). Guru yoga is the way to be blessed with the four influences *(dbang bzhi)*, which are the keys to understanding the four most important points of direct realization along the overall spiritual path.

Second, the blessing is also defined *post hoc* by "what necessarily follows from having meditated," namely the benefit (TN, p. 244).[247] The benefit of receiving the four influences is an initial taste of awakened wisdom *(ye shes)*, pertaining to the natural state of the enlightened mind according to the mahāmudrā tradition. Tashi Namgyel illustrates that the goal of guru yoga is to plant the seed of awakened wisdom:[248] "Pray to generate this precious understanding [of awakened wisdom] [directly] in your mental continuum...through getting the empowerment" (TN, p. 248).

Third, the lama bestows upon the initiate the blessing of complete assistance and support *(bsten;* WD, p. 64). A very special guru-practitioner relationship develops to support progress at all stages of the practice, and this continues even beyond full enlightenment.

In his brief root instructions Wangchug Dorjé illustrates all three aspects *(rnam pa)* of the lama's blessing described above:

> To practice guru yoga, meditate [as if the lama were] on top of your head, pray with fervent respectful admiration, and [then] the four influences will develop through the delight of the five [refuge objects]. If you take the lama's support, the signs of having penetrated empowerment, which arise from his compassion, will [eventually] come [to fruition]. (WD, p. 64)

The final phrase, "empowerment...out of compassion" *(thugs rje'i byin rlabs)*, signifies that guru yoga is a tantric practice. The lama is the embodiment of buddhahood, of all three buddha bodies—the emanation body, the enjoyment body, and the Dharma body.[249] Therefore, the lama, while appearing to the initiate in an ordinary human form, simultaneously acts on the level of the enjoyment body and the Dharma body. The lama is said to embody the complete understanding of emptiness in its subtlest form, namely the awakened wisdom of mahāmudrā. Out of his compassion, the lama manifests an emanation body so as to appear in an ordinary human form so that he or she can impart awakened wisdom to others. What began as a seemingly chance encounter with an extraordinary being culminates in guru yoga as a formal initiation (*dbang skur ba;* WD, p. 83) in order to quickly bring the practitioner to direct realization by means of the four influences.[250]

As a tantric practice, the refuge object (*yul*) used during the visualization is not the lama's ordinary form. The practitioner visualizes the lama in an extraordinary form, usually that of the cosmic buddha, Dorjé Chang, the primordial originator of the mahāmudrā lineage.[251] While, in a relative sense, it is the extraordinary condition of Dorjé Chang's mind, not the ordinary lama himself, who conveys the four influences, in an ultimate sense these are one and the same. Interestingly, Tashi Namgyel speaks of meditation upon the "as if" lama *(bla ma ji ltar):*

> For the benefit of all sentient beings, visualize the lama as if [he had] Dorjé Chang's [extraordinary mind], yet staying in his ordinary bodily form. (TN, p. 243)

Likewise:

> In reality, your guru may be an ordinary being or a manifestation of a Buddha or Bodhisattva. But if you can pray to him while meditating that he is the Buddha, all of the Buddhas, Bodhisattvas and yidams will enter the body, speech and mind of your Vajrayana master and work for the benefit of all beings. (Jamgon Kongtrul [1977], p. 126)

The practitioner adopts the attitude that his or her lama is Dorjé Chang himself. In actual practice he or she visualizes the entire Kagyü lineage—the tutelary deities, buddhas, bodhisattvas, and the remainder of the refuge objects—surrounding the root lama. After a series of ritual prayers and chants, "all the refuge objects are melted into the lama" (TN, p. 273). The visualized root lama symbolizes, in this absorbed form *(bsdu ba'i yul),* all the refuge objects as well as the three buddha bodies. To worship the lama during guru yoga is "the way to meditate upon yourself as being connected to *['dus]* all the buddhas" (TN, p. 243). Guru yoga is the means of pointing out the fundamental identity of the practitioner's own mental continuum and that of the enlightened refuge objects and lama.

The skillful means *(thabs)* or way *(tshul)* of practicing guru yoga is depicted by a number of technical terms such as: "generating the force of faith," "fervent respectful admiration," and "prayer." Faith is said to be the "highest vehicle." The type of faith required is stronger than the previous "unwavering faith," through which the practitioner took the lineage as a support of spiritual practice. Now the practitioner is instructed to "generate faith like the ancient ones" *(sngon po ji bzhin dad pa;* WD, p. 246). Such strong faith arises from the "force of longing" *(gdung shugs;* TN, p. 246), and also through "recollecting the kind words of your lama" (TN, p. 246).

Respectful admiration *(mos gus),* which is associated with "faith like the ancients," is the prerequisite to empowerment. Gampopa says:

> If you don't penetrate the lama's empowerment, it isn't possible to receive the transmitted truths of mahāmudrā. To penetrate the empowerment of the lama isn't difficult. If you have respectful admiration, then you penetrate it after finishing the prayers. (TN, p. 248)

Tashi Namgyel uses the adverb *rtag du,* which means "constantly." The initiate is advised to "constantly respect his lama." These adverbs distinguish the heretofore intensified version of respectful admiration from its predecessor. Other commentators use verbal nouns such as "earnest application" *(nan tan;* TN, p. 242) and "effort" *('bad pa;* TN, p. 245)[252] to convey the intensification of respectful admiration required.

The way to pray *(gsol ba' debs lugs;* TN, p. 248) for empowerment is to "pray over and over, uninterruptedly, when going, sitting, and sleeping" (TN, pp. 248–49). Empowerment as a skillful means eclipses the entire set of previous skillful means, and the effects of each are now qualitatively stronger due to the practitioner's progress in building the vessel. Table 4 illustrates how the practitioner completes the set of positive mental factors that potentiate enlightenment with guru yoga:

TABLE 4: SUMMARY OF SKILLFUL MEANS
USED TO BUILD THE VESSEL

Generating interest and causing faith to arise	
Interest; respectful admiration *('dun pa; mos gus)* Faith; depending on the lineage *(dad pa)*	

Preliminary practice	
Ordinary:	Earnest application *(nan tan)*
Extraordinary:	Visualization meditation *(dmigs pa)* (Refuge...maṇḍala offering)
Extraordinary: (Guru yoga)	Fervent respectful admiration *(mos gus drag po)* Faith of the ancient ones *(sngon po'i dad pa)* Earnest application *(nan tan)* Constant prayer *(rtag du gsol btab)*

The progress is summarized using the verb *rjes su brang ba,* which means "to pursue." In every way possible, the practitioner pursues the lama. When he is present, the practitioner sits at his feet. When he is absent, the lama is constantly visualized. Taking the lama to be a fully realized buddha, the practitioner generates him as the skillful means of empowerment.

The reason (*mtshan nyid;* TN, p. 244) for practicing respectful admiration is to "gain the delight of the lama by harmonizing with him" (TN, p. 245).[253] The lama, out of kindness (*'drin pa;* TN, p. 245), then empowers the practitioner to realize the fundamental view of the mind according to the mahāmudrā tradition.

Following respectful admiration is the actual visualization meditation. The basic structure is as follows:

1. It begins with the practitioner doing a generating visualization *[dmigs skye]* of himself or herself as a tutelary deity, usually Dorjé Phalmo. Failure to visualize oneself in the extraordinary form exemplifies lack of respectful admiration, through which the practitioner fails to receive empowerment. Next the root lama is visualized in the form of Dorjé Chang on top of the practitioner's own head. Finally, the five refuge objects and the entire lineage are visualized in the surrounding space.

2. The practitioner should then pray *[gsol btab]* to these for their blessing.

3. The practitioner then practices an absorbing visualization *[bsdu ba'i dmigs pa]*. In it, the five refuge objects and the entire lineage of extraordinary beings dissolve into light, and are then absorbed into the luminous body of the root lama, who retains the form of Dorjé Chang.

4. An offering is made, for example, the seven-limbed worship.

5. The practitioner prays for realization of the three buddha bodies. He or she may also make a number of additional prayers.

6. Next the practitioner prays directly for the empowerment. He or she visualizes the act of empowerment in which various colored lights emanate from specific locations of the root lama's body simultaneously, and touch the corresponding points on the practitioner's own body. Obscurations then disappear, and then the four influences are bestowed.

7. Finally the practitioner does a dissolving visualization *['jig ba'i dmigs ba]*. In this, the root lama dissolves into light, which in turn enters the head of the practitioner. Thereupon the root lama's [extraordinary] mind *[thugs]*, and also the [extraordinary] minds all the beings in the entire lineage and pantheon, become indistinguishable *[dphye med]* from the practitioner's own mental continuum [on some level]. The practitioner's mind is united *['dus pa]* to their [extraordinary] minds, and the practitioner's own mental continuum [becomes the vehicle for the eventual] manifestation of awakened wisdom.

8. The practitioner closes the visualization by dedicating the merit. The overall purpose of the meditation is to generate deep concentration influence *[ting nge 'dzin gye dbang]*. (TN, p. 249)

There are many versions of guru yoga, which, though sharing a basic structure, vary in length, wording of prayers, and also the particular extraordinary form in which the root lama is visualized. Dorjé Chang, the cosmic originator of the mahāmudrā lineage in primordial time, is commonly used.[254] With respect to more complex visualizations, Karma Kamtshang, for example, presents a version in which the root lama is imagined as having four bodies, corresponding with the four influences, respectively.[255] Wangchug Dorjé's expanded version of his root text illustrates the basic practices:

[1. Generating Visualization]

Guru yoga quickly helps you penetrate empowerment. To get the highest bliss, [generate] yourself as a tutelary deity. In the clear sky on top of your head is your very own root lama, your teacher of virtue, who appears with a gold and black hat, and holds a vajra and bell. He appears in order to bring forth [the realization in you] that wisdom and skillful means are nondual.... Pray to the precious lama to be quickly given the initiation of the four influences within you, and also the fruition of these four after you meet with them and have them ripen in your own mental continuum. Specifically, if you don't get the direct experience and understanding, then you have to establish the conditions for this lofty state and generate it [directly] in your mental continuum, thinking, "Now let it be transferred [directly] from these beings." Pray this way and, in a short time, it will come strongly and be known in its certainty.

[2. Absorbing-Visualization]

By absorbing the assembly of the lineage lamas, buddhas, bodhisattvas, ḍākinīs, and the Dharma protectors into your root lama, you [now] have the best of the three inner and outer secrets within you. So meditate on the [extraordinary] body that links you to the lama, Three Jewels, and all the rest of these. [Then] offer the seven-limbed worship. Pray like this: "I pray to all sentient beings equally throughout space, the lamas, and the precious buddhas [for blessings]. I pray for the omniscient Dharma body, for the perfect, great blissful enjoyment body, and for the compassionate emanation body." These prayers are made with respectful admiration when reflecting upon the [extraordinary] body that links [the three bodies] to the Three Jewels [and to yourself].

[3. Prayer and Empowerment Visualization]

When the four influences that the lama bestows manifest as white, red, and blue light emanating from the lama's forehead, throat, and heart, respectively, these light rays then strike the three corresponding locations on your body. They cleanse [dag pa] sin and obscurations from the three—body, speech, and mind—respectively. After that you get the four influences: (1)

vase, (2) secret, (3) special insight, and (4) wisdom. The first influence helps you with the generation stage meditation *[bskyed rim]*; the second, with the perfection stage meditation *[rdzags rim]*, using the energy currents; the third, with the meditation on nonduality *[snyom 'jug]* of wisdom and means and the four joys; the last, with direct realignment [of your mental continuum] with basis enlightenment, which then brings fruition [namely realization of the emanation, enjoyment, and Dharma bodies]. Now, each of these three kinds of colored light emanate from the respective locations on the lama's body, and when they strike your own body all over, they cleanse whatever propensities might still obscure the three gates [body, speech, and mind]. Then you attain the four influences [which establish a foundation for realizing the three moments of enlightenment: the basis, wherein awareness-itself and emptiness are nondual; the path, the power of which manifests the real-entity body of seeming substance, or the great-bliss body; and the fruit [enlightenment].

[4. Dissolving Meditation]
Then melt the lama into light and absorb him into yourself. [The mind] stays in non-artificialness, holding the perspective that "the body, speech, and mind of the lama, and your own body, speech, and mind are indistinguishable."

[5. Dedication]
Because this [meditation] is so very important, meditate using earnest application. (WD, pp. 83–84)[256]

Guru yoga has two main effects: what is given *(dbul ba)* and the benefit of that *(phan yon)*. The former pertains to cleansing *(dag pa)*. By visualizing the respective colored lights striking one's own body, sins and obscurations are cleansed. Tashi Namgyel specifically refers to cleansing suffering and fear. He says that guru yoga cleans not only emotional conflict *(nyon mong)* but also mistaken notions *(blo)*. "All kinds of [wrong] notions are taken away by the lama" (TN, p. 251). With such added clarity of mind, the practitioner's unfolding mental continuum for the first time begins to resemble a spontaneous meditative state. The commentator continues:

Generate the unborn meditation, and the gain arising from its generation is said to be the coarse effect coming from the empowerment. (TN, p. 242)

Such meditative clarity is essential to the subsequent development of awakened wisdom.

Each of the four influences[257] pertains to a specific level of meditation within the tantric tradition that corresponds to one of the various levels of attainment in the mahāmudrā tradition. For example, the tantric generation stage *(bskyed rim)* develops deep concentration using an extraordinary deity as the meditation object. The mahāmudrā concentration practices described in this book use a different meditation object, but the result is the same. The vase empowerment potentiates the development of each, respectively. The tantric perfection stage *(rdzogs rim)* consists of meditations utilizing subtle energy currents. The comparable mahāmudrā practices in this book for the secret empowerment pertain to the special-insight meditations regarding emptiness. Equalization *(snyon 'tug)* and direct realignment *(rten 'brel mngon du bya)* are extraordinary tantric practices potentiated by the insight and wisdom empowerments, respectively. These very advanced tantric practices are comparable to the one-taste and non-meditation extraordinary meditations in the mahāmudrā system. Tashi Namgyel says that the eventual fruition of these empowerments is a "state of omniscience" (TN, p. 247). With enlightenment the practitioner directly reconfigures the ordinary mental continuum into the three buddha bodies. Table 5 shows the correspondence between tantra and mahāmudrā practices as they pertain to the four empowerments or influences.

TABLE 5: RELATED MAHĀMUDRĀ AND TANTRIC PRACTICES WITH RESPECT TO THE FOUR EMPOWERMENTS

	Influence	Buddha-Body	Tantric Practice	Mahāmudrā Practice	Color	Gate
Beginning	Vase	Emanation	Generation stage	Concentration	White	Forehead
Essential	Secret	Enjoyment	Perfection stage	Special insight	Red	Throat
Concluding	Special insight	Dharma	Nonduality	One taste	Blue	Heart
Practice	Wisdom	Fruit	Direct realignment	Non-meditation	Blue	Heart

The four empowerments establish the necessary positive influence over the practitioner's ordinary mental continuum so as to increase the likelihood that the respective realizations will come from serious practice. The main benefit of empowerment is said to be the potential to realize emptiness *(stong ba)*, the fundamental realization upon which all advanced realizations depend. Tashi Namgyel says, "He who practices guru yoga holds buddhahood's benefit, namely emptiness" (TN, p. 250). Just as developing the enlightened attitude imparted compassion, guru yoga imparts wisdom. Through his kindness, the lama touches the practitioner with his light and in so doing directly points out emptiness as it manifests, or eventually will manifest, in the practitioner's own mental continuum. In this way the practitioner literally "changes his mind" about spiritual development.

Much earlier, when the beginner was given advice about the fundamental view, namely emptiness, it led only to an intellectual understanding *(go ba)* of it. With empowerment, the practitioner directly experiences *(nyams len)* this view as the basis of meditation practice. While the effects of guru yoga may be subtle at first, they nevertheless lead to a different experience of the mental continuum, which over time will ripen into genuine understanding *(rtogs pa)* of emptiness. Therefore if you have respectful admiration and then go into and penetrate empowerment, understanding of the mind arises (TN, p. 247).

The practitioner is empowered with the "wisdom of omniscience," the subtlest degree of emptiness *(kun khyen pa'i shes;* TN, p. 245). Even though the effects may not at all be obvious at first, Tashi Namgyel says, if you practice diligently following empowerment, "You will become enlightened even though you don't think about enlightenment" (TN, p. 247). These new propensities of empowered awakened wisdom progressively gain force and eventually ripen. The necessary groundwork has been laid. The subsequent advanced preliminaries, and after that the concentraton, special-insight, and extraordinary-meditation practices, are simply manifestations of the progressive ripening of this same wisdom. Furthermore, the three stages of enlightenment—basis, path, and fruition—are also manifestations of this same deepening wisdom. With the four influences the practitioner develops the potential to understand that "the body, speech, and mind of the lama and your own body, speech, and mind are indistinguishable." As Tashi Namgyel says, "You quickly become like the Ancient Ones" (TN, p. 246).

After empowerment it is as if the root lama's body, speech, and mind have penetrated those of the practitioner. There they are said to "stay" (*gnas;* TN, p. 249). Tashi Namgyel explains *staying* as follows: "The lama penetrates the top of your head. Then he constantly dwells in the center of your heart" (TN, p. 250). Taking the lama as the support of practice means that the propensities of his extraordinary mind constantly work their effect so as to allow their ripening in the ordinary mental continuum of the practitioner.

Staying implies that the entire lineage of extraordinary beings work their effect within the mental continuum of the practitioner:

> But if you pray to him while meditating that he is the Buddha, then all the Buddhas, Bodhisattvas and Yidams will enter the body, speech and mind of your Vajrayana master and work for the benefit of all beings. (Jamgon Kongtrul [1977], p. 126)

Through guru yoga, the practitioner establishes an intimate connection to the lama and the lineage. It is an absolute bond *(dam tshig),* one that cannot easily be broken. One common sign of this ripening bond is that the practitioner begins to think about the lama in very specific ways: (1) He is the very Buddha; (2) It is impossible to repay his kindness; (3) You constantly think about him or pray to him while moving, sitting, and sleeping; and (4) You have a deep longing, which sharpens your meditation and brings clarity (Jamgon Kongtrul [1977], pp. 128–29).

Although the practitioner's mind is yet very far from ripening into wisdom, he or she gets glimpses of positive changes through certain signs *(rtags).* Tashi Namgyel explains:

> Relying on guru yoga meditation, you retain closeness to the lama. You long to touch the lama's body. The lama has stolen all kinds of [erroneous] notions from you, so that he is, in fact, in close proximity to your mind. You long to pray day and night. Then, becoming illuminated through experience, you find understanding. When dreaming, you have auspicious dreams wherein you pay respect to your lama, and thereby get explanations of the teachings, get the initiations, etc. (TN, p. 251)

Empowerment radically, though subtly at first, transforms the practitioner's mind and behavior. One sign of progress is that the practitioner becomes more devoted to practice and more detached from the world (Jamgon Kongtrul [1977], p. 133). Yet another sign is that the practitioner begins to develop a new perspective on everyday suffering:

> In brief, imagine all pleasant experiences to be the guru's blessing. Meditate that all painful experiences are the guru's compassion. It is essential that you make use of such experiences to enhance your devotion and reverence and do not look elsewhere for a remedy [for suffering]. (Jamgon Kongtrul [1977], p. 123)

Furthermore, the practitioner may get spontaneous "glimpses of realization" (Jamgon Kongtrul [1977], p. 133) or "moments of calmness" (TN, p. 239) during meditation.

Formal meditation practice naturally follows from empowerment. The view establishes the necessary orientation for the meditation practice:

> When one practices meditation with the view,
> It is like a garuda fathoming space.
> The one who meditates without the view
> Is like a blind man wandering the plains.[258]
> ...Mahamudra meditation should not be practiced
> haphazardly, just sitting in the meditation posture without
> having the certainty of the proper view. It is very important
> first to acquire the proper view on the true nature of mind
> in order to practice meditation on this foundation.[259]

One of the signs of ripening is the urge to meditate more. The advanced preliminaries (khyad par) develop the spontaneous moments of meditative calmness now occurring into a solid foundation for formal meditation practice. Guru yoga opens the road to formal meditation practice, but only as these signs ripen over time. Therefore the advanced preliminary practices are designed to lay a solid foundation for formal meditation practice. Jamgön Kongtrül concludes *The Torch of Certainty* with the following advice:

> Do not run full tilt at tranquility and special insight. First, cultivate a fertile ground for positive qualities within yourself. (Jamgon Kongtrul [1977], p. 133)

Though some mahāmudrā texts skip the advanced preliminaries and go directly from guru yoga to formal meditation practice, this approach isn't recommended because the advanced preliminaries establish a solid foundation for concentration meditation.

III. The Advanced Preliminaries

The natural transition from guru yoga to the advanced preliminaries *(khyad par sngon gro)*[260] is an outgrowth of a number of signs—fleeting moments of special insight, spontaneous virtuous acts toward others, and refreshing moments of inner stillness. Such signs inevitably appear for the serious practitioner, and are said to be the "guarantee of the preliminaries" *(sngon 'dro'i dgos don;* KT, p. 711):

> With respect to the preliminaries, when the superiors explain these signs to you, the various signs should arise. Then, by settling into the essential [stage of practice], direct experience and understanding should arise without difficulty. Sometime following the preliminaries, these various [signs] manifest, and can be taken as what has been pointed out about the experience and understanding that arises. The right amount [of experience and understanding] will come. So it has been said by those who came before. Though the preliminaries are called preliminaries, the essentials depend upon their generation. The essentials depend on these for what does or doesn't occur during meditation. The masters have little disagreement concerning the many types of essential [practices]. From the preliminaries comes firmness, which brings forth the knowledge of certainty. The time that the signs come forth is extended. Then the practitioner can proceed to the essentials gradually. (KT, p. 711)

Before the practitioner begins the essential meditative practices, he or she must get experience *(nyams len)* with the benefits generated by the preliminary practices. It is especially important to get the right amount *(tshod rig pa;* KT, p. 711) of experience before proceeding to formal meditation. The right amount is said to be as much as is necessary to have an initial understanding of the fundamental view (emptiness), because it is difficult to meditate effectively without having the goal continually guide meditative practice. Although certain signs of progress are guaranteed, the result—firmness *(brtan pa)*—is not. "Firmness of mind" means uninterrupted awareness of the right view in all situations, in all activities.

The advanced preliminaries presume another shift in perspective. The ordinary preliminaries pertain to the "conditions [of the practitioner's everyday life and world] that cause attachment." The extraordinary preliminaries pertain to "the conditions of the Masters," that is, the lama and the refuge objects, who directly influence the practitioner's mental continuum out of their kindness. The advanced preliminaries pertain also to the practitioner's everyday life, but now to everyday life transformed by the fundamental view of the mind imparted through guru yoga.

Künga Tendzin says, "It is necessary to make effort *['bad pa]* to find the right amount [of experience] in your mental continuum" (KT, p. 712). Certain advanced practices, namely virtue practice *(dge sbyor)* and protecting *(skyong ba),* are designed to help the practitioner attain firmness. These practices are strenuous in that they strive toward the goal of uninterrupted practice, even in sleep (TN, p. 257). The practitioner uses diligence *(brtson 'dgrus),* which helps overcome laziness, and striving toward virtue and truth. When diligence gains momentum over time, certainty is said to arise in the mental continuum of its own power *(rang slobs).* The practitioner progresses from mere occasional signs to uninterrupted awareness of the true nature of the mind formerly pointed out during guru yoga.

A. Virtue Practice

Virtue practice brings to fruition the seeds sown during all of the previous stages of preliminary practice. Künga Tendzin says that virtue practice "consolidates the knowledge of the previous—that of the entire unit [of practice]" (KT, p. 712). Virtue practice is about firmness *(brtan pa).* The main goal of virtue practice is to make the practitioner's mental continuum firm, so that it will serve as a proper vessel to recognize certain truth *(nges don)* in whatever occasions and by whatever signs it arises. In this sense, virtue practice is a prerequisite for the later advanced preliminary known as *protecting,* in which certain truth initially manifests itself.[261]

There are two types of virtue practice—those exercises having to do with behavior and those having to do with mental training. The behavioral practices are usually done first. The positive propensities established by these behavioral practices subsequently manifest as certain mental qualities, which in turn make it easier to apply oneself to the mental training.[262]

B. The Behavioral Training: Ethical Training and Binding the Senses

Here is an example of the instructions mainly for the behavioral practices:

> To gain experience with ethical training is to become familiar with the mind-which-lets-go. Now, there is more to learn about increasing virtue through restraint, namely it is enhanced through mindfulness and intelligence. It becomes all the more necessary to let go of all immoral and evil behaviors and to carefully protect [the gains derived from] the ethical training.
>
> The interaction between the six sense objects—form, etc.— and the six sense organs—the eye, etc.—causes the six sense perceivers and the six [types of] sense consciousnesses to come forth. Through restraint [of the senses], the consequent [respective sense] consciousnesses arising within the mind, and also any attachment or aversion to any of these six sense objects, no longer occur. Nor do you grasp at any attributes *(mtshan ma)* of these [sense objects]. Because they are not taken to be manifest signs [of reality] *[mngon rtags]*, you protect the mind against the [ripening] action of attachment and aversion [to them], and you settle the mind *[sems 'jog]* in a virtuous or neutral state. (TN, pp. 252–53; cf. KT, p. 713)

It is clear from the passage that the effects of the behavioral restraint characteristic of ethical training *(tshul khrims)* is enhanced both by the act of sensory restraint *(dbang po'i sgo sdom pa)* and by mental training in mindfulness and intelligence *(dran shes)*. It is also clear that, though behavioral in nature, sensory restraint is primarily intended to generate a particular quality of mind referred to as *the mind-that-lets-go (spong ba'i sems;* TN, p. 252).

The behavioral form of restraint is well supported by such classic texts on ethical training as the *Bodhisattvabhūmi,* the *Śikṣāsamuccaya,* and the *Śīlasaṃyuktasūtra.* Citing a passage from the *Śīlasaṃyuktasūtra,* for example, Tashi Namgyel says that ethical training is "the foundation of all benefits...just as you do not see a form without eyes, you don't see the teachings without ethical training" (TN, p. 253). Elsewhere the ethical training is said to be "the foundation of all virtue."[263] Gampopa lists some of the benefits of ethical training. He says, "it is the way to meet the truth; it is the passageway to meditative calm."[264]

There are many different types of ethical training, which traditionally include the ordinary practice, such as the eightfold path and the *pratimokṣa* ethical code, and also the extraordinary practices of a bodhisattva, such as restraint from the eighteen basic faults, the four black deeds, and the forty-six ancillary deeds.[265] In the latter form the practitioner does not perform the restraints for his own sake, but for the sake of others.

Behavioral restraint is intended to simplify life. On the external level behavioral restraint reduces engagement in exactly those situations that might otherwise increase afflictive emotions *(nyon mong)* or attachment and aversion. Repeated practice of behavioral restraint leads to the development of an internal attitude, namely the mind-that-lets-go. The practitioner then protects the attitude that has developed through mindfulness training.

The complementary practice is sensory restraint. According to the Buddhist theory of perception, each of the five main sense systems creates its own sensory impression from contact of a sense object with its corresponding sense organ. For example, a form comes in contact with the eye, a sound with the ear, and so on. These sensory impressions, in turn, are interpreted by a sixth sense system, namely the mental perceiver *(yid shes)*, so that a specific sense consciousness develops for each sense impression. Through this cognitive appraisal process, raw sense data become associated with conceptualizing *(rtog pa)* and emotional states *(nyon mong)*. Distinct sensory preferences, notably attachment and aversion to certain sense objects, is an outgrowth of this process.

The practitioner is now instructed to reverse the perceptual process by which attachment and aversion develop by carefully observing exactly when the mind becomes attached to or averts from certain perceptual attributes *(mtshan ma)*. Sensory restraint entails observing moment-by-moment perceptual events with the attitude of the mind-that-lets-go, until the mind is less inclined to grasp *('dzin pa)* any given attribute of perception over another. Then the mind naturally settles inwardly "in a virtuous or neutral state." Sensory restraint is a method of protecting the mind from being afflicted by attachment or aversion.[266]

Behavioral and sensory restraint complement each other. Both can be practiced in the context of everyday living, but not if one's ordinary lifestyle is chaotic. For practitioners who live in a monastery or hermitage, the very environment aids the control of behavior and perception. Practitioners who do not live in such controlled environments need to work much harder to master behavioral and sensory restraint. The goal of both types of restraint is continuous practice in all situations:

> Whatever circumstances one may experience, either caused by himself or by others, he should zealously practice whatever rules apply just then. (BCA, 5:99)

The whole purpose of controlling external behavior and perception is to generate and then sustain a certain internal attitude, the mind-that-lets-go:

> After you have learned in the discipline, wherein you are prohibited and wherein you are commanded, you ought to act correctly for the purpose of protecting the mind in all situations. (BCA, 5:107)

C. The Mental Training: Mindfulness and Full Awareness

Reducing attachment to ordinary sensory experience is made easier by the practice of mindfulness *(dran pa)*. Mindfulness is the application of pure, nonreactive awareness to immediate experience, typically done within a meditative state. Full awareness *(shes bzhin)* is a similar application of pure awareness outside of meditation, in the context of everyday activity. In contrast to behavioral and sensory restraint, mindfulness and full awareness together *(dran shes)* are mental practices. They are a prelude to the intensive meditation characteristic of the essential practices. Mindfulness and full awareness provide a natural transition from restraint to formal meditative practice.

Tashi Namgyel cites the fifth chapter of the *Bodhicaryāvatāra* as the authoritative source on mindfulness and full awareness, which I have retranslated here:

> If you strive to protect the teachings, exert yourself to protect the mind. If you don't protect the mind, you won't be able to protect the teachings. (BCA, 5:1)

The practices of the bodhisattvas are said to be immeasurable. You must do these mental practices for certainty. (BCA, 5:97)[267]

Henceforth, the mind is to be well focused and well protected by you. Without correcting the "discipline of mind-guarding" *[sems bsrung brtul zhugs]*, what is the use of ethical training? (BCA, 5:18)

In the Mahāyāna Buddhist tradition, mindfulness and intelligence are the vehicles by which the signs of certainty ripen in the mental continuum and are the precursors to protecting:

> For those desiring to protect the mind, I fold my hands in prayer: With all zeal protect both mindfulness and intelligence. (BCA, 5:23)

Some commentators consider mindfulness to be the most important of all the preliminary practices. Jampel Pawo, for example, doesn't even discuss the range of other preliminary practices. He only emphasizes mindfulness.[268] According to the Buddhist psychological literature, the Abhidharma, all virtuous mental factors are said to depend upon mindfulness, because mindfulness has great influence upon other mental factors.[269] Therefore training mindfulness is the path to the development of many other virtuous mental factors. Neglecting mindfulness cuts off progress. Jampel Pawo cites a few famous passages from Nāgārjuna to stress the importance of mindfulness:

> "The Tathāgatha has taught the mighty ones that mindfulness of the body is the only path to walk. Intensify *[bsgrims]* and protect *[bsrung]* it directly. All teachings will be destroyed when mindfulness fails." (JP, f. 13b)[270]

Jampel Pawo explains this passage as follows:

> It follows that mindfulness is very important. Intensify it and protect it directly. Mindfulness is nonsectarian. It is the very same great path for entrance into the states leading to perfect buddhahood. For everything, it is the same support. This is called mindfulness that pertains to the body. (JP, f. 14a).

No matter what the meditation system—sūtra or tantra—mindfulness is the foundation of all meditation practice.

In Buddhist psychology mindfulness is classified as the third of five mental factors that make-the-object-certain *(yul nges lnga)*. Along a continuum of intensity leading to certainty, mindfulness surpasses the former two mental factors, interest and admiration, respectively. Interest and admiration signify progressively greater involvement with a perceptual object, so that the object makes a definitive impact upon the observer. With admiration the observer clearly distinguishes the object from other objects in the perceptual field and carefully discerns the object's qualities. Mindfulness includes these features and more. Mindfulness adds a temporal dimension to perception so that the object's qualities are known continuously over time. Jampal Pawo draws this temporal definition of mindfulness from the *Abhidharmasamuccaya:*

> If one were to say what mindfulness is, it is a nonforgetful *[brjed pa la med pa]* mind toward a familiar thing *['dris pa'i dngos po]*. It is a mind that is very undistracted *[rnam par mi gyen pa]* in its activity *[las]*.[271]

The term *mindfulness* is derived from the Sanskrit *smṛti,* which means "to remember." With mindfulness the object of awareness becomes familiar and stays familiar over time through continuous, nondistracted recollection of it. According to Gen Lamrimpa, "mindfulness refers to the mental faculty of being able to maintain continuity of awareness of an object."[272]

According to Jampel Pawo there are three very different types of mindfulness: (1) mindfulness that looks to the past *(bas pa la blta pa ba'i dran pa);* (2) mindfulness that is grasped by comparing the past to present objects *(don snga phyi sbyar nas 'dzin pa'i dran pa);* and (3) advanced mindfulness, which makes-the-object-certain *(yul nges kyi dran pa khyad par can)*. The first type of mindfulness confounds ordinary memory with present sense data. It is said to lead to attachment *(zhen pa)* and erroneous conceptualization *(rtog pa)*. The second type, recognition, relies on present sense data. Although less vulnerable to attachment, it also leads to erroneous conceptualization. The third type of mindfulness is known as *superior mindfulness,* or simply as *mindfulness.* Jampel Pawo says that when you practice superior mindfulness, "the former two types must cease" (JP, f. 14a–14b). Much like admiration, superior mindfulness pertains only to the immediate perceptual object and functions to make-the-object-certain. This is what the Abhidharma passage means when it refers to "a nonforgetful mind toward a familiar thing." Simply becoming familiar with the object in the past isn't enough. Mindfulness means being familiar with it in the immediate present,[273] because the word *familiar* pertains only to immediate perceptions *(snang ba)* arising in the mental continuum. Just as admiration was defined as an ability to distinguish the perceptual object from the stimulus field, mindfulness entails greater ability to distinguish an immediate perceptual object from the intellectual operations associated with it, such as memories, thoughts, and emotions. Mindfulness involves pure awareness of the immediate perceptual object without obscuration by other mental operations.[274]

At first mindfulness is difficult to practice. In the *Bodhicaryāvatāra,* the ordinary mind is likened to a wild elephant that, when agitated, causes great damage. When the wild elephant is tamed, great work can be done:

> Unsubdued and overwrought elephants do not effect that damage here which the unrestrained mind, an elephant roaming wild, does in the Avīci Hell and elsewhere. (BCA, 5:2)

Mindfulness literally means to "re-collect" *(dran pa)* mental events that otherwise unfold in a disorganized, scattered way. It is likened to taming a wild elephant by chaining it to a post:

> To recollect is to plant awareness deeply within the object as if planting a firm post in the ground.[275]

> If this elephant of the mind is bound on all sides by the rope of mindfulness, all fear disappears and virtue comes forth. (BCA, 5:2–3)

The distraction *(gyeng ba)* characteristic of the ordinary, wild-elephant mind continues to generate the emotional states.[276] Mindfulness is the first step toward putting order into the mental continuum, so that virtuous mental factors are more likely to arise. In this sense, mindfulness has influence over other virtuous mental factors. Gampopa says:

> Nondistraction is the path of all buddhas.

Nondistraction is our spiritual friend.
Nondistraction is the best of all advice.
Nondistraction, this mindfulness of the mental continuum, is
The middle path of the Buddha of the three times. (JP, f. 13a)

According to the Abhidharma literature, the Buddhist practitioner learns to observe the mind not as a continual flux but as discrete moments of awareness or mind-moments.[277] Each of these discrete mind-moments, however short in duration, can serve as a support for mindfulness. To forget *(brjed pa)* is to be unaware of the intended mind-moment even as it is present. To be distracted *(gyeng ba)* is to allow another mind-moment to draw awareness away from what is intended and toward something else.

From the perspective of the mind, mindfulness pertains to pure, nondistracted awareness. Jampel Pawo defines mindfulness as "continuous imagining—that is, a certain style of holding" (JP, f. 15a). Practicing mindfulness entails applying pure awareness to an immediate sense object without getting lost in thinking about the object, and then holding that awareness moment by moment without distraction. Once learned, mindfulness becomes a style of holding on *('dzin stangs)* to objects.

Whatever serves as the object of mindfulness is referred to as the support of mindfulness *(dran pa brten pa)*. Jampel Pawo draws upon the traditional *Satipaṭṭhānasutta* for his discussion of different types of supports.[278] According to that text, there are four types of supports: the body, feeling tone, state of consciousness, and contents of consciousness. The latter type includes the virtuous and nonvirtuous mental factors, perceptions, thoughts, and emotions. Each of these four is a distinct class of internal events within the mental continuum. Each can serve as a vehicle for mindfulness. Practicing mindfulness of the body is considered to be easier than the others, so it is often practiced first in the series. To fully master mindfulness, all four types are recommended.

A common way *(tshul)* of practicing mindfulness is to limit oneself to one type of support, for example, mindfulness only of body sensations, as recommended by Nāgārjuna and also by Śāntideva.[279] The practitioner applies pure awareness to the moment-by-moment unfolding of the array of bodily sensations, the moments of pain, itching, warmth, and so on. He or she focuses upon bodily sensations immediately as they arise as discrete events in the mental continuum. Another common way of practicing is to use various categories of consciousness as a support for mindfulness, such as thinking, sensing, feeling, seeing, hearing, and so forth. Then, moment by moment as events arise in the mental continuum, the practitioner applies pure, nonevaluative awareness to each event for as long as that event occurs. If, for example, a thought occurs, the practitioner notes that the process of thinking is occurring but does not focus on the specific content of the thought. If a sight captures awareness at any given moment, the practitioner notes that the process of seeing is occurring but does not think about the specific object seen. Moment by moment the practitioner catalogs the category of consciousness that is operative at that moment without thinking about the content being observed. This categorical approach to mindfulness is popular in the Burmese tradition.

A more difficult type of mindfulness practice, found in the Mahāyāna tradition, is to train moment-by-moment pure awareness of whatever arises *(gang shar)* in the mental continuum without the aid of categories or any notational system. While continually following the unfolding flux of discrete mental events in this type of practice, there is no such thing as distraction, because the distraction itself becomes the next support of awareness.

Regardless of the type of support used to train mindfulness, the primary goal is to develop continuous awareness without discontinuities or lapses in awareness. From the perspective of mind, the goal is uninterrupted mindfulness *(rgyun brnyan bar byed)* of everything as it occurs in the unfolding mental continuum. This is what Jampel Pawo calls *protecting the mental continuum* (*rgyun skyong ba;* JP, f. 15a).

Mindfulness training is an outgrowth of guru yoga:

> Through association with a lama, by fear, and an abbot's teaching, the satisfaction of mindfulness arises in those who are devoted to the pleasant ones. Brave-minded buddhas and bodhisattvas, whose sight is forever unobstructed, continually stand in the presence of them. (BCA, 5:30–31)

Guru yoga establishes a close affinity between the practitioner's mental continuum and the extraordinary minds of the lama and the refuge objects. This very awareness of being constantly connected to the refuge objects is a sign that mindfulness is already developing. In the advanced preliminaries the practitioner builds upon these developing signs by applying mindfulness as a technique until it becomes continuous and uninterrupted. Mastering mindfulness is said to require diligence. Laziness leads to loss of mindfulness, in which case the practitioner repeats the exercise on the sufferings of saṃsāra and continues practice again from that point.[280]

Mindfulness training has various benefits. Most importantly, mindfulness lays the foundation for the two essential meditative stages, concentration and special insight. Jampel Pawo calls mindfulness a limb of realization *(yang dag byang chub kyi yen lag)*, in which the practitioner comes to realize that all phenomena are empty. When mindfulness reduces the mental continuum to discrete moments of awareness, moment by moment, it becomes more difficult to locate a point of observation, or self, that is distinct from these mind-moments, and in this sense mindfulness lays the experiential foundation for direct understanding of emptiness:

> First, this series of skins is taken apart by one's own mind. Separate the meat also from the cage of bones with the knife of wisdom. Having taken apart even the bones, look at the inner space of marrow. Ask yourself, "What is the essence of this?" So if, even when you have searched carefully, you cannot see an essence to this by your manner of attachment, why then are you still protecting this body? (BCA, 5:62–64)

Full awareness *(shes bzhin;* Skt., *samprajaña)* is a counterpart to mindfulness.[281] Jampel Pawo and Tashi Namgyel both use the compound *dran shes,* which means "mindfulness and full awareness." Mindfulness pertains to periods of sitting meditation. Full awareness pertains to the application of pure awareness while going about daily activities *(las)*. Although it is hard to maintain the same level of precision with mindfulness in the context of everyday life that one can during sitting practice, most practitioners find that they can maintain some degree of awareness moment by moment while going about various activities. Tashi Namgyel defines full awareness as follows:

> When entering into whatever actions, bodily actions, and so forth, you practice these with concern *[bag yod pa]*. (TN, p. 254)

The classic definition of *full awareness* comes from the *Bodhicaryāvatāra:*

> Examine all the conditions of the body and mind over and over. Just this, briefly, is the definition of full awareness, protecting. (BCA, 5:108)

Tashi Namgyel gives examples of the kind of activities to which full awareness is applied: standing, sitting, eating, and sleeping. This is an abbreviated list of the seven activities found in the *Satipaṭṭhānasutta:* (1) going forward and backward, (2) looking to the front or to the side, (3) bending and stretching the limbs, (4) putting on clothes, (b) eating and drinking, (6) washing the body, and (7) walking, standing, sitting, sleeping, speaking, and remaining silent.[282] The aim of the exercise is to enlist all aspects of daily existence toward the same end, namely uninterrupted pure awareness of all mental activities and behaviors moment by moment, exactly as they occur.

Tashi Namgyel says that two additional virtuous mental factors potentiate the development of mindfulness and full awareness. They are concern *(bag yod pa)* and diligence *(brtson 'grus). Diligence* refers to strong effort to apply mindfulness/full awareness in all activities in order to overcome laziness and achieve the goal of uninterrupted mindfulness at all times. *Concern* means being sensitized toward virtuous thought and action so as to prevent reverting back to harmful thought or behavior. No matter what the circumstances, the practitioner continues to apply mindfulness and full awareness with diligence and concern:

> Apply it like this when standing—standing in a crowd of evil
>   beings, or even standing in a crowd of women. An ascetic's
>   firmness is never impaired.
> It is all right to be without property; it is all right to be without
>   honor or life of the body.
> It is all right for happiness to fall away too; but it is never all right
>   for the mind to be impaired.
> To those wishing to guide the mind with mindfulness and full
>   awareness, who protect accordingly, with all their efforts, I fold
>   my hands in prayer! (BCA, 5:21–23)

In the earlier Theravada Buddhism the primary benefit from mindfulness practice was special insight into the three marks of existence—impermanence, selflessness, and suffering. Direct observation of the mental continuum moment by moment leads to the discovery that the continuum is constantly changing. In this sense, direct special insight into impermanence naturally arises from mindfulness. Attempting to apply nonreactive, pure awareness to whatever arises also naturally leads to an appreciation of the mind's incessant reactivity to whatever comes into awareness. Mindfulness leads to direct experience of attachment and aversion as they operate moment by moment in the mental continuum. In this sense, special insight about how the mind generates suffering naturally arises from mindfulness practice. Furthermore, correct application of mindfulness, free from reactivity, leads to the observation of unfolding experience as a mere impersonal process. In this sense, mindfulness leads to the experience of selflessness.[283]

In the later Mahāyāna, including the mahāmudrā tradition, the benefits of mindfulness and full awareness are described as: (1) the eradication of erroneous concepts, (2) the deepening of certainty, (3) the attainment of firmness of mind, and (4) establishing this firmness as a foundation for formal meditation practice.

Tashi Namgyel describes the benefit of virtue practice as follows:

> If you continuously depend on mindfulness and full awareness,
> you will never go wrong, swayed by [perceptual] attributes and
> erroneous conceptualization. (TN, p. 257)[284]

The application of full awareness sows the seeds that correct false conceptualization (*log rtog;* TN, p. 254).

Eventually the signs of mindfulness and full awareness ripen in a new way, as the experience of certain truth in each of the moments of the unfolding mental continuum. The practitioner goes beyond mere intellectual understanding of the fundamental view and even beyond the arising of signs. Now the practitioner directly experiences these truths continuously in the very way the mental continuum unfolds in every moment, even while sleeping and dreaming. The right view has been established in the mind's very unfolding. Through the successive exercises of virtue practice the practitioner passes beyond external control of everyday behavior to cultivating an internal mental attitude of letting go, then to uninterrupted mindfulness practice, and finally back to experiencing everyday behavior in a new manner *(stangs).* Full awareness transforms everyday behavior into a continuous meditation. Each moment of awareness brings the same realization, the same certain truth.

A deeper understanding of certain truth, however, can only come through genuine meditation. Although mindfulness and full awareness prepare the mind for meditation, they are not a substitute for formal concentrative meditation. Mindfulness and full awareness are said "to generate" meditation (KT, p. 711). Śāntideva says, "I make the mind as firm in appearance as Mount Sumeru" (BCA, 5:58). In the subsequent protecting instructions, the practitioner learns to use this developing awareness to deepen the experience of the mind's real nature so that this truth will forever be a part of immediate awareness. Then, when going on to the essential practices, this truth will continuously guide the meditations.[285]

D. PROTECTING

Guru yoga sows the seeds for realization of the true nature of the mind. Mindfulness and full awareness, like sunlight and water, are the conditions that help the seed of awakened wisdom begin developing. The advanced preliminaries are practices designed specifically to plant the seed of an initial experience *(nyams len)* of certainty about the central realization of the mahāmudrā tradition, known as *the way the realized mind stays (gnas lugs)*,[286] although at this level of practice the realization is still very much cast within the framework of the conventional mind.[287] Wangchug Dorjé explains the last of these advanced preliminaries, called *protecting (skyong ba):*

> Don't mistake what is to be meditated. It is distinct from all [else]. It is the awakened way the mind stays. It is also known as [the mind] "settled into itself" *[rang babs]*,[288] which generates certainty of the teachings. You find certainty according to the conditions that represent it *[dmigs rkyen]* [when the mind itself is observed] in a nonattached way. Unfamiliar as such with certainty, practice the previous and current meditations to generate earnest application, and then firmness of mind *[snying rus]*. (WD, p. 84)

The term *skyong ba* means "to protect, guard, or defend," as if defending a fort. The same term also means "to care for, attend to, nurture." Protecting is a practice typically utilized at the formal conclusion of any unit *(thun)* of meditation practice, that is, at the end of the preliminaries, concentration, special insight, or extraordinary meditations, respectively. The introduction of protecting practice at this point signifies the conclusion of the preliminary practices.

Protecting signifies a review period, though a particular kind of review. In brief, the practitioner goes back over the unit of practices, paying particular attention to the view *(blta ba)* of the mind inherent in those practices. First, the practitioner tries to nurture this view in order to bring it more into direct experience in the unfolding mental continuum. Second, the practitioner tries to protect the practice from going astray *(shor sa)* or becoming defective *(skyon can;* TN, pp. 259–60) by comparing immediate experience of the unfolding mental continuum to the view imparted by the teachings. Protecting instructions sometimes contain descriptions of the common errors made by practitioners during a given unit of practice. Comparisons of current experience of the mind to these descriptions of the correct and erroneous view insures that the practitioner is on the correct path. Although meditation is a remedy for ignorance *(ma rig pa);* ignorance is pervasive. Even though the practitioner may have gained experience with a given unit of practice, and may have been guided by the right view, the power of ignorance is very great. Therefore protecting instructions are extremely important for keeping practice on the right track.

There are two kinds of protecting instructions: (1) ordinary protecting instructions, which are called *conditions that establish certainty (sgrub rkyen;* TN, p. 84), and (2) extraordinary instructions, which are called devotional prayers *(smon lam).*

1. Ordinary Protecting Practice: The Conditions That Bring Forth Certainty

As an example of the ordinary protecting instructions, Wangchug Dorjé says:

> Make no mistake about the conditions of the representations, the representations that are to be meditated, [for either] the conditions that cause nonattachment [the ordinary preliminaries] or the conditions of the masters that conclude with the lamas [the extraordinary preliminaries, ending in guru yoga].
>
> After that, you protect the conditions of immediacy of that [certain truth] in whatever happens to arise. These are protected without [any artificial activity of mind such as] hope or fear, taking up or letting go, obstructing or bringing forth. (WD, p. 64)

The two types of ordinary protecting practices are *the condition of the representations (dmigs rkyen)* and *the conditions of immediacy (ma thag rkyen)*. The word *rkyen*, "condition," refers to the doctrine of cause and effect. The cause *(rgyu)* of arising certainty is said to be mindfulness-intelligence, but it is not in itself sufficient. Just as a seed (the cause of a tree) must ripen into a tree by certain nutritional and climatic conditions, so also the cause of certainty must ripen into the experience of certainty by the respective conditions of representations and of immediacy. Conditions are secondary events that can influence an unfolding process. Therefore the practitioner uses whatever chances are available to insure the ripening of certainty. There are two such occasions: (1) periods when the mind is more meditative, and (2) all other times as the practitioner goes about daily activities. These two occasions correspond to the conditions of the representations and the conditions of immediacy, respectively.

The first exercise takes advantage of the increasing moments of meditative calm in order to produce *(sgrub pa)* certainty. From the perspective of the mind—that is, pure awareness—the unfolding, ever-changing content of the mind, moment by moment, with its various representations in consciousness *(dmigs pa),* is "what is to be meditated" as a reflection of mind. Despite ever-changing content, awareness is said to stay *(gnas ba),* moment by moment (TN, p. 260), and so becomes less distracted *(ma gyeng ba)* and less scattered (TN, p. 260). By taking awareness itself as the object of mindfulness, Wangchug Dorjé says, the mind "settles into itself." Likewise, Tashi Namgyel says that adopting this perspective, the practitioner is "guided straight to the center" (TN, p. 260).[289]

The term *primordial (gcnyud ma)* signifies a shift in perspective away from the mind's changing content moment by moment to the perspective of continuous awareness that stays prior to and throughout any and all discrete moments of unfolding events. Jampel Pawo summarizes his advice saying, "the [real] path is the nondistracted mind [itself], completely known in its [true] nature" (JP, f. 25b). The practitioner senses a fundamental affinity between the way the mental continuum now unfolds and the right view of the mind imparted by the teachings. Protecting entails a comparison of immediate experience and the teachings given. Wangchug Dorjé says protecting using the condition of the representations helps to "generate certainty" (WD, p. 85) because there is something about the unfolding experience of the mental continuum at this stage of practice that lets the view of the real nature of the mind shine forth *('char ba).*

Tashi Namgyel instructs the practitioner to review the set of virtue practices four times a day, until the benefit of the conditions of representation is "grasped with certainty," or at least until the "mind and body fall into perfect settlement" (TN, p. 258). The practitioner not only reviews the virtue practice but also looks ahead to the essential meditations. He or she is told to enumerate *(grangs)* and list in order *(go rim)* the previous, current, and future meditations in order to "protect [each stage of the overall practice] according to the way."[290] No matter what the stage of practice, the practitioner discovers that the mind works by exactly the same processes and yields the same special insight about its true nature. Certainty is not state-dependent, though understanding deepens at each successive stage of practice.

The second set of instructions, called *the conditions of immediacy,* take advantage of whatever opportunities arise in daily life that allow a view of the fundamental nature of the mind. The two sets of protecting instructions—representations and immediacy—parallel the distinction between mindfulness and full awareness, respectively. The term *shig ge* means "immediacy," or "only just now." Whatever discrete mind-moments arise in the mental continuum—perceptions, thoughts, emotions—all convey the same truth about the mind. All day long, without interruption, the practitioner develops direct experience of the same realization. Each and every distinct mind-moment reinforces the same certainty about the mind's real nature:

> Look to what has arisen as something merely arisen from causes
> and conditions. There is no knower, simply awareness-itself *[rang
> rig pa].*[291]

The flux of the mental continuum simply arises from causes and conditions. There is no self-existent self that can be taken as a point of observation toward it, no knower *(rig mkhyen).* What seems to arise as a self-existent substance *(dngos po)* is a mere emanation *(sprul tsam),* as if like a dream.

Since any and every moment of arising experience potentially brings the same realization, certain truth develops more quickly. Once realized with certainty, there is no further truth to seek. As Wangchug Dorjé says, "Protecting [is then] without hope [of gain] and fear [of not getting it]." He says, "There is nothing to search for" *(rtshol med;* WD, p. 85). There is no specific mental activity that can either obstruct or bring forth *(dgags grub)* what is already there with developing certainty. When the practitioner holds certainty in both meditation and daily activity, the protecting practice is said to be "well-rounded" *(hril por dge sbyor;* TN, p. 260).

2. Extraordinary Protecting Practice: The Devotional Prayer

Wisdom and compassion are aspects of the same nondual realization. Therefore the experience of certainty about the mind's real nature necessarily leads to a compassionate desire that others find this same truth. Tashi Namgyel explains the devotional prayer *(smon lam)* as follows:

> Without any elaboration [of the mind] pray that the highest realization will be known among all sentient beings, namely the virtue [of compassion] and the bliss [of awakened wisdom] coming from the virtue practice. Protecting sets the groundwork for the devotional prayer's perfect purification. Then, as it is said, you will greatly increase the roots of virtue, which is no small accomplishment. (TN, p. 261)

The "lofty ideal" is to desire to realize truth for the sake of all others. The devotional prayer is the standard method of protecting the ripening compassion at this stage of practice. Rangjung Dorjé's famous *Devotional Prayer on Mahāmudrā*, now translated into English, is a good example of the entire set of mahāmudrā instructions cast in the context of a devotional prayer.[292]

The preliminary practices are finished when the practitioner is capable of practicing each stage as a condensed unit *(thun bsdu'i tshe)*. Wangchug Dorjé gives the instructions:

> As a condensed unit, melting the refuge object, the Vajrasattva, the perfect maṇḍala, and the assembly of deities and lamas [of guru yoga] into yourself as light, so that you are indistinguishable from their body, speech, and mind. (WD, pp. 64–65)

He then explains the passage:

> These advanced preliminaries complete the preliminary stages. Each of these units, serving as the conditions that bring forth [certainty], are wrapped into a single unit [of practice]. (WD, p. 85)

As the practitioner reviews and repeats all the instructions as a single unit of practice, the realization ripens faster. However, it is generally acknowledged that only highly capable practitioners can practice the preliminaries as a condensed unit all at once, rather than in the more conventional stages.

To this end, special texts have been written that combine all the practices into one, for example Trophu's *Guidebook of the Five-Parts Mahāmudrā.*[293]

While the preliminary practices prepare the mind for the realization of certainty, true realization comes only after rigorous meditation. The advanced preliminaries properly prepare the mind for formal meditation practice. Contrary to popular opinion, meditation is the outcome, or fruit *('bras bu)*, not the beginning of spiritual practice. As one root text says,

> These preliminaries, which generate the yet ungenerated meditation, are called the yoga of calm.[294]

The profound changes in lifestyle and view of the mind that constitute the preliminary practices help to generate *(skye ba)* meditation, and open the way to the essential meditations that follow.

3. Contemplation

THE ABILITY TO EXPERIENCE and understand truth depends a great deal upon the quality of the unfolding mental continuum. In the protecting exercise, the practitioner discerns some similarity between the truth represented by the teachings and the qualities of his or her own mental continuum. Typically the practitioner's first attempts to protect only serve as a reminder of how far the emerging activity of the mental continuum has gone astray *(shor sa)* from any approximation of realized truth.

I. THE NATURE OF THE ORDINARY MENTAL CONTINUUM

William James once described the ordinary mind as a "blooming, buzzing confusion."[295] The Buddhist view of the ordinary mind is quite similar. The mind can be described from two perspectives: (1) from the perspective of the mind that observes these events, and (2) from the perspective of the observable events in the unfolding stream of experience.

From the perspective of the mind that observes, the ordinary mind fails to stay *(gnas ba)* on its intended object of focus for anything but very brief moments. Even when it stays on the intended object, the mind typically only partially stays on it, in that attention is divided between the intended object and the background noise of ordinary mental activity. The ordinary mind readily leaves its intended object of focus and easily becomes distracted *(gyeng ba),* going off in a number of directions in a disorderly fashion. Awareness of the unfolding stream of experience is discontinuous. There are frequent lapses in ordinary awareness, that is, episodes of mindlessness or unawareness *(ma rig pa).*

From the perspective of the unfolding events within the mental continuum, the very structure of the ordinary mind is disorganized. A mind that gets distracted from its intended object of awareness and gets lost in the construction of more and more mental content is said to become elaborated *(spros ba).*[296] Continuous elaboration is called "wandering" *('khor ba)* from one thing to another, with the mind attaching itself to one sensory object or thought after another. The ordinary mind constructs *(bcos pa)* images and ideas for the range of sensory stimulation *(reg pa),* and these mental constructions become more and more elaborate, in the form of ideas *(blo),* conceptualization *(rtog pa),* and conflictual emotional states *(nyon mongs).* These elaborations arise because the ordinary mind scatters in various ways with seemingly little order and control. This particular quality of the mind makes it extremely difficult to keep it focused upon protecting certain truth. Therefore the exercises are designed to help the practitioner "let go of [the mind's ordinary] activity" *(bya ba btang ba;* JP, f. 5a).

II. Contemplation: From the Perspective of Mind—Cultivating the Skills for Staying

The effects of meditation can also be described from these two perspectives: (1) from the perspective of the mind that observes these events, and (2) from the perspective of the observable events in the unfolding stream of experience. Both of these perspectives are critical to understanding contemplative and meditative experience. For example, the Tibetan term for concentration meditation is the compound *zhi gnas. Zhi ba* means "calm," and *gnas ba* means "stay." The compound term captures both perspectives on concentration meditation. From the perspective of the mind, the mind "stays" on its intended object without distraction. From the perspective of observable events, the events in the unfolding mental continuum become "calm." *Zhi gnas* literally means "calming/staying" from both perspectives. Gedün Lodrö defines *zhi gnas* as "a technique for setting the mind, without fluctuation, on a single object of observation."[297] According to Tsongkhapa, the purpose of concentration meditation is to bring the mind under control and make it serviceable. He says, "Serviceability means that you can direct your mind as you wish toward a virtuous object of meditation."[298]

Traditional Indian Buddhist accounts of contemplation and meditation emphasize the mind perspective. These classic accounts originate with the Indian master Asaṅga in his *Grounds of Hearers* and his *Summary of Manifest Knowledge* and from Maitreya's *Ornament of Mahāyāna Sūtras.* Kamalaśīla's *Stages of Meditation* is another commonly cited source. Asaṅga set forth the nine stages of staying, in which he described the progressive

degrees to which the mind stays on its intended object with greater meditation experience. Geshe Gedün Lodrö's *Calm Abiding and Special Insight*
and Lati Rinbochay et al.'s *Meditative States in Tibetan Buddhism* are excellent English-language summaries of these Indian Buddhist accounts of the
nine stages.[299]

The mahāmudrā tradition of meditation adopts the other perspective,
the perspective of the mind's events. Most mahāmudrā texts describe the
results of contemplation and meditation in terms of changes in the experience of the unfolding events in the mental continuum. Given the importance of both perspectives, the Indian mind-perspective will be discussed
first, followed by the mahāmudrā event-perspective.

At the very beginning of meditation, attempts to focus attention on the
intended meditation object cannot easily be separated from the coarse content of the mind, mostly elaborate thinking. The beginner easily confuses
attention with thinking. Since attention is confounded with thinking in
these early stages, they are referred to as contemplation *(bsam gtan)*, not as
formal meditation *(sgom ba)*. Nevertheless the attempt to isolate the act of
focusing attention from the background of elaborate thinking does produce a certain benefit with practice. From the perspective of mind, the
benefit is that the mind stays on its intended object, at least somewhat.
From the perspective of the mind's events, thinking becomes less elaborate—that is, it becomes a bit calmer.

A. Basic Skills for Contemplation and Meditation

Contemplation and meditation are learning processes, much like learning
to drive a car. Most student drivers feel completely overwhelmed the first
time they attempt to drive, because they must (1) steer to keep the car on
the road, (2) adjust the speed with the accelerator, (3) adjust the geer ratio
with the shift, according to the speed, and (4) constantly keep vigilant about
doing each of these tasks well. Once learned, or indeed overlearned, driving becomes second nature. Little awareness is needed to perform all of the
requisite driving skills quickly and effortlessly. Learning to meditate is very
similar, in that it requires four similar skills—*directing, intensifying, pliancy,*
and *intelligence.*

At the very beginning of contemplation the practitioner learns to focus
the mind on the meditation object and then to maintain that focus for a
longer and longer time without distraction or elaboration. The great weight

of the ordinary mind's negative momentum makes it quite difficult to keep the focus on the meditation object for anything but short intervals. The ordinary mind is described as a wild elephant on a stampede. Yet once calm, the elephant mind has great power to affect whatever it focuses on. Therefore Śāntideva describes the task as learning to tie up the mind, like tying a rope around the neck of an elephant. Every time the elephant wanders, it feels the pull of the rope, so over time the elephant learns to stay, without wandering. Likewise, tying up the mind to a meditation object is the primary strategy by which the mind learns to stay without distraction.

Once bound to the intended meditation object, the mind must be *directed (sems pa)* repeatedly back to that object time and time again, over and against the mind's great tendency to leave the intended object and wander somewhere else. Developing skill in directing the mind to stay is like learning to use the steering wheel of a car. Each time the momentum of the car starts to veer off the road, the driver directs it back to its proper course by skillful control of the steering wheel. Likewise, each time the ordinary mind gets distracted from the intended meditation object, the practitioner learns to direct it back until the mind stays on its object. With practice, smaller and smaller adjustments are necessary to make the mind stay there.

The degree to which the mind learns to stay on the intended meditation object is a function of another skill, *intensifying (sgrim ba)*. Just as progressing along the road while driving requires skillful use of the accelerator to supply more or less fuel to move the car along, progress in developing the skill of staying depends on similar skills of intensifying and easing up. Intensifying pertains to the degree of energy needed to direct the mind at any given moment. Imagine being told to look at a particular painting. Once you are given the instruction, the mental act of directing the mind toward the painting occurs. Then imagine being told to look at the painting much more carefully. What does the mind do at that point? Since the mind is already directed toward the painting, the act of directing the mind does not explain what else occurs. But something else does occur. The mind supplies more energy to the act of looking. From the event-perspective, the details of the painting become more salient than before. From the mind-perspective, the mind stays more closely on the intended object as a result of the additional energy supplied.

Meditators learn to adjust the degree of energy being supplied to concentration at any given point just like learning to adjust the accelerator while driving. From the mind-perspective, adding more energy—intensifying—

makes the mind stay better and decreases the likelihood of distraction. However, supplying too much intensity results in agitation of both body and mind, as a result of which the mind doesn't stay on anything. At that point, easing up on the energy increases the clarity *(gsal ba)* of the meditation object, from the event-perspective. However, easing up too much results in losing the degree of staying that has developed. The skilled meditator knows when to intensify and when to ease up depending on the quality of the meditation at the time, just as a skilled driver knows when to accelarate or deccelerate according to the conditions of the road.

There are two signs of progress. From the mind-perspective, the mind is said to stay longer and more completely on the intended meditation object. From the event-perspective, the mental continuum's coarse content comes forth with greater clarity. Visual objects are brighter, eventually becoming luminous.[300] Bodily sensations are felt more vividly. Staying and clarity are independent but complementary signs of meditation progress viewed from two perspectives.

Learning to direct a flashlight to an object and then holding the flashlight steady makes the light stay, but if the batteries are weak, the light will stay but have little clarity. Conversely, a flashlight may have strong batteries so that the object is very clear, yet the hand that holds it is unsteady so that the light fails to stay on the object. In this manner, intensifying and easing up are inversely related. Intensifying leads to more and more staying, but at the expense of clarity. Easing up leads to more and more clarity, but at the expense of staying. Therefore the skilled meditator first learns to intensify so that the mind stays longer and more fully on the intended object. Once the mind is able to stay on its own for some duration as a function of intensifying, the meditator then learns to ease up to bring out greater clarity. With experience the meditator knows precisely when to intensify and when to ease up so that both qualities—staying and clarity—are equally strong.

The third skill required of a driver is the ability to adjust the gear ratio, using the clutch and shift according to the car's speed. Most beginning drivers find this harder to learn than using the steering wheel or accelerator. Meditation entails a comparable set of skills, referred to as *pliancy (shin tu sbyangs ba)*. There are two broad types of pliancy—bodily and mental.

A rudimentary type of *mental pliancy* is the ability to stay on the intended meditation object despite marked shifts in mental content or state of consciousness. Geshe Gedün Lodrö defines pliancy as a "mental factor that removes...bad mental states...and takes to mind a true object...joyfully and the mind is light." A "bad mental state" is defined as a condition in which the mind during meditation "cannot bear...being aimed at its object of observation."[301] Another type of mental pliancy is the ability to generalize the gains of meditation to different meditation objects. A more advanced type of mental pliancy is skill in shifting perspective during meditation between the mind-perspective and the event-perspective.

Still another type of pliancy is the ability to stay on the intended meditation object throughout shifts in levels of the mind. According to Buddhist psychology, there are three levels to the mind. The coarse level pertains to ordinary content in the stream of consciousness, for example, thoughts *(rtog pa)*, percepts, bodily sensations, and emotions. On the subtle level there is no content. The skilled meditator learns to hold awareness on the mind's moment-by-moment fleeting movements prior to these movements being constructed into coarse content. At the very subtle level of mind the skilled meditator learns to hold awareness on karmic propensities prior to their manifestation in the time-space matrix of the ordinary mental continuum.

Mastery of the concentration stages of meditation opens up the subtle level of the mind. Mastery of the special-insight stages opens up the very subtle or extraordinary level of the mind. Advanced pliancy entails shifting through these levels of mind with considerable skill, much like shifting gears in a car. Overall, mental pliancy pertains to the developing skill of having the mind stay optimally on its intended object despite changes in mental content, state, or level of consciousness, or perspective of observation, just as adjusting the shift and clutch maintains an optimal level of a car's progress despite continous changes in speed and road condition.

The fourth skill required of the driving student is to keep watch that the other three skills are being performed well. Likewise, the skillful meditator uses *full awareness (shes bzhin)* to watch the meditation and insure that its best qualities are brought out for the duration of the session. A common beginner's mistake is to meditate for an entire session without ever reflecting on the quality of the meditation. Such beginners develop subtle and not so subtle bad habits of meditation, the accumulation of which will arrest progress at some point. A wise practitioner uses full awareness to assess the quality of the meditation.

There are several ways of applying full awareness during a given meditation session—the episodic method and the continuous method. Less experienced meditators episodically disengage from the meditation object, quickly assess the quality of the body posture and the quality of the meditation (degree of staying, ease of recognizing distraction, amount of effort needed to make the necessary correction and direct the mind back to the intended object, presence or absence of faults such as dullness, etc.), and then redirect the mind back to the intended meditation object. More experienced meditators reserve a small part of the mind to practice full awareness continually while the larger part of the mind remains bound to the intended meditation object.[302] It is important to apply full awareness in a balanced way. Trying too hard will only increase thought elaboration.[303] In addition to these standard strategies, the mahāmudrā tradition recommends utilizing a form of protecting practice at the end of each meditation session.

III. Contemplation: From the Perspective of Mental Events—Isolating Attentional Focus from Mental Elaborations and Enhancing Organization of the Mental Continuum

A. The Isolations and Points[304]

In the mahāmudrā tradition the instructions for letting go of ordinary mental activity are called *the three isolations (dben gsum),* or *the body and mind points (lus gnad dang sems gnad).* The term *dben ba* means "to separate or isolate." At the coarse *(rags)* level, the practitioner isolates himself or herself behaviorally from the noise and bustle (*'du 'dzi med pa;* JP, f. 7a) of the everyday world, the chaos of which becomes reflected in the unfolding mental continuum. The practitioner makes life simpler and becomes quieter. Moving *('gro ba)* about the world and looking *(mthong ba)* at one thing or another serves to sustain the inner chaos. At the more subtle *(phra ba)* internal level, the practitioner isolates or segregates an island of stable attention from becoming distracted by the chaotic ocean of disorganized mental elaborations *(spros ba).* The primary objective of the three isolations is to begin making the mind stay *(gnas ba)* on its intended object over and against its ordinary tendency to become distracted by ongoing thought. Milarepa calls this exercise *the three slayings (gnas gsum;* JP, f. 6a).

A common synonym for the word *dben ba* is *rang sar* (TN, p. 271; JP, f. 8a). In an active sense, it means "to put something in its own place,"[305] and in a passive sense it means, "to leave something alone." Both meanings are intended. The practitioner actively isolates attention from its ordinary overidentification with thinking and its incessant elaboration so that the mind stays in its proper place, unaffected by ongoing mental disorder. However, since at this stage of practice attention is still very bound up with thinking, this stage is called *contemplation* instead of meditation.

According to Jampel Pawo, there are three types of isolations: body isolation *(lus dben);* speech isolation *(ngag dben);* and mind isolation (*yid dben;* JP, f. 6a). Jampel Pawo explains:

> Now, it is improper to fail to practice the first of the meditations along this path. These are called the three kinds of settlement, or the three isolations, or the three immovables. The Lord of Beings, Milarepa, says, "The meaning of letting go of activity by the three isolations is as follows: Do not fall under the power of activity when the body moves or rests, when speech is spoken, or when the mind scatters by clinging to discursive thought. (JP, f. 4b)

Letting go of the influence of ordinary bodily activity starts by retreating to a meditation cell in a monastery, a quiet forest hermitage, or a cave and adopting a fixed, immovable posture. Letting go of the influence of ordinary speech starts with reducing normal chatter and perhaps by taking a vow of silence. Letting go of the great influence of ordinary thought is understanding that the act of focusing attention or applying awareness is fundamentally different from the act of thinking, so that the developing attention/awareness skills become increasingly segregated from the activity of ordinary thinking.[306]

Wangchug Dorjé and Tashi Namgyel call their comparable exercises *the body and mind points.* The word *gnad* means "point," that is, the essence of something, as in keeping track of the point of a conversation. Two verbs are used in conjunction with the object, or "point." First, the practitioner is said to rearrange *(sgrig pa)* the points. With respect to the body, various parts of the body are rearranged, or put in their proper order, during meditative sitting practice. Each part is adjusted according to an ideal model. With respect to the mind, an important benefit of attentional skill development is an increased sense of organization of the mental continuum. The unfolding disorder of the ordinary mental continuum eventually gives way to increasing organization and orderliness in the very way the events of the mental continuum unfold. In order to rearrange the body or mind, there are certain points to keep track of, as if reading a book by focusing on certain themes. The points must also be ordered according to some model, much like using a particular theme to guide comprehension of the book.

As a result of keeping track of these points, the practitioner *penetrates (snum ba)* them. Penetration results in a breakthrough in the way the ordinary mental continuum unfolds. It is rearranged in the sense that there is a noticeable shift in the unfolding events of the mental continuum so that they come forth in a more orderly manner, more like a slowly unfolding stream and less like mercury scattering in all directions. The overall effect of practicing the isolations or points is to increase the sense of organization of the unfolding mental continuum so as to establish it as a stable foundation for "entering into [formal] meditation" (PK, f. 2b; TN, p. 268; WD, p. 65). From the mind-perspective, it is able to stay on its intended object for some time. From the event-perspective, mental events become more calm and orderly in their unfolding. Because of these meditative-like changes, Jampel Pawo calls the three isolations the "first of the meditations," while Tashi Namgyel calls it "the [starting] point of meditation" *(sgom ba'i gnad;* TN, p. 267). These exercises are the natural transition to formal meditation practice. However, the overall effect is called contemplation *(bsam gtan),* not formal meditation, because at this stage of practice thought elaboration still dominates the events in the unfolding mental continuum. The subsequent essential *(dngos gzhi)* practices differ from the preliminaries *(sngon 'gro)* in that thought elaboration and other coarse mental content become less of a distraction during formal concentration meditation.

There are three progressive stages in this unit of practice, known as body isolation, speech isolation, and mind isolation, respectively. Mastery of one unit leads to the practice of the next:

> Cotton-clad Milarepa says, "When the body stays, that staying leads to speech-staying, when speech stays, that staying leads to mind-staying." (JP, f. 5b–6a)

1. The Isolation of the Body

Tashi Namgyel says that the reason the body points *(lus gnad)* are so important is that the act of learning control over the body's gross and subtle activity eventually ripens as greater control over unfolding mental activities. Body-point practice naturally leads to practice of the mind points, the outcome of which is a contemplative mind. Tashi Namgyel's root instructions for the body points say:

> In general, the points of this artifice, the body, are important [to keep track of] during any contemplation [exercise], and in particular the body points are very important to make the mind stay. So if you happen to put forth intense earnest application, you'll achieve partial staying. Then, it is good to protect the body points for at least a day. (TN, p. 654)

According to the law of cause and effect, a given action proliferates in its effects. The act of stilling the body eventually manifests its effect as mental calm. The ultimate design of the exercises is to re-order the body and mind so as to become a suitable vessel for the nectar of wisdom received by oral advice. The commentary illustrates the interrelationship between settling the body and settling the mind:

> The Ancient Ones call it *taming the artifice of the body when desiring the mind to stay.* You must rearrange the interconnected processes *[rten 'brel]* in the body, and by that, understanding arises in the mind. (TN, p. 268; JP, f. 9b)[307]

This passage contains a number of technical references to the Buddhist view of the body. The body is not solid, but rather consists of an elaborate system of interconnected processes *(rten 'brel).* The complex interrelationship between these processes makes the body seem solid, yet its seeming solidity is but an illusion. The body is an artifice *('khrul 'khor)*—that word itself is a compound. It is composed of the word *'khrul ba* (variation, *sprul ba*), which means "illusion, mistake," and the word *'khor ba,* which means "to wander." *'Khor ba* is the Tibetan word for saṃsāra. The term implies that attachment to the body, based on mistaken view, makes sentient beings wander in saṃsāra. Generating certain truth means penetrating this mistaken view of the body so as to view it as it really is, as nothing more than an insubstantial artifice of interconnected processes and activities *(bya ba).* Careful contemplative observation of the body reveals that the ongoing activities within it generally are disorganized.

The practitioner who wishes to tame *('dul ba)* the body attempts to put bodily processes in some order. Many Westerners have the mistaken view that contemplation and meditation lead to bodily relaxation. Contrary to the claim that meditation is a form of relaxation, scientific electromyographic studies of the striate musculature during meditation have shown that meditation postures do not result in relaxation but rather in an even output and distribution of muscle activity. Holding a meditation posture fixed for the duration of the meditation session requires continuous muscle work. The effort to hold the posture raises the energy level so that the mind stays alert, at the same time that it significantly reduces elaboration and wandering. By contrast, too much relaxation lowers the energy level and increases the mind's wandering.[308] Therefore, at the coarse level, taming the body entails sustaining the effort to hold the meditation posture fixed for longer and longer intervals, as a consequence of which the contemplative mind ripens. At the subtle level, the practitioner tries to create a new interconnectedness *(rten 'brel)* according to some ideal model.

According to the ordinary sūtra method of practicing the body points, the practitioner holds each of seven prescribed body points in the proper way according to the instructions, rearranging *(sgrig pa)* each of the main points of the body using the ordinary view of the coarse body. The instructions begin with advice on how to set up the body points (*lus gnad ji ltar bca ba;* JP, f. 6a). Because the purpose of the exercise is to re-order the body, the instructions are given in the form of a list *(spyir grags)* of body points to set up in certain ways and keep track of during sitting meditation (TN, p. 268).

Before beginning the body-point exercise, the practitioner must put everyday life in order. During this phase the practitioner must isolate himself or herself from the noise and bustle of the everyday world and retreat to a meditation cell or some comparable place. There the body-point practice begins, first working with the coarse level of the musculature and after that on the subtle, energy-current level. Coarse bodily control during sitting meditation begins with restriction of all movement. The practitioner sits still. Next he or she selectively focuses on ("isolates"; *dben ba)* certain key points of the body and realigns them according to the instructions. There are seven important points, called *the seven teachings of Vairocana,*[309] because Vairocana is said to be the perfect embodiment of the properly rearranged body during sitting meditation. The practitioner isolates "each and every one of these parts of the body." They include feet, spine, upper trunk, neck, tongue, hands, and eyes. Each must be ordered in a standardized way (JP, f. 6b–7b). Here is an example of Tashi Namgyel's root instructions for the body-point practice. Note their continuity with guru yoga:

> Do the preliminary yogas, the four [extraordinary] units as before, just for a little while, until each comes forth. Then, during guru yoga, pray fervently to generate the special samādhi. Then place your feet in Vairocana's cross-legged posture or Manu Sempa's cross-legged posture. Place the hands about four fingers below the navel in equipose posture [mnyam bzhag]. Straighten the spine and intensify your hold on the entire body. The shoulders and [upper] chest [are lifted and open] so as to expand the diaphragm. The neck is slightly bent. The tip of the tongue is turned upward just below the roof of the mouth. The eyes [are directed] toward the tip of the nose, so that the gaze is calm. Sit with these seven teachings of Vairocana. In general, the points of this artifice of the body are important during any contemplation practice, and in particular, the body points are very important to make the mind stay. So if you happen to put forth great earnest application, you will achieve partial staying. Protecting the body points for only a day is good. (TN, p. 654)

Pema Karpo's root instructions are very similar. Jampel Pawo adds a few comments in order to clarify some of the finer points. He emphasizes that straightening the spine is the most important of the seven points. The spinal column should be straightened "as if it were beads fastened together on a string" (JP, f. 6a). Keeping the spine straight is particularly important because it aligns the subtle energy channels in the body, especially the central channel, which in turn helps stabilize the mind.[310] Proper placement of the hands in the equipose posture means that the left hand is on the bottom. The chest is lifted slightly and expanded. The shoulders are pulled back so that the diaphragm is allowed to expand.[311] The neck is bent slightly like a fish hook or a cane. The tongue is held at the roof of the mouth, while the teeth and lips are left relaxed. The positioning of the eyes is very important. Tashi Namgyel recommends keeping them slightly open, unfocused at the tip of the nose. Jampel Pawo suggests looking, unfocused, "the distance of one yoke" (about four feet) in front. Either way an unfocused gaze "controls contact with the senses" (*reg pa dbang pos bsgyur;* JP, f. 6b). By fixing the gaze, the practitioner not only re-orders a point of the posture but restricts any interaction with and perception of the surroundings at the same time.

After setting up these seven body points,[312] the practitioner is told to practice according to a certain way (*tshul;* JP, f. 9b). Here is Jampel Pawo's explanation:

> You must make effort with earnest application but with no fault. This constitutes skillful means regarding the body points. (JP, f. 9b)

Most commentators agree that the way to make effort is by intensifying the hold *(sgrim ba)*. The word *sgrim pa* means "to intensify." It also means "to cram or stuff." Here it means to intensify the hold on the body points without allowing the slightest aberration from the standardized way of holding them. Jampel Pawo cites Nāropa's clear explanation of the way to practice:

> Intensify your hold [of the body points] inwardly, as if stuffing powder into a pill. Stay that way as if you were a big knot, and you will make great progress. (JP, f. 7b)

He adds that the practitioner should intensify holding the body points continuously (*rgyun du;* JP, f. 9b). Tashi Namgyel stresses that all seven body points must be held in this manner when he says, "Intensify your hold on the entire body." Effort *('bad pa)* and earnest application *(nan tan)* are familiar terms, introduced in the advanced preliminaries. Here they are used to stress the output of energy that is required both in and across meditation sessions to intensify holding the seven body points.

In the sūtra tradition the benefits *(phan yon)* of holding the seven body points and thereby taming the coarse activities of the body are as follows: (1) the immovable body *(lus mi gyo ba)*, (2) body isolation *(lus dben)*, (3) body staying *(lus kyi gnas ba)*, and (4) settlement of the body *(rang babs)*, (5) rearrangement *(sgrig pa)*, and (6) proper action *(las rung)*. *The immovable body* refers to the relative cessation of gross motor activity as well as to cessation of random spontaneous activity within the striate musculature. *Body isolation* refers to the skill of realigning the body points according to the standardized model and to the ease by which these points can be identified and held during sitting practice. *Body staying* refers to the developing skill in holding the seven body points fixed for the duration of the sitting meditation. Over time, holding the body perfectly in the seven-point posture becomes natural and easy. Such skill eventually develops that at the onset of each sitting meditation session the body naturally settles into itself *(rang babs)*. During the actual sitting session the coarse level of the body realigns itself more and more with the standardized model of the seven body points. Eventually a fundamental rearrangement occurs in the body at the coarse level. Following that, random activity of the musculature greatly decreases so that all that remains is the minimal activity of the musculature required to hold the posture to the desired length of the meditation session. This stage of skill is referred to as *proper activity (las rung)*. Once the body points stay and settlement and proper activity have occurred, the coarse activities of the body become sufficiently calm to allow the practitioner to focus more inwardly and to open awareness to the subtle activity of the body's energy currents.[313]

In the extraordinary tantric approach to the body-point exercise the practitioner imagines that the body holding the meditation posture is not his or her ordinary body but is actually the body of the Buddha, Vairocana *(rnam snang)*, who holds the meditation posture perfectly. As an extraordinary practice, the practitioner's ordinary body is eventually rearranged in such a manner that it actually becomes indistinguishable *(dphyug med)* from Vairocana's ideal form. Jampel Pawo explains the difference between the sūtra and the tantra methods:

> Does the [method of] the body points explained in the sūtras also bring about penetration *[snun pa]* of the body points? Even though these [sūtras] talk about the body points and know the essence of the body, yet they don't cause penetration of the points, so there is no penetration of the vajra body points. In our system, one depends on certainty, the certainty of the purified, purifier, and resultant purification [as indistinguishable and empty]. The thing to be purified is the teaching about the skandhas or body; the thing that purifies are the seven teachings of Vairocana; the process of purification is by the stages of entering, staying and dissolving of the energy currents [in the central channel]. The fruition of this process is [attainment of] the Vairocana's [buddha] realms. (JP, f. 10a–10b)

The tantra approach has two additional benefits over the sūtra method. *Penetration (snun pa)* refers to rearrangement of the subtle energy currents of the body, that is, to redirecting the usual chaotic energy flow within the body's subtle energy channels toward a single central channel. *Certainty (nges)* refers to the right view—emptiness—by which the practitioner's own body and that of Vairocana are viewed as empty in an ultimate sense while being one and the same manifestation in a relative sense. Just as the practitioner's mental continuum was seen as indistinguishable from that of the root lama during guru yoga, the rearranged coarse and subtle body becomes indistinguishable from Vairocana's body in this tantric body-points exercise.

As skill develops, the practitioner perceives the inner activity of the body as the manifestation of numerous energy currents *(rlung).* The term *rlung* literally means "moving air," such as the "wind," or the "breath." Here it refers to subtle energy currents that move throughout the body. They move in channels *(rtsa),* which become increasingly discernible with experience. The quality of movement of these currents as well as their direction are correlated with both the rhythm of the breath and the flow of events within the mental continuum. The more chaotic the elaboration of thought within the mental continuum, the greater the disorganization of energy flow within the body. There are five main channels *(rlung lnga)* as well as numerous subsidiary ones *(yan lag gi rlung)* described in the Buddhist tantras. Each of the five main channels is associated with one of the five elements *('byung ba lnga),* one of the five conflicting emotional states *(nyon mong),* one of the coarse bodily functions, and one of the body points. Table 6 gives these correlations.

TABLE 6: CORRELATION OF ENERGY CURRENTS WITH BODY POINTS AND PHYSIOLOGICAL FUNCTIONS[a]

Name of Energy Current	Related Body Points	Physiological Function
1. Inspiration *(thur sel)*	Crossed legs	Excretion
2. Expiration *(kyen rgyu)*	Hands in equipose	Speaking
3. Firelike *(me mnyam)*	Spine and upper trunk	Digestion
4. All-pervasive *(khyab byed)*	Neck and tongue	Muscular activity
5. Vital force *(srog 'dzin)*	Gaze	Breathing

a JP, f. 7b–8a.

Once coarse bodily activities "settle into themselves," the practitioner begins to discern the more subtle activity of the main and subsidiary energy currents within the body. Skillfully easing up one's hold on the body points at the right time makes these energy currents clearer. Because the body points are correlated with the activity of these energy currents, rearrangement of the body points necessarily causes alteration in the energy currents over time.[314] The primary benefit of the practice is said to be purification of these energy currents.

Wangchug Dorjé, in his expanded root instructions, is very explicit about the benefit:

> Unlimited benefit comes from the proper action of the currents and channels. (WD, p. 85)[315]

The first sign of change in the energy currents is that they are left alone *(rang sar)*. Rather than experiencing the activity of the main and subsidiary energy currents as inner chaos, the skilled practitioner is able to discern increasing internal organization of the currents and the discrete activity of each energy channel. The confusing activity of the subsidiary currents subsides so that the five main currents are easily distinguishable in their unique locations and activities. *Left alone* means "to discriminate the energy channel clearly from all other internal activity." As these energy currents become less and less affected by the vicissitudes of mental elaboration, their spontaneous activity is referred to as *purification (dag tshul) of the energy currents.*

With even greater skill, the energy currents undergo a fundamental rearrangement. They are said to *stay (gnas ba)*. This term covers several distinct stages through which the five main and subsidiary energy currents enter the central energy channel and dissolve there. These ordinary energy currents eventually enter *(zhugs pa)*, stay *(gnas ba)*, and dissolve *(shim ba;* JP, f. 10a) in the extraordinary central channel *(dbu ma)*. At some point, the five currents cease *(zin pa;* JP, f. 7b), thereupon causing a profound transformation of bodily and mental experience. The skilled practitioner's task is to make the ordinary currents "stay" within the central channel until they "dissolve." The activity of the ordinary energy currents then ceases, and with it all corresponding bodily and mental disorder. This fundamental body and mind rearrangement is called penetration *(snun pa)* of the body points. This fundamental transformation of the body-mind continuum greatly potentiates meditation practice. It establishes a solid foundation for the contemplative mind, known as *firmness (bsam gtan)*, which in turn properly prepares the vessel to become the enlightened mind *(byang chub kyi sems;* TN, p. 271).[316]

The result of this profound re-ordering of body and mind does not come immediately but ripens over time. Certain signs *(rtags)* manifest themselves:

> Having depended on that, the body's elements become balanced and [from that] you develop a strong constitution. (TN, p. 271; JP, f. 8b)

The practitioner notices better health and seems to have more energy. Jampel Pawo adds, "You don't experience fatigue and are able to stay for a long time in the same posture" (JP, f. 8b). These typical signs refer to the ordinary body. On the extraordinary level, the practitioner becomes Vairocana, embodying perfect realignment of the coarse and subtle body.

The most important benefit of either sūtra or tantra body-point practice pertains to transformation of the mental continuum. The chaotic construction of coarse sensory perception and mental elaboration diminishes so that certain properties of the mind's natural condition become manifest, as if the sun were beginning to shine after the clouds have dissipated:

> Since perception of sense objects doesn't occur, you generate the force of samādhi. Then there is little dullness or flightiness in the mind and awareness-itself, clarity, and brightness are said to come forth. (TN, p. 271)

Pema Karpo adds:

> The awakened wisdom of nonconceptualization arises. (PK, f. 2b)

Wangchug Dorjé also adds:

> First the energy currents flow less. Then they settle into themselves without searching. Then, left alone [in this way], bliss and clarity come forth at the coarse level of the preliminaries. (WD, p. 85)

There are three possible types of elaborated cognitions *(spros pa'i rtog pa)*: perceptions *(snang ba)*, emotional states *(nyon mong)*, and conceptualization *(rtog pa)*, such as thoughts, notions, and memories. The elaboration of each of these on the coarse level of the mind greatly diminishes with mastery of the body-point practice. Ordinary perceptions cease. Tashi Namgyel says that impressions *('jug shes)* no longer arise toward their sense objects *(yul)*. Negative emotional states also cease. When Wangchug Dorjé refers to "bliss" *(dbe ba)*, he is referring to the relative cessation of negative emotional states during contemplation. When Wangchug Dorjé says "without searching" *(rtshol med)*, and Pema Karpo speaks about nonconceptual stillness *(mi rtog)*, they are referring to the cessation of cognition at the coarse level of the mind.[317] The contemporary mahāmudrā master Bokar Rinpoche makes a distinction between correct and incorrect staying-calm practice. He explains that the relative cessation of elaborated thought and emotion in-and-of-itself is incorrect in that it can easily lead to further obscurity. Yet the relative cessation of thought and emotion combined with clarity becomes the way of preventing obscurity.[318] The respective terms *clarity (gsal ba)*, *bliss (bde ba)*, and *awareness-itself (rig pa)* refer to the corresponding aspects of the mind's natural condition that manifest once purified of coarse-level perceptions, emotions, and thoughts, respectively.[319] *Brightness (dwangs)* refers to a quality of mind that manifests once no longer obscured by elaborated thought. Table 7 summarizes these terms:

TABLE 7: TYPES OF ELABORATION COGNITIONS

Type of Elaboration at the Coarse Level of the Mind	Resultant Benefit
Perception	Clarity
Emotion	Bliss
Thought	Awareness-itself and brightness

As the passage says, you "generate the force *[shugs]* of samādhi" *(ting nge 'dzin)*. One of the first signs along the way to developing deep concentration or samādhi is partial staying *(gnas cha)* in that the contemplative can find a way through the chaos of elaborate events in the unfolding mental continuum in order to stay, more or less, on the intended object of awareness. Partial staying establishes a foundation that eventually ripens into contemplation *(bsam gtan),* which literally means "steadying reflections." Though the coarse activities of perceptions, emotions, and thought have far from ended, they are now less distracting, so that the practitioner voluntarily directs and controls awareness.

Incorrect body-points practice can lead to even greater mental disorder. Therefore the commentators warn of the "defect of disorderly body points" *(lus gnad 'chol ba'i skyon):*

> The defect of disorderly body points is like this: Although there may be clarity at first, if you move to the right, much thought about the object [of awareness] will follow. Although there may be bliss at first, if you move to the left, much thought about the subject [who observes the process] will follow. Although there may be a lot of partial clarity or even continuous clarity at first, if you lean forward, much dizziness will follow. Although there may be brightness and expansiveness at first, if you lean backwards, great distraction will follow. Now, if your gaze is unsteady, perceptions will come forth. The defect of each of these thought-elaborations comes forth like this. (TN, p. 271; JP, f. 9a)

These defects are introduced as a precaution so that the practitioner will hold each of the seven body points properly, apply intelligence skillfully, and make any necessary corrections throughout the contemplation session to insure that the appropriate benefits will ripen.

The ultimate purpose of this mind-body transformation via the body-points practice is to make the mental continuum a suitable vessel for the realization of awakened wisdom, the emerging initial signs of which are clarity, bliss, and awareness-itself. In the extraordinary, tantric version of the body points the practitioner not only realizes that his or her own body is indistinguishable with that of Vairocana, but also realizes that his or her own mind is as well, and he or she thereby gains a taste of Vairocana's enlightened mind.

Quoting the *Vajramālā Tantra,* Jampel Pawo says,

> First, the vajra body actually dwells in the form realm, then it is also said that certainty comes, which brings direct realization of the way the mind stays. (JP, f. 9a–9b)

Tashi Namgyel promises that "understanding arises," and Wangchug Dorjé says that "experience and understanding are illumined from just the body points" (WD, p. 85). These seemingly simple postural considerations establish a firm foundation for meditative special insight.

2. The Isolation of Speech

With greater proficiency, the body-points contemplation becomes more inwardly focused *(nang du)* on the quality of the unfolding mental continuum, and less focused on the more externalized virtue practices.

> Guru Pema [Karpo] says, "The root of all teachings is your very mind. Establish yourself inwardly, in samādhi, and understanding the truth will come forth. However, if you only cultivate the [external form of] body and speech virtue practice, it won't come forth. So leave aside these practices, if these alone are what you do." (JP, f. 11a–11b)

As the signs of ripening contemplation first appear, the practitioner has mastered attention control sufficiently to begin exploration of this inner world.

The beginner's first discovery is how little partial-staying has indeed been achieved.[320] Beginning contemplative experience is highly unstable. Jampel Pawo warns about the "danger of losing it" *(yal nyen yod pa;* JP, f. 11a). As the activity of the coarse body becomes calmer, the chaotic activity of the energy currents and mental continuum seem more salient. The problem of incessant mental elaboration seems more acute as the practitioner turns inward. The more the beginner tries to maintain a contemplative perspective, the harder, it seems, it is to do so. Jampel Pawo likens the problem of chaotic mental activity, and its interference with meditation, to an itching sensation that won't go away:

> About this time the beginner's meditation appears like an intolerable itch that can't be scratched. It is therefore very important to know both what happens to obstruct the generation or continuance [of contemplation] and also what conditions cause you to lose the very slight partial-staying that you have. (JP, f. 11b)

The main condition obstructing progress is the enjoyment of speech (*smra ba la dga' ba;* JP, f. 10b):

> Generally, enjoyment of speech is the gateway to poor [results].[321]
> So it becomes the foundation for generating all negative emotional states. (JP, f. 11b)

Enjoyment of speech produces chaotic mental activity and also lays the groundwork for emotional storminess during contemplation. Pema Karpo's root instructions say:

> The isolation of speech is called *stopping speech,* or *speech staying settled,* because of the silence that follows from expiring the breath and keeping quiet. (PK, f. 3a)

Two words are used for "speech." The former is *ngag,* which means "speech." According to the commentary, there are several aspects or types of speech, both internal and external. The external aspect of speech refers to speech on the coarse level, namely the spoken word *(smra ba).* Spoken words come in a disordered form, namely ordinary speech activity *(ngag byes),* and a more organized form, namely chants and recitations *(sngags bzlas;* Skt., *mantra; japa;* JP, f. 11b). On the subtle level, speech pertains to unspoken words, that is, a form of mental activity akin to an internal mental chatter. The latter word for speech is *rlung,* which means "breath." The coarse level of the breath pertains to the cycle of respiration *(dbugs pa),* while the subtle breath pertains to the energy currents. These in turn are correlated with internal mental chatter, as illustrated in Table 8:

TABLE 8: CORRELATION OF SPEECH, RESPIRATION, AND MENTAL ACTIVITY

Level	Mental Activity	Type of Speech	Breath
Coarse	Disordered Mental chatter	Spoken words	Normal respiration
Coarse	Ordered	Chants and recitations	Breath counting
Subtle	Mind-moments		Energy currents

Enjoyment of speech refers to all of these aspects of speech.

In order to master contemplation, the beginner must let go of the enjoyment of speech.[322] As the root text says, "It follows from expiring the breath and keeping quiet." The commentary explains the passage as follows:

> Amoghavajra says, "Not moving, not speaking, wherein the vowels and consonants become equalized, is the best kind of Recitation." To bring about the purification of the three poisons exhale three times. Then how much more of your foolish ordinary talk should there be? After a little while, don't even say the recitations you know by heart. (JP, f. 11a)

At the coarse level, the practitioner stops speaking. Abandoning the activity *(bya spang)* of speaking in a silent retreat is an intial step toward quieting mental chatter. Recitation *(bzlas ba)* of mantras puts order into speech, in place of the rambling quality of ordinary discourse. Next comes genuine silence *(smra bcad)*. The word for silence, *smra bcad*, is a compound consisting of *smra* ("speaking"), *bcad pa* ("perfect"), and *gcod pa* ("to cut off"). Literally, it means "speech that has been cut off." The practitioner cuts off all aspects of speech, from spoken words to mental chatter, because these cause the deterioriation of contemplation.

Having cut off the spoken word and recitation, the practitioner becomes intensely aware of mental chatter. The very effort to cut off this mental chatter generates more of it. The way to practice is to ease up *(glod pa)*:

> In the *Vajramālā* it says, "Ease up on the inspiration and expiration." With respect to this, Milarepa says, "When you practice mahāmudrā, don't get too invested in the body and speech virtue practices or else there is danger of losing the wisdom of non-conceptual stillness." (JP, f. 11a)

Easing up *(glod)* is the opposite of intensifying *(sgrim pa)*. The act of easing up is likened to the act of unstringing a taught bow. The practitioner eases up on trying to follow any given train of thought and simply recognizes that mental chatter is occurring moment by moment. Over time repeated easing up greatly diminishes the overall amount of mental activity during contemplation, so that mental chatter eventually becomes less of an obstruction.

There are several benefits to isolating speech pertaining to thought and attention. The cognitive benefits come from speech having settled into itself *(rang babs)*. When the practitioner eases up, mental chatter begins to settle. Though still present, the noise of mental chatter fades into the background and becomes less distracting. The flow of content in the mental continuum becomes more orderly. Discrete moments of thought occur with intervals of silence in between. Over time these moments of silence ripen into the relative cessation of mental chatter during contemplation, and the practitioner experiences a state of relative nonconceptual stillness *(mi rtog)*. Thinking still occurs, but mainly as fleeting moments of background noise.

As mental chatter settles, the practitioner is more able to stay on the intended object of meditation without distraction. The commentary explains:

> The *Vajrapīṭhatantra* says, "Breath and speech without movement. This brings forth the fruit, namely contemplation." (JP, f. 11a)

Isolation of speech[323] entails progressively cultivating the mind's capacity to stay on the intended object of contemplation and segregating this from the background of incessant mental chatter. In this way the effects of contemplation *(bsam gtan)* are enhanced.[324] The word *bsam gtan* literally means "steadying reflections." Reflections pertain only to present experience. The activity experienced moment-by-moment within the mental continuum becomes a bit calmer so that attention becomes more steady.

3. The Isolation of Mind

The practitioner carried out a specific mental action *(bya ba)* in both the body and the speech isolation exercises, namely intensifying and easing up, respectively. In the mind-isolation exercise *(yid dben)*, the practitioner is instructed to cease engaging in all arbitary mental activity, which includes not only going after certain thought elaborations but also trying to do specific things to meditate, such as intensifying or easing up. Instead of artificial mental activity, the requirement is simply to allow awareness itself *(rang rig pa)* to manifest itself. Wangchug Dorjé's root instructions say:

> The general mind points: cut off the three times, and whatever has arisen comes forth so purely. (WD, p. 65)

The references to "the three times" *(dus gsum)* and to "whatever has arisen" *(gang shar)* pertain to an acute awareness of the *process* of unfolding of events (not the content) in the mental continuum. The practitioner more and more experiences the mental continuum as an orderly flow of successive mental events. Though these events may vary in their respective content, each successive event is experienced as a discrete unit. One event occurs and ceases before another comes forth. Instead of the previous chaos of many conflicting trains of thought at once, events now unfold one at a time, moment by moment, in a regular succession. The phrase *whatever has arisen* signifies the shift from the disorder of the ordinary mind to the orderly stream of the contemplative mind. The phrase *gang shar* consists of the indefinite article *gang,* which means "whatever, anything," and also the perfect form of the verb *'char ba,* which means "to arise." The phrase indicates that attachment to specific mental content becomes less important. The content is simply "whatever." The process of how mental events come forth over time becomes much more important. At this point the mental continuum begins to rearrange itself *(sgrig pa)* in the form of an orderly temporal flow of discrete events.

In ordinary experience, thoughts *(rtog pa)* tend to get more and more complicated.[325] A thought arises and gives birth to further thought. Lost in a maze of increasingly elaborate thoughts, the mental continuum becomes disorderly. The process by which thought ordinarily proliferates so as to mask the succession of simple, discrete events is called *elaboration ('phro ba).* As elaboration intensifies, there is more mental content to distract *(gyeng ba)* awareness. Elaboration is to thought content what distraction is to awareness. Prior to speech isolation, mental chatter is so great that there is little opportunity to contemplate. During the mind-isolation exercise, ordinary thought elaboration is more circumscribed. The practitioner's awareness alternates between periods of somewhat continuous awareness of a discrete temporal flow and periods of distraction by thought elaboration.

The purpose of the exercise is to "cut off elaboration," that is, to strip the mental continuum of its disorderly content so that awareness is more likely to stay on its intended object. Various types of coarse mental content occur during a single contemplation session: thoughts, perceptions, sensations, and emotions. All are examples of cognitive elaboration. The mind-isolation exercise is about these cognitive elaborations of the mind *(yid kyi rtog pa'i 'phro;* JP, f. 5a) that distract awareness.

The reference to "the three times" indicates the categories of mental events likely to occur at this stage of contemplation. *Past elaboration ('das pa)* refers to personal memories. As the initial noise of the mind clears, spontaneous memories arise more frequently as a distraction to contemplation. *Future elaboration (ma' ongs pa)* refers to anticipation of certain experiences or future events. For example, the practitioner may hope for a certain type of experience from the meditation practice and look forward to this. *Present elaboration (da lta)* refers to labeling, categorizing, or otherwise reflecting on present experience. For example, the practitioner may try to figure out whether the meditation, at any given moment, is being done correctly according to the teacher's oral advice. Although each of these forms of elaboration vary in duration and intensity, each serves as a powerful condition *(rkyen)* for cultivating distraction and eroding contemplation, much in the same way that weeds become the reason a seed fails to ripen.

The advice for cutting off elaboration comes in two stages, each one of which is designed to allow mental processes to stabilize. Wangchug Dorjé's expanded root instructions present these stages in rudimentary form:

> [Step One:]
> Do not follow the past. Do not reflect. Do not anticipate what was past going into the future. Do not think, "I am doing or will do this." Let all categorizing about the present settle.
> [Step Two:]
> Establish what begins to arise only as present in the state of ordinary knowledge, bliss. Place your mind to stay without any activity whatsoever [in your mind, such as] abandoning or taking up, expecting or doubting. Don't artificially construct anything, but stay in the state of freshness, uninterruptedness, by-itself. (WD, pp. 85–86)

The first set of instructions come from the six yogas of Tilopa (*chos drug;* JP, f. 11b). These initial instructions involve a special type of activity, known as a cutting-off meditation *(bcod pa)* because the practitioner attempts to cut off the elaboration of certain types of thought. These meditations are also known as negation meditations. The use of the negative particle *mi* in conjunction with a verb signifies negation of the activity indicated by the verb. For example, *mi bsam pa* means "do not reflect." Whenever the practitioner recognizes reflections and other types of cognitive elaborations arising within the mental continuum, they are to be cut off or negated.

The first three of the six yogas pertain to the respective coarse cognitions—memories, anticipations, and present reflections. Jampel Pawo defines each of these in some detail. The first concerns memories:

> What is called "not recalling" *[mi mno]* is not following *[rje su mi 'brang ba]* thoughts about past objects *['das ba],* because, when pursued, the mind becomes distracted *[gyeng ba].* (JP, f. 11b)

The next concerns present reflections:

> What is called "not reflecting" *[mi bsam]* is not artificially constructing *[bzo bcos]* and categorizing *[rtsis gdab]* what appears presently *[da lta]* in the mind. By doing this, the mind goes astray under the influence of these conditions. Otherwise the mind would have become the cause of samādhi. (JP, f. 11b–12a)

Pema Karpo's root text gives several examples of specific types of reflections:

> Do not conceptualize *[blos btangs nas],*[326] nor hold [specific] views *[blta],* for example, about so-called emptiness as being nothing whatsoever. (PK, f. 3a)

These various reflections—categorization of immediate sense information, conceptualization, and adopting viewpoints—are all types of thinking. Simply opening to awareness is quite different from ordinary thinking.

The next of the six yogas concerns anticipation:

> What is called "not anticipating" *[mi sems]* is not advancing *[mi bsu ba]* a previous thought as [something] to do or be done in the future *[ma 'ongs ba].* If advanced, there is movement toward the object and [the mind] becomes unsteady. (JP, f. 12a)

As the practitioner becomes more able to recognize these types of thoughts *(rtog pa)* as they arise within the mental continuum, he or she becomes increasingly able to cut them off before they become elaborated.[327]

Jampel Pawo also explains the latter three of the six yogas. These pertain to subtle cognition. The latter practice is done only after some success has been achieved with the former coarse-level practice. He explains:

> What is called "not meditating" *[mi sgom]* is not meditating on anything that can be an object of notions *[blo]*, such as that which has or does not have attributes *[mtshan ma]*. If having meditated like this, subject and object will be taken to mind....
>
> What is called "not analyzing" *[mi dphyad]* is not using conceptualization *[blos brtag]* or reasoning *[blos dphyad]* once in the state of having calmed the elaborations....
>
> What is called "established settled-in-itself" *[rang babs bzhag]* is establishing the nature *[rang bzhin]* of the mind or the way of placing [the mind] *['dug tshul]* as it really is, without artificial construction. Otherwise, the truth of the way the mind stays will become corrupted. (JP, f. 12b–13a)

These more subtle forms of cognitions arise "once having calmed coarse-level elaborations." Attributes *(mtshan ma)* are the specific qualities of sensory experience that arise within the mental continuum. Pema Karpo says that practitioners should not think about whatever impressions arise from the sense systems, and above all should not try to think about whether or not these sense objects really exist. Rather, the practitioner should focus inwardly *(mand du)* so as not to become distracted by external sense impressions (PK, f. 3a). Once focused inwardly, thinking becomes more salient. If, however, the practitioner stays on the intended meditation object and resists becoming distracted by various types of thought, the foreground meditation object becomes more and more isolated from the background noise of thought elaboration. Eventually the mental continuum itself unfolds with increasing orderliness and regularity. From the event-perspective, arising events remain fresh in the moment and do not artificially become constructed into thought elaboration. Describing events as *settling into themselves (rang babs)* contrasts the ordinary tendency to elaborate upon immediate experience. From the mind-perspective, some skill develops in placing the mind readily on the intended meditation object. This "way of placing [the mind]" *('dug tshul)* occurs easily and quickly during contemplation and can be held uninterruptedly *(lhug par)*. Now partially free from artifical constructions and cognitive elaborations, the mind's true nature *(rang bzhin)* begins to manifest.

The second set of instructions come from Gampopa's "means to set up the mind" (*bzhag thabs;* JP, f. 11b). As the name implies, these instructions are practiced from the mind-perspective. The instructions are to establish the mind "easy" *(glod)*, "freshly" *(so ma)*, "self-contentedly" *(rang gar)*, and "uninterruptedly" *(lhug par;* JP, f. 13a).[328] Gampopa says that these latter instructions are to be practiced "when looking to the real nature of the mind itself" (JP, f. 13a). Successful mastery of the cutting-off instructions greatly reduces thought elaboration so that the natural condition of the mind shines forth in a new way. The practitioner no longer needs to make any effort to actively cut off thinking. By being *easy (glod)*, the true nature of the mind is revealed. The verb *'jog pa* ("perfect;" *bzhag pa*) means "to establish or set up." Here it means to establish certain necessary conditions *(rkyen)*. Cognitive elaboration and artificial construction of concepts about sense experience are improper conditions, which disorder the mental continuum and distract the mind. Over and against these conditions the practitioner establishes exactly those conditions that put order into the mental continuum. The mind remains in the moment without any need to think about the meditation *(fresh)*, focused on the intended meditation object and segregated from the background noise of thought elaboration, and focused continuously over time without distraction. The mind is established without effort *(rsthol med)* according to its own spontaneity.[329] In other words, no activity *(byas ba)* is needed, either in the form of intensifying or of easing up. When the mind is established self-contentedly *(rang gar)*, it remains on the intended meditation object completely apart from the background noise of thought elaboration. When it remains continuously on the intended object for some period of time without distraction, it is said to be uninterrupted *(lhug pa)*.[330] The mind in this natural condition is described as still, pure awareness, without any activity whatsoever associated with this awareness—either to intensify or ease up or to artifically construct anything from immediate experience. Wangchug Dorjé's phrase *stay so that you don't have any activity whatsoever* refers to the effortless, automatic quality of mind, from the mind-perspective.

There are two main benefits from mastery of the mind-isolation exercises. From the event-perspective, coarse-level cognitive elaborations greatly diminish in frequency and complexity so that the stream of unfolding experience begins to approximate a nonconceptual still *(mi rtog)* state.[331] There is a significant reduction in coarse mental activity from memories, anticipations, reflections of immediate experience, concepts, and other forms of thinking. The mental continuum unfolds as an orderly stream of discrete events. From the mind-perspective, awareness is said to stay *(gnas ba)* on the intended meditation object. Gampopa calls this benefit *undistraction (ma yengs pa):*

> Undistraction is the path of every buddha.
> Undistraction is the friend and teacher of virtue.
> Undistraction is the best of all advice....
> Undistraction, this mindfulness of the mental continuum,
>   is the middle path of the buddhas of the three times. (JP, f. 13b)

Undistraction pertains to mindfulness of the mental continuum *(rgyun gyi dran pa),*[332] that is, each discrete successive mental event that "has arisen" *(shar).* Uninterrupted awareness of each of these discrete moments of arising is called one-pointedness *(rtse gcig).* Jampel Pawo says, "the mind is an isolated mind with one-pointedness [from the event-perspective] or a non-moving mind [from the mind-perspective]" (JP, f. 5a). Awareness of the spontaneous unfolding of the mind free from cognitive elaboration is a step toward understanding the real nature *(rang bzhin)* of the mind (JP, f. 13a).[333] Another commentator says,

> ...established in samādhi, in a nonconceptual still state *[mi rtog],*
>   in the clear understanding of the present. (RD, pp. 4–5)

From the mind-perspective, what emerges is awareness-itself *(rang rig),* no longer obscured by conceptual elaboration. Such primordial awareness is unimpeded *(thags pa med).* This is what Wangchug Dorjé means by the mind being established purely *(dang du dzhag).*

4. FORMAL MEDITATION: CONCENTRATION WITH SUPPORT

. . . .

THE DEVELOPMENT OF CONCENTRATION *(sems bzhung)* is a necessary ingredient of the essential practice *(dngos gzhi)* of formal meditation *(sgom ba)*. The ultimate goal of concentrative development is to focus the mind fully and uninterruptedly on the intended meditation object for long periods without the slightest distraction *(gyeng ba)*. This is called *one-pointed concentration (rtse gcig du)*. The practitioner who attains one-pointed concentration masters staying-calm practice *(zhi gnas;* Skt., *śamatha)*. As was said in the previous chapter, the Tibetan word for staying-calm practice, *zhi gnas*, is a compound, which is composed of *zhi*, "calm," and *gnas,* "stay," and each of these words refers to one of the two perspectives on staying-calm practice. From the event-perspective, events in the mental continuum unfold in an orderly and calm manner, without cognitive elaboration. From the mind-perspective, awareness stays fully and uninterruptedly on the intended meditation object.

Staying-calm practice is the foundation of all subsequent spiritual development. Concentration occurs in several stages, each of which presupposes a variety of attention skills. Tashi Namgyel says that a practitioner must attend *(sems gtod)* properly in order to know the benefits of deep concentrative states *(ting nge 'dzin;* Skt., *samādhi* [TN, p. 266]). To make an internal representation of the intended meditation object *(dmigs pa)* requires not only attention but effort (*'bad pa;* TN, pp. 272–74).

Several technical words convey the variety of attention skills in question. *Attention (sems gtod)* is the more general term: *sems* = "mind"; *gtod pa* = "to turn, direct." The compound literally means "to turn or direct the mind to something," much like using a steering wheel in a car. *Concentration (sems gzung)* has a more specific meaning: *sems* = "mind"; *bzhung* = perfect tense of *'dzin pa* = "to hold." It means "having held the mind," specifically to hold on to something continuously over time. The phrase *sems 'jog* ("setting up the mind," or "placing the mind") is sometimes used instead of *sems gzhung* ("concentration"): *sems* = "mind"; *'jog pa* = "to set up; establish." It is used in a more specific sense pertaining to a quality of attention when there is no definitive object to hold. Although similar, these words are used in very specific contexts. *Attention* is used most often when speaking of initially directing the mind to the intended object of awareness or steering it back to the object after becoming distracted. *Concentration* is used when the mind has been held on the meditation object and has attained some degree of steadiness *(brtan po)* over time. *Placing the mind* is used when the intended meditation object is a subtle, not a coarse object.

Another very important technical term is *dmigs pa*. *Dmigs pa* refers to "making an internal representation." As a verb, *dmigs pa* refers to making a mental representation for any sensory impression from the six sense systems. As a noun, it refers to the resultant representation, or in the case of meditation, to the intended meditation object. It is equivalent to the Sanskrit *alambana,* which is sometimes translated as "the support or foundation for meditative concentration."[334] I have translated the verb as "to represent" and the noun as "intended meditation object." The intended object can come from any of the six senses—a sight, sound, smell, taste, touch sensation, or thought. Since a common approach to concentration training is to use a visual object, the term could also be translated as "visualization."

For each of the six sense systems described in Buddhist psychology the mind is said to take the shape of or reflect the qualities of its intended object as if it were a reflected image in a mirror *(snang brnyan;* Skt., *pratibim-bakam).* The term *attribute (mtshan ma;* Skt., *nimitta)* is often used in conjunction with the technical term *representation*. *Attribute* refers to various *(sna tshogs)* qualities of sensory experience. The act of making a representation during concentration meditation is a process by which the mind continuously holds *('dzin pa)* the sensory attributes of the intended object in awareness. As the attributes of each intended meditation object are unique, the mind particularizes only these attributes during concentration, and is not distracted by other events in the mental continuum. This is called *taking-to-mind,* or *mentally engaging (yid la byed pa),* the intended object. The term literally means "doing something in the mind" because concentration requires continuous, effortful mental activity to hold the attributes of the intended object over and against everything else that is and will occur in the unfoldig mental continuum. "Taking-to-mind" is an extremely important concept, because during the advanced, extraordinary practices in the mahāmudrā tradition the practitioner is given an instruction that is exactly opposite to that of the earlier concentration practices. That is to say, these extraordinary realizations occur only through *not*-taking-to-mind, through *not* doing anything to meditate. More will be said about this later.

The term *dmigs pa* is also used for the more advanced stages of concentration meditation—those without attributes *(mi tshan med)*, in which a subtle object is used instead of a coarse meditation object. Here the practitioner is said to place the mind in a certain way because there is no coarse sensory object to hold on to. Sometimes this advanced concentration stage is called *concentration without support*. Nevertheless the term *representation* is still used for this as well because the practitioner is considered to be actively making a representation for the intended meditation object. *Representation* is a key term used throughout all the stages of staying-calm practice.

Tashi Namgyel says:

> To meditate [in] samādhi, it is necessary to enter into making a representation because of the mind's tendency for elaboration. (TN, p. 272)

Representation is necessary because the ordinary mind wanders. Very advanced mahāmudrā practitioners, who have completely stopped mental elaboration, are capable of mastering *nonrepresenting (dmigs med) meditations*. Most beginners, however, practice making representations. Jampel Pawo defines it thus:

> It is impossible for ordinary people to learn quickly without an intended meditation object. The mental-perceiver must make a representation for some intended object, and that is why [the practice called] "having a support" is taught first. (JP, f. 26b)

To begin concentration training, the mind needs some object to serve as a support *(rten can)*. From the event-perspective, any sense object *(yul don)* could serve as a support for concentration training, according to Tashi Namgyel. From the mind-perspective, the supporting object is something intentionally produced *(sgrub pa; TN, p. 681)*. The mental act of producing an object results in the object being taken as apparently real and existent in its own right. Wangchug Dorjé explains that since this seemingly real sense object is taken to be something "other than the mind" (WD, p. 97), ordinary concentration training posits a subject-object duality. A true object *(don)* to be used in the more advanced, extraordinary mahāmudrā practice is not based upon this false dichotomy.

Rangjung Dorjé says that six different types of sense objects can serve as the intended meditation object, each corresponding to one of the six sense systems *(tshog drug)*. He relies upon the standard Abhidharma Buddhist psychology definition of *sense perception*. Each sense system has three components: an object *(yul)*, a sense organ *(dbang po)*, and a sense-perceiver *(dbang shes)*. For example, the visual system consists of the object appearing to the eye, the eye itself, and the mental apparatus that interprets the interaction. Each of the five sense systems functions so that its respective sense objects *(yul)* appear *(snang ba)* in the unfolding mental continuum. As each appearing object has characteristic attributes *(mthsan ma)*—shape, color, etc.—the array of sense objects ordinarily arising in the mental continuum over time are said to "appear as various" *(sna tshogs du snang)*.

Although each of the five main sense systems functions as a separate unit, the information between them is integrated by a sixth system, the mind-perceiver *(yid shes)*. In Buddhist psychology the mind is considered to be a sense system because the mind is said to take objects *(yul)*. Emotions *(nyon mong)* and the various types of thought *(rtog)*, such as memory, anticipation, reflection on immediate sensory experience, and conceptualization, are the mind's objects. Because the mind-perceiver functions as an integrator, sense perception, emotion, and thought get confounded in ordinary experience. Furthermore, ordinary experience posits a subject-object duality in that the sense and mental objects are believed to be objects *(yul)* distinct from the subject *(yul can)* or mind that perceives them. Table 9 gives the classification of mental events.

TABLE 9: CLASSES OF MENTAL OBJECTS

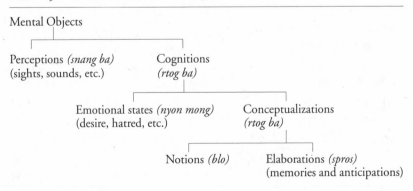

The most common objects used for concentration training are called substances *(dngos po;* Skt., *bhāva). Substances* are visual or other objects thought to be solid *(thas pa),* existing in themselves *(yin pa),* and enduring *(rtag pa).* From the perspective of ultimate truth, this ordinary belief is mistaken, because all substances are empty of any inherent self-existence and are also impermanent. Nevertheless substances are useful beginning concentrative objects because they allow the mind to grasp and hold something seemingly substantial. They are good supports. Tashi Namgyel defines *a support* as follows:

> Because you fix your mind on the supports of concentration—
> on the supports that are [internally] represented by the mind,
> for example, substances such as stones or pieces of wood, or on
> [insubstantial objects] such as seed syllables—we call it "having
> support." (TN, pp. 279)

During concentration training the act of internally representating the object properly is more important than the specific object used. The compound *dmigs rten* is often used. It means "supporting representation." The term *support (rten)* is merely an abbreviated form of the compound. A support is anything that the mind can use to learn how to make a representation during concentration training. The practitioner begins training with substantial supports, but must also learn to use insubstantial supports in order to complete the meditations with support *(rten can). Insubstantials (dngos med)* are objects generated solely by the imagination without a corresponding external stimulus. The practitioner who imagines a visual image does not necessarily take the image to be solid, self-existent, or durable. The same practitioner who stares at a tree takes it to be solid, self-existent, and durable. Substantial objects have the advantage of being easy to take hold of by the mind. Insubstantial objects are harder to take hold of as concentrative objects, yet have a different advantage. A practitioner who imagines the root lama seated on a throne on top of his head during guru yoga doesn't believe that the lama's physical body is present on his head. Insubstantial objects are considered to be better supports because the practitioner doesn't make the epistemological mistake of taking them to be solid, self-existent, and durable. In so doing he makes strides toward right view.

Concentration training is generally done in two steps. The initial step uses a substantial object, and the second step uses an insubstantial object.

Rangjung Dorjé recommends any of the five principal sense objects—sight, sound, and so on—as the starting, substantial object and then a mental object—an emotion or a thought—as the subsequent, insubstantial object. Pema Karpo and his commentator, Jampel Pawo, suggest ordinary *(ma dag pa)* objects for the first stage—a stone or piece of wood—and a sacred *(dag pa)* object for the second stage—an image of the Buddha, certain seed syllables *(yig 'bru)* or seeds *(thig le)* imagined in various bodily locations. Wangchug Dorjé says that the starting, substantial object is held in front *(mngon du)* while the subsequent, insubstantial object is represented inside *(nang du)*. No matter how the stages are named or described, there is general agreement that initial concentration training follows two distinct stages. (Kamalaśīla, however, in his *Stages of Meditation,* skips the former stage and starts concentration training using the Buddha's body as an insubstantial object.)[335] By contrast, Tashi Namgyel recommends that most ordinary practitioners start with a substantial object:

> It is difficult for less intelligent practitioners to use the features of the Tathāgata's body as an object for concentration, so they then concentrate on an ordinary substance. Since the staying-mind comes forth more easily this way, they must still do both [types] of concentration—ordinary representing using stones, sticks, and so forth, and representing using the Tathāgata's sacred body. (TN, pp. 274–75)[336]

Each stage, then, has a different goal. The former practice results in partial staying *(gnas cha)* in that the mind stays on the intended object at least for some duration. The latter practice results in great virtue *(dge ba chen po;* JP, f. 29b) because, from the mind-perspective, the mind stays *(sems gnas;* TN, p. 74) more fully and completely on the intended object; and from the event-perspective, the occurrence of negative emotional states and elaboration of thought in the unfolding mental continuum diminishes and becomes calmer.

I. Concentration-in-Front: Partial Staying

The goal of the initial stage of concentration, from the mind-perspective, is for the mind to stay relatively continuously over time on the intended meditation object. Nonetheless, at any given point in time, the mind will still be partially engaged in the background noise. The goal, from the event perspective, is to concentrate on the intended meditation object as a support, to such an extent that the background noise of thought and sense experience diminishes. These goals are referred to as *partial staying (gnas cha),* from the mind-perspective, and *concentration in front (mngon du),* from the event-perspective.

Any suitable (*'os pa;* WD, p. 86) object can be used to begin concentration training.[337] Objects are considered suitable if they are certain *(nges ba)* and clear *(gsal). Certain* objects are those grounded in immediate sensory experience. Such sense impressions are also *clear* if they are perceived directly by the given sense-perceiver *(dbang shes)* without cognitive elaboration by the mind-perceiver *(yid shes).* For example, when the practitioner looks at a stone and sees only the immediate sense object without thinking about its color, shape, classification, name, or meaning, the object is both certain and clear in immediate awareness. A stone or piece of wood is recommended because it has few distinctive perceptual features to distract away from concentration training.[338] If there is no stone around and the practitioner thinks about a stone he or she saw several hours ago, the representation is uncertain *(nges med).* If the practitioner sees a real stone, but elaborates on its shape or color, thinks about what it reminds him of, or has a memory or fantasy such that the mind wanders away from the immediate sense data, the representation is said to be unclear *(gsal med).*

While a wide range of objects are suitable for concentration training, visual objects (*gzugs can:* literally, "having form") are generally preferred at the onset of practice.[339] Tashi Namgyel suggests concentrating on a young plant if concentration doesn't develop easily using a stone (TN, p. 655).

Sometimes familiar objects are recommended. Some objects become more personally meaningful or familiar (*'dris goms;* JP, f. 30a) than others, and are held on to with greater force. Although caught up in attachment, it is actually easier to concentrate upon these objects because the mind naturally holds them. In the *Biography of the Eighty-Four Siddhas,* the tantric master Nāgārjuna II instructs a buffalo herdsman to take a buffalo horn as the starting, substantial meditation object. In a future life the buffalo herdsman gets reincarnated as a musician. This time the master instructs him to use his own guitar as the initial meditation object. Jampel Pawo summarizes the theme of the story:

It is easier to generate contemplation when someone relies upon something familiar that has the great force of habit. Generating contemplation is more important [than the particular object]. (JP, f. 29b)

This approach to practice is called *utilizing familiar propensities* (*'dris pa'i bag chags;* JP, f. 31a).

Tsongkhapa (2002) recommends selecting a meditation object according to the practitioner's personality. He says, "There is no single, definitive object; individuals require their particular object of meditation" (p. 42). For example, if the person thinks too much, the breath is the best meditation object. If the person is strongly attached to sense objects, then an unpleasant or ugly object is recommended. By selecting objects according to personality type, the meditator is able to remove impediments to meditation concurrent with training the mind to stay on the intended object (vol. 3, pp. 35–42).

The way *(tshul)* to practice concentration begins with setting up the body points and then preparing the mind by practicing guru yoga. Jampel Pawo explains the purpose of these preliminaries:

> First you make a representation using an ordinary support. In accordance with Atiśa's *Bodhipathapradīpa,* you won't attain samādhi, even if you practice over a thousand years, if you tamper with the limbs of staying-calm practice. Therefore, as it is explained in a chapter in the *Samādhivarga,* "Having represented the limbs we have talked about, the virtuous mind should be placed upon any of these intended meditation objects. You won't attain samādhi without the limbs of virtue because ordinary intended objects are used in the *Samādhivarga,* too. Master Jangchub Zangpo says, "With respect to concentration-in-front, there are two intended objects, the usual and unusual." The "usual" objects are the ones already cited above. Using these, start with the body points as previously done. Then fervently pray to the lama. This is considered the way to begin, namely with a respectful meditation to your understanding lama. And, Lord Maitripa adds, "Absolute truth occurs of itself through the very devotion that must be understood." Therefore the only entrance [to concentration] is through devotion. Now meditate with your lama on top of your head and visualize him surrounded by the

retinue of all the buddhas. As if all sentient beings were your mother, take refuge in your precious lama-Buddha. Pray that the precious understanding will come forth in your own mind. Pray for empowerment to realize the influence of the precious mahāmudrā. Having made your prayer and requested influence, let the lama melt into light, and absorb him into yourself. From the perspective that you and your lama's mind are united, non-dual, then place the mind on the support of a stone, piece of wood, or the like in front of you. Be with a straight gaze, with the light not too bright so as not to hurt the eyes. (JP, f. 27a–28a)

Having chosen a suitable object and performed the necessary preliminaries, the practitioner is now ready to begin training in concentration. Pema Karpo's root instructions for this are:

Place the mind in front on a small stone or stick as the intended
    meditation object.
Then familiarize yourself with the [object], but without any
    thought elaboration whatsoever.
Next [place the mind upon the intended object] inwardly without
    changing it. Look only to that one-pointedly.
Meditate on your lama on top of your head,
As if he were a realized buddha.
Pray to him with the prayer, "All beings are my mother."
Pray for the influence to attain the realization of mahāmudrā.
Having asked for the realization, absorb him into yourself.
Reflect that his mind and your mind [are now] mixed.
Then [continue meditating]. Enter into samādhi and stay in
    samādhi as long as possible.
Discuss with your lama the states of mind and discrete events [that
    you experienced] and [then continue to] meditate.
When there is dullness, raise the gaze or meditate where the earth's
    vast expanse can be seen.
When sluggish, do likewise, and be disciplined with your
    mindfulness.
When there is flightiness, sit [in an enclosed place such as] inside
    your meditation cell, lower your gaze, and try to ease up, above
    all. (PK, f. 4a–4b)

The intended object, the stone or stick, is set up in front (*mngon du;* TN, p. 655; WD, p. 86). The practitioner looks outward (*kha phyir bltas;* RD, p. 4). At the onset of concentration training the practitioner sits in a stable posture with eyes partly open and stares undistractedly at the intended object placed directly in front within the field of vision. The object is generally situated "the distance of a yoke," which is about an arm's length away.

Ordinary beginners are told to focus upon the external substance itself. Beginners with exceptional ability are reminded that grasping the substance as real or self-existent is a mistake. While seeming to gaze at the substance in front, they hold the mind on the internal reflected image (*snang brnyan;* JP, f. 30b) of that substance within the mental continuum. At a certain stage of proficiency, all practitioners are instructed to de-emphasize the outer image and focus only upon the internal reflected image. More will be said about this later.

Whatever way the substance is viewed—as an external substance or as an internally reflected image—the gaze (*lta stangs;* JP, f. 26b) is important:

> Because the practitioner has held the supporting intended object as the eyes nail it with an unflinching gaze, and has [then been able to] attend in an eased-up manner, there is no mental elaboration anywhere. This brings about mere undistraction [*ma yengs tsam*]. He also closely examines this supporting intended object, but doesn't resort to remembering, anticipating, reflecting, or analyzing with notions about its [immediate] color and form. In short, he doesn't lose the supporting intended object, and finds partial staying—staying wondrously connected with [the object], but without thought, without intention or anticipation. (JP, f. 28a)[340]

Jampel Pawo says the gaze is straight *(thad kar),* unflinching *(mi 'gyur ba),* nailed to *(brtod phur ba),* and wondrously connected with *(hu re lhan ne)* the intended object. The eyes (and also the mind) are held so as to not make any gross or subtle movements away from the intended object. The gaze is one of two necessary conditions for concentration. As a physical technique the gaze is one of the seven body points.

From the mind-perspective, directing and holding attention is the other necessary condition for concentration training. As a psychological technique, attentional skill is classified among the specific mind points (*sems gnad bye brag;* WD, p. 65). Concentration training entails repeatedly directing the mind to the intended object and holding it upon the object for longer and longer intervals. These attentional skills are rooted within the Abhidharma Buddhist psychology literature, especially its relation to the mind and mental factors (*sems dang sems 'byung*). Attention presupposes the five ever-going and making-the-object-certain mental factors.[341] The initial application of attention is not possible without these attendant mental factors, which serve to bring the object and its attributes into focus. Certain additional virtuous mental factors are necessary as well. Tashi Namgyel lists these as effort, diligence, faith, and pliancy:

> Staying: fervent interest that is zeal for samādhi. That is the effort of staying.
> Staying: being able to do so continuously. That is great effort or diligence.
> The outcome of which is faith, which steals away your heart, after becoming interested in and [then] seeing the benefit of samādhi. That is the result of effort.
> The overall outcome is the bodily and mental pliancy that develops. That is the effect of effort over time. Understand these and [then] direct the mind to the intended object. (TN, p. 273)

Faith *(dad pa)* is the prerequisite. Small faith takes an object, such as a god or Buddha. Great faith does not need an object. It is a quality of mind that does not need to evaluate the immediate perceptual experience nor anticipate what will happen next. Concentration training requires great faith. The practitioner does not allow thoughts to elaborate regarding the supporting object of meditation, but simply attends to it. The preliminary prayer lays the foundation for this type of faith.

Effort *('bad pa)*, diligence *(brtson)*, and pliancy *(shin sbyang)* are three closely related mental factors. Actually, they are varying degrees of the same quality of mind along a continuum. Tashi Namgyel explains that effort is the initial desire, diligence its continuance, and pliancy its effect, which ripens over time. Physical and mental pliancy serve to eradicate obstacles to the development of concentration training. The numerous attempts to hold the mind effortfully on the intended object have a cumulative effect. Intervals of undistracted concentration increase in duration. Furthermore, concentration can be held in an eased-up *(lhod de)* manner for some period without distraction.

The act of not staying on the intended object is called *distraction (gyeng ba)*. Distraction is defined by the interval during which the practitioner loses track of the intended object and has forgotten about holding the mind on it. At some point the practitioner recognizes that the mind has wandered from the intended meditation object, redirects the mind to it, and holds it once again. With experience the practitioner develops some skill in recognizing distraction closer and closer to the point where the mind strays from the intended object.

Distraction is related to *mental elaboration ('phro ba). Elaboration* was an important concept introduced during the mind-isolation exercise. Here again, elaboration is important, but the context of usage is slightly different. In the prior stage of practice, *elaboration* referred only to thinking processes within the mental continuum. Here, at this stage of concentration practice, mental elaboration is contrasted to perception. Mental elaboration occurs when the practitioner begins to think about the intended object (or something else) rather than simply attend to it. Ordinary sensory experience entails a great deal of mental elaboration. Simple sensory data are combined and categorized into elaborate constructions *(bcos pa)* about experience. Sensory data are interpreted, named, and given meaning. The process by which the mind constructs elaborate conceptual schemas from simple sensations is captured by the literal meaning of the term, which is "to spread out from, to elaborate, to proliferate." When the process of mental construction occurs spontaneously, it is called *elaboration.* When the practitioner purposely acts upon sensory experience so as to mentally construct something about it, it is called *making something happen (sgrub pa).*

The types *(rnam pa)* of mental elaboration in question here pertain to the latter three of the six yogas of Tilopa described in the mind-isolation exercise. At this stage of practice, the meditator may experience some residual difficulty with thinking processes such as memories, anticipations, and reflections, but these have generally become much less bothersome during meditation. As Jampel Pawo's passage reads, "[The practitioner] doesn't resort to remembering, anticipating, reflecting, or analyzing with notions about its [immediate] color and form." Likewise, Wangchug Dorjé says,

> The essence of the way to place the mind is to place it in staying-mode so that it doesn't produce anything nor hold on to notions

about anything.... Concentrate on whatever is suitable without doing any analysis, for example, is it good, bad, large, or small. These [ideas] don't belong to [the mind] settling-into-itself. During the interval that you stop these, [the mind] stays [and the unfolding mental continuum is recognized] with extensive clarity. Don't sustain defilement. Simply determine to be mindful of everything in the moment. Keep the body [points] going, the eyes—that is, the gaze—settled at the tip of the nose. Don't do any of the types of speech. Cut off anticipation, memory, and [reflections that] distort the [immediate perceptual] attributes in the mental continuum. (WD, pp. 86–87)

Wangchug Dorjé warns the meditator not even to think about meditating. This is another kind of mental elaboration. He says:

Entirely cut off all specific thoughts, such as the designations "I am meditating" or "I am not meditating" and the designations about expectation that the mind will stay, or fear that it won't stay. (WD, p. 86)

In the ongoing effort to counter mental elaboration, the practitioner learns to fix the mind upon the mere support *(rten tsam;* JP, f. 390). This necessitates some ability to distinguish between the supporting object and the mental elaboration. The mere support is to be examined closely *(btshir 'dzin;* JP, f. 28a; TN, p. 275). The root of *btshir* is *'tshir ba,* which means "to press out or extract." The context implies the act of extracting the supporting object from all other perceptual and cognitive events. The practitioner learns to separate *(dang gyes byas ba)* the intended meditation object from mental elaboration (TN, p. 276; JP, f. 28b; WD, p.87).[342]

The practitioner learns to hold only this support for longer and longer intervals:

With respect to the sense-perceivers, take the main one, the eye-perceiver, that apprehends the intended object. The practitioner relies upon this sense-perceiver when doing the gaze in such a way that the eye organ doesn't move, and in turn the sense-perceiver and even the many [usual] movements of the mind-perceiver don't [move either]. [After a while] the other sense-perceivers will also move very little. If they haven't moved, it is because of the fewer movements of even the mind-perceiver. [Now], it is easy to find [continuous, yet] partial staying because there is only the activity of attending and directing the eye-perceiver to the stone, stick, or whatever. Other than that, there are only the mere attributes of an undistracted mind. That is, [the act of] depending on the attributes (wherein the object is not forgotten) is being mindful of the object. (TN, p. 277; JP, f. 28b)[343]

As the activity of the mind-perceiver relatively ceases, the practitioner stops thinking about the attributes of the given supporting object, that is, its color, form, and so on. There is no thinking, "This is a blue object or this is a round object." The attributes are seen as they are sensed by the eye-perceiver with little mental elaboration. The practitioner perceives the mere attributes *(mtshan ma tsam)* of the object. For longer and longer periods, the practitioner holds attention only on the immediate sense data of the intended object.

The benefit of the concentration is described from two different perspectives.[344] From the event-perspective, the practitioner has mastered how to cut off mental elaboration. As a result, the intended object is no longer taken as a substance because a substance is thought to be solid, self-existent, and durable. Such ideas are cognitive elaborations of sense data. To the extent that such thoughts have ceased, the object is now said to appear as an insubstantial object *(dngos med)*. Thinking and perceptual processes have also become segregated from each other. Wangchug Dorjé calls the exercise *the particular mind points* because perceptual and conceptual processes within the mental continuum have undergone some rearrangement. Impressions from the five main sense systems now arise in a more orderly fashion within the mental continuum, and are segregated from the activity of the sixth, mental-sense system. Viewed negatively, concentration training cuts off mental elaboration. Viewed positively, concentration training helps the remaining events in the unfolding mental continuum to shine forth in a clear and orderly manner.

Clarity (gsal ba) is the technical term for the awareness of these mental events. From the event-perspective, there is recognition *(ngo bzhung)* of specific mental contents, and that content is said to have clarity. On the coarse level *clarity* means that the attributes of any object have acuity and sharpness. On the subtle level, *clarity* means that the object appears luminous.

From the mind-perspective, the practitioner has achieved the first approximation of the staying-mind *(sems gnas),* mastery of which will come only in the subsequent stages.[345] Tashi Namgyel introduces two terms to describe this level of attainment: *gnas cha,* "partial staying," and its synonym, *gnas bzhin,* "sort-of-staying." The verbal noun *gnas,* "staying," is qualified with the particles *cha,* "part," and *bzhin,* "sort of," respectively. The translations *partial staying* and *sort-of-staying,* which can be used interchangeably, come close to Tashi Namgyel's meaning. *Partial staying* is always used as a counterpoint to distraction. When a beginner tries to concentrate, the mind is incessantly distracted by thoughts, emotions, and external sense objects. Partial staying pertains to those moments during staying-calm practice when mental elaboration has greatly diminished and the mind stays relatively continuously on its intended object.[346]

The various intervals in which the mind is able to rest continuously in a state of simple undistraction and ease, without any cognitive elaboration whatsoever, are due to finding partial staying (TN, pp. 280–81). The term *partial staying* is always used in conjunction with one of several verbs, namely *searching ('tshol ba)* and *finding (rnyed pa).*[347] *Partial staying* describes the condition of the mind that is still largely distracted but that searched for and has found moments of relatively continuous staying on the intended object. From the perspective of viewing staying over time (temporally), staying is said to be relatively continuous. Yet viewing the degree of staying at any given point in time (cross-sectionally), the mind is said to be only partially on the intended object. In other words, the mind is perhaps 20 percent on the intended object, while 80 percent is still engaged in the background noise. Nevertheless it will appear to the practitioner at this point that the mind is staying relatively continuously on the object, and it is therefore imperative that the practitioner recognize the flaw of partial or patchy staying on the object at any given moment. The goal is to change partial staying into complete or close staying. Then the mind stays continuously over time, and 100 percent on the intended meditation object at any given time.

A second term, *simple undistraction (ma yeng tsam),* is used for the ripening of staying (TN, p. 275). The term *simple undistraction* is used with the verbs *protecting* and *recollecting,* which signify accomplishment. The practitioner is told to be very vigilant of any possible distraction so that these moments of more continuous and complete staying continue and develop further.

A third set of terms is used to describe the specific qualities of the staying-mind that resists the tendency toward mental elaboration. Such a mind is said to be "at ease," "fresh," "self-contented," and "uninterrupted" (WD, p. 86).

Relatively continuous and complete staying and *cutting off mental elaboration,* though differing in perspective, go hand in hand. For the beginner there can be no degree of staying as long as habitual mental elaboration occurs in the mental continuum. Once the practitioner has achieved some stability of staying, it is no longer necessary to make the effort to cut off elaboration, for whatever events arise in the mental continuum are less likely to cause distraction, and simply come and go with clarity. The practitioner is able to sustain concentration in a more eased-up manner without having to do anything to cut off mental elaboration. Tashi Namgyel summarizes:

> There is no need to block *[sna yang mi bskyi]* nor pursue *[rjes 'brang ba]* thought. The mind that has let go [of these] controls attachment and aversion. Then, the practitioner finds simple undistraction—a state in which there is neither [the act of] letting go of nor [the act of] producing [thought]. (TN, p. 281)

Though the practitioner need not act upon the remaining thoughts in any way, it is very important that he or she use intelligence to guard against the tendency toward mental elaboration so that staying does not diminish.[348] In order that the intervals of relatively continuous and complete staying increase in duration and frequency, the practitioner repeats short sets of concentration practice many times. Tsongkhapa (2002) recommends "numerous short sessions" wherein intelligence is used to sustain good-quality meditation sessions, and stopping at the point the meditation loses good quality (vol. 3, p. 54). Jampel Pawo explains:

> Moreover, if you find [continuous yet] partial staying for a mere moment, rest a little in that state of staying wherein mental elaboration has been cut off. Then place the mind to stay once again. Because you [are engaged in] a meditation that purifies, that cuts off mental elaboration, and that separates [elaboration] from the better [state of staying], you will want to repeat the meditation. If great fatigue comes at the very beginning, it is still possible to meditate without mental elaboration before being swept away by the fatigue. (JP, f. 28a–b)

Likewise, Wangchug Dorjé emphasizes the signs of pliancy that result from continued good practice:

> Because you have clarity, peace, and joy in the many little periods that you [are able to] separate the better [state of staying] from [elaboration] in meditation, it is important to learn to place yourself in samādhi again and again, and to be indefatigable in cutting off mental elaboration again and again. (WD, p. 87)

In this tradition it is commonly advised to concentrate for short periods of time while retaining a good quality of mind,[349] and repeating the practice again for a number of short sessions.[350] Concentration for longer intervals is not advisable because repeatedly sitting with a poor quality of concentration without making the necessary corrections trains a number of bad meditation habits that, over time, have the cumulative effect of making the benefit of concentration unattainable. Jampel Pawo warns:

> By continuing too long, the body points become restless, and sometimes you lose awareness of your body…. Then you lose control over protecting the staying-mind. So, rest. Offer a prayer as before, cut off mental elaboration, and protect [the state of continuous and complete staying] as before. (JP, f. 27b)

Once some proficiency is reached, the mind is kept firm *(brtan)* without wavering *(las shigs bshigs)*. The practitioner is able to easily sit in the meditation posture with the body points well aligned, to clear the mind of mental elaboration, to concentrate on the intended object without great distraction, and to hold that mind on the intended object continuously and completely for as long as desired. The practitioner attains some degree of physical and mental pliancy *(shin sbyangs).*[351]

II. CONCENTRATION-INSIDE: GREAT VIRTUE

The goal of the next stage of concentration training, from the mind-perspective, is to develop continuous and complete staying on the intended object with sustainable energy. The goal from the event-perspective is to do so in the relative absence of mental elaboration manifest as coarse-level elaborated thoughts, appraisals of sense experience, or conflictual emotional states. From the event-perspective this stage is referred to as *concentration-inside (nang du)*, or *great virtue ('dge ba chen ba)*. Since at this stage of concentration most of the mahāmudrā texts emphasize the event-perspective, both terms refer to the event-perspective.

Once the practitioner has attained some degree of partial staying using a stone, stick, or other suitable substantial support *(dngos po'i rten)*, it is advisable to switch to an insubstantial object.[352] Jampel Pawo calls this second stage of practice *great virtue*, while Tashi Namgyel refers to it as *the benefit (yon tan)*.[353] As the names indicate, this stage presupposes the ripening of effects of previous concentration training. According to Jampel Pawo, the entire sequence of concentration training is divided into three substages: (1) familiar propensities *('dris pa'i bag chags)*, (2) the substantial reflected image of the Conqueror's body *(rgya ba'i sku brnyan dngos bo)*, and (3) the insubstantial body *('dngos med;* JP. f. 31a). *Familiar propensities* refers to meditation on a familiar, substantial support toward the goal of achieving partial staying.

In the next stage the practitioner uses a "reflected [internal] image" instead of the external image with which it corresponds. As skill develops, the practitioner is able to hold the external image as an internal representation *(dmigs pa)*. Repeated concentration on this internal image develops relatively continuous and complete staying upon the internal image.

Both the Indian tradition associated with Kamalaśīla's *Bhāvanākrama* and the mahāmudrā tradition recommend a reflected image that is a sacred object *(dag pa)*. Instead of a stone or stick the practitioner places a statue of the Buddha in front. The gaze is fixed once again upon the external image until partial staying is attained. Then the practitioner makes an internal representation, a reflected image of the external statue, and holds the mind upon it until partial staying is attained using the internal image as a support.

The next stage of concentration training is called *concentration on the insubstantial body (dngos med)*. This entails making a representation of the Tathāgata's body *(de bzhin gshegs pa'i sku gzugs 'la dmigs)*. Jampel Pawo says, "Making a representation of the Tathāgata's body is said to be the most important representation for the mastery of the staying-mind" (JP, f. 27a). This meditation alone is said to be so powerful that it is possible to complete all the objectives of concentration training by means of it alone, without using the preliminary meditations on substances or insubstantial reflected images. In Kamalaśīla's *Stages of Meditation (Bhāvanākrama)*, the entire path of staying-calm practice is covered by just the single meditation on the Tathāgata's body.[354] In contrast, many mahāmudrā texts recommend the Tathāgata meditation only for a very circumscribed stage of staying-calm practice, namely concentration-inside.

The Tathāgata meditation is classified as an insubstantial meditation object because, using it, the practitioner learns to eradicate the mistaken view of taking the intended meditation object as substantial, external, and self-existent. Concentration, which separates immediate sense data from their mental elaborations, naturally leads to viewing the object as insubstantial. The practitioner becomes free from the ordinary tendency to take objects in the external world as substantial, and sets up an insubstantial, internally represented world as the support for concentration. In this way, concentration training lays the foundation for the eventual realization of the emptiness of phenomena.

There are two prerequisites to meditation on insubstantial objects. First, these internal visualizations require fair proficiency in concentrative ability. The preliminary concentration training in front was taught for this reason. Now the practitioner must learn to hold the mind continuously on the internal representation without distraction, even though there is no corresponding external image to support it. Second, such visualizations require virtuous propensities. Jampel Pawo says that such visualizations cannot be done by "those with bad devotional propensities toward the Three Jewels" (JP, f. 29b–30a) because they lack the necessary ingredients of mind to master the visualization.

Meditators with virtuous mental factors align their mind with a perfect template during the Tathāgata meditation. Through intense concentration the practitioner's unfolding mental continuum more and more approximates that of the perfect Tathāgata image—all of the good qualities. Because the meditator's mind progressively takes the form of the Tathāgata image as visualized, the outcome is called *great virtue:*

> Since you are able to concentrate on an intended object like the Tathāgata's body, you should attain great accumulation of merit from that. Such activity is to be praised! (JP, f. 30a)

Any object visualized repeatedly for a long time becomes more and more part of the practitioner's field of mental and perceptual experience. One interesting sign of the visualization's ripening is that the Buddha is experienced by the meditator as being actually present and is felt to be deeply connected with him or her (TN, p. 278; JP, f. 31a).[355]

The way *(tshul)* to practice the Tathāgata visualization comprises several stages. The root instructions are as follows:

> Having the support: a reflected image—maybe either a statue or a painting, the color of gold, adorned with [all the virtuous] attributes and qualities, [emitting] light rays, dressed in the three robes—is represented [first] in front and [then] taken-to-mind within your mental continuum. (PK, f. 4b-5a)

This icon is first visualized in front as a substance. Then the practitioner visualizes the same image as an internal reflected image. Repeated practice using this reflected image leads to staying with respect to the image.

The basic structure of the practice is as follows: (1) choice and placement of the intended object, (2) prayer, (3) generation of interest and related mental factors, (4) repetition of the body points and general and specific mind points, (5) taking-to-mind the attributes of the intended object, (6) the benefit, (7) protecting, and (8) repeating the practice. The following passage illustrates the stages quite clearly, though Jampel Pawo doesn't label them as such:

> [1] Take support of the reflected image of the [Tathāgata's] body. This is the first of three stages. Instead of an ordinary supporting intended object such as a stone as before, take a cast-metal statue or painting of the Tathāgata. With respect, place it in front, complete in all its parts, and without any defects such as its being old, broken, or deformed.
>
> [2] Develop the reflection. Having such a thing as a reflected image of the Conqueror is something of very great merit.
>
> [3] Then generate interest [and so forth], reflecting, "I take refuge in the body of the Tathāgata."
>
> [4] Next focus one-pointedly on that [image] so that the eye and mind are not distracted elsewhere.
>
> [5] Allow no thought toward the particulars, for example, the shape of the body, the impurities of the method, or its cause.
>
> [6] And so, you have taken [that reflected image] as a mere support, with undistracted mindfulness of that body.
>
> [7] Protect the mind that very much becomes settled into itself. Recognize any thought by being mindful of it. When distracted,

continue the practice with interest and so forth, and then protect [the gains you have made].

[8] If you continue for too long, the body points become restless or
you lose awareness of the body…. Offering a prayer, protect as
before. (JP, f. 30a–30b)

Jampel Pawo continues with the instructions for the meditation on the
insubstantial body. In this case concentration develops solely using the
internally visualized image without any object in front:

[1] In front [of your mind's eye] visualize: a jeweled throne adorned
with a lotus, sun, and moon; on top of that, the teacher, the body
of Shakyamuni, whose color is like a pure golden image encompassed by a rising sun; one face; two hands, [with one hand] having the gesture of equipoise and [with the other hand] the gesture
of earth-touching; adorned with the thirty [major] and eighty
[minor] attributes; made handsome by the three robes; sitting
with his feet in the vajra posture. Think that what you have visualized in your mind is the very Buddha in person. Stay with that.
Don't at all leave what is before your eyes.

[2–3] Generate faith and interest, being mindful of all the good
qualities.

[4] Now train concentration as before [using this image]…. (JP,
f. 30b)

Concentration inwardly on the Buddha's form is qualitatively more
intense than concentration on a stone in front. The practitioner is said to
be more interested *('dun pa)* in the sacred object. The meditator is required
to bring the internal image into focus and then to take-to-mind each of the
thirty major and minor attributes of the Tathāgata and to hold all of these
within the field of concentration. This visualization is far more complex
than concentration on a stone in front and requires a certain degree of
proficiency in concentration:

Take-to-mind a Tathāgata endowed with a perfect body. Meditate upon every single one of these [major and minor] attributes
of the Tathāgata. You'll generate increased merit, too. (JP, f. 31b)

There are several benefits to this visualization. Because this meditation demands more intense concentration, the ability of the mind to stay on the intended object is greatly strengthened. In earlier meditations the main technical term used for the practice was *attention,* that is, the act of directing the mind to its intended object. Now new phrases are introduced, such as *focusing one-pointedly (rtse gcig tu blta)* and *focusing with faith (dad pas blta ba).* These phrases capture the intensification of and subsequent increase in concentration. They depict a practitioner who is making progress in concentration training, toward the end state of perfect concentration or samādhi *(mnyam bzhag).* Jampel Pawo quotes the *Samādhirājasūtra:*

> Whosoever attends to that intended object—the very beautiful Avalokiteśvara, whose body is the color of gold—that bodhisattva effects what is called "samādhi." (JP, f. 32a)

Another way of describing this benefit is in terms of simple undistraction:

> By taking-to-mind the Buddha continuously—in and out of samādhi—you are never separated from [simple] undistraction. (JP, f. 32a)

The practitioner progressively approximates the staying-mind, wherein concentration never loses sight of the intended object.

According to Jampel Pawo, another important goal of concentration-inside is called *great virtue (dge chen):*

> Practice faithfully, focused upon the Tathāgata's body. That is called the "oceanlike heavenly samādhi." The sūtras say that mindfulness of the Buddha helps you attain great merit, washes away impurities, and perfects all the good qualities. Nāgārjuna says, "By taking-to-mind the Buddha, you hold the treasure of all good qualities and the weight and power of all the tathāgatas...whosoever takes-to-mind the Buddha Shakyamuni sits before him." (JP, f. 32a)

By doing the practice continuously, the meditator experiences the Buddha as always present. The practitioner has a friend *(grogs),* a continuous ever-present model for virtue who serves as a template for the practitioner's own unfolding mental continuum. When Jampel Pawo says, "Rearrange the interconnectedness in the mental continuum" (*rten 'brel rgyud la bsgrig;* JP, f. 34a), he means that the practitioner's own mental continuum begins to realign itself more with this perfect model through concentration training. Wangchug Dorjé calls the exercise a *specific mind point (sems gnad bye brag)* because the practitioner's mental continuum takes the shape of the specific points or attributes of the particular buddha being visualized. The practitioner who masters this meditation actually becomes the buddha being visualized. At this point the practitioner's mind is said merely to take on the good qualities of the visualized Buddha (*yon tan;* JP, f. 32a), but it does not yet become that buddha.[356]

When nonvirtuous qualities continue to arise in the mental continuum, the practitioner now has enough mental pliancy *(shin sbyangs)* to eliminate them at will. Emotions and thoughts arise less frequently. When they occur, they are easily recognized as such and are therefore less likely to interfere with staying.

Two problems, however, persist. These are dullness *(bying)* and its opposite, flightiness *(rgod)*.[357] Both are considered to be types of distraction because they function to make the practitioner lose track of the intended object. The former refers to consciousness receding from the object or losing its intensity with respect to it,[358] while the latter refers to the mind being unable to settle upon the object fully, even though the object is still present. These problems become more salient as mental elaboration decreases. According to Gedün Lodrö, three conditions contribute to the development of dullness: (1) sleepiness or lethargy, (2) withdrawal of the mind inwardly during meditation for long periods of time, and (3) failure to maintain sufficient intensity to the concentration.[359]

The instructions given to remove dullness and flightiness are as follows:[360]

> Now, if the problem of dullness or sluggishness arises, [first] elevate the gaze and the mental level and then eradicate it by [intensely] concentrating upon [a very refined point, such as] the hair tuft on the crown, the third-eye spot, or the round face of the Conqueror's body. Regarding the problem of mental elaboration and flightiness, [first] lower the gaze and the mental level, and then eradicate it by concentrating on the navel, the lotus-seated feet, and so on of the Conqueror's body. When there is

neither dullness nor flightiness, attend to the completely perfect [Tathāgata's] body. (JP, f. 32a)

Using the Tathāgata's body is sufficient because it contains the entire range of good qualities to generate the benefit. Visualizations of particular buddhas and bodhisattvas have more specific effects. For example, Jampel Pawo suggests visualizing the five wisdom buddhas. Each manifests a specific configuration of wisdom and specific beneficial qualities (JP, f. 33a). In the Drigung five-part mahāmudrā approach, specific deities, or *yidams,* are used—for example, Cakrasaṃvara or Heruka—and the meditation is done as if the practitioner manifested the virtuous qualities of the deity.[361]

While Jampel Pawo discusses the benefit almost entirely in terms of great virtue, Tashi Namgyel stresses the development of the mind's ability to stay on the intended object. The practitioner is getting a sense for what samādhi is like. This stage is likened to a thirsty person who senses water but does not yet drink (TN, p. 272).

Kamalaśila is the original source describing the benefits of concentration-inside.[362] It is interesting to note that he devotes no more than a few lines to discussing the benefits of concentration because Kamalaśila emphasizes the practice of special insight *(lhag mthong; Skt., vipaśyanā)*. Special-insight practice leads to conviction about the insubstantiality of the visualized image, and ultimately of all reality (Tib., *dngos med;* Skt., *bhāvānitū-parahitā*). Any reflected image like that of a visualized buddha runs the risk of seeming to become more real with greater concentration. Kamalaśila adds special-insight instructions as a precaution so that the practitioner does not mistake the view:

> To that extent see [the Tathāgata] more distinctly as sitting in front [of you]. Mindfulness arises from investigating the coming-and-going of this reflection of the Tathāgata. Thereupon investigate its attributes as follows. This very reflection of the visualized Tathāgata does not come from anyplace nor go anyplace, but is sitting, empty of any substantiality.[363]

In the mahāmudrā tradition, switching from stones (substantial objects) to reflected images (insubstantial objects) is used for the same purpose, namely to break the habit of grasping the meditation object as substantial.

III. SKILL IN VISUALIZING THE EMANATING SEED[364]

From the event-perspective, deeper concentration leads to a fundamental change in the perception of the meditation object. Since the practitioner has suspended the cognitive elaboration associated with ordinary perception, it becomes difficult to specify what sort of object is in question, what it is called, or whether it exists at all. The practitioner has cleaved the association between perception and thinking, so to speak. A new term is introduced, namely *simple appearance (snang ba)* to convey this experience of pure perception free from cognitive elaboration.[365]

According to Rangjung Dorjé, there are two kinds of simple appearances: *aggregated ('dus byas)* and *nonaggregated ('dus ma byas;* RD, p. 6). At the current stage of concentration the practitioner experiences the intended object as an aggregated simple appearance. These perceptual events are associated with several verbs: *occur ('byung ba), reveal itself (rdol ba), arise ('char ba),* or *appear (snang ba).* Later we will learn about even simpler perceptual events, namely nonaggregated simple appearances characteristic of more advanced meditation stages. Nonaggregated appearances are also said to *arise ('char ba)* or *occur ('byung ba).* In the case of aggregated appearances, something *(gang)* with particular attributes *(mtshan ma)* is said to appear *(snang ba),* but it is not elaborated beyond simple appearance. In the case of nonaggregated appearances, an event occurs *('byung ba),* but nothing *(gang med)* with any definable attributes appears. From the event-perspective, deep concentration results in a transformation from an aggregate to a nonaggregate type of object. In deep concentration the aggregate ceases *(zad pa)* so as to become a nonaggregate. Viewed from the reverse perspective, in ordinary perception a nonaggregate is said to be constructed *(bcos pa)* into an aggregate.

Examples of aggregated simple appearances occurring during concentration include: seeds *(thig le),* subtle attributes *(mtshan ma phra mo),* and light rays *(od zer gyi yan lag;* JP, f. 36b). These are all experienced as a consequence of visualization. Because they appear during meditation, they are classified as perceptual events, and are therefore considered to be supports to concentration training.[366] Seeds *(thig le)* are the most common type of aggregated simple appearance used in concentration training. A seed is a highly condensed perceptual event. In its simplest absorbed *(bsdu ba'i thig le)* form a seed is largely undifferentiated. A seed no longer pertains to a single sense modality like a visual form, but has "condensed the six sense systems into one" (RD, p. 6). A seed is the pool of sensory information occurring prior to the occurrence of a specific perception. A seed condenses all potential phenomena of saṃsāra and nirvāṇa within it. If it were thoroughly analyzed, the practitioner would find the seed ultimately to be the essential nature *(rang bzhin)* of all phenomena, namely space. Yet, just as something seems to arise from nothing, specific appearances come forth from a seed.

A seed also occurs in an emanating form *('char ba)*. At any given moment, a seed may manifest particular *(bye brag)* attributes, but as it changes over time, its attributes are varible *(sna tshogs)*. Just as a tree's seed is the potential unity behind the roots, trunk, branches, leaves, and fruit that grow from it, so also a seed meditation contains all forms, all colors, all sounds, all fragrances, all tastes, and all sensations. All the various perceptual experiences arise from the seed. Just as both a seed and a tree can be seen at different manifest stages of the tree's development, likewise the seed can be visualized in its rudimentary or condensed form or in its ripened form, in this case as the Tathāgata's body. As the potential unity of sensory information behind all complex perceptions or visualizations, the seed is likened to the mind *(thugs)* of the Tathāgata. It contains all of the thirty-two major and eighty minor attributes of the Tathāgata in their potential and unified form.

The instructions for practicing the meditations of this stage differ from those of the initial concentration instructions. Previously the practitioner was told to suppress all cognitive elaboration and keep the mind concentrated upon the intended object. Now he is told to take arising thought and perceptual events themselves as a concentrative support. Previously the practitioner was told to focus on a seemingly fixed and unchanging object. Now he is instructed to create the image in a number of ways and to allow it to keep changing. Such a shift in perspective—away from "binding the mind tightly to the pillar of its support" (JP, f. 35b), back to the normal flow of thought and perceptual events—is called *the skill of representation* *(dmigs pa'i rtsal;* JP, f. 35b). The word *skill* by no means suggests diminished concentration. It requires even greater mastery of staying. To paraphrase Saraha, it takes some effort to tie up a wild camel, but it takes skill to untie the camel and still keep him calm. The same holds for training the meditative mind.

Skill pertains to the thoughts and simple appearances as they arise *('char ba)* or have arisen *(shar ba;* TN, p. 411).[367] Rangjung Dorjé uses the verb *skye ba*, which means "to be born" (RD, p. 6). As these verbs imply, whatever arises within the mental continuum itself becomes the support of meditation as soon as it arises. Still the practitioner focuses upon these discrete events, one-pointedly. For example, emotional states are simple aggregates and serve as supports for skill development. If a feeling of anger arises at some point in the meditation, the practitioner takes it as a support of the meditation. He concentrates upon it, watches it unfold, and keeps his attention upon it until it dissipates. Then he takes the next feeling. Or he may focus on simple appearances arising from seeds, such as light rays, colors, and shapes emerging from the seed.

Because each moment of particular thought or simple appearance can be taken as a supporting object, in skill meditations the concept of distraction no longer applies. Recall that *distraction* was defined as those moments where awareness does not stay on the intended object because of mental elaboration elsewhere. However, here whatever the mind wanders to becomes a support to deepen conentration. The term *unobstructed (ma 'gag pa)* is used in this context to mean "allowing the thought or simple appearance to unfold in its own right without obstructing it, damming it up, or suppressing it," that is, simple awareness without doing anything to it.

At the earliest stages of concentration the mind wandered into elaborate fantasies, theories, and interpretations of perceptual events. Failure to intensify concentrative effort resulted in a persistence of ordinary mental elaboration. Now the opposite is true. Failure to ease up *(glod)* guarantees the persistence of certain kinds of negative propensities that may become constructed *(bcos pa)* into more elaborate thought patterns. From the event-perspective, easing up at this stage of practice functions to leave mental events in their nonconstructed *(ma bcos pa)* state.

When unobstructed, all forms of cognition arise and pass quickly. Conceptual habits dissipate without elaboration. Likewise, simple appearances, such as seeds, emit light rays and even complicated patterns, but these specific forms recede to their undifferentiated state quickly. Even the manifest Buddha body, with all its thirty-two and eighty marks, becomes absorbed back into the seed. Again, drawing from the metaphor of the camel, a bound camel is forever restless and paces to get loose. Once cut free, he settles down quickly. When the mind is eased up and its events come forth unobstructed, the practitioner tries to recognize *(ngo bzhung)* whatever arises exactly as it arises. From this stance the practitioner discovers, rather than ordinary mental elaboration, a natural tendency for the mind to calm itself and simplify its content. Viewing events in this manner is called *skill*. From the event-perspective, the events are said to *arise in clarity (gsal ba)*.

Skill presupposes a solid foundation in the staying-mind. By letting go of any attempts to obstruct or bring about the cessation of any cognitive elaboration or the construction of complex perceptual events, the practitioner attains even greater staying, so that concentration approximates a samādhi state. It is very difficult to master samādhi while continuing to act to bring about the cessation of mental elaboration. Samādhi arises when all mental events occur without obstruction, with simple recognition. Rangjung Dorjé says:

> Now, those who say it is so necessary to cause cessation of thoughts by letting go of them do not have the staying-mind. That practice makes it difficult to generate samādhi while still persisting in [doing something to make them] cease. (RD, p. 6)

Table 10 clarifies the difference in terminology between the concentrative and skill meditations:

TABLE 10: A COMPARISON OF CONCENTRATION AND SKILLED CONCENTRATION

Practice	Concentration	Skill
Intended object	Substances/insubstantials	Cognition (thought & emotions) or simple appearances (seeds)
Event-perspective	Mental elaboration	Clarity
Activity of mind, from the mind-perspective	Directing and holding attention	Simple recognition
Application of energy	Intensifying	Easing up
Skillful means	Undistracted	Unobstructed
Benefit	Partial staying	Complete staying

The way to practice skill involves using as meditation objects either simple appearances, such as seeds, or certain arising mental content, such as emotional states. Either alone is sufficient. If the purpose of the meditation were special insight into the nature of all classes of mental events, as in the subsequent special-insight skill meditations, the practitioner would be instructed to develop skill with respect to each class of mental events. The current concentration-skill exercises are designed only to calm the mind, so either type of meditation object is sufficient for this end. Preference of object varies. Pema Karpo, Jampel Pawo, and Tashi Namgyel recommend using simple appearances, especially seeds. Rangjung Dorjé recommends using emotional states. Wangchug Dorjé suggests using both appearances and mental states in the same unit of practice. A seed meditation is a representation meditation *(dmigs pa)*, in which the practitioner generates the meditation object. The use of emotional states entails utilizing spontaneously arising mental states *(sems 'byung)*, such as emotions, as the object for the meditation.

Jampel Pawo explains how to set up the seed:

> Rely upon the Tathāgata's mind, the seed. [Visualize] in the space in front of you, the distance of a yoke, a seed, shaped like a bird's egg, about the size of a pea, naturally pure, unobstructed, the five colors, blue, and so on, and the various light rays. Direct the mind to it as previously done. (JP, f. 35a)

After setting up the seed the practitioner allows various perceptual attributes to "emanate from and be absorbed back into it" *(sgro dang bsdu 'phro dang thim;* JP. f. 362). What emanates from the seed may vary in size, shape, intensity of light, color, fragrance, and so forth, but at any given moment of its emanation the seed has a particular set of perceptual attributes. These attributes quickly disappear and other attributes appear. The seed does not change its pure nature, even though various attributes arise and pass away moment by moment. When concentration is strong, the mind is fixed without distraction on the presence of the seed in such a way as to recognize its various ever-changing attributes, unobstructedly. Because of the level of concentration, ordinary mental elaboration is unlikely to occur, and the moment-by-moment activity of the seed comes under the practitioner's precise control and careful observation. Since the ordinary mental continuum has already become rearranged through concentration training, various perceptual attributes emanate from the seed moment by moment in a more or less orderly fashion.

The instructions continue:

> Having made the mind firm in this, visualize the seed about the size of a bird's egg, then as small as a grain of mustard seed, and so forth. Concentration then becomes the skill of representation. (JP, f. 35a–b)

Previous visualizations required fixing the mind on a particularly shaped and sized image that was held for long periods without apparent change in the object. Here the meditation object does not have the appearance of stability. It changes size, shape, and color. Various perceptual attributes emanate and recede in a somewhat orderly fashion. Yet, while observing these constant changes from the event-perspective, concentration is never lost. Thus the exercise is called *the skill of representation (dmigs pa'i rtsal)*.

To continue with the instructions:

> With regard to dullness and stupor, let the light emanating from the seed reflect in its clarity all the outer and inner [aspects] of your own body. When there is flightiness, direct the mind to the seed's darkness, and it will be removed. (JP, f. 35b)

At the moment of emanation the seed spontaneously emits light, which then transforms into a specific appearance with attributes. At the moment of absorbing these appearances, the seed becomes dark. This spontaneous appearance of light and darkness can be utilized as a remedy for sluggishness and flightiness, respectively. Intensifying concentration on the emerging light and clarity as it occurs eradicates sluggishness and dullness. Easing up and simply recognizing the disappearance of the various perceptual events into darkness eradicates flightiness. In this manner the practitioner is able to make the necessary corrections in energy level without ever departing from concentration on the seed.

As skill develops, the visualization task becomes more complicated:

> Visualize yourself as the deity and then visualize the seed. It is suitable to concentrate [first] on a blue seed in your heart, and then meditate on three seeds—white, red, and blue—and then

on five seeds, one at a time as before, and then on all five at once. (JP, f. 35b)

The benefit of the seed meditation is described as follows:

> The benefit is given in the *Vajraḍāka*. "The seed stays in the center of your heart. The seed's form never wavers. It has the array of wisdom's lights. Then meditate on its diamond aspect. Meditate using the maṇḍala method for selflessness. Then meditate on a ḍākinī at the tip of your nose as a white mustard seed that completely stays. All sentient beings are contained within that mustard seed. If your meditation is like that, you will greatly affect your influence."...And King Indrabhūti says, "Having amassed all of saṃsāra and nirvāṇa into a single seed, make it [then] expand into all three thousand [realms]. Then condense it into the size of a grain of mustard. From its center [emanate] all of the subtle and coarse [attributes], the three-diamond maṇḍala and the limitless diamond realms. From what is emanated and absorbed you essentially attain [both] the diamond-like samādhi and the force of the dancing emanations."(JP, f. 35b–36a)

These passages convey both perspectives on the seed meditation. From the event-perspective, the potential appearances of all the realms emanate from the seed. This is called *the force of dancing emanations (sgyu 'phrul gar;* WD, p. 89). From the mind-perspective, the mind stays concentrated "like a diamond" *(rdo rje lta bu)*. The mind stays fully concentrated even as various forms emanate and proliferate from the seed. This is called *completely staying (rnam par gnas pa)*.

Rangjung Dorjé describes a very different way to practice, called *skill using emotional states:*

> You meditate relying upon phenomena that appear as objects to the mind, the sixth [sense system]. There are two kinds: aggregates and nonaggregates. First [are the aggregates]. These are the phenomena of saṃsāra—cognitions you generally let go of [during meditation]. [But here,] whenever the mind is distracted by such cognitions such as the five [primary] afflictive emotions—attachment, anger, ignorance, pride, and [mistaken] view—and

the subsidiary afflictive emotions, too, you should meditate to hold one-pointedly whatever aspects of that cognitive object come forth in clarity. Now, because you had [previously] concentrated one-pointedly using thinking as a remedy to obstruct other thinking, [and then concentrated using] the mind's virtues, and [then] turned to whatever arises, the state of [complete] staying is generated. Being mindful of any cognition that arises in this manner is a way to know concentration, too. The main point is that [such mindfulness] isn't harmed by dullness or flightiness and you generate [at least] partial staying in the midst of these [seeming] distractions. (RD, pp. 5–6)

It makes little difference what kind of mental content arises. All coarse events arising in the unfolding mental continuum can serve as the intended meditation object once a certain level of concentration has been attained. All types of emotionally laden cognitions have to be calmed before samādhi is attained. From the event-perspective, by simply focusing upon these one-pointedly as they arise as discrete events within the mental continuum they quickly become calm. From the mind perspective, such skillful practice deepens the mind's ability to stay more continuously and completely on whatever the intended meditation object may be.

Wangchug Dorjé recommends a combined ('dres ba) practice using both a seed visualization and mindfulness of dullness and flightiness:

If dullness and flightiness arise for the inwardly concentrated practitioner, remedy these by means of praying respectfully to any tutelary deity or lama. [Visualize the lama] in your heart, or concentrate on the entity of the lama as a mass of light. If dullness or stupor occurs, [visualize] an eight-petaled white lotus in your heart, with a white seed about the size of a pea at your navel. Consider the appearance—extending from the heart to the crown of the head—to be pure, tranquil. When in a dense shroud [of stupor], get rid of it using the sun's or fire's heat. If you haven't digested your food yet, you won't find your supporting meditation object at all. So go throw a stick into the water, feel the breeze blowing, or look at the massiveness of the mountains. If flightiness or scattering occurs, visualize a black lotus in your heart, or discern a black seed as if it had streams of

[dark] water arising from it. Using the opposite of the above remedy for stupor, you can turn back the flightiness.

Practice with respect...then get rid of ordering these practices into definite stages—at first thinking to meditate like this with the seeds and so forth, and then ending in clarity. Afterward, when the clarity comes, it will be great. If there is no clarity, simply wait for it. Don't let the mind act toward sense objects, don't think, and so on. Hold the state without reactivity, in simple undistraction, with the mind settled into itself. Practice this way for many short periods and you'll get what has been called extensive clarity. (WD, pp. 87–88)

Here a complex visualization is recommended in which dullness and flightiness are viewed as just one type of mental event emanating and then dissolving into the seed. From the event-perspective, whatever arises gets transformed into clarity. Eventually every occurring event in the unfolding mental continuum that is simply recognized without obstruction reinforces the perception of the mind's natural state of clarity and luminosity. Thus the benefit is called *extensive clarity (gsal bde ba)*.

Another consequence of skill development is that perception naturally tends more and more toward the condition of the absorbed seed *(bsdu ba'i thig le)*. At first the seed arises like the "force of dancing emanations." Sense impressions arise initially as light rays from the seed, then particular sensory patterns and attributes emerge, and finally they dissolve again. As skill develops using the seed meditation, the emphasis naturally shifts from the arising to the cessation of each perceptual moment. Sustained perception of the seed in its condensed form constitutes a type of nonaggregated *(dus ma byas)* meditation object, in which no particular patterns or attributes are discernible. Perception is "empty of simple appearance" (RD, p. 6). No particular attribute remains in awareness long enough to serve as an intended object for concentration. "Nothing can be taken-to-mind" *(yid la ma byed pa)*. Taking-to-mind is a mental factor operative in ordinary perception that fixes particular attributes in awareness. At this stage of practice, not-taking-to-mind means that all of these attributes—whatever sizes, shapes, colors, sounds, fragrances, and so forth—arise, but quickly become calm so that none become the intended object:

First concentrate by absorbing whatever the object is (for example a form) into the one [seed], and then absorb the [objects of all] six sense systems into that one. The mind that represents whatever other objects occur like this comes very close to staying. (RD, p. 6)

By placing emphasis on the point at which any arising event becomes absorbed back into the seed, all the various *(sna tshogs)* impressions from the six sense systems emanating from the seed moment by moment become condensed into a single seed. At this point the seed is said to resemble a ball of light *(od kyi gong bu)* or a vast space (WD, p. 87).

At this stage the coarse form of the three poisons (anger, attachment, and ignorance) and the any subsidiary emotional states also become absorbed into the seed. These complicated affective patterns or aggregates become reduced to a simpler, nonaggregate condition. (RD, p. 6)

Experience with the seed meditation favors the absorbed over the emanating condition of the seed. At this stage, however, this condition is not yet firmly established. From the event-perspective, the seed continues to emanate specific attributes, though in a more orderly and simple manner. During the discrete moments of emanation, it becomes easy to direct attention to the process of arising. The specific emanation is recognized and comes forth with "extensive clarity."

From the mind-perspective, it becomes easier for the mind to stay concentrated upon the seed both during moments of emanation and during moments of absorption. It is unlikely that awareness will become distracted from the seed or its specific emanations. Awareness, then, is said to be "unwavering," and "diamond-like."

Because few moments of arising remain with stable, specific attributes, the practitioner's concentration is now without support *(rten med)* and also without representations *(dmigs med)*. Jampel Pawo and Rangjung Dorjé cite a famous passage from the *Secret Torch Tantra* to illustrate:

Having relied upon representing *(dmigs)* [a meditation object],
Do your best to generate not-representing it *[mi dmigs]*.
Having become familiar with not-representing,

you are without representations *[dmigs med]*
produced as entities. (JP, f. 36b–37a)

Jampel Pawo explains,

You rely on representations for the purpose of generating being
without representations [during deep concentration]. (JP, f. 37a)

IV. Being-Done-With the Absorbed Seed

When all simple appearance is reduced to its nonaggregated form, what
does the practitioner take as the intended meditation object? Any particular attributes that might be taken as a support as they emanate from the seed
become absorbed quickly back into the seed. At the lower limit of this
absorptive tendency there is nothing but an undifferentiated, nonaggregated seed. There are no seemingly real things, such as stones or sticks, to
take as supports. This condition of the seed is likened to vast space *(nam
mkha'i lta bu)*. Space cannot be considered a support for meditation, but
space can be taken as the intended meditation object. The practitioner is
ready to practice Tilopa's space yoga *(nam mkha'i rnal 'byor)*.

Because space is very difficult to comprehend as a subtle, nonsupport-
ing meditation object, space yoga is only practiced by highly capable individuals. Alternate objects may be used as supports in order to prepare less
capable practitioners for these more subtle staying-calm practices.[368] Concentration on the breath *(rlung cad)* is commonly recommended.[369] The
breath is considered to be a support *(rten)* by some, although it doesn't have
the solidity of a substance of a stone, for example. The breath is considered
to be a support because its coming-and-going movement *('ong ba dang 'gro
ba)* can be held on to by the mind. At a later stage of concentration on the
breath, when the coming-and-going movement of the breath settles into a
prolonged total stillness between the cycles of the breath, or when the breath
is intentionally held, focusing on the breath is like doing space yoga.

Any discussion of objects during this stage is a bit misleading. Not having a tangible perceptual or cognitive object is a boon, not a problem. The
practitioner is clearing away the disorderly mental debris. He is preparing
himself to observe the very functioning of the mind at its simpler levels.
The former two supporting stages were largely preparatory. Now the practitioner can capitalize on his efforts. For the first time he is able to see the

mind clearly. In the third of the preliminaries, the mind-isolation exercise, the practitioner got a glimpse of the natural state of the mind free from ordinary thought processes and mental elaboration. Here, in the third of the concentration exercises, the practitioner gets a deeper glimpse into the mind's natural state, free from its coarse-level content, such as ordinary appearances and emotional states.

These exercises are best described as *being-done-with* (*zad pa;* JP, f. 39b; *zin byed;* WD, p. 650; TN, p. 656). The word *zad pa* (variation, *zin pa*), is the perfect tense of the verb *'dzad pa,* which means "to be done." The word means "to be done with or finished with, to end, to cease." It would be misleading to translate *zad pa* and *zin byed* as "having ceased," because subtle cognitive and perceptual events continue beyond this stage.[370] They are "done with" more in the sense that they are no longer bothersome to intense concentration. They are not obstacles *(sgrib pa).*

The practice entails being-done-with both coarse cognitions *(rtog pa)* and perceptions *(snang ba)* that still emanate from the seed. The habitual tendency of the mind is to construct rudimentary sensory information into patterns with particular attributes, which take shape in the inner mind as well as in the outer world. From the event-perspective, this meditation is a way of being-done-with this habitual tendency for mental construction. From the mind-perspective, this meditation stops the mind from roaming to an object *(sems yul la 'pyan ba;* JP, f. 39b).

Even where simple appearances remain largely in their nonaggregated state, the mind, at a subtle level, is constantly active in response to sense objects. Only by refusing to permit even the most subtle engagement of sense objects can such movement be stopped. In being-done-with sense perception, the practitioner turns away from coarse-level sensory and thought contents toward empty space. Performing complex psycho-physiological breath manipulations is another way of making the breath like space. Using either method, the purpose is to close the doors of the mind (*yid kyi kha sbyor du byas;* JP, f. 41a). From the mind-perspective, closing the perceptual doors means that when events occur, they are much less likely to distract concentration. From the event-perspective, closing the doors of the mind does not mean that perceptual events no longer occur. Subtle cognitive and perceptual events persist, while coarse-level complex and simple appearances are no longer constructed.

Space yoga affects both coarse-level cognition and perception.[371] The occurrence of ordinary cognition is interrelated with the breath. By calming the breath, coarse-level cognitions, including any residual elaborated thinking and emotions, become relatively calm. The result is an experience of a relatively nonconceptual still state *(mi rtog pa)*. Residual, fleeting thoughts no longer hinder concentration, and pass quickly.

In a specific sense, *cognition* refers only to what are classified as cognitive processes: thinking and emotions. In a general sense, *cognition* is used to cover all ordinary types of coarse-level mental content, including perceptual and sensory experiences. A nonconceptual still state, in one sense, means to be-done-with all coarse-level cognitive, emotional, sensory, and perceptual events, especially thought content. Because both the activity of the sense doors and the coarse-level cognitions constructed from this activity are done-with, this meditation is sometimes called *stopping the mind (sems med)*.

As ordinary cognitive and perceptual events are done-with, concentration continues naturally without much distraction. Concentration remains one-pointedly and effortlessly on the intended object—space, the breath, or whatever. Trying to be undistracted and unobstructing in the former two stages of concentration, respectively, are types of artifical mental activity *(byas ba)*. So long as the practitioner is engaged in any such activity, a subtle disturbance in concentration develops, which prevents the full development of one-pointed concentration. When the mind becomes calmer, the practitioner learns that there is no need to do anything for unfolding experience to remain unobstructed. Events become calm quickly, and hence become less interesting. The practitioner has learned to let the coarse contents of the mind go their own way *(rang lugs)* while becoming relatively indifferent to this content. The term *rang lugs* is composed of *rang,* which means "self or own," and *lugs,* which means "way or manner." It literally means to let something go its "own way." The term usually refers to mental processes. For example:

> The mind is set up from the perspective of its own way, so that
> it is without any support and does not obstruct any cognition
> that may be taken-to-mind. (TN, p. 289)

Here "its own way" means that the mind's natural concentrative and observational tendencies continue uninterruptedly, relatively indifferent to any coarse-level cognitive or constructed perceptual events that might occur along the way. Consider the following metaphor. Before any concentration practice, the beginner is like someone drowning in the river of a distracted mind. The somewhat skilled practitioner begins to float by means of a supporting log held with concentration. Once accustomed to floating, the practitioner lets go of the supporting log and swims about in the very currents that previously threatened to drown him or her. At that point the practitioner swims with considerable skill, finally swimming to a calm, quiet shore. The practitioner can now see the entire stream, both its currents and its directions, from the perspective of letting it go its own way while remaining unaffected by it.

During the respective stages of skill practice the activity of coarse-level thought and perceptions were at first observed as emanating and then as becoming calm *(zhi ba)*. The former centrifugal tendencies predominated during the early phase of the skill practice, and the latter centripetal tendencies became somewhat apparent by the end of the skill practice. Predominance of the absorptive tendencies is a clear sign that the practitioner is transitioning to the done-with practice. Whereas the skill exercise focused upon the process of emanation, the done-with exercises focus upon the process of calming, as illustrated in Table 11.

TABLE 11: A COMPARISON OF THE SKILLED-CONCENTRATION AND DONE-WITH MEDITATIONS IN TERMS OF ACTIVITY

	Skill	Being-Done-With
Perspective	Event-perspective *(chos)*	Mind-perspective *(chos can)*
Vector of unfolding events	Emanating *('char ba)*	Calming *(zhi ba)*
Attributes	With *(mtshan ma)*	Without *(mtshan med)*

Recognizing arising events during the skill exercise brought forth a property of the mind's natural state known as *clarity*. A new term is introduced for another property of the mind's natural state that becomes more evident during the done-with practice, namely *awareness (rig pa)*. The term *rig pa* is difficult to translate. As a verb it is classified among many verbs pertaining to knowing. Yet, unlike most of these other verbs, such as *rtog pa,* which have negative connotations, *rig pa* always has a positive connotation. Awareness pertains to the mind-perspective. It is used wherever the events of the mind are calm enough to reveal the mind's natural way of knowing, that is, knowing through nonconceptual, nonreactive awareness. At the coarse level of the mind, *awareness* is used when purification *(dag pa),* cleansing *(sbyang ba),* or calmness *(zhi ba)* are being discussed. *Clarity* is used in the opposite way, namely when events arise *('char ba)* or are born *(skye ba)* in the mind. At this level, the term *awareness* is used in conjunction with the phrase *without attributes (mtshan med),* while *clarity* is used in contexts that imply the existence of perceptual or cognitive attributes (TN, p. 363). At the coarse level of mind, *awareness* is used for how the mind acquires knowledge, but only after a calm *(zhi ba)* state of mental activity has been achieved. As one text states, "At the time of calmness, there is simply appearance and awareness" (TN, p. 411). At the subtle level of the mind, once subtle cognitions *(phra ba'i rtog pa)* also become calm, the term *awareness* is used once again to convey the quality of the mind's direct knowing, once mental stability or equanimity has been achieved. At an even more advanced level of special-insight practices, the term *awareness* is used once again to convey the mind's direct knowing of dependent origination, namely the nontemporal or *always-here (ma skye ba)* condition of the natural mind. At the very advanced level of nonmeditation practice, the term *awareness-itself* is used to convey the quality of nonartificial, direct, and pervasive knowing that reflects the fully realized mind. Awareness, as the natural condition of the mind's knowing, is only possible when not obscured by the mind's content at either the coarse, subtle, or very subtle level. At the current level of practice when formerly coarse-level cognitions and constructed appearances become relatively calm upon arising such that they lose their attributive nature, the mind's natural awareness shines forth.

As a result of being-done-with coarse-level cognitions and perceptions, concentrative ability greatly increases. Jampel Pawo defines the result from the mind-perspective. He says:

> The duration extends in which the mind stays in a nonconceptual still state, blankness, or [simple] intention [prior to the construction of content]. (JP, f. 41b)

This is called *continuous staying (gnas ba'i rgyun),* the goal of concentration practice. Table 12 summarizes the shift in terminology.

TABLE 12: A COMPARISON OF THE SKILLED-CONCENTRATION
AND DONE-WITH MEDITATIONS IN TERMS OF TERMINOLOGY

Practice	Skill	Being-Done-With
Intended object	Thought & emotion Simple appearances	Space Breath
Quality of the mind's natural state	Clarity	Awareness
Means	Unobstructed	Own way
Benefit	Staying	Continuous staying

Concentration on the breath is the most widely recommended object to begin the done-with stage of concentration. It is the only object recommended by Pema Karpo and Jampel Pawo. Tashi Namgyel and Wangchug Dorjé recommend using the breath first and then doing space yoga.[372] The breath is an easier object to hold because it is an ever-present activity independent of the practitioner's awareness of it. Furthermore, concentration on the breath is a useful starting object because it is a direct way of controlling the coarse-level activity of the mind:

> Lord Tilopa says, "If you don't want to stay in a state of stupidity, hold the breath points and throw yourself into the nectar of knowledge.... Since the mind rides upon the carriage of the breath, binding the breath is the same point as binding the mind." (JP, f. 37b; TN, p. 282)

Because the breath is a different type of object from the previously used substances—insubstantials, simple appearances, and thought—the practitioner has to become familiar with it. Each of the previous stages of the concentration practices must be repeated using the breath as an object before the breath can be used for the done-with meditation. Many commentators divide their exercises into two parts, the diamond recitation and the breath-holding exercise.[373]

A. The Diamond Recitation

Jampel Pawo teaches the diamond recitation, otherwise known as the breath-counting meditation *(dorje'i bzlas ba)* as a preliminary to the done-with meditation. It is included to help students become familiar with breathing as a meditation object (JP, f. 38a). Breath meditation is especially well suited to practitioners who tend to think too much during meditation.[374] Tashi Namgyel says that the diamond recitation repeats the gains of the concentration (in front and inside) and skill stages:

> This way trains in concentration and skill as before—wherein you attain the staying-mind. (TN, p. 285)

Although Jampel Pawo and Tashi Namgyel use the diamond recitation as a preliminary to the done-with meditation, the diamond recitation itself is said to be sufficient to stop the mind in the tantric *Pañcakrama* tradition.[375] The commentators are certainly not unaware of this. Their purpose, however, is different. They intend for the meditator to review and strengthen accomplishments before proceeding. As the practitioner is required to view the mental continuum in a radically new way beyond this point, the commentators wish to insure that the practitioner has laid the proper foundation.

According to Jampel Pawo, the diamond recitation has three stages: (1) counting *(grangs ba)*, (2) following, or pursuing *(rjes su 'gro ba),* and (3) practicing coming-and-going *('gro 'ong la slob pa)*.[376] According to the *Abhidharmakośa,* there are additional stages, but these three are sufficient to bring forth skill.[377] Counting and pursuing correspond to the in-front and inward substages of concentration. Practicing coming-and-going corresponds to the skill stage.

Counting each breath aids the practitioner's development of concentration. One number is used for each full cycle of respiration (inhale, hold, exhale). After counting to a certain number, the practitioner begins counting again. Becoming distracted during concentration causes the practitioner to lose track of the count. Being able to count without losing track is a good indicator of the degree of concentration. Jampel Pawo first describes the preliminary instructions and the instructions for setting up the breath as the intended object:

Make the body points, the seven dharmas, perfectly. Pray to your lama and the protective circle, and your connection to them will purify the three poisons. Remove the stale breath three times. Then inhale air into the nostrils so that it enters silently and gently. As the breath comes inside, it settles into itself and goes on by itself with ease. Fix your awareness on this very movement. Continue this way with the breath and mind intermingled. (JP, f. 37b–38a)

Next come the instructions for counting:

Count to 7 and begin the count at 1 again.
Count [this way] from 21 up to 21,600 [breaths].
When the mind becomes distracted through being unfamiliar with this [intended object],
The body points or breath may become faulty.
So remove the stale breath, correct the [body] points, and continue as before.
As for how to count, take the three—inhaling, holding, and exhaling—as one [unit] and count, "One, two," etc.

Finally, the primary and secondary benefits of the diamond recitation are described. As with concentration on a stone in front and then inside, the diamond recitation lays the foundation for the staying-mind:

Then you will attain the main thing you expect, namely the staying-mind. After counting any number of breaths for a whole day, you attain confidence and certainty as a secondary benefit. (JP, f. 38a)

Next Jampel Pawo gives the instructions for following the breath. Instead of focusing on the breath as it is inhaled at the tip of the nostrils, the practitioner now tries to follow the movement of each successive breath farther and farther into the body:

Examine and analyze by following the inhaled and exhaled breath. Does the breath circulate through all parts of the body, or does it move in only one direction? After a while it seems as if the breath doesn't move either through parts of the body or in any one direction,[378] and you have the experience of the attributes of the breath becoming reorganized. (JP, f. 38a)

The commentator cites a passage from the Abhidharma to show that following the breath entails the act of representating *(dmigs pa)* the intended object:

Following: represent how it goes out throughout the entire body and comes back. Does it move through the entire body or in some [area]? (JP, f. 40a)

Representation of the inner breath eventually leads to the discovery of the main and tributary energy channels and currents inside the body. The breath lasts for a different duration in each channel. Each channel has a different color, element, syllable, and seed associated with it. The respective attributes of each energy channel become distinct through repeated representation of the inner breath:

Then concentrate on the separate currents. Hold each for its respective duration, with its color and unique element [associated with it]. For example, when the earth current circulates from the right nostril, the earth current appears yellow. (JP, f. 38b)

In preparation for the practice of coming-and-going, the practitioner sharpens his or her representative and concentrative ability by visualizing a seed syllable *(yig 'bru)* corresponding to each of the three components of the breath:

Visualize a group of seed syllables: when the breath leaves the nostrils, a garland of white syllables, *Oṃ,* so that it has the vibration of *Oṃ* as the breath leaves; when the breath comes inside, a garland of blue syllables, *Hūṃ,* having the vibration of *Hūṃ;* and when the breath stops, a red syllable, *Āḥ,* having the vibration of *Āḥ.* These distinct vibrations [eventually] transform into one. [Then] reflect on its staying below the navel. (JP, f. 38a–39b)

The practitioner relies on the deepening concentrative and representative ability to mix *('dres ba)* these distinct energy vibrations into one.

In the next stage, coming-and-going, the practitioner is told to ease up concentration on the breath. As a result, the breath comes and goes of its own accord. The commentator says, "Don't bother to count your breath." (JP, f. 38b)

This is another way of describing unobstructed practice on the breath. As each breath naturally comes and goes, the breaths eventually begin to mix *(bsres ba)*. The practitioner is able to discern all five energy currents at once, even when focusing on only one of them:

> Insofar as you have meditated on the [earth] current to the point of mixing it with the others, then you get the power and capacity of [all] five currents, their attributes and elements,[379] when you get the power and capacity of the earth current. (JP, f. 39a)

The currents also begin to come forth in a new way. The flow of energy in each current emanates and then becomes absorbed. During emanation, colors, light rays, sounds, and so forth can be recognized. In this sense, successful practice of coming-and-going is very similar to the previously described skill meditation:

> Don't bother to count your breath. The breath and mind become mixed. Trying to follow the substance of the breath going from the navel to the tip of the nose and also coming from the tip of the nose to the navel, respectively, helps establish undistraction and one-pointedness [as the main benefit from the mind-perspective]. The subsidiary benefit [from the event-perspective] is that you get to see the colors of the five currents. Now, there is the yellow earth current, the white water current, the red fire current, the black air current, and the blue space current. (JP, f. 38b–39a)

The main benefit of the practice is increased staying, from the mind-perspective. From the event-perspective, sensory events from each of the sense systems are combined, as is typical of seed meditations. Here, without doing a specific meditation to create the seed, the seed comes forth spontaneously in conjunction with the rhythm of the circulating currents. Upon inhalation, the five main and tributary currents emanate *('char ba)*, each with its specific color, light, sound, seed syllable, and so forth. Upon exhalation, the distinct currents, colors, and so on become absorbed into an undifferentiated state. Just as the emanating condition of the seed predominated at the onset of the skill meditation, here, too, during the diamond recitation the coming *('ong ba)* component of the breath, along with its concomitant attributes, predominates over the going *('gro ba)* component and its attributes.

If the practitioner continues to watch the unfolding experience from the event-perspective, the experience changes over time. The breath tends to stay for longer periods within the body, and the exhalation gets shorter. Circulation of the staying-breath *(gnas ba'i rlung)* decreases in intensity and variability. The attributes associated with each distinct current emanate less frequently until the breath remains in its absorbed condition:

> Then you learn to hold the duration of the currents: the space current goes out from the nostrils no more than 16 counts; the air current, 15; the fire current, 14; the water current, 13; the earth current, 12. Each of these, then, goes out for shorter and shorter intervals and stays longer and longer inside the body. (JP, f. 39a)

With each cycle of inhalation/exhalation, the creation and dissolution of the variably patterned and ever-changing inner world is reenacted again and again. The emanating content is more and more immediately followed by absorption. Tashi Namgyel says, "The [coarse-level] mind goes to sleep" *(sems rnal du pheb;* TN, p. 285). Exhalation becomes shorter and shorter until the outer breath totally ceases, as do the corresponding attributes of the energy currents. In short, both the coarse-level mind and the breath stop. Quoting the *Vajramālātantra,* Jampel Pawo explains:

> The fruit of the latter [practice] is called "being-done-with the movement of the breath." Being-done-with occurs when neither the energy currents move to the outside nor the mind that depends on them roams to sense objects, so that a threshold is established by which the external is cut off. (JP, f. 39b)

The tantric *Pañcakrama* adds that purification of the energy currents clears away the coarse-level cognitive activity so that the mind's real nature can shine forth:

> Representation of the mind through the diamond recitation
> results in staying, but its real objective is complete purification
> [of the energy currents]. In this samādhi the mind stays, and [its
> appearances] are like a mirage. Achieving this real objective, you
> will attain the wisdom of nonduality.[380]

It is clear from the passage that the diamond recitation alone can accomplish
the goal of the being-done-with meditation if practiced thoroughly, but in
the mahāmudrā tradition Jampel Pawo and many of the others limit the diamond recitation to a type of skill meditation and thereby see it primarily as
a technique for setting up the emanating seed with its corresponding rhythm
of the breath. If used in that way, the diamond recitation is no more than a
review of the skill stage, but with regard to a new intended meditation object,
namely the breath. Having mastered the coming-and-going of the breath,
the practitioner is instructed in a second exercise specifically designed to
affect being-done-with. This meditation is called *vase breathing*.

B. VASE BREATHING

In the mahāmudrā tradition vase breathing (*bum ba can;* Skt., *kumbhāka,*
literally, "having a pot") is the most important exercise to affect being-
done-with. The name is literally descriptive of the condition of holding
the breath after having filled (*dgang ba;* TN, p. 285) the lower lungs. The
diaphragm protrudes so that the abdomen looks like a pot. With respect
to the psycho-physiological exercise, there are four steps to vase breathing.
The practitioner inhales and fills the lungs with air. Next the practitioner
visualizes filling the two side energy channels. After that the abdomen is
extended like a pot, the diaphragm is tightened and pushed down, while
the practitioner visualizes directing the air from the two side channels into
the central channel. This occurs while holding the breath as long as it is
comfortable. Finally, during the exhalation, the air is imagined shooting
up the central channel. Progressively holding the breath for longer periods amplifies the tendency for the breath to become absorbed into the
central channel following mastery of the breath's coming-and-going. Vase
breathing merely quickens the process of absorption that comes with
repeated practice of the diamond recitation, especially when some
proficiency is reached directing the energy currents into the central channel and projecting it upward and out through the crown of the head.[381]

The second part of vase breathing is meditative. The practitioner observes the mind in the stillness while the breath is being held. This latter step is called *the power of mindfulness (dran pa'i stobs)*. According to Khenchen Thrangu Rinpoche, "vase breathing does not involve forceful breathing. Its purpose is to allow the mind to rest, and so it is very relaxed and gentle."[382]

The vase-breathing exercise begins with a series of preliminary breathing exercises designed to purify and energize the system. Jampel Pawo suggests, "Take the body points and remove the stale breath three times" (JP, f. 41b).

Elsewhere he suggests a more rigorous way to do this, namely through alternate nostril breathing:

> …clean air from the right nostril, stale air from the left; clean from the left, stale from the right; inhale from both, cleared out from both. (JP, f. 42a–42b)

This cleansing breath brings energy *(shugs)* to the system. The more vigorous the practice, the more energy develops. After the cleansing breath comes the main physiological exercise. The practitioner draws the air down and holds the breath:

> Completely draw in the outside air from both nostrils. Slowly draw it down just below the navel. Draw up only a little of this air, close off, and hold it, so long as you are not uncomfortable. Then let it out softly and silently. (JP, f. 41b)

While the breath is held, the practitioner does the following meditation:

> So, for the entire duration of inhaling from the outside, holding [the breath] in, and letting it out, the mind and its activity is viewed without any distraction, from the perspective of mindfulness and intelligence, respectively. Specifically, for as long as the breath is being held inside, the duration of time increases in which the mind stays wondrously still, in a nonconceptual still state. (JP, f. 41b)

There are numerous benefits to the vase-breathing exercise. Vase breathing helps to "stop the mind," in the sense that coarse-level cognitions *(rags pa'i rtog pa)* are done-with. Wangchug Dorjé says, "You do not contact anything that resembles the previous coarse cognitive events" (WD, p. 90). Thinking processes involving elaborate content stop. Emotional states and shifts in arousal such as dullness and flightiness characteristic of the skill stage of concentration are also done-with (JP, f. 42a). Likewise, coarse-level perceptual events are done-with.

To understand what is meant here, it is important to know something about perceptual functioning. The subtle activity of the mind is constantly roaming *('pho ba)*. The term *'pho ba* means to "roam, change," or better, "constantly roam from one thing to another." Roaming is a subtle form of the mind's activity *(bya ba),* and is classified as a subtle cognition *(phra ba'i rtog pa).* Roaming occurs with respect to impressions *(reg pa)* from the different sense systems. The activity characteristic of the subtle level of the mind is its roaming about *('phyan pa)* and attachment to various sense objects *(yul).* In order for a given sense impression to arise *('char ba)* to the point of recognition, the door *(sgo)* of a given sense system must move *(rgyu ba;* JP, f. 43a). The compound *'char sgo* (JP, f. 39b)[383] literally means "door of arising";[384] *'char sgo* also has the sense of something shining forth in a new way. Used in this context, it implies that any activity that appears through the door of the sense systems shines forth in a new way, given the fact that it is viewed with pure awareness from the perspective of the non-elaborated or subtle level of mind.[385]

Once a sense door moves, the subtle-level roaming activity is translated into a coarse-level sense impression that arises as a recognizable event in the mental continuum. The sense impression is subsequently constructed *(bcos pa)* into a more elaborate appearance with an associated matrix of conceptualization about it. The incessant subtle activity of roaming and the operation of the sense doors usually occurs automatically in ordinary perception. These otherwise high-speed perceptual processes normally operate outside of awareness and voluntary control, but the meditator progressively learns to bring these operations into full awareness and voluntary control. The meditator becomes the gatekeeper *(sgo yi bu ga 'gag pa)* of the senses.

> In the *Vajraḍākinī* it says, "Filling the body [with air] purifies and cleanses it of poisons and diseases. Hold the breath and energy currents. Through vase breathing you become the gatekeeper." (JP, f. 40b–41a)[386]

Mastery over the instability of the ordinary mind comes from "closing the door of the [coarse-level] mind," "stopping the movement of its doors" (*sgo rnams kyi rgyu ba 'gags nas;* JP, f. 43a), or "closing the mouth" *(kha sbyor ba;* JP, f. 41a). "Closing the mouth" is an idiomatic expression for closing off or shutting something, in this case stopping the breath and doors of the mind at once.

Once closed, sense impressions neither arise nor become constructed into recognizable coarse-level content. Specific attributes no longer emanate during the seed meditation. Simple appearances do not come forth in the unfolding mental continuum. The coarse-level mind stops, and for those moments even the absorbed seed is done-with. All that remains in awareness is the mind's subtle-level activity, its incessant roaming. During meditation such subtle activities no longer become constructed into coarse-level perceptions, because these fleeting movements of the mind do not become assemblies *(tshogs).*[387] Such movements are often called mind-moments.

Jampel Pawo describes the entire process as one of purification *(dag pa).* There are two kinds of purification: (1) purification of obscurations to knowledge, and (2) purification of obscurations with respect to emotional states *(shes sgrib dang nyon sgrib dag pa;* JP, f. 44a). The concept of obscuration *(sgrib pa)* is introduced at this point to illustrate that the purpose of the meditation is to clear away coarse-level obstructions that block an understanding of the workings of the mind at a more subtle level.

The development of mental pliancy enables the meditator to hold concentration at the subtle level of the mind for increasingly extended periods. At the initial stages of the shift from coarse- to subtle-level mental activity, the practitioner needs to be "aware of any forms of elaboration and to [intensify the] mind's staying [at the subtle level]" (TN, p. 656). Jampel Pawo explains:

> From the perspective of mindfulness and intelliegence, don't go into [coarse-level] cognitions, [but keep awareness at the level of] the fleeting movements below. As these subtle cognitions arise, don't apprehend them incorrectly. Generate the force of mindfulness as you have done before, and out of the depth of this knowledge, the now-inactive [coarse-level] passions will easily be destroyed! (JP, f. 42a)

Clearing away the coarse-level content of the mind allows the practitioner to discern the workings of the mind at the subtle level.[388]

Jampel Pawo warns the reader not to misunderstand the concept of being-done-with. Being-done-with does not imply cessation of all coarse-level mental content during concentration meditation. Coarse-level content is done-with only in the sense that it no longer becomes an obscuration to holding awareness at the mind's subtle level. In a relative sense, coarse-level thinking and perception ceases during vase breathing. At other times during concentration meditation it may not entirely cease. The skilled practitioner is able to voluntarily shift from coarse- to subtle-level mental activity and vice versa and to hold awareness continuously at either of these levels, much like shifting gears in a car.

> During [the subtle level of] staying-calm practice, most concur that there is occurrence ['byung ba], and therefore so-called being-done-with doesn't mean that it goes to nothingness. Those practiced in the skill of unobstruction don't give up this skill [when shifting to the subtle level], and therefore [from the mind-perspective there is] continuous staying and [from the event-perspective there is realization of the subtle-level] nature [of the mind's ongoing subtle activity]. (JP, f. 43a–43b)

Moment-by-moment fleeting activity still occurs ('byung ba), and this incessant roaming activity prior to any cognitive elaboration itself can serve as the intended meditation object. Since, in ordinary consciousness, this subtle level of the mind's activity generally operates outside of awareness, the skilled practitioner who holds concentration at this level is said, from the event-perspective, to realize the mind's nature. From the mind-perspective, the being-done-with meditation greatly increases the capacity to stay on the intended object. Therefore Jampel Pawo refers to this stage of concentration as staying continuously (gnas ba'i rgyun). Tashi Namgyel warns about the danger of losing continuous staying if concentration is not accompanied by leaving the mind in its own way (rang lugs):

> At first it is necessary to do something to make the mind unceasing or to make it cease in order to find partial staying. After a while, it is as if many fleeting movements of the mind occur, and there is very little partial staying. This is because you are no

longer aware of all the elaboration as a continuous chain [of constructed coarse-level cognitions] the way you once were. Now you are aware of one thought arising, [then] a second arising. You may lose your assurance and find very little partial staying, so don't hold it incorrectly. By making a little effort to set the mind up in an eased-up manner, so that you neither block nor go after any of these thoughts, staying arises. (TN, p. 656)

With practice the meditator becomes able to find some stability while holding the mind at the subtle level. From the mind-perspective, the mind stays more completely and uninterruptedly on the object. From the event-perspective, the unfolding mental continuum is held at the subtle level, experienced as a rapid flow of fleeting movements, and each of these rapid movements can be observed as a discrete mind-moment. Each mind-moment, in turn, has a [dual] distinction *(rnam dbye)*. That is, it can be viewed either from the mind-perspective *(chos can)* of the mind that stays continuously and completely, or from the event-perspective, namely the mind's observable moment-by-moment activity or movement *(chos):*[389]

> Now, what is this distinction between staying/moving and temperament/harmony that perfects the realms of knowing the nature [of the mind's natural condition]? It is only that which conforms to the explanation of being-done-with practice. (JP, f. 44a)

C. SPACE YOGA

The more difficult way of calming coarse-level cognitions is called *space yoga*. Rangjung Dorjé cites Tilopa as the original source of space yoga, but the meditation is apparently much older because it appears in earlier mahāmudrā source material. Here is the version reported in Tilopa's *Ganges Mahāmudrā*:

> For example, if you block seeing by staring into space,
> and the mind is likewise viewed by the mind itself,
> having blocked the elaboration of thought,
> you attain the highest realization.[390]

This very brief and compact verse contains the entire instructions. There are two parts: (1) stare into space, and (2) view the mind by the mind itself. The first instruction pertains to the intended object. Space as an intended object is categorized as a nonsupport *(rten med)*. One way of eradicating the habitual tendency to construct and elaborate coarse-level cognitions is to turn away from objects and stare into space. The second instruction concerns how to observe the mind. The mind becomes aware *(rig pa)* of its own functioning at the subtle level. According to Khenchen Thrangu Rinpoche, the objective is for "the mind…to rest without resting on any object."391 The benefit of space yoga pertains to "blocking the construction *(tshogs)* of thought." The tendency of the mind to construct coarse-level cognitions is done-with through space yoga.

Tashi Namgyel, Rangjung Dorjé, and Wangchug Dorjé each include the space yoga meditation, and all follow Tilopa's model. Tashi Namgyel and Wangchug Dorjé suggest practicing space yoga following vase breathing. Wangchug Dorjé's space yoga is a typical example:

> Now, concentrate on what is without support as follows: Consider that the duration of earth, water, fire, wind, and space, respectively, become absorbed into each other and become Great Emptiness. Direct the mind to the intended object by staring blankly into the peaceful, blissful void of open space. Don't take-to-mind anything whatsoever—thinking neither that things exist nor not exist—and sustain it for as long as you are undistracted, unhurried, carefree, and let-go. When distracted, reestablish the partial staying as if putting a thread into the eye of a needle, like a waveless ocean without agitation, like the effortless flight of the garuda, without hope or fear, peaceful and cool. And when remaining undistracted, there won't be any [coarse-level] cognition. You have one genuine thought—a moment of simple undistraction. You recognize immediate occurrence. Besides that, you are not to do anything—the nonvirtues of attachment, aversion, and ignorance; the virtues of giving and the like; what is taught in the oral readings; any conceptualization similar to these; abandoning taking up; abandoning and producing; joy and misery! Establish it in undistraction. Look with the eyes of special insight. Take that [one genuine] thought as a support of concentration. Act free from the defect of fervent

intensifying and fervent easing up, and establish it, too, so that you don't lose it! (WD, pp. 88–89)

Wangchug Dorjé views space yoga as a concentration practice that has an affinity with later, advanced practices regarding meditation on the natural condition of the mind itself.[392]

Rangjung Dorjé combines the coming-and-going instructions of the diamond recitation and space yoga into a single meditation:

> You should turn both eyes to the space in front of you. Don't move your body. Establish the coming-and-going breath freshly, leisurely, silently.... (RD, p. 6)

Wangchug Dorjé's space yoga can be broken down into the same structure as Tilopa's. First, staring into space is the same as taking an object without support. Just as the distinct currents and their attributes become absorbed during the vase-breathing exercise, Wangchug Dorjé says the same for space yoga. Likewise, Tashi Namgyel says that no outer forms, sounds, and so on, not even the coming-and-going of the breath, can serve as a support for space yoga (TN, p. 656).

Second, Wangchug Dorjé gives instructions for how to view the mind. He says, "Don't take-to-mind" *(yid la mi byed pa)*. Rangjung Dorjé qualifies this by saying, "Don't take-to-mind anything, not attributes, not thoughts" (RD, p. 6). That is, the practitioner does not act in any way with reference to the mental events. He holds the mind to relaxation with a very special quality so that it is unable to act toward or engage whatever arises in the continuum. Various words are used to describe the quality of mind: *unhurried ('hol le), carefree (lhod de), eased up (glod),* and the three similes, "threading a needle," "waveless ocean," and "Garuda's flight," respectively. Without these qualities it becomes difficult to get a glimpse of how the mind works behind its content, just as it is difficult to thread a needle when hurried. These qualities are summed up in the term "in its own way" *(rang lugs)*.

Leaving the mind in its own way leads to a major shift in awareness. One-pointed concentration is able to proceed without interruption. The mind continuously stays, not getting involved with distractions. Just as a talkative person becomes silent when realizing that no one is listening, so also mental events become calm *(zhi ba)* when the mind is left in its own way. The effect is different from the previous skill meditation in that here thoughts tend to become calm, according to Wangchug Dorjé. Rangjung Dorjé says that space yoga suppresses emotional states (RD, p. 7). Though subtle cognitions may occur, they are less likely to become constructed, or as Tilopa says, "the assemblage of cognitions is obstructed."

Wangchug Dorjé says little about the perceptual changes from space yoga. On the other hand, Tashi Namgyel stresses these:

> If you are firm, being immovable, without [coarse-level] cognition, the various indications of absorbing the inner and outer breath arise instantaneously, and you are said to be liberated from the substances of saṃsāra.... The way to find the staying mind of what has and has not breath is, therefore, to be without a support that appears in the form and color of a stone or stick. Those in the lineage make the designation "without support." (TN, pp. 290–92)

Both vase breathing and space yoga bring about being-done-with both thought and perception. However, peace *(sing ne)* of the mind is not the main benefit of the exercise. Awareness of the workings of the mind is the essential benefit. According to Wangchug Dorjé, the practitioner "recognizes immediate occurrence" (*ma thag;* WD, p. 88). The practitioner becomes aware of an event exactly as it happens, at the moment that it arises. All such immediately occurring events pass almost as quickly as they come forth. Rangjung Dorjé says, "Movement, impermanent, is quickly abandoned" (RD, p. 7). What has been-done-with are the obscurations to becoming aware of the mind's spontaneity, the subtle levels with which it "acts" to make experience come forth in the continuum.

5. Concentration Without Support

.....

As a consequence of the done-with instructions the practitioner has stopped the mind, in the sense of its coarse-level content. More specifically, the doors of perception have been closed so that percepts remain at the level of the subtle roaming activity without being constructed into coarse-level content. Coarse-level cognitions, such as discrete emotional states and patterns of thought, still have a tendency to arise, but they immediately proceed to self-calm. Neither percepts nor thoughts are constructed (*bcos ma*) out of the movements and roaming activity of the subtle-level mind. Therefore no specific attributes remain to serve as the intended meditation object. As all mental content virtually remains in its unconstructed (*bcos med*) state, this stage of staying-calm practice is called *concentration without attributes (mtshan med)* from the event-perspective and *concentration without support* from the mind-perspective. From the mind-perspective, concentration without support is more about the process and quality of meditation than about the intended meditation object *per se*.[393]

Jampel Pawo begins his discussion of the problem of the status of the represented meditation object (*dmigs pa*) by quoting a play on words from the tantras:

> Having depended on insubstantials as the substance,
> Then take non-support as the substance.
> Taking no-mind as the mind,
> There is also no-reflection, not even a little bit. (JP, f. 44b–45a)

He begins his explanation of the passage by defining *non-support (rten med)* as "having nothing whatsoever to practice concentration upon" (JP, f. 45a). He then explains the final two lines of the passage as follows:

> Do not conduct your practice in a way that holds on to any-
> thing, that is, attends to an external supporting intended object,
> to the coming-and-going of the inner breath, or anything else.
> Let the mind be [instead] without any basis that supports [the
> concentration], and too, don't be obscured by thinking that you
> have to take-to-mind anything. You should set up the mind *[sems
> 'jog]* in its [natural] disposition, in its own way *[rang lugs]*. More-
> over, so that you don't think at all about the past—that is, "it was
> done or it happened before"—and so that you don't let the mind
> even elaborate on the future—that is, "it will be done, or is being
> done at a later time"—you should set up the mind [this way]:
> solitary *[rang gar]*, at ease *[lhod de]*, and vibrant or pulsating *[shig
> ge ba]*. (JP, f. 45a–b)

The above passage explains the final two lines of the passage in two parts.
First, Jampel Pawo clarifies the meaning of *no-mind (yid med)* by explaining that at this stage the meditator does not perceive perceptual objects
(snang ba) because he or she does not act *(byas ba)* to construct perception
from the activity of subtle-level cognition. The practitioner does not take-
to-mind any particular perceptual event. The use of the verb *holding ('dzin
pa)* in such a context usually refers to making a false subject-object
dichotomy. The ordinary subject-object differentiation between the practitioner's own mind and external objects is eliminated when the practitioner does not act to take-to-mind any particular sense impression.

Second, Jampel Pawo explains the meaning of *no-reflection*. Coarse-level
cognitions (in this case, thoughts about the past, present, or future) have also
been eradicated, in a relative sense. In short, little of the ordinary mental content remains, nor can it serve as an adequate support for meditation. Only
the subtle, attributeless activity of the mind remains, its incessant roaming.

At this stage of practice the intended object of concentration is none
other than (1) the mind itself, operating in its own way *(rang lugs)*, or (2)
some of the natural mind's more salient qualities, which Jampel Pawo
describes with such adjectives as *solitary (rang gar)*, *at ease (lhod de)*, and
vibrant or pulsating (shig ge ba). At this stage a major shift in the type of represented meditation object *(dmigs pa)* occurs. The reason for Jampel Pawo's
lengthy commentary concerns the intangible quality of the natural mind
as the object of concentration. How can this natural mind be used to deepen
concentration when it cannot serve as an adequate support? At this stage

of concentration the mind-as-object is neither perceived nor thought about. From the event-perspective, not even the subtle-level fleeting moments *('phral ba)* can be considered appropriate supports for concentration because they are impermanent and cannot be definitely taken-to-mind *(yid la ma byed pa)*. From the mind-perspective, the subtle mind itself becomes the object of concentration.

Tashi Namgyel also devotes considerable attention to the various problems associated with using the natural mind as an object of concentration. He writes a prefatory section entitled "Why It Is Important to Know the Point *[gnad]* of Intensifying *[sgrims]* and Easing up *[glod; lhod]*."[394] From the previous meditation the subtle processes of the natural mind shine forth in their own right. From the mind-perspective of staying *(gnas)*, the mind is pure expanse *(gu yangs)*. From the event-perspective, the moving *('gyu ba)* aspect is merely fleeting movement *('phral ba)*. Though the natural mind is all-pervasive, this very pervasiveness enhances the difficulty of using it as a concentration object. Therefore Tashi Namgyel describes the most common faults *(skyon)* for practitioners who meditate upon such an intangible object. Referring to traditional sūtric sources, he lists the typical faults as flightiness, grief, obscurity, sleepiness, doubt, too much desire, too much interest, and generating harm for oneself. For example, the practitioner may get restless when trying to concentrate upon the natural mind, or may doubt that he or she has focused upon the right object. Tashi Namgyel subsumes all of these faults under two main categories, dullness *(bying)* and flightiness *(rgod)*. He then defines each of these faults:

> In brief, with regard to the faults of the staying-calm samādhi, there are two necessary things: (1) having intense clarity *[gsal ngar]*, in which the mind [in its natural state remains] very purified; and (2) partial-staying *[gnas cha]*, in which you rest one-pointedly in a nonconceptual still state *[mi rtog]*. The fault that obstructs the former is dullness. The fault that obstructs the latter is flightiness. Therefore because dullness and flightiness cause obstruction, and because they are the worst of all problems in regard to protecting the samādhi, the means to remove them are essential: In the sūtric meditation texts it says to hold in the mind a substance that is lofty and joyous, to hold the [specific] attributes of any percept, and so forth when dull. It also says to represent and view the harmful consequences of distraction, to meditate on

impermanence, and so forth, when flighty. However, relying on intensifying *[sgrims]* and easing up *[glod]* is the most important of these [sūtra instructions]. This is how you search for the flaws of samādhi to remove any dullness and flightiness. You understand the main point *[gnad]* when you think, "There isn't any [real] problem of dullness after a little bit of intensifying, nor is there any [real] problem of flightiness after a little bit of easing up." (TN, pp. 293–94)

Drawing from traditional Abhidharma sources, Tashi Namgyel defines *dullness (bying ba)* as "slipping away from" and *flightiness (rgod pa)* as "becoming distracted from" the intended object.[395] Because the intended object is technically a non-support, it is easy to become oblivious to it, or become restless trying to pin it down. Dullness and flightiness become more of a problem as the intended object increases in subtlety.

After the done-with meditation, the two conditions of staying and moving form a pair of simultaneous perspectives that exist concomitantly in every discrete mental event, whether coarse or subtle. Whenever any event occurs, the practitioner becomes aware of *both* the observable event (mental content at the coarse level and movement at the subtle level) and the point of observation (the mind staying). Looking from the event-perspective results in clarity *(gsal ba)*. Looking from the mind-perspective deepens the degree of staying *(gnas cha)*. If the mind slips away from its awareness of subtle-level activity or movement by becoming dull, clarity is lost. If the mind becomes unsettled through flightiness, *partial*-staying is lost. The central problem at this stage of concentration is how to preserve the very fine balance between the concomitant perspectives of clarity and staying in each discrete mind-moment, over and against dullness and flightiness. The above passage also contains the central recommendation for eradicating dullness and flightiness, namely by intensifying *(sgrims)* and easing up *(glod)*, respectively. When dull, exert more effort to intensify; when flighty, relax the effort and ease up.

According to standard Abhidharma definitions, dullness and flightiness belong to a class of transformable mental factors *(gzhan 'gyur bzhi;* literally, "change into another"). *The four transformables* represent a distinct class of mental factors, in that all other mental factors are either entirely positive, such as faith *(dad pa)* and effort *(rtsol)*, or entirely negative, such as hatred *(zho stangs)* and attachment *('dod pa)*. In contrast, the four transformables are neither totally positive nor totally negative. According to the *Adhi-dharmasamuccaya*, they can be either positive or negative depending on the nature of the mental state:

> The reason for calling dullness, flightiness, general examination, and focused analysis "the four variables" is that they become positive, negative, or indeterminate according to the level and quality of the mental situation.[396]

The first pair of transformables is dullness *(bying)* and flightiness *(rgod)*. When dull, the practitioner manifests the negative aspect, and can remove it with the positive aspect of the opposite, namely intensifying. Likewise, the negative aspect flightiness can be removed with the positive aspect of the opposite, namely easing up.

The second pair of transformables is general examination *(rtog)* and focused analysis *(dpyod)*. Both of these have a coarse and subtle form. One may make a coarse general examination, as in philosophical speculation, or a subtle general examination by using a certain thought to guide meditation.[397] General examination and focused analysis can be used positively at this stage of practice. For example, dullness and flightiness cannot be transformed into their positive conditions without some ability to discriminate them as faults. How could the practitioner detect these as faults if all discriminative abilities had ceased? At this stage of practice thoughts have not actually ceased but merely become calm quickly.

It now becomes a bit clearer why the commentators are so careful to define the nonconceptual state as a state in which cognition still occurs. When Tashi Namgyel recommends that the practitioner think about *(snyams ba)* the faults of dullness and flightiness, he means for the practitioner to discern the negative condition of dullness and flightiness so that he will be able to stay in tune with the intended meditation object. The practitioner uses the positive condition of general examination *(rtog)* to discern dullness and flightiness. Cognition is thus effectively harnessed insofar as it no longer becomes elaborated very far beyond the practitioner's control. The skilled practitioner can use rudimentary cognition in a limited way as a means of detecting faults and can thus remove any remaining obstructions to attaining a perfect samādhi. In the present stage the practitioner uses a fairly unelaborated cognition, namely a subtle cognition *(phra ba'i rtog pa)*, as the skillful means for detecting faults. Jampel Pawo likens the act of eradicating the entire array of negative thought with a single positive thought to the act of removing water from the ears by adding more water to them (JP, f. 46a).

It is possible to group all previous content of experience—the coarse-level cognitions *(rags pa'i rtog pa)* such as thoughts, negative emotional states, and perceptions—under the general category of *mental content.* Transformable objects (intensifying and easing up) and subtle cognitions— are best categorized as *mental processes.* These latter events are more dynamic and subject to constant change. Such changes in the status of the meditation object are expressed with new verbs: *to change ('gyur ba), to occur ('byung ba),* and *to happen ('dug pa).*

The practitioner has carried awareness beyond coarse-level mental content to take the very subtle workings of the mind itself as the object. The method of meditation and the object of meditation are one and the same. The practitioner now observes the subtle changes *('gyur ba)* of the mind on each occasion that he slips into dullness or flightiness. He likewise observes the very activity *(bya ba)* that intends to intensify or ease up and also the events *('byung; 'char),* and also any subtle cognitions that become elaborated as a fault of meditation. In taking dullness, flightiness, or subtle cognition as the intended object, one is watching the mind unfold in its own way. Tashi Namgyel's method, which is essentially the same as Jampel Pawo's, is summarized in Table 13:

TABLE 13: TASHI NAMGYEL'S INSTRUCTIONS FOR CONCENTRATION WITHOUT SUPPORT

	Natural Mind Qualities	Fault	Sūtra Way to Remove	Mahāmudrā Way to Remove
Event-perspective	Clarity	Dullness	Meditate	Intensifying upon joy
Mind-perspective	Staying	Flightiness	View a flaw of distraction, meditate on impermanence	Easing up result

I. INTENSIFYING

Tashi Namgyel calls the first meditation on mental processes *the representation of intensifying (sgrim ba'i dmigs pa).* Pema Karpo and Jampel Pawo call it *completely cutting off arising as it happens (thol skyes rab gcod)*. Intensifying normally precedes easing up. According to Jampel Pawo, the intensifying exercise comes first because of the problem of "slipping away from" the less tangible subtle cognitions that have now become the intended meditation object. Jampel Pawo adds that the easing up exercise can only be done once a continual stream of subtle cognition "remains clear" and there isn't any coarse-level dullness.

There are different gradations of dullness. Tashi Namgyel explains:

> Dullness: If you have connected to some degree of staying, wherein the mind is in a nonconceptual still state, and have protected this, then the power of mindfulness is the way to hold that degree of staying. However, this may fade, and after that the intended object may drift *[shor ba]* or become unclear. The mind may also become tired. This condition is great or coarse-level dullness. Sometimes, while in a nonconceptual still state, even though the intended object may not drift, you stay on it only faintly and dreamily. That is, you are without any degree of clarity, yet by definition you are still holding the intended object. Such faint even momentary dullness is the worst because it is subtle dullness. With regard to this latter, subtle dullness, inexperienced practitioners might [mistakenly] think their staying-calm [practice] is flawless. If they try to protect their gains but haven't yet eradicated subtle dullness, even though they may have protected these for a long time, the mind's intense clarity never shines forth, mindfulness becomes dull, you become forgetful, and so forth. Your practice becomes greatly flawed. (TN, pp. 294–95)

Tashi Namgyel introduces a definition of subtle dullness *(bying ba phra mo)* to show that the meditation may become lax without the practitioner knowing it. Geshe Gedün Lodrö defines *subtle dullness* as a state in which there is some degree of brightness to the mind but not intensity.[398] Tsongkhapa adds that *clarity* refers both to the perceived clarity of the object from the event-perspective and to the clarity of the mind's way of apprehending the intended object from the mind-perspective. *Subtle dullness* and *laxity*, conversely, refer to the lack of clarity of both the perceived object and the mind's way of apprehending it.[399] According to an oral explanation, subtle dullness results from a sense of internal relaxation that comes when meditation gets easier.[400] From the perspective of ordinary experience, these subtle mental processes have never been anything but dull. Less advanced practitioners have generally been asleep to the workings of their own mind. The intensifying instructions help awaken the practitioner.

Both Jampel Pawo and Tashi Namgyel agree that the practitioner is able to advance because of proficiency in having some degree of staying. At this level of practice the subtle workings of the mind rarely slip completely from awareness, although they may remain dull even while staying on them. It is like focusing a flashlight very carefully, yet with low batteries so that while the focus remains steady, the object is nevertheless dim. Yet awareness generally stays on the subtle movements of the mind, moment-by-moment. The practitioner is reminded to "hold the staying-mind every single moment" (PK, f. 11a; JP, f. 47a).

The intensifying instructions have two essential components. From the mind-perspective, the technical term *sgrim pa* has several meanings: "to stuff, to pack, or to cram," for example, to stuff a suitcase. It can also mean "to tense the body or hold it tightly." In this context intensifying refers to a mental attitude, namely holding the mind tightly, or specifically, supplying more energy to concentration, much like stepping on the accelerator while driving a car. A skilled practitioner intensifies to make the mind stay more closely on the intended object.

From the event-perspective, the other dimension of the practice is called *recognition (ngo 'dzin pa)*. Jampel Pawo describes the goal of the meditation from the event-perspective:

> Under these conditions the always-here stream of subtle cognition becomes manifest. So it is called *the state of recognizing subtle cognition in the knowledge of the arising and passing away of perceived events.* (JP, f. 47a)

The verb *to recognize* was also used in the previous skill meditation, during which the practitioner was instructed to recognize distracting coarse-level mental content as it occurred. The resultant knowledge was described with the term *clarity (gsal ba)*. In the present meditation the same verb, *to recognize,* is used, but in this case it refers to the activity of subtle-level cognition. Subtle cognitions or mind-moments are to be recognized "as they arise." The resultant knowledge at this stage is described by somewhat different technical terms. Jampel Pawo uses the term *brightness (dwangs cha)*, and Tashi Namgyel uses the term *intense clarity (gsal ngar)*, instead of the simpler term *clarity (gsal)*. Both terms refer to the mind-perspective, in that they refer to the vividness and sharpness by which the mind becomes aware of an object, rather than to the clarity of the perceptual attributes of the object itself.[401] The mind is bright and clear prior to any activity that occurs. Gen Lamrimpa uses the term *strength of clarity*. He explains:

> This does not refer to the clarity or lucidity of the object. It refers to the mode in which the mind apprehends the object. The distinction between the clarity of the object and the clarity of the mind is an extremely important one. If the mind is very vividly apprehending its object, strength of clarity is present.[402]

At this stage more than just the mind's coarse-level mental content becomes clear. From a certain perspective, the luminosity of the natural mind has always been there, although this realization has become obscured by the habitual negative tendencies of the ordinary mind. Since this natural luminosity is always present, Tashi Namgyel calls this realization *intense clarity* (literally "fore-clarity," in that the practitioner discovers what has always been there).

At this stage of meditation, the practitioner generally suffers from subtle dullness—that is, the way the mind focuses on the intended object lacks intensity or brightness.[403] Intensifying is a method for making the subtle mental processes more clear. By continued practice of intensifying, the practitioner is able to recognize subtle cognition closer and closer to its actual moment of arising, and before any elaboration. The final attainment is a new form of intense clarity far beyond any previous clarity. Furthermore, because intensifying also enhances the capacity of the mind to stay on the intended object, staying becomes more complete and continuous. The practitioner approximates a fine balance between intense clarity and staying in each mental event. Awareness stays continually and uninterruptedly while the mind's subtle activities are bright and luminous. Because of the great progress, it is called *the first staying-place*, the first genuine approximation of samādhi. Technically, from this point onward the term *staying* is used instead of *partial-staying* to describe progress from the mind-perspective.

Tashi Namgyel's comments on the intensifying instructions are very brief. His instructions are both similar to and different from traditional sūtric instructions on dullness and flightiness. They also differ somewhat from those of Jampel Pawo, specifically with respect to the recognition instruction. Tashi Namgyel begins his comments with a review of sūtric methods for removing obstructions to samādhi:

> Therefore the way to remove flaws is as follows: Set up the body points as before—turn the gaze upward, the eyes straight forward, and so on. Then concentrate the mind as before. [The practitioner] is said [in the sūtras] to be able to remove dullness and turn back from faint-heartedness and heaviness by taking peaceful expanse from the mind-perspective. In the *Pāramitā* literature [it says], "Lofty joy when faint-hearted..." In *The Great Compassion of the Middle Way [U ma snying po]* it says, "If meditating upon an intended object that is in some degree faint-hearted, make it expansive." (TN, p. 296)

Then he gives his own intensifying instruction for the more subtle form of dullness:

> If you haven't removed coarse and subtle dullness by that [sūtric method],[404] then generate a firm mind, intensifying in order to be undistracted every single moment. Fix the mind one-pointedly, serenely, and sharply so that it is without any inclination toward aversion or attachment. (TN, p. 296)

Most practitioners find it unnatural to hold the mind so closely on the intended object at first, so it will predictably wander. When this happens, Tashi Namgyel adds,

> In not a long time it will waver. So intensify earnestly again. Practice to fix [the mind] nakedly, so that it is undistracted every single moment. (TN, p. 296)[405]

Once the practitioner gets skilled in keeping the mind free from distraction moment by moment, Tashi Namgyel gives the next part of the mahāmudrā instruction, namely not only to recognize subtle dullness at the moment it occurs but to recognize it from the perspective of the natural mind, not the ordinary mind:

When practicing, if the staying mind has become exhausted, faint, sleepy, weak, or spoiled, you must recognize [this condition] serenely, vigilantly, transparently. (TN, p. 296)

The adjectives *transparently* and *serenely* are used to describe how subtle dullness appears to the natural mind when viewed from the perspective of the mind that stays closely and vigilantly.

Tashi Namgyel summarizes the result of this practice as follows:

In short, from the perspective of a nonconceptual still state, you must hold the mind sharp, wherein the mind is both (1) sharp and vigilant when the flaw of [subtle] dullness or flightiness occurs, and (2) can also recognize it as it occurs.... In the *Differentiating the Middle and the Extremes [Dbus mtha]* it says, "Understand dullness and flightiness." In the *Second Bhāvanā-krama* it says, "See the mind as dull and anticipate dullness; see the mind as flighty and anticipate it to be flighty." By using these methods, you may still find short intervals of some dullness and flightiness. However, if you have (1) a mind that has generated intense clarity and also (2) stay in a nonconceptual still state, and (3) do not view it as a problem, then you should repeat this practice over many short sessions until flawless staying/calm arises. If after such practice you lose some degree of staying, then do your protecting practice, [that is, learn from your mistake;] for example, especially know when to ease up, [so that you don't lose staying by being too intense, but in a way] that the intense clarity simply doesn't go astray. (TN, pp. 296–97)

When dullness and flightiness are recognized immediately as they arise, they dissipate quickly so that the mind's natural clarity is never lost. Tashi Namgyel says, "The mind anticipating dullness has intense clarity." Tashi Namgyel warns, however, that intensifying can be overdone and can result in its negative counterpart, flightiness. To prevent this, the skilled practitioner knows when to ease up so as to find just the right balance.

Jampel Pawo's instructions about intensifying take subtle cognition, not dullness, as the point of reference. Jampel Pawo instructs the practitioner to recognize subtle cognition immediately as it arises to prevent its elaboration:

> Although there is still [activity in the mind] to let go, because you think to yourself, "Now I am not going to produce any [subtle] cognition," this practice is called by some people *mindfully holding [gzung dran]*. In this text, such a meditation turns back all the former [thoughts]. Therefore you think, "From its very onset, I am not going to let any thought elaborate," and when it elaborates, you remain mindful of it. Holding it in this manner, you cut off the elaboration. So, we define it as *entirely cutting off arising [as] immediately as it is born*. (JP, f. 46a)

The above passage illustrates how subtle cognition in its positive condition can be taken as a remedy for all other distracting thought. At this stage the practitioner can still think, but skillfully uses only a single, unelaborated thought, namely to permit no elaboration of thought whatsoever beyond its immediate occurrence. Granted that even such a single-minded thought constitutes a subtle form of grasping, nevertheless it is very useful to turn back the strong habitual tendency for elaborate thought construction. Jampel Pawo calls this method *the path that abandons [all thought by taking] thought as the remedy, as if wiping away dirt with [more] dirt* (JP, f. 45a–46a). In other texts, the technique is likened to using poison to counteract poison. The Abhidharma sources explain that such a meditation is effective because cognition *(rtog pa)* is a transformable mental factor that can be used positively as well as negatively.

Jampel Pawo explains the results of the cutting-off practice from the event-perspective:

> You proceed as before with an intense resolve not to produce even a single moment of [elaborated] thought, and then the mind's brightness shines forth each time the various thoughts and the perception of external objects, and so on, arise moment by moment. You meditate to cut off the elaboration of whatever thought happens to arise more and more immediately. By extending the duration of these [sessions] in which you cut off the thought more and more immediately, you eventually generate immediate [subtle] cognitions moment by moment, and these "events" *['byung]* [or mind-moments] can be taken as an [ongoing] stream that need not be cut off [because it doesn't become elaborated]. (JP, f. 46b)

In the first attempts at cutting off, the practitioner is only able to recognize cognition after it has become elaborated to some extent. Once intelligence is sharpened, elaboration can be cut off more immediately. Holding mindfulness closer and closer to the very moment thought arises alters the way subtle cognition appears, in that the frequency of mind-moments seems to greatly accelerate. To use a metaphor cited in the commentary, "[subtle] cognition breaks out in an uninterrupted succession like a ball rolling down a steep incline" (JP, f. 47b) or like a waterfall going over a cliff.[406] Subtle cognition comes "faster and faster" (*'phral 'phral*), yet each as a distinct mind-moment, until it is as if there were a continuous stream *(rgyun)* of subtle mind-moments—a hundred thousand mind-moments in the blink of an eye, as described in the sūtras.

Jampel Pawo likens the single, positive thought that is the intent to cut off to the master of a household, and the stream of subtle cognitions to the possessions of the household. Dullness is likened to a thief. As a thief steals away all the possessions when the house is empty, so also dullness steals away all the subtle cognition that could serve as the intended object. But if the master, a single-minded positive thought, "stays inside" and catches the thief of dullness, he is assured of keeping his possessions. He is assured that the ongoing fluctuations *(mang nyung)* of subtle cognition will shine forth brightly, completely free of any subtle dullness. The natural luminosity of the subtle level of mind, its inherent brightness *(dwangs cha)*, shines forth in place of subtle dullness.

Jampel Pawo explains that from the event-perspective the main intent of intensifying is to bring out certain properties of the natural mind, specifically to manifest the clarity of subtle cognition in the form of a rapidly unfolding stream of fleeting, luminous mind-moments. He likens the practice to damming up a stream:

> The necessity [of cutting off] is for the purpose of easy recognition of [subtle] cognition. For example, it is like damming up a pond because you wish the fields to be watered. (JP, f. 47b)

The effect of obstructing *(dgag pa)* the elaboration of subtle cognition brings forth the acceleration of unelaborated, fleeting mind-moments. At an earlier stage of meditation, intense concentration, a type of obstructing, was used to prevent coarse-level cognition from elaboration. Subsequently skill, a type of nonobstructing, resulted in the initial realization of clarity.

In the present exercise, the situation is reversed. A new form of subtle clarity, *brightness,* comes forth by obstructing the elaboration of subtle cognition through intensifying and/or vigilantly cutting off. This current meditation will be followed by easing up, a type of nonobstructing, wherein all tendencies toward elaboration of subtle cognition will cease. Table 14 summarizes the differences between these practices:

TABLE 14: THE OPPOSITE EFFECTS OF OBSTRUCTING-TYPE
PRACTICE IN CONCENTRATION WITH AND WITHOUT SUPPORT

	Stage of Practice	Obstructing	Clarity
Coarse cognition	Concentration	+	-
	Skill	-	+ Clarity
Subtle cognition	Intensifying	+	+ Brightness
	Easing up	-	-

The processes of the mind left in its own way, with brightness and staying, shine forth in every fluctuation of subtle cognition, moment by moment.

How does the process shine forth? Jampel Pawo cites Pema Karpo's root text to illustrate:

> Because the mind stays moment by moment, you come to know the [immediate] arising and passing away of [subtle] cognition. Based on this, it seems as if [subtle] cognitions have become much more numerous. It doesn't really occur [this way], because [subtle] cognitions are always there in a continual stream-of-arising of discrete moments *[rgyun chags],* and there is no [real] change to them. What arises in the former moment goes; that coming in the latter does the same, and on and on, and is hence the [true] Dharma. (JP, f. 47a)

Jampel Pawo comments on the result of the exercise in three parts. First he comments on the continual stream-of-arising of discrete moments *(rgyun chags),* or the not-cut-off-flow *(rgyun mi chad),* from the event-perspective. *The not-cut-off flow* is a technical term for a special quality of the subtle level of mind that has been restored through the exercise, namely the immediate, momentary stream of subtle cognition prior to its elaboration into coarse-level cognition. Pema Karpo's root text states, "[Now] the practitioner really sees the enemy" (the incessant activity of subtle cognition), yet learns to have the mind stay in the face of that. If the staying-mind is able to remain stable in the midst of the not-cut-off flow of subtle cognition, then staying likewise gains a new level of strength. To stress this advance, Pema Karpo says it is the first time the mind is really staying. He therefore calls it *the first staying-place.*

Jampel Pawo also describes the benefit from the mind-perspective. He uses the verb *rig pa,* "to become aware," to describe the resultant knowledge:

> Furthermore, since this is the first time there is the staying-mind, then all [coarse-level] perceptions, thoughts, and events are inactive, except for discrete moments of [subtle] cognition in awareness. The brightness [of awareness from the mind-perspective] and the impurities [from the event-perspective] are not separate. So it is important to protect your realization [of the stream of subtle mind-moments shining forth in awareness] because knowing this is the remedy [for any flaws in concentration]. (JP, f. 470)

Engaging in artificial activity to make the meditation happen guarantees only partial-staying. Once such artifical activity is made calm, complete and continuous staying comes forth. From the mind-perspective, awareness *(rig pa)* is a fundamental property of the natural mind, and awareness is not associated with any type of artificial activity. Refining the degree of staying becomes an opportunity to grasp the nature of the mind that stays, that is, to learn something about the natural mind's awareness. Along with this realization comes the opportunity to realize the fundamental nonduality of the mind's events and the awareness that reflects them. This is what Jampel Pawo means by his comment "The brightness and the impurities are not separate."

II. Easing Up

The second meditation on mental processes is simply called *the representation of easing up (glob ba'i dmigs pa)* by Tashi Namgyel, and *not reacting to what has arisen (gang shar bzom med)* by Pema Karpo and Jampel Pawo. Easing up follows intensifying. The staying that has been attained amid the stream of mind-moments is precariously balanced. Both commentators say that it is difficult to maintain. Wangchug Dorjé says it is "like walking across a single-poled bridge" (WD, p. 90). The practitioner is in danger of over-doing intensifying and losing the staying-mind altogether by becoming flighty *(rgod pa)*.

Jampel Pawo does not devote much time to defining flightiness. It is to be understood from the previous meditation that the not-cut-off stream of subtle cognition contains a kind of subtle flightiness. It is easy for the mind to become unsettled with respect to seeming fluctuations of subtle cogni-tion. Tashi Namgyel, on the other hand, carefully defines flightiness. He defines it in general terms as a kind of distraction, and in specific terms as a kind of attachment. By the latter he means to imply that the practitioner has made a mistake in the previous meditations by being attached to one aspect of meditative experience over another—whether dull or clear, with or without subtle cognition. These preferences are a form of subtle flight-iness. Tashi Namgyel implies that the practitioner has *always* seen the intended object in a flighty manner. His definition follows:

> Coarse flightiness is when coarse-level cognition arises and thereby distracts the practitioner from concentrating upon the intended object. Subtle flightiness is when subtle cognition occurs. It is a condition in which the practitioner either tries to prevent something from happening or to make something happen.[407]

The practitioner engages in a lot of subtle meditation strategies, all of which constitute subtle flightiness. For example, he or she may wish to let go of all subtle cognition or to produce a single-minded positive subtle thought, or may wish to intensify at this point. Tashi Namgyel's comments again indicate that the meditation is unsettled even when the practitioner doesn't perceive any flightiness and thinks that he is proceeding without fault. This, then, is all the more reason to practice easing up. Gen Lamrimpa explains that coarse flightiness makes the mind lose the intended object completely, whereas with subtle flightiness "the mind can be wandering around and at the same time still be focused on the object."[408]

Because the extent and activity of the continuum of subtle cognition has become clear, the practitioner is now able to see all the subtle activity of the mind with respect to the meditation. The practitioner has attained enough proficiency in holding the mind at the subtle level that all the activity of mind-moments remains perfectly clear. So now Jampel Pawo gives easing-up instructions to cut off all the subtle activity involved in doing something to make the meditation happen. He begins his instructions with a reminder that easing up takes place only because the stream of mind-moments has arisen *(gang shar):*

> Because one subtle cognition after another has been produced, then you should think to ease up so that you cut off the elaboration. (JP, f. 48a)

The easing-up instructions contain two essential components. First is the technical term *glod* and its synonym, *lhod. Glod* means "to ease off pressure, or slacken," as, for example, to unstring a bow. It also means "to relax." In the present context the term *glod* has two referents. It refers to a type of directed activity, namely letting up on intensifying, much like letting up on the accelerator while driving a car. It also refers to an attitude of mind, namely being easy. From the mind-perspective, the practitioner still suffers from a subtle type of unsettledness, namely subtle flightiness. The act of doing something *(byas ba)* to bring about the intended meditation effect creates this subtle flightiness. Such artificial activity involves the mind's averting from or attaching to any state, the mind's expecting or worrying about a certain outcome, or the mind's trying to produce or prevent any given state. The practitioner learns to ease up and let go specifically of all such distinctions. Since no activity of mind is necessary to produce the effect, Tashi Namgyel refers to easing up as an unobstructing *(ma 'gags pa)* type of practice. The result is a great increase in the degree of staying, referred to in the texts as "simply not going astray," "staying one-pointedly," or "becoming immovable."

The second technical term is *making calm (zhi bar bya ba).* From the event-perspective, the more the practitioner is able to ease up the mind, the more the events of the unfolding mental continuum are made calm. *Making calm* specifically refers to the tendency toward cognitive elaboration. The practitioner learns to make calm any potential elaboration of subtle cognition before it can become a distraction, simply by the very quality of mind generated. Moreover, the skilled practitioner predominantly sees potential events as immediately becoming calm upon arising as opposed to seeing their habitual momentum to become elaborated. As long as the attitude of the easing up is maintained, no occurring mental content becomes elaborated. *Making calm* also signifies a fundamental rearrangement of the mental continuum in that events occur in a regular orderly manner without any scattering or elaboration.

The way to practice easing up as specified by both Tashi Namgyel and Jampel Pawo will now be further explained.

A. THE REPRESENTATION OF LETTING GO

Tashi Namgyel contrasts his instructions with those found in the sūtras. He explains that the sūtra method is only able to make calm the coarse form of flightiness, known as distraction. The sūtra approach uses intelligence to detect coarse flightiness as a fault when it occurs. According to Tashi Namgyel, these methods generally do not eradicate subtle flightiness, wherein the practitioner acts artificially to make the meditation happen and makes subtle discriminations between desirable and undesirable states while concentrating. All of these activities and distinctions, according to Tashi Namgyel, are based on attachment *(zhen pa)*. His method of easing up is designed to make calm all forms of artificial actions and subtle discriminations. The instructions are summarized by the compound "not make happen nor prevent" *(dgag sgrub med):*

> Although easing up is not called that in the sūtras, it is mentioned there for the purpose of correcting the problem of flightiness. In those texts [sūtric] flightiness is eradicated by representing it as the intended object and keeping it close to heart. Flightiness is said to be a kind of attachment. Herein it is removed by making calm any kinds of elaboration that are not calm—grief, doubt, and harm—and that are included under the category of flightiness. This is called the "way of making calm the problem of [coarse-level] distraction, in general, and the problem of [subtle] distraction, in particular. This [approach] uses mindfulness." In the *Stream Sūtra* it says, "By realizing the harm of distraction, you make calm that unpleasantness; similarly, you make calm the attached mind, the worried mind, and so forth." In the *Essence of the Middle [Way]* it says, "When caught up in some kind of distraction, represent it as a fault again and again." Our approach uses easing up. You make calm [any

tendency of mind to] make something happen or prevent something from happening, and you remain in a nonconceptual still state toward the intended object. (TN, pp. 297–98)

Next Tashi Namgyel gives his own method in greater detail:

> While the mind's awareness is expansive and pure, ease up. Be without attachment and aversion [to any state of meditation]. Do not think that you are or are not meditating, or that you are happy when the mind stays and unhappy when elaboration occurs. Hereafter let there be no artificial construction, such as producing or preventing, based on such thoughts. Instead set up the state eased up and slow, so that the mind is settled into itself. Then resolve yourself that there will be no distraction besides that [one positive thought]. From this perspective, protect [the gains] and you will generate great calm. If you try to pursue and master any event, coarse thoughts sometimes arise. Don't hurry after them with the mind or you'll get distracted. Don't try to block the [sense] doors-of-arising or anything like that. Just pray to continue mindfulness and you will wisely know a [continuous] life-stream [of mind-moments] without any distraction. Be mindful also when those fleeting subtle cognitions arise. Don't become upset and try to produce or supress them. Just be mindful with the intention to ease up. You simply won't go astray, and [the duration of] this state will be extended. (TN, p. 298)

Next come the easing-up instructions. These are designed to eliminate all subtle discriminations within the state—for example, evaluations of good and bad events, discrimination of the quality of awareness within meditation, or emotional reactions to the process. As the mind eases up, it naturally settles into itself *(rang babs)*. Next Tashi Namgyel gives the instructions for making calm *(zhi ba)*. Both coarse and subtle cognitions become calm. The attainment is described in terms of greater and greater staying. That is, with less and less subtle distraction there is less chance to go astray *('chor ba)*. Independent of the activity of subtle cognition, the mind becomes totally undistracted.

Next Tashi Namgyel contrasts the easing-up instructions to the previous intensifying instructions in order to show that the resultant degree of staying is much greater:

> Protect [the practice] as before. The mind stays, pure and eased up. It stays with very little wavering. When you previously intensified, you acted so as to obstruct all the coarse and subtle cognition. Then, for the mind to be completely pure, it seemed necessary to be in a nonconceptual still state and to make an effort to be one-pointed, but because of that the mind wasn't at all peaceful. Now, confident that you simply won't go astray, it is only necessary to set up the mind in bliss, wherein it settles into itself. When eased up, there is [continuous] undistracted mindfulness. (TN, p. 300)

Finally Tashi Namgyel summarizes:

> [a] When coarse and subtle cognitions arise, you [previously] tried to be done-with them or became mindful of them. [b] By easing up you make calm the various former [coarse] and latter [subtle cognitions] so that you don't go astray in the face of these cognitions. After that everything becomes slow.[409] [c] [Now] because you no longer fear attachment and aversion or any other [(artificial activity)] that isn't associated with mindfulness, the mind is as before, but becomes like a vast expanse. [d] The eased-up mind is flawlessly aware, staying purely and serenely, and the benefit of easing up comes forth. (TN, p. 300)

The letters refer to: (a) cognition described from the perspective of the natural mind's intense clarity; (b) easing up and making calm, the actual practice; (c) an explanation of making calm, specifically with reference to calming artificial activity, that is, doing things to make the meditation happen; and (d) the benefit. The resultant state is described in greater detail:

> Know the way to protect [the gains] and how to eradicate any flaws. By protecting in this way, [each mind-moment] comes forth [from two perspectives] concomitantly and close together, [both] from the perspective of the [the mind] staying stabilized with mindful awareness and [from the event-perspective] of the

clarity, pureness. In that state wherein staying/calm is generated, various unceasing perceptions—forms, sounds, and so on—may arise in a discrete yet slow manner. (TN, p. 302)

The benefit is the achievement of a fundamental rearrangement of the stream of events in the mental continuum. Each arising subtle event is discrete. Discrete events arise slowly *(cham me)* so as to be discernible at the very moment of occurrence. Furthermore, each discrete event is discerned from both the event- and the mind-perspectives. The mind-perspective (staying) and the event-perspective (clarity) become two concomitant *(lhan ne)* perspectives taken to each mind-moment, and the succession of mind-moments arise slowly *(cham me)* and close together *(shig ge)* as an orderly stream of flowing mind-moments. According to the oral tradition, the metaphor of a slowly flowing mountain stream best illustrates this rearrangement in the mental continuum.[410]

B. Not Reacting to Whatever Has Arisen

Jampel Pawo gives his instructions in terms of the intended object, subtle cognition. The exercise is called *not reacting to whatever has arisen (gang shar bzom med).* He begins with an explanation of the root instructions:

> Here is the skillful means for not inhibiting the moment-by-moment arising *[thol skye].* Think about slackening [the mind] so that the progression of one [subtle] thought after another isn't cut off. Then, except for that one thought, ease up, relax, and allow thoughts to do whatever they will, and they won't affect you. Be mindful without either [trying to] prevent or not prevent them. Act only like a shepherd. Once you set it up like this, don't allow any thoughts to elaborate. During this staying-calm practice, from the mind-perspective, staying one-pointedly becomes somewhat firm as these occur. (JP, f. 48a)

He uses a single positive thought—thinking about slackening the mind—to guide mindfulness during meditation. The instruction to ease up, so as to neither prevent nor not prevent, is similar to Tashi Namgyel's instruction to neither supress nor make something happen. In both instances the practitioner is instructed to relinquish any form of artificial activity to make the meditation happen. The instruction is essentially a negation of all such types of mental activity *(bya ba ma yin pa):*

> In meditation, there is to be no [such] activity. When set up in-its-own-way, great bliss comes. (JP, f. 48a)

The metaphor of the sheep and camel illustrate this kind of easing up:

> Saraha says, "By intensifying, the mind becomes bound. When easing up, you no doubt become free...when tied up, a camel tries to wander in all ten directions. When freed, it stays immovable and firm. I have come to understand the mind to be like a stubborn camel." (PK, f. 7a)

Easing up itself is a kind of activity, which, however, approximates the limit of nonactivity with practice. The ripened, less-active quality of easing up is called *unconcern (bag pheb;* JP, f. 48b).

According to Jampel Pawo the benefit is a more complete form of staying:

> By nonchalantly letting go, staying comes forth. Thought neither becomes elaborated nor moves. When you tie up a camel with a rope, it makes him want to go somewhere else. He paces back and forth and pulls on the rope. When you remove the stake, he doesn't go anywhere else. The stubborn beast sits unconcerned. (JP, f. 48b)

In addition, the quality of moving events undergoes a change:

> Furthermore, Buddha Padampa says, "Try to prevent any negative thoughts and they come forth like gushing water...."

> Siddhidvopa says, "When [the mind] is set up without artificial construction, [suble] cognitions arise freshly, like the flow of a river. Then protect it like this." (JP, f. 48b)

> Furthermore, Milarepa says, "Meditate until you have destroyed [the artificial construction of] cognitions."

> According to these sayings, the meaning of the meditation that
> destroys [artificial] cognition really is about the way to protect
> [the gains], so [stabilize the concomitant perspectives of] stay-
> ing and the [fresh] activity, too, wherein each [subtle] cognition
> moves like a meteor. (JP, f. 49a)

From both the mind- and event-perspectives significant changes occur:

> By meditating like this, there is continuous staying and greater
> and greater movement. This is called intermediate staying, like
> a river calmly flowing. (JP, f. 49a–49b)

From the mind-perspective, staying becomes complete and continuous,
no longer partial and discontinuous. From the event-perspective, there is a
reorganization in the way the mental continuum comes forth, like a calmly
flowing river. This metaphor is comparable to Tashi Namgyel's description
of slow and discrete events. The tendency to construct subtle cogniton into
elaborate perceptions and thoughts is destroyed, yet "thoughts do not cease"
(JP, f. 49b). Finally, both the mind- and event-perspectives occur simultaneously, as two distinct perspectives. Jampel Pawo expresses this concomitance with a metaphor. He likens the movement from the event-perspective
to a river and the staying from the mind-perspective to a piece of driftwood.
No matter what the course of events within the mental continuum, the
staying perspective remains distinct from that of the moving event as if a
piece of driftwood were kept afloat on the water (JP, f. 49b). Both perspectives come forth at the very moment an event occurs. The progression
of events come forth as moment-by-moment arisings *(thol skye)* from the
event-perspective, seen from the locus of the mind itself *(sems rang mal du)*
from the mind-perspective.

III. Balancing: The Means to Set Up

The practitioner has learned to remove subtle dullness by intensifying,
thereby attaining intense clarity of all subtle mental processes, and has also
removed subtle flightiness by easing up, thereby attaining continuous staying concomitant with the occurrence of moment-by-moment subtle cognitions. Nevertheless a subtle problem persists: How can the practitioner
ever completely remove the faults of subtle dullness and flightiness when

the very activity to remove either one creates the conditions for the other to arise? Pema Karpo states the problem:

> In meditating, if you intensify too much, you will stray into thought; if you ease up too much, you get exhausted. (PK, f. 7a)

The intensified mind is less likely to settle upon its intended object and becomes flighty. The eased-up mind may slip from its intended object, and subtle dullness arises. Intensifying to remove subtle dullness can lead to subtle flightiness, and easing up to remove subtle flightiness can lead to subtle dullness. The problem is one of balance.

The solution is similar to the tactic taken in the done-with meditation. Recall that distractions in relation to supporting objects were done-with by totally changing the strategy, that is, by changing to a different class of intended objects. Rather than using another coarse-level support, the practitioner switched to the mind-in-its-own-way. Now, by a similar strategy, the remaining flaws of samādhi are circumvented by switching to a different class of intended object. Continued attempts to intensify or ease up generates further imbalance. Focusing upon the mind itself *(sems rang gi ngang gis byung)* becomes the means of finding balance. The practitioner takes as the intended object the mind that recognizes subtle dullness or flightiness, or that knows when there is neither. To focus on the mind-itself is to focus on what knows *(shes ba)* or what acts *(bya ba)* to eradicate subtle dullness or flightiness during the meditation.

Taking the mind-itself as the intended meditation object is at first difficult. It becomes easier if the practitioner performs a preliminary operation of balancing out subtle obstructions so that the mind itself, its samādhi-nature, can shine forth.

The objectives of the present meditation are (1) balancing intensifying and easing up, and (2) letting the samādhi-mind shine forth. Only when a perfect balance of concentrative energy is maintained can the samādhi-mind come forth. Therefore even though the samādhi-mind is the central goal of the meditation, the preliminary issue of balance occupies a good portion of the instructions.

Although the practitioner is no longer distracted by coarse-level thought and perceptions, subtle discriminations *(rtog)* are still made during meditation. Based on these discriminations, the practitioner still tries to act in certain ways to make the meditation happen. For example, to recognize subtle dullness or flightiness entails a subtle discrimination between the two conditions. Even to recognize an interval in meditation when there seemed to be neither subtle dullness nor flightiness is to make a subtle discrimination. According to Jampel Pawo, these subtle discriminations are caused by grasping (*'dzin po;* JP. f. 51b–52a) and by artificial construction. The main problematic artificial constructions at this stage of meditation pertain to the sense of doing something to meditate *(sgom byed)* and to the sense of the observer *(shes ba).* Tashi Namgyel mentions three flaws: mindfulness going astray, using effort, and relying on memory impressions (*'du shes)* from previous meditations.

So long as there is any artificial activity, the mind is imbalanced. The goal of the present meditation is to clear away such obstructing artificial activity so that the natural samādhi-mind can shine forth. When there is no artifical activity, the mind-itself settles in equanimity. Tashi Namgyel recommends equanimity *(btang synoms)* as the way to eradicate artificial activity. The way to remove artificial activity is called the way of equanimity *(snyoms lugs),* which Tashi Namgyel defines as follows:

> In short, be wise in protecting according to the way of equanimity, a dimension of intensifying and easing up. This way is the sacred main point of all the ways to protect concentration. In short, it is a mind having continuous mindfulness following the intended object, without the slightest excess of any subtle dullness or flightiness, and having the joy of settling into repose. This is called "samādhi." The intended object on this occasion has a nonconceptual still quality *[mi rtog]*, clarity *[gsal]*, and awareness *[rig pa]*, and within the context of mindfulness and intelligence *[dran shes]* there is a continual stream-of-arising [mind-moments]. (TN, p. 311)

According to Tashi Namgyel, continuous mindfulness is the way to achieve equanimity.[411] Effortless mindfulness is the next step after acting to eradicate subtle dullness and flightiness:

> Equanimity comes from having made calm the fault of [subtle] dullness and flightiness. When intensifying and easing up are equanimous, the mind comes to rest. (TN, p. 312)

The word *btang synoms* is composed of *btang,* the perfect form of *gtong ba,* which means "to abandon," and *synoms,* which means "equal." The compound expresses the intended abandonment of subtle discriminations and artificial activity, as well as the outcome, equanimity. Neither commentator uses verbs or participles to describe the practice that brings forth equanimity. Tashi Namgyel uses the noun *lugs,* "style or manner." Jampel Pawo uses the noun *thabs,* "means or way." Equanimity results from a particular style of awareness that has no artificial activity associated with it. These commentators do not wish to suggest that any artificial activity or discriminatory knowing can lead to equanimity.

One contemporary meditation teacher suggested the analogy of a complex electronic system, such as the control panel of a modern jet airliner. If the pilot wishes to land the jet manually, he must make many intricate, immediate decisions and actions so that the jet lands smoothly at a very high speed. However, if the pilot wishes to land it automatically, using its computerized controls, he merely has to set up the instruments. Then he settles back, without any need to think about the landing process nor to take any immediate actions. The plane lands itself, very smoothly. Likewise the practitioner simply sets up the conditions *(rkyen)* for this balanced state and lets it unfold. Once set up, there is no decision to be made nor action to perform. Just as the plane is able to land itself with its own automatic controls, the mind also knows exactly how to proceed once set up correctly. Just as the plane lands smoothly and perfectly, so does the mind peacefully go to repose.[412]

All the previous meditations inherently carried subtle value judgments, such as elaborating, losing mindfulness, becoming dull or flighty. The very act of taking the mind-itself as the intended object equalizes all such subtle discriminations. Tashi Namgyel calls the intended object the mind-object-of-awareness *(yid dmigs pa;* TN, p. 302). Whether the practitioner intensifies or eases up, it is still the same mind. Whether dull, flighty, or balanced, it is still the same mind. Seen in this way, all such discriminations disappear.

Similarly, Jampel Pawo cites several passages from the tantras and mahāmudrā source material to show that the real intended object is the natural Dharma body *(gnyug ma chos sku),* or the simultaneous mind *(lhan cig skes sbyor).* He uses various technical terms for the natural mind derived from the mahāmudrā tradition.

The mind-itself is a subtle object. When intensifying or easing up, it is especially important to focus upon the mind-itself that is acting either to intensify or to ease up. The mind-itself also can be seen during unfolding thought and perception. Both Jampel Pawo and Wangchug Dorjé use coarse-level mental content as a device to set up the mind-itself. The practitioner learns to focus on the mind-itself when thought or perception manifests. By switching to the mind-perspective like this, any subtle discrimination between one type of mental content over another—coarse or subtle—is balanced out. Likewise, the mind-itself can be seen in reference to the observer during meditation. The practitioner can use one or all of these intended objects to achieve equanimity because in each case the mind-perspective is adopted. By switching to the mind-itself as the object, the meditation finds more and more of a natural course, and subtle discrimations and/or artificial activity become less of a problem.

The final attainment is called *samādhi*. In samādhi all subtle discriminations calm themselves because their very moment of arising and their self-recognition occur concomitantly:

> When all the coarse and subtle cognitions no longer break out, or when even the slighest instant of subtle cognition that has broken out becomes self-calm *[rang zhi]* and self-purified *[rang dag]*, it is like a river meeting a great ocean. (TN, p. 314)

Calm (zhi ba) does not mean *cessation ('gag pa)*, it simply means that no discrimination or artificial activity is associated with whatever arises, like an ocean whose waves become calm. Wangchug Dorjé calls this meditation *reverse meditation* (WD, p. 65) because it is no longer necessary to do away with thought. Subtle cognition still occurs but is no longer acted upon nor discriminated in any way.

Pema Karpo's "four means to set up" *(bzhag thabs bzhi)*, and Jampel Pawo's commentary upon them, are a very detailed set of instructions for balancing the mind. They were originally derived from various metaphors in the oral tradition and then compiled into a coherent set of practices. The four metaphors are the Brahman's thread *(bram ze skud pa)*, the straw rope *(sog phon thag pa)*, the child viewing a temple *(bu chang lha khang blta)*, and the elephant pricked by thorns *(glang po che la tsher ma btab pa)*. Each metaphor refers to a different type of intended object wherein the perspective of the mind-itself is taken. Each metaphor also refers to a specific type of flaw that must be eradicated in order to balance the mind. Table 15 summarizes:

TABLE 15: THE FOUR MEANS TO SET UP SAMĀDHI

Means to Set Up	Flaw	Intended Object	Benefit
Brahman's thread	Acting to intensify/ ease up	Transformables	Equanimity
Straw rope	Effort in applying mindfulness	Coarse thought	No acting or observing mind
Child in temple	Attachment to internal perceptual features	Coarse perception	Great seed
Elephant	Failure to establish the concomitant perspectives	Mind-moments (subtle cognition)	Nondual staying & moving

A. BRAHMAN'S THREAD

The most important of the four means is the Brahman's thread. The root instructions are:

> It is necessary for intensifying and easing up to become balanced, so set it up as if spinning a Brahman's thread. If there is too much intensifying when meditating, thoughts go astray. If there is too much easing up, you get slothful, so make intensifying and easing up balanced. Moreover, a beginner initially intensifies to cut off moment-by-moment occurences and then, when overdoing it, ease up and tries not to react to whatever has arisen. After alternating between one and the other of these, try to make intensifying and easing up balanced. Intensifying and easing up the mind again and again like this is called "spinning the Brahman's thread." (PK, f. 7a–7b)

According to Jampel Pawo, the Brahman's-thread instructions are designed to correct the mistakes of the former two exercises—intensifying and easing up. Acting to intensify or ease up is based on the presumption that subtle dullness or flightiness and also elaborated cognitions are an enemy (*rnam rtog dgra langs;* JP, f. 50a). To consider these to be enemies is to make a subtle discrimination. The practitioner is now told to abandon the false discrimination by "…meditating mixing intensifying and easing up together" (JP, f. 50b).

By mixing intensifying and easing up, the practitioner does not alter the meditation in any other way. Subtle dullness and flightiness still occur on occasion. The practitioner continues to use the respective transformables. As Jampel Pawo says, "Remove one by the other as needed" (JP, f. 50b). The beginner, however, tends to intensify or ease up too much whenever detecting dullness or flightiness. The way to prevent this problem is eventually to switch awareness to something else once the application of intensifying and easing up is proceeding smoothly. Here the intended object becomes the mind-itself:

> Phagmodrupa says, "The meditation of the natural Dharma body is like spinning a Brahman's thread. Set up the mind freshly, nonartificially, continuously. As it is set up, it wanders high and low. When these vile defilements come, [switch perspectives and] meditate upon the simultaneous mind." (JP, f. 50b)

When the practitioner is no longer concerned with subtle dullness and flightiness as a problem, he or she is less likely to strain too much or become too lax when they occur. The terms *freshness (so ma), nonartificially constructed (ma bcos),* and *continuous (lhug pa)* refer to progression toward less activity on the part of the meditator.[413] The comparable term *rang sor* means "to leave alone." The practitioner who is only interested in the mind-itself and not in its particular events is more likely to leave subtle dullness and flightiness alone when they occur. Dullness and flightiness still occur, but the practitioner is able to make more and more subtle refinements in intensifying and easing up in order to remove them without making the subtle discrimination of viewing them negatively nor trying too hard to eradicate them. The metaphor of spinning a thread captures this process. The commentator explains:

> The meaning of this [metaphor] is as follows: When weaving, the thread doesn't get tangled when it is tight. It doesn't fall apart nor break when loose. Likewise, the best way of knowing intensifying and easing up as they really are when weaving the mind is when intensifying and easing up are balanced. (JP, f. 51a–51b)

The less experienced weaver hesitates to examine whether the thread is in danger of becoming tangled or breaking, and such subtle discriminations prevent the natural flow of weaving. The skilled practitioner continues to intensify and ease up evenly without evaluating the process. The experienced weaver spins the thread quickly and evenly.

B. STRAW ROPE

The second and third metaphors deal with the two classes of mental content, thought and perception, respectively. The straw-rope instructions pertain specifically to artificially using effort and trying to do something to affect the meditation. Artificially acting in one way or another must be cut off. The root instructions are:

> Set up as if sundering a straw rope. All the previous remedies actually generate thought, such as the thought that it is necessary to do something to become undistracted. Thoughts do not cease, nor do remedies come from trying, and the activity of struggling to bring forth mindfulness just strains the meditation. Give up [both] trying to be mindful and to think about these [flaws and remedies] accordingly. Set up the mind so that it settles into itself, in the very state of staying/calm. The mind that is set up without activity, without effort, is called "sundering a straw rope."(PK, f. 7b)

Just as the metaphor of the Brahman's thread was used to correct the flaw of making a subtle discrimination as to when subtle dullness or flightiness occurs, so the metaphor of the straw rope is used to correct the flaw of making a subtle discrimination as to when distraction and mental elaboration have occurred. In the previous meditations thought elaboration was considered to be a distraction. Trying to be undistracted through intensifying in order to hold the intended object was recommended as a remedy. The practitioner maintained concentration upon the intended object over and against any thoughts that may have occurred. Maintaining concentration required effort. Jampel Pawo now shows that the flaw made in these previous meditations was that of being too active *(bya ba)* and that this was based upon grasping *('dzin pa)*. Now the practitioner lets go of all such discriminations altogether by switching perspectives and taking the mind-itself as the intended object while leaving thought to occur in its own way *(rang lugs):*

> After this, give up putting effort into mindfulness and any grasping. Set up the mind in its own way. (JP, f. 51b)

Another important form of subtle discrimination pertains to the ordinary self-representation or observer *(nga)* during the meditation. The instructions address letting go of this also:

> Candragomin says, "If you make [the mind] firm through trying, flightiness is generated. If you give that up, dullness comes. So it is hard to find balanced awareness. When my mind is so disturbed, what shall I do?" That's the point. You can only go in the direction of not putting in effort to be mindful. Vajradhara says, "Completely let go of duality. Be free from [distinguishing] thought, and stay. The thought to act [in any way during meditation] is based on an 'observer.' So completely give it up." The citation means that holding on to an observer that is being mindful must be given up once you consider that this is an aspect of the [ordinary] self, [which is empty]. (JP, f. 51b–52a)

Turning to the mind-itself in its own way as the intended object helps the meditator let go of the sense of doing something, of the ordinary self-representation, and of the reference point for the meditation. This radical shift in perspective cuts the link to the meditator's usual way of going about and observing the meditation. It is like cutting a rope. Once cut, there are two pieces of rope. Once the ordinary sense of agency and observer are given up, pure effortless awareness stays in its own way as the point of observation for the meditation.

C. CHILD VIEWING A TEMPLE

The third metaphor pertains to correcting subtle discriminations associated with perception. The root instructions are:

> Set up [the mind] like a small child viewing a temple. Because the elephant of the mind has been tied to the stake of mindfulness

and knowledge, the energy currents have been done-with and stay in their own place. Whatever [still] arises is neither to be grasped if liked nor obstructed if disliked. Because of the influence of [holding the energy currents], the experiences in a nonconceptual still state are such that empty forms arise like smoke, and a bliss arises that almost makes you faint and in which you don't feel like you have a body or mind, as if you were floating in space. Not grasping and not obstructing these kinds of perceptions is called "setting up like a small child viewing a temple." (PK, f. 7b–8a)

Jampel Pawo devotes considerable discussion to this metaphor because of the unusual perceptual experiences that occur when deep concentration results in rearrangement of the energy currents. The five main energy currents and the subsidiary currents become intermingled, and some energy flows into the central channel. Likewise, corresponding perceptual attributes—colors, elements, seeds—also become intermingled. If this rearrangement continues over a number of sessions, *the ten signs of clarity* will manifest themselves. The first five of these to come forth are *the five signs of purification (dag rtags lnga)* after the ordinary energy currents begin to enter the central channel. Each sign corresponds to a given energy current and its associated element, as illustrated in Table 16:

TABLE 16: THE FIVE SIGNS OF PURIFICATION

Energy Current	Sign	Description
Earth	Smoke	Swirling smoke
Water	Mirage	Vibrant rays of light; drizzling rain
Fire	Glow-worm	Alternating emanation and cessation
Air	Burning torch	Lighting a series of torches; dawn arising
Space	Clouds	As if passing through a sieve or grating

(JP, f. 52a–53a)

The latter five of the ten signs of clarity are *the five signs of dwelling ('jug rtags lnga)*, and they come forth once the intermingled currents remain in the central channel for an extended period of time, as illustrated in Table 17:

TABLE 17: THE FIVE SIGNS OF DWELLING

Energy Current	Sign	Description
Earth	Burning radiance	Great fire of wisdom
Water	Waxing moon	Great light
Fire	Rising sun	The fire along the path
Air	Eclipse	Torch of wisdom
Space	Lightning flash	Clear light

These intense experiences occur as a result of deep concentration in general, and the vase breathing exercise in particular:

> Because the mind has been bound, every possible outer and inner attribute [of these signs] arises. (JP, f. 52a)

If the practitioner were to make even the slightest subtle discrimination when these events occur, strong hallucinations might occur. The meditator is specifically warned not to hold on or become attached to whatever of these experiences are pleasant, nor to obstruct or prevent those that are unpleasant. The skilled practitioner simply lets them be, letting them go their own way, and takes in the experience with a kind of simple wonder.

When even the slightest bit of reactivity to these experiences is eradicated, the five signs of purification become complete:

> These come forth more completely. They are self-clear, in that they are neither associated with any middle or extreme [discrimination] nor are they in any way impure. (JP, f. 53a)

Later the five signs of dwelling become more lucid:

> When unclear, they arise like a dream, but when clear, it is as if
> they were real (JP, f. 53a)

These inner sensory experiences, when left alone, appear to be as real as
the stone or stick that initially was used to support concentration. There is
one important difference, however. After mastering the straw-rope instructions, wherein the natural mind's awareness is cut away from the ordinary
sense of agency and of self-observation, here the link between ordinary perception and awareness is cut by learning to be nonreactive to very powerful perceptual experiences. Perception and its awareness become two
concomitant perspectives, ones that no longer affect each other. Perceptual
experiences just pass through the mind. Awareness stays completely on
them but does not react to them, nor is affected by them. Just as thoughts
became calm in the straw-rope exercise when not interfered with, likewise
even these compelling perceptual experiences pass quickly.

Jampel Pawo goes on to describe how these perceptual experiences
become self-calm (rang zhi). With respect to coarse-level perception, specific
perceptual attributes arose and subsequently became absorbed through the
skill and done-with meditations, respectively. Now with respect to subtle-
level perceptual events, any subtle discrimination between the emanating
and absorbed conditions of the seed is eradicated. In each potentially discrete moment of perception the seed is seen simultaneously in its emanating and absorbed aspects. To distinguish between the previous and present
conditions of the seed, Jampel Pawo now calls it the great seed (thig le chen
po). From its emanating perspective, infinite possible inner experiences
shine forth from all the sense systems. From its absorbed perspective, the
great seed is like black empty space. These two perspectives become one and
the same, "like the moon arising from the blackness [of night]" (JP, f. 54b).
As the great seed contains all potential experiences of saṃsāra and nirvāṇa,
the practitioner is aware of the great variety of all potential experiences in
every moment of perception:

> Once the ten signs have arisen, then the experiences of the great
> seed also arise. Along the stages of the way that have no certainty,
> staying and skill of the six realms arise. Then you will experience
> the three hell worlds, either as if you were awake or in a dream
> [depending on the clarity]. Then you'll see these change into
> something else. You'll experience the enjoyment body of the three

god realms. Others who see these experiences see them as the aspects of saṃsāra, but you'll correctly understand all these aspects as they arise to tend you in the direction of nirvāṇa [by seeing them as empty]—the many larger and smaller buddha fields, the center of the maṇḍala, the greater and lesser buddha bodies dwelling in a luminous circle, all surrounding the embracing couple, the stūpa and its letters, etc. (JP, f. 53b–54a)

Śabari says, "Once you have understood the ten signs, the perceptions of the great seed arise. From one perspective this great seed has a great variety [of perceptual experiences associated with it]. From another perspective it is a kind of blackness. But you'll see all six realms, many subtle emanation bodies and many enjoyment bodies, and all the great variety [of perceptions] as clear light." (JP, f. 34a)

The contrast here is between the variety *(sna tshogs)* of potential perceptual experiences from the emanating perspective and the blackness *(nag po)* from the absorbed perspective.

A profound transformation of perception begins to take place. The commentator explains:

In the *Torch of Experience* it says, "Moreover it is self-perception, in which the propensities of holding the currents and the tendencies of the mind no longer exist. Therefore whatever appearances arise in this state—the miserable state of the three lower realms and the desirable realm of gods and men, or the buddha fields and lotus gardens—are the way the realized mind appears." (JP, f. 54a–54b)

The particle *rang,* "self, own," is added to the noun or verb *snang ba,* "appearance, perception." When the ordinary sense of an observer is seen as empty and any reactivity to these various perceptual displays has been eradicated, appearances arise by themselves without interference.[414] Appearances are transformed into the way that they are seen by the mind in its natural state. *The way the realized mind appears (snang tshul)* is a technical expression in the mahāmudrā tradition for direct nondual perception by the natural mind.

If perception in general changes character, body perception in particular also changes. At this stage there is no consciousness of having a solid body:

> Something exists in space, yet you do not perceive yourself as
> having a [solid] body or mind. (JP, f. 154b)

This passage describes the body both from the absorbed perspective (not
having a solid body) and also from the emanating perspective (something
exists) simultaneously.

Another benefit is the experience of strong physical pliancy:

> Having attained physical pliancy, you move with bliss, much
> like the collapse at the height of sexual climax, as if you were
> stunned by bliss. (JP, f. 154b)

Both perspectives on the body exist simultaneously.[415] The description
"unchanging bliss" *(mi gyur ba'i bde ba chen po)* captures both the absorbed
("unchanging") and emanating ("bliss") perspectives on bodily experience
simultaneously.

Because the all-inclusive absorbed and highly particularized emanating
conditions of the great seed come into awareness concomitantly, this state
of perception is likened to the sense faculties of a buddha. It is also likened
to a child's perception. The child metaphor is explained as follows:

> You walk along the path described above that is known as the
> path of equanimity. Because you walk along that path in such a
> way that you have no intention to hold on to or let go of the
> aforementioned joy, this is like a child viewing a temple. A small
> child brought into the temple does not pick out perceptual
> events. Even when shown many different and specific works of
> art and icons, the child neither thinks about them nor desires
> them. This is an example of bliss. (JP, f. 56a)

When the great variety of potential perceptual events comes into awareness all at once, "the status of everything that arises is equal" so that the
mind doesn't act in favor of any one event over another (JP, f. 56a). This is
called *the transformation of illusory samādhi* (JP, f. 8a).

D. The Elephant Pricked with Thorns

The final metaphor is the elephant pricked with thorns. It is designed to correct any artificial activity that might interfere with the concomitant perspectives of the moving events and staying-mind coming forth as discrete mind-moments, moment by moment. As a consequence of the previous meditations, the two perspectives—the event- and mind-perspectives, or moving and staying—come forth in their own right *(rang sa)*. The elephant metaphor is designed to eradicate any activity that does not allow it to come forth in its own way.

The root instructions are:

> Set up [the mind] like an elephant pricked with thorns. When staying, the [dual perspectives of the] arising thoughts and the mindfulness that recognizes them come simultaneously. Then that which is to be abandoned and its remedy become the same, and one thought does not elaborate into the next. Therefore it is unnecessary to produce any remedy or to make any effort to do so. This is called "self-occurring mindfulness," in which it keeps to its own place.[416] Setting up [the mind] so as neither to prevent nor to produce the occurring and recognized thoughts is the meaning of the metaphor of the elephant pricked with thorns. (PK, f. 8a)

Jampel Pawo explains each of the two perspectives that come forth distinctly. First, the quality of staying is perfected:

> It says in the *Bhāvanākrama,* "Letting [the mind] go inwardly, continuously, and in its own way toward its intended object, staying. Such a mind has joy and pliancy. This is called 'staying/calm.'" (JP, f. 157b)

Mental pliancy is the effortless quality that arises when subtle dullness and flightiness are eradicated and complete balance is attained.[417] When complete and continuous staying happens naturally, there is no need to artificially do anything to produce any remedy nor to attempt to prevent thoughts from arising in order to guarantee that the mind will stay:

> Even though coarse and subtle movements occur while staying,
> it is unnecessary to rush for any remedy, to effortfully produce
> any remedy, or to deviate into practices not taught in the oral
> readings, such as letting one thought continue into a second as
> a chain. (JP, f. 58a)[418]

Without any artificial activity, awareness stays, while moving events are left
in their own right. They are self-occurring *(rang byung)*. The commentator introduces the term *mere self-recognition (rang ngo shes)*. The qualifier
mere is used to stress noninterference:

> With mere self-recognition it is no longer necessary to struggle
> to be interested nor intend to meditate. (JP, f. 58a)

The thoughts and perceptions that move within the unfolding mental continuum are seen as they really are. They are left to move in their own way
without the ordinary sense of any meditator *(sgom byed)* to recognize or
artificially act upon the movement. The mind's movement occurs naturally, and awareness stays continuously upon it as concomitant event- and
mind-perspectives. The particle *rang* is added to stress the lack of an ordinary observer. Awareness *(rig pa)* lets events unfold in their own way, unaffected by them, much the way a thick-skinned elephant would react if
pricked by a thorn.[419]

These concomitant perspectives come forth in each discrete event. Though
differing as perspectives *(nang du)*, they nevertheless pertain to one and the
same event. Ultimately these perspectives are realized to be nondual:

> It is like pouring water into water: [the mind-perspective] staying, and [the event-perspective] self-clarity and staying-in-its-own-way. It isn't necessary to distinguish staying and movement
> as being different. The duality between staying and moving falls
> away.... (JP, f. 58a)

> At that point, the staying and that which recognizes the
> moving is called "taking-to-mind the way it really is" or "special insight into awareness-itself in each and every event." It is
> also called "self-clarity without the effort to produce or hold
> on to." In the *Samputa* it says, "From beginning to end,
> thought [from the event-perspective] is liberated. [Staying from

the mind-perspective] is like space. Wise ones meditate like this." (JP, f. 58b)

Each and every mind-moment brings both nondual perspectives. Awareness-itself saturates each mind-moment. Events arise moment by moment in self-clarity, free from the interference of artificial activity. From the perspective of the natural mind, the mind's activity has always been like this "from beginning to end."

Tashi Namgyel's method is called *protecting the way of equanimity* (TN, pp. 302–10). Like Jampel Pawo, he acknowledges the "faults of samādhi," namely dullness and flightiness, as the main problem to overcome in attaining equanimity. He also sees subtle discrimination as central to the problem. He attributes this discrimination to the analytical nature of the mind:

> Those who are too analytical will try to hold the intended object one-pointedly, [thinking that they are holding it] with mindfulness and intelligence, but fail to generate a nonconceptual still state because of the subtle discrimination made to examine the mind as staying or not-staying or as occurring or not occurring with respect to the intended object. Failing to generate [a nonconceptual still state], they also fail to let [genuine] mindfulness and intelligence come forth as the way to understand [subtle] dullness and flightiness. Because of their subtle discriminations they think they should [artificially] do things like this, but such stupid practitioners hold it defectively. (TN, p. 304)

Whereas Jampel Pawo breaks the instructions into four units, Tashi Namgyel combines them into one combined instruction that addresses the mistakes that interfere with perfecting samādhi.

First he addresses the mistakes typically made by less experienced meditators, such as allowing mental elaboration of the intended object, failing to make the mind stay mindfully, and failing to develop the mind's natural clarity:

> In samādhi the mind stays in a nonconceptual still state, concomitantly with both necessary perspectives—staying one-pointedly, wherein mindfulness and intelligence are maintained; and recognizing in intense clarity. On the other hand, the flaws

of samādhi are as follows: elaboration with respect to the intended object; letting mindfulness of the object deteriorate even when there isn't elaboration; and maintaining just mindfulness of subtle cognition, while having the mind stay blankly, with no mental clarity. (TN, p. 302)

Next he discusses the problem of artificial activity, specifically with reference to subtle attachment or aversion to any given state. To alleviate such tendencies to do something to change one's mental state, he recommends switching perspectives and holding awareness on the mind-in-its-own-way:

Therefore the ways to remove the flaws of [subtle] dullness and flightiness are very important. They are briefly explained here. When dull, there is a great desire to generate mindfulness, intelligence, and the mind's [natural] intense clarity. When flighty, ease up on any attachment or aversion, wherein the mind is [overly] intensified with respect to the intended object. When intensifying and easing up are balanced, you hold the mind-in-its-own-right, the mental continuum doesn't deviate, you don't make any other discriminations, and this state is extended. (TN, pp. 302–3)

This passage is very similar to the Brahman's-thread instruction. Subtle distinctions are eradicated by turning to certain qualities of the samādhi-mind-in-its-own-right.

Finally he shows that a certain quality of effortless mindfulness and intelligence, one that has no artificial activity associated with it, is the means to set up samādhi:

Regarding both mindfulness and intelligence, mindfulness is how the mind remains undistracted from the intended object; intelligence is how the differences between distraction and undistraction, especially between that of [subtle] dullness and flightiness, is known. (TN, p. 304)[420]

Mindfulness is the way to know the natural samādhi-mind continually without interruption. Intelligence is the quality of effortless awareness capable of recognizing flaws. In previous meditations, mindfulness and intelligence corresponded to the staying and moving perspectives on the mental continuum, respectively. Here mindfulness and intelligence become one and the same. Tashi Namgyel uses the compound *dran shes,* "mindfulness/intelligence," to express the collapsed distinction:

> Various sayings distinguish between the coarse and subtle or rough and fine types of both mindfulness and intelligence, but the quality of intelligence comes when mindfulness is strong and clear, and vice versa. (TN, p. 304)

Furthermore, Tashi Namgyel wishes to correct another common subtle discrimination. Many commentators give these instructions in stages (*rim pa;* JP, f. 50a), using the four metaphors, for example. Tashi Namgyel has combined these stages into a single unit of practice so that the practitioner is less likely to make any subtle discrimination between stages or various methods used to attain balance of mind. When combined, these distinctions collapse.

The outcome of the cumulative instructions of each stage of concentration is described in the root text as follows:

> The final stage of staying is said to be like a waveless ocean. When an event occurs, there is recognition that it's moving while [continually] staying; and when that event is done-with, there is still staying-in-its-own-right. So it is called "the collapse of the separation between staying and moving." It is pointed out as one-pointedness. When an event occurs, such knowledge of staying and moving is called "taking-to-mind the way it really is," "the special insight of each and every moment," and "awareness-itself." In the *Elegant Sūtra* it says, "Once the body and mind have found considerable pliancy, then you can come to know taking-to-mind and analysis [next in the special-insight practices]." (PK, f. 8b)

The metaphor of the waveless ocean (*rgya mtsho rlabs dang bral*) is the most common description used for the final stage of concentration. Another common metaphor is a stream. Events now come forth as a stream of discrete mind-moments, each of which arise and pass away quickly with little chance of elaboration. Tashi Namgyel uses the arising-stream *(rgyun chags)* metaphor:

> What is a one-pointed mind? Mindfulness remains naturally on its intended object over and over again within the mental continuum in a continuous manner [with equanimity] but not joy. This is called samādhi, the one-pointed virtuous mind. (TN, p. 307)

Furthermore, each successive mind-moment comes forth from two perspectives *(sgo nas; nang du),* yet each of these perspectives "stays in-its-own-right," and the duality ordinarily separating these two perspectives begins to lose its distinction. Rearranging the mental continuum so that these two perspectives on each mind-moment are first distinguished and then seen as nondual is a necessary precursor to the special-insight practices.

From the event-perspective, moving mental events have two kinds of spontaneous activity *(bya ba)* associated with them. Such events are *self-occurring (rang byung), have their own power* (*rang shugs;* WD, p. 90), and *have their own way of arising* (*'char tshul;* TN, p. 315). These terms refer to the arising *('char ba)* dimension of mental events, specifically when not obstructed by any ordinary self-observer who tries to know them or artificially act upon them. Another cluster of terms refers to the ceasing *(dgag pa)* dimension of the same events. Events that are not obstructed quickly *become self-calm* (*rang zhi;* TN, p. 309). It is perhaps easiest to appreciate the experience of self-calm with reference to powerful emotional states:

> Because powerful negative emotional states (e.g., pain and misery) that arise are seen as they really are, they become self-calm. (WD, p. 90)

The same holds true for all other coarse-level thought content and perception. Just as a great ocean absorbs its waves back into it, the moving events of the mind become calm of their own accord.

From the mind-perspective, staying is *continuous (rtag du), immovable (mi gyo ba), equanimous (snyoms ba),* and *expansive (gu yangs).* One-pointedness changes into equanimity. Equanimity is the upper limit of the samādhi state, the goal of staying-calm practice. Jampel Pawo defines this last stage of concentration as follows:

> Ninth, samādhi comes from familiarity with the eighth stage, one-pointedness. Set up [the mind] effortlessly, spontaneously,

in its own perspective. Give up the habit of relying on memory impressions *['du shes]* to develop this, and let the mind come under its own [direct] influence. (JP, f. 60a)

The generic term for the concentrative practices is *staying/calm (zhi gnas)*. The compound captures the benefit in both perspectives. From one perspective, the mind stays like a vast ocean of continuous and complete awareness; from another perspective, its events become calm, like an ocean without waves.[421]

The practitioner must enter samādhi again and again and learn to protect the gains. Playing a musical score perfectly one time does not guarantee that it will be played perfectly the next time. Playing it perfectly once at least insures that the musician knows the proper way to play it so as to attempt to play it perfectly again. Likewise the meditator who plays the musical instrument of the mind perfectly once must then protect what has been learned so as to be able to do it again. After one has repeated the success a number of times, great mental pliancy *(shin sbyangs)* is developed, thereby enabling the meditator to enter samādhi with greater and greater ease. The technical term *shin sbyangs* is composed of two terms. *Shin* means "very much," and *sbyangs* means "to master." The compound term literally means "very much mastery."[422]

IV. THE STAGES OF CONCENTRATION

The Indian Buddhist concentrative meditation tradition originating with Asaṅga and Maitreya has customarily divided concentration training into nine discrete stages. Gedün Lodrö's *Calm Abiding and Special Insight: Achieving Spiritual Transformation Through Meditation* is an excellent synthesis of these works available in an English translation. Another excellent source is Tsongkhapa's chapter on serenity in *The Great Treatise on the Stages of the Path to Enlightenment*. According to Gedün Lodrö, *the nine stages of the mind staying (sems gnas dgu)* were originally developed by Asaṅga. Maitreya is said to be the source of a more detailed method for attaining these nine stages through eradicating the five faults and the eight remedies.[423] Gedün Lodrö adds that Maitreya discussed the nine stages primarily in terms of stages of improvement in concentrative stabilization, while Asaṅga discussed the stages mainly in terms of eradicating faults.[424]

According to Asaṅga, the nine stages are likened to a winding road that the meditator walks along. There are five bends in the road and six straight roads between each bend. The five bends symbolize difficult transition points, each of which requires application of a special method. The six straight roads symbolize the six powers of concentrative stability along the way. According to traditional sūtric metaphors, the elephant of the ordinary mind is running wildly down the road, being led by the monkey of attachment. The meditator follows after the elephant with two tools—the rope of mindfulness and the elephant prod of intelligence. Tsongkhapa says, "Your mind is like the untamed elephant; you bind it with the rope of mindfulness to the sturdy pillar of an object of meditation such as I explained above. If you cannot keep it there, you must gradually bring it under control by goading it with the iron hook of vigilance."[425] On the first straight road, known as *the road of hearing*, the meditator uses the teacher's instructions to repeatedly place the mind on the intended object. The first of the nine stages occurs along this road; it is called *directing the mind (sems 'jog pa)* because the meditator follows the instructions by tying the rope of mindfulness to the intended meditation object and then repeatedly redirecting the mind to the object. At this initial stage the meditator becomes acutely aware of incessant coarse-level mental elaboration and the tendency to become repeatedly distracted from staying on the intended object. The meditator has to forcibly place the mind upon the intended meditation object for it to stay even for a short while, and has little control over distraction. The first skills to develop are the skill in recognizing distraction and the skill of recovery from distraction. At this stage the mind is much more distracted than not.

The second straight road is called *the road of reflection* because the meditator thinks about and has applied the teacher's instructions in such a way as to try to reflect, as if in a mirror, the instructions directly in the experiences that unfold in the mental continuum. This road corresponds to the second stage, called *continuously directing the mind (rgyun du 'jog pa)*. At this stage the meditator is still easily distracted, yet is able to apply the rope of mindfulness to the intended object with some success. Nonetheless some force must still be applied to bring the mind back. At this stage both the duration of staying on the intended object and the duration of getting lost in mental elaboration are increased. The skills arising out of this stage are the achievement of some continuity of staying and a marked reduction in mental elaboration.

The third and fourth of the nine stages—*resetting (slan te 'jog pa)* and *setting closely (nye bar 'jog pa)*—correspond to the third straight road, known as *the road of mindfulness,* because now the meditator rarely completely loses track of the intended object. At the resetting stage the meditator is able to recognize distraction more immediately after it has occurred and is able to redirect the mind back to the intended object with less forcible effort. Recovery of focus occurs shortly after becoming distracted. There is much greater continuity to the mind's ability to stay on the intended object over time. The main problem at this stage, however, is the problem of patchy or partial-staying, in which a part of the mind stays on the intended object while the rest of the mind engages in mental elaboration. Therefore the meditator is at risk of developing the illusion of staying continuously on the meditative object. Redirecting the mind, intensifying to stay on the intended object, and/or focusing on more refined details of the intended object are the typical methods for overcoming patchy staying. The result-ant staying is both more continuous over time and more complete, less patchy at any given moment.

At the fourth stage, *staying closely,* the meditator has developed very pow-erful mindfulness, so staying is relatively continuous and complete, and he or she rarely fully loses track of the intended object. It is called staying closely because staying is more complete, less partial. The main problems at this stage are coarse flightiness and dullness and their derivatives, sleepi-ness and heaviness. Coarse-level dullness actually seems to increase at this stage because concentration is much more inward than outward.[426]

The fifth and sixth of the nine stages—*disciplining (dul bar byed pa)* and *calming (zhi bar byed pa)*—correspond to the fourth straight road, *the road of intelligence.* The three turns between each of the first four straight roads are negotiated by the flame of intensifying. Intensifying is vitally important because it effects the shift from the road of hearing to the road of reflect-ing, from the road of reflecting to the road of mindfulness, and from the road of mindfulness to the road of intelligence. Once attaining the road of intelligence, the meditator rarely loses track of the intended object. Along this road concentration is pleasurable and uplifting, and at times intensely blissful. During the fifth stage, disciplining, coarse-level flightiness settles down, but subtle dullness is very strong. Therefore the meditator needs to use intelligence to recognize it and to use intensification to eradicate it in a disciplined manner. The practitioner must stay very alert and keep the mind bright and sharp. At the sixth stage, calming, subtle dullness has disappeared, but subtle flightiness remains a problem, in part because the ordinary mind remains habitually attached to sensory experiences, in part because the meditative mind has become attached to the uplifting sense[427] of the road of intelligence, and in part because in order to get this far, the practitioner has held the mind very tightly. Thus at this stage the skill is to calm subtle flightiness.

The seventh and eighth of the nine stages correspond to the fifth straight road, *the road of perseverance.* Along this road the meditator has sustainable energy to continue meditating for long periods without distraction or fatigue, and without any coarse-level flightiness or dullness. At the seventh stage, *thoroughly calming (nye bar zhi bar byed pa),* neither subtle flightiness nor dullness pose any real risk, but the meditator is still distracted by these states. Both mindfulness and intelligence operate automatically with little need to do anything to bring them about. Geshe Gedün Lodrö says, "If one has a vibrancy *(thu re)* of meditative stabilization with respect to remaining on the object of observation, it is possible to tell when laxity or excitement is about to arise."[428] However, at the seventh stage the meditator still needs to apply considerable effort to get the mind to stay continuously and completely, and must continue to apply such effort until it becomes automatic.[429] During the eighth stage, *one-pointedness (rtse gcig tu byed pa),* effort is only needed to set up the meditation session, but it becomes automatic after that. At this point the meditator is confident that easing up on the effort will not cause distraction from the intended object, nor will subtle dullness or flightiness be a problem. Concentration is never interrupted, moment by moment, for the entire meditation session, and flows continuously and automatically.[430]

The ninth stage, *equanimity or balance (mnyam par 'jog pa),* corresponds to the sixth road, *the road of mastery.* At this final stage staying is complete and continuous and events arise with intense clarity. It is also effortless and spontaneous, and great mental pliancy is developed. Mastery of both the ninth stage and mental pliancy leads to mastery over calming/staying practice. The signs of genuine mastery include continuous meditative stabilization during both waking and sleep; being done-with coarse-level appearances and negative emotional states during meditation; the sense of having acquired a new body upon waking from meditation; the occurrence of pure, illusionlike appearances and meditative visions.[431]

Tashi Namgyel reviews Maitreya's and Asaṅga's nine stages in his massive commentary on the mahāmudrā (TN, pp. 305–7) but does not correlate these sūtric nine stages with the stages of concentration found in the mahāmudrā tradition.[432] In fact none of the mahāmudrā texts used as sources for this book attempted to correlate the stages of concentration of the Indian sūtra tradition with those of the mahāmudrā tradition. Table 18 represents my own attempt to show both the similarities and the differences between these two concentrative meditation traditions. Although the stages align quite well across both traditions, the major difference is one of perspective. The Indian Buddhist sūtric tradition discusses the nine stages primarily from the mind-perspective, that is, in terms of degrees of staying and the problems interfering with staying. The mahāmudrā tradition discusses comparable stages primarily from the event-perspective, that is, in terms of how events seem to unfold along a continuum from seemingly ordinary events to the way they seem to unfold as the mind's natural condition is progressively revealed. However, in an attempt to preserve continuity with the sūtric tradition, the mahāmudrā texts also include some discussion of the mind-perspective, that is, the degree of staying. These similarities and differences are illustrated in the table below:

TABLE 18: A COMPARISON OF SŪTRA AND MAHĀMUDRĀ STAGES OF CONCENTRATION

Sūtra Nine Stages	Problem with Staying	Mahāmudrā Stages	Result: Mind-Perspective	Result: Event-Perspective
1. Directing	Little staying	Isolation of speech	Danger of losing partial-staying	Increased orderliness of continuum
2. Continuously directing	Increased duration of staying and distraction	Isolation of mind	Undistraction	Cut-off elaboration
3. Resetting	Patchy, partial-staying	Concentration in-front	Partial-staying	Insubstantial object
4. Staying closely	Continuous staying; Coarse dullness & flightiness	Concentration-inside	Staying faithfully	Great virtue
5. Disciplining	Subtle laxity	Skill	Unwavering staying	Unobstructed clarity

6. Calming	Subtle flightiness	Done-with	Continuous staying	Calming elaboration; Nonconceptual stillness
7. Thoroughly calming	Mastery of effort, not yet automatic	Intensifying	No mind; Brightness of awareness	Always there stream; Intense clarity
8. One-pointedness	Less effort required for automatic staying	Easing up	Locus of mind-itself	Calmly flowing river; Making-calm artificial activity
9. Equanimity, balancing	Spontaneous staying	Equanimity, balancing	Spontaneous staying; Mind-itself	Concomitant perspective of mind-moments

6. SPECIAL INSIGHT

THROUGHOUT THE STAGES of concentration, the practitioner has gained considerable insight into the workings of the mind. Mental elaborations and coarse-level mental content that obscure seeing the mind in its natural state have been made calm. The practitioner has also stabilized noneffortful awareness as the point of observation of the events in the unfolding mental continuum. Notwithstanding these accomplishments, the stages of staying/calm practice are merely preparatory to those of special-insight practice *(lhag mthong;* Skt., *vipaśyanā).* Staying/calm practice merely suppresses the coarse-level cognitions that happen to occur within the mental continuum. Inactive negative emotional states *(bag la nyal;* TN, p. 327), those that ripen from propensities *(bag chags)* over time, have not been suppressed. Therefore upon completion of a meditation retreat and returning to everyday activities, the practitioner typically discovers that the "root and subsidiary [conflictual emotions] arise following that" (TN, p. 328).

Special insight is designed to eradicate the manifestations of the negative emotional states once and for all by destroying their very propensities. To illustrate, Tashi Namgyel opens his comments in the following manner:

> To attain certainty, you must do the special-insight meditations pertaining to the varieties of emptiness. If you don't meditate on that, you have merely conquered [manifest] negative emotional states but have not destroyed their propensities, and you won't become liberated from saṃsāra. (TN, p. 326)

Only awakened wisdom *(ye shes),* which arises during enlightenment, can completely purify defilements *(yongs su dang pa'i shes;* TN, p. 327). Special insight is a precursor of that wisdom because it cuts off the root *(rtsa bcod)* of all nonvirtuous propensities by eradicating wrong view *(blta log),* namely the view of the self as a self-existent entity *(bdag nyid).*[433]

In general, special insight practice pertains to analyzing the nature of the mind itself.[434] Specifically it is the skillful means to understand right view, namely the view of emptiness (stong ba). Kamalaśila defines special-insight practice as follows:

> By means of special-insight practice the light of genuine wisdom arises by correctly understanding the true nature of all dharmas.[435]

Special insight differs from perception (sems; Skt., samjña) and conceptualization (rtog pa; Skt., vijña)[436] because it is a form of direct awareness that leads to certainty (nges ba). Perception is a form of knowledge about the sensory impressions that arise—for example, color and form—but one that does not lead to certainty about ultimate truths, such as impermanence and emptiness. Conceptualization is a form of knowledge that involves subject/object duality and obscures certainty.[437] According to the Abhidharmakośa, special insight enables the practitioner to distinguish between certain and defective aspects of knowing. Special insight is a form of direct knowledge (mngon du) that eradicates ignorance because it permits the practitioner to grasp the fundamental view that all phenomena, everywhere, are empty.[438]

Without special insight, meditative experience (nyams len) cannot ripen into understanding (rtogs pa). The practitioner is like a blind man who is unable to find where he or she is going.[439] Special-insight practice complements staying/calm practice. Gampopa likens the two to eyes and feet, which lead a traveler to a city. Staying/calm practice provides the feet and special-insight practice provides the eyes, both of which are needed to enable the practitioner to reach the destination of enlightenment.[440]

In a section entitled "Supports for the Practice of Special Insight," Tashi Namgyel discusses how special-insight practice is built upon the solid foundation of the preliminary practices:

> Preliminaries:
> Depending on holy beings who are skillful in staying/calm and
>   special-insight practice;
> Seeking to hear [i.e., seeking oral advice].
> Reflecting on their way in order to get direct experience.
> Discovering the general truth, the truth of certainty, in your own
>   mental continuum. (TN, p. 331)

The propensities for special insight were established through guru yoga. Following that, contemplative practices are necessary to cultivate special insight "through one's own effort" (TN, p. 332). Attainment of special insight brings closure to these previous practices. Special insight that leads to wisdom is the culmination of the six perfections and is also the last in the list of the five making-certain mental factors.

Just as each of the units of practice of the preliminary and staying/calm practices are described in terms of stages *(rim gyis),* likewise special-insight practice also follows a sequential development. There are three main subdivisions of special-insight practice. The technical descriptions of these stages are: (1) putting in order the entity; (2) resolving the aspects, the skill that cuts off doubt; and (3) the yoga of the unelaborated, always there [mind]. A simple way of conceptualizing these three stages is to see them as pertaining to the emptiness of ordinary constructions for self-representation, reality-perception, and ordinary time-space experience, respectively. All three stages pertain to the real basis *(dngos gzhi)* or ultimate view *(yang dag pa'i blta ba),* namely to a deeper and deeper insight into emptiness through thorough analysis of the events that occur, moment by moment, during meditation.

In the first stage the practitioner tries to understand what serves as the basis for the experience of the ordinary self-representation in discrete moments of experience. In the second stage, the practitioner tries to discern the causes and conditions of each type of mental event as it occurs within the mental continuum, moment by moment, as these events pertain to the construction of external reality. In the third stage, the practitioner tries to understand the very process by which events seem to arise and pass away within the unfolding mental continuum, as it pertains to the construction of the seeming stream of temporal events. Common to all three stages is the perspective that the mind-itself is the intended object of special insight. In the oral tradition special insight is called a meditation on mind *(sems sgom;* TN, p. 338). Tashi Namgyel summarizes the importance of special-insight meditation:

> In general, all phenomena are said to be mind. Many have explained the benefits of meditating upon the mind's truth, as well as the faults of not meditating upon this. In short, since all existing problems of saṃsāra arise from the mind and depend on the mind, it is important to meditate by taking the mind as the intended object. (TN, pp. 334–35)[441]

Special-insight meditations take the mind as the intended object. This type of meditation is described as knowing the mind, or knowing the secret of the mind [sems shes]. (TN, p. 335–36)

The first part of the above passage refers to the doctrine of mind-only.[442] This passage sets forth the basic view, namely that all phenomena are merely the appearance of one's own mind.[443]

The second part of the passage discusses both the way to meditate (sgom tshul) and the benefit (yon tan) of it. Guided by an intellectual understanding (go ba) of the correct view, the practitioner sets out to meditate (sgom ba) by taking the mind and its seeming attributes as the intended object. The intended object (dmigs pa'i yul) is the mind, and the fact that it seems to have attributes such as being an independent, self-existing entity is the object's attributes (rnam pa'i yul).[444] Attributes are designations made about objects based on conceptualization. Making such designations obscures understanding of the mind's natural condition of emptiness and leads to ignorance. According to Gen Lamrimpa, the root of ignorance is "grasping onto self" (bdag 'dzin), and sometimes it is referred to as "grasping onto true existence" (bden 'dzin).[445]

The mind can be seen from two perspectives. The practitioner may meditate on the event-perspective of mind, namely on what arises from (las byung ba) the mind, or may meditate on the mind-perspective, that is, upon what these events depend on (la brten pa), namely the observational point of awareness that stays. The practitioner views (blta ba) either the mind-itself or each discrete mental event from either or both perspectives to see if either has any independent, self-existing nature. The fundamental task is to determine whether or not the mind (or any of its events) is an entity (ngo bo), that is, something substantially and independently existent.

The main realization is that no such entity can be found. The arising events, as well as the mind that stays on them, are both found to be empty, to be mere constructs without a substantial, self-existent nature. Somewhere during the search for an entity of mind, the practitioner gets the point and gains special insight into emptiness. Emptiness (stong ba) is synonymous with nonentityness (ngo bo nyid med; TN, p. 341). Geshe Gedün Lodrö calls this process "observing the limits of phenomena" because the practitioner realizes that phenomena are "not existing from their own side."[446]

The experience of emptiness opens the door to enlightenment. Emptiness is said to be the "way to liberation" (TN, p. 339), the "cause and effect of nirvāṇa" (TN, p. 328), and the "way to become a primordial buddha" (TN, p. 337). There are two basic kinds of emptiness that the practitioner must understand: emptiness of the person *(bdag nyid stong ba)* and emptiness of phenomena *(chos stong ba)*. These two correspond to subject and object:[447]

> The essential view [of emptiness] is to be without subject and object *[blta ba dngos gzhi ni gzung 'dzin gnyis med]*. (TN, p. 97)

When the mind is viewed from the perspective of the observer, no inherent, self-existing self-representation can be found. This is emptiness of the person.[448] When the mind is viewed from the event-perspective, the events are found neither to be solid, inherently self-existent, nor durable. This is emptiness of phenomena. "No external object can be grasped" *(gzung pa'i yul med;* TN, pp. 96-97).

I. Putting in Order the View

A. Attaining the View by Stages

Tashi Namgyel discusses special insight in a chapter entitled, "Putting in Order the Root," or "Viewing the Entity of the Mind" *(sems ngo bo lta)*. The chapter has two subsections. The first is on emptiness of the person, the second is on emptiness of phenomena. He writes about the fundamental meditations on emptiness, so his comments are not especially different from other Mahāyāna texts. Each of these two meditations is further subdivided into four stages by which special insight into emptiness ripens.[449]

The first type of meditation is called an examination meditation *(dpyad sgom)*. It is described as a way of finding the view *(lta ba rnyed pa;* TN, p. 152) and is therefore very important. Without a means of discovering the correct view, it is impossible to generate special insight and thereby master the meditations on emptiness. An examination meditation is the type of meditation done by logicians or paṇḍits. It relies upon the transformable mental factor of analysis *(dpyad pa;* PK, f. 36a), which thereby leads to an intellectual understanding *(go ba)* of emptiness. Analysis lays the foundation for finding the right view.

The first step of an examination meditation is for the practitioner to listen to the oral readings on emptiness and then to reflect on them. These oral readings on emptiness are generally included as part of the preliminary practices (TN, p. 127). For those who have not yet heard such oral readings, Tashi Namgyel recommends Nāgārjuna and the inspirational stories of Saraha and Śabarapāda as sources (TN, pp. 125–26). He warns against listening to advice that is not given directly by the lama or listening to erroneous views (TN, p. 141).[450] Tashi Namgyel devotes much discussion to proper listening because this view, whether understood correctly or incorrectly, lays the foundation for the special-insight practice. Next the practitioner must examine the view with the power of reason.

The way to do an examination meditation is to "take the mind as the intended object," at least in thought. In other words, the practitioner makes emptiness a matter of philosophical reasoning (TN, p. 333). The practitioner should come to "know it with notions" (TN, p. 340). It is not enough simply to rely on what has been heard in the oral readings. The practitioner must take the notion of self *(bdag nyid)* as an object of direct reasoning. For example, the practitioner might try to locate the self in each or any of the five skandhas.[451] By such careful reasoning, the practitioner discovers that no such entity exists independent of the five skandhas. The self is found to be a mere construct *(btags pa),* empty of being substantial.

Once certain about the emptiness of self, at least on an intellectual level, the practitioner begins the actual meditation in order to transform this intellectual understanding into direct meditative experience. This is accomplished through a samādhi meditation *('jog sgom).*[452] Whereas an examination meditation is the means to find the correct view on an intellectual level, a samādhi meditation is the means to examine the view in each and every moment *(so sor rtog pa)* of the unfolding mental continuum (TN, p. 153). The practitioner searches *(rtshol ba)* for the self *(bdag nyid)* in the events within the unfolding mental continuum until directly discovering that no such entity exists in any of these arising moments.

The examination meditation and the samādhi meditation form a set of practices (TN, pp. 129–30). The examination meditation must be done first to establish the propensities for correctly understanding the view. Without a proper foundation for viewing the mind correctly, the practitioner, like the kuśali meditators, is in danger of mistaking meditative stillness for genuine insight into emptiness (TN, p. 128). Conversely, without samādhi meditation the practitioner, like the pandit, has only an intellectual understanding but no direct experience of emptiness.[453] The scholar falsely believes he or she knows the truth. Emptiness becomes certain *(nges ba),* however, only through direct meditative experience that builds upon a foundation of philosophical understanding.

According to Jampel Pawo, the three stages of initial special insight are (1) that arising from attributes while taking a reflected image, (2) completely searching, and (3) examining each and every moment (JP, f. 25b). The four stages of initial special insight, according to Tashi Namgyel are (1) the common explanation, (2) the essential meditation stages, (3) connecting to the oral tradition to bring forth the special insight, and (4) the way to put in order the mind (TN, p. 339). These two models for initial emptiness practice are very similar, though expressed differently, as illustrated in Table 19:

TABLE 19: A COMPARISON OF TASHI NAMGYEL'S AND JAMPEL PAWO'S STAGES OF INITIAL SPECIAL INSIGHT[454]

	Tashi Namgyel	Jampel Pawo
Examination Meditation	(1) Common explanation	
Samādhi Meditation	(2) Essential meditation	(1) Taking a reflected image
Continual Practice to Get Special Insight	(3) Connecting to bring forth special insight	(2) Complete searching
Benefit	(4) Way to put in order	(3) Examining each and every moment

The actual meditation instruction is divided into two parts. The first includes the instructions for setting up the meditation. The second gives the instructions for how to bring about special insight.

Attaining special insight necessitates the use of the transformable mental factors of general examination *(rtog pa)* and focused analysis *(dpyad pa).* These mental factors can be either positive or negative depending upon the configuration of other mental factors and on the level of practice. With mastery of the staying-calm practice, general examination and focused analysis manifest their positive aspects. Staying-calm practice alone cannot lead to special insight. Completely making calm all coarse-level cognition, including examination and analysis, as in the practice of the formless samādhis, makes special insight impossible. After being done-with most coarse-level mental elaboration the practitioner learns to maintain concentration at an optimal level—one where examination and analysis still operate. The positive form of focused analysis is used in the examination meditation, while the positive form of both general examination and focused analysis are used in the samādhi meditation, as illustrated in Table 20:

TABLE 20: USE OF TRANSFORMABLE MENTAL FACTORS DURING AN EXAMINATION MEDITATION AND A SAMĀDHI MEDITATION

Examination Meditation	Samādhi Meditation
Focused analysis of a concept	General examination of each and every unfolding event [so sor rtog]

Note the change in adverbs used to indicate the positive dimension of these transformable factors. The term *so sor rtog pa* is composed of the verb *rtog pa*, which means "to cognize" or "to generally examine," and the adverb *so sor*, which means "each one." Because the term applies to meditation, it is qualified. Balanced meditation occurs as a progression or slowly moving stream of discrete mind-moments in the mental continuum. The adverb *so sor* refers to "each and every one" of these discrete mind-moments for the entire duration of the meditation. Each of these mind-moments occurs with two concomitant perspectives, the arising event and the mind's effortless awareness that stays with that event. Each and every mind-moment must be examined from these two perspectives. Therefore *so sor rtog pa* is translated as "to generally examine each and every one." Such meditative examination cannot occur when concentration is distracted, but only when awareness continuously stays, enabling each mind-moment to be examined at its exact moment of occurrence. Therefore "examination of each and every one" is said to pertain to immediately occurring *(glo bur)* mind-moments.

The samādhi meditation capitalizes on the "firmness of samādhi" (JP, f. 63a) that comes from mastery of the nine stages of concentration. Two qualities of samādhi are essential for special-insight practice: mere undistraction and a nonconceptual still state (TN, p. 342). To practice special insight, awareness cannot lose track of its object, in this case the mind-itself, as it manifests itself moment by moment, and awareness must be purified of coarse-level perceptions, thoughts, and emotions that lead to distorted conceptual elaboration. A relatively nonconceptual still state is required for initial special insight, with one exception. In order to generate special insight, the practitioner uses a single concept *(rtog gcig),* namely the concept of self, and compares this concept to the immediacy of mind-moments arising within the mental continuum. This method is said to be one by which "concepts are removed by concepts" (JP, f. 15b) or by which "the mind is examined by itself" *(rang sems la brtag pa;* TN, p. 342). The mind's own conceptual processes are used to generate special insight. The mind is designed for its own realization, and this realization can come forth as a continuous experience in each unfolding mental event. To illustrate:

> The mad elephant of the mind [is bound] to the pillar that reflects on the Dharma [that is, takes the mind as an object]. There is no escape when it is examined in this way. Be diligent, use every effort during the examination in samādhi. As there is no escape, even for a single moment, ask yourself, "Where is this mind, this self?" Examine each and every moment as if it were this mind accordingly.... You enter the practice through the staying/calm practice. Even a little bit of staying/calm practice brings its force, so that the staying/calm practice, with its nonconceptual still state, becomes special-insight practice, with its examination of each and every moment. (JP, f. 63a–63b)

Staying/calm and special insight are practiced simultaneously when there is optimal balance in meditation. Staying/calm practice provides the experience of the mental continuum as a stable, undistracted moment-by-moment slowly unfolding stream of discrete mind moments. Examining each and every one of these mind moments for knowledge about the mind is special-insight practice. According to Jampel Pawo, both staying/calm and special-insight practices are different "activities" of the mind that are "indistinguishable" from the right perspective (JP, f. 63b). According to Tashi Namgyel, both form an inseparable pair called samādhi/special insight *(mnyam par pa'i shes rab;* TN, p. 138).

The actual meditations can be very complicated because they are often done as a series of simultaneous special insights into emptiness. The root texts often give a combined *('dres pa)* form of instruction, wherein emptiness of the person and emptiness of phenomena are practiced simultaneously. Tashi Namgyel gives the instructions for the easier stages form of practice *(rim gyis)*. He gives the instructions on emptiness of the person and emptiness of phenomena in two sequential stages. Then, after giving instructions on each separately, he gives the combined form of instruction. For the sake of simplicity this book follows Tashi Namgyel's method of presentation. After learning about each emptiness practice the reader will be better prepared to understand the highly condensed combined form of root instructions, such as those used by Pema Karpo.

1. Emptiness of the Person
a. Examination Meditation

Tashi Namgyel's initial instructions on emptiness are called "putting in order the root *[rtsa ba gtan la phebs]* regarding the mind as an entity." The initial examination meditation is entitled "the common explanation" (TN, p. 239) because the correct view must first be explained to the practitioner. The practitioner also relies on general knowledge of the philosophical tenets *(grub mtha')*,[455] especially the doctrine of mind-only *(sems tsam)* and the Madhyamaka works on emptiness. Tashi Namgyel takes it for granted that the practitioner is already well versed in these tenets. Therefore his instructions are little more than vignettes from well-known sources. He summarizes:

> In general, examine all phenomena as mind [only], and [ordinary] mind as being a nonentity.... Where do we find the way to meditate this special-insight view that cuts off doubt? In the sūtras it says,
>
>> You are aware of the notion that it is none other than mind.
>> So understand the mind is nonexistent.
>> With such a notion you come to know the nondual and stay
>>   in the dharmadhātu that has no duality. (TN, pp. 339–40)

The phrase "you are aware of the notion" signifies an examination meditation. This examination meditation is composed of two parts. First the practitioner reads the scriptural sources and intellectually considers all phenomena of saṃsāra to be generated by the mind. Then the practitioner goes about daily experience constantly reflecting on this idea "as if all the phenomena encountered depend on the mind *[sems la brten]* in order to be cognized at all" (TN, p. 335).[456] This notion is said to guide awareness *(rig pa)* so that intellectual understanding leads to direct observation of all phenomena as mind. Practice is repeated until the ordinary mind continually stays with the mind-only notion.

When the mind is in its ordinary distracted state—not staying on the mind-only notion—the verb *sgrub pa* is used. It means "to affect, bring forth, or produce." The verb is transitive. Its objects include the "various" (TN, p. 340), "substances" (TN, pp. 347, 399), "self-existent [perceptual] attributes" (TN, p. 365), and "self-sufficient entities" (TN, p. 380). The common element in this list of objects is that they all imply epistemological realism, in which the ordinary mind is said to act *(byas ba)* in an artificial way to produce *(sgrub pa)* the illusion of seemingly real, self-existent entities *(ngo bo)* apart from the mind. Likewise the mind itself can be produced as something seemingly real. All such mistaken views are due to false conceptualization *(rtog pa),* that is, the negative aspect of the transformable mental factor cognition. In a negative sense, the ordinary mind acts upon itself to produce the illusion of a seemingly substantial, self-existent world and sense of self. In a positive sense, the well-reasoning mind can stay with the view of mind-only and/or emptiness and thereby lay the foundation for special insight:

> In a commentary on bodhicitta it says, "Having stayed on mind-only, bhikṣus purify that [mind]." This is spoken of as perfect knowledge. The various [phenomena of the world] are produced by the mind. What is the nature of consciousness? It is what is explained: all these [phenomena] are mind-only, just as the Mighty One taught. (TN, p. 340)

The second part of the examination meditation is to intensify the examination specifically with respect to the mind. The practitioner may still hold the eternalist view that the mind exists in itself. This part of the examination meditation entails representing the mind *(sems dmigs;* TN, p. 334). The practitioner considers whether the mind exists as an independent, self-existent entity *(ngo bo)* or whether it is merely a designated construct *(gdags pa).* Through examination the practitioner is unable to locate any substantial entity, mind, anywhere in the field of experience and becomes convinced that no such entity exists.[457] Representing the mind through discursive examination continues until the practitioner is convinced of the mind's nonentityness *(ngo bo nyid med)*, or that the mind is a mere construct (TN, p. 340). Having intellectually understood the right view, the practitioner protects what has been learned in everyday experience (TN, p. 336).

b. Samādhi Meditation
(1). Putting in Order the Entityness of the Mind

Determining the mind to be a nonentity is said to "cut off the root" *(rtsa bcod)* of the ordinary mind (TN, p. 336). The misery of saṃsāra is said to be produced by the mistaken view of a seemingly real, objective world and a self-existent, subjective sense of self, whose interaction leads to attachment, aversion, and ignorance. After gaining an intellectual understanding of emptiness, the practitioner begins formal samādhi meditation in order to make the transition from intellectual understanding to direct experience. The practitioner sets up the usual meditative routines—the body points, and so on— until entering the highest samādhi possible *(sgom gtso che ba)*, namely a relatively nonconceptual still state with a calmly flowing stream of subtle mind-moments (TN, p. 342). Formless samādhi states, wherein even subtle cognitions are quieted, are not used for special insight. Nevertheless a stable samādhi state is required, in which there is an optimal balance between undistracted staying and some degree of thought and analysis still occurring.

Ongoing awareness takes two perspectives *(ngang)* on each unfolding event within the mental continuum—movement *('gyu ba)* and staying *(gnas ba)*. From the event-perspective, discrete events fall into two categories: thought *(rtog pa)* and perception *(snang ba)*. Coarse-level arising events have aspects *(rnam pa; mthsan nyid)*. Aspects are the specific qualities of events that the practitioner becomes aware of. Ultimately, all aspects are represented by the mind. Because the mental continuum is ever-changing, aspects appear as various *(sna tshogs)*. For example, there are different types of perceptual aspects, such as color *(kha dog)* and form *(dbyibs)*. In ordinary experience the mind roams about and becomes aware of a panorama of various attributes. The term *rnam' gyur* literally means "changing aspects." Here it refers to the various patterns of ordinary experience that these aspects make. When aspects are viewed by the ordinary mind, they appear as various, and also appear as external substances. When aspects are viewed during special-insight practice, they are no longer defiled by misperception or an erroneous view. Depending upon the level of special insight, aspects may appear as mirage-like images or as clear light.

Aspects first came into play during the initial stage of staying/calm practice, where the visual aspects—such as roundness and roughness—of that which is seemingly substantial are first recognized *(ngo bzung)* along with the pattern *(rnam 'gyur)* that these attributes manifest, for example, earth, stones, mountains. During samādhi the internal world becomes progressively insubstantial, and instead a flow of successive but discrete mind-moments occur *(byung ba)* in which the various aspects arise and become calm quickly. Each moment of appearance *(snang ba)* is seen in clarity.

Concomitant to each moment of appearance that moves *('gyu ba)* in the mental continuum, there is a moment of awareness that stays *(gnas ba)*. The mind-perspective is the intended object of the initial samādhi meditation. The staying-moment of awareness is said to recognize in and of itself *(rang ngo shes ba)* both the mind and its seeming appearances. To the ordinary individual it seems as if there were some basis to the staying [mind] *(gnas sa)* or some basis that supports *(brten sa)* the movement of mind-moments. These terms refer to the mind. The objective of the meditation is to try to locate the basis *(sa)* of the mind with respect to both the staying-awareness and its occurring events. The practitioner tries to locate such a basis seemingly outside the body within some ideal essence *(bcud pa)* or within the seeming external substances *(dngos po)*, and also tries to locate the basis both within the parts and the whole body, and within each discrete arising event, and also within the entirety of the mind.

The practitioner utilizes the mental pliancy characteristic of the developed samādhi state to perform a rather complicated meditation "from many perspectives" *(sgo du ma nas;* TN, p. 344). The emptiness-of-the-person meditation emphasizes the mind-perspective while utilizing both the event- and the mind-perspectives. Discrete events within the mental continuum are examined only from the perspective of their possible support, the mind, or operationally, of that which stays to recognize the aspect of these events. This is not to say that the aspects are not taken into account. The practitioner is aware of the aspects as they arise, but emphasizes the mind-perspective that stays to recognize these aspects.

To make this clearer, consider the verbal compound *brtag cig dpyad*. It is most often found in the phrase "examine and analyze the mind-itself, by the special insight that examines each and every one *[so sor rtog pa'i shes rab kyis rang sems la brtag cig dpyad]*" (TN, p. 342). *Brtag* is the perfect form of the transformable *rtog*, the general term for "examination," as opposed to *dpyad pa*, which is more "focused analysis." After generally becoming aware of both the event- and the mind-perspectives as concomitant dimensions of each discrete event, the practitioner then makes a more focused analysis of the latter only. The compound is used to illustrate that both perspectives are equally present but that one is emphasized over the other for a more detailed analysis. The opposite emphasis is taken in the emptiness-of-phenomena meditation, as illustrated in Table 21:

TABLE 21: TRANSFORMABLE MENTAL FACTORS AND PERSPECTIVE IN THE EMPTINESS-OF-THE-PERSON AND EMPTINESS-OF-PHENOMENA MEDITATIONS

	Emptiness of the Person	Emptiness of Phenomena
General *(brtag cig dpyad)*	Aspects Staying	Aspects Staying
Specific *(dpyad)*	Staying	Aspects

Tashi Namgyel uses the respective compounds *way-of-clarity (gsal lugs)* and *way-of-emptiness (stong lugs; nyams lugs)*. Due to staying/calm practice, aspects arise with clarity. Due to special-insight practice, the staying- or mind-perspective is not found to have a basis and is therefore empty. As staying/calm practice and special-insight practice are combined, special-insight meditation leads to both clarity and emptiness, as illustrated in Table 22:

TABLE 22: THE COMBINATION OF STAYING-CALM AND SPECIAL-INSIGHT PRACTICE AND THEIR RESPECTIVE ATTAINMENTS

Way-of-clarity	Staying/calm practice *(śamatha)*
Way-of-emptiness	Special-insight practice *(vipaśyanā)*

The initial examination meditation helps the practitioner to see that appearing and staying are both conditions of the mind. As Tashi Namgyel says, "The mind is examining the mind." As this examination is done for every discrete mind-moment in the unfolding stream, he adds, "you should examine to the last extreme the mind by the mind" (TN, pp. 344–45). The way to practice this focused analysis is illustrated by the compound *dran rig*. It is composed of *dran pa*, "mindfulness," and *rig pa*, "awareness." The compound is translated as "mindful awareness." *Mindfulness* is defined as "not forgetting the intended object," and *awareness* as "direct knowledge of the mind." By combining these terms, Tashi Namgyel conveys the point that the practitioner is to become aware of the workings of the mind-itself, as known through its discrete events, by mindfulness upon these events moment by moment, without the slightest distraction from the task.

The task in this first meditation is to become aware of what supports each of these events moment by moment. For each discrete event that occurs in the mind the practitioner seeks out its basis or support. The process is likened to that of following a snake along its path in order to discover its hole.[458] Since ultimately no support is found, awareness is said to come forth of its own accord. The term *awareness-itself (rang rig)* employs the preverb *rang* in order to make this point.

The root instructions for the meditation follow:

When doing staying/calm practice, the samādhi with the best nonconceptual still state brings forth the best meditation. From the perspective of staying/calm practice, when there is mere undistraction, clarity of mind is generated. This is different from the representation in the special-insight meditation. The examination that examines and analyzes the mind-in-and-by-itself by the special insight that examines each and every moment is the best special-insight meditation. Putting in order the entity of the mind, discussed herein, is the same as putting in order the selflessness of the person, discussed in the sūtras. The way to do this is to practice the body points and so forth as before.... (TN, p. 342)

In staying-calm practice, characterized by a nonconceptual samādhi, from the perspective of knowing clarity take the aspects—viewed either externally or internally—to be bliss in the mind that views in-and-by-itself. View them nakedly in the mind as they come forth as color or as form. Can you find any basis to the staying *[gnas sa]* or any basis that supports *[brten sa]* them? You should examine in stages *[brtags]* generally both of these perspectives and then analyze *[dpyad]* specifically using the latter [mind-perspective]. Examine in general what happens to be recognized and its [particular] pattern. Examine how the recognized form is round, square, or whatever, and how the pattern is a particular earth, stone, mountain, or a particular person or animal. Examine how the color directly comes forth as white, black, red, and so forth. Then examine specifically [to find any] basis to the staying or basis that supports. [From the mind-perspective] examine what stays looking at the substance. Is there some nectar in this vessel [of mind, some secret essence]? Is there something outside the mind? Examine what stays, what may seem to support [the mind] in the body. If you think the entity of the mind stays in the body, examine whether it stays in particular parts of the body, in its cells, or whether it pervades the entire body from the soles of the feet to the crown of the head. If you think it might pervade the entire body, examine whether it stays inside the body, outside the body, or both. If both, examine whether it stays when the mind elaborates on sense objects and their outer forms. (TN, pp. 343–44)

The foregoing passage depicts a technically complicated meditation that includes a general examination done from both concomitant perspectives—appearing-aspects (recognition of aspects, patterns, color, and form) and staying-awareness, and also a more detailed analysis specifically focused on the mind-perspective to "examine what stays [the basis to the staying, the basis that supports]."

From this kind of meditative analysis comes a special insight about the natural conditions of emptiness and clarity in the mind:

Thoroughly examine like this with respect to recognition and patterns. Examine the cause of recognition: Is the mind empty or does something exist? Examine the recognition: Does the mind come forth in clarity or does something exist? If you find it to be empty, examine whether this emptiness is the emptiness of nothingness or emptiness that is like space. If you find it in clarity, examine whether this clarity exists—and if so, is it like the light emitted from the sun or a lamp or is it like the clarity that has no light or color? If you simply examine sense objects arising in the mind according to what you have heard, reflected upon, and intellectually understood, you won't be mistaken. All error is shut out with respect to the mind. You should examine to its limits the mind by the mind-itself. Having examined it as such, put it in order so that it no longer produces seemingly real things *[rdzas],* such as the particulars of external and internal substances. As you do this, don't forget to meditate on the mind's events as concomitantly staying from [both] perspectives of emptiness and clarity. When emptiness stays, whatever has arisen in the mental continuum will no longer be mistaken but seen as the mind really staying. Pray fervently and with respect. (TN, p. 344)

A very important technical term is introduced in this emptiness meditation: *ngo bo,* "entity" or "thing." The term *ngo bo* is difficult to translate. It is almost always used in conjunction with active, transitive verbs such as *search, put in order, try to find,* and *attain.* Generally, an entity is like an essence or a thing-in-itself. Hypothetically any phenomenon could have an *entity.* For example, sugar has a "thing" called "sweetness." The ordinary mind is believed to have a "thing" called "the self." Viewed as discrete moments in the mind, all phenomena that occur in the mental continuum might also be taken to have their own individual entities (TN, p. 98).

However, there are two different kinds of entities. When the term is used in an unqualified manner, it pertains to a false-entity (TN, p. 341). A *false-entity* is like a thing-in-itself. Buddhism considers it a mistaken perception to think that any phenomenon exists as a "self-existent, real thing" *(rdzas).* Consider the following usages:

> Finding an independent entity is a mistake. (TN, p. 380)
> There is no self-sufficient entity. (TN, p. 380)
> There are no different entities. (TN, p. 380)

The term *false-entity* refers to particularity and entityness. Such a false-entity is said to be an artificial construction (*bcos pa;* TN, p. 93), merely a mental construct (TN, p. 340) that is not self-existent in its own right (RD, p. 8). Entityness, or thingness, results from artificial activity to produce the mind's experiences as seemingly real.

When the term *entity* is used in a qualified manner, it refers to real-entities *(rang ngo bo).* A *real-entity* is not defiled by the false distinction of duality, as illustrated by the following phrases: *empty entity (stong ngo bo), clear entity (gsal ngo bo), real-entity (rang ngo bo).* Used this way, the term is difficult to translate as "entity." The term *real-entity*, or *real thing*, is a play on the word and is a synonym for *emptiness*. The distinction between false entities and real-entities sets forth a fundamental philosophical position within Mahāyāna Buddhism.

The object of the meditation is to eradicate the view of any single entity, or many false entities. The skilled practitioner discovers that mind is a nonentity *(ngo bo nyid med)*. At the time of each discrete mind-moment, the practitioner looks not so much to its appearing-aspect but to the staying-awareness in order to find out the basis or thing upon which this awareness depends. Moment by moment, the practitioner tries to discover the hypothesized entity known as the mind. The practitioner tries to locate it both outside and inside his or her own body. Moment by moment, the same conclusion is drawn. No such entity can be found. The true nature of the mind is realized—the mind as an empty thing.

(2). Bringing Forth Special Insight in the Samādhi Meditation by Searching

As the examination continues, the practitioner enters the next stage of practice, which Tashi Namgyel calls "connecting with the oral readings to bring forth special insight [directly] in this [mental continuum]" (TN, p. 346). As the name implies, the objective is to link what the practitioner has read or heard or intellectually understands about emptiness to the actual experience of the unfolding mental continuum during meditation so that direct experience of emptiness is realized. The way the meditator accomplishes this is by the use of a searching mind *(sems 'tshol)*. The perfect form of the verb *tshol ba*, "to search," is used in conjunction with the adverb *yong su*, "thorough." The phrase *yong su tshol ba* means "having sought thoroughly" (TN, p. 347). The phrase is meant to convey the thorough nature of this direct inquiry into the mind. The practitioner now examines each and every discrete moment of experience within the mental continuum in exactly the same way the previous analysis was conducted. The practitioner searches for the mind everywhere *(sems kun tu 'tshol ba;* TN, pp. 347–51), both inside and outside.

In the sūtras it says that the practitioner will not be satisfied with this search until all phenomena of the six realms and the three times have been examined.[459] Ordinarily the search need not be that extreme and is continued only until special insight dawns. Thus the searching-mind meditation is the upper limit of the examination *(dpyad pa'i mthar)* and concludes the samādhi meditation.

In the Indian Buddhist meditation tradition Kamalaśīla similarly calls this stage of special insight the "limit of things" (Skt., *vastuparyantata*).[460] The fruitless search for a fictional entity culminates in the dawning of genuine special insight—what Kamalaśīla calls "accurate realization of the nature of all phenomena" (Skt., *sarvadharmānamyathā-vatsvabhāvānagamat*).[461]

The technical expression for this realization is *nonrepresentation* (*dmigs med; ma dmigs;* TN, p. 350; JP, f. 64b). The mind-itself was taken as the intended object for the samādhi meditation, but the practitioner was unable to verify that such an entity exists:

> The kaśyapa mind[462] cannot be represented on the outside, the inside, nor both the outside and the inside. The kaśyapa mind cannot be explained, nor can it be taught. It does not have a support. It does not appear. It is not something of which you can became aware. It does not stay.... The kaśyapa mind, when sought everywhere, cannot be found. Not finding it anywhere, it cannot be represented. Not represented anywhere, it can have no past, no present, no future. Having neither past, present, nor future, it transcends the three times. Transcending the three times, it neither exists nor non-exists. (TN, p. 350)[463]

This passage uses typical negation instructions to convey the futility of the search. Special insight can be considered in two ways. Negatively, the practitioner gives up the search for an illusory entity. Positively, the practitioner attains proper understanding of the nature of all phenomena. H.H. the Dalai Lama calls this type of search an "affirming negation."[464] On the one hand, the instructions are designed to negate the ordinary habit to construct the idea of the mind as a self-existent entity. On the other hand, after thoroughly negating this convention in direct experience something still remains, namely the mind's natural awareness, although conceptualizing about or assigning attributes to that awareness is also empty. Negating the false view of the mind clears away what obscures realizing or affirming its natural condition, which is awakened wisdom.

With respect to what has been negated, the mind is no longer represented in direct experience as an entity. It can no longer be seen as real (*yang dag par rjes su mi mthong;* TN, p. 351),[465] but is simply a construct or mere designation:[466]

The mind is a mere name. It is none other than a name. As a mere name, it is only an idea. As such, a name has no self-existent nature. Whenever they search for it inside, outside, and both, the Conquerors never find the mind. The mind's self-existent nature is an illusion. (TN, p. 355)

Tashi Namgyel summarizes the purpose of the exercise as follows:

In order to understand the mind to be empty of a self-existent nature, do not produce the mind as something substantial but search for it with examination and analysis. In the description of the meditation stages given in the *Jewel Cloud of the Āryas,* it says, "After many meditations on emptiness wherein you have thoroughly sought [to find] the thingness of the mind, both in its elaborations here and there [from the event-perspective] and also when it stays [from the mind-perspective], you will come to understand emptiness and directly experience its joy. If you have examined everything occurring in the mind, you understand emptiness, and by understanding it as such, you experience the yoga that has no attributes." (TN, p. 348)

This passage illustrates how the initial insight into emptiness ripens into full understanding. During formal meditation each and every *(so sor)* moment of arising becomes another occasion to seek and discover the nonentityness of the mind. To realize emptiness directly in a single mind-moment is to realize the inherent emptiness of all potential mind-moments, so it is not necessary to examine all phenomena in existence. It is only necessary to examine successive mind-moments until direct experience of emptiness dawns. This is what "reaching the upper limit" of the examination means.

An important distinction is made between the terms *entity (ngo bo)* and *nature (rang bzhin).*[467] The term *entity* pertains to the initial stage of the samādhi meditation, while the term *nature* pertains to the concluding stage, where special insight ripens. The term *entity* is often the object of transitive verbs, as in "something not found." The term *nature* is used in apposition to the term *mind* and is usually defined by a list of qualifying adjectives. The term *nature* refers to how the mind is experienced *after* giving up the search for an entity. It refers to the type of affirmations that can be made about the mind's natural condition.

The negative use of the term *nature,* like that of *entity,* pertains to the mistaken view of the mind as seeming to have a self-existent nature *(rang mtshan).* Unqualified use of the term refers to *false-nature.* The *real-nature* of the mind is always qualified by a negative (for example, "without a nature" *[rang bzhin med]*) or is sometimes marked by a negative adjective. For example, consider the previously cited passage on the kaśyapa mind:

> It does not have a support. It does not appear. It is not something that one can become aware of. It does not stay.... The kaśyapa mind, when sought everywhere, cannot be found. Not finding it anywhere, it can have no past, present, nor future, it transcends the three times. Transcending the three times, it neither exists nor non-exists. (TN, p. 350)

Nothing definitive can be said about the mind as a nonentity. Therefore the exercise is sometimes called *the yoga that has no attributes (mtsha ma med pa'i rnal 'byor;* TN, p. 348). The real-nature of the mind is not expressed in negative terms. Certain metaphors are used to indirectly affirm it, the most common being *awareness-space* and *clear light.* Since the mind's real-nature is similar to vast space (except that it has the property of awareness), the emptiness meditation is sometimes called *space meditation* (not to be confused with space yoga; TN, p. 119). Because the adjectives are not always used in the Tibetan texts to mark the term *rang bzhin,* in this book the term will be translated as "nature," but whether the false-nature or the real-nature is meant will be marked respectively, according to Table 23:

TABLE 23: QUALIFICATIONS AND USAGE OF THE TECHNICAL TERM *Rang bzhin*

	Qualification	Descriptors
False	(Self-existent) nature	Nonexistent, nonappearing, not taught
Real	(Real) nature	Space, clear light

The outcome of the meditative search process is a direct experience of emptiness. Tashi Namgyel explains:

If you have analyzed in all the ways I have explained with respect to the mind as an entity, and have searched for it, you won't find any attributes that can be produced as its basis. Even the elaboration of notions about a searcher become calm in and of themselves and cease. Here lies the absolute truth wherein phenomena become thoroughly calm. This is called emptiness. (TN, p. 407)....

In so many sayings like those I have cited, the nature of the mind is said to be clear light. It is called "clear light" because of its purity. It is not obscured by elaboration, even [the illusion of] arising and passing away. Neither do the skandhas and dhātus have any material basis. The mind is stainless like space, whose aspects are nowhere really existent, and space's [real] nature is called "nonduality." (TN, p. 408)

The search meditation brings genuine insight into the mind's real-nature. For the first time the practitioner is in a position to comprehend the negative and positive assertions made about the mind in the oral tradition, because the mental continuum has now become a manifestation of that same realization. What was heretofore knowledge on the intellectual level has now deepened into an experiential truth about emptiness.

(3). The Outcome: Putting in Order Emptiness

The following exercise begins with the dawning realization into the real-nature of the mind, which is where the benefit *(yon tan)* comes forth (WD, p. 95). Tashi Namgyel explains:

If you have searched according to the way of the searching mind as just explained, then at its conclusion the mind is said to shine forth without having content (form, color, and so on); without having any basis to the staying [from the mind-perspective] or any basis that supports appearance [from the event-perspective]; without recognition; without patterning; and not obscured by any kind of elaboration. It is like the metaphor of space. (TN, p. 356)

The real-nature of the mind *(rang bzhin)* is said to shine forth *('char ba)*, as described by the space metaphor *(nam mkha' lta bu)*. Tashi Namgyel elaborates on the metaphor:

O Bodhisattva, how does one view the inner mind? He answers, "The mind has no form; it is like space." (TN, p. 356)[468]

Space as a metaphor conveys the nature of emptiness, in that it can only be defined as an absence. Space is not something that can be represented. It "cannot be seen" (*mthong med;* TN, p. 356). It has no form, nor can it obstruct form. Space, though all-inclusive and all-pervasive, cannot be considered "existent." It is impervious to the changes of time and to the law of impermanence.

Tashi Namgyel is careful to qualify the metaphor. Emptiness is not exactly space. It is only "like space." The term is qualified so that the practitioner does not make the mistakes of either grasping space as an entity (TN, p. 358) or failing to realize that, unlike space, something exists. The space metaphor is limited by being merely a designation. "What is called seeing space *(nam mkha' lta ba)* is merely a sentient being's expression" (TN, p. 362).[469] The essential difference between emptiness and space has to do with the capacity for knowledge:

In the beginning, you examine with the special insight that examines each and every one. At the end, having calmed conceptualization, the wisdom of a perfect nonconceptual still state is said to shine forth. If you don't think that the mind and space are or are not a little different, they indeed are! Space doesn't lead to knowledge. Awareness-in-and-by-itself does. [Genuinely] understanding the mind does lead to awakened wisdom, [and the mind is experienced as] awareness-in-and-by-itself. (TN, p. 359)

The mind, unlike space, has the potential to know itself.

Another important technical term is introduced at this point, *rang rig,* as well as its related terms *rang gyis rang rig* and *so sor rang rig.* They mean "self-awareness," "awareness-in-and-by-itself," and "self-awareness of each and every moment," respectively. *Rig pa,* "awareness," is used when seeing the real-nature of the mind no longer obscured by content. Therefore *rig pa,* "awareness," is used in conjunction with such phrases as "without aspects" (TN, p. 412), "beyond all thought" (TN, p. 360), and "stainless" (TN, p. 412).[470] Once the obscurations to the correct view of the mind have been removed, special insight occurs.

> Now let me explain the ineffable truth, which is called "awareness-in-and-by-itself." After analyzing the mind-in-and-by-itself there is awareness, which is the way the realized mind stays in its awakened state. It is self-purified in that it is free from any elaboration and all attributes. It is given the simple designation "self-awareness." (TN, p. 361)

It is not entirely correct to say that the practitioner becomes aware of the mind's real-nature. Who does the knowing? Who has the awareness? It is more accurate to say that awareness-itself shines forth of its own accord once obscurations are removed. True knowledge just *is*. It is a property inherent in human existence, which may or may not shine forth under certain conditions. Awareness-itself can shine forth in each and every moment of experience, given the proper conditions. This is what is meant by the term *so sor rang rig,* "self-awareness of each and every moment" (TN, p. 413). Each successive event comes forth in the mental continuum immediately known by the same special insight.

When such realization comes forth, the practitioner experiences a profound transformation of view. The technical term for this change is called *putting in order (gtan la phebs) the mind.* The term *gtan* refers to a "system" or "arrangement." The verb *phebs pa* means "to come or put." The entire phrase means "to put in order, rearrange, or transform." The term *put in order* signifies both a profound transformation as well as its expression or manifestation. The practitioner not only experiences a profound change of view but literally changes his or her mind. That change will become manifest in every successive mind-moment in the mental continuum and will permeate behavior in the everyday world. The term *put in order* is similar to the concept of rearrangement of body and mind during the body- and mind-point instructions. The common factor is rearrangment in the direction of greater orderliness. At this stage of practice the entire makeup of the mental continuum undergoes a more comprehensive and profound rearrangement because the practitioner has cut off the root *(rtsa bcod)* by no longer viewing the mind and its aspects as substantial, self-existent things.

Special insight purifies *(dag pa)* obscurations and clears the way for the eventual ripening of awakened wisdom (TN, p. 356). To cite Tilopa:

Viewed from the heart of space,
Seeing is brought to cessation.

Likewise when viewing the mind by the mind-itself, the practitioner attains perfect enlightenment and the cessation of various
aspects and conceptualization. Just as fog and clouds evaporate
into the realms of space yet don't go anywhere nor stay anywhere,
likewise various thoughts arise from the mind, but those
thoughts, like waves, evaporate by seeing the mind-itself.... For
example, what is designated as "empty space" is not really like
space. Likewise what is designated as "clear light," which is the
mind-itself, although found here, doesn't have any basis. So the
real-nature of the mind is like space. (TN, pp. 357–58)

The fog of ignorance lifts. All views based on erroneous conceptualization *(rtog pa),*[471] which, at a more fundamental level, are all views based
upon duality, cease. Like space, emptiness is everywhere the same. Mind is
the same as the mind-perspective. There is no difference between the
searcher *('tshol mkhan)* and that which is sought *(tshal;* TN, p. 362), no difference between the viewer and that which is viewed (JP, f. 64a), no difference between the knower and that which is known (JP, f. 64a).
   Tashi Namgyel's four exercises for putting in order the root of the mind
are primarily practiced from the mind-perspective, which with special
insight is specifically called the *way of emptiness (stong lugs).* Although the
practitioner focuses the detailed analysis from the mind-perspective, he
or she is never entirely unaware of what appears *(snang ba; 'gyu ba)* in each
moment of experience. Therefore the term for this change of view from
the event-perspective is *clarity-itself (rang gsal).* As obscurations disappear,
what arises in the mind shines forth with luminosity. Yet it is not exactly
correct to say that "something" shines forth. When there is no subject-
object duality, what can shine forth? It is more accurate to say that the
mind-as-appearance-itself shines forth. It's seeming coarse-level content—
perceptual aspects, thoughts, and emotions—just *are.* They are properties
inherent in being human that spontaneously occur under certain conditions by the force of ripening karmic propensities. The term *clarity-itself*
or *self-illumination* illustrates the spontaneous way these events come forth
once the habit of subject-object duality is alleviated.
   The corresponding metaphor that describes the realization from the

event-perspective is clear light *(od gsal).* To emphasize that clear light is not different from the mind from the perspective of nonduality, the full expression of the metaphor is expressed in the genitive phrase "clear light that is the mind-itself" (TN, pp. 357–58).

In the next series of exercises, having to do with the emptiness of phenomena, the perspective will be reversed. The event-perspective, or way of clarity *(gsal lugs),* becomes the focus of specific analysis *(dpyad),* while the mind-perspective, or way of emptiness, is adopted only as the preliminary general examination *(rtog pa),* as illustrated in Table 24:

TABLE 24: DOMINANT PERSPECTIVE
IN THE EMPTINESS-OF-THE-PERSON MEDITATION

| | Emptiness of the Person | |
	Dominant	Subsidiary
Name	Way of emptiness Way the realized mind stays	Way of clarity Way the realized mind appears
Specific analysis	Staying	Appearing aspects
Knowledge	Awareness-itself	Clarity-itself
Benefit/outcome	Emptiness	Clarity
Metaphor	Like space	Clear light

In a relative sense, a distinction can be made between the way-the-realized-mind-stays and the appearing-way perspectives. From an ultimate perspective, special insight into nonduality *(gnyis med)* collapses the distinction between these perspectives. Aspects and mind-itself, appearing and staying, become indistinguishable *(dpyed med).* Their distinctions disappear because special insight shines forth, as if consuming two sticks by the fire that is generated from rubbing them together:

> Fire comes from rubbing two sticks together so that both are consumed. Likewise, both the sense faculties and the special insight that are generated become consumed as they arise. (TN, f. 9a; JP, f. 65a)
>
> Rub two sticks back and forth. Stir the burning pieces together, and both are consumed simultaneously by the resultant fire. They become mere ashes. Likewise, once you have analyzed

both the staying and the moving with the examination of each and every moment, the special insight of understanding emptiness is spontaneously generated. (JP, f. 65a)

At this stage the practitioner only begins to eradicate the habit of duality. The power of the erroneous view of subject-object duality is very great and takes considerable opponent force to overcome. Although the practitioner has had the first genuine special insight into emptiness, the force of habit of old views is very strong. Therefore Tashi Namgyel concludes his instructions on emptiness of the person with comments on protecting the realization:

> Now, I've told you that the beginner is to have nothing but [direct] experience of mindful awareness and a certainty of knowledge that is difficult to express in words. In the *Sūtra of the Holy Dharma,* and also in the *Likeness to the Dharma,* it says, "By setting up the mind accordingly, experience arises, unobstructed by words." Tilopa says, "Phenomena remain unelaborated, the experience is mindful awareness, [and both of these] occur spontaneously." (TN, p. 363)

The reference to mindful awareness signifies a protecting instruction. The term *spontaneously occurring* (*glo bur du 'byung;* [variation, *skye*]; JP, f. 65a; TN, p. 363) means that the practitioner, without the slightest distraction from continuous mindfulness, experiences the exact same insight into emptiness at the very moment that any discrete event begins to arise in the mental continuum.

2. Emptiness of Phenomena

a. Examination Meditation

Tashi Namgyel's commentary on the emptiness-of-phenomena meditation is called "putting in order that which is sought, the entity of thoughts and appearances" (TN, p. 371). It has three parts: (1) "learning that all appearances are the mind," (2) "the way to understand appearance by understanding the mind," and (3) "explaining the representations in the meditation stages" (TN, p. 363).[472] Each successive exercise leads to deeper and deeper awareness of clarity *(gsal ba).* Clarity from the event-perspective corresponds to emptiness from the mind-perspective, as illustrated in Table 25:

TABLE 25: CORRESPONDING PERSPECTIVES TAKEN IN THE EMPTINESS-OF-THE-PERSON AND EMPTINESS-OF-PHENOMENA MEDITATIONS

	Emptiness of the Person	Emptiness of Phenomena
Attainment	Emptiness	Clarity
Perspective	Staying	Appearing (moving)

The initial examination meditation begins with a series of vignettes setting forth *the doctrine of appearance-only (snang tsam)* in contrast to the erroneous views *('khrul lugs)* of believing in self-existent attributes *(rang mtshan)*, grasping things as real *('thas par gyur ba)*, holding things to be substantial *(dngos po)*, and grasping appearances as seemingly external *(phyi rol snag ba'i 'dzin pa)*. These mistaken perceptions occur because the mind artificially produces *(sgrub pa)* elaborations of actual perceptual experience and some form of subject-object dichotomy is posited. The right view, appearance-only, comes from the negation of that ordinary habit of mind, as illustrated by Tashi Namgyel's instruction to "be completely without external appearance" (TN, p. 364). In the oral tradition the correct view is pointed out in a series of aphorisms that signify the nondual *(gnyis med)* activity of the mind-as-appearance. Typical examples include "mind-arisen as various" *(sems ni sna tshogs rnams su shar;* TN, p. 363) and "all [phenomena] are emanations of the mind" *(thams cad sems kyi rnam 'phrol;* TN, p. 365).

Tashi Namgyel begins his instructions by contrasting the correct and erroneous views of appearance:

> To those who are ignorant of the mind's thatness, all types of thoughts and perceptions (forms, sounds, and so forth), which have [correctly] arisen through the mind's skill, become erroneous in that they are artificially taken as self-existent aspects that are believed to be independent of the mind. Yet the ultimate truth is that these [thoughts and appearances] are the very mind itself. (TN, pp. 363–64)

Tashi Namgyel goes on to explain the origin of this erroneous view:

> Now, how is it that external substances (forms, etc.) appear? It

is because you haven't been done-with the "[two] selves," so that self and other are held to be a duality, and you haven't understood the mind-in-and-by-itself or the way the realized mind stays. Due to the erroneous conceptualization of holding that [view] through the [habitual] accumulation of such erroneous propensities [over lifetimes], objects seem to appear as external.

Now, how is it that substances are artificially produced as self-existent aspects seeming to be solid, hard, and so forth, and not taken as appearance-only? It happens through the habit of very many erroneous propensities in which things have been held to be real and external so that now substances appear as self-existent aspects with solidity, hardness, and so forth. (TN, p. 365)

The first step in the examination meditation is to intellectually understand the correct view, appearance-only. The practitioner negates the habitual outward orientation inherent in ordinary perception and adopts an inward orientation, as if all appearances were none other than an emanation of the mind. Negating the habit of projecting a seemingly external world is difficult due to the tremendous power of ordinary dualistic perception. In ordinary experience every thought and every perception, moment by moment, establishes additional propensities to reaffirm the same mistaken view. Karmic propensities pertain to actions *(las)*, in this case mental actions, namely the mental action of artificially producing dualism.

The second, critical part of the exercise is to turn back appearance *(snang ba ldog ba;* TN, p. 366). Briefly, the practitioner negates any mental action that reinforces the habitual view. As an affirming negation the negation part of the instruction is known as *not artificially producing (sgrub med).* The affirming part of the instruction is known as *experiencing the way the realized mind appears (snang lugs).* Just as the mind has been realized to be a nonentity, so now appearance is seen as no real thing. It is a mere construct. Mind and appearance are one and the same, "indistinguishable." When there is no artificial activity, the natural condition of the mind shines forth without obscuration. From the event-perspective, the way of appearance of the natural mind manifests as clarity or luminosity *(gsal ba).*

The equation of the way the realized mind stays and the appearing-way is emphasized in a special section entitled "The Way to Understand Appearance by Understanding the Mind" (TN, p. 367):

Therefore the root of all the calm realms is said to be mind only. Whatever worlds are elaborated by mind—whose real-nature is the master of all the realms or whose real-nature is that of space—are the same as the mind. Are water and waves different? All that becomes elaborated in or that has arisen from the mind is just the mind's real-nature. In the sūtras it says, "The mind is nonexistent; the real-nature of the mind is clear light." The real-nature of the mind described in the passage is emptiness as clear-light. So if you understand the mind's [real-]nature as emptiness, you will be able to understand appearance's [real-]nature as emptiness. (TN, pp. 367–68)

So once you have practiced all the ways to examine and ana-lyze to put in order the mind's entity, as I have explained, you will also know the way to put in order the all appearances' entity. (TN, p. 369)

Since mind and appearance have already been experienced as nondual, the practitioner essentially already understands the emptiness-of-phenomena meditation. If the mind is a nonentity, then every appearance is also a nonen-tity. The real-nature of the mind is expressed in the metaphors *space* and *clear light*, depending on the perspective taken at the moment. From the mind-perspective, it is like space. From the event-perspective, it is like clear light that can move *('gyu ba)*, shine forth *('char ba)*, spread *('phro ba)*, or appear *(snang ba)*. Table 26 illustrates the use of these metaphors:

TABLE 26: CORRELATION OF BENEFITS AND THEIR METAPHORS
IN SPECIAL-INSIGHT MEDITATION

Perspective	Way the Realized Mind Stays	Way the Realized Mind Appears
Benefit	Emptiness	Clarity
Metaphor	Like space	Clear light

The emptiness-of-phenomena meditation is conducted from the event-perspective. The practitioner focuses on thoughts and perceptual aspects as they arise or have arisen *(shar ram 'char)*, but knows that adopting this perspective is no different from that of the mind-perspective of awareness-itself. As the practitioner shifts perspective, there is some risk of mistakenly reinforcing subject/object duality. Tashi Namgyel gives a special set of instructions to correct going astray *(shor sa)*. These instructions will be addressed later in this book.

b. Samādhi Meditation
(1). Putting in Order the Entityness of Phenomena

Having intellectually understood *(go ba)* the doctrine of appearance-only, the practitioner then conducts the formal samādhi meditation in order to experience the realization directly.[473] For each discrete mind-moment in the stream of the unfolding mental continuum, the practitioner generally examines both concomitant perspectives but specifically emphasizes the event-perspective. He or she specifically focuses upon the content as it arises moment by moment. Tashi Namgyel recommends specifically analyzing a wide range of mental content that includes both cognitions and perceptions. Cognitions include both (a) coarse-level cognitions, especially emotions such as attachment and aversion, thought content; and (b) fleeting subtle cognitions. Perceptions comprise three aspects: (a) the movement associated with the sense doors in response to pleasurable and unpleasurable sensations (TN, p. 375); (b) the coarse-level perceptions themselves *(snang ba)* from each of the six sense systems (sights, sounds, and so forth); and (c) the parts of perception *(snang cha),* that is, the incessant cognitive judgments made about perceptions so that these seem to be part of the perception itself (for example, good/bad, helpful/hindering, internal/external) (TN, p. 661). According to Khenchen Thrangu Rinpoche, "Because it is easier to investigate the nature of thoughts than the nature of appearances, we start with investigating the nature of thoughts."[474]

The objective of the meditation is to specifically analyze mental content as it moves. In order to maximize the realization, an optimal level of samādhi is required. The emptiness-of-the-person meditation required a high level of samādhi, namely nonconceptual samādhi. The emptiness-of-phenomena meditation requires a different level of samādhi, as illustrated by the phrase "nonrecognition from the perspective of a clear and empty mind." *Nonrecognition samādhi (ngo bzung med)* refers to a special-insight samādhi wherein staying-calm practice and special-insight practice are combined.

A refined level of calmness is no longer needed. If the mind is too calm, the flow of discrete mind-moments will neither arise nor become sufficiently elaborated to serve as a focus for special insight. Some teachers recommend using the transitional period waking from samādhi *(rjes thob)* as the ideal time to do the emptiness-of-phenomena meditation (JP, f. 63a). Others, such as Tashi Namgyel, recommend shifting to a lower level of samādhi, wherein thoughts and perceptions do not so readily calm themselves. If thoughts and perceptions fail to arise or become elaborated, he suggests bringing forth a little distraction in order to generate them (TN, p. 372).

In this samādhi state the practitioner focuses moment by moment upon the arising mental content and lets it become somewhat elaborated. For example, if a thought arises, it is allowed to become elaborated until it becomes intense *(ngar;* TN, p. 661). If a specific perceptual event occurs, the sight or sound is allowed to manifest its various shapes or patterns. The terms *'char tshul* ("arising-way" TN, p. 372) and *snang tshul* ("appearing-way" TN, p. 367) are used when a given thought or perception occurs. Either way, the practitioner views whatever has arisen *(shar ba)* nakedly. Table 27 summarizes.

TABLE 27: DOMINANT PERSPECTIVE IN THE
EMPTINESS-OF-PHENOMENA MEDITATION

	Appearing-Way	Arising-Way
Dominant Event-Perspective (Aspects)	Perception	Thought
	Outer appearance (round, square)	Elaboration
	Pattern (earth, stone, mountain)	Intensity
	Color	
	Form	
Subsidiary Mind-Perspective (Mind-itself)	Basis to the staying	

As before, the practitioner examines each discrete event, moment by moment, using the transformable mental factors *(brtag dpyad)*. The instructions are as follows:

First, put in order cognition. Practice as usual with the body points and so forth. Now, nonrecognition is practiced from the [event-]perspective of the clear instead of the empty mind. Set up the samādhi, moment by moment, without the slightest bit of distraction. From this perspective, very intense coarse-level cognitions (such as aversion) may happen to have arisen or will arise, and after that become very intense. If you let them arise just the way they are, you only look at these nakedly. So conduct the examination and analysis as you did before according to the stages so that the meditation will ripen. Examine [generally] what comes forth seemingly as form and color as to whether or not it has any basis to the staying or basis that supports it. Then analyze [more specifically] the cause of recognition of any [seeming] entity and its aspects.

Now, when no cognition arises, you won't have any object upon which to conduct the examination and analysis. So think about the harm your enemies have brought you and let yourself become a little distracted. Examine the thoughts of hatred that are thereby generated. In the same way examine all coarse-level cognitions. For example, examine thoughts of attachment to desired sense objects. Likewise, examine the subtle cognitions that also happen to arise or have arisen by the very examinations you just did on coarse- and subtle-level cognitions. All these [categories]— form and color, basis to the staying and basis that supports—are understood to be nonexistent *[yin par med]*. (TN, pp. 371–72)

The objective of the meditation is to "search for the entity of appearance [moment by moment]" (TN, p. 368). Using negation instructions, the practitioner does not grasp *(ma 'dzin)* or does not recognize *(mi ngo bzhung)* appearance as self-existent in whatever arises or has arisen.

(2). Bringing Forth Special Insight in the Samādhi Meditation by Being Assured

As the examination continues over many sessions, the practitioner enters a second phase of the samādhi meditation called *the meditation to become assured* (*'phrug tshul;* TN, p. 373). The term is meant to convey the exhaustive, thorough nature of the inquiry. Over and against the great power of karmic propensities to perceive the world dualistically, the practitioner carries on with the analysis until reaching a point of assurance, when genuine insight dawns. This is called *the special insight of nonrecognition.*

The technical expression used to describe full assurance is called *unobstructed* (*ma 'gag pa;* TN, p. 372). This means letting whatever has arisen (*gang shar*) occur in its own way without interfering with it. The practitioner need not act to artificially produce mental content of any kind nor to create any subject-object distinction. Thoughts just happen (*'dug pa*). Emotions just happen. Perceptions just happen. Colors, forms, attributes, and patterns are essentially non self-existent (*yin par med;* TN, p. 372). Whatever the content, the practitioner becomes assured of its real-nature as ultimately empty. Though no self-existent thing occurs, nevertheless something occurs. What occurs is likened to an illusion. Gen Lamrimpa defines illusion-like perception as "the awareness of the *appearance* of the phenomenon, and…an awareness that despite appearances, the phenomenon does not truly exist."[475] So that nonrecognition isn't confused with the nihilistic view of cessation, terms such as *unobstructed* are used to imply that something does occur. The practitioner becomes assured of the natural mind's real way of arising and real way of appearing.

Tashi Namgyel continues his instructions:

> Now, because you haven't yet cut off doubt about cognitions, you have to examine the seeming clarity in such a way as to not let either the potential arising of perceptions to cease or the potential arising of any thoughts to cease or get eradicated. It is necessary to gain experience about this and above all to become assured. Don't generate the activity of [negative] thought in such a way as to hold things as being real, because they aren't at all like the above [valid] cognition [of emptiness]. The [direct] experience you'll have is difficult to describe. It is called recognition of the [real] entity. When assurance [ripens], you'll thereby put in order the cognitions through the [direct] experience that comes forth. After that you must protect what has come forth without distraction, that is, protect the seeming clarity and nonrecognition of whatever coarse- or subtle-level cognitions have arisen. (TN, pp. 372–73)

Events spontaneously occur because of the accumulation of karmic propensities, causing the mind to manifest events within the unfolding·

mental continuum. When they occur, they are essentially the mind-as-appearance expressing itself moment by moment (TN, p. 367). Tashi Namgyel defines *clarity* by saying, "The mind's clarity is merely one's own experience as it is arising" (TN, p. 411). Whatever arises shines forth and reflects the mind's real-nature. Tashi Namgyel uses the metaphor of clear light to capture something of the nature of clarity. Light is intangible. It does not have material substance. It is nowhere existent but is all-pervasive (TN, p. 408). Yet light seems to spread (TN, p. 403). It seems to arise or emanate. Likewise, the natural mind's way of arising shines forth, but what shines forth is neither real nor self-existent, yet seems to arise as various *(sna tshogs)*.

Tashi Namgyel summarizes the arising-way as follows:

> Moment by moment in your experience the mind's aspects, which were [once] nowhere certain, now arise as various without ceasing. They arise [spontaneously] by the power of infinite propensities. They arise "like true objects" *[don ltar]* but are not real external objects. So appearance-as-such occurs, and is thought about as arising by the activity of the propensities according to certain causes and conditions. Just as dye changes [the color of] wool but the wool's essence does not change, likewise the aspects become various but their real-nature, clear light, does not. (TN, p. 417)

The clear-light metaphor needs some qualification. Mind-as-appearance or appearance-as-such, unlike light, has the capacity to know itself, which is why the technical term *clarity-itself* or *self-illumination(rang gsal)* is used. Genuine clarity occurs only when the mind's events are unobstructed.

Assurance occurs when seeming clarity *(gsal bzhin)* ripens into the full experience of clarity *(gsal)* with continued practice. Each moment of arising becomes another occasion to directly experience the natural mind's clear light.

(3). The Outcome: Putting in Order Clarity

In the concluding part of the meditation the practitioner deepens the understanding of the arising-way so as to experience a fundamental change, namely putting in order cognition and perception (TN, p. 363). Here again a rearrangement occurs in the mental continuum. This change of view is expressed in the term *nonrecognition (mi ngo bzhung)*. Thought still arises, but the practitioner "no longer generates the activity of [false] conceptualization, which holds things to be real" (TN, p. 373). Any obscuration to understanding the arising-way lifts. There are no distinctions between what appears and what observes the appearance:

> Because you have put in order the grasping mind, objects that were [held to be real] become self-liberation after that. So the examination that you should do in this text is primarily an examination of knowing the appearer.
>
> Thus examine the mind accordingly from the perspective of clarity and emptiness, this mind wherein potential arising perceptions do not cease, become clear, and then become calm. Enter the proper samādhi and calm the mind's potential arising and also any tendency to hold on to [false] concepts. Then you must examine and analyze appearance—in every single appearance, when the various appearances happen to come forth—so that you don't mistake the appearance and the appearer. In short, when all of the various aspects of appearance do not cease, then the mind-as-appearer comes forth as empty, without a [false] nature. This is nonrecognition. (TN, p. 375)

Tashi Namgyel encourages the practitioner to become familiar with the new point of view by doing the meditation again and again. Sounds, tastes, fragrances, and sensations are to be nonrecognized as empty in the same way as sights are known (TN, p. 375). If a moment of perception comes forth in a vague or indiscrete manner, the practitioner learns to adjust the level of samādhi. Successful mastery of nonrecognition is followed by protecting the gains (TN, p. 376).

B. Attaining the View by a Condensed Form of Instruction

Tashi Namgyel presents a set of careful, systematic instructions for directly experiencing emptiness in stages *(rim gyis)*, beginning with emptiness of the person, and ending with emptiness of phenomena. Both exercises conclude with a fundamental rearrangement of the mental continuum. The advantage of the stage presentation is that it leads to clear comprehension of a complicated meditation. The disadvantage is that the stage model may encourage a dualistic view.

Few root texts follow that format. The root texts do not encourage such dualism. They combine or mix *('dres ba)* the emptiness-of-the-person and emptiness-of-phenomena meditations into a single exercise. Below are two such examples of mixed instructions. In the first, Pema Karpo uses the terms *staying* and *moving (gnas dang 'gyu)* to refer to the concomitant perspectives inherent in each moment of arising. *Moving,* in this case, refers only to subtle-level cognition. Pema Karpo recommends a different level of samādhi than does Tashi Namgyel to bring forth the same insight. In each discrete mind-moment the practitioner experiences the concomitant perspectives of staying-awareness and moving events. The practitioner searches for the mind-as-entity in the staying-awareness concomitant to developing assurance of nonrecognition of the movement. The outcome is realization of the "nonduality of viewer and viewed" (PK, f. 9b). To ensure proper understanding, the instructions end with the famous fuel-and-fire metaphor to protect against false duality:

> Let the awakened wisdom, which comes forth from staying-calm practice in a nonconceptual still state, examine each and every moment. Then [specifically] analyze as follows:
>
> > When staying, what thing stays?
> > How does it stay?
> > How does it move from staying?
> > When moving, has it been distracted from staying or does it move while still staying?
> > Is what moves different from what stays, or is it not?
> > What is the thing that is moving?
> > Finally, how does moving become staying?
>
> Now, since movement is found to be none other than staying, and staying none other than moving, you won't find any thing [either] staying or moving. Examine this with the eyes of awareness-itself and you won't find any [entity] as such, and you'll understand that which is viewed and that which is doing

the viewing as indistinguishable *[blta bya lta byed dphyer med]*. Because you can't find any entity of these, this view is beyond all ideas, beyond all philosophizing. The Lord of the Conquerors said,

> Views based upon what has been heard, however noble, are
>   eradicated.
> This view beyond ideas cannot be given a name.
> The truth found when that which is to be viewed and that
>   which is doing the viewing are indistinguishable.
> It comes from the lama's kindness.

Śāntideva gives the means to conduct this examination:

> In a stable samādhi,
> not going astray for a single moment,
> Examine your own mind.
> Examine each and every moment of the mind accordingly.

In the *Sūtra of Kāśyapa's Questioning* it says:

> Fire comes from rubbing two sticks together…[as before].
> (PK, f. 8b–9b)

The reader now familiar with Tashi Namgyel's four stages of the respective emptiness-of-the-person and emptiness-of-phenomena meditations should find these root instructions fairly straightforward. They constitute a samādhi meditation held at the nonconceptual level. In short, the instructions require the practitioner to find any seemingly self-existent entity of moving and staying, from both the event- and the mind-perspective simultaneously. No such thing is found. Duality is eradicated. That viewed and that doing the viewing become the same. Because of the impossibility of attaining this realization at a conceptual level, Pema Karpo says that it only comes about through the cumulative effect of the lama's empowerment and subsequent meditation conducted through "the eyes of awareness-itself."

Jampel Pawo's commentary on the root text underscores how staying/calm practice and special-insight practice are combined in the same meditation. Whereas Pema Karpo explains how to set up the samādhi meditation, Jampel Pawo explains the outcome in greater detail. He discusses how the mind's natural condition of awareness-itself shines forth once false notions have been eradicated:

> In consideration of this, Āryadeva says, "If you want to know whatever is blissful, [ask yourself] what is awareness? Indeed, the mind makes awareness, but there can't be any defilement of knower and known because it has no [false] nature." (JP, f. 64b)

In one respect the outcome is described in terms of purification of all false cenceptualizations. They become relatively calm:

> Through special insight you purify the entire mass of [false] conceptualizations, clinging to duality, and this leads to certainty. This is how they became relatively calm. (JP, f. 64b)

He concludes with an explanation of *relative calm:*

> Most sentient beings are permanently trapped, but you with a nonconceptual state become free by mastering whatever [valid] concept [of emptiness] turns back [the rest of false] concepts as the fruition of thorough analysis. (JP, f. 65b)

In short, conceptualization does not exactly cease. Only invalid or false conceptualization ceases. More accurately, concepts are purified of their false or erroneous aspects.

Rangjung Dorjé's root instruction is also a combined instruction based on an analysis of the six sense systems:

Fourth Unit of Practice:

Now, here's what is pointed out in order to generate special insight. Tilopa once said,

> "Behold this! The awakened wisdom of awareness-itself that is beyond words, has no sphere of activity, and cannot be taught even by Tilopa."

You should know whatever has been set forth in-and-by-itself in a nonconceptual state, from the perspective of staying and clarity. Concentrate on the truth of that passage, and then examine the six sense perceivers and any elaboration about them. Examine as follows:

> Where do [elaborated] concepts about appearing external
>   objects come from?
> Are the sights, sounds, tastes, smells, and sensations
>   generated by the aspects of these phenomena?
> Do they arise from the eye, ear, tongue, nose, and body?
> When so examined, no [false] concepts arise about any
>   of these.

Resolve the [examination of] sense objects and the five main sense faculties [with the experience of] clarity, nonconceptualization, and nonentityness. Now examine the five sense perceivers—consciousness of the eye apprehending its form; consciousness of the ear apprehending its sound; of the tongue, its taste; of the nose, its smell; and of the body, its sensations. When you find these not supported by the [respective] sense objects and sense faculties, then whatever appears even for the moment comes forth in clarity, nonconceptualization, and nonentityness, and you will cut off the root, which is the sixth sense perceiver, the mind only.

Now to see that the mind that directs itself toward things and the five sense perceivers are the same, you must remain in clarity and in a nonconceptual state for longer than a moment.

[After a while you] become assured about the real-entity *[rang ngo]* of the sixth sense perceiver [the mind]. A moment of consciousness arises, then ceases. Yet, what seems to arise is always there. Since whatever appears becomes clear as it appears in the present moment, you don't cast aside relative truth. Furthermore, such clarity is not artificially produced when it becomes a form or color, because any self-agent seeming to do anything, even the sense faculties themselves, does not exist alone. They are empty of any nature, and you don't cast aside absolute truth. It is best to consider whatever appears as both appearance and emptiness because they are indistinguishable. This and subsequent appearances become the vehicle of perfect enlightenment.

So try to understand Tilopa. This is called the awakened wisdom, awareness-itself gaining understanding in any mistake [that is, thought and perception] that comes forth, because it enables you to know the way the realized mind stays, which is perfect staying. Now, stupid people are ignorant about what has been directly pointed out. There is no locus of activity to the dualistic thoughts by which the ordinary mind becomes entangled. It can't really be taught to you unless you experience it for yourself. As it says in the *Dohās:*

Let water and oil come to clarity by themselves.
No self takes up or lets go of what arises and passes away.
    Yes! This is awareness-itself.
And so, it can't be taught in any substantial way.
So, don't be mistaken.

Also, in the *Prajñāpāramitā Saṃcayagāthā* it says,

Awareness-itself, unelaboration.
Empty when appearing; appearing when empty.
Emptiness and appearance are indistinguishable,
Like the moon reflected in water. So also,
Nonduality is put in order.

These scriptures, oral readings, and many others like them are sufficient to put in order [the mind], so long as the [real-nature of the] sixth, the mind-perceiver, has been pointed out and [then] you have [conducted your meditation] by placing the mind in [the state of] clarity and nonconceptualization. Then use awareness-itself to become familiar with its [seeming] entity until appearance and emptiness become indistinguishable. Then staying/calm practice and special-insight practice are generated [as a pair], through which you eradicate all the coarse-level emotions and enter into the true path. The ancient lamas [directly] point out this [truth when saying], "See the mind's entity." The stages are as follows:

> By means of special-insight practice combined with the best
>   of staying/calm, the complete eradication of negative
>   emotional states can be known.
> First find staying/calm practice.
> The fruit, direct understanding, comes forth when you give
>   up attachment to the words [of the saying, and meditate
>   on it instead].

So, these sayings teach you directly. (RD, pp. 7–9)

As the root text indicates, it is possible to use a single class of mental content, in this case, sense perception, as the medium to realize emptiness. In each moment of appearance, moment by moment, the three components of each sense system are examined and found to be without any self-existent thing. They are simply aspects of an interdependent process. For example, when seeing a form with the eyes, consciousness of that form has no support beyond the interdependence of the components of the sense system. A new technical term is introduced, *spyod yul,* which means "locus of activity." No sphere or locus can be found that generates this interdependent process. The term *locus of activity* is to the sense systems what the term *entity* is to the mind. Just as the meditative search does not discover an entity within the mind, so also it does not yield a locus of activity for the five main sense systems. There is only emptiness. Yet perceptual content continues to arise. Following direct experience of emptiness, it now arises free from the habit of making false conceptual elaborations, and it arises in clarity. Rangjung Dorjé describes the results using three terms to depict the natural mind's condition—*clarity, nonconceptualization,* and *nonentityness.* Appearance and emptiness shine forth as two concomitant but nondual perspectives in the same discrete moment of perception, as if the moon were being reflected in water. The nonentityness of the ordinary perception's locus of activity has been likened to that of a mirror.[476]

These three forms of instruction are all means for understanding the two truths, no matter what perspective or what content is used at the moment to generate special insight. The mind is brought to its own realization in many ways. The message of the root texts is the stark appreciation of the interdependence of mind and its events moment by moment. The metaphor of fuel and fire is enormously instructive in this regard. One stick—mind—when rubbed against the other—appearance—ignites the fire of special insight that grows into awakened wisdom, wherein the seeming thingness of both are consumed. The practitioner has fundamentally reorganized the mental continuum so that emptiness and clarity shine forth in direct experience, without any false concepts about them. Events still occur, moment by moment, but are unobstructed. The practitioner is now in a position to wonder about how these events occur at all. This is the topic of the next set of meditations.

II. The Skill of Recognition

As a result of putting in order the view, neither the mind nor its events are taken to be self-existent entities. Nevertheless the practitioner is still able to recognize *(ngo bzhung)* that something happens *('byung ba)* and that events seem to arise as various *(sna tshogs)*. Now the practitioner shifts awareness away from the search for entities and toward events as they immediately occur. Tashi Namgyel calls the new stage of special-insight practice "skill, cutting off doubt," and Jampel Pawo calls it "recognition" or "reverse meditation." I have combined these into the single term *skill of recognition*.[477]

Putting in order the view does not eradicate the great number of karmic propensities that have accumulated over aeons of rebirths. These propensities inevitably ripen according to the doctrine of cause and effect. The flow of the events in the mental continuum is the manifestation of these ripening propensities. The practitioner must allow the mental continuum to unfold naturally, and with each event he or she must come to the same realization about emptiness and clarity and their nonduality. This is the only way to cut off doubt *(sgro 'dogs bcod;* TN, p. 377). The phrase *cut off doubt* means that the practitioner becomes convinced about the same truth with respect to any mental event—past, present, or future. After that an even more fundamental rearrangement of the mental continuum occurs, which is expressed by the term *ma skye,* meaning "unborn" or "always here." Both realizations—cutting off doubt and always here—come from continual meditation experience subsequent to putting in order this view.

Now the meditator focuses on whatever happens to arise or to have arisen *(shar ba'am' char do bcug nas).* As an event arises, the practitioner specifically analyzes how it happens to occur, and also why successive events are various. The meditation presumes a previous intellectual understanding *(go ba)* of the doctrine of cause and effect. In short, each discrete event arises in accordance with particular causes and conditions. Apart from these causes and conditions, no self-existent entity—whether person or phenomenon—exists. Tashi Namgyel explains:

> Now, as the emptiness and appearance of staying and moving [respectively] seem to have the mind's same [real] nature, what are the causes of and conditions for each and every arising [event]? Because of the dependent origination *[brten 'brel]* of the breath (causing appearances to arise) and the three [parts of the sense systems] (object, organ, and sense perceiver), various events arise as a support from the sense doors *['char 'sgo]*. They occur from the actions of residual propensities and their immediate ripening. The actions of conflicting emotions occur likewise. (TN, pp. 384–85)

Drawing from the early mahāmudrā source material, Tashi Namgyel explains the passage using a seaweed metaphor:

> Seaweed in an ocean does not have any "mind," yet its branches appear to move. What moves them? The currents of the ocean. Likewise, what is called mind, though not a thing, appears to move. It arises as various due to currents generated in the body, the breath, and the fluctuations of the mental continuum, all due to ripening propensities. (TN, p. 385)

The doctrines set forth in the above passage establish the relative existence *(kun rdzob)* of all phenomena as they arise. Most mahāmudrā teachings draw upon the Madhyamaka distinction between absolute *(don dam)* and relative *(kun rdzob)* truth.[478] In a relative sense, events arise as various in the mental continuum during meditation, and appear as various in everyday life. In an ultimate sense, all events are empty. Unless the relative existence of events is acknowledged, it is easy to fall into the extreme view of nihilism. The skill-of-recognition meditations pertain to the relative existence of events. However, the practitioner must keep emptiness constantly in view during the practice. As Tashi Namgyel states, the meditation must be done "from the perspective of the clear and empty mind" (TN, p. 378).

Skill of recognition, as a special-insight exercise, bears some resemblance to the skill of representation of the staying/calm series. At that stage of concentration the practitioner, after intensifying focus on a single seed *(thig le)*, eases up and recognizes the various events as the seed emanates. Whatever happens to emanate is viewed in such a way that it brings forth clarity. The current special-insight exercise has the same structure. After an exhaustive search for the mind's entityness the practitioner eases up on this search and views whatever happens to arise with (special insightful) clarity.

The phrase "whatever happens to arise or has arisen *[shar ba 'am 'char du bcug nas]* "[479] implies a more relaxed stance. The perfect form of the verb *'jug pa* (perfect, *bcug pa*), "to take place; to happen; or to enter," is added to the verb *char ba*, "to arise, emanate," thus making a causative verb-form, "cause to arise." In this context causes from the remote past established as propensities ripen and are experienced as effects in the immediate present, as observed in the unfolding mental continuum. The translation "happens to arise" captures the immediacy of the event, though losing the precise verb structure. In any case, the phrase suggests allowing awareness to go whatever way it will, according to its own karmic conditioning. Though there is consensus on the use of the phrase "whatever happens to arise," different authors use other technical phrases to illustrate an eased-up perspective: "not abandon" *(ma spang;* PK, f. 9b), "not abandon nor take up" *(spang blang;* JP, f. 69b; TN, p. 384), and "neither prevent nor make happen" *(dgag sgrub;* TN, p. 384). Wangchug Dorjé uses "eased up" *(lhod;* WD, p. 66). Here are Pema Karpo's root instructions:

> In that you neither abandon *[ma spang]* nor let yourself be influenced by *[de' dbang du mi bstang ba]* thoughts or emotions as they are born, you establish whatever has arisen *[gcug shar]* without artificial construction. You therefore recognize *[ngo shes bar byas]* the concomitant [mind and appearance] as indistinguishable *[do gar]* at the very moment it is born *[skye ba'i skad cig]*. Not abandoning that, it is empty as it arises and becomes purified as it stays *[gnas]*. This is exactly how all the conditions *[rkyen]* [which have previously been] obstacles are carried along the path, and therefore the method is called "using the conditions that have previously been obstacles along the path." (PK, f. 9b–10a)

The instruction calls for a major shift in approach. The practitioner is to neither abandon nor be influenced by the content of the mind-as-it-arises. Without any reactivity the practitioner simply recognizes *(ngo shes)* whatever arises at the moment that it arises. Wangchug Dorjé uses the term *rang babs,* "settled into itself," to illustrate that the search for the correct view can ease up, because otherwise at a certain point the search itself becomes an obstacle. Similarly, Jampel Pawo uses the verb "to prevent" plus a negative (*mi' gogs par byed;* JP, f. 66a). "Not preventing whatever arises" means that the mental continuum is allowed to unfold in its own right. Tashi Namgyel describes the shift in instruction with two compounds. The former term, "neither prevent nor make happen" *(dgags grub med),* refers to artificial activity (or reactivity) at the subtle level immediately as an event arises. The latter term, "neither abandon nor take up" *(spang blang med),* refers to the resultant elaborated coarse-level mental content after it has arisen. Both compounds refer to artificial activity directed toward mental content at different levels of its elaboration. The terms convey that the practitioner must cease acting upon or reacting to mental events in any way. The only permissible action, which is really nonaction, is mere recognition *(ngo bzhung tsam),* moment by moment.

Stopping artificial action upon or reactivity to mental content insures that the ripening of past propensities moment by moment in the present mental continuum will not be contaminated by present actions or their propensities. One immediate result is a change in the way unfolding events are experienced. The phrase "unceasing signs" *(ma zin gyi rtags;* WD, p. 65) conveys that events seem to be experienced more rapidly and with greater clarity by a practitioner, who is able to look nakedly *(gcer gyis bltas ba;* JP, f. 65b) at the events-as-arising, moment by moment. The variety of arising events includes both subtle- and coarse-level cognitions and perceptions. In a brief meditation period the practitioner may experience a rapid turnover of many various discrete events: a thought, an instant of pain, a sound, a moment of impatience, an image, and so forth. The signs *(rtags)* of genuine skill practice *(rtsal sbyor;* RD, p. 9) are that moments of bodily pain seem more intense than before and perceptions flash with greater vividness. It is unnecessary to suppress whatever arises, because these events become very useful in deepening the direct experience of emptiness and clarity. As Pema Karpo says, "Skill means using previous obstacles as a vehicle to realization." The verb *'khyer ba* means "to ride along or be carried on." Special insight is inevitable as the practitioner simply lets awareness ride along *('khyer ba)* the unfolding mental continuum, moment by moment. Since what arises is unceasing *(ma 'gag pa),* there is unlimited potential to deepen direct insight.

At this stage of meditation the practitioner is likely to experience a series of shifts in the way events seem to arise and pass away in the mental continuum, as if the temporal organization of events itself were changing. Four such rearrangements occur in stages:

(1) Awareness of the initial phase of arising only. Mind-moments arise so rapidly that one appears to arise just as the previous one ceases. The practitioner is aware of only the moment events arise and is not aware of their duration or cessation. This awareness of the immediate arising is expressed in Pema Karpo's phrase "at the moment it is born," as well as in Tashi Namgyel's phrase "happens to arise."

(2) The tripartite unit of arising, staying, and ceasing *(byung, gnas, song)*. During the next stage the practitioner notices not only the initial moment of arising *(byung)* but also some discernible duration *(gnas;* literally, "staying") of the event, followed by its cessation *(song)*. The entire unit—arising, staying, ceasing—constitutes a single discrete mental event, irrespective of the category of mental content.

(3) At the next stage, the practitioner experiences another shift in temporal experience, characterized by awareness of only moment-by-moment arising and passing away *(skye 'gag)*. Mind-moments are experienced to be very short-lived without much discernible duration. They arise and pass very quickly. Tashi Namgyel calls this stage "momentary arising" *(thol ba)*.

(4) During the final stage the practitioner comes to realize that the idea that discrete events arise and pass over time is itself a mere construct of the ordinary mind. All distinctions concerning the seeming temporal unfolding of mental events are found to be empty, and the practitioner develops a new realization of the mind's real nature as always here *(skye med)*.

The first three experienced rearrangements in the temporal unfolding of the mental events pertain to the skill exercises, while the fourth pertains to the subsequent yoga of unelaboration. Although the three parts of the skill meditation are said to be experienced in stages *(rim pa)*, this distinction is not always explicit since the actual root-text instructions are typically given in a combined form.[480]

Pema Karpo and Jampel Pawo's instructions emphasize immediate arising. Of the various types of mental content that might arise, Jampel Pawo recommends focusing on certain emotions and moments of attachment or aversion. These are meant only as examples because the entire range of mental formations can be used, as indicated by the generic term *rnam rtog,* "mental events."[481] Here are the actual instructions:

From the standpoint of samādhi, [subtle] cognitions—such as immediate attachment to or aversion toward something—happen to arise with both clarity and some intensity, which has some affinity to joy and happiness. When they have arisen like that, view them nakedly in their very way of appearing. You'll come to see fleeting moment after moment of these kinds of cognitions in emptiness and in clarity as you recognize these fleeting moments in their real-entityness, the emptiness of no thing whatsoever. Come to experience both thing and emptiness as indistinguishable—both moving and empty—so you don't generate any duality by mistaking [that which has arisen] as real. You'll see the real nature of simultaneously born cognition. Special-insight recognition is the recognition of whatever has arisen. Establish awareness and clarity and then examine the awareness in what arises as various, likewise the [kind of] clarity that doesn't prevent the aspects of these cognitions' arising-way.... The perspectives of both emptiness and recogniton are indistinguishable. Experiencing emptiness and moving, and nonmoving and emptiness, is seeing the simultaneous-born, the real-nature of cognition. Consider water and waves. When water arises as waves, the very water in question does not become other than water. Being nothing other than water even though it has arisen, these thoughts likewise do not become other than their real-nature [when arisen]. After concluding the [previous] meditation on emptiness, these now arise as mere aspects of thought through the interdependence of certain causes and conditions. (JP, f. 65b–66b)

The practitioner turns awareness to events, which happen to arise. As the practitioner refrains from artificially acting upon them in any way, being especially careful not to prevent them from arising, these events arise with clarity and seem to ride along by their own intensity *(nar dag bcar)*. Certain signs, such as joy *(dga)* or happiness *(skyid pa)*, indicate successful practice. In defining recognition *(ngo bzung)*, Jampel Pawo begins with an explanation of how mental events are experienced temporally. They are "viewed nakedly in their very way of appearing." The practitioner becomes aware of the exact moment of arising of a given mental event but is not generally aware of its duration beyond that point. As a result the practitioner is aware of the seeming proliferation of immediately arising moments, as Jampel Pawo illustrates using the distributive form *cha na gru ma cag gru ma,* "fleeting moment after fleeting moment."

This initial moment of arising is experienced from two nondual yet concomitant perspectives—emptiness and clarity. Although the practitioner experiences the temporal nature of arising moments differently in the current exercise, the special insight about emptiness and clarity is the same as in the previous emptiness meditations. To illustrate the more developed realization of emptiness, the term *mere aspects (mtsan tsam)* is used. To emphasize the growth of special insight, several additional new terms are introduced. The terms *simultaneous-born (lhan skyes)* and *concomitance (do mar)* signify that awareness of each mental event carries two nondual perspectives, as illustrated in Table 28:

TABLE 28: THE RIPENING OF NONDUAL SPECIAL INSIGHT DURING SKILL SAMĀDHI

Perspective	Moving (immediate)	Staying
Insight	Recognition of real-entity	Seeing real-entity
Benefit	Clarity	Emptiness

Although the practitioner still becomes aware of each mental event from one of two perspectives, there is no duality. Therefore Jampel Pawo introduces the term *mi phyod pa* ("indistinguishable"; JP, f. 65b). To insure that no mistake is made, he adds the term *rang ngo bo* (literally, "thing-itself" or in this context, "the same entity," a synonym for *simultaneous-born*). To illustrate the seeming paradox, Jampel Pawo draws upon a famous metaphor from the oral tradition, water and waves. Both are the same entity yet appear in different ways at the same time—as a body of resting water and as waves. Each wave also seems different from the previous wave. Likewise the mind at once stays at rest and arises as various subtle and coarse movements. Yet both conditions are the same (empty) thing.

Tashi Namgyel's instructions emphasize the tripartite unit of a discrete mental event—arising, staying, and ceasing.[482] He focuses on a later stage in the awareness of the temporality of mental events, wherein the practitioner is able to discern beyond the immediately arising moment and more carefully notice the entire duration of any mental event—from its arising, staying, and ceasing—before the next discrete event is noticed in the same way.

Tashi Namgyel distinguishes the skill meditation from previous meditations used to put in order the correct view:

> Now, what is the difference between this [set of exercises] and putting in order thoughts and appearances? The previous examinations analyzed form, color, and so on to find the entity of thought or perception, only to find them to be without a [real, self-existing] nature. The current examination analyzes the three [temporal moments] (arising, staying, ceasing) of these thoughts and appearances, only to find them to be indistinguishable from the mind's entity. You must analyze each and every mental event *[so sor zhib tu]* with precision, as explained here and elsewhere. (TN, p. 377)

The instructions call for a shift in awareness away from searching for an entity in mental content, toward a more precise analysis of the very process of arising of this content, in the form of each discrete temporal unit (arising, staying, ceasing). Table 29 illustrates the difference between the previous emptiness meditation and the current skill meditation, and also the difference between Jampel Pawo's and Tashi Namgyel's instructions:

Table 29: A Comparison of How Tashi Namgyel and Jampel Pawo Illustrate the Differences Between Special Insight and Skilled Special Insight

	Concomitant Arising-way = Way the realized mind stays
Jampel Pawo	Movement (immediate arising only) = Emptiness
Tashi Namgyel	Movement (arising, staying, ceasing) = Real-entity of mind

Of the various types of mental events Tashi Namgyel selects two—thought and perception—and repeats the instructions for each separately. Here are the instructions for thought:

> Now, first resolve thoughts to be mind. This samādhi is done from the perspective of [both] the mind's clarity and emptiness whenever thoughts or emotions, such as anger, are just arising

or have arisen. It is done by analyzing the tripartite unit (arising, staying, and ceasing) of this [event]. Begin by examining (1) that which is arising for any basis to, or cause of, that thought. Consider whether it arises from taking another thought as its basis of arising [from the event-perspective] or whether it arises from the mind [from the mind-perspective].... After that try to find (2) what stays in the same way. Consider whether you can find some other way to its staying or whether the staying arises as an aspect of the thought of hatred itself.... Finally, examine the (3) cessation as such. Consider whether you might find any basis to where it goes or whether where it goes lacks any substance.... Practicing this way, precisely examine and analyze all other coarse and subtle cognitions.... By examining as if [the entity were something different] you won't find this to be your [actual] experience of the tripartite unit (arising, staying, ceasing). All concepts based on duality and any false conceptualization about a mind/body split, the body's inside/outside as different, or the body and limbs as different will be experienced as clarity and emptiness. You won't recognize any entity. You can also know the mind and its events as indistinguishable, like water and waves. (TN, pp. 377–79)

As the passage illustrates, this exercise deepens special insight into nonduality. The term *indistinguishable* and the metaphor "water and waves" depict the natural mind-as-arising, then elaborated as thought content. The mind's thoughts seem various because of the natural mind's own skill *(rang rtsal)*.

The instructions for perception are as follows:

Next, resolve perceptions to be mind: This is done from the perspective of the same samādhi state. Along this path you can use whatever suitable aspects happen to arise in clarity, such as a visual form, and so on, but it is especially important to examine the tripartite unit as above (arising, staying, ceasing). Examine whether the visual form and the mind come forth as different or identical. If seeming different, examine whether these seem to be opposites or seem the same inside and out, above or below. Examine whether these are artificially produced as two separate entities, or whether the visual form is the mind coming forth as appearance-only. When you think that the visual form is the mind-as-appearance-only, examine whether the mind is something artificially produced as a seemingly different [entity], as if by something other than the activity of this very same mind. If the visual form and the mind seem the same, examine precisely whether the mind is the same because it has become the visual form or whether the visual form is the same because it has become the mind. After practicing this way, examine all other coarse and subtle perceptions, for example, sounds, smells, and so forth, [primarily using] opposite perceptions such as beautiful and ugly or familiar and unfamiliar. The beginner who has examined the aspects of both such [opposite] perceptions, in the final analysis, examines whether each has a different entity so as to be either beautiful or ugly. If these perceptions and mind seem different, examine whether these seem to be opposites or seem the same inside and out, above or below. If you don't examine them like this, you'll hold on to duality. Then, you'll experience all the various perceptions[483] (and their aspects, too, such as visual forms), as appearance and emptiness, without any recognizable entity. You must come to know mind and perception as indistinguishable, like the mind of the dreamer and the dream's appearances. (TN, pp. 380–83)

The same special insight is experienced as with the examination of thoughts. A new metaphor is used, also from the early mahāmudrā source material—dream and dreamer:

Just as dream content is not thought to be different from the dreamer who creates it, so also appearances are not different from mind. They *are* the very mind as it emanates. (TN, p. 382)

Table 30 illustrates the respective metaphors used for skilled special insight of thought and perception:

TABLE 30: CORRELATION OF METAPHORS WITH THE NONDUAL PERSPECTIVES OF SKILLED SPECIAL INSIGHT

Event-perspective:	Mind-perspective:
Way of arising or Way of appearing	Staying
1. Cognition (arising, staying, ceasing)	Mind
Waves	Water
2. Perception (arising, staying, ceasing)	Mind
Dream content	Dreamer

At a later stage the practitioner's awareness of the temporal nature of mental events undergoes another rearrangement, so as to become aware of only the moment-by-moment arising and passing away of mental events, without any sensed duration of these events. Mental events at this stage seem so short-lived that it is no longer possible to discern the tripartite unit (arising, staying, ceasing). Tashi Namgyel calls this practice "cutting off the root of the moving/staying mind" because only at this advanced stage does the practitioner become completely certain about the same special insight—clarity and emptiness—in every single event of the mental continuum.

The instructions are as follows:

> From the standpoint of a nonconceptual samādhi, with the mind in clarity and emptiness as before, look nakedly, concomitantly, with awakened wisdom to examine what stays each and every moment. First see through this to examine if the tripartite unit (arising, staying, and ceasing) [has any entity] as before. Then examine any available thought that happens to move, seeming to suddenly come forth. You find neither any entity nor cause of recognition in either the tripartite unit or the [immediate movement], even though in that state the concomitant perspectives of staying and appearance (wherein movement seems to suddenly come forth) seem to be different. Examine what seems to be different in both of these as you did previously—whether they are with or without a cause of recognition, are empty or not empty, are good or bad—until they

cannot be found to be different. When your manner of inquiry discovers that there is no difference nor any distinction whatsoever, nevertheless you should examine whether the staying and movement are no different because they are [genuinely] the same, or no different because they are [really] different but [seem] identical. If you think they are the same, examine whether they are the same during the beginning, middle, and end [of any discretely arising event]. If different but [seeming] identical, examine precisely how they could at all be identical. These are errors caused by taking or holding staying and moving in the mental continuum as different from each other. Staying and moving are not to be taken as a duality. All the various thoughts that have arisen and the mind [which stays upon each of these] are one and the same. When you examine them accordingly, you'll experience them as one taste. This is called "awareness-itself of whatever moving aspects arise so as to be not recognized [as entities]." You'll know the self-skill of the mind through the metaphors of water and waves, or the sun and its rays. (TN, pp. 383–84)

The meditation is very much like that of arising, staying, and ceasing, only the duration of the temporal process has shifted. Table 31 illustrates the transition to the arising-and-passing-away samādhi:

TABLE 31: A COMPARISON OF SHIFTS IN THE DURATION OF TEMPORAL PROCESS

	Simultaneous Perspectives	
Previous	Movement (arising, staying, ceasing)	Staying
Current	Movement (suddenly coming forth, then passing)	Staying

Tashi Namgyel introduces the phrase "happens to move, seeming to suddenly come forth" (*rtog na cig thol gyis 'gyu ru bcug nas;* TN, p. 383). The perfect form of *thol ba,* "to come forth," is used. When used in conjunction with the verb "to be" *(thul byug),* or in this case with the verb structure "happen to move," the verb takes on the added meaning of "immediacy or suddenness." Other similar terms used are *momentariness* (*glo bur;* JP, f. 68a), *immediate mind* (*ma thag yid;* RD, p. 1), and the arising and passing away (*skye 'gag;* JP, f. 67a) of mental events.[484] A line from the mahāmudrā source material states:

> "Unarisen, arises; arisen, ceases. From what's always here, all arises." (JP, f. 67a)

These terms are meant to convey the extent to which the practitioner has become acutely aware of the immediacy of events at their exact moment of arising. The practitioner is also aware of the very short duration of these mental events. The practitioner senses not only the immediacy of events but also their impermanence.

This set of meditations—from the initial phase of arising to the current arising-and-passing-away examination—results in being able to "cast off doubt" regarding the nonduality of clarity and emptiness in any possible mental event. The concomitant perspectives on any given mental event—a happening that moves, and a mind that stays to recognize this movement—are simultaneously born yet indistinguishable, because ultimately both are found to be the same nonentity.[485]

These complex dialectical instructions are designed to facilitate realization of "sameness" of what "appears to be different" (TN, p. 387). For example, Jampel Pawo comments as follows:

> These are a pair—staying/calm and special-insight practice—wherein mind, whose nature is emptiness, and emptiness, whose aspects are mind, are in short, indistinguishable as mind/emptiness or as emptiness/mind. So the thoughts have arisen and are set free as the dharmakāya. (JP, f. 66b)

The juxtaposition and interchange of the mind- and event-perspectives in the passage uses the written or spoken form of instruction itself to illustrate the desired realization, in a manner comparable to metaphors such as water and waves.

Another important term is *one taste,* a term that will have great significance in more advanced stages of practice. *One taste* is an allusion to the dawning realization of sameness or equanimity (*snyoms ba*) of all mental events. There are a number of stages that deepen the special insight into the equanimity of all events. Skill practice is brought to completion when the practitioner begins to realize the equanimity of each and every arising-and-passing-away moment.

At some point the practitioner begins to realize that this special insight is generalizable to all past and future events, which comprise the mental continuum. This dawning realization is called *grasping the mental continuum (rgyun 'dzin pa)*. At this point the practitioner directly generates certain knowledge (*nges shes;* TN, pp. 384 and 685), and has finally "cut off doubt" (WD, p. 83). Truth is certain because it is discovered in the immediacy of directly experienced events within the mental continuum. The verb most often used in conjunction with the skill exercises is *resolving (thag bcad pa),* which means either "to sever or disconnect" or "to resolve or become certain about." The practitioner resolves once and for all the same truth in each mind-moment of the unfolding continuum, and at the same time severs all ties with erroneous views henceforth.[486]

Tashi Namgyel and Jampel Pawo give a detailed explanation of the outcome. Here are Pema Karpo's root instructions:

> Because all these thoughts become liberated *[grol]* by their mere recognition *[rang gyis ngo shes pa tsam],* this is the understanding in which that which is to be abandoned and its remedy are indistinguishable. This is called reverse meditation *[bzlog pa'i sgom pa],* the heart of the tantra path experience. From this, great compassion is generated toward all those sentient beings who do not understand the nature of their own mind. There are lots of practices, such as the stages of generation of body, speech, and mind, for the benefit of all sentient beings, but practicing special insight leads to powerful purification of any flaw with respect to the truth, as if being unaffected by poison [charmed by] a mantra. Being familiar with such experience is called "not abandoning or taking up *[spang blang]* whatever arises on the path." (PK, f. 10a–10b)

The practitioner does not artificially act upon the arising mental events. These events need not be abandoned nor taken up once elaborated on the coarse level, nor prevented or made to happen on the subtle level. One need only allow awareness to be carried along spontaneously. This is called *mere recognition by itself (rang gyis ngo shes pa tsam).* The instrumental *rang gyis,* "by itself," and the intensifier *tsam,* "mere," have been added to the verb "to recognize," a verb used throughout all the skill exercises. At this stage, recognition just happens. Jampel Pawo comments:

> Be aware of the sameness of these, and all the distinctions between such dichotomies as wisdom and means, and so forth become the same special insight [shes rab rkyan pal]. Apart from that there is only great error. So all thoughts and emotions through mere recognition by itself become self-liberated, when there is only not abandoning nor taking up whatever has arisen on the path. (JP, f. 69a–69b)

Special insight becomes automatic. Tremendous momentum builds as every arising mind-moment carries the same truth.

A new term, *self-liberated (rang grol)*, is introduced. It contains the perfect form of *grol ba*, "to became liberated or set free," and the preverb *rang*, "by itself." Another term, *understanding (rtogs pa)*, is used. The practitioner's experience ripens into full understanding as special insight proliferates.[487] Jampel Pawo draws upon a metaphor from the mahāmudrā source material—"like a forest fire"—to illustrate how rapidly special insight grows. Every mental event shines forth with the same special insight immediately as it arises, and in this sense every mental event effects its own liberation.

Certain signs *(rtags)* indicate the dawning of certain truth. Clear light *(od gsal)* is the most common indicator (JP, f. 67b). At its very moment of arising any given mental event shines forth like clear light. As mental events now arise and pass away very quickly, the mental continuum is experienced as great light itself *(rang grol)*.

The mental formations themselves become the vehicle of special insight. In all previous meditations of the staying/calm and special-insight meditations, arising mental events were viewed as obscurations to special insight. At this stage the very same mental events become the vehicle of special insight. This radical shift in viewpoint is called *reverse meditation* (*bzlog pa'i bsgom pa*; PK, f. 10a).

Jampel Pawo calls the outcome of reverse meditation *the cognition Dharma body (rtog pa'i chos sku)* to emphasize that a fundamental transformation has taken place by which the ordinary events in the mental continuum become transformed into the natural condition of Buddha-mind. He defines *the cognition Dharma body* as follows:

It is the understanding wherein mistakes arise as awakened wisdom *['khrul na ye shes sor 'char ba]*. (JP, f. 66b)

As special insight deepens and ripens into wisdom, previous obstructions become useful, or as Pema Karpo says, "One uses the conditions [that have previously been obstacles] along the path." Emotions such as attachment and aversion generate special insight, as do erroneous concepts:

> Desire is said to be nirvāṇa; habit, hatred, and ignorance likewise. These very realizations are the very way the realized mind stays. There is no duality between realization and attachment. (TN, p. 679)

All mental events bring the same realization because ordinary consciousness *(rnam shes)* and awakened wisdom *(ye shes)* are understood to be one and the same. Therefore saṃsāra *('khor ba)* as it is experienced directly in the mental continuum and nirvāṇa *(mya ngam 'das pa)* are indistinguishable:

> There is little difference between what has the form of true wisdom (nirvāṇa) and saṃsāra's conceptualizations. What is called "saṃsāra" is also the very same as that called "nirvāṇa." These phenomena of saṃsāra—attachment and aversion—are nirvāṇa. (JP, f. 69b)

Ordinary mental events become very important as the real active producer *(sgrub byed)* of enlightenment. Jampel Pawo says, "Just as poison can be a remedy for poison, thought can serve as a remedy for thought" (JP, f. 69b). Likewise, "One can draw water from the ears with more water" (JP, f. 69b).

Jampel Pawo comments extensively upon reverse meditation in order to carefully distinguish the realization from what he calls "the other path" (JP, f. 69b). A fundamental difference between the Hīnayāna and Mahāyāna styles of meditation becomes evident at this point. In Hīnayāna meditation, the stage of arising and passing away is followed by dissolution *('gog pa;* Skt., *nirodha)*, which in this case means the moment-by-moment dissolution of all mental formations.[488] In the Mahāyāna system,[489] mental events need not and should not cease. What ceases is artificially acting upon them so as to prevent their spontaneously manifesting special insight. These events are not ceasing *(ma zin pa)* and not dissolved *('gags med pa)*. As they do not cease, the ordinary mind *(tha mal)* becomes the vehicle of awakened wisdom.

Skilled special insight concludes with a review of the possible errors *(ldog;* TN, p. 387) of misunderstanding the true nature of the mind. According to Jampel Pawo, the practitioner must protect the gains so that genuine understanding reflects "staying in the Dharma body" *(chos skur gnas)*. Understanding the real-nature of the mind stays, even though various formations continue to ripen at a rapid pace:

> The real-nature of thought stays in the Dharma body. As it now seems, some people doubt thought to be the Dharma body. They believe thought cannot become the real active producer *[sgrub byed]* of the Dharma body. Such practitioners do not prevent thought, yet still fail to correctly understand the ultimate nature of thought. Therefore no special insight comes. Other people don't understand staying in the Dharma body, the real-nature of thought. They look to understand it but doubt its value and so are ignorant. They expect some transformation to occur manifesting the Dharma body and the real-nature of thought, but they cut off thought from arising in the mental continuum. Although these practitioners know the difference between understanding and ignorance, they still prevent cognition and therefore won't come to realize the cognition Dharma body. Drawing an example from the oral readings, can the sun maintain the light without rays? [So also, can awakened wisdom come without thought?] (JP, f. 68b)

The two main errors are failing to understand but not preventing thoughts from occurring, and understanding but preventing thoughts from occurring. Tashi Namgyel adds two other types of errors made by those who do not prevent thought from occurring:[490]

> (1) Taking either one of the two perspectives—staying or moving—but not the other, (2) trying to take moving as staying and staying as moving, without practicing skill, which is the way to realize them as the same thing. (TN, p. 386)

Once free of these errors, the very content of the mind, its moment-by-moment formations, become the means to liberation. As Jampel Pawo says, "What binds us liberates us" (JP, f. 70a).

III. The Yoga of Unelaboration

Skillful recognition of the moment-by-moment arising and passing away of mental events, each carrying the same special insight, cuts off doubt and brings with it the certainty *(nges)* of understanding emptiness. Yet even with special insight ripening there is still a strong propensity to make distinctions, for example, the distinction that something either exists *(yod pa)* or does not exist *(med pa)*.[491] Mind-moments are also distinguished as one *(gcig)* or many *(tha dad)*. These conceptual distinctions are known as *the four extremes and the eight concepts*.[492]

Such distinctions—exist/not-exist; one/many—depend on a third, even more fundamental distinction, a temporal distinction. The fundamental problem of the yoga of unelaboration *(spros bral gyi rnal 'byor bsgom pa)* is the ordinary convention of time *(dus)*. The verb *phro ba* (perfect, *spros ba*) means "to spread or become elaborated"—within this context, to spread over time in the mental continuum.[493] The seeming observable reality of moment-by-moment arising-and-passing-away events in the mental continuum is in itself a false distinction. As the name of the exercise suggests, the instructions are designed to put an end to the seeming reality of ordinary temporal experience, to the seeming unfolding or elaboration of the mental continuum. With this collapse of the ordinary temporal distinction itself, all other extreme views collapse. Through the yoga of unelaboration the practitioner aligns his or her own mental continuum directly *(mngon du)* with the philosophical views of the Buddhist Middle Path *(lam dbu'i)*.

The main problem confronting the practitioner at this stage is the ordinary propensity to make time into a thing or an entity, much the same way that the mind and its various arisings were taken as entities prior to the special-insight meditations. The ordinary habit of representing *(dmigs pa)* time causes the mind to be experienced as discrete, through momentary events of various content, which arise and pass away in succession as a mental continuum *(rgyun)*.[494]

The actual instructions designed to negate the ordinary representation of time are not so very different from those of previous emptiness meditations, which were designed to view the mind as a nonentity:

[You thoroughly search] as before in what occurs
that is past, future, or present.
Now, whatever is a past mind is done-with.
Whatever is a future [mind] is unborn.
Whatever occurs in the present does not stay.
Don't represent the mind anywhere.
Not representing anything, there is no past,
There is no future,
There is no present occurrence.
You really pass beyond the three times so as to be without the past,
without the future, and without the present hereafter. (JP, f. 70b)[495]

Time, like mind, is a mere construct *(btags pa tsam du)*,[496] a construct
without any real substance. Intellectual understanding *(go ba)* is not
sufficient. The practitioner must eradicate the false view *(log lta)* of time
directly in the mental continuum during samādhi. In so doing, the practitioner experiences the "final purification of the conditions [necessary for
thoroughly] holding emptiness" (TN, p. 712).[497]

The time meditations complete a set of instructions pertaining to a rudimentary understanding of emptiness, and pave the way for a new set of special insights into the subtle understanding of emptiness.[498] With the collapse
of the ordinary convention of time, the practitioner experiences radically different states of consciousness, known as *the extraordinary samādhi states.*[499]

An important technical term in the yoga of unelaboration is *awareness-
itself each and every moment (so sor rang rig).* A similar term, *rang rig* ("awareness-itself"), was used at the end of both the concentration-support and the
concentration-without-supprt series of meditations. In both these cases the
term signified a shift in perspective, away from the respective intended
objects and toward knowledge of the mind itself in its natural state. Here
again, in these latter ordinary emptiness meditations, the practitioner now
turns away from the temporal events of the unfolding mental continuum
and toward the unborn or always-here *(ma skye)* nature of the mind.
Through this, the practitioner's understanding of emptiness is said to stay
and, more, to become certain,[500] irrespective of the elaboration of mental
events. When special insight into emptiness penetrates the always-here
mind, the practitioner is in a position to understand the way the realized
mind stays at all times *(gnas tshul)*. Jampel Pawo cites a famous passage
from Śabari:

The three times, not represented, without arising and passing away,
do not change into anything else.
This is the way the realized mind stays,
Whose real-nature is great bliss. (JP, f. 70b)[501]

Most commentators concur that the purpose of the yoga of unelaboration is "for the sake of generating certain knowledge" (JP, f. 70b). Time
must be done-with in order for certain knowledge to come forth:

> According to such sayings [as Śabari], when you analyze as such
> for the sake of generating certain knowledge, ask whether this
> knowledge-itself in question is contained within the three times
> —the knowledge of the past, future, or present. You will dis-
> cover that this moment of knowledge is not found to be con-
> tained in either all three times together *[car gyis],* nor is it
> thought to be contained in any single one *[gcig du]* of the three
> times whatsoever. (JP, f. 70b–71a)
>
> In short, directly experience that all dualistic phenomena, in
> absolute truth, are empty of anything such as the three compo-
> nents of ordinary time (arising, staying, and ceasing), and culti-
> vate the special-insight practice in this text toward the goal of
> having certain knowledge. (TN, pp. 395–96)

Discerning the emptiness of any representation of time enables the practitioner to attain an uncorrupted perspective of knowledge. Certain knowledge is not associated with ordinary temporal processes. According to
Madhyamaka philosophy, certain knowledge is free from extreme views
(*mtha' 'bral;* JP, f. 73a), such as existence/nonexistence, or one/many. These
extremes can only be eliminated through the eradication of the ordinary
habit of representing time, in the form of seemingly unfolding events in a
mental continuum.

The interplay between the eradication of ordinary time representation
and the dawning of certain knowledge is inherent in the various names
given to the meditation. The most common name, *the yoga of unelaboration* (TN, p. 707; JP, f. 70a), captures both the instruction (yoga) and the
attainment (unelaboration), respectively. Other titles emphasize the attainment only. For example, the meditation is also called *the always here [mind]*

(TN, p. 337) and *the benefit coming forth* (RD, p. 9). Tashi Namgyel defines the yoga of unelaboration in atemporal terms:

> Because the way the realized mind stays (like space) is that there is no elaboration of the three [units of time] (arising, staying, ceasing), [nor any dualities] (eternalism/nihilism, coming/ going), it is called "unelaboration." (TN, p. 707)

The term *unelaboration* suggests the eradication of successive mental events, so that neither self-existence nor substantiality is imputed to the seeming arising and passing away of events. In a general sense, the yoga of unelaboration is the eradication of all related distinctions and extreme views.

The actual instructions for realizing the emptiness of temporal distinctions are complicated. Pema Karpo uses a dialectical approach. Tashi Namgyel uses an affirming negation.[502] Both approaches are designed to eradicate the ordinary tendency to represent time as an entity.

A. THE DIALECTIC ON THE THREE TIMES

Pema Karpo's root instructions are given in three successive stages: (1) three times, (2) substance and nonsubstance, and (3) one and many. The first meditation gives the essential instructions for the eradication of ordinary time representation. This meditation leads to the realization of the natural mind as unborn, or better, as always here. The second meditation is an outgrowth of the first. Once time representation is eradicated, there can be no distinction between something existing and nonexisting in a given moment within the continuum. The seeming events that arise within the mental continuum neither happen nor not happen. The final meditation leads to the realization of the always-here mind as the primary outcome. When the mental continuum is no longer experienced as an ordinary temporal flow, both the mind and the various events arising within it are understood to be unborn or always here.

The root instructions for the three-times meditation have two parts. The first part contains the actual instruction in dialectic form:

> Analysis from the perspective of the three times:
> The past mind stops and is gone;

The future mind is not yet born nor does it exist;
The present mind cannot recognize anything [as real]. Examine
    this way.
This is the way of all phenomena as they really are.
Although all [phenomena] occur, they do not exist as real,
And are thereby found to be mere concepts [constructed]
    by your own ideas. (PK, f. 10b)

The latter part gives the attainment:

You become aware:
There is no artificial production of any arising, staying,
    or ceasing [as real].
Saraha says,
"That [which seems to] arise as a substance becomes calm, like
    space.
Having abandoned substance, what arises after that?
Bring forth the real-nature of the beginningless always-here mind
And you'll understand what was taught by lamas throughout history."
    (PK, f. 10b)

Jampel Pawo's commentary on the three-times meditation is largely
aimed at criticizing the Hīnayāna approach to the arising-and-passing-away
samādhi. The Hīnayāna texts describe a total breakup of the mental formations moment by moment, until no events occur within the mind.[503]
This is known as a *dissolution experience ('gags pa)*. While not questioning
the authenticity of dissolution as a legitimate meditation experience, Jampel Pawo cautions that a dissolution experience does not lead to the generation of certain knowledge, because it is based upon a failure to
understand the emptiness of ordinary time representation. According to
him, those advocating for the ultimacy of the dissolution experience manifest the extreme view of nihilism. If mental formations were actually to
cease, they would be nonexistent:

You may think that the way to generate certain knowledge is by
[actively] letting the past mind stop or by eradicating it. When
doing so, you come under the influence of the false view of the
mind [seeming] as an entity, as if you should be without the

three [times] from beginning to end. When doing so, you also come under the influence of [the false view of there seeming to be self-existing] outer appearances, as if these must [somehow] stop or be eradicated. This is not the way to generate certainty. When you understand the truth [of the mind's real-nature] and its outer appearances to be unelaborated, then you'll find it easy to bring forth the direct experience of [the mind's] real-nature. In this guidebook you won't get it using any of these other methods. (JP, f. 71a–71b)

Ordinary temporal experience cannot lead to the generation of certain knowledge, because believing in the seeming reality of a succession of arising-and-passing-away events exemplifies the extreme view of eternalism, that is, the presumption that something occurs or exists in time. On the other hand, believing in the cessation of all mental formations during meditation exemplifies the extreme view of nihilism. Pema Karpo's root instructions together with Jampel Pawo's commentary are designed to refute both the eternalist affirmation and the nihilist negation of ordinary temporality so that Middle Path view directly comes forth.

As the mind-moments neither arise nor not-arise, the correct Middle Path view of the mind-moments is captured in the technical phrase *skye med* ("unborn" or "always here")—a term chosen to negate the great karmic weight of the propensities by which time is taken to be an entity and events seem to arise. Nevertheless something seems to happen *('dug pa):*

Now, the way to do the analysis when coming under the influence
of [a false, seeming] nature or entity is as follows:
From where does the first mind-moment arise?
Then, where does it stay?
Finally, where does it go when it stops?
Use the above sayings in such a way that all the appearing
phenomena of saṃsāra don't go into dissolution anywhere
and are not artificially produced anywhere.
Then there is no arising that depends on the past.
There is no intention that depends on the future.
There is no recognition that depends on the present.
Then you understand it to be free from any beginning or end.
When it is always here, what stops?

When it does not arise or pass away, what stays?
Understand it to be free from the three—arising, staying,
    ceasing—so that it only seems to exist everywhere because
    of certain conditions.
The truth is not wrong when you say time is both with and
    without recognition.
[Each mind-moment] that [seems to] arise and its liberation
    come at the same time.
Then you see the real-entity of the unelaborated. (JP, f. 71b–72a)

Something "happens," but the various events are not taken as real, substantive events in time.

According to Jampel Pawo, the actual practice comes in two stages—an examination meditation followed by a samādhi meditation, both employing dialectical instruction. The latter is a search meditation, similar to the initial meditation on emptiness. In this case the practitioner searches for the locus of arising, staying, and ceasing, as if to find a thing. At some point the search becomes exhaustive and the practitioner realizes that there is no locus nor any substance to the seeming arising, staying, and ceasing. The ordinary convention of time is realized to be empty, and the always there condition of the natural mind is affirmed.

The dialectical meditation on time is inextricably bound to the dialectic on existent and nonexistent substances. If nothing ultimately arises, then nothing comes into existence; if nothing ultimately passes away, then nothing goes to nonexistence. Pema Karpo's root instructions follow with a meditation on substances and nonsubstances. First come the actual instructions:

Analysis from the perspective of substance and nonsubstance:
Are these mind-moments produced as self-existing,
    as substances?
Are they produced as nonexisting, as without substance?
If they are produced as substances, is it because they are
    produced to be subject and object?
If they are produced as objects, where are their form and
    colors?
If they are produced as subjects, is it because of being done-
    with appearances?

If it is found to be without substance, how come it acts by its many
   various appearances?
Examine it this way.

Next is a description of the outcome:

If it existed and could be produced as an entity, you would have
   been able to establish it to be a substance in samādhi.
Awareness shows that the truth of this examination is not anything
   produced whatsoever.
Therefore you can't establish nor find any existent, substantial
   phenomena.
Because awareness-itself comes forth from awakened wisdom's locus
   of activity, it can't be nonexistent nor insubstantial.
Don't go toward toward either extreme of substance and nonsubstance.
Then, when you are free from [viewing it as] either substance or
   nonsubstance, you won't fall into either extreme view of eternalism or nihilism and will enter what has been called the Middle
   Path. (PK, f. 11a)

Jampel Pawo's commentary reduces these complex dialectical instructions to a single phrase, *sgrub med* ("not produced," or "not made to happen"). All distinctions stem from the artificial mental activity of producing,
constructing, elaborating on, and then reifying certain thoughts and perceptions. When the mental continuum is reduced to its simplest condition
during samādhi—the arising and passing away of subtle mental events,
moment by moment—the practitioner is in a good position to eradicate any
tendencies to artificially act upon or construct more complex cognitions
from these fleeting mind-moments. If the practitioner lets the mental continuum be, without trying to do anything or make something happen, and
allows awareness-itself to become the point of observation, then the spontaneous unfolding experience becomes the Middle Path, and all possible
obscurations to certain knowledge are removed. Not artificially producing
anything entails a certain way of being *(lugs)* with unfolding experience.
Adopting this way of being toward the seemingly unfolding mental continuum prevents extremism.

The outcome of this meditation is the elimination of all extreme views so that certain knowledge in its more developed state can shine forth (JP, f. 73a). Certain negative terms—for example, *nonsubstantial* and *unborn*—are linguistic devices designed to prevent extremism, especially the extreme view of realism of appearances and time.

Tashi Namgyel's root instructions focus on the still-distinguishable concomitants—staying and arising. In contrast to Pema Karpo, he employs negation as the primary strategy to negate the convention of time. First are the actual instructions, then a description of the outcome:

> Continuation of skill:
> The mind takes the perspective of clarity and emptiness as
> before.
> When there are various cognitions and perceptions,
> this very mind manifests the skill of being unobstructed.
> When the mind happens to manifest appearance,
> look nakedly and consider that this very mind is settled
> into itself.
> Then go on to analyze:
> what seems to arise from many causes, the way it stays, and
> the way it seems to cease.
> If you make a mistake during this [skill exercise], go on to ana-
> lyze the correct doctrines in order to prevent extremism.
> Then, in the very first mind-moment, experience what happens
> as if it were (1) not arising from causes and conditions nor
> born from any basis, but without any root or ground of exis-
> tence; (2) not staying as any [seemingly self-existent] distinct
> form nor any outer appearance, but without a cause of recog-
> nition; and (3) not ceasing likewise, but without being
> obstructed.
> [Experience what happens as if it were] self-cleansed, self-
> purified, and self-liberated.
> As such, this is a way of being, so that there is nonrecognition
> of the [conventional view of the] three—arising, staying,
> and ceasing.
> This is awareness-itself and emptiness, so it is unnecessary to rely
> upon any artificial construction.
> Do not corrupt it by trying to make it good or spoil it by trying
> to make it bad. Do not change it in any way.

You must simply resolve it as self-purified, self-aware, and self-liberated.

So study all the texts and commentaries, and then set up the body points and so on. Examine and analyze the mind's clarity and emptiness from the best possible level of samādhi. Then you'll experience what's special about the special-insight practices. (TN, p. 666)

These instructions begin with a review. The meditation to set up the always-here mind naturally follows from the ripening of the skill meditation—at the point when the mind appears in an unobstruced manner, moment by moment. Then the same special insight comes forth: clarity and emptiness. As each moment brings the same special insight, the meditation proceeds with less and less effort. The mind settles into itself *(rang babs),* which implies that mind-moments arise and pass away very quickly. At this point the practitioner is ready to begin the emptiness of time meditation. As the meditation presupposes a sophisticated intellectual understanding of Madhyamaka philosophy, it is advisable to review the dialectical treatises of the Middle Path.[504] Tashi Namgyel introduces a preparatory examination meditation in order to "prevent extremism."

The actual samādhi meditation begins with the passage "Then, in the very first mind-moment." In brief the practitioner looks to the three temporal divisions of each discrete mind-moment (arising, staying, and ceasing) and negates their reality respectively. The autocommentary elaborates that no entity can serve as the basis for any of these three components of each mind-moment. There is no constructor *(bzo bo)* nor agent *(mkhan po)* to bring any mind-moment about. What seems to occur over time, when correctly negated as unborn, affirms the always-here *(skye med)* dimension of the mind's real nature. The outcome is captured in the term *always here:*

You resolve it to be always here. It is not born from causes and conditions. It has no basis. It is without a root. (TN, p. 388)

Likewise the staying component, or duration, of each mind-moment—either as a seeming perceptual object or as a thought—is negated, because no thing can be recognized that stays. The ceasing component of each mind-moment likewise is not found to have any basis:

You resolve it to be without eradication and without cessation. (TN, p. 388)

Table 32 lists the respective negations of each of the three seeming temporal components of each mind-moment:

TABLE 32: NEGATIONS USED FOR EACH OF THE TEMPORAL COMPONENTS (ARISING, STAYING, AND CEASING)

Arising	Unborn; always here
Staying	Without a cause of recognition Without a basis to the staying
Ceasing	Without annihilation Without cessation

Tashi Namgyel's root instructions then continue with a description of the outcome. This begins with the phrase "As such this is a way of being." The natural mind emerges after the proper negation of extreme views and is best depicted as a way of being *(yin lugs),*[505] because the meditator doesn't have to do anything artificially to bring this about. According to the root text, this way of being is summed up in three terms: *nonrecognition of the three* (arising, staying, and ceasing), *awareness-itself,* and *emptiness.* The first of these terms, *nonrecognition,* illustrates that conventional temporal experience is found to be empty. Negation of the conventional experience of temporality leads to a profound rearrangement of the mental continuum. The term *awareness-itself* indicates that the mind is purged of all extreme views. The mind becomes the very expression and manifestation of the Middle Path. The third term, *emptiness,* illustrates how, with the negation of the conventional experience of time and any remnants of extremism, the set of meditations concerning the rudimentary understanding of emptiness is completed.

Tashi Namgyel couples the verb *to recognize* and the phrase "the three (arising, staying, and ceasing)" within a genitive phrase in order to capture the interplay of temporality and existence. When the negative particle is added to make the phrase "nonrecognition of the three," the entire phrase negates both the extreme views on temporality and those on existence at once. He explains:

By not being able to analyze where the three times come from, you are also free from the extreme [view] of existence, because nowhere are they made to happen. Furthermore since everything seems to arise [conventionally] and becomes the root of saṃsāra and nirvāṇa, you are free from the extreme [view] of nonexistence. [Ultimately] no substance or attribute is produced. This has been explained by a number of metaphors. Above all, [remember] that [the three] does not arise from causes, so that it is [ultimately] unborn. Nothing can be recognized that stays, and nothing comes to cessation, so it is without [a real] end. [With respect to arising and passing away], it does not arise from causes, nor does it pass away by conditions. Therefore it is all-at-once time, nonoccurrence, all time. To be free from the three (arising, staying, ceasing) does not mean to cut off the mental continuum. Stay so that nothing is good or bad, understood or not understood, and without increase or decrease. Don't try to have either recognition nor nonawareness. Don't try to attain anything nor go astray. And so, at all times, be without change, without any decrease, and so on. Examine and analyze the truth of the unborn with the special insight that examines each and every moment. Examine it to its final limit, until you have the experience that cuts off the power [of mistakenly viewing] a basis or root to the mind. Having analyzed accordingly, your experience is beyond thought and beyond words. It is the way the realized mind stays. In summary, examine each and every moment so as to bring about the effect of the analysis, [namely that all the mind-moments] go to self-calm, self-absorption, and self-dissolution. This is explained as the generation of nonconceptual wisdom. (TN, pp. 389–90)

Not only do the three conventional components of a single mind-moment collapse, but so also do the extreme views of existence and nonexistence. Furthermore, the experience of a mind-moment as arising and passing away is also negated.

These instructions condense Pema Karpo's root instructions—the three times and substance/nonsubstance—into a single meditation. The goal of Tashi Namgyel's meditation is the same, but the method is different in that it relies heavily upon a negation style. This method directly attacks the most likely extreme, that of eternalism, by which time and space are taken to be self-existent realities. Negation instructions are less complicated than dialectical instructions, but run the risk of leading to the opposite extreme, namely nihilism. Tashi Namgyel is not unaware of this. He is careful to say that although the conventional components of temporality do not exist from an ultimate perspective, something still happens *(byung)* from a conventional perspective. Statements such as "does not mean to cut off the mental continuum" and terms such as "all-at-once time" and "all time" used in juxtaposition to "nonoccurrence" are designed to prevent the nihilistic view.

B. The Middle Path Without Extremes

Because these meditations eradicate extreme views, the benefit is called *the experience of the Middle Path (dbu ma'i lam; JP, f. 73b).* Events neither arise nor not arise; they neither exist nor not exist. These views are summarized in Nāgārjuna's famous *Eight Extremes:*

> You will also give up the eight extremes, as master Nāgārjuna has said,
>
> "Based on dependent origination something occurs, yet
> There is no arising nor passing away.
> There is no nihilism nor eternalism.
> There is no coming nor going.
> There are not many nor one event(s).
> Whatever tends to be elaborated becomes almost calm again and
>   again." (JP, f. 73b)[506]

In Mahāyāna Buddhism extreme views are summarized by the terms *nihilism and eternalism (rtag pa dang chad pa).* These views are closely associated with the extreme views on time and existence. As the passage shows, the key to the correct view lies in the direct experience of dependent origination[507] as a replacement for conventional temporality. Things neither exist nor not exist, and yet they seem to happen through their interconnectedness *(rten 'brel).* The use of this term, *interconnectedness,* is designed to show that a fundamental rearrangement of the mental continuum has taken place.[508]

Jampel Pawo cites a passage from the tantras:

Realization has no beginning or end. This is calmness. Calmness has no beginning or end, so that the [natural] mind is without arising or passing away. This is what is called "being without beginning and without end." (JP, f. 71a)

The phrase *thog ma mtha med pa'i pa* ("without beginning and without end") is designed to negate both extreme views. "Without beginning" negates the extreme in which seeming events unfolding in time are taken to be a real occurrence. "Without end" negates the extreme view in which cessation is seen as a real event. The phrase *zhi ba* ("calmness") signifies a fundamental rearrangement. Temporal experience comes forth in a new way, as the interconnectedness of everything all at once, as captured in the phrase *unborn*, or *always here from the beginning (gdad nas skye med)*. The term *skye med* can be translated as "always here" from the mind-perspective, and as "unborn" from the event-perspective. Time as an event is negated, while the mind's real-nature as always-here awareness-itself is affirmed. The term *skye med* is designed to negate the eternal view of time, while the phrase *from the beginning* is designed to negate the nihilistic position on time:

Saraha says, "That born as substance becomes calm, like space.
Abandoning that, what can arise hereafter?
It is always here, from the beginning.
So understand what is taught by your lama." (JP, f. 72a)

The new experience is expressed by the verb *zhi ba,* which means "to calm." Elsewhere, the verb is qualified, "nearly calm" (JP, f. 71b). Nāgārjuna qualifies the term even further. He says, "almost calm again and again." Tashi Namgyel uses the terms *self-calm (rang zhi), self-absorbed (rang bsdu),* and *self-dissolved (rang thim).* These terms are meant to imply that whenever conventional temporal experience seems to come forth in its habitual way—as a seeming succession of discrete mind-moments—these events quickly become calm, over and over again and dissolve into emptiness.[509]
Another way of expressing the state is with the term *emptiness:*

Through many meditations on emptiness, emptiness stays everywhere even when the mind becomes elaborated [in time] again and again. You'll understand emptiness when you have thoroughly searched for the entityness of both what seems to become elaborated and what seems to stay. Then the mind's bliss comes forth. You'll understand emptiness when you have examined whether the mind [really] exists. You'll understand emptiness when you have searched for this thing everywhere. (JP, f. 77a)

The mental continuum itself becomes a manifestation of a continuous understanding of emptiness. This is certain knowledge. This is what is called the real-entity (*yang dag pa'i ngo bo;* TN, p. 392). The right view of emptiness stays throughout ripening experience.

C. Nondissolution

It is important to realize that some happening *('dug pa; 'byung ba)* continues. Experience still ripens. The experience is neither a genuine experience of discrete mind-moments nor is it genuine dissolution. In order to express this extraordinary outcome, certain qualified phrases are used. Jampel Pawo uses the phrase "not completely staying" (*rab tu mi gnas;* JP, f. 71a). The reason for the qualification is so that the always-here condition is not confused with a dissolution experience. Tashi Namgyel contrasts his definition of the always-here mind with the two most common mistaken views of unelaboration:[510]

> Those who assert that the meaning of unelaboration is to be without conceptual elaboration (based on a subject and object duality) and those who assert that the meaning of unelaboration is certain knowledge that recognizes all phenomena as empty are both wrong. The former just experience the nonconceptual state of staying/calm practice. The latter become attached to [the idea of] emptiness as a form of certain knowledge, which is also wrong. The real meaning is a [proper] understanding of the mind's elaboration of time, so that the real-nature of the mind is [affirmed], like space, never changing, never substantial. (TN, p. 708)

This passage refutes the nihilist position, which adheres to the dissolution experience. It also refutes the eternalist position, which misunderstands emptiness as if knowledge of it were some entity. As the state involves neither dissolution nor nondissolution, the practitioner is "without hope and fear" (TN, p. 708).[511]

Another way of expressing the experience is with phrases such as "never changing, never substantial" *('pho 'gyur med pa'i 'dus ma byas)*. The resultant very subtle or extraordinary level of mind is experienced as if it is unchanging, in that it is no longer subject to ordinary rules of time. The experience is also as "never substantial" in that it is no longer subject to ordinary mental construction and elaboration. A similar term used to describe the extraordinary outcome is "produced en masse" *(lhun gyis grub;* JP, f. 73b). This term is made up of the verb *sgrub pa,* which means "to produce," or "make happen" at the very subtle level of mind and the noun *lhun,* which means a "mass." The term is often used idiomatically. It is sometimes translated as "spontaneity" or "spontaneous presence."[512] However, the literal meaning is quite accurate, namely "to manifest everything all at once." Rangjung Dorjé uses the term *kun gzhi* (Skt., *alāya).* This term has often been translated as "store consciousness." The literal Tibetan meaning is "basis of everything." Each of these terms is meant to express a profound rearrangement of the ordinary mental continuum. Rather than a temporal succession of discrete mind-moments, the practitioner experiences the entire causeless, groundless, interconnectedness of everything. Everything, in the form of very subtle karmic propensities *(bag chags),* comes forth at once. The practitioner realizes the "basis of everything" and grasps the entirety of all potential experiences—past, present, and future, of all of the realms throughout space—in the same instant. He or she becomes aware of the vast interconnectedness that makes up potential consciousness, as opposed to the narrow, conventional flow of elaborated events in the ordinary temporal mental continuum. This profound and sudden experience of the atemporal interconnectedness of everything is called *the nondissolution experience (ma 'gag pa)* to delineate it from the Theravada path.

Though comparable in profundity to the Theravada dissolution experience, the Mahāyāna experience of nondissolution or unelaboration is very different, both experientially and philosophically, which is why the commentators are careful to refute the nihilistic dissolution position.

The commentators also carefully refrain from describing the nondissolution experience in positive terms. They are cautious to use terms such as "produced en masse" or "basis of everything" because of the potential danger of adopting an eternalist position. Rather than using such terms, the commentators try to express the experience metaphorically. The following metaphors are used: "son of a barren woman" (JP, f. 73a), "space" (JP, f. 52a,

73a), "salt in the ocean" (TN, p. 390), and "treasure in the palm of your hand" (JP, f. 73b). For example:

> You cannot put it in order by going after or turning away from its attributes. It only comes through the lama's oral advice, and so it is called a greatness that is like seeing a treasure that remains in the palm of your hand. (JP, f. 73b)[513]

The terms *nearly calm* and *unborn* capture the experience from the event-perspective.

The practitioner has learned to downshift experience from the subtle to the very subtle level, which is composed of a vast network of interconnected (but not amassed) karmic propensities *(bag chags)* deposited on the ground of phenomenal existence. These propensities have their own spontaneous activity (but not artificial activity), and that activity is unobstructed. Based on causes and conditions, yet unborn propensities within this vast network have the potential to ripen. Through dependent origination certain propensities at the very subtle level ripen into subtle movements within the temporal mental continuum, which in turn become constructed into and elaborated as coarse-level thoughts and appearances. Through mastery of the yoga of unelaboration the meditator learns to shift skillfully from the subtle to the very subtle level of mind and then to view the process of dependent arising from the perspective of the very subtle or extraordinary level of mind. From the perspective of the very subtle level, virtual events occur en masse, as a vast network of very subtle propensities all there at the same instant yet unborn as actual experience. Yet from this perspective specific events can arise in the temporal mental continuum through the process of dependent origination, and when they do, they almost immediately become calm. In this sense the experience is both unborn and nearly calm, both atemporal and temporal. Tashi Namgyel tries to illustrate the experience using the paradoxical phrase "meditate unelaboration while mixing it with various appearances" (TN, p. 715). At the extraordinary level all propensities are unconstructed, nonaggregated, nonarising, and empty from the beginning. The skilled meditator can view events transforming from very subtle propensities to specific subtle mind-moments and constructed coarse thoughts and appearances seeming to arise and pass in the temporal mental continuum through a process of dependent origination. However, because the perspective is now vastly different, each specific mind-moment that arises automatically carries emptiness and clarity from the beginning.

Pema Karpo makes an important distinction between the samādhi state and the postsamādhi state. During the samādhi state *(mnyam bzhag)* the practitioner eradicates extremes, such as the convention of time, and directly experiences an extraordinary state of the interconnectedness of all potential experience. Due to the sheer power of past karma the ordinary temporal way of experiencing the mental continuum returns at the end of the meditation session and the practitioner enters the postsamādhi state *(rjes thob)*. Once again, discrete mind-moments seem to occur, at least in a relative sense. Because these events occur, however, the practitioner becomes more convinced of their emptiness. Pema Karpo explains the outcome:

> When you understand accordingly, during samādhi nothing whatsoever appears other than the awakened wisdom, which is awareness-itself of each and every thing. This is called nonappearance. During the postsamādhi, everything appears like a magic show because you have purified [the mistake of] holding all the phenomena along the path as being real. (PK, f. 11b)

Because of the extraordinary nature of the nondissolution samādhi, the state deepens certain knowledge *(nges shes)* so that it becomes the precursor to awakened wisdom *(ye shes)*. The certain knowledge that comes forth at this time is not to be confused with enlightenment, where awakened wisdom comes to perfection. So as not to generate confusion, terms such as *certain knowledge,* as opposed to *awakened wisdom,* are used to convey attainment. When the term *awakened wisdom* is used at this stage, it is always qualified. Tashi Namgyel uses the phrase "locus the activity of awakened wisdom" (TN, p. 390). With a shift to a causeless, groundless experience of the entirety of all potential phenomena, the practitioner passes beyond the realm of discrete temporal mind-moments to another locus of very subtle activity of mind, which works by a different set of rules. These conditions eventually guide the mind toward full enlightenment. At this point, however, conventionally experienced awareness has not yet crossed over to the locus where awakened wisdom operates.

It is very important that the practitioner experience continuous emptiness, both within and without the samādhi state. According to Tashi Namgyel, the nondissolution experience comes forth in lesser, intermediate, and greater forms. Therefore the practitioner needs to "protect it again and again" in order to strengthen this extraordinarily new experience of the mental continuum.

Tashi Namgyel suggests four ways of protecting the new realization. First is prayer. The practitioner established the appropriate conditions as far back as guru yoga. Now the practitioner is told, "Pray to the lama and to the assembly" (TN, p. 714)[514] in order to reinforce the appropriate conditions for the ripening of awakened wisdom. Next the practitioner reenters the nondissolution samādhi and eases up. As Tashi Namgyel says, "Ease up during unelaboration and the outcome will come forth" (TN, p. 714). As a result the practitioner experiences the entire interconnectedness of all phenomena of the three times and six realms over and over again and has a number of nondissolution experiences. Finally the practitioner takes advantage of the "intensity" of the rearrangement of the ordinary mental continuum to protect the experience by means of continuous, undistracted staying on emptiness. Once the practitioner gets some sense of emptiness pervading the interconnectedness of all times and realms, it becomes easier to persist with a continuous focus on emptiness when leaving the samādhi state and reentering ordinary daily experience.[515]

Table 33 summarizes the terms used in the yoga of unelaboration:

TABLE 33: NEGATIONS AND METAPHORS USED IN THE YOGA OF UNELABORATION

	Negation of Eternalism	Negation of Nihilism	Metaphor
Mind-perspective	No entity	Way the realized mind stays always here	Space
Event-perspective	Unborn Never substantial Never changing	Produced en masse; basis of everything	Son of barren woman; treasure in hand

7. EXTRAORDINARY PRACTICE

THE NONDISSOLUTION EXPERIENCE marks a profound shift in consciousness. From the event perspective, the ordinary mental continuum is experienced in a radically new way—no longer as discrete coarse- or subtle-level successive mental events, but as a vast atemporal network of very subtle, interconnected propensities *(bag chags)*, seemingly produced en masse. The practitioner begins an entirely new set of exercises, called *the extraordinary practices (thun mong ma yin pa)*. According to Jampel Pawo, the extraordinary practices build upon the foundation of the ordinary staying-calm and special-insight practices.[516] These practices are especially designed to reveal the real nature of the mind. [517]

There are a number of versions of extraordinary meditations within the Mahāyāna tradition, each one giving these advanced stages of practice a unique flavor. The technical language and extraordinary practices specific to mahāmudrā distinguish it from other advanced Mahāyāna meditations such as those of the bodhisattva bhūmis, the completion-stage tantras, and the Great Perfection practice *(dzog chen)*. The practices presented here constitute an approach and technical vocabulary that is entirely unique to mahāmudrā.[518] There are two substages in the mahāmudrā cycle of extraordinary meditation: the yoga of one taste *(ro gcig gi rnal 'byor)* and the yoga of nonmeditation *(sgom med kyi rnal 'byor)*. Both are designed to set up the conditions "to generate enlightenment" (JP, f. 77b).

I. THE YOGA OF ONE TASTE

The word *taste (ro)* in *the yoga of one taste* is analogous to the term *great desire ('dod chags)* used in the early mahāmudrā source material (JP, f. 78a). The nondissolution experience is such a profound shift in consciousness, from the coarse and subtle to the very subtle level of mind, that it seems that the practitioner finally gets a taste of what the spiritual path is about. This experience increases the desire for enlightenment. No matter what level of mind, all experience becomes the great desire for enlightenment. Yet this desire need not be another form of attachment. To the extent that the practitioner has correctly entered the Middle Path, the taste of enlightenment is not so much an artificial expectation as it is a self-occurring *(rang 'byung)* given of the extraordinary samādhi state.

The yoga of one taste, as the name implies, is concerned with equanimity *(btang snyoms)*. From the event perspective, the shift to the very subtle level of mind—experienced as a ground or great network of interconnected karmic impressions of potential experience—puts the practitioner in a position to experience the equanimity of all potential phenomena. From the mind perspective, the vast ocean of awareness-itself *(rang rig pa)* pervades *(khyab)* this massive network of very subtle propensities and is guided by the same truth—emptiness—with respect to the entirety of all karmic propensities within this network. In this sense, knowledge of emptiness is said to stay *(gnas)* as awareness-itself pervades the network of all karmic propensities throughout all virtual realms and times. In a certain sense, awareness-itself stays because it never leaves. Awareness-itself is a property of the natural mind at the deepest level of mind from the beginning.[519]

A distinction is sometimes made between coarse and subtle special insights about emptiness,[520] where the ordinary special-insight meditations correspond to coarse emptiness and the extraordinary meditations correspond to subtle emptiness. It is called *subtle emptiness* because, viewed from the perspective of nonaggregated, unborn propensities, all experience at the very subtle level is inherently empty. Emptiness is a property of the natural mind from the very beginning.

The yoga of one taste is designed to deepen one's experience of the natural condition of the mind. Staying-calm practice helped do away with coarser-level mental content, and special insight helped cut off the root of the ordinary representations of self, external appearances, and time. These ordinary practices were designed to clear away the coarser levels of mind so that they less and less obscure the mind's natural condition. With the shift to the extraordinary level the mind's natural condition is revealed. From the perspective of mind at the extraordinary level, awareness-itself is always there from the beginning and is never discontinuous or partial. The technical term for the mind's pristine awareness is *the way the realized mind stays (gnas lugs)*. From the mind perspective at the extraordinary level, a radical shift in point of observation takes place:

With Mahāmudrā meditation, we are focusing neither on what the flashlight is illuminating nor on being the person holding the flashlight. Instead, we are looking from the point of view of the flashlight itself. In a sense, we are focusing on being the flashlight.[521]

From the perspective of events at the extraordinary level, the spontaneous activity of the vast network of karmic propensities (in contrast to the artificial activity of trying to make experience happen) remains clear and unimpeded.[522]

While the yoga of unelaboration opens the door to the mind's extraordinary or very subtle level and brings forth the initial taste of equanimity, the yoga of one taste is the actual means *(thabs)* or way *(tshul)* to practice using the extraordinary level of mind as the point of observation. The meditator learns to stabilize this extraordinary level of samādhi from the perspective of the way the realized mind stays so as to observe the spontaneous activity of karmic propensities dependently arising as specific coarse-level mental events such as appearances, thoughts, or emotions. From the perspective of the way the realized mind stays, however, these events reflect the natural mind's karmic tendency to give rise to things,[523] that is, to its event-making function. Whatever seems to arise, no matter how diverse and various, is already saturated with the natural mind's inherent emptiness and clarity. All these various seeming events have the same taste of emptiness/clarity.

The realization in the sūtric tradition is comparable to that of one taste. There the practitioner meditates on the relationship between emptiness and dependent origination. The meditator comes to realize that each and every dependently arising event is naturally imbued with emptiness,[524] and that emptiness and seeming appearances arise simultaneously.[525]

From the extraordinary perspective, the natural mind and its event-making function are inseparable. Jamgön Kongtrül explains:

> One Taste is the union of external objects with the internal awareness that experiences them. Distinctions between subject and object no longer occur.[526]

However, this fundamental nonduality between the mind and its appearances at the extraordinary level does not mean that events don't really occur.

To protect against the extreme of nihilism, Alexander Berzin, in *The Gelug/Kagyü Tradition of Mahamudra,* says:

> Non-duality does not render the mind and its objects totally identical—one and the same thing. Experience always has contents.... Non-dual, then, means that at any moment, these two things—mind and its objects, or experience and its contents—always come together as one entity.[527]

The word *zung 'jug* ("pair") literally means "to enter into a connection" or "to link together." One-taste practice is the way to establish the natural connection between the mind and its experiences at the extraordinary level so that this connection can be discerned at the ordinary level of seeming appearances. Extraordinary practice signifies a coupling together of relative truth and absolute truth so that both are held in a nondual relationship:

> The object, the many [seeming appearances] as great bliss; the subject, the highest refinement of emptiness; and the pair, bliss and emptiness, simultaneously born; also relative truth in its illusory body; absolute truth in its clear light; and both truths, nondual—are one taste. They are the simultaneously born, the pair. All phenomena when appearing in [ordinary] time are not artificially made to become [self-existent] things, and therefore are found to be empty. Although they are not made into anything, nevertheless appearance happens, and therefore these are found to be a [nondual] pair—appearance and emptiness, or one taste. Therefore since you know bliss and emptiness, clarity and emptiness, and awareness and emptiness to be [nondual] pairs, you understand what is called "many as one taste." (JP, f. 79a)[528]

Pema Karpo defines the one-taste meditation with a single aphorism:

> The yoga of one taste is making the same taste out of all phenomena, appearing/mind, so that they are indistinguishable. (PK, f. 12a)

This definition is worded in such a way as to be continuous with the previous set of meditations and also introduce new discontinuous elements.

The word *indistinguishable (dbyer med)* is reminiscent of skill insight meditation, where the distinction between appearance and mind was eradicated. The phrase "making the same taste out of all phenomena" shows continuity with the yoga of unelaboration, especially in terms of the dawning equanimity. However, the participle form of the verb *snyoms pa* ("to equalize") is used in conjunction with an object, *ro* ("taste"), to make the phrase "making the same taste out of." This linguistic construction conveys the nature of the one-taste practice. Equanimity of all potential mental formations is not the result of a passive, all-at-once realization but of an active, cultivated practice, according to the doctrine of cause and effect.

Even though seemingly ordinary phenomena of the mind are encountered anew as bases of wisdom, it is extremely important to keep in mind the vastly different perspective through which these phenomena are experienced. In fact one of the most critical questions of the one-taste meditations concerns itself with qualifying just how ordinary events are experienced, and also with developing a technical language to express this. Are the seeming events experienced over time as a succession of discrete events, or are they experienced at once, as an interconnected network of all the potential experience? According to the protecting instructions for this practice, it is incorrect to say that phenomena come forth either as discrete temporal events or as an emergent mass. Both positions are extreme. The events are neither one nor many. In an ultimate sense these conceptualizations are empty. Yet in a relative sense it may seem both as if many single mind-moments occur and as if there is one entire interconnected network of very subtle propensities. Pema Karpo's phrase "all phenomena, appearing/mind" captures this paradox. "All phenomena" alludes to the nondissolution experience in which the mind's network of very subtle propensities is manifested en masse. "Appearing/mind" alludes to the temporal succession of discrete mental events with their concomitant perspectives of moving and staying. Pema Karpo's placement of these words in apposition expresses the paradox in which events seem to come forth both, and neither, temporally and simultaneously.

Each seemingly discrete mind-moment contains the very subtle imprint of the entire network of interconnected propensities comprising all saṃsāric realms. Therefore Jampel Pawo compares the one-taste meditation to tasting saṃsāra:

> The [many] tastes of saṃsāra and the one taste of meditation are
> the very same. That is what is meant. (JP, f. 79b)[529]

A. The View

1. Simultaneous Mind

The key technical term in the mahāmudrā tradition is *lhan cig skye sbyor* (Sanskrit, *sahaja*). It means literally "arising together" or "simultaneous." *Simultaneousness* has a number of technical meanings: (1) In one sense, it means that when awareness-itself is taken as the point of observation at the extraordinary level, the mind's awareness and the content of its experiences arise together as inseparable aspects. (2) The vast network of all potential experience and the occurrence of seemingly discrete events arising in the temporal mental continuum come together in each moment of experience. (3) From the point of observation of awareness-itself, clarity and emptiness arise together in each seeming moment of experience. (4) From the mind perspective, the extraordinary level of practice invites a remarkable realization about awareness-itself. Awareness-itself begins to seem less and less like the practitioner's ordinary awareness packaged in ordinary patterns of thought or self-representation or even packaged in the practitioner's seemingly unique individual consciousness. When such constructions of mind are cleared away, each seeming moment of awareness-itself is linked to the dharmakāya, the ground or body of awareness saturating all existence. In this sense, each moment of awareness arises together with awakened wisdom. The simultaneous mind is the direct experience of awareness-itself (both the practitioner's seeming individual consciousness and the universal ground of awareness-itself) and the seeming objects of experience arising together as an inseparable pair from the beginning. Tashi Namgyel's root instructions capture the technical complexity of the simultaneous mind:

> [From one perspective] the ordinary mind is connected to the awakened wisdom of the simultaneousness of appearance, or [from the other perspective] the simultaneousness of emptiness is connected to the mind that [seemingly] arises as attributes and self-existent attributes. In short, awareness/emptiness, clarity/emptiness, appearance/emptiness, and the emptiness of the simultaneous itself—none of these couplings differ in their meaning. (TN, p. 425)

The inseparability of the mind's awareness and the content of experience is captured by the phrase *clarity/emptiness* and, when that content pertains to seemingly external appearances, by the phrase *appearance/ emptiness.*

Tashi Namgyel further explains how direct experience of the simultaneous mind occurs at all levels of mind:

> The real nature of the simultaneous [mind] is when support *[brten]* and movement *[gyo]* are transformed by awareness-itself, which pervades, in its own way *[khyab bdag]*, all of saṃsāra and whose nature is like [vast] space [from the mind perspective] and clear light [from the event perspective]. (TN, p. 418)

This passage illustrates how the deepest level of awareness-itself pervades or saturates all levels of the phenomenal world at the very subtle, or extraordinary, level as well as at the subtle ("movement") and coarse ("support") levels of the seemingly ordinary temporal mental continuum.

Tashi Namgyel elaborates on his definition with a citation from the *Hevajra Tantra,* commonly referred to as the *Two Signs:*

> The simultaneous can't be spoken about by other people. [You must experience it yourself.] This is what the word means: (1) The entire ground of phenomena, as well as each particular moment of experience included [in the coarse and subtle categories], support and movement *[chos]*, and (2) that [awareness] of these phenomena *[chos dan]*—stay together from the beginning so as to be without the former [objects] and the latter [subjects]. This is called *simultaneous.* (TN, p. 419)

The word *simultaneous* is more accurate than its synonym, *pair,* because it has both a seeming temporal referent, "arising together with," and an atemporal referent, "stay together from the beginning." The qualifiers *together with (lhan cig)* and *at the same time (dus mtshungs par)* signify the absolute emptiness of time and substance, so that at the very onset of any seeming moment of conventional experience, its ultimate truth—emptiness—arises together with that moment of experience.

When the extraordinary level of mind is taken as the point of observation, every seeming moment of conventional experience brings the same realization. The attainment of one taste, then, is the appreciation of the equanimity and emptiness of all seeming mental events that constitute the conventional mental continuum as well as the vast network of potential experience. Technical words such as *self-pervasion (khyab bdag)* are meant to capture the realization about awareness-itself as a property of the natural mind. From the extraordinary perspective, awareness-itself saturates all phenomena because this awareness ultimately is the dharmakāya. Tashi Namgyel quotes the *Hevajra Tantra:*

In the *Two Signs* it says,

"This profound wisdom,
as the ground, stays everywhere.
It is the way that is neither dual nor nondual,
neither with nor without substance. This supreme state
stays, pervading all that stays and moves." (TN, p. 418)

Awareness-itself permeates all events in the seemingly ordinary temporal mental continuum as well as the extraordinary interconnected network of very subtle propensities. At the ordinary level of experience each seeming occurrence brings the same truth, which resounds throughout all the realms and throughout all time.

In the *King of Samādhi [Samādhirāja]* it says that the real nature of all phenomena—equanimity—permeates all its aspects:

Form teaches realization…
Form, realization, and equanimity,
Are not found to be different…
When equanimous in nature,
All phenomena [of saṃsāra], everywhere,
Are the same as nirvāṇa.
In the *Samputa Tantra* it says,
"When viewing [specific] forms,
When hearing sounds,
When speaking
When you experience these various [events in meditation]
and when you do all your activities [after meditation],
the [natural] mind likewise does not move."
For the practitioner who knows this, yoking

[the relative and ultimate] will forever be generated.
This is the ultimate enlightened attitude.
It is the indestructible diamond of Vajrasattva.
It is the perfect enlightenment of Buddha. (TN, pp. 445–46)

In the oral tradition certain metaphors illustrate the coupling of the relative and ultimate:

> The simultaneousness of the mind and the simultaneousness of appearance are said to be indistinguishable, like the sun and its light or a sandalwood tree and its scent. Nāgārjuna says, "Like an herb and its scent and the essence of fire and its heat, the [real] nature of all phenomena likewise is said to be empty."...Relative truth is said to be empty, and emptiness is also relative truth. If it does not happen that way, then you do not have certainty. If it does, the seeming relative experiences are impermanence. (TN, p. 422)

Tashi Namgyel warns that the seeming reappearance of ordinary experience is not in itself simultaneousness. Relative experience must be yoked with awareness-itself (*rang rig pa;* TN, p. 423). Technical terms such as *always there* and *from the beginning* signify that the point of observation is awareness-itself held at the extraordinary level of mind, so that relative experience is always coupled with emptiness from this perspective. The metaphor "like the sun and its light" is misleading because the sun does not have awareness. Phrases such as "wisdom of the simultaneous" illustrate that the illuminating or wisdom dimension of awareness-itself must be coupled with each seeming moment of conventional experience (JP, f. 81b).

2. The Return of Conventional Appearance

Jampel Pawo cites Milarepa to explain how the mental continuum is experienced differently in the yoga of unelaboration from that of one taste:

> When practicing unelaboration, appearance and emptiness are found to be indistinguishable, but external appearances generally do not arise in that meditation. When practicing one taste, they do arise exactly in the way that appearance and emptiness come directly as the simultaneous. Moreover, when practicing

appearance-only, nothing is [artificially] made to happen, so that not being [artificially] made into anything, it arises as appearance only.... All these phenomena [seemingly] appearing in time are not made into entities and are found to be empty. Although they are not [artificially] made into anything, nevertheless some sort of appearance happens, and therefore these are found to come as a pair—"appearance and emptiness" or "one taste." (JP, f. 79a)

Likewise Tashi Namgyel says:

Appearance and mind, ultimately empty, are said to occur during the great one-taste meditation. (TN, p. 443)

These passages illustrate a meditative analysis of conventional appearance viewed from the extraordinary level of mind's natural awareness-itself, or illuminating wisdom. Following the negation of ordinary temporal experience in the yoga of unelaboration, the practitioner affirms in the yoga of one taste that something still happens *('dug pa)*. As Jampel Pawo says, "some sort of appearance happens" *(snang gyi 'dug pa),* although it is no longer taken to be real. Appearances come forth as seeming events *(snang ba bzhin),* in a relative sense, yet each appearance carries the concomitant realization of its ultimate emptiness, so that each various-seeming appearance deepens the realization of emptiness. The truth of emptiness, for all possible experience, becomes absolutely certain only when such phenomena are allowed to ripen spontaneously and are "neither prevented nor made to happen" (TN, p. 470).

The yoga of one taste addresses the mind's ordinary phenomena—both its seeming happening content, such as coarse-level cognitions, perceptions, emotions, and their seeming elaboration. According to Gampopa, the yoga of one taste pertains to knowledge of the ordinary (*tha mal gyi shes ba;* TN, p. 468). In Mahāyāna Buddhism it is just as incorrect to say that ordinary events don't happen as it is to say that they are real. It is more accurate to say that the phenomena of the ordinary mind "seem to happen" *('dug pa)* but are "not made into entities" (JP, f. 79b).

Tashi Namgyel comments that one taste revisits conventional phenomena:[530] "In essence [coarse-level] appearance and [subtle-level] movement are said to occur at the time of the great one-taste meditation" (TN, p. 443). He adds, "Once you realize emptiness, you illuminate the [mind's] real nature only when its aspects arise unobstructed everywhere" (TN, p. 406). In other words, realization of emptiness greatly deepens when meditation focuses on dependent arising.[531] Tashi Namgyel likens the one-taste meditations to a skill meditation. He calls the one taste an exercise leading to supreme clarity *(gsal steng)*, by which the mind's seeming events can be recognized "nakedly" (TN, p. 669). Since emptiness is guaranteed to stay from the beginning, the practitioner is in a position to ease up and allow ordinary experience to ripen spontaneously according to karmic propensities. In order to achieve the highest clarity possible in human experience, the practitioner must allow the ordinary mind to manifest experience on all three levels— the coarse, subtle, and very subtle. Revisiting ordinary experience as a vehicle for wisdom is unique to extraordinary practices *(thun mong ma yin pa)* such as mahāmudrā. The use of ordinary experience as a vehicle for enlightenment is also a manifestation of the enlightened attitude's resultant action, by which the relative and the ultimate enlightened attitude are linked.

3. Mistakes Become Wisdom

Holding awareness-itself at the extraordinary level as the point of observation by which to examine conventional experience as it seems to arise results in profound purification of any residual defilements that might otherwise obscure the realization that the ordinary mind is itself the carrier of the Mahāyāna enlightenment experience (TN, p. 416). The fundamental obstructions to such a realization are false conceptual distinctions, taking phenomena and the mind to be real, and subject/object dualities *(rtog pa)*. Realizing all phenomena and mind to be empty and nondual at the subtlest level of mind eliminates all such obscurations.

A famous saying in the mahāmudrā is "mistakes arise as wisdom."[532] Once viewed as an obstacle to special insight, the ordinary *(tha mal)* workings of the mind now become the very means to deepen the realization of emptiness and bring about awakened wisdom. Thoughts, perceptions, and emotional states become the primary vehicle for wisdom:

> All three realms, without remainder, transform into one great desire. (JP, f. 78b)

The verb *kha dog bsgyur ba* ("to transform," literally "to change color") signifies a fundamental transmutation of the ordinary mental continuum so that what was previously considered to be a hindrance becomes the means to enlightenment. Other verbs, notably *gtan la dbap* ("to put in order") likewise suggest a fundamental transformation of the practitioner's view of unfolding experience, as if finally getting it right (JP, f. 78b). As one commentator says, "All phenomena included in saṃsāra and nirvāṇa become the potential means of self-liberation" (TN, p. 447). Perceptions, thoughts, emotional states, and sensations were once described with such adjectives as "enemies," "poisons," or "mistakes." Now these same phenomena are given different descriptors. They are called "friends" *(grogs).* As one commentator says, "When recognized-in-itself [at the extraordinary level]…everything arises as one's own friend" (JP, f. 78).[533] The practitioner revisits ordinary mental content, but now welcomes it as if meeting a familiar friend along a road.[534]

4. Pointing Out

The extraordinary instructions—both one taste and nonmeditation—are usually marked by the verb *ngo sprod pa,* "to point out." The complete realization of nonduality in the one taste and the subsequent realization of enlightenment in the nonmeditation practice cannot be attained by any artificial activity or method the practitioner may adopt. For these realizations to occur, the natural condition of the mind must be directly pointed out by teachings or a teacher. Pointing out signifies an identity or tautology. The lama helps the practitioner realize the identity between his or her own mental continuum and the oral advice given about the natural condition of the mind. Certain negative propensities are likely to persist that might obscure realization, and these can only be removed by the lama's direct influence:

> Mahāmudrā is awakened wisdom that comes from [the lama's] influence. Stupid people cannot meditate on the awakened wisdom that comes from influence. Stupid people cannot become a vessel for this influence bestowed through the lama's empowerment. (TN, p. 457)

Saying that the nature of the extraordinary practices must be pointed out is another way of saying that it depends on empowerment. Pointing out pertains to direct instructions about the nature of mind. Chokyi Nyima Rinpoche defines *pointing out* as follows: "Pointing-out instruction…means that all the teachings have been condensed into just a few essential lines of text which contain the vital point, the key point regarding the nature of mind."[535] Tashi Namgyel defines it this way:

> Behold! Without clouds the sun spreads its light everywhere, but
> To those who have no eyes, only darkness comes.
> Even though everything is pervaded by the simultaneous [mind],
> Those who are obscured will forever not get it. (TN, p. 424)

> [Valid] cognition is yoked to the four [buddha] bodies. Thoughts (seemingly arising from subject/object duality) and mind, phenomena and emptiness, [both perspectives arise] simultaneously, from the beginning, as nondual. As those who have walked the path know, understanding the way does not come by holding the mind and its appearances to be different, nor thinking the simultaneous [mind] to be good or bad. It comes from the oral advice of the true-hearted ones and from their [directly] pointing out that these are simultaneous while your mind stays [at the extraordinary level of samādhi]. (TN, p. 424)

In the above passage, Tashi Namgyel first sets out two definitions of the simultaneous mind. At a lower level of realization, *simultaneousness* refers to the fundamental nonduality of the mind and its manifest appearances and thoughts, so that appearances and thoughts are realized to be the display of the spontaneous activity of awareness-itself. Therefore clarity and emptiness are natural conditions inherent in the mind's manifestations as they occur in awareness. At a higher level of realization, awakened wisdom and the buddha bodies emerge, simultaneously linked to each moment of conventional experience with the mental continuum. Tashi Namgyel adds that direct experience of the simultaneous mind comes from: (1) its first being intellectually understood via the oral readings, followed by an examination meditation, and (2) then directly experienced after being pointed out by the lama while the practitioner holds the mind at the extraordinary level in a samādhi meditation.[536]

The following description of the natural mind is typical of pointing-out instructions:

The *Sūtra on View [Dṛṣṭisaṃkṣepta]* gives the way:

"That [natural mind] freed from the stains of false
    conceptualization is
Awareness-itself, without any elaboration,
Is nonstaying, nirvāṇa
Is Vajrasattva himself,
Is the six wisdom buddhas,
Is the six wisdoms,
Is the young Mañjuśri,
Is the world appearing in its entirety,
Is the dharma-body and great bliss,
Is that known as the pair, staying/calm
Is the outcome of the fourth [empowerment],
Is the very simultaneous mind itself,
Is its innate nature,…
Is the ultimate enlightened attitude,
Is the buddha families,
Is the Sugata's heart.
This self-occurring awakened wisdom
Is great bliss.
Awareness-itself is luminosity.
Awareness-itself is the nonconceptual still state.…
Awareness-itself is complete freedom from elaboration.
It is the basis of saṃsāra.
It is also nirvāṇa.
It is the great Middle Path.
This is what you observe.
This is what you meditate on.
This is what you realize." (TN, pp. 431–32)

There are many different types of pointing-out instructions, all of which share the common feature of describing the natural condition of the mind. There are two basic types of pointing-out instructions. Tashi Namgyel's root text and autocommentary exemplifies one approach, namely using passages much like those exemplified by the above passage from the *Sūtra on View*. By listening to and then reflecting on such scriptural descriptions of the natural mind, the practitioner intellectually understands the fundamental nondual nature of the mind and its appearances and the linkage of this natural mind with awakened wisdom and buddha bodies that become manifest with enlightenment. Pema Karpo and Jampel Pawo exemplify the other approach found in the oral tradition, namely the use of metaphors such as dream/dreamer, water/ice, and water/waves. These metaphors suggest the essential nonduality and emptiness of the natural mind and its manifestations.

B. The Way to Practice

While pointed-out instructions lead to an intellectual understanding of the natural condition of the mind and sow the seeds for direct realization, the practitioner must match the lama's influence with his or her own meditation practice. There are two stages to the actual practice. The first is an examination meditation regarding the natural mind. Next is the formal samādhi meditation. This is subdivided into two substages. The former substage sets up the extraordinary samādhi to realize simultaneousness, and the latter substage is a continuation of the meditation until the three levels of one-taste realization have ripened. Tashi Namgyel presents these practices in stages *(rim pa),* while Pema Karpo gives three brief aphorisms to be used for either stage or combined *('dres pa)* practice. The stages approach is presented first, followed by the combined form.

1. The Way to Practice by Stages
a. Examination Meditation: Appearance as Mind
Tashi Namgyel calls the one-taste examination meditation instructions "putting in order the way the realized mind stays." Just as the ordinary special-insight examination meditation was designed to establish the propensities for an entirely new realization about the mind—as being empty —likewise the extraordinary examination meditation is designed to establish the propensities for the realization of the mind's natural state and its awakened wisdom. To establish the foundation for this even more radical vision of the mind, the practitioner must prepare by conducting an *examination meditation.* As the name indicates, this meditation results in a profound rearrangement in the way the mind is experienced. The new point of observation for meditation becomes the always-here mind in its natural state from the beginning, that is, the way the realized mind stays. The same verb, *to put in order,* that was used for the special-insight practices is used here, but the object of the verb has changed. During the ordinary special-insight practices the ordinary mind *(sems)* is put in order;

during the extraordinary one-taste practice the way the realized mind stays *(gnas lugs)* is put in order.

Tashi Namgyel divides his examination meditation on the way the realized mind stays into three beginning instructions and one advanced instruction. The three initial instructions pertain to the entity *(ngo bo)*, real nature *(rang bzhin)*, and aspects *(rnam pa)* of the mind. He begins:

> Generally, from the perspective of the way the realized mind stays, the designation of each of these three—entity, nature, and aspect—are none other than the mind's real nature. (TN, p. 404)

Tashi Namgyel went to considerable length in the ordinary special-insight exercises to carefully develop a technical vocabulary with terms like *entity, nature,* and *aspect.* Though related to emptiness, each word had a significantly different usage. Here in the extraordinary meditations Tashi Namgyel does away with his own distinctions. From the perspective of the way the realized mind stays, the previously important differentiation between entity, nature, and aspect collapse. Whether one considers the mind as a possible entity, by its resultant nature, or by its manifest aspects is of no consequence from the perspective of the way the realized mind stays. By deconstructing the terminology, Tashi Namgyel means to convey the equanimity of all perspectives on experience.

Tashi Namgyel's initial instruction, called "Entity," is a review of the practitioner's understanding of emptiness, now looked upon from the extraordinary level of the always-here mind. Not only is the mind an empty entity, "it is also a thing free from arising and passing away" (TN, p. 405), and therefore emptiness is an inherent property of the natural mind that is always there, irrespective of temporal unfolding. Generally speaking, the natural mind is "free from [all] elaboration" (TN, p. 407), so it is impossible to lose sight of emptiness. As a result of this review, the practitioner comes to know the meaning of really staying *(ye nas gnas pa;* TN, p. 407). The new technical term, *ye nas gnas pa* ("really staying"), suggests a fundamental shift in perspective.

In the next instruction, entitled "[Real] Nature" *(rang bzhin;* TN, pp. 408–13), Tashi Namgyel points out the mind's natural condition, or real nature. The very subtle level of mind is also referred to as clear-light mind from the event perspective:

Numerous sayings convey that the "real nature of the mind is said to be clear light." The term *clear light* means "pure, not obscured by the elaboration such as arising and passing away," and not [producing] particles into elements or aggregates. Clear light has no impurities. It is like space, with aspects nowhere existent. So this explains the real nature, said to be like space and nondual. (TN, p. 408)

Tashi Namgyel explains that the correct experience of clear light is not cast in a subject-object duality. Clear light is not something that has objectified perceptual characteristics, such as external color or form or an internal state of great light. Clear light is simply a manifestation of the natural mind's appearance-making or self-clarity *(rang gsal):*

Now, what about the practitioner's experience of the way the realized mind arises? Doesn't the [natural] mind, being beyond the appearance of color and form, self-appear, as if by its own light? This is the knowledge of [nondual] awareness-itself and self-clarity. (TN, p. 411)

Comparable to the term *mind-only,* this appearance-making function of the natural mind is called *arisen-only (shar tsam):*

The experience of the mind's [nondual] clarity and awareness is one of its having arisen-only. (TN, p. 411)

Tashi Namgyel's final instruction, entitled "Aspects" (TN, pp. 413–18), points out the immutable purity of the natural mind despite its many coarse-level manifestations or self-appearing aspects *(rnam pa).* Tashi Namgyel explains how the ordinary mind's momentary defilements *(glo bur dri ma),* such as false conceptualization and emotional states, seem to obscure the inherent condition of the natural mind as completely purified *(rnan byang).* Appearance comes forth as attachment. From the point of view of the way the realized mind stays, the natural mind is inherently pure from the beginning, and from that perspective there has never been impurity, so that appearance comes forth as a mirage or as the illusory embodiment of the natural mind:

Know that the way the realized mind stays is free from any
momentary defilements and that there is complete purification
even when things dependently arise. [From that perspective] all
phenomena are the embodiment of absolute truth, so that even
if it seems that different appearances directly come forth, these
appearances are like a mirage. In the *Sūtra on View [Dṛṣṭisaṃ-
kṣepta]* it says, "Alas! The six illusory realms, all the infinite realms
throughout space, become a fabrication and bring unthinkable
misery for those with a defiled mind. Alas! These appear as sublime realms all condensed into the illusory body with all the
maṇḍala's various illusory forms, and as so many wondrous, illusory emanations that pervade infinite space for those with an
undefiled mind." (TN, p. 414)

The practitioner puts in order both the way the realized mind stays and
the way the realized mind appears as one and the same (TN, p. 418). From
this extraordinary, nondual perspective the natural mind is found to be
completely purified. When there are no impurities whatsoever to obscure
the mind's natural condition, awakened wisdom is there for the realization.
From the perspective of the way the realized mind stays, the seeming
unfolding of ordinary experience is a necessary condition for understanding ultimate reality (TN, pp. 418–26), and ordinary experience becomes
the vehicle or carrier of awakened wisdom.

The advanced section of Tashi Namgyel's examination-meditation
instruction, entitled "Explaining the Definitive Meaning *(rnam nges)* of
the Simultaneous" (TN, pp. 418–26), points out the nature of the simultaneous mind:

> The essence of the simultaneous mind is a mind whose real nature
> is like space and clear light, firm and moving, self-pervading all
> of saṃsāra. (TN, p. 418)

Tashi Namgyel introduces a new technical term, *khyab bdag* ("self-pervad-
ing"), to illustrate that the mind at its subtlest level is all-encompassing.
The simultaneous mind's vast awareness saturates all phenomena like
infinite space, while the simultaneous mind's appearances encompass all
the phenomena of saṃsāra. Tashi Namgyel calls these two perspectives
mind-simultaneousness and *appearance-simultaneousness,* but he is quick to

point out that they are inherently nondual, like the sun and its light or a sandalwood tree and its scent (TN, p. 422). Quoting Gampopa, he says, "Mind-simultaneousness is the dharmakāya, and appearance-simultaneousness is the light of the dharmakāya" (TN, p. 423). Direct realization of the simultaneous mind is important because it establishes the foundation for enlightenment through which buddha bodies come forth (TN, p. 424).

Completing the extraordinary examination meditation yields an intellectual understanding of the simultaneous mind. Next the practitioner must translate that understanding into direct realization of the simultaneous mind through a samādhi meditation. Tashi Namgyel calls this samādhi *the yoga of simultaneousness.*

b. Samādhi Meditation on the Simultaneous
(1). Setting Up the Simultaneous Mind

Tashi Namgyel explains the actual samādhi meditation in a section called "What Needs to Be Accomplished After Pointing Out the Simultaneous Mind" (TN, pp. 426–48).[537] Direct realization of what has been pointed out comes only from meditation. Tashi Namgyel divides the samādhi meditation instructions into three parts. The first part pertains to the mind perspective. It is called mind-simultaneousness. The second and third parts pertain to the event perspective. They are called cognition-simultaneousness and appearance-simultaneousness, respectively. He explains that the latter two instructions, "though considered slightly different are the same" (TN, p. 421).

The instruction on *mind-simultaneousness (sems nyid lhan skyes;* TN, pp. 426–33) presents the way to set up the samādhi of simultaneousness *(lhan skye kyi mnyam gzhag)*. As the name suggests, the emphasis is on the mind perspective, in this case the absolute or ground condition of the mind in its natural state. The mind-simultaneousness picks up where the yoga of unelaboration left off, namely with awareness-itself of the way the realized mind stays in its always-here condition from the beginning. Here are the root instructions:

> When practicing according to the pointing-out instructions, if you haven't listened to your lama or some important teacher, your mind may not settle into itself, and therefore elaboration occurs. From that perspective you will become obscured and you haven't learned the oral readings. In that case do all of the previous points.

However, if you are able to set up your mind nonartificially, in its own way, then all coarse- and subtle-level cognitions become calm in their own right *[rang sa]*. When the mind happens to stay in its own way, or when viewed with equanimity *[mnyam pa zhog]*, this is called [real] staying/calm practice.

Now view that which seems to cause the experience, but which does not cause the experience [namely the mind-itself]. From the [extraordinary] level of samādhi, take this view [of the mind's natural condition]: [The natural mind] can't be elaborated by such concepts as "the mind's entity" and can't be reflected because it is beyond any [ordinary] recognition. Awareness-in-and-of-itself contains the understanding and the unobstructed clarity. This is called [real] special-insight practice.

Yet both practices mentioned here are not essentially different. Staying/calm practice happens to be the same as special-insight practice when there is awareness-itself and self-clarity, beyond all [ordinary] recognition. To put it another way, special insight happens to be staying/calm when [the natural mind] stays in its own way and is not obscured by [coarse- or subtle-level] cognitive or perceptual attributes. To put it another way, from the [extraordinary] level of samādhi, you take what seems to be a "view," and this "view" is called "the coupling of staying/calm and special-insight practice." Both of these occur at once. Experiencing this is called "generating the meditation of recognition [of the mind's natural condition]." There are many ways of referring to this: "a sentient being's mind contemplating the mind of a buddha," "the intrinsic way the realized mind stays," "the unborn dharmakāya," and "knowledge of natural mind-simultaneousness." The practitioner attains the highest teachings of all the sūtras, tantras, shastras, and oral advice, and really knows them. Taking these oral readings into consideration generates certain knowledge. Even with many more sayings like this, nothing further is necessary because not even the slightest idea could possibly deceive you. So set up the mind so as to settle into itself and all thought becomes liberated in its own right *[rang sa]*. The mind's awareness-itself *[rang rig]* and its self-clarity *[rang gsal]* are beyond [ordinary] recognition. Set up the mind one-pointedly from the perspective of mind-simultaneousness. (TN, pp. 667–68)

Tashi Namgyel explains the practice in terms of finding just the right balance between staying calm and special insight. The practitioner stabilizes the meditation at the extraordinary level of samādhi and takes the way the realized mind stays *(gnas tshul)* as the point of observation. Tashi Namgyel explains, "Set up the mind in the way the realized mind stays" (TN, p. 426). The staying-calm portion of the instruction refers to holding the mind at the right level of samādhi, namely the extraordinary level. The right level of samādhi is necessary because once the correct view of the simultaneous mind has been pointed out, any kind of artificial mental activity *(las)* on the part of the practitioner only serves to obscure the mind's inherent self-purity. The technical term *bzhag pa* ("to establish or set up") is meant to convey that while the meditator cannot make the extraordinary samādhi happen through any kind of artificial activity, it is nevertheless possible to establish just the right conditions for the extraordinary samādhi to occur on its own. The special-insight portion of the instruction refers to viewing the mind and its appearances not from the perspective of the ordinary mind but from the perspective of the way the realized mind stays. From that perspective, when the natural mind settles into itself *(rang babs),* then all illusory, unobstructed coarse- and subtle-level cognitions and appearances quickly become self-cleansed *(rang sang),* self-purified *(rang dag),* and self-calm (*rang zhi;* TN, p. 426), and the practitioner directly realizes the inherent purity of the natural mind. Tashi Namgyel calls this insight "recognizing the [natural] mind" (TN, p. 428). Citing the *Tantra of Mahāmudrā, Not Completely Staying [Phyag rgya chen po rab tu mi gnas pa'i rgyud],* he adds:

This is mahāmudrā.
This is not covered by stains.
It is neither rejected nor made to happen.
It is not found by any path nor by any remedy.
This is all the buddha bodies.
This is the basis of all benefits.
This is spontaneously present. (TN, p. 433)

The meditator sets up just the right conditions by settling into the extraordinary level of samādhi, allowing awareness-itself to stay as the uninterrupted point of observation and then letting the mind go its own way *(rang lugs).* Tashi Namgyel comments that this term, *in its own way (rang lugs),* means that awareness goes its own way *(rang lugs)* and also that clarity goes its own way (*rang gsal;* TN, p. 427), so that the mind's seeming events are not different from the mind itself and therefore are not obstructed (*ma bkag;* TN, p. 426). He adds that "no real content can be recognized" (TN, p. 426) in that all content is inherently empty. Even so, the practitioner is said to "take what seems to be a view" *(ltos dang zhes ltar byed),* and in this case the view is the extraordinary level of the mind-itself. No longer operating from the ordinary self-representation as the point of observation, "the mind changes heart" (TN, p. 420). The new, extraordinary point of observation is called *the simultaneousness dharmakāya* (TN, p. 428) and is also called *the supreme mind (sems nyid gyi thog tu;* TN, p. 428). The meditation is like a mind-only meditation, except that the experience of mind is remarkably different. Tashi Namgyel emphasizes this difference by calling the meditation "recognizing [the true nature] of mind" (TN, p. 428). He says,

> In the *Sūtra of Mahāmudrā, Awakened Wisdom [Jñānamudrā Sūtra]* it says,

>> Phenomena unfold by mind.
>> They are set up in the mind as empty.
>> Recognize the mind in whatever occurs,
>> This is the practice of yoga.

> In the *Saṃdhinirmocana* it says,

>> How does a bodhisattva meditate?
>> The answer: by taking-to-mind the stream as it arises,
>>   you take-to-mind
>> the [real] nature of mind. (TN, p. 429)

(2). Bringing Forth Awakened Wisdom by Cognition- and Perception-Simultaneousness

(a). Cognition-Simultaneousness

Taking the extraordinary mind as the point of observation, the practitioner looks at emerging thoughts and perceptions. The seeming ordinary mental continuum with its coarse-level cognitions and perceptions is allowed to unfold unobstructedly as a consequence of the spontaneous activity *(las)* and ripening of previous karmic propensities (TN, p. 434). Therefore the exercise is entitled *cognition-simultaneousness* and *appearance-simultaneousness*. The root instructions for cognition-simultaneousness are as follows:

> Do the body points directly as before. Set up the mind in its own way, so that thought [and emotions] are made calm, from the perspective of undistraction. From the perspective of supreme clarity *[gsal steng]* look nakedly at the natural condition[538] of the mind, wherein no [substantial entity] can be recognized. Then stay nakedly [continuously] in clarity and emptiness. From the perspective of supreme clarity also look nakedly at the natural condition of this [clarity and emptiness] and generate the path of transformation, by which the very intensity of thought seems to bring real bliss.
>
> You happen then to take what seems to be a view of:
> 1. Thoughts, which happen nakedly in supreme [clarity]
> 2. The mind, whose natural condition is simultaneousness, with clarity and emptiness that are beyond recognition
> 3. Both of these as nondual
>
> This is called "happening to be in nondual clarity and emptiness."...Whenever you put in order thought's natural condition, as said previously, and likewise whenever you cut off the root of staying and moving, the [natural] mind, beyond recognition, is awareness-itself *[rang rig]* and clarity-itself *[rang gsal]*. It is neither one nor many. It is like the metaphor of water and its waves.... It is no longer necessary to obstruct thoughts in order to protect [the realization]. In whatever seems to arise, when it arises, both staying and moving become inseparable. What is true for those thoughts you [actually] experience is true for all thoughts. Whoever walks along this path of thought protects the [mind's] natural condition even as those previously unborn thoughts seem to become elaborated thereafter. Furthermore, if you are afraid you might get distracted when seeing thought's natural condition, you should meditate regularly to master what is called "protecting during occurrence" *['byung la skyong]*. Once you consider the oral readings, certain knowledge is generated when there is elaboration. (TN, pp. 669–70)

In this meditation the extraordinary mind observes its own nature, in this case the nature of the spontaneous activity of karmic propensities ripening as coarse-level thoughts and emotions. According to the commentary, the meditator holds the mind at the extraordinary level of samādhi, wherein staying-calm and special-insight practice are perfectly balanced. In the root text the passage "from the perspective of undistraction" refers to staying/calm and the passage "from the perspective of supreme clarity" refers to special insight, respectively. In other words, in the extraordinary level of samādhi, awareness-itself is never distracted because it is a continuous property of the natural mind. Furthermore, in this extraordinary state the meditator taps into the mind's inherent capacity to illuminate itself to itself as a continuous property of the natural mind. This is called *supreme clarity (gsal steng)*. After setting up this extraordinary samādhi the meditator is told to "look nakedly" and thereafter to "stay nakedly." Looking nakedly refers to adopting a view of the coarse-level thoughts and emotions that seem to arise in a way that is completely free of any artificial activity, such as trying to make something happen or suppressing what is happening. From the perspective of the natural, always-here mind these previously elaborated thoughts *[khrul rtag]* seem to arise in a new way. They are now directly experienced as inherently empty, diverse manifestations that result from the spontaneous activity of the natural mind's condition. The commentary explains:

> Mistaken concepts, such as holding things to be real *[a'thas kyi bden 'dzin]*, simply do not occur. There is [only] emptiness. There is no basis whatsoever for recognizing an entity or self-existent nature in any concept. There is no difference between the clarity of thought's aspects and the emptiness beyond recognition. When you directly experience that movement is emptiness and emptiness is movement, you see the very face of the cognition-simultaneousness itself, as captured by the metaphor of water and waves. The polarities "movement is emptiness and emptiness is movement" are meant to illustrate the equanimity of thought's relative movement and the ultimate emptiness of the staying-mind. The coupling of thought and emptiness is called *cognition-simultaneousness [rtog pa'i lham skye]*. Just as water and waves are the same, likewise every single wave of thought remains completely untainted by mistaken concepts. (TN, p. 433)

All coarse-level thoughts and emotions arise unobstructed as inherently empty.

The outcome of this samādhi meditation is described as permanently putting in order *(gtan la phebs)* coarse-level cognition, such as thought and emotion. Tashi Namgyel uses the term *path of transformation (zhig' gyur chags la de lam)* to illustrate how every seeming wave of thought (relative truth) simultaneously and continuously displays the natural mind's inherent emptiness (absolute truth). Another way of describing the outcome is to say that "mistakes arise as wisdom" (TN, p. 440). In his commentary Tashi Namgyel cites various passages from the sūtras, tantras, and oral readings to illustrate the certain knowledge that comes from the meditation:

[In the sūtras]
In the *Sāgaramatiparipṛcchā* [Lodro Gyatso] it says,

> O Bhagavan, is this [extraordinary] samādhi difficult to attain?

Bhagavan answers:

> It comes from realizing that [coarse-level] aspects and awakened wisdom are the same. When you understand all phenomena to be the same, you reach enlightenment. Bodhisattva, don't try to figure this out if you want to get enlightened.

In the *Sarvadharmapravṛttinirdeśasūtra* [Sūtra Wherein All Phenomena Are Said to Be Non-Events], it says,

> Attachment is said to be nirvāṇa.
> Aversion and ignorance, too.
> Because these *are* enlightenment,
> Enlightenment and attachment are nondual.

In the *Saṃputa [Tantra]* it says,

> Saṃsāra and nirvāṇa are without difference.
> Knowing saṃsāra's real nature is nirvāṇa....

[In the oral readings] Maitripa says,

> "Moment by moment thoughts arise from that which is
>   always here.
> These very thoughts are the supreme condition of the
>   natural mind.
> Both are inseparable from the beginning.
> I point out both of these as 'one taste.'" (TN, pp. 435–38)

Tashi Namgyel summarizes these passages by saying that correctly understanding cognition-simultaneousness is the realization that all coarse- and subtle-level thoughts are "recognized as the dharmakāya," that is, as the embodiment of enlightenment (TN, p. 438).

(b). Perception-Simultaneousness

The root instructions for perception-simultaneousness follow suit. Essentially the practitioner allows perceptions to come forth. However, they arise in a new way. According to the commentary, "Perception-simultaneousness is not different from that of cognition" (TN, p. 441). The same extraordinary level of samādhi is used. The natural mind is taken as the point of observation to view the diverse manifestations of coarse-level sensory experiences as reflective of the simultaneous mind's spontaneous ripening of karmic propensities. These diverse perceptual events, for example seeing a mountain or a house, are taken to be inherently empty from the beginning while at the same time the inherent clarity of the diverse perceptual qualities of these sensory experiences is appreciated. Therefore such perceptual events arise in a new way, as mere appearances *(snang tsam)* inseparable from the mind that generates them. Tashi Namgyel calls this insight seeing *appearance as it really is (yang dag par snang;* TN, p. 443):

> In short, these [diverse] perceptual aspects [inherently] have
> both clarity and emptiness (without recognition of an entity),
> and [both the clarity and the emptiness] are inseparable. There-
> fore any perception [that seems to come forth] is directly expe-
> rienced as appearance-emptiness or as emptiness-appearance.
> (TN, p. 442)

Here again, the juxtaposition of seeming polarities—appearance-emptiness and emptiness-appearance—is a linguistic device meant to show the inseparable nature of relative perception and ultimate emptiness. Direct realization of the mind's empty appearance-making activity as an inherent property of the natural mind is called perception-simultaneousness. In the oral tradition perception-simultaneousness is captured by the metaphor of the dreamer and the dream's content, which are inseparable (TN, p. 442). What holds true for visual forms, such as mountains and houses, holds true for all perceptual experience, sounds, smells, and so on (TN, p. 442).

The outcome of the samādhi meditation on perception-simultaneousness is described as putting in order *(gtan la 'bebs)* perception. Tashi Namgyel says that all sensory experience is realized to be the embodiment of the dharmakāya (TN, p. 444). Tashi Namgyel uses the term *walking along the path of perception* to illustrate how every seeming sensory event (relative truth)—sights, sounds, and so on—simultaneously and continuously displays the natural mind's inherent emptiness (absolute truth). Various passages from the oral tradition illustrate the realization:

> Nāgārjuna says,
> "Seeing any substance as it really is
> is seeing all substance as it really is." (TN, p. 443)

> Śabari says,
> "All saṃsāra is like an illusion, a mirage,
> Like a reflection [in a mirror].
> Substance without attributes
> The agent of perception, the mind, like space, is an illusion,
> Without either an extreme or a middle [view], who can know it
> [conceptually]?" (TN, p. 447)

From the perspective of perception-simultaneousness, all the diverse manifestations of sensory experience, being inherently empty, are illusory. They are experienced as "mere appearances," much like dream content, which is inherently inseparable from the mind that dreams it. Ultimately all sensory experiences are the natural appearance-making activity of the dharmakāya, the embodiment of enlightenment.

(c). Removing Faults and Recognizing Flawless Meditation:
Knowledge of the Ordinary

Through the one-taste meditations the practitioner is introduced to a truly extraordinary level of mind, far beyond ordinary experience. Therefore it is especially important that the meditations be done correctly. To insure this, Tashi Namgyel ends with a very detailed set of protecting instructions. These protecting instructions come in two parts. The first part reviews the various problems that occur during the one-taste meditation that may prevent a complete or accurate experience of the extraordinary simultaneous mind. The second part describes the desired outcome in terms of certain knowledge of the ordinary mind, and how the ordinary mind, properly understood, becomes the foundation for awakened wisdom. After recognizing and correcting any faults occurring during the extraordinary samādhi meditation, the practitioner "sees the benefit" or "recognizes the true aim of the meditation" (TN, p. 448–49).

1'. Removing Faults

Tashi Namgyel begins his protection instructions with advice on removing faults *(skyon sel).* The faults of one-taste meditation are divided into two categories: (1) fundamental faults *(nor sa),* and (2) biased or partial samādhi *(phyogs re ba,* var. *phyogs ris ba;* literally, "skewed in a particular direction"). The basic faults are the most common mistakes that serve to obscure correct understanding of the natural mind. These faults occur through "pride generated in the meditation" *(rlom pa;* TN, p. 450). The special samādhi constitutes a profound shift that carries a sense of conviction, as if one has reached full enlightenment itself. However, the practitioner has merely begun to set the mind right.

There are two categories of basic faults: (1) not setting up the special samādhi state properly, and (2) not receiving proper pointing-out instruction.

a'. The Fundamental Faults of Samādhi

The first type of fault pertains to deficiencies in the extraordinary samādhi state. There are two subcategories of faults: (1) failing to perfectly balance staying/calm and special insight, and (2) engaging in artificial activity during the extraordinary samādhi meditation in a way that interferes with full manifestation of the simultaneous mind. The yoga of one taste requires perfect balance between staying/calm and special-insight practice. The samādhi is faulty when there is an imbalance in one or the other, that is, when there is staying/calm without sufficient insight or when there is insight without sufficient staying/calm. Such an imbalance makes it impossible to directly experience the simultaneous mind. Table 34 lists the most common flaws of the samādhi state and their respective deleterious effects.

The first two flaws pertain to a samādhi state skewed in the direction of staying/calm. First, Tashi Namgyel explains that the meditator may have developed a very strong capacity for staying/calm that has no dullness or flightiness, and is so strong that visions and psychic abilities occur. However, if that samādhi state lacks special insight and the direct realization of emptiness, then it cannot serve as a foundation for enlightenment (TN, pp. 448–50). Second, he explains that a very strong samādhi is likely to have the three characteristics of bliss, clarity, and nonconceptual stillness, but that if it lacks insight practice, then it is impossible to realize emptiness, and therefore the practitioner fails to establish the foundation for enlightenment (TN, pp. 454–56). However compelling the respective states of bliss, clarity, or nonconceptual stillness may seem, they are nevertheless "uncertain appearances" (*snang la mi nges pa;* TN, p. 455) with respect to their potential to yield special insight.

TABLE 34: FLAWS OF THE SAMĀDHI STATE

Imbalanced staying/calm and special insight	1. **Staying/calm without special insight** a. Strong staying/calm with visions & psychic abilities b. Strong staying/calm with bliss, clarity, & nonconceptual stillness	Can't serve as cause or foundation for enlightenment
	2. **Special insight without staying/calm** a. Special insight without strong staying/calm b. Mindfulness without special insight	Obstructs cognition, so it arises as an enemy. Or does not obstruct cognition, which remains indistinct Clinging to emptiness

The next two faults pertain to a samādhi skewed in the direction of special insight. First, without a strong foundation in staying/calm the practitioner may completely obstruct the appearance of any object from any of the six sense systems. This experience is like fainting, intoxication, or a deep sleep (TN, p. 453). Sometimes attempts at cutting off thought do not entirely cut off the thought, so that whatever arises is seen as an enemy. Sometimes the intended object does not become obstructed but remains indistinct. These experiences are "not meditations intent on emptiness" (TN, p. 454). Second, the practitioner with strong special insight may develop continuous mindfulness in such a way as to develop a subtle attachment to emptiness. In this case no special insight develops and pride is mistaken as emptiness (TN p. 455). Proper balance of staying/calm and special insight in the extraordinary samādhi insures the correct realization of the simultaneous mind in a way that includes both certain knowledge of the natural mind's spacelike awareness as empty, and nonobstructed manifestations of appearances and cognitions as the natural mind's clear light.

b'. The Faults of Pointing Out

Table 35 lists the most common faults of pointing out:

TABLE 35: FAULTS OF POINTING OUT

Deficient Sources	(1) Use of unsuitable sources
	(2) Hearsay
Deficient Development	(3) External interferences
	(4) Seeking other means

Pointing out is an act of empowerment, performed by a lama employing instructions that have been established by tradition as effective in evoking awakened wisdom in students. The student, in turn, must respect the lama and have sufficient faith in the instructions so as not to seek elsewhere for means to effect the desired realization. Using unsuitable sources or secondhand knowledge runs the risk of developing a faulty understanding of the simultaneous mind. Even when the correct sources are used as part of the examination meditation, the samādhi meditation may go astray if the practitioner tries to do some other sort of meditation or if the meditation is influenced by external sources.

c'. Biased or Partial Extraordinary Samādhi

The basic faults prohibit direct experience of the simultaneous mind. Having experienced the simultaneous mind, further problems may occur. These are called *the faults that skew the simultaneous mind in a particular direction*

(phyogs re ba, var. *phyogs ris ba).* These faults typically occur because of residual artificial activity occurring during the extraordinary samādhi meditation, which creates a bias toward either the mind- or the event-perspective
of the simultaneous mind, so that the practitioner fails to realize the ultimate inseparability of the natural mind and its various manifestations.

One problem is that staying/calm practice may be very strong so that a
nonconceptual still state predominates and all seemingly occurring events
immediately become calm. The meditator may artificially act in such a way
during the meditation as to become attached to this stillness, and in so
doing thought and appearances become obstructed (TN, pp. 460–61). As
a consequence the state becomes biased toward mind-simultaneousness
and there can be no certain knowledge about cognition- and appearance-
simultaneousness. While this is a typical beginner's *(dag po pa)* extraordinary meditation, it lacks the characteristics of genuine mastery with respect
to the "end state" simultaneous mind (TN, p. 461).

Another problem is that some practitioners approach the extraordinary
samādhi by trying to maintain uninterrupted mindfulness/awareness *(dran
rig)* by intensifying. They become attached to the idea that the mind
should stay with clarity and emptiness every moment. According to Tashi
Namgyel, this approach is acceptable at the beginning so long as the practitioner maintains the focus on the mind's real nature. Other meditators
fail to clear up their doubts *(sgro 'dogs)* about the emptiness of thoughts
and appearances, so that they appear as enemies rather than as nondual
manifestations of the natural mind. However, skilled practitioners overcome this "lower state" problem once they become more familiar with
cognition- and appearance-simultaneousness (TN, pp. 461–63).

Table 36 lists the faults that skew the simultaneous mind so as to dilute
full realization of its nondual nature. According to Tashi Namgyel, the
best remedy for these faults is to become familiar with all three samādhi
meditations on simultaneousness—mind-, cognition-, and appearance-
simultaneousness, respectively. Of these three, greater emphasis is given to
cognition- and appearance-simultaneousness:

> Chiefly, pointing out and understanding cognition- and
> appearance-simultaneousness is very important. (TN, p. 463)

TABLE 36: FAULTS THAT SKEW THE SIMULTANEOUS MIND

Problem	Bias Favors	Remedy
Attachment to a nonconceptual still state	Mind-simultaneousness	Cognition- & appearance-simultaneousness
Intensified mindfulness/awareness	Mind-simultaneousness	Cognition- & appearance-simultaneousness
Continuing (i.e., not cut off) doubt about events	Cognition- & appearance-simultaneousness	Cognition- & appearance simultaneousness

2′. Recognizing Knowledge of the Ordinary: Initial Awakened Wisdom

In the second part of the protecting instruction, Tashi Namgyel gives a careful description of the end state of the one-taste meditations so that the practitioner can compare his or her experiences in order to insure being on the right track. If the practitioner completes the extraordinary samādhi meditation with a correct view of the simultaneous mind, then the way the realized mind stays is known as *ordinary knowledge* (*tha mal gyi shes pa;* TN, p. 463). Tashi Namgyel clarifies that ordinary knowledge is not intended to mean the ordinary, everyday dysfunctional mind. He says that there are two definitions of *ordinary*—the ordinary confused mind and the ordinary natural mind *(rang bzhin)*. Ordinary knowledge refers to a proper understanding of the natural mind. The properties of the natural mind include the following:

> The meaning of the natural mind is the mind's (1) staying, in its self-nature, in its own way, and (2) its clear-light nature when the mind is settled into itself, undefiled, nonartificial. (TN, pp. 463–64)

From the mind-perspective, the simultaneous mind stays continuously in its own self-nature *(rang gshis)* and in its own way *(rang lugs)*. From the event-perspective, the appearance-making function of the natural mind is its illuminating clear-light nature, which remains undefiled *(ma 'bag pa)* by any misconceptions, completely free of any artificial activity *(ma bcos)*, and remaining calm or settled into itself *(rnal du phebs)* upon manifesting itself. Another technical term for undefiled is *fresh (gnyug ma)*, which means "free of any false conceptions." The main points in understanding the ordinary mind are that the ordinary mind is completely free of any artificial activity and any false conceptions about it. When the special samādhi is properly set up, ordinary knowledge settles into itself. The term *setting-up* refers to finding the exact balance of conditions, free from artificial activity, so that a desired effect can manifest.

Tashi Namgyel devotes a lengthy discussion to "recognizing how this seeming ordinary mind is special" *(khyad par;* TN, p. 465). Consistent with his pointing-out style, he describes the special view of ordinary mind by citing a passage from Gampopa for those who "fail to recognize" the ordinary mind properly (TN, p. 465):

> "Well, if you desire to be liberated from saṃsāra, you must recognize the ordinary mind because it is the root of all phenomena. Further, you must set up the mind freshly: (1) in what has been called ordinary knowledge; (2) in knowledge-itself, wherein the aspects of phenomena are not defiled by anything; (3) in knowledge about the aspects of the world, undefiled by anything either; (4) not covered by dullness, obscurations, and false concepts either; (5) but set up freshly. Then you'll recognize the ordinary mind. (6) Then awakened wisdom will come, which is self-awareness in and by itself. If you are unaware of that, you are ignorant of simultaneousness. If you understand it, you recognize the natural mind and its ordinary knowledge, and are familiar with its experience and description. Then, as these experiences increase, they are more special than typical [meditative] outcomes."
>
> (1) The term *ordinary knowledge* means "awareness-itself," "the natural mind," "the awakened wisdom of simultaneousness, freshness, unelaboration, and clear light." (2) the phrase "knowledge-itself wherein the aspects of the phenomena are not defiled by anything" pertains to when the mind is not corrupted by its habit of using concepts, getting preoccupied with concepts about the [philosophical] tenets, or clinging to the [meditative] states of clarity, bliss, or nonconceptual stillness. (3) The phrase "knowledge of

the aspects of the world undefiled by anything" pertains to when the mind is uncorrupted, separated from emotional states such as desire and hatred and from the turbidity of concepts about what is to be done [in the meditation] and who seems to be doing it. (4) The phrase "not covered by dullness, obscurations, and false concepts" pertains to when one is no longer obscured, but manifests the way the realized mind stays and the way the realized mind happens along the path, even when distracted by obscurations, dullness, or clouded by [seeming] self-existent [external] attributes or by elaborated false concepts, or by flightiness. (5) The phrase *set up freshly* pertains to the way the realized mind happens when it comes forth as it is, in its natural condition or temperament [emptiness], and when it is not corrupted by any effort to prevent anything or make anything happen. [The mind] is set up [naturally] in the very way the realized mind happens by itself. (6) On that occasion or anytime after that, too, if your practice manifests awakened wisdom, completely free of conceptualization, you speak the [true] words of the Dharma. If you manifest ordinary knowledge, nakedness, you don't talk like a foolish ascetic. These [that is, awakened wisdom and ordinary knowledge] are one and the same truth. (TN, pp. 465–67)

The passage is a highly condensed description of how ordinary knowledge ripens. The first part of the instruction is a description of how to set up the extraordinary samādhi. *Freshness* refers to the absence of any conceptual elaboration whatsoever. Under that condition the meditator is able to "recognize the ordinary mind." Because of the shift away from any ordinary point of observation during the extraordinary samādhi, it is more accurate to say that the always-here mind recognizes itself *(rang ngo shes)*. What is recognized are the properties of the simultaneous mind, namely awareness-itself and clear light. The next part of the instructions pertain to intrinsic knowledge about subtle-level meditative experiences (such as the respective states of bliss, clarity, and nonconceptual stillness) and coarse-level emotional states and thought patterns, respectively, as they are understood in direct experience at the level of the natural mind, and in such a way that they are not corrupted by any false concepts. Such content and experiences come into awareness nakedly *(rjen pa)*, that is, free from false conceptualization. These experiences are simply manifestations of the natural mind's appearance-making. The technical term used to describe these spontaneous manifestations, from the event-perspective is *the way the realized mind happens by itself ('dug tsul)*. The technical term used for the point of observation of these manifestations is called *the way the realized mind stays (gnas lugs)*. The next part of the instructions describes the ripening of ordinary knowledge. As recognition-itself of the ordinary mind gets stronger, it will no longer be obscured by any type of potentially distracting experience, such as dullness, flightiness, elaboration of thought, or taking external appearances to be self-existent.

These instructions contain a description of skillful means *(thabs)*—or better, non-means *(thabs med)*—by which ordinary knowledge is attainable. The key phrase is "to set up freshly" *(rang sor)*. This passage refers to the absence of any artificial activity to try to bring about ordinary knowledge. Recognition-itself is an intrinsic property of the natural mind. It is *not* a type of cognitive activity, because it doesn't involve activity *(byas ba)*, and it certainly doesn't involve artificial activity, such as trying to prevent certain experiences from occurring or trying to make certain experiences happen. When set up freshly, the natural mind's intrinsic staying as well as the way it makes experience happen by itself occur without any artificial activity to obscure it. Even though recognition of the ordinary mind is free of any conceptualization, this does not mean that the meditator needs to establish a nonconceptual still samādhi state, because such an attempt might introduce artificial activity and/or false ideas about the natural mind. Tashi Namgyel defines *recognition-itself* as a "way of seeing" *(mthong tshul)*, or more specifically as "seeing the real nature of the mind" (TN, p. 470). It is as if the mind recognizes its own intrinsic nature. This profound insight into the natural condition of the mind must also ripen "again and again" through "familiarity" (TN, p. 471).

The last part of the instructions contain a description of awakened wisdom *(ye shes)* that has the potential to develop during the latter part of the one-taste or in the subsequent nonmeditation practice. Tashi Namgyel says that awakened wisdom develops "on such an occasion or anytime after that" (TN, p, 467). More will be said about this later. For now suffice it to say that refined knowledge of the natural mind establishes the foundation for enlightenment. Ordinary knowledge becomes the cause *(rgyu)* or foundation *(bsten)* from which enlightenment ripens. Ordinary knowledge ripens into awakened wisdom under appropriate conditions *(rkyen)*. The culmination of the one-taste meditation sets the threshold for enlightenment. It is the "dawning of mahāmudrā meditation" (TN, p. 469), the precursor to full enlightenment. For perfect enlightenment *(rdzogs byang)* to come about,[539] the "causes and conditions" for its ripening must be present. The cause *(rgyu)* of awakened wisdom is emptiness; the essential conditions *(rkyen)* are: (1) generating the extraordinary samādhi state, (2) correctly understanding the oral readings that have been appropriately pointed out, (3) recognition-itself of the simultaneous mind and ordinary knowledge, and (4) mastery of the yoga of nonmeditation.

If the intrinsic condition of the ordinary mind is recognizing correctly, then awareness never strays from that realization. Therefore Tashi Namgyel ends the protecting instructions by saying that "mahāmudrā meditation is explained as [continous] undistractedness" (TN, p. 472). The two technical terms introduced are *the mindfulness of awareness-itself (rang rig pa'i dran pa)* and *the undistracted perspective (ma yengs pa'i ngang nas)*. Prior to this point in the overall meditation practice, mindfulness entailed some degree of artificial activity. At this stage mindfulness is pointed out to be an extension of awareness-itself, that is, an intrinsic property of the mind's natural condition. The term *recognition-itself* pertains to the natural mind's capacity for it own realization, while the term *mindfulness of awareness-itself* pertains to the natural mind's ongoing awareness of its own true nature.

Tashi Namgyel explains how ordinary knowledge deepens:

> Recognition-itself of this ordinary knowledge is the basis for the mindfulness of awareness-itself, and this in turn forms the basis for the deepest meaning of mahāmudrā meditation, namely the undistracted perspective. (TN, p. 472)

Once having achieved the undistracted perspective, awareness-itself never departs from continuous awareness of the mind's nondual intrinsic nature, and the meditator need not do anything to sustain that continuous realization. This is the true meaning of the technical term *the way the realized mind stays (gnas lugs)*. There is no special state nor any particular attainment to protect, as was the case in previous protecting exercises:

> The *Tantra of the King of Secret Nectars* says,
>
> > By meditating on the [natural mind's] real nature—
> > emptiness and clear light—there is nothing to attain.

By not meditating there is nothing to attain.
Meditation is a false concept.
Nonmeditation is a false concept, too.
There isn't even the slightest cause to meditate,
Nor [the slightest] movement of distraction.

The Meditation on Perfect Truth says,

Don't meditate on anything when meditating.
Meditation is a mere designation. (TN, p. 473)

Tashi Namgyel redefines the traditional term for concentration, *undistraction (ma yengs pa),* as an intrinsic property of the natural mind that is devoid of any artificial activity or grasping.

2. The Condensed Way to Practice the Yoga of One Taste

Pema Karpo uses a condensed style of instruction, and points out the entire practice of one-taste yoga as a single unit. Nevertheless, discrete stages of one-taste yoga are implied. The brief instructions are given in the form of three metaphors, which correspond to an examination meditation, samādhi meditation, and the outcome, respectively.

The first metaphor, *sleep and dreams,* is designed to point out the correct view of the simultaneous mind. The root instructions are:

First, pointing out appearance to be mind by the metaphor of sleep and dreams: Just as whatever appears during sleep is none other than the mind, likewise, all waking appearances are the dreams of waking state's ignorance and are none other than the mind. Set up [awareness-itself] in an eased-up manner on whatever appears, so that the seeming external sense objects that appear and the mind-itself become inseparable and transmuted into one taste. Milarepa, the lord of yogis, says,

Experiencing last night's dream carries the same realization as the teacher who pointed out appearance to be mind. Is this not so?

In the *Hevajra Tantra* it also says,

> Transmute all three realms, without remainder, into one great
> desire. (PK, f. 12b)

Pema Karpo's metaphor utilizes a pointing-out style of instruction characteristic of the oral tradition. A brief metaphor is given to the actively meditating student in order to empower the practitioner to develop a correct
view of the extraordinary, simultaneous mind. The central instruction is
"pointing out appearance to be mind." The main technical term pertains
to the nonduality *(gnyis su med pa)* of the mind and its manifestations. *Nonduality* is synonymous with *simultaneousness.*

Jampel Pawo explains the pointing-out instruction to mean that "the
mind-itself and its appearances are inseparable" (JP, f. 77b). The term
mind-itself (rang gi sems) refers to the extraordinary level of mind wherein
awareness-itself is taken as the point of observation. Using this point of
observation brings the realization that the mind and its seeming manifestations are fundamentally inseparable, like a dreamer and his dreams. Consistent with a pointing-out style, the commentator explains the passage
by citing a few famous passages from the mahāmudrā source material:

Śabari says,
> Understanding the mind-itself is mahāmudrā.
> The mind-itself and its appearances are inseparable.
> Appearance is that which has the form of the mind-itself.

Saraha says,
> Wind agitates calm water. Calm water then forms into waves.
> Likewise, Saraha [points out to you], O king! that appearance,
>   though one, takes many forms. (JP, f. 77b–78a)

The first passage illustrates how an understanding of the mind-itself leads
to an understanding of appearance as the nondual form *(gzugs can)* of the
mind-itself. The second passage reverses the order. An understanding of
seemingly manifest appearances leads to realization of the mind-itself as
the one calm, nondual backdrop to whatever seems to appear. Both the
mind-itself and its appearances are empty. Jampel Pawo says they are "without independent existence" *(rang skyu thub ba med par):*

It is easy to recognize whatever has arisen—good or bad, joyful or miserable, beneficial or harmful—as mind-itself, without independent existence other than [mere] appearance. (JP, f. 78a)

Note the switch in verbal object. The object of the verb *to recognize* is usually some sort of appearance. Here it is the mind-itself. This linguistic device, as well as others, is meant to convey the inseparability of the mind-itself and its appearances. The metaphor of sleep and dreams is designed to convey the same realization.

Correctly understanding the simultaneous mind leads to the realization that it is unnecessary to obstruct the relative activity of the mind. The practitioner sets up the meditation in an eased-up manner and allows the relativity activity of the mind to proceed according to its own causes and conditions, until the relative activity and the mind-itself are found to be inseparable. The result is that each and every potential event carries with it the same realization—as the root text says, "one great desire."

The second part of the one-taste instruction is for the actual samādhi meditation:

Second, pointing out appearance and emptiness as a pair using the metaphor of water and ice: Since all the appearing phenomena are not made into false-entities, they are found to be empty. They are not made into anything [real], yet some appearance happens. Thus, appearance and emptiness are considered a pair, or one taste, as in the metaphor of water and ice. [Practicing] that way, you will know that awareness and emptiness, clarity and emptiness, and bliss and emptiness are also pairs. This is known as "understanding everything as one taste." It is said, "When you understand all [phenomena] as Thatness, you will not find anything other than Thatness. What you read about is Thatness. What is apprehended is Thatness. What is meditated on is Thatness." (PK, f. 12b–13a)

The core of the instruction is "pointing out appearance and emptiness as a pair."

This passage briefly describes how to set up the extraordinary samādhi. First, the meditation rests upon the direct experience of emptiness of all phenomena. From the extraordinary perspective of the mind-itself, the manifestations of the mind are not made into *(ma sgrub pa)* false-entities. They are not artificially constructed into seemingly real, self-existent phenomena but are found to be empty. Yet something nevertheless occurs. The root instructions are careful to avoid the extremes of eternalism and nihilism, respectively.

Second, the samādhi meditation is designed to bring about the direct experience of the nondual nature of the simultaneous mind. Pema Karpo uses the technical term *pair (zung 'zug)*. When he says, "Appearance and emptiness are considered to be a pair," he is pointing out simultaneousness. Just as water and ice are seemingly different manifestations of the same element, likewise the natural mind's seeming appearances and the mind-itself are an inseparable pair. From this extraordinary perspective, seeming appearances no longer serve as objects of attachment but become "friends of the mind" *(sems kyi grogs;* JP, f. 78b) and remain as "mere appearance" *(snang tsam;* JP, f. 79a).

Third, the root instructions introduce three sets of pairs: awareness and emptiness, clarity and emptiness, and bliss and emptiness. These very brief instructions refer to the three main dimensions of the one-taste samadhi meditation, namely mind-simultaneousness, appearance-simultaneousness, and cognition- simultaneousness, respectively.

The last part of the one-taste instruction refers to the outcome. The description of the benefit is given only by a brief metaphor, water and waves.

The root instructions conclude:

> Third, put in order all phenomena as one taste using the metaphor of water and waves. Just as water's waves have arisen from the water itself, likewise all phenomena come from the mind-itself. Understand this so as to practice in such a way that emptiness has arisen in every [seemingly manifest] aspect. Saraha says, "So long as [manifest perceptual] aspects become elaborated from the mind[-itself], the natural mind is your teacher." Herein it is explained that every single phenomenon becomes the entire dharmadhātu, or that one taste manifests as many. For the practitioner who realizes this, emptiness comes forth encompassing all [phenomena of all realms and times], which is the end-state knowledge. (PK, f. 13a)

The use of the verb *put in order* signifies a fundamental rearrangement as a result of the extraordinary samādhi meditation. Emptiness pervades all experience. Like water and waves, the mind-itself and its various manifestations are intrinsically inseparable. Jampel Pawo explains that genuine mastery of the samādhi meditation, or skill *(rtsal)*, occurs when there is absolutely no obstruction *('gags med)* nor any false conceptualization, so that "absolutely everything arises as a friend," just as we welcome the rays of the sun but don't obstruct them (JP, f. 80b).

The passage "every single phenomenon becomes the entire dharmadhātu," alludes to the potential to realize awakened wisdom at this stage of the meditation:

> To the extent that one taste has arisen as many [phenomena], then awakened wisdom will develop. (JP, f. 80a)

The practitioner enjoys the "taste" of the spontaneous dance of all potential phenomena. Seeming events are not obstructed but blissfully welcomed as the dance of emptiness. The term *end-state knowledge* implies there is nothing beyond this other than the realization of awakened wisdom, which is already present as a property of the natural mind.

Sometimes the one-taste meditation is subdivided into three levels of attainment: (1) At the first level, awareness-itself recognizes all the phenomena of saṃsāra and nirvāṇa as the same taste of emptiness. All false conceptualization is eradicated. Freshness becomes the stance toward whatever arises. (2) At the second stage the nonduality or inseparability of the mind-itself and its manifestations is realized, as if water is being poured into water. The root of all forms of subject-object duality is cut off. (3) At the third and final stage the realization of vast equanimity or one taste becomes stable. Continuous mindfulness and an undistracted perspective, free from any artificial activity to sustain the realization, are intrinsic properties of the natural mind-itself, so that all seeming appearances arise as manifestations of the same taste of emptiness.[540]

II. THE YOGA OF NONMEDITATION: CROSSING OVER TO ENLIGHTENMENT

The yoga of one taste is the means by which awakened wisdom dawns and ripens into full enlightenment. Through the yoga of one taste the practitioner has set the mind right so that it has the potential to conform to the enlightened mind. Though the previous practice proceeded through many meditational stages, the practitioner is only now ready to begin the real path of meditation, that is, the path that leads to perfect enlightenment.

A seed only ripens when conditions are appropriate. The seed must first be planted in proper soil. Then it must slowly germinate. Finally a sprout breaks through the ground. Then, if the nutritional and climatic conditions are suitable, it will blossom. As far back as the preliminary practices the lama empowered the practitioner and established the propensities for awakened wisdom within the practitioner's mental continuum. It is as if a seed were planted then. The meditation experiences at each of the many stages of the preliminary and essential practices are manifestations of the slow germination of this seed. The first glimpse of awakened wisdom becomes especially possible at the end of the one-taste meditation, like a seed breaking through soil. The yoga of nonmeditation establishes the appropriate nutritional and climatic conditions so that the sprout of awakened wisdom blossoms into perfect enlightenment. Jampel Pawo explains:

> The practitioner does not generate the ground of [completely] unelaborated awakened wisdom directly in the mental continuum until the yoga of nonmeditation. Along the stages from mastery of one-taste yoga through the subsequent stage of non-meditation yoga, awakened wisdom is perfected. (JP, f. 82b)

The one-taste samādhi only serves to set up the conditions by which awakened wisdom is able to come forth. In the yoga of nonmeditation the practitioner "proceeds from the perspective of having seen the benefit" (TN, p. 499). For most practitioners awakened wisdom initially dawns as a sudden, brief, yet very compelling shift in the locus of awareness, or glimpse of the dharmakāya mind, like rays of light suddenly appearing in a deep canyon. For some the clear light of awakened wisdom shines more intensely and for a longer time, like the sun breaking through the clouds. For the exceptional practitioner the initial dawning of awakened wisdom immediately becomes full enlightenment, like the sun arising in a cloudless sky.[541] For most practitioners, however, this initial fleeting glimpse of awakened wisdom doesn't last, and may not even be appreciated for what it is. For these practitioners new conditions must be established for awakened wisdom to ripen. The yoga of nonmeditation is the fulfillment of a very long meditational path that began as far back as interest in spiritual teachings. The exercise is called *understanding the way the realized mind stays* (TN, p. 499), *seeing the bene-fit* (JP, f. 80b), or *experiencing mahāmudrā* (PK, f. 13b) because the outcome of nonmeditation yoga is enlightenment.

Pema Karpo reduces his definition of *nonmeditation* to a single aphorism:

> Having put in order all phenomena of the simultaneous mind as the innate dharmakāya, you [directly] experience the yoga of nonmeditation. (PK, f. 12a)

The verb *put in order* indicates that another significant reorganization of the mind takes place during nonmeditation. This is the final and most profound rearrangement, namely full enlightenment.[542] Several new technical terms are introduced. *Innate (gnyug ma)* is the antonym for *artificial construction (bcos ma)*.[543] Once realizing the simultaneous mind, there is no need to act *(bya ba)* during the extraordinary samādhi meditation, outside of letting the mind manifest its own spontaneity.[544] The term *innate* is related to other terms, such as *settled into itself, not prevent nor make happen,* and *not artificially construct.* In this sense the term *innate* is continuous with the state of mind characteristic of the one-taste meditation.[545]

The other term, *dharmakāya,* suggests discontinuity with the previous one-taste meditation. Through nonmeditation yoga the practitioner's individual consciousness is linked directly to the ground of existence, namely the dharmakāya. The dharmakāya is the ultimate embodiment of Buddha-mind. Sometimes nonmeditation yoga is called *crossing over (la la dza; la bzla ba).* The verb *la la dza* literally means "to cross over (a stream or a mountain)." This verb is used because the practitioner's point of observation during meditation crosses over from seeming individual consciousness to the infinite ground of awareness-space known as the dharmakāya. Another way of saying this is that the seeming ordinary mind reorganizes itself so as to become a manifestation of the four buddha bodies, of which the awakened wisdom body *(ye shes chos sku)* is the most important. The awakened wisdom body is a manifestation of omniscience *(thams cad mkhyen pa),*[546] and is inclusive of the other three buddha bodies—the emanation, enjoyment, and dharma bodies (JP, f. 82b).[547]

The nonmeditation yoga is as concerned with the conditions under which awakened wisdom may or may not ripen as it is with the actual fulfillment of this process in full enlightenment. According to Tashi Namgyel, nonmeditation yoga consists of an elaborate set of protecting instructions followed by three substages of practice. These stages are as follows: (1) recognizing wisdom, (2) setting up wisdom, and (3) the outcome, enlightenment. Returning to the seed metaphor, the grower must recognize when the seed has sprouted. Then new conditions must be established to insure its further growth, such as providing water and sunlight. Finally, the plant blossoms. Likewise the practitioner must first recognize *(ngo bzhung)* awakened wisdom as it comes forth during the special samādhi. Just as a sprout breaking through the soil manifests a new dimension of itself, likewise dawning awakened wisdom distinctly transforms the mind as if lifting a lamp to the darkness.[548] In light of this transformation the practitioner must proceed in such a manner as not to lose sight of the dawning awakened wisdom. Therefore careful instructions are given to protect this nascent realization. These practices are called "the way to protect the meditation experience" (TN, p. 477) because the practitioner can easily stray *('chor ba)* from awakened wisdom or lose it.

The skilled practitioner becomes concerned *(bag yod pa)* about the exact conditions that allow awakened wisdom to ripen. There are two general types of conditions: (1) pointing-out instructions and (2) setting up awakened wisdom. If a grower does not know how to cultivate a plant, he must ask a more experienced grower for assistance. Likewise, the practitioner must ask for oral advice and pointing-out instructions from an enlightened lama. The lama communicates the exact conditions under which full enlightenment may come forth, and warns against conditions likely to obstruct its development. Therefore nonmeditation yoga, more than any other previous meditation, relies heavily upon the oral readings given by the great masters of the mahāmudrā tradition. These instructions are used to transmit directly the exact conditions under which enlightenment was found to develop in previous masters. For example, oral readings from early Indian mahāmudrā masters, such as Saraha, Śabara, and Maitripa, as well as those of the Tibetan source tradition, such as Tilopa, Nāropa, Marpa, Milarepa, and Gampopa, are invaluable. Without their pointing-out instruction, the practitioner would find it very difficult to recognize the true nature of the mind and reach perfect enlightenment.

Once the real nature of the mind has been correctly pointed out, the practitioner must set up *(bzhag pa)* the exact conditions for enlightenment within the extraordinary meditation state. These critical instructions are called *the means to set up (bzhag thabs)*. The issue of skillful means at this point in practice becomes problematic in that any artificial activity used during meditation to establish a foundation for enlightenment makes it difficult, if not impossible, to realize enlightenment. The special samādhi must be free of any artificial activity, such as trying to prevent certain experiences or make others happen (TN, p. 468). In other words, the practitioner does not act in any way whatsoever upon the natural spontaneity of the mind. Jamgön Kongtrül adds, "There should be no trace of deliberateness" to the meditation.[549] Nonactivity *(byas med)* itself is a necessary condition of practice. The problem is this: If a practitioner cannot act in any definitive way to set up the enlightenment experience, then how is it possible to set up the exact conditions by which it occurs? Does the practitioner totally rely upon the pointing-out instruction? Is there nothing that can be done during meditation to bring forth enlightenment? It is in part true that the practitioner depends heavily upon the pointing-out instruction. This fact does not, however, exempt the practitioner from playing the critical role in bringing forth the enlightenment experience. The skillful means *(thabs)* to this end are called *nonmeans (thabs med)*[550] because they do not involve any artificial activity during meditation. Unlike a grower who acts by watering a plant or changing its lighting conditions, the practitioner cannot use activity. Paradoxically, however, there are two "nonactive means to set up" enlightenment. These include (1) very specific protecting instructions and (2) a set of nonmeditation practices. Each of these steps will be discussed following Tashi Namgyel's stage model.

A. The Stages Way to Practice Nonmeditation Yoga

1. Protecting the Realization about the Simultaneous Mind

As the practitioner discovers the true nature of the mind, it becomes extremely important to consolidate and protect the realization.[551] Having directly realized the extraordinary nature of the nondual mind, it would be extremely unfortunate if the practitioner regressed back to ordinary experience. The oral tradition describes such regression as being like a king who relinquishes his throne to work among the common people or a lion that roams with stray dogs (TN, pp. 477–78). On the other hand, the meditator who remains attached to certain meditative states has failed to correctly understand the natural mind. When the natural mind is correctly understood, there no distinction made between times meditating and times not meditating. The natural mind remains the same under all conditions. Therefore the skilled practitioner maintains mindfulness of the true nature of the realized mind at all times and under all circumstances. This condition of continuous mindfulness of the mind's true condition is called *virtue practice (dge sbyor)*. The skilled practitioner is also able to recognize the conditions that prevent true realization or make it go astray. The protecting instructions of nonmeditation yoga fall into two categories: (1) those that maintain the realization flawlessly and continuously under all conditions (virtue practice), and (2) those that deal with flaws that either prevent the realization or make the practitioner lose it.

2. Virtue Practice: Maintaining the Realization

Tashi Namgyel's instructions are entitled "After Pointing Out Comes Virtue Practice, the Way to Protect" (TN, pp. 477–95). These instructions reverse the order of pointing out and virtue practice as used in the extraordinary preliminaries. There virtue practices, such as mindfulness, were followed by pointing-out instruction. Here pointing-out instruction is followed by virtue practices, such as mindfulness, albeit a different kind of mindfulness. Moreover, the term *virtue practice* is used in a very new way. Tashi Namgyel now calls the previous virtue practices "inferior acts" and contrasts them to a new understanding of virtue practice. A practitioner who relies solely upon these former practices fails to set up the exact conditions for enlightenment:

> It is said that staying in the ordinary and becoming involved in inferior activities after generating this [extraordinary] meditation causes the benefit to decline, so that you become just like any ordinary sentient being and are chained to saṃsāra once again. The Great Brahman [Saraha] says,
>
>> Ah! After understanding the way the realized mind stays, the king who becomes involved in lowly activities such as sweeping falls from his throne. Relinquishing inexhaustible great bliss, he is chained by contact with the pleasures of saṃsāra over and over again....
>
> Je Gyara says,
>
>> Being without this meditational condition once it has been generated is like having your jewels swept away by a storm, a

lion roaming with dogs, or a precious gem thrown in the mud....

The practitioner who artificially acts toward this supreme state with [meditative] representation or with the previous [ordinary] virtue practices of body, speech, and mind is described as one who goes astray after attaining the true view, which never ceases and is never elaborated. That would be like seeking a fake stone after finding a precious gem. (TN, p. 478)

The earlier preliminary virtue practices—for example, ethical training—and concentration meditation practices are now considered to be inferior precisely because they involve artificial activity. Artificial activity contradicts direct experience of the innate, awakened mind. To rely on these is to thoroughly misunderstand the extraordinary samādhi and its fulfillment in awakened wisdom. It is not that these virtue practices are wrong in themselves, but rather that they are practices directed toward a particular goal. Any representation of a goal or any artificial activity to bring about this end becomes a hindrance at this stage of practice. There is nothing to do once awakened wisdom begins to arise, beyond correctly seeing it for what it is and allowing it to ripen. To do otherwise would be to throw away something valuable, as if falling from a throne. Genuine virtue practice cannot involve arbitrary activity.

Consistent with a pointing-out style of instruction, Tashi Namgyel cites the oral readings to explain real virtue practice:

Tilopa says,

Truth derived from reflection does not lead to [real] truth that transcends reflection, nor does truth derived from activity. If you think otherwise, you don't understand!

Atiśa says,

When your mind is firm, set it up one-pointedly toward the supreme, but don't do the [ordinary] body and speech virtue practices.

The Reverend [Milarepa] says,

> At the time the unelaboration has come forth in the mind,
> do not pursue words. There is danger in proclaiming the eight
> [ordinary] dharmas.... Don't make the effort to practice the
> body and speech virtues. Otherwise, there is danger that non-
> conceptual awakened wisdom will decline. Firmly hold the
> perspective of nonartificially constructed naturalness. (TN,
> p. 479)

The Tilopa passage is designed to negate the usual conception that ordinary virtue practice and/or meditative reflection leads to wisdom. The latter two passages present a new conception of virtue practice, namely
"firmly" and continuously holding direct realization of the innate, simultaneous mind. The words *natural perspective (ngang),* are substituted for
practice (sbyor ba) to illustrate that maintaining this realization, or better,
being that realization, does not depend on doing anything, and that doing
something to maintain it contributes to losing it. Real virtue practice is not
a practice in the sense of artificial activity but a state of being, a state
strengthened only by continuing to be that way.

Real virtue practice is synonymous with protecting, that is, undistracted
mindfulness of the way the realized mind stays, both in the special samādhi
and outside of it, too. The practitioner does not do anything outside of
firmly sustaining that perspective, both when remaining in samādhi and
after coming out of samādhi.[552] He should return to the special samādhi
many times over:

> So now practice this kind of meditation on the [natural] mind,
> on the [realized] truth, continuously. (TN, p. 479)

So that the practitioner properly understands the distinction between
activity and nonactivity, Tashi Namgyel carefully defines the kind of protecting practice that lays the ground *(mthil)* for enlightenment.[553] He
begins by redefining the usual protecting practices—mindfulness, intelligence, and concern—in light of the extraordinary perspective on the
innate, simultaneous mind. As used in the preliminary and concentration
practices, the term *mindfulness* was defined as "not losing track of the
intended object." The intended object of the extraordinary practices is not

a particular representation but rather a particular view, in which the mind-in-and-of-itself is both the vantage point of the meditation and the object of the meditation, yet nondual. Even though the intended object is remarkably different, the basic definition of *mindfulness* as "undistractedness" is retained. However, instructions about extraordinary practices pertain to a different type of mindfulness. It is called *real mindfulness* (*yang dag pa'i dran pa;* TN, p. 481). This type of mindfulness is "beyond speech" and therefore difficult to define. Nevertheless the commentator defines it as that which "protects against nonvirtuous practices and develops virtuous practices accordingly" (TN, p. 481). The adverb *accordingly* refers to firmly holding the view of the simultaneous mind. Real virtue practice is synonymous with continuously and uninterruptedly protecting that view. Real mindfulness is said to be a "limb of enlightenment" (TN, p. 482).[554] Not only does the practitioner protect the new realization but in so doing he or she sets the stage for enlightenment. In this sense, real mindfulness is *special* (*khyad par;* TN, p. 482).

Real mindfulness is further qualified as being closely established mindfulness (*dran pa nyer bzhag;* TN, p. 483) because once awareness-itself is set up firmly as the intended object, it stays very close to that view, ideally never departing from it. Real mindfulness is also called "mindfulness of the way the realized mind stays" (TN, p. 675).

Intelligence is also redefined in the context of extraordinary practice:

> Intelligence separates [perfect] staying from [the artificial activity of coarse-level] taking up and abandoning.... It protects the way the realized mind stays and leads to the outcome [enlightenment]. (TN, p. 483)

Here, intelligence has been redefined in terms of the total absence of artificial activity, especially coarse-level artificial activity, such as becoming attached or aversive to certain thoughts, emotions, or perceptions. When the practitioner ends the extraordinary meditation session and returns to everyday experience, no particular experience needs to be intentionally engaged, neither made more of nor less of. When all such experiences are the same taste and awareness continuously reflects the way the realized mind stays, the practitioner protects the practice.

The inclusive term for the perfect balance between mindfulness and intelligence is *concern (bag yod pa)*. A practitioner who manifests concern, in the ordinary sense of the term, is said to:

…watch the mind everywhere in all defiled phenomena, and completely watch its worldly and nonworldly virtues. (TN, p. 485)

A practitioner who has real concern, at the extraordinary level of practice:

…has no cause of misconceiving the way accordingly and has no cause of misconceiving the truth as defiled or nonvirtuous. (TN, p. 484)

No matter what the relative activity of the mind, however seemingly defiled, no false discrimination is made between its being nonvirtuous and virtuous. From the perspective of the extraordinary simultaneous mind, all experience is a mere empty manifestation of the mind's spontaneous activity. This collapse of any ultimate distinction between virtue and nonvirtue is not, however, a license for unethical behavior. Therefore Tashi Namgyel qualifies *concern* as "having respect," "removing pride" (TN, p. 486), and "generating compassion" (TN, p. 675). *Real concern* is a synonym for the ripening of the ultimate enlightenment attitude. Real concern is both a prescription for how to protect the extraordinary realization and how to lay the foundation for enlightenment. Real concern "brings forth the [final] outcome of the meditation" (TN, p. 487), namely enlightenment.

Protecting practice at the extraordinary level of mind requires that the practitioner firmly keep the view of the simultaneous mind uninterruptedly on all occasions. The indispensable ingredient of extraordinary protecting is mindfulness (TN, p. 487). Therefore Tashi Namgyel gives a very detailed explanation of extraordinary mindfulness. He says that there are four types of mindfulnesss *(dran pa bzhi po)*. Two of these are effortful *(rtsol bcas)* and two are effortless *(rtsol med)*.[555] The former two pertain to the ordinary meditation practice and the latter two to the extraordinary practices. Table 37 summarizes this:

TABLE 37: THE FOUR TYPES OF MINDFULNESS

Ordinary Effortful	Extraordinary Effortless
1. Mindfulness while taking things as real or when caught up in the world *('a thas; 'zur)* Staying/calm practice; initial special insight (putting in order the view)	3. Mindfulness of the pair, that is, real mindfulness *(yang dag pa'i dran pa'i zung 'jug gi dran pa)* One-taste yoga
2. Mindfulness that recognizes or holds emptiness *(stong nyid bzung dran nam ngo shes kyi dran pa)* Special-insight practice (skill)	4. Inconceivable mindfulness *(blo bral lam blo 'das kyi dran pa)* Nonmeditation yoga

The first type requires considerable effort to set up the mind so that the practitioner can generate beginner's special insight into emptiness. Once the practitioner is directly putting in order this view of emptiness in the unfolding mental continuum, effort is still required "to recognize and resolve emptiness in every [thought and appearance] that has arisen and to hold the view of certain knowledge [directly] in the mental continuum" (TN, p. 490). The third type, real mindfulness, refers to the yoga of one taste:

> Once you realize awakened wisdom, there still may be subtle, effortful grasping at certain knowledge, but you don't need to grasp in order for the force of understanding the pair to come about. (TN, p. 488)

Once realizing awakened wisdom, effortful mindfulness is not only unnecessary but becomes a hindrance. The fourth type, inconceivable mindfulness, refers to nonmeditation yoga:

> After purifying all [dualistic] notions (such as what is to be meditated and who is doing the meditation) stay in the innate, natural condition of great equanimity. This uninterrupted mindfulness becomes the mandala of awakened wisdom. (TN, pp. 489–90)

Inconceivable mindfulness remains completely uncorrupted by dualistic conceptions or by any form of artificial activity, and can never be interrupted.

Establishing this form of spontaneous mindfulness, along with the ultimate enlightened attitude,[556] lays the foundation for perfect enlightenment.

Perhaps the most perplexing instruction concerning what to do to reach enlightenment is that of instructing the practitioner to "do" nothing. The habitual propensity to do something during meditation is very difficult to overcome. Moreover, the entire meditative path leading to nonmeditation yoga has been presented in terms of exercises, or prescriptions for action, which have in fact reinforced the karmic propensity to make something happen *(sgrub pa)*. Now, as enlightenment is "close by," only the condition of "nothing but inactivity" *(byas med tsam)* can set up enlightenment. Ironically the many stages of meditation, which have brought the practitioner to the very threshold of enlightenment, now become obstacles to its attainment. *Nonmeditation (sgom med)* means precisely this: doing away with any artificial activity that can be considered meditation. From the perspective of the extraordinary mind, the whole concept of meditation is an artificial construction, just as ordinary virtue practice was. The practitioner must relinquish the idea of "acting to meditate on emptiness" (TN, p. 517) or "representing" the mind in a certain way according to a given exercise (TN, p. 478). In order to set up the exact conditions for enlightenment, the practitioner must stop meditating in any arbitrary sense. Those who think they can achieve enlightenment by any form of activity during meditation misunderstand the pointing-out instruction. The practitioner systematically dismantles all of the previous practices and gives up trying to do something. The practitioner simply protects the realization by continuously locking onto the extraordinary view.

A negative particle, *med,* has been added to the verbal noun, *sgom,* ("meditating"). The use of the negative particle is a typical linguistic device of the nonmeditation yoga. Common negations include: *not artificially constructed (bcos med), nonrepresented (dmigs med), mindfulness-without (dran med),* and *not-taken-to-mind (yid la mi byed pa)*. According to the early mahāmudrā source material, as made popular by Maitripa, the master who gave only two simple pointing-out instructions to a practitioner in a receptive state could quickly bring about enlightenment. It was said that the master could literally sing the student into enlightenment using a brief pointing-out poem called a doha. These two critical instructions, found in every doha were (1) mindfulness-without *(dran med)* and (2) not-taking-to-mind, or not mentally engaging anything *(yid la mi byed pa)*. Later in the tradition these two instructions became the fundamental ingredients of nonmeditation yoga given to the practitioner while protecting the special samādhi. They are two of the most important terms in the specialized vocabulary of the mahāmudrā tradition.[557] Each is designed to negate any propensities toward artificial activity with respect to the absolute and relative dimensions of truth. Table 38 illustrates the usage:

TABLE 38: USAGE OF THE TERMS *Not-Take-to-Mind* AND *Mindfulness-Without*

Stage of Practice	Term	Perspective on Truth
Nonmeditation	Not-take-to-mind	Relative truth
Nonmeditation	Mindfulness-without	Absolute truth

These terms are used strictly only when real mindfulness approximates being free of any artificial activity and ripens into continuous, uninterrupted protecting of the realization regarding the innate, simultaneous mind. According to the commentator, these apply:

> ...after the special samādhi state has been perfected, and after closely established mindfulness. (TN, p. 491)

Once continuous awareness of the simultaneous mind becomes natural, the practitioner is in a better position to comprehend the nonmeditation instructions. However, if the practitioner misinterprets the instruction and prematurely believes he should stop meditating before reaching this advanced stage, he has thoroughly misunderstood the pointing-out instruction.

Not-taking-to-mind is defined as follows:

> Likewise, the meaning of not-taking-to-mind is also defined in the *Avikalpapraveśadhāraṇī [Force of Entering into a Nonconceptual State.]* It says,
>
>> [Question:] O sons of the lineage, why is anyone who enters the nonconceptual realms said to be not-taking-to-mind? [Answer:] Because one really passes beyond the attributes of all mental events. He who does so learns how to really pass

beyond all [dualistic] mental events. This is the meaning of not-taking-to-mind.

The *Bhāvanākrama* says,

> Not-taking-to-mind is to abandon [mental engagement of] all attributes such as form.

If you try to explain the meaning of this passage in terms of special insight, you'll [incorrectly] consider the meaning of not-taking-to-mind to be whatever is not represented. This view of not-taking-to-mind is simply incorrect. The passage intends to mean (1) abandoning the movement of the mind and (2) any false conceptualization. This is the [real] meaning of not-taking-to-mind. It does not mean being without mental activity.

> The Great Brahman says,

> O yogi, practice one-pointedly on the innate mind *[gnyug ma'i yid]*.

Śabara says,

> At all times realize the innate mind.

Moreover, the *Śrāvakabhūmi [Ground of Hearers]* says,

> There is neither any intention to act toward any attribute nor any distraction whatsoever. (TN, p. 493)

Not-taking-to-mind is the negation of one of the five ever-going mental factors, each of which is necessary for ordinary perception. Taking-to-mind functions in close conjunction with another of the five mental factors, namely attention *(sems pa)*. Attention pertains to directing the mind in general toward an intended object. Taking-to-mind pertains to a more specific form of active mental engagement and selective fixation on the intended object.[558] When taking-to-mind any object, a dualistic distinction is made. Taking-to-mind disrupts the mind's natural condition by selecting or particularizing this or

that object. By focusing upon a particular object, the continuity of awareness across all phenomena is disrupted and one becomes distracted from
the general awareness of the one taste of all phenomena. This fundamental
intentional act is the basis of all forms of discrimination, which leads to
false conceptualization and then to mistaken views. When the mind does
not move toward any seemingly appearing object, and more specifically
does not-take-it-to-mind, the most rudimentary basis for any discrimination falls away, and the practitioner completely transcends all false conceptualization. Mastery of not-taking-to-mind completely purifies the mind of
any tendency to move toward or away from seeming objects. More
specifically, it eradicates any movement of the mind-perceiver *(yid shes)* and
clears the way for undistracted awareness of the natural mind.[559] When the
mind-perceiver is still, awakened wisdom comes forth. From an absolute
perspective, there is no "mind" *(yid)*. There is no basis nor support for any
artificial activity other than the spontaneous unfolding of the mind's relative activity due to karmic causes and conditions. Not-taking-to-mind is the
negation of any artificial activity associated with the relative activity of the
simultaneous mind. The way the realized mind appears *(snangs lugs)* is not
associated with any artificial activity, including the artificial activity inherent in every moment of ordinary perception.

Likewise, mindfulness-without *(dran med)* is the negation of activity associated with the ultimate dimension of the simultaneous mind. *Mindfulness-
without* is shorthand for continuous, uninterrupted mindfulness without
any artificial activity associated with it. It is defined as follows:

> The meaning of mindfulness-without is when any aberrant
> mindfulness or associated distracting thought becomes calm.
> Mindfulness-without does not mean forgetting the truth, or any
> kind of straying (for example, becoming obscured, fainting, or
> falling asleep). (TN, p. 492)

The term *mindfulness-without* does *not* refer to the negation of mindfulness, but is a pure type of mindfulness. As with previous types of mindfulness, mindfulness-without implies undistracted awareness. The technical
term *mindfulness-without* is designed to negate any artificial activity, any
false conceptual discrimination, and also any particular intended object
other than the natural mind itself in its entirety. The real object is the simultaneous mind in its absolute dimension. No form of activity can bring forth

enlightenment other than continuous, uninterrupted awareness of the natural mind's awareness-itself. Lesser forms of mindfulness are sometimes called *falsely conceptualized mindfulness (dran rtog)* because these forms of mindfulness discriminate specific content over the entire simultaneous mind and its innate awareness (TN, p. 497).

Real virtue practice is a state of being, not a state of doing. The skilled practitioner establishes continuous, uninterrupted mindfulness with the innate, nondual simultaneous mind as its object. Supreme truth *(don thog)* is the object of this mindfulness (TN, p. 497). From this perspective real or inconceivable mindfulness is no longer limited to formal meditation sessions. Real mindfulness occurs all the time irrespective of context. It is customary to make a distinction between formal meditative samādhi and the practice after leaving a meditation session. However, once the practitioner stabilizes mindfulness at the extraordinary level of mind in samādhi *(mnyam gzag)*, this mindfulness generally does not cease when sitting meditation ceases. The practitioner carries the same level of mindfulness and the same realization about the simultaneous mind into the everyday world after leaving the meditation session. The aftereffect of this profound realization on everyday life is known as the postsamādhi state *(rjes thob)*. The skilled practitioner locks onto continuous, uninterrupted mindfulness of the simultaneous mind in the postsamādhi as well as in the extraordinary samādhi state. From the perspective of real mindfulness, "seeming thoughts and appearances have no substance and arise unobstructedly as the inseparability of appearance and emptiness" (TN, p. 497). Tashi Namgyel adds, "The meaning of mahāmudrā is to maintain the perspective of the way the realized mind stays in whatever arises without discriminating 'this thought is false' and 'this is not false,' and then firmly maintaining that unceasingly without taking up or abandoning anything that occurs" (TN, p. 498). Real virtue practice occurs at all times, in all contexts, until formal samādhi and postsamādhi practice are also inseparable.

3. Setting Up the Conditions for Enlightenment
a. Recognizing Wisdom
Tashi Namgyel calls the two stages prior to experiencing enlightenment *recognizing awakened wisdom* and *setting up awakened wisdom*. One-taste yoga establishes the foundation for awakened wisdom to emerge. In non-meditation yoga the practitioner:

...proceeds from the perspective of having seen the benefit of the aforementioned [special] samādhi. Generate a fervent desire for this [awakened wisdom] to increase and continue once you have eradicated all the pain from the mind. (TN, pp. 499–500)

Early nonmeditation yoga entails setting up and stabilizing the simultaneous mind as the vantage point of the extraordinary samādhi practice, up to the point where direct experience of the great same taste of emptiness of all experiences within and outside of the meditation session is both automatic and continuous. Later on, the way to proceed is by protecting the correct view of simultaneousness with effortless mindfulness until awakened wisdom is recognized.

The root instructions for recognizing wisdom are as follows:

It is necessary to carefully protect what has not yet fully arisen in meditation. As you stay on ordinary [knowledge, awakened wisdom] arises during meditation. The practitioner who doesn't protect it or who does other practices with other intended objects turns away from the truth, like a king becoming a common subject, or a lion roaming with dogs. So continue the practice, being inclined only toward emptiness but without attachment even to that. Otherwise it will serve as the basis of flawed meditation. [In this state you are] free from the miseries of saṃsāra brought by self-grasping and free from life's impermanence. Generate the view by which [all mental] activity becomes equanimous. With no need to suppress everyday ideas about the meditation nor make anything happen in the meditation, such mental actions become equanimous. Because you have respect and desire for this supreme meditation and its realization, say a prayer deep within your heart to keep the [correct] view moment by moment, maintaining it as if you had the consciousness of your own [root] lama and the genuine Kagyü buddhas.[560] Since [real] mindfulness is the main point or essential ingredient of this meditation, never relinquish it during this stage of practice by thinking about anything other than this. At all times and in all situations practice never to be without [real] mindfulness of the way the realized mind stays. The work of this meditation is also to make compassion a distinct part of the practice. Meditate

upon the [ultimate] enlightened attitude with love and compassion toward all sentient beings. Continue with the refuge
prayer and the [special mahāmudrā] devotional prayer [and
awakened wisdom will come]. If you don't reach the goal of this
meditation, you've pursued some other truth or other teachings.
[The flaws inherent in such] views may now increase so that what
you hold to be the truth is really Mara's deception. First set up
the mind inwardly, and then continue this supreme meditation
until the initial flames [of awakened wisdom appear]. Beyond
that point, practice with even greater intensity, meditating from
the perspective of a firm conviction [to experience awakened
wisdom, based on the fact that you have previously] shaped [the
vessel of mind properly], and have mastered all the stages [of
meditation]. Don't be ashamed of taking the lama, Three Jewels, and spiritual fellowship as your guides [in finding this]. (TN,
pp. 674–75)

The phrases "not yet fully arisen in meditation" and "until the initial flames"
are references to the initial-flash awakened wisdom that arises in this
extraordinary samādhi.[561] Awakened wisdom is the first condition *(rkyen)*
necessary for perfect enlightenment. Therefore its realization must be
appropriately protected. Tashi Namgyel quickly adds the qualification that
protecting is not a form of activity. If so, the practitioner would "turn away
from the truth" or lose the wisdom gained.

Next the passage alludes to some of the changes that follow from a deep
understanding of emptiness and the simultaneous mind. These are (1) non-
attachment, (2) freedom from saṃsāric misery, and (3) freedom from impermanence and death. The commentary merely alludes to these changes with
the brief passage from Gampopa, "once you have eradicated all the pain
from the mind" (TN, p. 500). These and other changes, however, are
described in much greater detail in the oral tradition, especially by
Rechung.[562] Rechung says that the practitioner "unties the chakra knots
that prevent the full experience of mental and divine bliss, respectively."
Attachment *(zhar ba)* is transmuted into great enjoyment *(dga 'chen)*. The
practitioner finds great bliss *(bde chen)* simply from experiencing ordinary
phenomena as they arise in their own way. The natural spontaneity of the
mind is freed. Bliss replaces misery.

The remainder of the root text describes the exact conditions that establish the likelihood that awakened wisdom will develop. First, the practitioner must have real mindfulness at all times and in all situations. Second, that mindfulness must be relatively free from all forms of artificial activity, such as trying to prevent or make things happen *(dgags grub)*, or from taking particular experiences to mind. Third, the object of real mindfulness is not any particular experience but the mind-itself, namely the way the realized mind stays.[563] Fourth, awakened wisdom *only* ripens when a proper foundation has been established with the relative and ultimate enlightened attitude. The root-text allusion to identifying compassion as the real work of the meditation makes it clear that compassion, more specifically the ultimate enlightened attitude, is a necessary ingredient for enlightenment. Fifth, the skilled practitioner realizes that the point of observation during the extraordinary samādhi is not necessarily his or her seemingly unique, individual consciousness. The instruction to "to keep the [correct] view moment by moment, maintaining it as if you had the consciousness of your own [root] lama and the genuine Kagyü buddhas," points out how the practitioner can displace seemingly unique, individual consciousness with enlightened consciousness as the "observer" mindfully holding the view.

The practitioner who (1) previously established the correct view, built the vessel of mind properly, and has mastered all the stages of meditation; and (2) has also carefully established the nonmeditation conditions need only continue this meditation uninterruptedly and the initial experience of awakened wisdom will dawn. Nevertheless the skilled meditator must recognize awakened wisdom as it arises *(ngo shes)*. Those practitioners who have taken the lama as a guide and have properly understood the direct pointing-out instructions are much more likely to recognize wisdom as it dawns than those following some other path or teaching.

b. Setting Up Enlightenment

Enlightenment sometimes occurs as a momentous, onetime transformative event, like a rapidly encompassing forest fire, at least for very highly capable practitioners skilled at recognition. Most practitioners, however, get small glimpses of awakened wisdom, like a flame immediately igniting and then going out. Provided that the conditions are just right, the frequency and duration of these flames of awakened wisdom ripen over time, eventually evolving into full enlightenment. These practitioners are given a special set of specific *(khyad par)* instructions designed to set up *(bzhag)* the exact conditions so that these glimpses of awakened wisdom ripen into perfect enlightenment. In addition to the specific conditions outlined above, an essential ingredient is awareness-mindfulness *(dran rig)*. The term *dran rig* is a compound composed of "mindfulness" and "awareness." At this stage of nonmeditation, awareness turns back on itself. The practitioner maintains continuous, uninterrupted mindfulness, without any artificial activity, with the intended object being the natural mind's awareness-itself. This inconceivable mindfulness is continuous at all times and in all situations, during both the samādhi and the postsamādhi states, until full enlightenment occurs. And even when particular events seem to arise, they are viewed from the vantage point of that vast ocean of awareness, as awareness self-illuminating itself to itself without particularization.

Tashi Namgyel's root instructions to set up enlightenment are as follows:

> Here are the specific instructions to protect this meditation during samādhi and in the postsamādhi state. Start by doing the samādhi and postsamādhi practices in their own right. A distinction between the samādhi and postsamādhi state generally is applicable from the beginning of meditation practice up through [mastery of] one-pointed [concentration] but no longer applies now. During this [current] protecting meditation you generally meditate on everything [in and out of meditation] with undistracted awareness-mindfulness.
>
> Start with the [extraordinary] samādhi as the basic unit of practice and then combine the samādhi and postsamādhi practices. Practice one-pointedly to protect the mind's real nature in a manner free from any [artificial activity], such as taking up or abandoning [any type of coarse-level meditation practices], and during any session the realization may occur. Then practice the same way during the postsamādhi interval so as to be carried along the path of thought and appearances [automatically].
>
> So come to realize what the lineage holders intended! Great yogis have mastered each of these [previous ordinary] meditations, but this [supreme protecting meditation] appears to be the best. So it is explained as follows:
>
> The skillful means to protect the mind's real nature is described as setting it up three ways: freshly *(so mar)*, self-evidently *(rang thang)*, and uninterruptedly *(lhug par)*. There are nine points to make about these: (A) *freshly:* (1) the body points are inwardly

relaxed, (2) the speech points are such that the breath is not forced, and (3) the mind points are such that there is no intention to take anything as its support; (B) *self-evidently:* (4) set it up in its own way, (5) set it up without [any activity associated with] recognition, and (6) set it up undistractedly; (C) *uninterruptedly:* (7) set it up without preventing anything from happening or causing anything to happen, (8) set it up effortlessly, and (9) set it up so that the six sense systems settle into themselves. Sometimes the following three points are made about these: (1) Set it up free from mental elaboration, that is, freshly; (2) set it up self-contentedly, that is, without artificial construction and without preventing anything from happening or causing anything to happen; and (3) set it up uninterruptedly, that is, without making any effort. The metaphors used to describe [these exact conditions] are as follows: (1) Set up appearances as if they are part of the vast, still expanse of infinite space; (2) set up mindfulness so that it completely saturates everything, solid as the great earth itself; (3) set up the mind without the slightest movement or agitation, like a massive mountain; (4) set up [simultaneous] appearance and emptiness in luminosity and brightness, like a bright lamp; and (5) set up the realization [of awakened wisdom] clear and still like the nonconceptual still state, as if it were a flawless crystal. Three other metaphors used to describe how to set up the mind in equanimity pertain to the three special states. The instructions are as follows: (1) Set up [the bliss of seeming emotions], without recognition, like still space free from the shrouds of darkness, like a cloudless sky; (2) set up the nonconceptual still state, immovable, completely undistracted, like a waveless ocean; and (3) set up the clarity [of seeming appearances] peaceful and bright, like a bright flame motionless in the wind.

To continue, keep the body and mind inwardly eased up without any effort. After you stabilize this, set up the mind freshly and nonartificially. After that realize that all seeming mental events are unborn [in ordinary time] and that they become self-liberated. This is called *protecting.* Realize that all seeming mental events are unborn [and that the real nature of the mind is always here]. Seeming appearances are immediately apprehended from the perspective of awareness-mindfulness in such a way that they are transmuted into the bliss of liberation every time they are not made into a false thing with the three [ordinary temporal characteristics]—arising, staying, and ceasing. Once you realize [temporal unfolding as] unborn [and the real nature of the mind as always here] so that self-liberation comes on all occasions, there is nothing beyond this. So protect what isn't yet [fully] recognized. It is extremely important to protect this realization [of awakened wisdom] single-mindedly, as if you were throwing a spear straight at its target, because any of these points [of meditation] could be set up incorrectly, you could try to artificially construct [awakened wisdom], you could be without [great] equanimity, or you could even have [coarse-level] dullness and flightiness.

As you continue, there may also be flaws of the postsamādhi interval: Practice awareness-mindfulness with respect to everything [seemingly] arising in the mental continuum. Undistractedly protect [both] the [subtle-level] doors of arising [or movements of the mind] and the actual [coarse-level] appearances for [both] perception and thought, just as a wise shepherd watches his cattle. It is unnecessary to round up cattle that graze contentedly, but is sufficient simply to follow them with your eyes.[564] Likewise, it is unnecessary to obstruct or block any of these [seeming] appearances or thoughts—either at the [level of the subtle] doors of arising or [at the coarse level of] those [seeming] appearances [and thoughts] that have already arisen. Awareness-mindfulness is [continuously] watchful of whatever has arisen. In other words, uninterruptedly protect whatever has arisen without [the artificial activity of] recognition [of any self-existent entity].

When such undistracted awareness-mindfulness becomes the foundation, then the arising mental continuum becomes the support [of awakened wisdom]. At first it may seem that distraction greatly increases, but real mindfulness gradually gets much stronger. Seemingly ordinary appearances and thoughts arise more and more as clarity and emptiness. However, if this protecting practice gets difficult, return to samādhi practice, and [go back and] put in order the real-entity of whatever suitable thought or perception happens to arise. After that continue the protection practice [in the postsamādhi state once again].

Practice in such a way as to protect [uninterrupted mindfulness of the real nature of the mind] in both the samādhi and the postsamādhi states, wherein everything, at all times, is penetrated by awareness-mindfulness. All [seeming] thoughts and perceptions have arisen, those that [now seem to] appear, shine forth as clarity and emptiness, without [any artificial activity of] recognition [of any false entity], by virtue of seeming to merely have arisen or merely to be now appearing.

Furthermore, in addition to protecting [the view of the real nature of the mind in] everything, [both] in samādhi and in the postsamādhi state, protect it freshly and nakedly, because both types of protecting practice are inseparable.

The [special] states—bliss, clarity, and nonconceptual stillness—still occur, but now you have to become familiar with these states as potential obscurations to the way the realized mind stays. Yet, when you come to meet awareness-mindfulness as inherently saturating these [special] states, you'll realize them as truly marvelous over and over again. (TN, pp. 675–78)

The root instructions begin with a description of the objective of the protecting practice. It says that if the extraordinary samādhi and postsamādhi intervals are set up correctly, then "during that session the realization may occur." As the text indicates, realization of awakened wisdom occurs during protecting meditation once the general condition of continuous, uninterrupted awareness-mindfulness (as opposed to effortful mindfulness) has been established, with the simultaneous mind as both the intended object of awareness-mindfulness and the vantage point of observation. According to the commentary, the realization of awakened wisdom is the supreme thing *(ngo thog;* TN, p. 514), and once realized, it is advisable to "bring out the force of this supreme thing during samādhi" (TN, p. 541). Awareness-mindfulness continues uninterruptedly throughout the postsamādhi interval, wherein the "arising mental continuum is taken as the support," as the root text says, so that the allurements of all relative events deepen the realization of emptiness and clarity. Such seemingly ordinary experiences are known for the first time "without ensnarlment" (TN, p. 542). This realization of seemingly ordinary events is called the "postsamādhi magic show" or "the wordly wisdom of postsamādhi" (TN, p. 542).

The majority of the root instructions are dedicated to the skillful means to set up *(bzhag thabs)* the realization of awakened wisdom. Instructing the practitioner at this point in practice to relinquish all activity is such a radical departure from all previous meditation instructions that Tashi Namgyel goes to considerable length to make his point very clear. The yet-missing precondition for enlightenment is the complete eradication of all forms of artificial activity associated with meditation itself, along with any attempt to conceptually represent enlightenment.[565]

The skillful means discussed are all ways of negating residual artificial activity. These instructions are so subtle and difficult to comprehend that many different types of oral instructions for the purpose of pointing them out exist within the tradition. Tashi Namgyel points out a variety of skillful means in the root text alone, which include Gampopa's skillful means to set up, along with a number of metaphors taken from the oral tradition. These instructions are directly transmitted to the practitioner during the appropriate stage of the nonmeditation yoga, when the practitioner is likely to understand the instruction.

Because these particular instructions contain the most difficult yet most critical preconditions for enlightenment, Tashi Namgyel goes to great length in his commentary to review the "many means to protect," though in his root text he offers only Gampopa's method (TN, p. 514). The expanded commentary reviews one of the most famous pointing-out instructions, namely Tilopa's six means to set up:

> *mi mno/mi bsam/mi sem/mi sgom/mi dpyad/rang bzhin.*
> Do not recall/ do not reflect/ do not anticipate/ do not meditate/
> do not analyze/ settle into the real nature.[566]

The recurrent use of the negative particle *mi,* "do not," is designed to negate artificial activity. Tilopa's oral instruction is a classic example of a negation-type, or nonmeditation type, of skillful means. These instructions emphasize the negation of artificial activity, but fail to affirm that awareness-mindfulness continues as such activity diminishes.

The first three Tilopa instructions form a unit in themselves. The reader became familiar with these during the preliminary mind-isolation practice. There the instructions were used to eradicate mental elaboration specifically in the form of thinking. At the current stage of practice the same instructions are used to eradicate notions *(blo)* about how to set up enlightenment and about enlightment itself.

The latter three Tilopa instructions form another unit, specific to non-meditation yoga. These are designed to negate all forms of artificial activity *(byas ba)* occurring during the extraordinary samādhi meditation, especially with respect to taking-to-mind or using effortful mindfulness. The meaning of the passage "do not meditate" is explained as follows:

> Don't meditate upon anything that becomes an object of thought, such as whether it has or does not have certain characteristics. When you meditate like that, you take-to-mind dualism. (TN, p. 503)

Meditation *(sgom ba)* as an activity is negated because the very notion of meditation presupposes a subject-object duality and rests upon discriminations that prevent enlightenment. "Something" is to be meditated on, using some point of observation. Some sort of attainment is expected. Such erroneous ideas *(blo)* about meditation reflect subtle forms of dualistic self-grasping:

The Great Brahman says,

> Ah! It is not considered to be meditation upon that which is free from [false] nature. If you conceive the duality between that meditated and that meditating, you abandon the [ultimate] enlightened attitude. Such people bring afflictions upon themselves… The mind free of such a false thing is also free from [dualistically distinguishing] that meditated and that meditating. The [real] attainment, beyond any expectation [of attaining it] or fear [of not attaining it], is the non-dual mind. (TN, pp. 503–4)

Second, analysis *(dypad)* was an important ingredient of special-insight practice. This also is negated during nonmeditation yoga because the very notion of examining and analyzing presupposes some dualistic distinction between the events in the mental continuum, for example, as either arising or staying and as elaborated or made calm. Analysis is also a subtle form of dualistic self-grasping, therefore don't analyze. Don't perform any examination or analysis, as done previously with ideas about what is elaborated or made calm. When you act artificially, based on such ideas and erroneous thoughts, you generate dualistic appearance and become attached to [perceptual] attributes. (TN, p. 504)

The basis for the negation of analysis is the source mahāmudrā instruction of not-taking-to-mind.[567] As a result, the mind's natural condition settles into itself *(rang babs),* so its innate, real nature *(rang bzhin)* becomes evident:

> The real nature is set up without artificial construction, as both the mind's real nature [absolute truth] and the way of happenings [relative truth]. Unless you set it up like that, the way the realized mind stays becomes corrupted by artificial activity and ideas *[blos byas].* The Great Brahman says, "So long as you set up the real nature of the mind, the unobstructed fruition stays from the perspective of its always having been there.... Do not corrupt the mind, whose real nature is seen by contemplation as pure. Stay in the bliss-itself. You won't fail" (TN, pp. 505–6).

Table 39 summarizes Tashi Namgyel's discussion of the instructions:

TABLE 39: USE OF TILOPA'S SIX MEANS TO SET UP ENLIGHTENMENT

		Negation	Definition	Mistake
No artificial activity or false ideas	No elaboration	Do not recall	No pursuit of past object	Distraction
		Do not reflect	No artificial construction, no categorization of present	Losing samādhi
		Do not anticipate	No advance to future	Unsteady
	Not-take-to-mind	Do not meditate	Subject/object duality	Grasping
		Do not analyze	Activity of ideas	Grasping
	Mindfulness-without artificial activity	Real nature settled into itself	Setting up of real nature in nonartificiality	Artificial construction

Tashi Namgyel then sets forth another famous oral instruction, Gampopa's four means to set up from his *Dharma Collection,* of which the root instructions give an abbreviated version:[568]

> Look to the real-entity, the mind-itself.
> Set it up by easing up.
> Set it up freshly.
> Set it up self-contentedly.
> Set it up uninterruptedly. (TN, p. 507)

Gampopa's oral instructions are a classic example of nonmeditation instructions. Though not directly negating artificial meditative activity, as in Tilopa's negating instructions, Gampopa's affirming instructions specify exactly how to set up the mind once artificial activity has been negated. These instructions pertain to awareness-mindfulness of the mind's real nature. Tashi Namgyel gives a brief definition of each, followed by citations from early source material:

> Of the four above, the first is "set it up by easing up" *(glod).* When you know how to ease up the mind, the mind's way of happenings comes spontaneously and effortlessly. This is a very profound means to cut off any doubt about the nonartificial, real nature of the mind. (TN, p. 507) …Tilopa says, "Set up the mind nonartificially, taking its innate nature as the vantage point. When eased up, there is no doubt that whatever has been bound becomes free,… The mind, like the vast expanse of space, goes way beyond any object of thought. So set it up by easing up, without preventing anything from happening or trying to make anything happen.
>
> Such continuous concentration is mahāmudrā." When familiar with that, you'll attain perfect enlightenment. (TN, p. 508)
>
> The instruction "set it up freshly" *(so mar)* pertains to setting it up in equanimity, free of any conceptualization about it, according to the way the realized mind stays, from the beginning.[569] This is the [real nature of the] mind that the lamas have pointed out to you, the real thing or real nature, completely unelaborated. The real meaning of the instruction "set it up freshly" is recognition without [either artificial activity or erroneous conceptualization

about it]. The way the realized mind arises is already there from the beginning, just as fine gold doesn't lose its luster through the process of melting or molding it. (TN, pp. 508–9) Biravada says, "With simultaneousness, from the beginning, you don't search elsewhere. The real nature of the mind, when empty of any [conceptual] designations and free from any thought elaboration, *is* mahāmudrā."(TN, p. 509)

The instruction "set it up self-contentedly" *(rang gar)* means to set up the mind in bliss, in its own way, simply as the way the realized mind stays [from the mind-perspective] and as the mind's way of happenings [from the event-perspective]. [Ordinary] concentration meditation gets the mind all tied up with attachment and aversion, and the mind doesn't want to stay very easily, just as a man taken prisoner wants to run away. When you set it up self-contentedly, the [unbound mind] stays in whatever bliss there is, in its own way. The Great Brahman [Saraha] says, "Whenever the mind is bound, it wants to roam in all ten directions, but when it is set free it stays, firm and immovable. I understand the mind to be like a camel." (TN, p. 510)

…The instruction "set it up uninterruptedly" *(lhug par)* means being unwavering, without artificially acting in a way that grasps and binds [you to erroneous, dualistic concepts such as] existence/nonexistence, good/bad, or preventing something from or making something happen, as if you were untying the rope that binds a bundle of straw. (TN, p. 510)[570]

If you practice nonartificial protecting, then the doors-of-arising by which appearing conditions come forth are transmuted into self-liberation by the mind's naturalness and its spontaneous presence. (TN, p. 511)

Table 40 summarizes the root and commentarial discussion of Gampopa's skillful means:

TABLE 40: GAMPOPA'S FOUR MEANS TO SET UP ENLIGHTENMENT

Means	Definition	Simile
Eased up (glod; lhod)	No artificial activity, e.g., either preventing or making happen	Untying something
Freshly (so mar)	Unelaboration; natural	Gold
Self-contentedly (rang thang; rang gar)	Unbound, in its own way	Camel; prisoner
Uninterruptedly (lhug par)	Natural, without grasping or binding	Untying a straw bundle

According to the root text, each of Gampopa's skillful means is seen along a continuum from greater to lesser artificial activity. *Easing up* requires the most effort, as if taking the effort to unstring a bow. *Freshness* is the resultant state, after having eased up on activity to some extent. With this decrease in artificial activity, real mindfulness does not waver *(tshom tshom)*. *Self-contentedness* is a consequence of inactivity further ripening, so much so that the practitioner becomes acutely sensitive to *any* artificial activity potentially disturbing the meditation. *Uninterruptedness* is the fruition of the complete eradication of artificial activity, so that the spontaneous unfolding of the natural mind remains unbound. This is another way of describing self-liberation.

There are many other types of protecting instructions.[571] Sometimes they are given in the form of metaphors, as in the oral tradition. No matter what form of instruction is used, Tashi Namgyel says that "the distilled essence of all of these practices includes: (1) not meditating, that is, not-taking-to-mind particular events; and (2) being undistracted from the supreme way..." (TN, p. 515). In other words, the two essential ingredients of Tashi Namgyel's nonmeditation yoga are the same two ingredients found in the early mahāmudrā source material, beginning with Saraha. These are not-taking-to-mind and mindfulness without artificial activity, with both the point of observation and the object of awareness being none other than awareness-itself, and not any specific object within the ordinary mental continuum.[572] There can be "no distraction from the truth" (TN, p. 520) if enlightenment is to occur. The first ingredient, described in terms of nonmeditation in general, or not-taking-to-mind in particular, is a negation-type of instruction. The second ingredient, mindfulness-without, is an affirming negation or protecting instruction. These two types of pointing-out strategies are exemplified by Tilopa's and Gampopa's instructions, respectively. Here is a definition of the non-meditation or not-taking-to-mind instruction:

First, the nonmeditation way is when no ideas [about meditation] are taken-to-mind. While setting up this mahāmudrā meditation and its protecting practice, if you were to: (1) meditate having artificially constructed any ideas and their elaborations, or (2) engage in any other [mental] activity, except for that which never strays from holding that perspective [of the simultaneous mind] characterized by the mind-in-its-own-way [from the mind-perspective] and by the way of happenings [from the event-perspective], then you'll discover all sorts of reasons why the truth of the way the realized mind stays has become flawed. Some of these flaws have been discussed already but will be emphasized here. The mind is to be in its own way. With respect to the way the realized mind stays, this meditation should be free from any attachment to or aversion toward anything that moves at the sense doors, other than awareness of appearance and emptiness. Similarly, since the mind's real truth does not entail recognition of any [self-existent entity], then don't meditate on the mind's real truth as if trying to recognize something as either existing or not existing, or as if something is to be prevented from happening or made to happen. When nothing seems certain about the mind's real truth, don't meditate to try to recognize something, either by trying to direct attention or by trying to prevent something from happening or making something happen. While being [continuously mindful of] the mind's real truth, you should remain free from all the incessant switching and changing [characteristic of ordinary meditation]. Furthermore, don't meditate with any particular motivation or expectation [of a certain gain] or fear [of a certain failure]. You'll find nothing either good or bad about the mind's real truth, so don't try to do anything in the meditation to artificially construct anything, nor try to prevent something like this from happening nor try to make something like this happen during meditation. You'll also find that the mind's real truth cannot be represented or visualized, so don't meditate with the kind of effort to produce a particular representation of it during meditation. In summary, "nonmeditation" is when there is *nothing* to meditate on, just the mind-itself staying in the way the realized mind stays. If you meditate on *something,* you only generate the mind's [coarse-level] components of consciousness—the mental-perceiver, the intended object and its characteristics, attachment to these, and clinging to [dualism]. These are mistaken when in real meditation, [uninterruptedly mindful] of the view of the way the realized mind stays. (TN, pp. 515–17)

The use of the negative in a preverbal position, *mi sgom,* "do not meditate," instead of a postverbal position, *sgom med,* "there is no meditation," is designed to negate incorrect meditative activity while affirming correct awareness-mindfulness *(dran rig).* The use of either negative depends on whether or not some counterpoint is intended. If the negative were used in a post-position, no other means would be implied, thereby signifying enlightenment, that is, the end stage *(sa med).* These two uses of the negative are drawn from debate-style discourse:[573] *mi* + verb = "it is not X"; verb + *med* = "there is no X." The strategic use of the negative particle, *mi,* in the pre-position is designed to negate only artificial activity: "there is no" *(mi)* artificial activity in extraordinary meditation, but "there is" *(yin)* real mindfulness in extraordinary meditation. Tilopa's six skillful means uses the same preverbal negative as does Maitripa's famous not-taking-to-mind instruction (TN, p. 517). The use of any of these nonmeditation-type instructions is intended to offset the great propensity to conduct samādhi meditation using various forms of artificial activity and making a dualistic distinction between the meditator and that meditated.

Next is Tashi Namgyel's definition of the protecting, or undistraction-type of instruction, exemplified by Gampopa's skillful means and by the oral tradition metaphors:

> Second, being undistracted from the supreme truth is the way. Even when your meditation is not guided by artificially constructed ideas, you must above all have undistracted mindfulness [of the mind's real nature], and never deviate into the [seemingly] ordinary mental continuum. (TN, p. 518)

Undistracted mindfulness is mindfulness without any artificial construction associated with it, one that is continuously and uninterruptedly directed toward the mind's real nature, with awareness-itself as both the vantage point and the object of the meditation. Undistracted mindfulness never loses sight of this view during the extraordinary samādhi meditation and does not deteriorate into an ordinary form of meditation.

So that absolutely no dualistic distinction is made between these two forms of nonmeditation instruction, Tashi Namgyel concludes by saying that not-taking-to-mind and undistracted mindfulness are an "indistinguishable pair," as illustrated in Table 41:

TABLE 41: THE INDISTINGUISHABLE PAIR OF MEANS TO SET UP ENLIGHTENMENT

Type	Source
Nonmeditation	Tilopa
Protecting	Gampopa

Practitioners unfamiliar with nonmeditation practice use both types, although an advanced practitioner uses only the latter instruction (TN, p. 525).

4. The Postsamādhi State

The practitioner who masters continuous, uninterrupted real mindfulness with the simultaneous mind as the object of mindfulness never really leaves that state. Awareness-mindfulness is no longer a function of the extraordinary samādhi state but persists after the formal meditation session is terminated. This postmeditative continuance of awareness-mindfulness with respect to "everything, at all times" (TN, p. 677) is called *the postsamādhi state* (*rjes thob;* literally, "knowledge after"). Combining samādhi and postsamādhi practice, wherein awareness-mindfulness of the simultaneous mind is continuous and uninterrupted, establishes one of the prerequisite conditions for the ripening of awakened wisdom into full enlightenment.

Tashi Namgyel calls this practice "recognition of the postsamādhi mindfulness." Having had at least some glimpse of awakened wisdom, the practitioner proceeds with real mindfulness "from having seen the benefit." The special quality of this mindfulness must be appreciated if the practice is to be perfected. Tashi Namgyel calls it "still, expansive mindfulness" because of the vast spaciousness of awareness at the extraordinary level of mind (TN, p. 528). He explains:

> After you directly experience the supreme simultaneousness of mind previously pointed out, mindfulness and intelligence become the cause of a kind of really intense mindfulness that has its own force. (TN, p. 528)

Undistracted mindfulness of the simultaneous mind becomes a given. It continues as if caused by itself, because there is neither artificial activity nor false conceptualization to obscure it. After terminating the formal meditation session the practitioner continues the same special mindfulness under four behavioral conditions *(spyod lam),* namely walking, sitting, engaging in the world, and sleeping. Beginners frequently get distracted, but skilled practitioners *never* leave undistracted mindfulness regarding the mind's real nature (TN, p. 530). Tashi Namgyel says, "maintain undistracted mindfulness of clarity/emptiness and appearance/emptiness for every thought and appearance, respectively" (TN, p. 530).

He explains that "the postsamādhi experience isn't even a bit like the previous [meditations]" (TN, p. 528). It occurs as something beyond *(steng du)* the previous extraordinary samādhi practice. The relative activity of the mind spontaneously occurs without obstruction, without any artificial activity toward it. Coarse- and subtle-level perceptions and thoughts seem to appear as a manifestation of the natural mind's spontaneity or appearance-making capacity. This is called *the arising continuum (rgyun chags).* These "clear appearances" are:

> Recognized as supreme [wisdom] without holding them to be real and without trying either to prevent appearances from happening or to make appearances happen...the perspectives of both virtue practices—cognition- and appearance-simultaneousness— previously pointed out must be protected. (TN, p. 528)

Thus, a necessary precondition for setting up enlightenment is continuous, uninterrupted mindfulness/recognition of the simultaneous mind's vast awareness and its self-illumination as everything that seems to arise at all times and under all circumstances.

The reappearance of the mind's spontaneous relative activity at this extraordinary level of practice brings continuous supreme bliss *(bde steng)*. Because mindfulness/recognition now has its own force *(shugs)*, it goes on by itself without any effort whatsoever. Tashi Namgyel likens postsamādhi practice to the mind state of a wise cowherd who watches his cattle wander about and graze contentedly. He feels no need to interfere with the cattle in any way outside of merely being aware of them. Likewise, coarse- and subtle-level thoughts and perceptions shine forth as the clear-light mind, but are not acted upon—neither obstructed *(dgag pa)* nor held back *(bkug pa)*, neither made to happen *('grubs pa)* nor chased after *(rjes su 'brang ba)*. To take such trouble *(dka' tsheg bya)* with any particular seeming experience only serves to entangle *('jur ba)* the practitioner, and thereby distract him or her from uninterrupted mindfulness/recognition of the mind's real nature. This might lead to mistaking these occurrences as real *('thas ba)*, rather than as illusory-like clear appearances *(snang gsal bzhip pa)*. During postsamādhi practice the practitioner need only ease up and protect the realization the same way as in extraordinary samādhi practice. Therefore this postsamādhi exercise is sometimes called *the way of protecting as if meditating*. Although the relative events of the mind seem to appear and the practitioner seems to return to everyday experience, the practitioner does not really leave the meditation as long as he or she maintains the realization with uninterrupted awareness-mindfulness.

According to the commentary, there are three levels of postsamādhi practice. The first is called "meeting and destroying" *(phrad 'joms)*. It occurs when the practitioner has little experience *(chug zad goms pa)* with postsamādhi practice.

> For example, if you were to meet acquaintances and intimate friends you once knew along a path, you would recognize them as soon as you met them, without having to examine or analyze who's who. Likewise, it is not necessary to examine and analyze just what thoughts and perceptions have merely arisen. From the perspective of the always-here mind, these lead to liberation. As the Great Brahman says,
>
> "In the ten directions, back and front of you,
> whatever you see, again and again...

whatever becomes elaborated *is* the mind's real nature.
Are water and waves different?"

Maitripa says,

"Mahāmudrā is when you simply meet with the mind's real
nature, which manifests in every appearance in such a way
that you don't make it happen." (TN, pp. 532–33)

The second stage is called "not chasing after" *(phyi bsnyag)*. It occurs
once there is more than a little experience *(cung zad ma goms pa)* with postsamādhi practice:

When a snowflake falls on a warm rock or into a lake, it melts and
becomes water. Likewise, even if you become a little distracted
from the conditions of [perfect] mindfulness, look to any thought
or perception as it first comes, so that from the perspective of the
always-here mind it becomes one taste…. Śabara says,

"Just as a crow who flies from its ship circles in all [ten] directions, and flies back to the ship again, [because it doesn't sight
land], likewise, the desirous mind pursues thought, but its
initial intention [quickly] settles itself into the innate
mind."(TN, p. 533)[574]

The mind may still be somewhat desirous to crave after sense objects or
thoughts at this stage. However, awakened wisdom has ripened sufficiently
that all seeming desire, at the most rudimentary level of its initial intention,
immediately becomes calm, and even the simplest momentary impulse to
act artificially upon any seeming experience becomes eradicated as it occurs.

The third stage is called "the emanation of nothing" *(med sprul)*. It occurs
once there is considerable experience *(shin tu goms pa)* with postsamādhi
practice:

Burning wet wood in a small fire presents little danger. Yet, burning dry shavings in the wind unleashes a great forest fire that you
can't help but notice. Likewise, [seemingly] ordinary thoughts

and perceptions arise as the always-here mind. The previous mental mire of thought and miserable perceptions become manifest and emanate, but now arise as the [spontaneous] play of the always-here mind. The Great Brahman says, "Like tongues of fire that destroy the forest as they advance, all appearances are found to be simultaneousness, with their root being emptiness." (TN, p. 534)

At this final stage awakened wisdom spreads rapidly so that all possible emanations of the mind become the embodiment of awakened wisdom. The term *emanation of nothing* captures both the relative and the ultimate dimensions of truth, respectively. All the mind's relative activity becomes the play *(rol du)* of the always-here mind. Where ordinary thoughts and perceptions once were, "only the great fire of understanding burns" (TN, p. 536).

This realization is sometimes called "the wisdom of the world" (TN, p. 542), wherein experience occurs like a mirage *(sgyu ma lta bu)*. He explains that a master magician is able to create impressively convincing illusions, such as that of a horse or an elephant. The spectator mistakes these as real, but the master magician knows them to be an illusion. Likewise, the practitioner who masters blending samādhi and postsamādhi practice is like the master magician for whom every moment of experience is a wondrous illusion (TN, pp. 538–39). The practitioner experiences continuous great bliss *(bde chen po;* TN, p. 536), wherein all the stains *('dri ma)* of misconception disappear. All thought and the entire world of appearances arise as a magic show only after all artificial activity has been eradicated. Tashi Namgyel explains that all spontaneously manifested experience is "not made to happen, yet appears as relative truth" (TN, p. 538).

When postsamādhi practice fully matures, there is no difference between the state of realization during formal meditation and the state after it. These become inseparable. Tashi Namgyel calls this "bringing together both the allurements and the certainty" (TN, 542). He explains:

> Blended practice occurs when you are forever mindful of the real nature/clear-light mind throughout the four behavioral conditions. (TN, p. 547)

He adds that the essence of blended practice meets two criteria: "(1) immediately knowing the cause and effect of any karmic impulse without getting caught up in it, and (2) knowing all phenomena as the certain knowledge of emptiness without any self-existent nature" (TN, p. 542).

Tashi Namgyel's root text explains how nonmeditation yoga ripens in three stages:

> At the lowest level, it becomes possible to maintain undistracted mindfulness of the simultaneous mind at any time, so that it is unnecessary to limit the practice to formal meditation sessions. Seeming appearances arise "like a mirage." At the middle level, awareness-mindfulness continues day and night. The subtlest flow of shapes that arise is the mind's self-illumination. At the highest level, awakened wisdom stays even throughout all these subtle forms. Continuous awakened wisdom in the face of everything experienced is great nonmeditation. (TN, p. 697)

Blending samādhi and postsamādhi practice greatly increases the likelihood of enlightenment, if it has not already occurred. Quoting some meditation master, Tashi Namgyel concludes:

> He who first masters samādhi and then postsamādhi [practice] is a bodhisattva. He who blends them is a perfect buddha. (TN, p. 547)

Karma Chagme also discusses the three substages of nonmeditation yoga: (1) At the lowest level, the practitioner eradicates any distinction between meditator and the object of meditation. (2) At the middle level, the practitioner finds total spontaneity, without any artificial activity or any mental engagement or taking-to-mind. However, subtle obscurations sometimes remain at this level that may interfere with full realization. (3) At the highest level, the seeming individual consciousness of the practitioner (son or daughter consciousness) and the ground consciousness or dharmakāya (mother consciousness) merge as one, thereby bringing full enlightenment in the form of the three buddha bodies.[575]

5. Crossing Over

Crossing over (la bzla ba) pertains to how the initial glimpses of awakened wisdom become full enlightenment. The word *la bzla ba* means "to walk across or go beyond." This expression is often used for crossing over a mountain. The meaning here is similar. Once the practitioner gets a glimpse of awakened wisdom as the ground of existence, it becomes possible to shift the locus of observation from seeming individual consciousness to the ground of existence by literally crossing over to it. Once having crossed over, the practitioner, in one sense, maintains an absolute perspective of awareness that both totally transcends ordinary reality and saturates it. Crossing over refers to the shift from individual consciousness to the vast perspective of awareness characterized by the enlightened mind. Tashi Namgyel says, "crossing over is the natural disposition of the way the realized mind stays" (*la bzla sa'i gshis kyi gnas lugs;* TN, p. 590). Once having crossed over, he adds, "it is the way to resolve everything as the always-here mind" (*thams cad skye med du thag bcad;* TN, p. 590). Crossing over is the final skillful means to "gradually let go of everything except for the fundamental way the realized mind stays" (TN, p. 617). Crossing over is the final shift of mind by which the practice reaches its end state, perfect enlightenment. Yet crossing over is not an action in the mind, in the sense that any attempt to make it happen *(sgrub pa)* or otherwise artificially act in any way makes it very difficult to cross over.

Tashi Namgyel begins his commentary with a discussion of the likely time *(dus tshad)* for crossing over (TN, p. 590). The likely time occurs independent of temporal unfolding and independent of any ordinary mental activity (*mi bsam;* TN, p. 591). Crossing over is most likely to occur when there is "continuous meditation" (*sgom khor yug;* TN, p. 590) that lasts all day and night "at least for a day" (TN, p. 592). The practitioner sets up the extraordinary samādhi; establishes just the right conditions for awakened wisdom, especially strengthening the ultimate enlightened attitude; locks into continuous, uninterrupted inconceivable mindfulness with the way the realized mind stays as both the vantage point and the object of mindfulness; carefully protects the practice from even the slightest forms of artificial activity or from faults; and continuous flawless meditation until crossing over. Crossing over will just happen by itself, but only when "not reflecting [on a meditation object], not taking to mind, not directing the mind, and [having real mindfulness without artificial activity]" (TN, p. 592). Tashi Namgyel's crossing-over instructions are as follows:

> The likely time is when the practitioner has refined any intense experiences of nonconceptual stillness, clarity, or bliss, and then (1) continuously meditates, having attained certainty letting the

mind's [natural] brightness and clarity come forth in awareness, with the view being clarity [from the event-perspective] and emptiness like space [from the mind-perspective]; or (2) continuously meditates with unobstructed [real] mindfulness on (a) various appearances coming from movement within the six sense systems, as well as on (b) the movement of thought in such a way that clarity/emptiness [at the coarse level] or movement/emptiness [at the subtle level] arise, throughout the day and night. In short, crossing over happens at the time when every single sensory experience—appearance and thought—are viewed as clarity/emptiness and movement/emptiness with absolute certainty. (TN, pp. 592, 690)

Tashi Namgyel cautions that intense samādhi experiences, such as the respective states of strong bliss, clarity, or nonconceptual stillness, are not to be confused with crossing over and may actually interfere with crossing over due to attachment to them. Once "refined" in the sense of having no attachment to or artificial activity associated with these special states, crossing over becomes more likely. Irrespective of these special states, crossing over is primarily the result of continuous, inconceivable mindfulness of the simultaneous mind, either with respect to the simultaneous mind's vast awareness-itself or with respect to its seemingly unobstructed, self-illuminating appearances and thoughts, so that every seeming moment manifests absolute certainty about its innate emptiness/clarity. Other than that there is nothing else.

According to Tilopa, such uninterrupted, effortless mindfulness finds no refuge (gtad so) in any particular events of the mind because of their inherent emptiness/clarity, so that awareness-itself turns back on itself and naturally crosses over. Crossing over is most likely to occur when there is absolutely no artificial activity associated with meditating or with mindfulness of the simultaneous mind. Crossing over cannot occur when a dualistic distinction is made between meditator and that which is meditated upon. The practitioner cannot use even valid concepts or views to secure crossing over (TN, p. 608). There is nothing to "generate" (TN, p. 608). There is nothing to "meditate" on (TN, p. 609). Expectation of crossing over or fear of not crossing over prevents the realization (TN, p. 609). There is only "awareness-itself of the way the realized mind stays" (TN, p. 609), only the "awakened wisdom that cannot be reflected [in meditation]."

Awakened wisdom is self-occurring *(rang byung)* and self-staying *(rang gnas)*.

Crossing over is a way to return to the mind's natural temperament *(gshis; TN, pp. 594–97)*, which is explained in terms of the way the realized mind stays *(gnas lugs)*. Crossing over is called "the great penetration of the always-here mind" *(skye med zang thal chen po; TN, p. 592)*. When crossing over occurs, seeming individual consciousness is displaced by the Buddha-mind. This enlightened mind is also called *the dharmakāya (chos sku)* or *the awakened wisdom body (ye shes sku)*. After crossing over, the practitioner's mind is no different from the mind of the enlightened master who originally empowered the practitioner to attain this supreme realization. Tashi Namgyel emphasizes that the practitioner must correctly recognize *(ngo shes)* that crossing over has occurred (TN, pp. 597–606). Crossing over is a way to "separate the dense from the pure mind" (TN, p. 598), so that what is recognized is that the practitioner's own consciousness is now identical to that of all the enlightened masters, and that this consciousness is the "dharmakāya [saturating] all saṃsāra" (TN, p. 598).

B. The Outcome: The Nature of Enlightenment

Contrary to the slow ripening of meditative experience throughout the preliminary and essential stages of meditation, and even the gradual ripening of awakened wisdom during extraordinary meditation, crossing over to enlightenment is an immediate and compelling event, wherein the mental continuum undergoes a series of fundamental and enduring reorganizations. One implication of the term *nonmeditation* is that the "journey ends." There are no more stages. Pema Karpo says,

> The journey ends. Going by stages stops. There are no stages that go anywhere else. You find the perfection of everything that came before, without stages. (PK, f. 13b)

There are no stages *(sa med)* beyond this point. Enlightenment in the mahāmudrā tradition results in two kinds of perfection. First is the perfection of awakened wisdom *(ye shes)*. The term *ye shes* is composed of the noun *shes pa,* "knowledge," and the particle *ye,* "complete." Enlightenment completes the search for knowledge. Second is perfect purification. The term *thar ba,* "liberation," is derived from the same root as *mtha',* "final, last." The practitioner becomes completely free of all defilements, false concepts, and negative emotional states. Whether enlightenment is considered in terms of either knowledge or purification, completion is implied in either case. The technical terms for enlightened knowledge are *omniscience (thams cad mkhyen)* and *awakened wisdom (ye shes)*. The terms pertaining to purification are *liberation (grol ba)* and *final liberation (thar ba)*.

Enlightenment as liberation predominated the earlier Buddhism of the Theravada tradition. Enlightenment as the perfection of wisdom and compassion, in addition to liberation, is characteristic of the later Mahāyāna tradition. The Mahāyāna perspective on enlightenment introduces the three buddha bodies as an aspect of enlightened omniscience. More will be said about this later.

1. The Stages of Enlightenment

The enlightenment experience does not occur exactly as a momentary event, though it happens within a relatively short span of ordinary time. It is experienced as three very distinctive shifts in consciousness, which follow immediately upon each other. These are called: (1) basis *(gzhi)*, (2) path *(lam)*, and (3) fruition *('bras bu)*.

a. Basis Enlightenment

The first enlightenment moment is sometimes called samādhi-enlightenment *(mnyam bzhag)* because it typically occurs during continuous, uninterrupted mindfulness. When the conditions of the extraordinary meditation are exactly right, crossing over occurs. A profound shift occurs during which seemingly individual consciousness, and all ordinary sense experience and all false concepts associated with it, drop away.[576] The vast awareness-space of the dharm-akāya becomes the point of observation. Seemingly individual consciousness *(yid)*, the point of observation throughout the entire path of meditation, is now found to be a mere concept *(btags pa)*, which drops away. Basis-enlightenment is said to be "beyond all notions," "beyond examination," "beyond representation," and "beyond false concepts" (TN, pp. 519–20). Tilopa says,

> When the mind comes to an end,
> The three realms become absorbed therein....
> Through the nonduality of self and other you become the
>   blessed Buddha.

> The mind becomes absorbed through the force of the ripening
> perspective of [vast awareness-]space.
> Then, the five sense systems and their objects, the aggregates, and
> the elements also dissolve in the perspective of space.

The seeming reality of individual consciousness along with its functions
and activities gives way, leaving only an infinite ocean of awareness-space.
Basis enlightenment leads to a very "new view of the way the realized mind
stays" (TN, p. 517). When the concept of individual consciousness or
"mind" is finally eradicated, a profound rearrangement takes place. Awakened wisdom now comes forth unobstructed, no longer as a brief glimpse
or flash but as that which saturates all experience. It has no real support
(brten), yet serves as the ground or basis for all experience. Therefore the
first moment of enlightenment is called *basis enlightenment.*

During the ordinary special-insight meditations the practitioner searched
for certain knowledge within arising events of the ordinary mental continuum. During the extraordinary samādhi meditations the practitioner
located the simultaneous mind as the source of certain knowledge. Now,
with basis enlightenment, knowledge takes on a new epistemological locus
of knowledge. Awakened wisdom comes forth but not in association with
either the ordinary or the simultaneous mind. Awakened wisdom has no
basis. It is without coming *('ong med)* and without going *('song med),* in that
it does not arise from the seeming activity of the relative mental continuum.
Awakened wisdom is self-originated *(rang 'byung).* It is simply there, and
with basis enlightenment, stays there. Basis enlightenment is called, "wisdom beyond the world" (TN, p. 542).

b. Path Enlightenment

Immediately following basis enlightenment, a second profound rearrangement takes place on top of *(steng du)* basis enlightenment. Basis enlightenment puts in order the absolute dimension of truth. Path enlightenment
puts in order the relative activity of the mental continuum. Awakened wisdom seems to shift its locus, now saturating every potential experience (TN,
p. 527). The experience of path enlightenment is profound. In a single
instant *(dus skad cig)* or flash of clear light the entire seeming content of the
relative mental continuum in all its interconnectedness—all realms,
throughout all times—"arise as self-liberation."[577] Path enlightenment is
marked by the instantaneous return of cognitions and perceptions, now

completely unobstructed. *All* of the content of the saṃsāric realms, the entire potential of relative activity, is "let loose" (TN, p. 497) and becomes elaborated" (TN, p. 498). The experience of path enlightenment sharply contrasts the moment of vast awareness-space characterizing basis enlightenment after individual consciousness, sensory experience, and false concepts dropped away.

Path enlightenment marks another shift in perspective. Rechung says, "Worldly phenomena themselves are considered to be the basis for self-liberation."[578] Whereas awakened wisdom had no support during basis enlightenment, the entire relative activity of the ordinary mental continuum and its interconnectedness to virtual, storehouse consciousness now becomes its support. Path enlightenment is called "wisdom of the world" (TN, p. 542). The entire ordinary, temporal stream, as well as the extraordinary, interconnected network of all potential mental content, become the embodiment of wisdom. The mind's manifest spontaneity is the very expression of awakened wisdom.

This second fundamental rearrangement is called "entering the path,"[579] because the entire potential content of all realms and times is "let loose" as if "undamming" it (*bskyil na ma 'gag pa;* TN, p. 529). Yet, the practitioner no longer "clings to" (TN, p. 529) nor "becomes entangled in" (TN, p. 529) in any particular mental content because there is no artificial activity or reactivity associated with it in any way. The practitioner traverses the path *(lam 'khyer)* of all potential content in an instant, as if swept along by the miraculous play of the natural mind's spontaneity. From the new locus of unceasing awakened wisdom, all relative activity becomes the manifestation of truth. Awakened wisdom spreads "like fire in a forest" among all the relative content of existence in its entirety. As a result of this catapult along the flow of content, the practitioner achieves perfect understanding of all relative events of all realms and all times. The practitioner masters path awareness *(lam rig)* and all that is not knowable *(shes bya med)*. There is nothing particular to know because everything is known.

Because path-enlightenment immediately follows basis-enlightenment, the practitioner does not corrupt this wisdom about the manifest relative content of experience with any false cognitions (thought and emotion) nor artificial activity (trying to prevent the experience from happening or making it happen). Traversing the path of all relative experience, without taking-to-mind anything and without any reactivity whatsoever, brings complete liberation from suffering and from false views.[580] The great weight of potentially corrupting karmic propensities is completely erased by rapidly going through all relative content with this enlightened nonreactive awareness. Path enlightenment is sometimes called "the great cutting off" (TN, p. 499). The seemingly ordinary mental continuum becomes stainless *(dri med)*. However, it is important to understand that the dharmakāya "is the ground for purification but not itself the object to be purified, for within its own nature there is not a single established atom that might be purified."[581] The Tibetan word for *buddha* is the compound *sang gye,* which contains *sang* ("purified") and *gye* ("to arise or blossom"). The word literally means the blossoming of complete purity.[582]

c. Fruition Enlightenment

In a flash, the entire mental continuum of cognition and perception becomes nondual awakened wisdom, basis and path enlightenment become "mixed" *('dres ba).* As the practitioner is swept along this path, a third enlightenment moment follows, namely fruition enlightenment. As the name indicates, this brings closure to enlightenment. It is the final and most profound rearrangement of the mind.

The necessary condition by which fruition enlightenment comes forth is, once again, protecting practice, completely free of artificial activity:

> When there is [absolutely] no artificial construction regarding thought and emotion, what follows is the way the realized mind happens across all the three realms of saṃsāra.
> Not artificially constructing this experience is cause for being born in the supreme god realms.
> Not artificially constructing the way the realized mind stays is letting the mind stay in its ground as nirvāṇa.
> Not artificially constructing this inconceivable attainment is an attainment that originates by itself and occurs by itself.
> It means none other than being without [any] effort and without making anything happen.
> This is mastery of the fruition enlightenment, beyond what can be taught. (TN, p. 544)

Fruition enlightenment, as the name indicates, is the perfection or fruition of the practice. Fruition enlightenment is buddhahood:

> Regarding the samādhi and postsamādhi [nonmeditation prac-
> tice] that you did, they are called boddhisattvahood. When you
> go beyond these, it is called buddhahood. (TN, p. 547)

Path enlightenment puts an end to any and all stages of meditation. The practitioner whose enlightened mind continuously traverses the path of all experience no longer needs to meditate, in the formal sense of meditation sessions, yet meditates all the time. Fruition enlightenment is an expression of the fulfillment of all practice. The practitioner once again returns to the world, to a world that is "like a mirage." How to act in that world becomes the primary concern. The enlightened mind is the mind of compassion. When every potential experience is interconnected to all other potential experiences, and all such experiences are reflections of awakened wisdom, ethical behavior is the natural consequence of this realization. The enlightened master acts according to the four services (spyod lam) day and night. Yet these actions arise out of a very different state of mind:

> ...not without single-minded samādhi, yet familiar with thought,
> as if seemingly not in samādhi. (TN, p. 548)

The most important feature of fruition enlightenment is that the practitioner's seemingly individual consciousness is realized to be the three buddha bodies; (1) The dharmakāya, or truth body, represents the level of the fully enlightened mind, namely its vast awareness-space, unstained by artificial activity and false concepts. (2) The sambhogakāya, or enjoyment body, represents the extraordinary level of all potential propensities for experience. (3) The nirmāṇakāya, or emanation body, represents thought, emotion, sensation, and perception seeming to unfold in the temporal mental continuum at the coarse level of mental content. During fruition enlightenment these three levels of mind, or buddha bodies, become manifest simultaneously. Sometimes the term ye shes pa'i sku ("awakened wisdom body") is used in the mahāmudrā tradition to signify the fundamental nondual unity of the three buddha bodies. The full ripening of awakened wisdom is the realization of the three buddha bodies.

Fruition enlightenment in the Mahāyāna mahāmudrā tradition is very different from the Theravāda conception of enlightenment, or nirvāṇa. Theravāda enlightenment is described by the Mahāyānists as a form of dissolution experience that leads only to liberation. Mahāmudrā enlightenment is the culmination of nondissolution, wherein the seemingly ordinary coarse-level experiences of the mind are not obstructed. This leads, in addition to liberation, to the realization of the three buddha bodies. The seven qualities of the buddha bodies are as follows: (1) nonduality, (2) never-ending bliss, (3) delight in the Dharma, (4) deep compassion, (5) pervasiveness, (6) uninterruptedness, and (7) emptiness.[583] The five qualities of the completely purified mind are as follows: (1) emptiness, (2) clarity, (3) unobstructedness, (4) always here or continuous from the beginning, and (5) staying.[584] Buddhahood also brings special ways of seeing and paranormal abilities.[585]

In other words, mahāmudrā enlightenment leads to both liberation and omniscience. Because mahāmudrā enlightenment very much includes the seeming relative activity of the ordinary mental continuum, this type of enlightenment is called *nirvāṇa not-staying*.

Yet a perfect buddha in the mahāmudrā tradition is not affected by the seeming stains of the mind's ordinary relative activity. The mind's seeming relative activity itself becomes the embodiment of wisdom and compassion. The Tibetan name for mahāmudrā, *phyag rgya chen po,* means "great gesture." As the enlightened practitioner returns to what seems to be the everyday world, his or her return in the form of an emanation body becomes the great gesture of wisdom and compassion.

C. The Condensed Style of Pointing-Out Practice

Pema Karpo's root instructions on nonmeditation are highly compact. Consistent with the style of pointing-out instruction, he does not want to give elaborate explanations that could easily lead to conceptual grasping *(blo yis 'dzin pa)*. Tashi Namgyel's extensive commentary offers a detailed explanation of nonmeditation practice. However, these explanations are somewhat misleading in that the actual instructions are seldom given in such a manner. With some knowledge of the practice, the reader is now in a better position to understand the usual condensed form of instruction. Here are the complete root instructions:

> Second, after putting in order all phenomena as the natural, simultaneous, dharmakāya, you experience nonmeditation yoga. After doing away with suffering, you do away with the need for any remedy, which presupposes trying to let go of something.

Then the path comes to an end. Proceeding [by stages] also comes to an end. There are no stages that go anywhere else. Then you master everything coming before, without stages, the nirvāṇa of not-staying, the siddhi of the supreme mahāmudrā. Further, in the *Cycle of Energy Yogas [Bsre skor]*, Naropa quotes Tilopa, saying:

> "Well, this is awareness-in-and-by-itself, ineffable awakened wisdom, without a locus.[586] Tilopa can say nothing about it. Its characteristics are self-evident by themselves.... Set it up by not recalling, not reflecting, not anticipating, not meditating, and not analyzing, [but rather] by being settled into itself." As the saying goes, this is truth. (PK, f. 13b)

Jampel Pawo explains the opening line "you experience the 'yoga of nonmeditation.'" He says the juxtaposition of the words *natural, simultaneous,* and *dharmakāya* pertain to basis, path, and fruition enlightenment, respectively. Through enlightenment, the practitioner "reaches the limit" of the two truths. The respective names for perfection of each of the two truths are *great abandonment (spangs ba chen po)* and *great understanding (rtogs pa chen po)*. The former term pertains to relative truth, in which entanglement with negative emotional states and erroneous conceptualization is permanently eradicated. *Great abandonment* means "liberation." The latter term pertains to ultimate truth, namely to awakened wisdom. The profound and permanent rearrangement that occurs through enlightenment is distinctly different from putting in order the simultaneous mind in one-taste yoga. Therefore it is given a new designation, the "simultaneousness of crossing over" (JP, f. 82b), because awakened wisdom saturates all of saṃsāra and ultimately transcends the type of understanding possible to the ordinary mind.

According to the commentator, nonmeditation yoga is the perfection of both the relative and the ultimate enlightened attitude. Wisdom and compassion form a nondual pair. Therefore the realization of awakened wisdom is also the realization of deep compassion. He cites Saraha to explain:

> The sacred tree of the nondual mind [ultimate truth] saturates the entire three realms. Hold the benefit and fruition of each, namely through the flower of compassion [relative truth]. That is more useful than the former. Both the sacred tree of emptiness

as well as the flower [of compassion] develop. The nectar of that flower of compassion is found in the [coarse-level perceptual] aspects. Its subtle fruition is spontaneous presence. Bliss is none other than mind. (JP, f. 80b)

The spontaneous presence of the ordinary mental continuum becomes the basis for continuous and uninterrupted compassion.

The commentator calls the meditation a "causeless meditation" that is "free from effort." Pema Karpo's root text uses Tilopa's now-familiar non-meditation instructions, which are designed to negate artificial activity and thereby set up the exact conditions for enlightenment. The enlightenment experience is called *nirvāṇa not-staying* in that it manifests both ultimate and relative truth as a simultaneous pair. Relative events are not obstructed. The commentator concludes with a discussion of the types of simultaneousness as experienced during each moment of enlightenment, as illustrated in Table 42:

TABLE 42: JAMPEL PAWO'S COMMENTARY ON MIXED ENLIGHTENMENT

Samādhi	Simultaneousness of mind	Basis	Ultimate truth	Temperament	Tree
Post-samādhi	Simultaneousness of cognition/ perception	Path	Relative truth	Harmony	Fruit
Mixed	Simultaneousness of crossing-over	Fruit	Pair		Nectar

D. PROTECTING PRACTICES FOR CORRECTING MISTAKES THAT PREVENT ENLIGHTENMENT OR CAUSE THE PRACTITIONER TO LOSE IT

It is customary for advanced protecting practices to include instructions that review the types of mistakes that prevent enlightenment from occurring or cause the practitioner to lose it partially or fully after it has occurred. Initial enlightenment is not necessarily a stable experience for certain practitioners. Genuine enlightenment becomes the very real possibility for overcoming the entire force of karmic propensities, which perpetuate ignorance and suffering. Sometimes the great weight of residual karmic propensities serves to either prevent or cause the loss of enlightenment. These special protecting instructions are designed to correct these potential problems. The "fate" of enlightenment depends upon the configuration of the conditions *(rkyen)* that establish and maintain it (TN, p. 590).

Consistent with the style of pointing-out instruction, the conditions that establish and maintain enlightenment are carefully set forth in the oral tradition. The oral readings precisely specify the optimal conditions for both the pre- and post-enlightenment practice. It is very important for the practitioner to accurately understand the oral readings and pointing-out instructions. Any misunderstanding may lead to a failure to develop enlightenment or to losing it. It should now become clear to the reader why the exact wording of the pointing-out instructions is so important, and why the ceremony of direct transmission of these instructions must be preserved.

There are three types of improper conditions that affect enlightenment: (1) An attempt may be made to maintain the correct view but missing it *(shor sa)* in a way that prevents enlightenment from occurring. (2) Meditation experience may be in error *(gol sa)* in a way that prevents enlightenment from occurring. (3) An initial enlightenment experience may have occurred, but certain obstacles *('geg pa)* may cause the practitioner to partially or fully lose it or otherwise prevent its subsequent stabilization as a permanent condition of mind.

1. Missing It [587]

The first general *(sphyi)* condition that prevents enlightenment is called *missing it (shor sa)*. Tashi Namgyel defines straying in terms of "losing the supreme view" and/or "turning to bad view" (TN, p. 555). There are two categories *(tha snyad)* of missing: (1) completely going off the track *(ye shor)*, and (2) having meditative experience trail off into a mistake *(nyam su len lugs 'khrul pa la 'phral shor)*. In the former case the practitioner never develops the fundamental realization of one-taste yoga, namely the "emptiness and clarity of all phenomena" (TN, p. 552). This is considered to be a "very big mistake" (TN, p. 555). In the latter case the practitioner attains the correct view of emptiness/clarity but loses it during subsequent meditation practice. Some commentators disagree as to the importance of these distinctions. Jampel Pawo feels that all types of missing are equally negative and does not distinguish between them (JP, f. 85a).

In either case most commentators concur that there are four subtypes of missing. All four types pertain to "not understanding emptiness correctly" (TN, p. 560; JP, f. 85a). While each subtype differs in emphasis, all four share a common feature, namely that the highest view *(go yul)* of emptiness has not been established correctly. Establishing the highest gradation of emptiness is a prerequisite to enlightenment.

To maximize the likelihood of attaining enlightenment, these four types of missing emptiness must be "corrected through [correct] realization" (PK, f. 14b). The practitioner who recognizes the simultaneous mind properly will not stray far from a refined view of emptiness (TN, pp. 551–52). Careful attention to protecting practices establishes the proper conditions for the realization of awakened wisdom and its fruition in the enlightenment experience.

Pema Karpo's brief root instructions delineate four types of missing *(shor sa bzhi)* and the skillful means for removing them *(sel pa'i thabs):*

> The four [ways to] miss:
> 1. Missing the natural condition of emptiness. This is corrected by emptiness being compassion.
> 2. Missing how to seal [emptiness on all phenomena]. This is corrected by understanding the way the realized mind stays as it really is.
> 3. Missing the remedy stops by taking that to be abandoned and its remedy to be inseparable.
> 4. Missing the path stops by understanding that what has arisen and liberation come at the same instance. (PK, f. 14a–14b)[588]

The former two types of missing—natural condition and sealing—pertain to the ultimate truth, while the latter two—remedy and path—pertain to the relative truth.

The natural temperament of the mind is emptiness/clear light. The technical term, *gshis,* means "temperament," here translated as "natural condition." Completely missing or straying from the mind's natural condition after having realized its intrinsic condition is said to be a "very big mistake" (TN, p. 555). Jampel Pawo adds that a refined understanding of emptiness is the realization that emptiness and compassion are one and the same. Failure to realize the inseparability of emptiness and compassion can lead to a subtle or not-so-subtle attachment to emptiness:

You become attached to emptiness when you don't know emptiness and compassion to be inseparable. Then emptiness, which
previously destroyed cause and effect, becomes an enemy. You
may have held on to the main realization, but now your meditation becomes flawed. The best [truth] becomes the worst
flawed view. (JP, f. 85a–85b)

This subtle attachment to emptiness suggests a failure to give proper cre-
dence to relative truth so that a proper understanding of the simultaneous
mind goes astray. This is the worst kind of mistake because the practitioner
believes that he or she has found awakened wisdom but gets farther and farther away from it.

The skillful means to not completely miss *(mi 'chor ba)* the mind's natural condition is to cut off *(bcod pa)* the possibility of missing it by directly
realizing awakened wisdom, so as to eradicate all ideas about emptiness at
the subtlest level and also to allow awareness-itself to continuously reflect
both the ultimate and the relative dimensions of the simultaneous mind.

Sometimes this flaw can be very subtle in a way that causes the realization to trail off into a mistake. Tashi Namgyel explains:

The highest view of emptiness, though not really flawed, does
not entirely develop because it has been resolved primarily as an
idea and not with [direct] meditative experience. (TN, p. 552)

The practitioner has mastered only the extraordinary examination meditation, but has not fully mastered the samādhi meditation on the simultaneous mind, which brings direct realization of the natural mind and its
inseparable manifestations, that is, direct realization of the most refined
level of emptiness and clarity. Tashi Namgyel explains that the practitioner
"does not understand the real nature of the mind at its highest level, and
has no awareness-itself of the way the realized mind stays" (TN, p. 553). By
having such an experience, the practitioner at least has not completely
missed the correct view. However, the extraordinary samādhi meditation
may deviate into a subtle attachment to emptiness, which is remedied by
mastering the cognition- and appearance-simultaneousness samādhi meditations. This type of missing is corrected by realizing that emptiness and
compassion are inseparable. *Compassion* here refers to the relative aspects
of existence. When not seen as inseparable, "the view of emptiness goes

bad" (TN, p. 555). Once they have been properly understood, the practitioner keeps from deviating from the right view by "very careful protecting" (TN, p. 556).

Next is the mistake of missing how to seal *(rgyas 'debs)*. According to Tashi Namgyel, the practitioner "fails to realize how to use awareness-itself to establish that all phenomena stay in their real nature" (TN, p. 557). In other words, he has had some realization of emptiness but has failed correctly to put the seal of emptiness on all phenomena. If this had been done correctly, there would be no need to artificially act in any way to bring the realization. There would be no means by which enlightenment could be produced. "The means and realization of this meditation are inseparable" *(sgom thabs shes dbyer med;* TN, p. 554). The practitioner completely misses the point when failing to correctly put the seal of emptiness on all phenomena and therefore thinks that enlightenment is somehow different from what has already been realized.

The more subtle form of missing the point occurs when the practitioner's protecting practice is inadequate *(ma grig),* so that the practice is not in harmony with the mind's relative activity (TN, p. 555). As a result the practitioner becomes distracted from continuous mindfulness of the natural mind as he or she searches for some realization elsewhere.

The way to correct this type of missing is by "understanding the way of existence as it really is." Tashi Namgyel explains:

> Know the naturalness, mahāmudrā, the self-saturation of all phenomena.... Then you will know the reason for never leaving emptiness. So don't stray from sealing. Don't act on that with ideas about emptiness as you once did. (TN, pp. 558–59)

The practitioner lets awareness-itself penetrate all realms and all times and seals all phenomena as being emptiness as they seem to arise. When reality is thoroughly known as sealed as empty, there is no desire to intellectualize. All seeming appearances, once sealed with the realization of emptiness, are known as merely the play *(rol pa)* of the natural mind (TN, p. 559).

The third type of mistake is missing the remedy *(gnyen po).* This way of completely missing the point occurs when the practitioner thinks that emptiness serves as a remedy for all the mind's afflictions and thereby makes a false, dualistic distinction between emptiness and affliction. Jampel Pawo explains:

> If you fail to intellectually understand their real nature as insep-
> arable, you might become attached to [thinking that] the emo-
> tions to be overcome and their remedy, awakened wisdom, are
> somehow different. In that case you might try to prevent the for-
> mer and make the latter happen. (JP, f. 85b)

Here the practitioner fails to realize that both seeming emotions and any possible remedy for them are nondual. Tashi Namgyel says, "you might grasp the emotions and emptiness dualistically and [then try to] prevent these emotions" (TN, p. 554). The more subtle type of trailing off into a mistake occurs when, during samādhi meditation, the practitioner "uses ideas to analyze how to not make emotions happen so as to realize the real nature of the mind" (TN, p. 554).

The correction for missing the remedy is "realizing that [which has] arisen and its remedy to be inseparable" (JP, f. 85b). As such, there is no further need for any artificial activity. Once the correct view has been estab-lished, nothing needs to be done to bring about liberation from emotional suffering. Emotional states become self-liberated *(rang grol)* as they arise. As emotions arise, awareness-itself shows them to be nondual, relative man-ifestations of awakened wisdom (TN, p. 558).

The last type of missing is missing the path *(lam)*. Jampel Pawo explains:

> Not being aware that the truth of the four paths,[589] and the path
> and its fruition are inseparable, you think each path has a dif-
> ferent fruition. In this way you become corrupted by a desire to
> taste each [path] and you strive to do so. (JP, f. 85b)

Tashi Namgyel says that fruition is spontaneous presence *(lhun gyis grub)*. No effort can bring it forth. A practitioner completely misses the path by "desiring to attain something other than this fruition—the three bodies and five wisdoms" (TN, p. 553). Fruition is the upper limit of the path. Some practitioners fail to understand this and "seek elsewhere" *(gzhan du 'tshol ba)* in hope of finding something else. This is because the practitioner is "loaded with ideas," has "failed to understand that emptiness stays as the real nature of all phenomena," and therefore "doesn't realize that awakened wisdom and skillful means are inseparable" (TN, p. 554). Having ideas about other kinds of possible wisdom only kindles greed and sets in motion harmful karmic propensities. This kind of practitioner is only representing *(dmigs pa)* enlightenment, which makes it impossible actually to attain enlightenment.

This final type of missing enlightenment is corrected by "understanding that what has arisen and liberation, being inseparable, stay as the self-manifestation *(rang chas)* of the three buddha bodies" (JP, f. 85b). Another way of saying this is that the practitioner "reaches the upper limit of under-standing, wherein the mind's manifestations are realized to be the three bud-dha bodies" and that "basis, path, and fruition are inseparable" (TN, p. 553).

In short, it is necessary to have a correct understanding of mahāmudrā *(rnam rtog phyag rgya chen po)* in order to correct these four ways of miss-ing the realization. Such understanding comes from "knowing the oral read-ings and pointing-out instructions" and using these to guide the meditation, so that their advice "is transmuted into mahāmudrā" (TN, pp. 560–61). After hearing the correct view, the practitioner reviews the state in formal meditation practice so that the realization properly ripens. The practitioner who does this correctly will not completely miss the realization.

2. Errors in the State[90]

The errors *(gol sa)* pertain to extraordinary samādhi practice, that is, to the quality of the samādhi state *(nyams)* within which enlightenment ripens. Pema Karpo warns against attachment to various meditative experiences in his brief root instructions:

> There are three errors regarding attachment to staying/calm states. Remove these by sticking to the special-insight practices. (PK, f. 14a)

Attachment to particular experiences *(bye brag)* of the extraordinary samādhi state is an error. The three compelling experiences of the extraor-dinary samādhi are bliss *(bde ba)*, clarity *(gsal ba)*, and nonconceptual still-ness *(mi rtog)*. These three particular attainments correlate with the categories of sensation and emotion, perception, and thought, respectively. A practitioner may become fascinated with any one or all of these states and mistake them for realization. Jampel Pawo comments:

> These three errors come from attachment to the state of bliss, clarity or nonconceptual stillness associated with staying/calm practice. Baravada says,

"Once you have taken-to-mind the way the realized mind stays and then become attached to any of these states or [try] to represent the truth of the meditation as being any of these, you make an error. The consequence of bliss as an error [is rebirth] in the desire realm; of clarity, the form realm; and of nonconceptual stillness, the formless realm." (JP, f. 85a)

The first part of the passage lists the type of the samādhi experience that leads to the error and the second part gives the consequence. Tashi Namgyel gives a much more detailed commentary. He says there are three kinds of extraordinary bodily bliss:

(1) Your body is filled with bliss. (2) Bliss comes forth from every [seemingly external] sensation. (3) You lose any sense of your body and get the bliss of not feeling anything. (TN, p. 564)

There are also three kinds of extraordinary mental bliss: (1) Mental joy spreads like a fire. (2) You have only happy thoughts, day and night. (3) Since you don't find anything to be substantial, bliss spreads everywhere. (TN, p. 564)

These powerful experiences result from a fundamental rearrangement of the interrelationship between the body, the energy currents, and the mind. (TN, p. 566)

Powerful perceptual experiences also occur, all classified as examples of clarity:

The mind's clarity is like a crystal [reflecting] a perceptual state [characterized by] various [emanating visions]. In this state, if you try, you'll see things at considerable distance during the night. Even when there are no [perceptual] attributes to see, you'll [still] be aware, and [all] appearance comes forth as clear light; In addition to these perceptual experiences extrasensory perception also occurs, for example, reading someone else's mind. (TN, p. 564)[591]

There is also the nonconceptual stillness:

Form sometimes arises from karmic propensities as if out of a void from nowhere, and this can be taken to be emptiness. At times all of the sense objects (sights, sounds, and so on), when not obstructed, will arise very little. At other times all perception seems to arise as empty patterns, whether [you thought of it to be] self-existent or not. Then there is what occurs when even subtle cognition becomes absorbed, leaving only something like vast, pure space, and this can be taken as emptiness. Each of these [experiences] [runs the risk of] generating a kind of attachment to [false] emptiness with respect to any staying or moving phenomena. (TN, pp. 564–65)

These states are not inherently harmful. Wangchug Dorjé, for example, describes how these three states, properly understood, lay the foundation for awakened wisdom.[592] These states are simply manifestations of the changes that sometimes accompany extraordinary samādhi practice. The instructions only address the "way these [might] become errors" (TN, pp. 567–79). Jampel Pawo's passage explains that the error occurs from becoming attached to the meditation state or by representing it *(dmigs pa)* through some idea as a way of trying to re-create the experience. Tashi Namgyel explains:

> In short, any attachment or desire and any resorting to representation is said to make these states an error. (TN, p. 568)

The two ways of bringing about error are as follows: (1) becoming attached *(zhen ba, chags)* to the meditative experience, or (2) resorting to representation *(dmigs gtad)* as a way of re-creating it. The former error pertains to trying to hold on to *('dzin pa)* the samādhi experience. The latter pertains to "examining [the state] with ideas" (TN, p. 568).

The last part of Jampel Pawo's passage alludes to the consequences of making such errors. Those who become attached to bliss, clarity, or nonconceptual stillness open themselves to the desire realms, the form realms, and the formless realms, respectively. These three realms are included in the enjoyment body *(longs spyod;* TN, p. 570). Such sublime experiences generally are accessible only to those within the divine realms. Yet the pleasures do not last. Practitioners who become attached to these experiences are said to "fall into the lower realms" and experience "endless wandering" in future lifetimes (TN, p. 569). By not following the pointing-out instructions carefully the practitioner runs the risk of losing sight of the emerging realization of awakened wisdom, or of confusing sublime meditative states with this realization. The practitioner "no longer sees the way the realized mind stays" (TN, p. 573). He "does not see the truth" (TN, p. 579).

There are two consequences of making errors. First, the practitioner misunderstands *(mi rtogs pa)* the truth. According to Tashi Namgyel, "analysis has become defective" (TN, p. 586). Failure to acquire knowledge differs from erroneous knowledge. In the former case, the practitioner knows that something is missing. In the latter case, the practitioner does not know that he has misunderstood the truth, and persists with practice as if enlightened. Erroneous knowledge is more harmful because the practitioner has become deluded or has developed "very great pride" (TN, p. 563). Second, erroneous practitioners are said to "depend on special means" *(thabs khyad par can la brten pa;* TN, p. 562) and consider themselves to be "advanced saddhus" (TN, p. 562). They devote most of their time to practicing special yogas, such as the tantric energy yogas *(brse 'pho),*[593] instead of following the natural, spontaneous course of realization. Such practitioners are forever preoccupied with seeking some perfected state of body and mind (TN, pp. 562–63).

There are other kinds of errors besides these enjoyment-body errors. There are the errors of the four contemplative states *(bsam gtan bzhi),* wherein the practitioner becomes attached to certain sublime qualities associated with samādhi states, namely joy, bliss, rapture, and equanimity.[594] There are the errors in the sense fields *(skye mched),* wherein the practitioner loses the functions of perception, thought, or consciousness (TN, pp. 572–73). There are also "errors caused by thinking." A practitioner may try to make enlightenment an object of thought, and in so doing has "not listened to the oral readings" (TN, p. 572). Such a practitioner continues the practice mistakenly believing that the truth has been realized:

> You may have no attachment and find equanimity. You may even have a lot of knowledge. Yet if you don't know the oral readings, you'll [still] be in error when you're trying to correct problems in meditation because you haven't considered these sayings. (TN, p. 579)

The consequence of erroneous understanding is "not seeing the way the realized mind stays" (TN, p. 573).

All these errors develop from an imbalance between staying/calm and special-insight practice. As Pema Karpo's root text says, the way to correct them is "by sticking to special-insight practice." The commentator explains:

> These are corrected by generating certain knowledge about the truth of emptiness, which cuts off their root, the means to inciting these [errors]. Gampopa says, "From the perspective of the always-here mind, the three—bliss, clarity, and nonconceptual stillness—become certain [knowedge]." (JP, f. 85a)

No such attachment to any of these sublime experiences will occur when the practitioner properly realizes the emptiness inherent in any of these unusual experiences. Careful adherence to special-insight practice corrects these errors. Tashi Namgyel summarizes:

> When there is continuous mindfulness of certain knowledge about the always-here mind, in all situations, there is no error. Protect so as not to start holding on to or become attached to the truth. (TN, p. 580)

3. Obstacles to the Continuance of Enlightenment [595]

Missing it pertains to misconceptions about absolute truth, while *making errors* pertains to clinging to relative experiences associated with samādhi practice. These two complementary types of hindrances establish conditions that prevent enlightenment from occurring. *Obstacle (gegs pa),* on the other hand, pertains to some condition occurring *after* enlightenment that might cause the practitioner to fully or partially lose enlightenment. Obstacles are related to inadequate protecting *(skyong ba)* and are said to cut off the continuance *(bar du gcod pa)* of enlightenment.

Obstacles occur when certain conditions *(rkyen)* block the ongoing enlightenment experience. At that point certain experiences may become enemies *(dgrar langs).* For example, thought is a welcome friend *(grogs)* to the enlightened individual. Yet if one leads one's life in certain ways after enlightenment, thoughts may become an enemy.

Various commentators differ in their presentation of the types of obstacles. Tashi Namgyel lists two categories: general and other (external and internal). Jampel Pawo lists three: perception, emotion, and physical discomfort. The combined list is given in Table 43. According to Tashi Namgyel general obstacles occur during samādhi, while the other obstacles occur during everyday life (TN, p. 586).

TABLE 43: TYPES OF OBSTACLES
TO THE CONTINUATION OF ENLIGHTENMENT

General	Emptiness	Absolute perspective
	Clarity	Relative perspective
Other	Perception	External
	Thought, emotion, physical discomfort	Internal

The practitioner may have learned to correctly protect the state so as to be no longer attached to its particulars (TN, p. 586). Then, Tashi Namgyel says:

1. Clarity that is not covered by obstacles comes forth.
2. This clarity is not moved by the slightest distraction. It remains very firm.

Even though enlightenment unfolds, it is possible to lose it. The former obstacle happens by drifting into dullness. The latter obstacle happens by drifting into flightiness. Dullness and flightiness are considered to be the most common root obstacles for those with nascent enlightenment experience. The enlightenment experience itself usually serves to remove them:

> To purify these and come to direct realization, you should have become aware of the real nature of all phenomena, which includes becoming aware of the real nature of dullness and flightiness as they arise in meditation. (TN, p. 586)

When properly understood, dullness and flightiness manifest as the seeming self-illuminating aspects of the simultaneous mind rather than as obstacles to ongoing enlightenment.

Pema Karpo mentions another obstacle. His root instructions are as follows:

The obstacle wherein emptiness becomes an enemy [because of too much emphasis on compassion] is remedied by knowing appearance and emptiness to be [an inseparable] pair. (PK, f. 14a)

His commentator, Jampel Pawo, explains the instruction, citing Saraha:

Saraha says,

If you have emptiness without compassion, you won't master the supreme path. Meditating on compassion alone similarly does not lead to liberation. Staying, here in saṃsāra…whatever arises through dependent origination is found to be empty.

As the saying goes, it is remedied by realizing that certain truth regarding emptiness and dependent origination are inseparable. (JP, f. 84b–85a)

Saraha's reference to meditating illustrates that this obstacle pertains primarily to samādhi practice. A very common obstacle occurs when there is an imbalance between emptiness and compassion so that one or the other perspective is lost, thereby affecting the enlightenment experience.

Yet another type of obstacle is physical discomfort or sickness that might cause the practitioner to lose enlightenment unless such experiences are seen as manifestations of the natural mind's experience-making function.

The second main category of obstacles pertains to experiences encountered in the seeming external world. Pema Karpo's root instructions continue:

The obstacle in which perception becomes an enemy is removed by knowing perception to be mind-only. The obstacle in which thought becomes an enelmy is removed by knowing thought to be the dharmakāya. (PK, f. 24a)

According to Tashi Namgyel, certain types of ordinary experiences can become a seemingly external *(phyi)* obstacle. These obstacles are likely to occur while engaging the everyday world. There are two kinds of external obstacles—those pertaining to relationships with others and those pertaining to everyday life events *(spyod yul)*. He explains:

Once you become intensely obsessed with nirvāṇa and saṃsāra, you become obsessed with various worldly experiences. Tormented by these thieves, you may abandon [real] virtue practice. Mara is backed up by the incessant support of her emanations, such as demons and hungry ghosts. She can stop you with lions and other beasts of prey, and once you come under her influence, you cut off the continuance [of enlightenment]. (TN, p. 588)

When encountering difficult life situations, it is possible to forget about service and compassion or to lose sight of the inherent emptiness of such experiences. In either case one or the other of the inseparable dimensions of the simultaneous mind is blocked, as illustrated in Table 44:

TABLE 44: EXTERNAL OBSTACLES

Category	Mistake	Skewed truth dimension
Relationships	Compassion without emptiness	Relative truth
Life events	Stress of everyday events	Absolute truth

Engaging in the eight wordly dharmas increases the likelihood of losing enlightenment. The eight wordly dharmas are pleasure from gain, displeasure from no gain; happiness from worldly pleasure, sadness from displeasure; pleasure from praise, displeasure from criticism; pleasure in gossip, displeasure in gossip.[596]

There are two general categories of skillful means to remove these obstacles. Tashi Namgyel recommends strengthening the protecting practices by "repeating guru yoga many times over" (TN, p. 590). Jampel Pawo recommends "various remedies." Here are some of them:

The skillful means to remove the first obstacle [regarding appearance] is by knowing that any ideas about perceptual experience are none other than the mind and also by understanding the mind to be empty. As the [root] passage says, "remedy that by certain knowledge so that perception is the embodiment of mind." The skillful means to remove the second [regarding thought] is by realizing thought to be the supreme awakened wisdom that is inseparable from the dharmakāya itself. Saraha says,

"Thought's supreme wisdom dries up the ocean of saṃsāra." It is remedied by realizing the truth. (JP, f. 84b)

The passage "knowing that any ideas about perceptual experience are none other than the mind and also by understanding the mind to be empty" refers to reestablishing a correct understanding of the simultaneous mind.

Carefully protecting the enlightened experience strengthens it against any residual effects of the ripening of previous karmic propensities. Enlightenment is no longer affected by the laws of cause and effect in an absolute sense, yet it may still seem to be subject to their influence in a relative sense. Carefully correcting the conditions that may cause the practitioner to lose it serves to stabilize enlightenment as a permanent condition of mind.

8. Practice After Enlightenment

.....

I. Path Walking: Enhancing the Realization[597]

JUST AS CERTAIN CONDITIONS serve as obstacles to maintaining enlightenment, other conditions, properly understood, serve to enhance it. The term *path walking (lam 'khyer)* pertains to the type of lifestyle, behavior, and specific practices engaged in after enlightenment that serve to enhance and consolidate the realization as an enduring condition of mind.[598] The term *lam 'khyer* means "to walk along a path." A traveler who crosses over a mountain needs a plan for discovering the new territory. Likewise, the practitioner whose mind crosses over from seeming individual consciousness to the enlightened mind is more likely to stabilize and consolidate the realization with a plan for everyday behavior and activity. The path-walking instructions provide that plan.

According to Tashi Namgyel, path-walking instructions are given only *after* realization and are applicable to encountering "strong difficulties that arise along the path" (TN, p. 620). The "ideal time" to practice path walking is "after the real nature of mind-simultaneousness in general, and cognition-simultaneousness and appearance-simultaneousness in particular, have been pointed out, and when there is undistracted [inconceivable] mindfulness within postsamādhi practice" (TN, p. 619). Tashi Namgyel lists a variety of everyday situations that best serve to enhance the realization. These include when there is attachment to ordinary experience, when the practitioner is caught up in passion and hatred, when the practitioner is meditating and is finding it very difficult to settle the mind, and when the mind is so much at rest and happy in everyday life that he or she is less likely to recognize the real nature of idle thoughts (TN, pp. 619–20). The best time to practice is when there are passions *('khu phrig),* and especially when these passions are intense *(drag po;* TN, p. 619). In short, *any* difficulties *(dka ngal)* encountered in everyday life become good vehicles for consolidating the realization, and the more intense the better.

Some authorities add that certain spiritual practices can be used for path walking. These could include advanced tantric practices, dzogchen, or the oral mahāmudrā practices (TN, p. 620). They could include guru yoga and giving-and-taking practice.[599] Tashi Namgyel says that these traditional spiritual practices can be adapted to path walking, but he emphasizes that using adverse life circumstances is better precisely because such circumstances evoke more intense emotions.

The ideal place to practice path walking is any place that is uncomfortable. Monasteries and towns are not suitable because strong passions and deluded thinking are less likely to occur there. Best are places where "intense passions" are likely to occur. These include forbidden mountain peaks, cemeteries, and places where evil forces and hungry ghosts lurk about (TN, p. 624). According to Tashi Namgyel, one month of practice in a rough area characterized by terrifying conditions and evil forces is equal to three years of practice in a secluded meditation retreat (TN, p. 624).

Path-walking instructions are not intended for everyone. The Ninth Karmapa explains:

> For those who are exceptionally sharp-witted, there is no need to enhance [their practice], for they are in [the enlightened state of the dharmakāya], in which there is no longer anything to meditate upon or anyone to meditate. For those who are not like this, there are many methods to enhance [their practice].[600]

For most practitioners, path walking is recommended in order to consolidate enlightenment as an enduring condition of mind and to prevent the possibility of partially or fully losing it.

However, testing the realization under adverse circumstances must be done correctly. The practitioner must use these situations as a way of enhancing the same, fundamental realization, and not straying from it. Tashi Namgyel explains:

> The reason for path walking is not to increase sense desire but rather to recognize, through the way the realized mind stays and through knowing that the real nature of thought is the cause of path walking, that all staying and moving phenomena have the real nature of one taste. (TN, p. 621)

Whatever the circumstances, it is especially important to maintain undistracted, continuous mindfulness with the nondual, simultaneous mind as the object of the mindfulness.[601] In order to use difficult life situations correctly as vehicles to enhance the realization, the practitioner must (1) have observed the precepts, (2) demonstrate an ability to apply remedies while remaining free from dualistic thinking, (3) have realized the pointing-out instructions, (4) have strong faith, and (5) know how to purify very subtle karmic propensities (TN, pp. 624–25).

The essential meaning of path walking is defined as follows:

> Use every single seemingly clinging and deluded thought [precisely] because these are the cause for entrapment in saṃsāra. When this very thought doesn't go astray as a result of path walking, its real nature arises as awakened wisdom. (TN, p. 627)

Path walking leads to "complete liberation" (TN, p. 627). During meditation it becomes relatively easy for the skilled practitioner to transform subtle cognition into awakened wisdom. However, it is much harder to transform coarse-level thought into wisdom, especially when this thought has become elaborated (TN, p. 628). Path walking is the way to transform even the most passionate and deluded coarse-level states of mind into awakened wisdom, provided there is "continuous mindfulness of the way the realized mind stays" (TN, p. 629).

Tashi Namgyel says that path walking entails "three important points" (TN, p. 630). These are (1) recognizing every dualistic cognition for what it is so as not to stray, (2) completely letting go of clinging to a self or having ideas about a self, and (3) letting go of hope for benefit or fear of failure (TN, p. 631). An enlightened practitioner who is able to walk the path keeping in mind these three points is said to experience five benefits *(spyod dngos la lnga)*. Tashi Namgyel explains the five-benefits approach to path walking. Each is introduced through a metaphor:

> 1. *Yoga Like a Wounded Deer.* Like a wounded deer, the practitioner does not associate with others. He does not engage in thought about anything. He stays by himself. He protects the mind's real nature and cuts off both the enemy and its remedy. He no longer needs advice nor does he need friendship.

2. *Yoga Like a Lion.* Like a lion that is never frightened of the game [it seeks] nor of other beasts of prey, the practitioner has no terror in his mind. Whatever the conditions of thought that move internally, or the [seeming] appearances externally, he finds no obstacle. He never sheds tears.

3. *Yoga Like the Wind Through Space.* There is no substance to the winds throughout space. The hawk spreads its wings [and soars above all]. Likewise, the practitioner penetrates [the real nature of the mind] when he walks. The enjoyment body is the bliss of practice that has let go of all attachment and all deluded ideas. There is nothing to take up, nothing to hold on to.

4. *Yoga Like Space.* Space has no support. The practitioner does not take support in any intended meditation object, does not direct attention, does not utilize ideas to act or intend to act in a certain way or to think that this or that has or does not have certain qualities.

5. *Crazy Yoga.* The practitioner is like a madman who has nothing fixed in his experience. He finds nothing "good" and nothing "bad." He neither prevents any experience nor makes any experience happen. He neither takes up nor abandons anything. (TN, pp. 625–27)

This section concludes with three very different texts on path walking. The first text, by Pema Karpo, uses the most difficult situations—the passions—as a vehicle for path walking. The most difficult situations of life, according to Pema Karpo, are (1) difficulties of genuinely praying; (2) the greatest difficulty of all, false conceptualization or ordinary dualistic thinking; (3) influences set upon humans by gods and demons, namely the greatest temptations and the greatest terrors; (4) the state of human misery; (5) pain and sickness; and (6) the time of death.

The second text, by the Eighth Situpa, uses the rhythm of waking and sleeping and the periods of the day and night as a vehicle for path walking. The quality of consciousness in general, and of thought and perception in particular, undergoes various transformations throughout the full sleep-wake cycle. Situpa uses these conditions as an opportunity for path walking.

Whereas these first two texts emphasize awakened wisdom, a third text, by Rangjung Dorjé, emphasizes compassion as the vehicle for path walking. The instructions found in his *Devotional Prayer* constitute the bodhisattva's unique approach to path walking.

Path walking is an expression of the ultimate enlightened attitude. Pema Karpo and Situpa's texts are an expression of a quest for the perfect wisdom that will allow the practitioner to become genuinely compassionate toward others. All life situations become an expression of the ultimate enlightened attitude. Taken as a unit, all three texts depict the balance between nondual wisdom and compassion at the heart of path walking. Path walking uses life's greatest difficulties as well as virtuous spiritual practices in order to help self and others. Self and others, nondual, are contained within the realized state of the dharmakāya. The term *mahāmudrā* literally means "great gesture." Mahāmudrā enlightenment is said to be the "great gesture" of wisdom and compassion.

II. Walking the Path of Passion: The Oral Transmission of "Same Taste" by Pema Karpo

Following are the "rolled into a ball"[602] instructions of the six cycles of same taste:

> Homage to the holy lamas.
>
> Homage to the glorious [enlightened] minds [of those lamas] who have pointed out the supreme realization to the School of Elephant Siddhas by the skillful means of the five faces of supreme wisdom. Stay in samādhi undistracted, dwelling in the mind's inner forest.
>
> Here are the instructions about the mahāmudrā, same taste, given in the form of two sets of three instructions over a "cycle of six same tastes," or "liberation rolled into a ball":
>
> I. Prayer [Guru Yoga]
> There are two instructions about the chronicles of the lineage. The first pertains to offering prayers to the lineage. The second [has two parts]—the preliminaries and the basic [practice]. First, pray to release all sentient beings from the prison of saṃsāra. Fix the mind on the supreme realization. To accomplish this, think, "I should meditate on this profound realization, the one taste, that purifies the depth of suffering." Set up the body virtuously,

as if it were Vajrayoginī. In general, pray to those lamas of the tantric stages. [Specifically,] offer a prayer for the one-taste [realization]. Second, dissolve [those lamas] into light, and absorb them into yourself. Next, turn back the mind's movement toward sense objects and set up the mind in samādhi.

II. Thought and Emotion

The second of the six cycles. First come the path-walking instructions to experience evil as a blessing by viewing thought. There are three parts. First, the preliminaries, [which] consist of the seven [-limbed prayer]. Second, the basics, [which] consist of establishing [the mind] in emptiness. Third, the conclusion, [which] consists of same-taste practice. These instructions are explained:

First [of the preliminary practice]. Seemingly ordinary thought is the basis for saṃsāric existence. Not wishing for that to occur, you might abandon thought. This [is wrong]. You are ignorant of path walking. You won't master the supreme purity, [because you] cling to that [which has been] abandoned and its remedy [as dual]. So don't do that. Do the reverse meditation [and let thought remain unobstructed]. In one-taste meditation the special insight is that seeming ordinary appearance occurs as the one taste of awareness-itself. [Correctly seen this way,] the foundation of awakened wisdom will increase by as much thought as comes forth, like fire and fuel coming together in flames. Thus, when thought occurs, it is the activity of only joy!

Second [of the preliminary meditations on thought] is as follows:

Whenever thought has arisen, if it is merely recognized, then what has arisen turns to liberation. Awakened wisdom is known by turning away from ignorance. If thought is not recognized [correctly], this very thought keeps you ignorant. In previous practice you were more or less attached to some idea of using a remedy for thought. Now free yourself of that [dualistic attachment]. Whatever is to be abandoned and its remedy are inseparable. Here the practice is one taste for a life of inner peace called "the thought-dharmakāya." Through that [practice] the mind is able to stay in awareness-itself and yet take a perspective on [thought]. How can there be any other path? In the *Showing of the Oral Readings on Inner Contemplation,* it says, "the first movement of the mind brings staying/calm practice. Seeing thought's elaboration from the unborn mind brings what is called special-insight meditation." Here we explain how to combine staying/calm and special-insight practice [as inseparable]. This is bliss, the root of the experience of the ear-whispered [tradition].

Third [of the preliminary meditations on thought] is as follows: One taste is beyond both the knowledge of recognizable sense objects and that which acts to grasp them [as a duality]. It is like pouring water into water. If [a given] thought is not elaborated, then you become distracted from the [true] path of non-artificiality. If a given thought is elaborated, it doesn't continue into a second thought and you can recognize [each distinct thought as empty] at the very moment in which it has arisen.

Second, [the essential practice regarding thought]:

First, path walking with emotions. Meditate in such a way as to let go of any desire to find an entity and [since you see them as empty]: (1) arising emotions, (2) their [ongoing] agitation, (3) and your getting caught up in their influence are all transmuted into extraordinary experience.

The second basic practice is to remain established in emptiness. If all the primary and subsidiary emotions were condensed, they would contain five emotions. Take, for example, the emotion of confusion that occurs during sleep, especially at the deepest point of sleep. Establish undistracted [mindfulness throughout sleep]. Then during the stage when sleep disappears, [upon awakening] liberation will manifest itself. The mind's fundamental clear-light nature causes the experience of any mental event to recognize itself. Thus the mind sustains its familiarity [with truth] at all times, [even during deep sleep], as in your meditation. So realize this clear light. As another example, whenever you tend to get lost in any of the ten kinds of attachment (such as the emotion of desire), merely recognize the attachment for what it is, and you won't get lost. The great bliss of just-this is called "awareness-itself." With respect to hatred, when hatred occurs, it recognizes itself [with clear light], and great clarity comes forth. Thus [these emotions hold] the potential for their transformation into both (1) direct practice and (2) guidance [in realizing the truth]. Now that the instructions on these [three primary] emotions have been given, [the other two,] pride and jealousy could also be explained [in the same manner].

Third, [the conclusion]. Through emotion's becoming mere emptiness, by itself comes self-liberation. Thus it is called "the awakened wisdom of emotion."

III. Gods and Demons

Third [of the cycle of six] is the last of the first set of three path-walking instructions. This instruction transmutes the influences put forth by the gods and demons into special psychic powers. The first occurs in those places typically associated with intense fear and shuddering, such as a mountain chain, the site of a latrine, a cemetery, or, briefly, anyplace associated with intense fear. Whether going or staying, if this seemingly real influence is not fear [because it is realized to be empty,] you can abandon the advice of the Joyous Ones because this influence has [now] been transmuted into the foremost of all special psychic powers.

Second are the seeming dangers caused by the influence and deception by the gods of those sites. When these have arisen and you are afraid, examine if you are afraid of body or afraid of mind? If afraid of body, visualize your body as a sacrifice to all [suffering] sentient beings, and give it away. Give your body over to all those gods and demons. When the mind is empty, they are not able to harm the body either. If you are afraid of Māra, feed this fear-inspiring being with your body, since you have cut off the root of that which makes the fear. Knowing her real nature brings self-liberation. What appears as fear is transmuted into virtue practice.

Third, viewing them as gods and associated demons is a mistake, and results in seeming divine influences occurring in this lifetime. When recognizing [the act of] holding them to be gods and demons [as empty], then the lineage of Māra arises to protect the dharma, and these influences become transmuted into special psychic powers.

IV. Misery

The next instruction has two parts: (1) training in the ideas of relative truth as an enlightened attitude and (2) training in the idea of absolute truth as an enlightened attitude.

(1) There are many sentient beings who are tormented by all sorts of bodily misery. Take on the misery of all these [beings] and let all of them be endowed with bliss by thinking, "As much [torment] as all these beings carry, that much must be carried by me!"

(2) By recognizing the entity of the misery [to be empty], you and they will not fail to enter into purification itself, in that you don't try to make the experience of either misery or bliss happen. Since there is no other bliss than [that found in] purifying misery, it is called "misery transmuted into bliss."

To conclude [the practice], enter into the [ultimate] enlightened attitude, which gives the same weight to the misery of self and other. This becomes the highest skillful means of practice on this path.

V. Same Taste

Fifth [of the cycle of six]. There are three instructions for same-taste pathwalking.

The first is that while purifying inner obscurations and becoming acquainted with bad and virtuous conditions, meditate joyfully!

The second instruction is that when you get sick, try to associate your sickness with all the diseases and all the illnesses [suffered] by sentient beings and let them have the bliss. Think, "They must not be affected by all these [illnesses], and it is better for me to carry them. They should have only bliss!" Never lose this thought. Here, meditate on "the compassion that reverses." After cutting off the root of all disease and illness as well as the master who is the agent of illness [that is, self], there is no representation of these [as self-existent]. You set up the mind immovably so as not to make anything happen. Here this is called "the emptiness that reverses." If any illness seems to flare up, meditate to increase both meditations, namely, the compassion that reverses and the emptiness that reverses.

The third instruction assumes that since emotions are the cause of disease, then the teachings are the cause of path walking. Since the conditions [of disease] are based on false concepts, you can remove disease by divine path walking. Learn to use this suffering. The effect is that you can destroy [it] by practicing skillfully. Come to know all disease as the same taste [of emptiness]. This is the way to greatly elaborate special insight. Come to see every one of the hundred diseases, as well as the seeming [various] aspects of each [as empty]. In the *Thirteen*[603] it says, "Embrace the conditions that [seem to] go against the [teachings of the] kind lamas, and those conditions become precious." So it is said.

VI. Death
Sixth, [of the cycle of six]. There are three parts to the instructions on path walking with death. They pertain to pointing out how the mother [enlightened consciousness] and the son [seemingly individual consciousness become the same].

The first is that if [you] know that you are dying and don't view it as a problem, think, "Through death comes the clear-light dharmakāya!"[604]

The second instruction has two parts to the path walking—the subtle and the coarse-level death. The subtle instruction pertains to moment-by-moment arising and passing away, because [at] death, the very passing away of the former moment does not lead to the arising of another. Whatever thought happens to arise at the time is self-illuminated as clear light, according to the pointing-out instructions. They are the same. When this is recognized in subtle death, there is only mother and son [consciousness merged]. The Reverend [Mila] says, "The former and the latter thoughts are the same. Here lies the blessing. They are awakened wisdom." The stages of coarse-level death also [serve as a source of awakened wisdom] when illuminated by this clear light at four points [in the process of dying]: (1) the moment of dissolution during dying, (2) the end of individual consciousness, (3) the cessation of the outer breath, and (4) how the inner breath stays. After recognizing these stages of dissolution by that [clear light], purification comes. Once you purify all the propensities through realizing this ground clear light, you enter buddhahood.

Third, due to recognizing the clear light of death, then death is no longer represented [as an idea to fear], and you thereby link yourself to the truth of naturalness, beyond death!

These are the life situations that teach you how to practice the six cycles. Therefore blend your own mind and that of your lama whenever you practice, and protect the samādhi. Then, from every thought you have up until your death there are no further stages. When anything whatsoever is encountered, it becomes the means to develop [the same] skill, and so it is called "one-practice session."

Composed by Master Pema Karpo

III. Path Walking Using the Conditions of the Everyday Perceptual World

The following comes from *Oral Advice on Path Walking* by Situ of the Drikung Kagyü sect, which is related to the Five-Parts school *(lnga ldan)* of Mahāmudrā Transmission:

...Lastly, the conclusion, how to seal [the practice] with prayer. Set up the two assemblies [of buddhas] on the maṇḍala. [Generate] your spiritual teacher as awareness-itself in your heart, and reap the two accumulations of virtue. Petition for as much virtue as the three times: Once establishing the object of your prayer, absorb the agent and activity [of prayer] into one. All sentient beings, self and other, become liberated from the prison of saṃsāra through the view of emptiness, wherein nothing is represented across the three realms. Pray single-mindedly for the sake of realizing the state of mahāmudrā, wherein simultaneousness and awakened wisdom become a nondual pair.

Now, what does this extensive virtue accomplish? When you correctly view these three realms, they are done-with. So the Conqueror [Buddha], said in sūtras like the *Prajñāpāramitā* that [this view] is like being blind or like mixing food with poison. Such stainless liberation has no cause. Therefore what [kind of] virtue practice should you, who are forever endowed with realization, do? Should you practice generation or perfection yoga? By your efforts you have already sown the seeds of enlightenment. Henceforth, the seeming five units [of practice] will become the same with time. The initial purification experiences came from concentration practice. Through the essential practices you became familiar with this realization [primarily] while the [samādhi] meditation was settled into itself. Other than the yoga of the pair [simultaneousness], nothing else needs to be elaborated [about the view]. However, hereafter the best time to practice is [not in formal meditation but] when events occur in the following ways:

1. The Yoga for Setting Forth Clear Awakened Wisdom at Daybreak
Immediately upon coming out of sleep, there comes the samādhi whose natural condition is awareness-itself, along with recognition of the pair—emptiness/clarity—in a way that is unimpeded by false concepts. Meditate intensely on compassion toward all those sentient beings who do not understand this. Only virtue practice comes. As you gain more experience, this realization comes correctly from the [very] moment you begin [to practice upon awakening]. This is the oral advice for entering into the habit of virtue practice.

2. The Yoga That Seals Perception During the Day
All [seeming external] perceptions are the mind's mistakes. They are like dreams when you are unmistaken about their real nature. View them accordingly, as emptiness, because you can't hold a dream to be substantial. Henceforth, meditate on the seal [of emptiness]. Once you complete the search [for an entity], you'll no longer come under the power of false concepts. The skill of awareness-itself arises. This is the oral advice for protecting the rest of the day.

3. The Yoga in Which Things Desired Are Carried as "Friends" in the Morning and the Evening
Train yourself to absorb all phenomena into themselves. Know the real nature of food, drink, clothing, and resting-place to be emptiness. Do not be attached [to them]. Not only that but train yourself to [give things away and] make offerings to the gods

and the lamas. This is the oral advice about the perfect assembly [of buddhas] who are not bound to things desired.

4. The Yoga in Which [Five] Main Sense Faculties Are Gathered in at Dusk

Practice mindfulness on the [seeming] mistakes [of thought and perception] that have arisen during the day. View their real nature nakedly so as not to increase any elaboration [as you leave aside the day's practice and prepare for sleep]. This is the oral advice for guiding virtue practice during the night toward liberation.

5. The Yoga in Which Knowledge Resides in the Pot at Midnight

Meditate on your lama in the center of your heart and pray. Enter into sleep just as you did in the samādhi of unelaborated phenomena [in which you] cut off all the false concepts. Henceforth, in this [initial] state [of sleep], and [also] in very deep sleep that is like death, you'll practice the oral advice about blending the mother and son clear-light consciousnesses.

6. The Yoga for Penetrating Awakened Wisdom at Death

Abandon attachment to everything. Confess all the sins and harmful deeds of this and previous lifetimes to the lineage. After praying to those of virtuous nature, meditate joyfully and pray for perfect enlightenment. When you get agitated [at the early stage of dying], make an offering of the skandhas [that comprise your body and mind]. Firmly resolve that what will occur in your mind is beyond death. Observe all of the stages of dissolution, but don't act upon the many shifts by trying to take an intended meditation object. Just stay in the samādhi with mahāmudrā, settled into itself [as the point of observation], which is without even the slightest trace of meditating or not meditating, and it transforms itself into the expanse of the dharmakāya. The [sense] doors [controlling] what has taken or will take rebirth in a lower existence [will forever] cease. [This] destroys any attachment to mistakes [in either] saṃsāra in general or in the specific bardo [planes]. [This] is the oral advice for realizing death to be the dharmakāya.

This has been a brief elaboration of the advice from the Five-Parts school of mahāmudrā. I pray before the great master of virtue. This advice came from the mouth of the intelligent Drepo Chosong. By exhorting [his words], I speak in serenity, unattached to practicing mindfulness on anything and unattached to virtue practice. [This explanation] is called "the arising of Dharma science."

IV. PATH WALKING WITH COMPASSION: *The Mahāmudrā Devotional Prayer* BY RANGJUNG DORJÉ

Here is the mahāmudrā devotional prayer, certain truth:

> Homage to the teacher, lamas, yidams, and maṇḍala deities,
> proliferating in the ten directions and three times, [yet]
> contemplated as a [single] point inside me. Here is my devotional
> prayer.
> Please bring your influence so that I might realize the [sublime] state
> of the siddhas.
> Let me enter into the stream of accumulated virtue, undefiled across
> the three realms, which arises from the snowy mountain
> of virtuous action and then becomes the ocean of the four
> buddha bodies, so that all sentient beings—self and others—
> those not yet born and those already born—can reach
> that state.
> Let me practice to remove every instance of sin and misery, while
> filling the ocean with bliss and virtue.
> I have taken support in good spiritual friends [that is, lamas] and
> taken the nectar of their advice.
> Now, having special insight into this precious opportunity, so
> difficult to attain, let me practice the holy Dharma at all times
> until I obtain realization, according to the way.
> Let me increase my perception of the three special insights:
> Liberation from the defilement of ignorance through hearing the
> oral readings,
> Cutting off the bewildering doubt through reflecting the oral advice,
> Clarity about the way the realized mind stays through the [clear]
> light arising in meditation.

Let me meet with the Dharma, without any error, for realizing:

The basis, the two selflessnesses, free from the extremes of eternalism and nihilism,

The path, the two accumulations, beyond hope and fear,

And the fruition, the two truths, free from the extremes of saṃsāra and nirvāṇa.

Let me directly realize the pair, clarity-emptiness of mind, the basis for purification.

Through the great yoga of mahāmudrā, the agent of purification,

May the stains, the moment-by-moment mistakes, become purified,

And that which becomes purified then becomes stainless fruition [enlightenment].

Let me be able to set forth the practice of meditation on the deities: setting up the deities [in meditation] to cut off doubt about the basis, the points of meditation, the skillful means for realization of the truth of the meditation, remaining undistracted about that, and protecting that at all times.

Let me cut off the root, after understanding well that all phenomena are but emanations of mind.

To the mind, there is no mind; the mind is empty of any [self-existing] entity.

Being empty, there need not be any obstruction of its [seeming] appearances.

Let me eradicate nonawareness, the root of mistakes.

Do not mistake appearance-itself, so that there is no experience of self-existent, [seemingly external] sense objects.

The [bad karmic] influence of mistaking awareness-itself for a [seemingly self-existent] self, leads to nonawareness and dualistic grasping, which leads to being lost in saṃsāra.

Let me understand the mind's phenomena, free from extreme [views]:

By fearlessly mastering that there is no "existence," and that there is no "nonexistence," which serves as the basis of all saṃsāra and nirvāṇa, then comes the Middle Path, the simultaneous pair, without [dualistic] contradiction.

Let the resulting certain truth genuinely be realized:

Wherein there is no assertion, "this exists."

Nor the assertion "this is nonexistent."

These phenomena, beyond all ideas, are nonaggregated.

Let me become aware of the fundamental error, which is the basis
   of all phenomena.

If I have not understood this, I shall wander in the ocean of
   saṃsāra.

If I have understood this, I am none other than a buddha.

All [phenomena] neither exist nor not-exist.

Let me cut off all doubt in the mind.

Not only appearances but also the mind's emptiness is the
   [very] mind.

The mind's understanding, as well as its mistakes, are the
   very mind.

What arises and what passes away in the mind is also the
   very mind.

Let me realize awakened wisdom and then protect my [direct]
   experience of the mind's truth, so that I am never corrupted by
   the kind of meditation that artificially acts based on ideas or uses
   effort, and so that I am not agitated by the commotion and noise
   of the ordinary [world], but rather, know how to set up the
   nonartificial, natural, self-originated [simultaneous mind].

Let staying/calm practice be immovable and firm like the ocean.

The waves of coarse and subtle cognition become calm in their
   own right.

The mind's mental continuum viewed from the perspective of the
   immovable, staying [awareness-itself], free from the defilements
   of dullness and heaviness.

Let there be recognition-itself, which is never mistaken:

When viewing the mind that cannot be viewed, over and over
   again,

When having special insight about a truth that cannot be seen,

And when cutting off doubt about a truth that cannot exist.

Let me understand the mind's clear light and the way the realized
   mind stays:

By viewing sense objects, but seeing them not as sense objects, but
   as mind,

By viewing the mind, not as mind, but as an empty entity,

By viewing both, so that there is self-liberation from holding on
to duality.
Let me become assured about my understanding of this supreme
omniscient truth:
What is not-taken-to-mind becomes mahāmudrā, free from
extremes, the great Middle [Path].
This is called the great perfection, beyond everything.
Let my experience be effortless and may I not obstruct the mental
continuum:
I do not cut off the mental continuum of the great bliss of
nonattachment,
I do not cut off the clarity and luminosity of not grasping
attributes, so as to be not covered by the sin [of attachment],
I do not cut off the nonconceptual still state, spontaneous presence,
beyond ideas.
Let me understand the truth of phenomena to be unelaborated:
Holding this blissful state without attachment becomes self-
liberation in its own right.
Any attachment to harmful, mistaken concepts becomes purified
in the realm of the mind's real nature.
This is the knowledge of the ordinary, free from taking up and
abandoning, without anything to attain.
The real nature of all beings is buddhahood.
Let it come forth evermore for all sentient beings who wander
endlessly in saṃsāra, and who, through their ignorance and their
incessant misery, can no longer stand it!
Let compassion arise with the mental continuum for all of them!
Let there be continuous meditation, inseparable from the [relative]
attributes.
This is the supreme path, the pair, without straying,
And when unobstructed, there comes the skill of infinite
compassion.
When this kindness has arisen, do [not] forget the truth—
emptiness.
Let there be ripening of enlightenment, reaching maturation
with the well-purified buddha fields,
With the special psychic powers that arise from the force
of meditation,

With the complete purification of buddhahood, whose actions
   ripen [for the sake of all] sentient beings,
And with the perfect devotional prayer, which produces the
   Buddha's teachings.

Following enlightenment and path-walking there is no need
for further spiritual practice, outside of living daily life fully.
"Once one finds the elephant, one does not need to search for
the footprints."[605]

NOTES

1 Toulmin (1972).
2 Snellgrove (1959), p. 37.
3 Wilbur, Engler, and Brown (1987).
4 Maitreya (2000), p. 15.
5 Tsele Natsok Rangdrol (1989), p. xiii; Chokyi Nyima Rinpoche (1989), pp. 68–69.
6 Chokyi Nyima Rinpoche (1989), p. 35.
7 Dalai Lama and Berzin (1997), pp. 71–93.
8 See Rangjung Dorjé in Eighth Situpa Tenpa'i Nyinchay (1995), pp. 131–33, for a discussion of different types of individuals and their capacity for realization.
9 Buddhaghosa (1976).
10 Maitreyanātha/Āryāsaṅga (2004).
11 A very good description of the standard Tibetan approach to ordinary concentration and insight is available in Geshe Gedün Lodrö (1998).
12 For a biography of the original Jamgön Kongtrül, Lodrö Tayé, composed by Bokar Tulku, see Jamgön Kongtrül (1992), pp. 105–14.
13 Kalu Rinpoche speaks of three essential, simultaneous qualities of the natural mind: (1) openness: like space, the mind can never be located; (2) clarity: "both the lucidity of mind's intelligence and the luminosity of its experiences"; and (3) sensitivity or unimpededness: "the mind's freedom to experience without obstruction [that results in] the mind's perceptions of each thing as being this or that." Kalu Rinpoche (1997), pp. 21–23.
14 "The inner truth of mind is unborn from beginningless time like the center of the sky. One should keep the mind without any positive or negative dualistic conceptions. The realization of the nature of mind, which is non-existent and unborn, is called Mahamudra." Gyaltsen (1986), p. 78.
15 Dowman (1985), p. 3.
16 Taranatha (1970).
17 Dowman (1985), pp. 71–72.
18 Karma Trinlepa's biography of Saraha, as translated in Guenther (1969), p. 7.
19 The Heart of Siddhi cycle of texts by Saraha is found in the anuttarayogatantra section of the Tibetan canon. Peking Edition. Suzuki (1962), pp. 3068, 3110, 3111.
20 Phyag rgya chen po'i chos bskor bcu. pp. 3068, 3110, 3111, 3115, 3116, 3117, 3118, 3148, 790, 2334.
21 The absolute view is described as "thatness" (de yin). This view must be pointed out "from the mouth of the lama" (bla ma'i zhal las). This extraordinary level of mind is said to be the mind's natural condition (gnyug ma).
22 Saraha uses the word "bliss" (bde ba) when referring to the relative activity of the mind seen correctly.

23 *People's Songs,* v. 32. For an example of protecting instructions, see *King's Songs,* vv. 29–33.

24 'Gos Lo-tsā-ba Gzhon-nu-dpal (1949–53), p. 839ff.

25 Dowman (1985), p. 72.

26 'Gos Lo-tsā-ba Gzhon-nu-dpal (1949–53), p. 866.

27 Bhattacharyya (1964), pp. 65–69.

28 For a very clear explanation of generation-stage and completion-stage practices, see Cozort (1986), pp. 41–114.

29 A lucid contemporary account of tantric mahāmudrā can be found in Gyatso (1982).

30 Panchen Lama, First (1976), p. 8.

31 See 'Gos Lo-tsā-ba Gzhon-nu-dpal (1949–53), pp. 839–66, for a detailed discussion of the three waves of the source translation lineage.

32 Evans-Wentz (1928), p. 7.

33 Ibid.

34 The *Ganges Mahāmudrā* has been translated into English by Chögyam Trungpa in *The Myth of Freedom and the Way of Meditation* (1976), pp. 157–63. A commentary by Drikung Kyabgon Chetsang Rinpoche appears in *The Practice of Mahamudra* (1999), pp. 77–88.

35 Tilopa, *Treasury of Songs,* vv. 22–23.

36 Kagyu Thubten Chöling (1999), p. 7.

37 Nāropa, *The Aphorisms of Mahāmudrā,* v. 5: "The way-of-realizing the mind's natural condition is the truth of mahāmudrā. Set up the conditions without artificial activity, without representing [an object of concentration] nor searching, with uninterrupted mindfulness of the dharmakāya. This is [real] meditation. Meditation that involves searching is a mistaken idea."

38 Drikung Kyabgon Chetsang Rinpoche (1999), p. 9.

39 Eighth Situpa Tenpa'i Nyinchay (1995), p. 133.

40 Marpa, *A Miracle Story of How Marpa Attained the Four Letters Mahamudra in a Dream from Saraha.* The author is not mentioned, but the text is attributed to Marpa. *Mga' bdag mar pa lo tsā bas dpal sa ra ha las gsan pa'i phyag rgya chen po yid la mi byed snying po don gyi gdams ngag yi ge bzhi pa'i don rdo rje'i mgur du bzhengs pa,* in 'Jam mgon Kong sprul (1971) 5:63–66.

41 Chang (1962).

42 'Jam mgon Kong sprul (1971), vol. 5.

43 Re chung Rdo rje grags pa. *Bde mchog snyan brgyud kyi phyag rgya chen po ye shes gsal byed,* in 'Jam mgon Kong sprul (1971), 5:443–55.

44 The reader wishing to learn more about this lineage should consult Kagyu Thubten Chöling (1999).

45 Eighth Situpa Tenpa'i Nyinchay (1995).

46 Wangchuk Dorje, Ninth Karmapa (1981).

47 Dalai Lama and Berzin (1997), pp. 263–64.

48 See Gyaltsen (1986), pp. 22–26, for a biography of Pagmodrupa.

49 For a biography of Jigten Sumgön, see Gyaltsen (1986), pp. 29–43.

50 Jigten Sumgön's five-parts teachings can be found in Gyaltsen (1986).

51 Gyaltsen and Rogers (1986).

52 Dalai Lama and Berzin (1997), pp. 264–67.

53 Ibid., p. 262

54 Ibid., p. 270.

55 Ibid., p. 262.

56 *Buddhahood in the Palm of Your Hand: The Union of Mahāmudrā and Dzogchen* has been translated into English in two works: *A Spacious Path to Freedom: Practical Instructions on the Union of Mahamudra and Atiyoga* [Karma Chagmé (1998)], and *Naked Awareness: Practical Instructions on the Union of Mahāmudrā and Dzogchen* [Karma Chagmé (2000)] with commentary by Gyatrul Rinpoche. A series of twenty talks by Chökyi Nyima Rinpoche on this important work is available in *The Union of Mahamudra and Dzogchen* (1989). Another English translation, Tsele Natsok Rangdrol's *Lamp of Mahamudra* (1989), also comes from this tradition.

57 Karma Chagmé (2000), pp. 165–66.

58 Ibid., p. 267.

59 The lineage is: Tsongkhapa, Jampel Gyatso, Baso Chökyi Gyeltsen, Chökyi Dorjé, Gyelwa Ensapa, Sangyé Yeshé, and Panchen Lobsang Chökyi Gyeltsen. For the life stories of these figures, see Willis (1995). For the Panchen Lama's root text and its autocommentary, accompanied by a commentary by H.H. the Dalai Lama, see Dalai Lama and Berzin (1997).

60 "The main point in the Gelug/Kagyü tradition of Mahamudra is meditation on voidness...as an object realized by primordial clear light mind." Dalai Lama and Berzin (1997), p. 223.

61 Bahr et al. (1974); Frake (1964).

62 The criteria used to assess whether a text is authoritative were (1) the extent to which the text is cited or cross-referenced in other mahāmudrā texts and (2) whether the text was included in important anthologies.

63 Bkra shis rnam rgyal, in 'Jam mgon Kong sprul (1971) 5:651–702.

64 Bkra shis rnam rgyal (1974). English translation in *Mahāmudrā: The Quintessence of Mind and Meditation,* Tashi Namgyal, Takpo (1986).

65 Rang byung rdo rje (Third Karmapa) in 'Jam mgon Kong sprul (1971), 6:1–16.

66 Jamgön Kongtrül (1994), pp. 100–101.

67 Dbang phyug rdo rje. These three texts are *Phyag rgya chen po lhan cig skyes sbyor gyi khrid kyi spyi sdom rtsa tshig,* in 'Jam mgon Kong sprul (1971), 6:62–69; *Phyag rgya chen po lhan cig skye sbyor gyi khrid yig zin bris snying po gsal ba'i sgron me bdud rtsi nying khu chos sku mdzub tshugs su ngo sprod pa,* in 'Jam mgon Kong sprul (1971), 6:7–104; and *Sgrub brgyud kar tshang pa'i phyag rgya chen lhan cig skye sbyor gyi sngon 'gro bzhi sbyor sogs kyi ngag 'don 'phags lam bgrod pa'i shing rta,* in 'Jam mgon Kong sprul (1971), 6:105–22.

68 Wangchug Dorjé's *Ocean of Certainty* is mentioned as the main mahāmudrā text used for three-year meditation retreats in Jamgön Kongtrül (1994), pp. 77–78.

69 *Phyag chen gyi zin bris bzhygs.* See also the expanded practice manual *Chos rje 'brug pa'i lugs kyi phyag rgya chen po lhan cig skyes sbyor gyi khrid yig,* in 'Jam mgon Kong sprul (1971), 7:19–33. This text has been translated into English three times, first in "The Nirvanic Path: The Yoga of the Great Symbol," in Evans-Wentz (1935), pp. 115–53. The most recent translation is by Ven. Anzan Hoshin Sensei in Padma Karpo Ngawang Norbu (1991).

70 'Jam dpal dpa' bo (1969).

71 *Phyag chen sngon 'dro bzhi sbyor dang dngos gzhi'i khrid rim mdor bsdus nges don sgron me.* For an English translation, see Jamgon Kongtrul (1977).

72 Kun dga' bstan 'dzin (1974).

73 Padma dKar po. *Ro snyoms skor drug gi nyams len sgong du dril ba;* Chos kyi 'byung gnas, Eighth Situ (1699–1774), *Phyag chen lnga ldan gyi khrid yig.*

74 Wylie (1959).

75 Cf. Künga Tendzin's "generating interest by explaining the benefit and advising one to listen" (KT, pp. 8–11) to Tashi Namgyel's "the certainty of generating belief" (TN, pp. 163–207).

76 KT.

77 Consider the following contemporary oral commentary from Dhargyey (1974):

> Someone, owing to a sudden passion to renounce what he thinks to be Samsara, might abandon all belongings and escape to a mountain retreat, only to return a week or two later feeling very discouraged and weak. Such "renunciation" is generally insincere and rarely lasts for more than a short time. (p. 63)

78 The complete expression is *dge ba' i bshes gnyen.* Consider also the following passage: "In each of the three yanas the teacher has a different role. In the Hinayana he is an elder (Skt., *sthavira*), or wise man. In the Mahayana he is the good spiritual friend. In the Vajrayana he is the master—almost a dictator—who tells you what to do" (Jamgon Kongtrul [1977], p. 15, from a transcribed interview with Chögyam Trungpa Rinpoche). A very accurate description of a spiritual teacher can be found in Berzin (2000): "For spiritual teachers to be and to act as spiritual mentors, they need to be weighty with positive qualities and need to combine compassion and bodhichitta with a deep understanding of reality. Moreover, they need to have the power to uplift and to inspire disciples to achieve the same. They need to be spiritual friends in the sense that they act, speak, and think constructively in ways that never cause long-term harm, but only ultimate benefit. These ways are always free of greed, attachment, anger, or naivety as their motivation. Instead, they arise from love and compassion and come from wisdom. Further, spiritual mentors lead disciples to constructive behavior, like friends who have become trusted, close family members. Ultimately, spiritual mentors lead disciples to liberation and enlightenment" (p. 48).

79 According to the Mahāyāna tradition, a practitioner takes refuge in the Three Jewels—the Buddha, the Dharma, and the Saṅgha. In the Tibetan tradition, particularly, the lama is thought to be the incarnation of all Three Jewels. The lama is the very Buddha, the teaching, and the community. To gain the title of lama, however, teachers must have perfected their own practice to such an extent that they have realized buddhahood in their own mind.

80 The six perfections *(phar phyin drug)* include giving *(sbyin pa),* ethical behavior *(tshul khrims),* patience *(bzod pa),* diligence *(brstom 'grus),* contemplation *(bsam gtan),* and special insight *(shes rab).* These comprise the standard training of a bodhisattva, as found in numerous sources, e.g., Gampopa (1971). The first perfection, giving, is the basis for compassion.

81 The description of mental factors is from Vasubandhu (1975) and Asaṅga (1950). See Yeshe Gyeltsen's commentary to the "Mind and Mental Factors" section of the Abhidharma literature. It is available in an English translation in Guenther and Kawamura (1975). See also Lati Rinbochay and Napper (1980).

82 According to Lamrimpa (1992), p. 15, negative emotional states are the main obstacle

to liberation, and erroneous conceptualization is the chief obstacle to realization of
buddhahood.

83 For example, Rangjung Dorjé explains as follows:

> Let me increase the appearance of the three special insights.
> Hearing the oral readings liberates one from the defilement of ignorance.
> Reflecting on the oral advice cuts off the muddlement of doubt.
> The light of the resultant meditation makes clear the way the realized
>   mind stays.

> *lung rig thos bas mi shes sgrub las grol*
> *man ngag bsam bas the tshom mun nag bcom*
> *sgom byung 'od kyis gnas lugs ji bzhin gsal*
> *shes rab sum gyi snang bryas par shog.* (RD, f. 2)

Note that Rangjung Dorjé sees the destruction of ignorance as an ongoing process.
This process is set in motion by hearing *(thos)*, further thinking about or reflecting
on what was heard *(bsam)*, and finally, meditating upon it *(sgom)*. There is no arbitrary decision to meditate. At some point in the unfolding process, the inclination to
meditate naturally arises. It all starts with hearing *(thos)*. The technical correlation of
stages of mental activity (hearing, etc.) with the stages of the relative ignorance or
special insight is implicit in the structure of the passage. See also Tashi Namgyal (1986),
pp. 121–24.

84 Understanding *(rtogs pa)* is an effect that ripens over time, as a result of practicing the
Dharma correctly and diligently. In the mahāmudrā system, the final realization is
called the way *the realized mind stays (gnas lugs)*, the absolute truth, the finest understanding of emptiness that is possible. The relative truth, *the way the realized mind
arises*, or more simply, *the way the world appears*, is given by the metaphor "clear light."
Therefore the passage illustrates that both the absolute and the relative dimensions of
truth are attainable through oral advice (TN, pp. 205–7).

85 *slob dpon gyi kun slong lhag pa'i sems bskyed dang ldan pas 'di ltar gdams par bya ste* (KT,
p. 8).

86 Intellectual understanding *(go ba)* ripens into direct meditative experience *(nyam len)*.
When one's own mental continuum becomes a direct manifestation of the intended
philosophical view, the experience is said to ripen into understanding *(rtogs pa)* (PK,
f. 14b).

87 TN, 5:652.

88 The complete passage is:

> ...this path quickly yields the nectar in the heart, which brings forth the
> complete realization of mahāmudrā, the entirety of the Dharma, the pro-
> found seed. This discourse is difficult to understand for those who have ears
> for reason. One [who hears] reaches the endpoint of the mahāmudrā [path]
> as the victorious Vajradhara himself. (JP, f. 2a)

89 "Of the roar of a lion in the forest, thus, all the little animals will be afraid, but the
lion cubs run about with joy! Those seeing this great bliss, always there from the beginning, will forsake the obscurities of false conceptualization. The Blessed One's hair will
bristle with joy!" From Śabari, in Suzuki. (1962), p. 3112, f. 95b.

90 Lobsang P. Lhalungpa says that *mahāmudrā* "stands for the ultimate nature of mind" (Tashi Namgyal [1986], p. xxi).

91 This argument is given in a section entitled "The True Characteristics and Famousness" *(mtshan don dang rnam grangs)* (TN, pp. 163–68).

92 This explanation continues in a section entitled "The Real-Entity and Its Special Distinction" *(ngo bo dang rab dbye)* (TN, pp. 163–68).

93 *Khyab bdag:* literally "pervading itself," but translated as "all-pervasive." Consider also the following passage: "The way the realized mind stays transcends objects of reflection or speaking and is the foundation of mahāmudrā" *(gnas lugs bsam brjod kyi yul las 'das pa ni gzhi phyag don)* (TN, p. 169).

94 From a section entitled "The Fault of Ignorance and the Benefit of Knowledge" *(ma shes pa dang shes pa'i skyon yon)* (TN, pp. 168–71).

95 Skt., *Vajrasattva.*

96 Tashi Namgyel gives a lengthy review of the way truth is explained in the sūtras and tantras in general (TN, pp. 172–80) and in anuttaratantra in particular (TN, pp. 175–97). He sets forth the view in a section entitled "The Way, Which Is the Profound Truth in All the Sūtras and Tantras" (TN, pp. 197–207). This has two subsections. The first is on recognizing truth. Here the commentator urges his listeners to distinguish the profundity of his advice from mundane, inferior teachings. Next he summarizes the teachings for those who have recognized their value.

97 Jampel Pawo's commentary is likewise written for Buddhists with some previous meditative experience.

98 Notice how the root text condenses the entire argument into a single line: "this pervading secret of certainty, which is difficult to understand, by any other path." The commentary expands the passage into several sections, entitled "True Characteristics, Famousness, and Its Special Distinction" and the "Flaw of Ignorance." This condensation style is very typical of Tibetan root texts. The reader will encounter this throughout the chapters.

99 "In a healthy relationship, we seek our mentors' advice only concerning important matters that would affect our spiritual development and practice. Asking our mentors to make all our decisions, especially concerning trivial matters, indicates a lack of maturity." Berzin (2000), p. 134.

100 Dayal (1970); Schmid (1958); Dowman (1985).

101 According to the *Abhidharmakośa,* there are fifty-one mental factors; according to the *Abhidharmasamuccaya* there are fifty.

102 Künga Tendzin devotes a number of subsections of his text to an analysis of the stages by which interest ripens. The outline *(sa bcad)* of the stages follows:

    A. Generating interest
       1. Generating an open, interested mind (KT, pp. 8–11).
       2. Generating interest and admiration by explaining the benefit of hearing the teachings that were given.
         a. The benefit of explaining the teachings (pp. 11–14).
         b. The benefit of hearing the teachings (pp. 14–18).
         c. The benefit of both explaining and hearing (pp. 18–19).
       3. The benefit of listening to spiritual teachings (pp. 19–21).

103 Rangjung Dorjé's title to his devotional text uses a common appositional structure:

nges don phyag chen ("mahāmudrā, certain truth"). Here the final goal of mahāmudrā practice is given in the epithet *certainty*. The exact meaning of this term will be explained later in the text.

104 The five object-certain mental factors are interest *('dun pa)*, admiration *(mos pa)*, mindfulness *(dran pa)*, deep concentration *(ting nge 'dzin)*, and special insight *(shes rab)*. See Guenther and Kawamura (1975), pp. 29–38.

105 Ibid., p. 31.

106 A paraphrase of the definition of *mos pa*, as cited, ibid.

107 Ibid.

108 According to Pema Karpo, all perceptual objects are classified as either sacred or mundane *(dag pa dang ma dag pa)*, although the mental factors involved in the perception of either type of object are identical (PK, f. 4a).

109 For an additional explanation of listening, see Tsong kha pa (2000), vol. 1, pp. 55–67.

110 From a section entitled "The Benefit of Listening to the Teachings" (*chos nyam pa'i phan yon;* KT, pp. 14–18). The five benefits are "(1) knowing the unknown, (2) relinquishing erroneous views, (3) grasping the certainty of what may otherwise be doubted, (4) taking what is uncertain to the teacher [for clarity], and (5) opening one's eyes to supreme awakened wsdom" (KT, p. 17).

111 The text lists twenty benefits: "mindfulness; right ideas, [etc.]; intelligence; admiration; special insight; understanding otherworldly things; nonattachment; nonhatred; non-ignorance; not being obstructed by māra; buddhahood; gaining protection from spirits; having a healthy, godlike body; not having encounters with mean-spirited people, etc." (KT, p. 13) The three particular Mahāyāna benefits are the three emptinesses—self, world, and time, respectively.

112 The commentator concludes his explanation section entitled "The Benefit of Listening to Spiritual Teachings" (KT, pp. 19–21). He says:

> On all occasions, now and evermore, it is necessary to take up the immediate cause of effecting happiness [the teachings] and to abandon that arising from misery [i.e., mundane life], respectively. To do that, it is necessary to know the spiritual teachings. To know the spiritual teachings, it is necessary to listen to them. After listening it is necessary to see the benefit of what you have heard.

113 The commentator begins a new section entitled "Explaining the Reason for Specifying [the Act of] Listening." The first two of five subsections discusses the special qualities of a lama, which distinguish him or her from an ordinary person (KT, pp. 22–26). The third subsection is entitled "Commonly Presented Teachings" (KT, pp. 26–35). That section reviews the main teachings that the beginner is now in a position to understand.

114 See "The Qualities of the Buddha" in Dhargyey (1974), pp. 68–74.

115 Ibid., pp. 66–67 and 219–27.

116 Dalai Lama and Berzin (1997), p. 6. For a more detailed discussion of the progressive levels of realizing emptiness, see Gyamtso (1986).

117 According to Khenpo Tsultrim Gyamtso Rinpoche, this highest level of emptiness, exemplified in the Shentong approach, developed as a reaction against the Prāsaṅgika system, which was designed to "silence completely the conceptual mind" (p. 66) but which failed to adequately account for the manifestation of appearance. The Shentong

system argues that "non-conceptual Wisdom Mind is not the object of the conceptualizing process and so is not negated by Madhyamaka reasoning."(p. 76) Beyond the negation of mind and its appearances as empty, this affirmation of awakened wisdom is unique to the way emptiness is understood in traditions such as the mahāmudrā. See Gyamtso (1986), pp. 65–88. However, for the Prāsaṅgika response to this argument, see Lamrimpa (1999), pp. 75–76.

118 The beginner has only established propensities for acting according to Buddhist teachings. Over and against the sheer weight of unvirtuous karma, the virtuous propensities will not ripen into manifest action without subsequent reinforcement. The beginner is as yet unaware of any difference in his actions at this time, thus he has not been taught anything that can be made evident.

119 Berzin (2000), p. 183–94.

120 The commentator is using one of several terms for "mind." The term *yid* is used when referring to the activity of the mental perceiver *(yid shes)*. It is this very activity, which creates ideas *(blo)*, cognitions *(rtog pa)*, and emotional states *(nyon mong)*, that constitutes ongoing events in the mental continuum. Another term, *sems pa,* refers specifically to direct perception without corresponding mental activity. By using the former term, the commentator wishes to show that respect involves both increased activity on the part of the listener and a specific kind of activity, that is, cognition over mere perception. Consider also Künga Tendzin's use of the same term elsewhere in the same section: longing mind *(yid la gdung ba;* KT, p. 45) and compliant mind *(dang la yid;* KT, p. 43).

121 Berzin (2000) explains that mental respect entails "two mental actions: feeling deeply convinced of the good qualities of their mentors and appreciating their kindness" (p. 117).

122 The metaphor of a ripening seed is the classic metaphor to illustrate the doctrine of cause and effect. It is found in the *Abhidharmakośa* as well as in numerous other works.

123 Tilopa says, "Do not recall, do not anticipate, do not reflect" *(mi mno, mi sems, mi bsam).* According to Jampel Pawo's commentary on this famous set of cutting-off instructions, *recall (mno ba)* refers to past objects; *anticipation (sems pa),* to future objects; and reflection *(bsam pa),* to present objects (JP, f. 11b–12a).

124 According to the doctrine of cause and effect, all actions ripen. The ongoing activity of one's mental continuum is a type of inner action. Repetitive thoughts ripen and become fixed views over time. Outward behavioral actions also ripen. All actions begin as inner actions, and as they increase their force, they eventually manifest as behavior. Künga Tendzin introduces certain behavioral consequences at this point to indicate the increased momentum of virtuous propensities that have been set forth by the mental act of listening.

125 The commentator's rationale for dividing up the section on building the vessel is based on the doctrine of cause and effect. The six defilements pertain to the correcting of coarse actions. The easiest way of interrupting the continuation of nonvirtuous actions is by altering coarse actions. The three faults pertain to the more subtle control of inner mental activities. It is not possible to control mental activity until a beginner has made some progress in restraining himself from harmful coarse actions and previous efforts have ripened somewhat. Finally, the practitioner experiences the benefit of purifying the vessel, but nevertheless must guard against further error. The action is divided up as follows:

Little ripening: six defilements

Moderate ripening: three faults

Much ripening: error of not grasping

126 Berzin (2000) emphasizes the behavioral dimension of respect. He suggests, "We may help our mentors, for example, by making travel arrangements, driving them to appointments, writing letters, or transcribing and editing their teachings" (p. 131).

127 Künga Tendzin uses a compound here, "admiration-respect" *(mus gus)*, to signify the condensation style of practice *(bsdu ba)* at the conclusion of the chapter.

128 This table clearly demonstrates how seemingly common words, such as *hearing* and *listening*, are used in a very specific context and have highly refined technical meanings. Translators all too often assume such words to be synonyms. Such translations neglect the authors' subtle precision.

129 Guenther and Kawamura (1975), p. 74.

130 According to the doctrine of cause and effect, all actions ripen over time. These actions first become manifest in the mental continuum as signs *(rtags)*, later as full experiences *(nyam len)*.

131 The text reads *gol ba*. It makes more sense as *'gol ba*, "to be separate from," i.e., to leave behind one's ordinary state of existence.

132 Guenther and Kawamura (1975), p. 39.

133 Guenther (1974), pp. 63–64.

134 Ibid., p. 62.

135 Ibid., p. 63.

136 Ibid., p. 62.

137 For a detailed explanation in English, the reader is referred to Guenther and Kawamura (1975) or Lati Rinbochay and Napper (1980).

138 Guenther and Kawamura (1975), pp. 38–41.

139 The eleven positive mental factors are faith *(dad pa)*, self-respect *(ngo tsha)*, poise *(khrel yod pa)*, detachment *(ma chags pa)*, nonaggression *(zhe sdang med pa)*, nondeludedness *(gti mug med pa)*, diligence *(brtson 'grus)*, pliancy *(shin tu sbyang ba)*, concern *(bag yod)*, equanimity *(btang snyoms)*, and sympathy *(rnam par mi 'tshe ba)*.

140 *Influence* (Tib., *dbang po;* Skt., *indriya*); *power* (Tib., *stobs;* Skt., *bala*). Consider Guenther and Kawamura's (1975) explanation:

> Qualifying these functions by "dominance" [influence] and some of them also by "power," as we shall see later on, does not mean that a value, either ethical or intellectual, has been imparted to them. It simply means the determining power which is manifest in the specific operation of these functions, i.e., their nature and "effects." The difference between "dominance" [influence] and "power" is that the former *(indriya)* is variable in intensity and may subside as other functions gain in strength and begin to exert their dominance, while the latter aspect *(bala)*, once the specific function has been established, will not subside or give way to other functions by way of a change in energetic value. (p. 61)

141 Guenther (1963); Evans-Wentz, ed. (1969).

142 According to Schmid (1958, pp. 1–171), the occupations of the siddhas are given in the iconography. Saraha was a brahmin; Śabari was a forest-dwelling hunter; Padmavajra

was a fisherman; Tilopa was an oil presser; Indrabhūti and Lakṣminkara were royalty. According to their biographies, Nāropa was a scholar, and Mila was a shepherd. Also see Dowman (1985), pp. 33–384.

143 "Pray incessantly for the seed of omniscience. It must be distinguished from interpreted truth *[drang don]* and the lower vehicles…. It is profound, the Dharma of the mahāmudrā wherein the real nature of the mind, from the beginning, is understood with certainty *[nges don]*." (KT, p. 94)

144 Thrangu (1993), p. 67.

145 This distinction was clarified by E. Gene Smith, personal communication, Chicago, Illinois, 1975.

146 More advanced practitioners do not always need the lama to be present. The advanced practitioner may visualize the lama as if being present.

147 *gzhi, lam, 'bras bu* = basis, path, fruition. *Fruition* is an epithet for "perfect enlightenment." The beginner is given an explanation of the basis. This will ripen in time. The beginner will become a fully enlightened being if the conditions of practice are correct.

148 "Thereupon the mind *(thugs)* of the root lama, also the mind of the entire lineage and pantheon, become indistinguishable *(dphye med)* from the practitioner's own continuum. The practitioner becomes connected to *(dus pa)* them." (KT, p. 88)

149 See the section on settling the view in Gyaltsen and Rogers (1986), pp. 72–79.

150 For an explanation of the process of generation, see Beyer (1973), pp. 66–67 and 103–4.

151 According to the Buddhist understanding of the body, the relative views of the body are twofold. The gross body consists of organs, muscles, etc. The subtle body consists of energy currents, which flow through energy channels. Ultimately, the body is an empty construct. The subtle view of the body becomes the basis of an entire set of energy practices. These are called *bsre 'pho* exercises, or energy yoga.

152 The three buddha bodies are the emanation body, the enjoyment body, and the Dharma body. See Dhargyey (1974), pp. 202–8.

153 Tib., *lhan gcig skyes sbyor;* Skt., *sahaja.* This is a technical term that is difficult to explain in a few words. Briefly, it refers to a perspective in which the ultimate dimension of truth (emptiness) and the relative dimension of truth (the seeming appearance of the ordinary world) are coupled in each moment of experience. I translate it as "simultaneousness." This term will be explained at great length in chapter 7.

154 Another version reads "lose."

155 The complete text is found in two versions: JK (1971), 5:28–33; and Suzuki (1932), p. 3112.

156 Berzin (2000) explains that the Tibetan term for "disciple" is *dge phrug.* He says, "*Ge* means constructive and *trug* means a child. A *getrug* is a child raised by a spiritual mentor to be constructive—along the way as an increasingly balanced, ethical, and positive person, and ultimately as a Buddha" (p. 53).

157 The term *yid,* like *sems,* has been translated as "mind." Several translators have quite correctly rejected such a translation. Bharati (1965), pp. 47–48, points out that *yid* refers to that which operates as the interpreter of sense data and generates cognition about them. Guenther translates *yid* as "mental activity" (see Gampopa [1971], p. 74, n. 3). Both translators are in part correct. Since interpretation is a form of mental activity, I agree that the term should be translated as "mental activity." It is nevertheless convenient at times to simply translate the term as "mind."

158 *yid 'byung bskyed pa 'khor ba'i nyes dmigs* (KT, p. 96). Notice how Künga Tendzin places the "generation of the restless mind," and the "bad result of saṃsāra" in apposition. He means to convey that although one leads to the other, both are the same. The restless mind produces the suffering world. According to the doctrine of cause and effect, all mental activity ripens and subsequently manifests in behavior. Incessant mental activity guarantees everyday suffering.

159 Jamgön Kongtrül (1992), p. 43.

160 From a contemporary oral account of the four notions by Dhargyey (1974), p. 25.

161 Ibid., p. 46:

> The difficulty of obtaining this form is illustrated in examples. The classic example is a vast ocean on which a golden yoke drifts about, moved by the wind and the currents. Once every hundred years a blind turtle surfaces, for a moment, then again submerges. The chances of the turtle surfacing with its head inside the yoke are likened to those obtaining a fully endowed human body. In this example, the golden yoke symbolizes the Buddhadharma, and its motion refers to the fact that the Dharma moves from one land to another according to the needs of the people. The turtle's blindness symbolizes the inability of creatures in the lower realms to discriminate between virtue and non-virtue.

162 B. Alan Wallace (2001) says that the precious opportunity for meditation "increases appreciation for free time" and how we use it.... Leisure and opportunity mean having the time, motivation, and circumstances to engage in spiritual practice" (pp. 18–21).

163 Jamgon Kongtrul (1977), p. 44.

164 *Certainty (nges)* is a term meant to signify a "direct experience," i.e., something that a person can identify directly within the mental continuum. See Gampopa (1971), p. 45.

165 The technical term *dmigs pa* means "to make a mental representation of." It can refer to a sensory representation from any of the six sense systems. When used in a circumscribed context, e.g., the visual system, it has the meaning of "to visualize" or "to make an image of." I translate it as either "visualize" or "represent," depending on the context. Note how the commentators move beyond simple reflection *(bsam pa)* to more complicated, systematic visualization *(dmigs pa)*. The beginner is directing more and more of his or her mental processes toward spiritual development.

166 Dhargyey (1974), p. 56.

167 Gampopa (1971) cites the following passage from Mila:

> "This life is passing like the shadow of the setting sun. The farther the sun has gone, the longer the shadow has grown; I have not seen liberation won by running away" (p. 52, n. 23).

168 Dhargyey (1974), p. 56.

169 Jamgon Kongtrul (1977), p. 47; RD, p. 3.

170 *las dkar nag gi rnam gzhig* (TN, pp. 228–29). Most commentators make a distinction *(rnam gzhig)* between black *(nag)* and white *(dkar)*, i.e., nonvirtuous and virtuous karma *(las)*.

171 Two technical terms are used. The term *las,* in a general sense, means "karmic action." In a specific sense it means any original action. The term *byes ba,* the perfect form of

byed pa, signifies the result of that original action. The term *byes ba,* cannot be used without assuming the former use of *las.*

172 Dhargyey (1974), p. 76.

173 Jamgon Kongtrul (1977), p. 93; Dhargyey (1974), p. 93.

174 Tashi Namgyel, in traditional condensation style *(bsdu ba),* mentions the "three effects," but does not elaborate. He assumes the reader understands based on knowledge of Buddhist tradition. For elaboration see Dhargyey (1974), p. 93; Gampopa (1971), pp. 84–88, n. 7–9.

175 Dhargyey (1974), p. 94.

176 (1) *srog gcod,* (2) *ma byin,* (3) *mi tsangs spyod,* (4) *rdzun du smra ba,* (5) *phra ma,* (6) *tsig rtzub,* (7) *ngag 'chal,* (8) *brnab sems,* (9) *gnod sems,* (10) *log lta.*

177 The verb *sems pa* is used in reference to the future, in contrast to *bsam pa,* which refers to the present.

178 Wallace (2001), pp. 61–62.

179 Ibid., p. 49.

180 Gampopa (1971) says: "…because of evil deeds committed…, there arises in their minds the appearance of such hellish beings" (p. 60).

181 "The preliminaries [are] the conditions for the cause of non-attachment" *(sngon 'gro ma zhen rgyu yi rkyen;* WD, p. 95).

182 According to the doctrine of cause and effect, each stage of practice begins with an action that then ripens. The result is first manifest as a sign. This sign further ripens into the full benefit *(yon tan; dgos pa).*

183 *'khor ba'i nyes dmigs sgom* (WD, root text, p. 63).

184 This analogy was provided by Geshe Wangyal, personal communication, Washington, New Jersey, 1975.

185 Dhargyey (1974), p. 63.

186 *shes rab rgyas byed pa ni thos pa ste*
    bsam pa clang ni gnyis po yod gyur na
    de las sgom pa la ni rab tu sbyor
    de las dngos grub bla na med pa 'byung. (TN, p. 222)

187 Pema Karpo's root text says, "The extraordinary preliminaries are the preliminaries, from refuge and the [enlightened] attitude up to guru yoga" *(thun mong ma yin pa'i sngon 'gro ni skyabs sems nas bla ma'i rnal 'byor gyi bar sngon du 'gro bas;* f. 2a). The following section of the book is an expansion of these lines according to other root texts and commentaries, which give the complete set of exercises. Pema Karpo's passage is another good illustration of the condensation style of root texts.

188 *shin sbyangs,* "pliancy," is one of the eleven virtuous mental factors. See Guenther and Kawamura (1975), pp. 53–54.

189 *thun mong ma yin pas rgyud rnam par sbyong ba* (KT, p. 7).

190 Recall the discussion of the relative influence *(dbang po)* of certain mental factors. The tantric term *dbang* has certain affinities with the Abhidharma term. Here, an extraordinary being, present or visualized, can bestow influence. In a special ceremony, he can influence the entire makeup of the practitioner's mental continuum so as to clear away obstructions to the practitioner's realization. The influence is, however, short-lived. Unless the practitioner follows up with his own efforts after the ceremony, the influence gradually diminishes. Breaking a vow is said to immediately annihilate the influence.

191 "The unique method of Secret Mantra…is to cause one's own mind, absorbed in the realization of emptiness, to appear in the form of the very enlightened being—a Buddha—that one is destined to become upon enlightenment" (Cozort [1986], p. 27).

192 "Viewing one's teacher as Vajradhara is a way of uniting one's mind with the Vajradhara state" (Gyaltsen and Rogers [1986], p. 16).

193 *jigs shig skrag* = "fear and terror" (TN, p. 230).

194 Gampopa (1971), pp. 99–100:

> …it may be asked whether we should take refuge in such asylums as the powerful deities…The answer is that since they all are unable to protect us they provide no refuge…Should we then take refuge in father or mother, in friends and other persons who are dear to us and who rejoice at our well-being? The answer is that they are unable to protect us…You may ask why they all are unable to protect us. The reply is that a protector must himself be free from fear and not suffer from misery.

195 Tantric texts speak of six objects of refuge. These include the Three Jewels—Buddha, Dharma, and Saṅgha—to which are added the lama, tutelary deities, and sky walkers (Jamgon Kongtrul [1977], pp. 54–56).

196 Gampopa (1971), p. 101.

197 Ibid., p. 102.

198 Ibid., p. 99.

199 Dhargyey (1974), p. 67.

200 *rgyud snod du rung zhig ci bya that pa'i lam du 'gro ba skyabs 'gro.* Cf. WD, p. 78, to JK, 7:1–18.

201 Gampopa (1971), p. 99.

202 Gampopa lists eight benefits. Tashi Namgyel adds a ninth: "taking refuge in the Mahāyāna." Cf. Gampopa (1971), p. 106.

203 For examples of the refuge ceremony, cf. Gampopa (1971), pp. 103–4; PK, pp. 13–14; and WD, pp. 107–9. For an English translation of the ceremony, see Jamgon Kongtrul (1977), pp. 53–66.

204 *'on 'khor ba'i sdung bsngal de las thar ba'i thabs dang skyabs thub pa gang yin na/ yul dkon mchog gsum la brten nas sang rgyas la ston pa chos la lam dge 'dun la lam gyi grogs so bzhung nas lam bgrod dgos la* (WD, p. 78).

205 For example, see Prebish (1975) and Nyanamoli Thera (1969).

206 "Engendering the Enlightened Attitude [bodhicitta] accompanies Taking Refuge" (Jamgon Kongtrul [1977], p. 60).

207 Gampopa (1971), p. 112.

208 Ibid., pp. 133–34.

209 Ibid., p. 116.

210 Dhargyey (1974), p. 112; Jamgon Kongtrul (1977), p. 61.

211 The *Bodhisattvabhūmi* says, "Immediately after he has formed this attitude he enters upon a course of unsurpassable enlightenment." This passage is found in Gampopa (1971), p. 134.

212 For the entire list of similes and their explanation, see Gampopa (1971), p. 112. These include: earth, gold, moon, fire, treasure, jewel mine, ocean, diamond, mountain, medicine, spiritual friend, wish-fulfilling gem, sun, king, treasury, highway, carriage, reservoir, echo, river, and cloud.

213 Dhargyey (1974), p. 121.

214 Gampopa (1971), p. 136.

215 Ibid., p. 134.

216 "A fish will take to water but not to dry land; realization will not arise in the absence of compassion.' Just so, ultimate bodhicitta, realization of the undistorted true nature of things, depends on relative bodhicitta." (Jamgon Kongtrul [1977], pp. 60–61)

217 Cf. Gampopa (1971), p. 144; and Jamgon Kongtrul (1977), p. 61. All the texts mention the same procedure.

218 There are other ways of practicing. These use elaborate ritualized visualizations. Gampopa reviews a well-known practice attributed to Śāntideva. It consists of three parts. The preliminaries include making offerings, confessing violations of the ethical code, generating joy for others' gain, requesting Buddha to turn the wheel of Dharma, vowing not to enter into nirvana, and dedicating the merit. The "essential practice" consists of repeating the bodhisattva vow many times. The "concluding practice" consists of a prayer and a final dedication of merit. Most commentators follow Śāntideva's model.

219 Dhargyey (1974), p. 122.

220 Ibid., p. 133.

221 Ibid., p. 122.

222 Gampopa (1971), p. 149.

223 The main work is that of Gampopa (1971), pp. 148–231; see also Dhargyey (1974), pp. 139–72.

224 "Fixed order means the succession in which the perfections arise in our life. By liberality [giving], not counting how much enjoyment we give, we bow to ethics and manners. Following these rules we grow patient and so become strenuous. This in turn develops the power of the meditation concentration. When we enter the latter state we acquire discriminating awareness born from wisdom and see things as they are" (Gampopa [1971], p. 149).

225 Dhargyey (1974), pp. 125–26.

226 Ibid., p. 127.

227 This is a passage from the The Realization Story of Avalokiteshvara [Spyin Ras gZigs kyi rTogs brJod].

228 Liberation (thar pa), path of omniscience (thams cad mkhyed pa'i lam), and fruition (bras bu). These terms refer to the three stages of enlightenment: basis, or ground; path; and fruit. See the section of this book entitled "Crossing Over" for a detailed description.

229 See pp. 79–82.

230 Willis (1972), p. 83.

231 Tashi Namgyel cites a passage from the Subahupariprccha Tantra (Dpung bzangs kyis zhus pa'i rgyud):

> Like flames leaping out as a fire spreads through a dry forest, completely burning everything, the fire of recitation is inflamed by the wind of
> ethical training.
> Like a glacier that melts by the clear light of the sun, so also brightness comes to those tormented, as if it were melted by ethical training,
> whose clear light is recitation.

When [one is] tormented, [recitation] consumes the glacier of sin.

Putting the tiny lamp to the black mass of obscuration removes the
entire mass of sin.

The obscurations and sins that have accumulated from previous lifetimes
are quickly removed by the lamp of recitation. (TN, p. 240)

232 See Beyer (1973), p. 144.

233 Retranslated from Willis (1972), p. 86.

234 For an English translation of this ritual, the reader is referred to ibid., pp. 83–86; Beyer (1973), pp. 434–36; or Jamgon Kongtrul (1977), pp. 80–82.

235 Jamgön Kongtrül qualifies this statement. For him "complete purification" only pertains to minor and moderate misdeeds. Major misdeeds, though suppressed, are not completely purified (Jamgon Kongtrul [1977], p. 87).

236 "So it is necessary to have confessed these [sins and obscurations] again and again" (TN, p. 241).

237 Goldstein (1976).

238 Dhargyey (1974), pp. 130–61.

239 Cf. TN, p. 236; Jamgon Kongtrul (1977), p. 93.

240 Wangyal (1973), pp. 200–26.

241 From "Practice and Theory of Tibetan Buddhism," pp. 11–13. Part of a translation from Tsongkhapa's *The Three Principal Aspects of the Path of the Highest Enlightenment.* See Sopa and Hopkins (1976).

242 Jamgön Kongtrül lists "five refuge-objects"; Künga Tendzin uses a sixth, the sixth being the root lama who encompasses the other five objects.

243 The reader is referred to an English translation of the entire ritualized meditation in Jamgon Kongtrul (1977), pp. 95–105. For Tibetan texts see WD, pp. 81–84, or for the full liturgy text see pp. 111–13.

244 According to B. Alan Wallace (2001), preliminary practices such as guru yoga are designed to bring "shape and meaning to conceptual thought by refining the way we view the world" (p. 16).

245 Kalu Rinpoche (1997), p. 184.

246 See Beyer (1974), pp. 127–43, 452–54, for an explanation of the "process of perfection."

247 Tashi Namgyel often uses the term *dgos ba* synonymously with terms for "benefit" such as *yon tan.* The term *dgos ba* literally means "to be necessary; must." Tashi Namgyel wishes to emphasize here the importance of the doctrine of cause and effect. If a practitioner follows the instructions for a given practice, the benefit "must" follow according to the laws of cause and effect. Although the term *dgos ba* is translated as "benefit," according to its context, the semantic field of the term is lost in the translation. For example, consider the commentator's use of this passage from Nāgārjuna:

So if you find the path of benefit by the kindness of your lama, liberation
must come even though you don't think of liberation. (TN, p. 247)

248 H.H. the Dalai Lama (2000) defines *ye shes* as the "mind free from dualistic perceptions" (p. 32).

249 Dhargyey (1974), pp. 206–8.

250 *byin rlabs myur du 'jug par byed pa bla mati rnal 'byor;* WD, p. 82; TN, p. 244.

251 Wangchuk Dorje (1978) recommends visualizing the lama as Vajrayoginī (p. 17).

252   Cf. TN, p. 242; WD, p. 84.

253   This passage is from the *The Gathered Secret [gSang 'Dus]*.

254   Cited by Wangchug Dorjé, Jamgön Kongtrül, Tashi Namgyel, Pema Karpo, and Jampel Pawo.

255   JK, 6:269–93. This is a text on guru yoga by Mikyo Dorjé.

256   Tashi Namgyel uses the same structure, but his text is somewhat condensed; cf. TN, p. 249.

257   The four influences are cited in all the major root texts and commentaries. According to Tashi Namgyel, these four influences come from Gampopa (TN, p. 250).

258   Jamgön Kongtrül (1992), p. 5.

259   Ibid. p. 49.

260   Jamgön Kongtrül (Jamgon Kongtrul [1977]) also included a section on advanced preliminaries, but they were not translated. Cf. also TN, pp. 252–58; KT, pp. 711–14; WD, p. 65; and WD, pp. 81–85. Künga Tendzin adds his own introduction and then cites Tashi Namgyel's text, almost line by line. This is one of the few instances in which a major commentary has cited a passage from another major commentary for the mahāmudrā tradition.

261   Neither Wangchug Dorjé nor Jamgön Kongtrül includes a section on virtue practice. They include only the more fundamental section on protecting. Certain root texts, notably that of Tashi Namgyel, take virtue practice for granted. Though not included in the root text, the autocommentary devotes a section to the explanation of virtue practice (TN, pp. 252–58).

262   Only the larger commentaries, but no root texts, include a section on behavioral virtue practice. Tashi Namgyel and Künga Tendzin both explain behavioral-virtue practice in their respective commentaries. Tashi Namgyel is the source from which Künga Tendzin draws.

263   Gampopa (1971), p. 164.

264   Ibid.

265   Ibid., pp. 165–67.

266   "Restraining means protecting the mind from being afflicted, and then setting it on something that is ethically neutral or virtuous" (Tsong kha pa [2000], p. 102).

267   Matics translates 5:97 of Śāntideva's *Bodhicaryāvatāra* as follows:

> The role of conduct taught by Bodhisattvas is immeasurable; but one should always practice that conduct which leads to the purification of the mind.

Matics misses the reference to *certainty (nges bar)* in his translation. See Śāntideva (1970), p. 171.

268   JP, f. 13b–15b.

269   "...since any attainment of concentration, be it on the basis of the sūtras or tantras, must be attained by virtue of this." This is a passage from the *Abhidharmakośa*, quoted in Guenther and Kawamura (1975), p. 33.

270   Ibid., p. 32.

271   Ibid.

272   Lamrimpa (1992), p. 38.

273   Ibid.

274   The Burmese call this "bare attention." Nyanamoli Thera (1969), pp. 30–45.

275 Soma Thera (1967), pp. xviii–xix.

276 See BCA, 5:27–29:

> Because of that thief, lack of intelligence, loss of mindfulness follows;
> Even those who have accumulated merit go to a lower state, as if robbed by a thief.
> The community of thieves, the emotional states, search for an opportunity.
> Having seized upon the opportunity, they rob virtue and also destroy the blissful life.
> So, never let the mind go out far from the mind's door.
> Even when it's gone, it can be restored by recollecting the harms of the hell worlds.

277 The Indian advocates of the *Yogasūtras* disagree. For them, the continuum unfolds as continuous, uninterrupted change, not as discrete events. See Patañjali (1914), 1:32.

278 Pema Karpo's root text refers to "mindfulness of the body." This is only one of the four objects of mindfulness. For a more detailed explanation, see Soma Thera (1967), pp. 43–130.

279 Shantideva (1970), 5:60–65, pp. 167–68; Nāgārjuna cited in PK, f. 3b.

280 Shantideva (1970), 5:29, pp. 164–65.

281 Although Jampel Pawo discusses mindfulness in great detail, he does not discuss full awareness. By contrast, Tashi Namgyel discusses full awareness in great detail, but not mindfulness. It is evident that both commentators, though differing in their relative emphases, are aware that mindfulness and full awareness form a pair. Both use the compound *dran shes* (mindfulness/full awareness).

282 Soma Thera (1967), p. 58.

283 Ibid., p. 54.

284 Cf. KT, p. 714.

285 Jampel Pawo discusses the thirty-seven *bodhipākṣadharmas* at length. These include four supports of mindfulness, four factors effecting gain, five foundations for miracles, four influences, five powers, seven limbs of perfect enlightenment, and the eightfold path. The commentator correlates the list with mindfulness and presents a complete unit of advanced preliminary practices composed of the *bodhipākṣadharmas*. This set of practices is comparable to Tashi Namgyel's virtue practice.

286 *The way the realized mind stays (gnas lugs)* is the most common epithet for the central realization of the mahāmudrā tradition.

287 Panchen Lama (1976), p. 23.

288 Keeping the mind "settled into itself" without any artificial activity establishes the exact conditions for realizing mahāmudrā. "Meditate, leaving the mind in a state of total presence.... If the mind remains like this 'as it comes from itself, as it is in itself,' this is what we call natural mind, *rang babs* in Tibetan....When realized, this is the mind of Mahamudra" (Kalu Rinpoche [1997], p. 234).

289 "Let me increase my perception of the three wisdoms: First, liberation from the defilement of ignorance by hearing the oral readings; second, cutting off the muddlement of doubt by reflecting on the oral advice; third, the clarity of the way the realized mind stays by the clear light of the arising meditation" (RD, f. 2).

290 Cf. KT, p. 717; TN, p. 258.

291 JK (1971), 6:531.

292 RD, f. 1a–4b.

293 JK (1971), 6:530–32.

294 Ibid., 6:513.

295 James (1950).

296 Duff (1999–2003) translates *spros ba* as "elaboration." Literally, it means that the mind "spreads out" to more and more elaborate thought constructions. As Duff correctly says, the English verb *to elaborate* best approximates the Tibetan meaning. The outcome of such elaboration is that the content of the mind becomes more and more complex.

297 Lodrö (1998), p. 14.

298 Tsong kha pa (2000), vol. 1, p. 99.

299 Lodrö (1998). The nine-stages model for concentration is attributed to Maitreya and Asaṅga. See also Lati Rinpochay et al. (1983), pp. 58–72.

300 According to the Third Jamgön Kongtrül ([1992], p. 57), *clarity* refers to "a totally clear apprehension of sense perceptions, including the ability to distinguish the minutest details quite clearly." According to Lodrö (1998), the clarity refers not only to events but also to the mind, in which case the term *dwangs ba,* "brightness," is used.

301 Lodrö (1998), pp. 97–101.

302 Personal communication in 2002 with Ven. Denma Locho Rinpoche, Washington, New Jersey. Lamrimpa ([1992], p. 74) also recommends that "one part of one's awareness should be devoted to intelligence," but warns that overdoing this may make "your whole practice deteriorate."

303 Bokar Rinpoche (1993), p. 11.

304 The term *three isolations* is used by Pema Karpo and Jampel Pawo. Wangchug Dorjé and Tashi Namgyel use the term *body and mind points.* The content of the respective sections, despite the different titles, is remarkably similar; cf. JP, f. 4b–17d; WD, pp. 65, 85–86; and TN, pp. 267–72.

305 ...*rlung bcu rang mal du 'ching nas:* "having fixed the energy currents in their own place." *Rang mal du* is a synonym for *rang sar* (JP, f. 8a).

306 Thrangu ([1993], p. 18) reviews the external conditions that aid the development of concentration. These are as follows: finding a favorable place, being relatively free of attachments, being content with whatever you have, having completed all business so that nothing is left unfinished, having developed the ethical training, meditating in the right way, and avoiding distractions and thoughts during meditation.

307 Jampel Pawo and Tashi Namgyel cite identical passages. It is unknown whether one commentator draws from the other or both draw on some other source entirely; cf. TN, p. 268; JP, f. 9b.

308 Akishige (1970).

309 Jampel Pawo also mentions the eight constant practices *(kun spyod brgyad).* He correlates these to the "seven dharmas of Vairocana." They include the seven, but also add the breath *(rlung)* as an eighth (JP, f. 7a).

310 Karma Chagmé (2000), p. 204. Lamrimpa (1992) adds, "Pay special attention to the coccyx. There is a natural tendency to let it roll forward a bit.... Tuck the pelvis forward and think of the coccyx as an arrow pointing into the earth" (p. 49).

311 "The shoulders should he held back a bit, opening the chest. This is said to be like a soaring bird with its wings stretched back"(Drikung Kyabgon Chetsang Rinpoche

[1999], p. 38); "shoulders are open like the wings of a vulture" (Bokar Rinpoche [1993], p. 65).

312 According to Kamalaśila, there are eight, not seven body points. He adds the breath as the eighth one. See Thrangu (1993), pp. 24–25. See also Panchen Lama (1976): "Your in-breath should be of the same length as your out-breath. The two should be neither too deep nor too shallow, and you should not hold your breath" (p. 14).

313 "Vairocana means 'what illuminates, what makes clear.' So Vairocana is the physical posture of sitting that helps one develop a meditative state and makes the mind stable and clear" (Thrangu [1993], p. 21).

314 "Because the body, channels, and mind do not exist self-sufficiently but are in a dependent relationship, when one is straightened all are straightened, and when one goes bad all follow" (Lodro [1998], p. 25).

315 Beru Khyentze Rinpoche's commentary to this root text says, "Therefore, if your rough body is straightened in the correct posture, your energy-channels will also be in a proper position. Then the energy-winds can flow freely through them and, when properly channeled, your mind will be fully focused. For this reason the bodily posture of Vairocana is essential" (Wangchuk Dorje [1978], p. 41).

316 In the special texts entitled *Moving and Mixing the Energies [bSre 'Pho]* it says that you can become liberated by simply doing the body points (JP, f. 8b).

317 The translation of *mi rtog* as "nonconceptual [stillness]" follows Geshe Gedün Lodrö's ([1998], pp. 182–83) recommendation that, from the event-perspective, there is a relative absence of elaborated conceptual thought, but he adds that, from the mind-perspective, awareness is still.

318 Bokar Rinpoche (1993), p. 81.

319 "The most difficult task is to differentiate between ordinary mind and *rig pa*...there is a danger that you could end up meditating on the clear, empty qualities of your ordinary mind" (Dalai Lama [2000], p. 49).

320 Jampel Pawo still considers the practitioner a beginner *(las dang po pa)* at this point. At the onset of the isolations, the practitioner still has little or no meditative experience.

321 *nyes = nyes dmigs.*

322 "Activity of speech, the formation of sounds, also depends on the activity of the winds. Talking too much disturbs them and increases the productions of thoughts, while remaining silent aids the meditation. In this way, tranquility of speech and body creates the conditions for inner calm by avoiding the production of excessive thoughts" (Bokar Ripoche [1993], p. 6).

323 Though neither Tashi Namgyel nor Wangchug Dorjé include a section on the isolation of speech, they do make reference to contemplation *(bsam gtan)* as an outcome of practicing the body points.

324 Thrangu (1993, p. 30) makes a distinction between coarse-level thoughts that cause the practitioner to "forget that one is meditating and loses one's mindfulness and awareness" and subtle-level thoughts wherein "one does not forget that one is meditating, but remains there thinking."

325 *rtog pa* (Skt., *vikalpa*) is used in a general sense to cover all types of activity within the mental continuum. The word is also used in a more specific sense to refer to thinking processes, those based on making distinctions. I have translated *rtog pa* as "cognition," which has a similar dual usage in Western psychology, when it is used generically. Cognition refers to the mental operations in general, and to the thinking

processes more specifically. Sometimes I translate it as "conceptualization" or as "thought," depending on the specific context of usage.

326 *blos btangs nas* literally means "examined by notions," which I have translated as "conceptualization."

327 There is inconsistency in the use of the verbs in Wangchug Dorjé's and Jampel Pawo's texts:

> Wangchug Dorjé: *'das pa'i rjes mi gcod mi bsam/ ma 'ongs pa'i sngun bsus te 'di bya'o byed de zhes mi mno*

> Jampel Pawo: *mi mno…rjes śu mi 'brang ba mi bsam…bzo bcos dang rtsis gtab mi byed pa*

Verb usage by Pema Karpo, Rangjung Dorjé, and Tashi Namgyel is consistent with that of Jampel Pawo. Only Wangchug Dorjé differs. Therefore I have followed Jampel Pawo. The word *bsam pa* is translated as "reflecting," which pertains to present *(da lta)* experience, while *mno ba* is translated as "recalling," which pertains to past experience *('das pa)*. Wangchug Dorjé has reversed these.

328 See TN, pp. 675–79, for further explanation.

329 Cf. TN, root text, p. 675.

330 Pema Karpo's root text only uses *lhug pa*. Likewise, Jampel Pawo stresses the importance of *lhug pa* over the other "means to set up." The other terms are simply lesser degrees of the function described by the term *lhug pa*.

331 "Nonconceptual stillness"*(mi rtog;* Skt., *nirvikalpa)* is a complicated word with several meanings. Here it means "to be without elaborated notions or concepts." The term often refers to a level of deep concentration relatively free of coarse-level thought content, i.e., a nonconceptual state.

332 "Saraha says: 'Set up the real nature, thatness, stay in fruition itself, which is unobstructed from the beginning'" (JP, f. 13a). The issue here pertains to the perspective taken. Ordinary mindfulness pertains to mindfulness of the mental continuum. Extraordinary mindfulness takes the perspective of awareness-itself, as part of the natural condition of the mind's extraordinary nature, as the point of observation from which mindfulness operates.

333 Jampel Pawo adds a very long section on mindfulness, which he correlates with the thirty-seven *bodhipākṣadharmas*. The location of the discussion of mindfulness practice is seemingly out of place. Most authors speak of mindfulness as part of the preliminary virtue practice. Jampel Pawo, however, qualifies the type of mindfulness in question. It is "mindfulness of the mental continuum." The practitioner, for the first time, is able to perfect mindfulness with the unfolding stream of the mental continuum as the object of mindfulness.

334 Lodrö (1998), p. 34.

335 Jampel Pawo says, "Since unenlightened beings are not able to do without a representation, then the mind-perceiver must represent some intended object. Therefore concentration with support is taught first" (JP, f. 26b). Kamalaśila, in his *Bhāvanākrama 3*, skips concentration-in-front and begins with concentration-inside, that is, visualization of the Buddha's image. Though Kamalaśila still suggests the use of a supporting object, the use of an external, substantial support is not always necessary.

336 The discussions of concentration-in-front are found in TN, pp. 272–82; TN, root text, p. 654; JP, f. 26b–30a; RD, pp. 4–5; and WD, pp. 85–87.

337 Bokar Rinpoche (1993) makes it very clear that the ultimate object is the mind's natural condition, but that since most practitioners have insufficient concentration ability, it is better to start with a supporting object. He says, "In effect, while one is learning to meditate, it is often very difficult to place the mind in its own essence, and so one uses supports to guide it to inner calm. Any external object can be used.... By regularly concentrating like this on objects, we are preparing ourselves to meditate on the mind" (pp. 32–33).

338 Thrangu (1993), p. 32.

339 The mahāmudrā texts generally recommend a stone *(rdeu)* or piece of wood *(shing)* as the initial substantial object. This is in contrast to the use of auditory objects such as mantras, which are much more common in Hindu yoga and in certain Buddhist tantras. The Tibetan Mahāyāna, especially the mahāmudrā, makes more use of substantial and insubstantial visualized forms at the onset of concentration training, for example, the image of the Buddha. The one important exception is Wangchug Dorjé, who also explicitly suggests the use of an auditory object (WD, p. 85).

340 Tashi Namgyel cites the exact same passage in his commentary, but leaves off the first sentence, "...as the eyes nail it...gaze." The rest of his passage is the same. The commentators may be citing from a common source here, cf. JP, f. 28a; TN, p. 275.

341 See chapter 2.

342 Jampel Pawo reads, *'phro gcod pa la sgom dang bzang gyis byas bas.* There appears to be a spelling mistake here. Tashi Namgyel's comparable passage reads, *'gzang gyes byas bas.* Wangchug Dorjé's paraphrase also reads, *bzang gyes. gyes + dang* means "to separate from." Cf. JP, f. 28a–b; TN, p. 276; and WD, p. 87.

343 For a discussion of sense restraint, see Conze (1967), pp. 64–66.

344 *sems gnas ngo bzung* (TN, p. 280). The title of this section, "Staying-Mind and Recognition," has two terms in it. The former term is from the mind-perspective, the latter pertains to the event-perspective, specifically to recognition of cognitions. Together, these terms refer to the two "benefits of concentration."

345 TN, p. 274: *mdo dang ka ma la shi la'i sgom rim rnams su thog ma'i dmigs pa de bzhin gshegs pa'i sku gzugs dmigs nas sems gnas sgrub par bshad.*

> "One is said to effect the staying-mind through having visualized the Tathāgata's Body, above all the visualizations of the sūtra and the *Bhāvanā-krama* of Kamalaśīla."

346 "...and the [practitioner] who is staying therein should not scatter the fixed mind" (Kamalaśīla [1971], 3:3). This is the standard definition given by Kamalaśīla and others.

347 Regarding the passage *gnas cha 'tshol ba,* cf. TN, p. 276, to TN, root text, p. 657. For example, the root text reads, "If you have found partial staying, you should remove any fatigue when you waver from the state whose real nature is staying" (*gnas cha rnyed na gnas rang bzhin gyi nang las shigs bshigs la chung zad tsam ngal gso'*; TN, root text, p. 655).

348 "...and should observe when inwardly he sees the mind tended toward elaboration outside, then, having made calm this elaboration by means of attention to the real-entity of that, and only then, should once again direct the mind continuously" (Kamalaśīla

[1971]), 3:3). For Kamalaśila, *recognition* means to view the "real-entityness" of elaboration *(ngo bo)*. Kamalaśila is advocating a combination of special insight and concentration practice, whereas the mahāmudrā texts are simply advocating concentration. At this stage of practice in the mahāmudrā, recognition does not imply special insight.

349 Lamrimpa (1992) recommends beginning with sessions fifteen minutes in duration but stresses that "the point here is to cultivate a high quality of awareness, to try to extend the duration of that high quality, and to avoid sitting around with a muddled awareness for a very long time" (pp. 76–77).

350 Rangjung Dorjé suggests that you repeat the entire practice five times for each of the five main sense systems. After finishing with a stone, the practitioner takes a mantra, then a fragrance, and so forth (RD, p. 5).

351 Lodrö (1998) says that "if a yogic practitioner is able to maintain clear observation of the object for a four-hour session, calm abiding can be achieved" (p. 67).

352 There are differences of opinion. Geshe Gedün Lodrö (1998), for example, says, "In general, it is not suitable to change the object of observation until calm abiding is achieved" (pp. 67–68). He adds that it is better not to change until at least the first third of the nine stages of concentration is mastered.

353 The discussion of the practice of concentration-inside can be found in JP, f. 30a–34a; TN, pp. 278–80; and WD, pp. 86–87.

354 Kamalaśila (1971), 3:3.

355 The commentator cites a passage from a sūtra to summarize the purpose of the visualization of the body of the Tathāgata. The passage reads, "Samādhi is pointed out in [the text entitled] 'The Samādhi for Standing Present Before the Generated Buddha'" (Kamalaśila [1971], 3:3).

356 H.H. the Dalai Lama calls this progressive identification with the qualities of the virtuous object through meditation "divine approximation." See Dalai Lama, Tsong kha pa, and Hopkins (1981). This book contains a detailed discussion of tantric visualization by which the meditator approximates the virtuous qualities of the visualized object.

357 This translation for *rgod* is taken from Dalai Lama and Berzin (1997), p. 135.

358 Geshe Gedün Lodrö (1998) defines *dullness* as resulting from "the mind's withdrawing too much inside" (p. 35).

359 Ibid., p. 78.

360 These instructions are taken from Kamalaśila.

361 Gyaltsen and Rogers (1986), pp. 49–57.

362 Jampel Pawo and Tashi Namgyel acknowledge Kamalaśila as the source for their meditation. See TN, p. 274; and JP, f. 33b.

363 Kamalaśila (1971), 3:2.

364 Comparable discussions of skill practices can be found in JP, f. 35a–37a; TN, p. 277; RD, pp. 5–6; and WD, pp. 86–87.

365 The qualifier *simple* is not used in the Tibetan. According to the context, it is understood that whatever appears in the mental continuum during this stage of meditation is in a simple form. See Dalai Lama and Berzin (1997), p. 73. In that book, *appearance* means "the manifest occurrence, not a visual aspect" that is experienced by simply engaging an event merely as it arises.

366 For a discussion of "supports," cf. JP, f. 36a, and TN, p. 277.

367 The word *skill* is used at several stages of the overall practice. Here it refers to the skill of concentration. There is also the skill of special insight. In both cases the events of the mental continuum come forth in an unobstructed manner and are recognized in clarity.

368 Tashi Namgyel considers the breath to be a "support" (TN, p. 234), while Pema Karpo, Jampel Pawo, and Rangjung Dorjé consider it a "nonsupport" (PK, f. 5b). Because the breath has only "subtle attributes," there is some disagreement as to whether or not it is classified as a support.

369 *rlung cad* = "having breath/energy currents." At this stage of practice, the word *rlung* refers to both the coarse breath and the subtle energy currents. The exact translation "breath/current" is cumbersome. The reader is to understand that both meanings are intended.

370 The commentators are very careful to say that cognitive and perceptual events, though less bothersome, do not exactly cease. To say so would be to adopt the extreme view *(mthar blta)* of nonexistence *(med pa)*, by which the Middle Path goes astray.

371 These two categories of mental events, *rtog* (cognition) and *snang* (perception), are most always kept separate in discussions. Cognition includes all forms of thinking and also emotional states *(nyon mong)*.

372 For a discussion of space yoga, see TN, pp. 289–92; WD, pp. 88–89; and RD, p. 6. For a discussion of breathing exercises, see TN, pp. 282–89; WD, pp. 89–90; and JP, f. 37b–40b.

373 For a discussion of the diamond recitation, see PK, f. 5a–5b; JP, f. 37b–40b; WD, p. 89; and TN, pp. 282–85. For a discussion of breath-holding, see PK, f. 5b–6a; JP, f. 40b–44b; WD, pp. 89–90; and TN, pp. 285–89.

374 "The breath is the object of meditation recommended for those who are strongly inclined to conceptualization or imagination" Lamrimpa (1992), p. 67.

375 Suzuki, ed. (1962), p. 3061, f. 51a.

376 Tashi Namgyel gives identical instructions, but Jampel Pawo's comments are longer and more detailed; cf. TN, p. 285; JP, f. 37b.

377 The stages are counting *(bgrang ba)*, pursuing *(rjes 'gro ba)*, establishing *('jog pa)*, discerning *(rtog pa)*, transforming *(bsgyur ba)*, and complete purification *(yong su dag pa)*. Cf. JP, f. 40a–40b; TN, p. 282.

378 The practitioner gives up any ideas about the direction of the currents and thus no longer depicts these currents in any fixed manner. Although the energy channels have been realigned, the currents are constantly changing within them.

379 *mtshon 'byung lnga'i rlung gi stobs nus zin par 'gyur ro.* There appears to be a spelling mistake. *mtshon* = *mtshan*, "attributes" (JP, f. 38b).

380 Suzuki, ed. (1962), p. 3061, f. 51a.

381 Wangchuk Dorje (1978), p. 55. For a more detailed description see Yeshe (1998), pp. 121–27.

382 Thrangu (2004), pp. 106–7.

383 The usual translation for the term *'char sgo* is "concept or theory." This does not seem to be the meaning here. According to the context, the commentators are describing the activity associated with perceptual processes at the subtle level of mind.

384 *phyir chad kyi 'char sgo zad par* is best translated as "to be-done-with the door of arising, that cuts off externals" (JP, f. 39b).

385 Duff (1999–2003).

386 There is an identical passage in TN, p. 286.

387 This passage is found in Tilopa's *Gangama*, in JK, 5:33, verse 3.

388 Even though Tashi Namgyel speaks of "awareness of any forms of elaboration" and Jampel Pawo speaks of "fleeting subtle cognitions," there is no real inconsistency. The former takes the perspective of coarse-level cognitions in the process of "construction" *(bcos ma)*, while the latter focuses on the process of "deconstruction" *(ma bcod pa)*. Though taking different perspectives, both commentators are describing a stage during which coarse-level cognitions are done-with *(zad pa)*.

389 This dual distinction marks the beginning of what has been called *access concentration* in the Theravada Buddhist tradition.

390 Tilopa, *Gangama*, in JK, 5:33, verse 3.

391 Thrangu (2004), p. 108.

392 Wangchuk Dorje (1978), p. 51.

393 Drikung Kyabgon Chetsang Rinpoche (1999), p. 44.

394 TN, pp. 292–94.

395 Asaṅga (1950), p. 10.

396 Guenther and Kawamura (1975), p. 103. This is a paraphrase from Guenther because he translates these terms somewhat differently than I do. He translates the terms as "drowsiness," "worry," "selectiveness," and "discursiveness," respectively.

397 A single thought can be used against other thoughts. For example, the single thought of emptiness can be used against the entire continuum of false concepts. The act of using a single [positive] concept against the remainder of [false] concepts is analogized to fighting fire with fire or curing sickness with poison (JP, f. 46a).

398 Lodrö (1998), p. 80.

399 Tsong kha pa (2001–4), vol. 3, p. 52.

400 Drikung Kyabgon Chetsang Rinpoche (1999), p. 45.

401 Gyatso (1982) defines *brightness* with respect to "the intensity with which our mind holds onto th[e] object" (p. 160).

402 Lamrimpa (1992), p. 69.

403 Ibid.

404 *sol ba.* There appears to be a spelling error: *sol ba = sel ba*, "to remove" (TN, p. 296).

405 *tsen gyis.* Again, probably this is a spelling error: *tsen gyis = rjen gyis*, "nakedly" (TN, p. 296).

406 Thrangu (1993), p. 55.

407 "With gross flightiness of mind, the mind actually loses its mental hold on its object of focus. With subtle flightiness, on the other hand, the mind maintains its hold on its object, but because the accompanying attention is weak, there is either an underlying current of thought or, even more subtly, a restlessness or 'mental itchiness' to leave that object and focus on something else that we find more attractive" (Dalai Lama and Berzin [1997], p. 136).

408 Lamrimpa (1992), p. 82.

409 *Cham me;* root text uses *bol le*.

410 Thrangu (1993), p. 55.

411 Equanimity is the fourth and last point *(gnad)* of staying/calm practice. It is the culmination of the series: body point, mind point, breath point, and equanimous point. The practitioner's awareness passes respectively to the body, mental content, mental

processes, and finally the mind-itself. Therefore the equanimous point is called the "sacred point." When the mind is balanced, there are no more obstructions. The natural condition of the mind comes forth (TN, pp. 306–8).

412 Personal communication, Robert Hoover, Bucksport, Maine, 1976.

413 See the nonmeditation yoga section in chapter 7 of this book for a more detailed discussion.

414 *Rang snang ba = rang mtshan ma. Self-appearance* refers to the way events come forth once the mind is balanced. Although events still seem to come forth in a relative sense, they are empty of any self-existing nature. The latter term, *self-existent (rang mtshan ma)*, refers to events that are mistakenly believed to exist in the external world.

415 Wangchug Dorjé's explanation of transformed perception is very much like Jampel Pawo's. He captures both the simultaneously absorbed and the emanating perspectives of the body, perceptions, and cognitions, as does Jampel Pawo. Wangchug Dorjé further adds that this condition lays the foundation for the later practice of special insight:

> As if going into an altered state, he sees the various conditions of bliss, clarity, and nonconceptual stillness. There are also many emanations and psychic abilities *[mngon shes]*. Because knowledge, such as that of the ten signs and so forth, arises, it becomes the basis of producing all the benefits of special insight and so on, when [such knowledge] is produced in the mental continuum. (WD, p. 91)

416 *Rang jung ba'i dran pa tshur bcangs par zhes bya ba.*

417 Asaṅga's *Abhidharmasamuccaya* defines *pliancy* as "a serviceability of the body and mind due to the cessation of the continuum of physical and mental dysfunctions, and it has the function of dispelling all obstructions." Cited in Tsong kha pa (2000–4), vol. 3, p. 82.

418 This refers to keeping the mind-moments discrete, as opposed to letting them unfold as a continuous flow of events. The argument is with the Hindu practitioners, who see the mental continuum as an uninterrupted flow of continuously changing events that flow into each other, but not as discrete events. The Hindu-Buddhist debate revolves around the difference between continuity *(ekattatva)* and discontinuity *(kṣanika)* of mental events. The debate is actually mentioned in commentaries to the *Yogasūtras* 1:32. See Patañjali (1914), pp. 66–70.

419 Chogyal Namkhai Norbu (1996) describes the "three bodies of the path" of dzogchen. These are *gnas ba, 'gyu ba,* and *rig pa,* which we have translated as "staying," "moving," and "awareness." He further defines *rig pa* as "the pure recognition without judgement, of either the calm state or the movement" (p. 56).

420 This is a passage from the *Śrāvakabhūmi.*

421 "Calm abiding is that mind which has overcome distraction to external objects, and which spontaneously and continuously turns toward the object of meditation with bliss and pliancy." This definition of *staying/calm practice* comes from Kamalaśīla, as described by Dalai Lama (2001), p. 107.

422 Thrangu (1993), p. 58.

423 The five faults originated with Asaṅga's *Śrāvakabhūmi.* The principal flaws of concentration meditation are laziness, forgetfulness, dullness or flightiness, failure to apply the remedy, and over-application of the remedy. The eight remedies include four pertaining to laziness (faith, concern, exertion, and pliancy), mindfulness to

remedy forgetfulness, vigilance [intelligence] to correct for dullness and flightiness, application to correct for failure to apply the remedy, and equanimity to correct for over-application. See Lodrö (1998), pp. 69–95.

424 Ibid., p. 69.

425 Tsong kha pa (2001–4), vol. 3, p. 49.

426 "...there is great danger of laxity [dullness] because the mind is strongly withdrawn inside." Lodrö (1998), p. 78.

427 Geshe Gedün Lodrö also mentions a sense of "haughtiness" *(rgyags pa)*, or self-inflation, that derives from the uplifting sense of the meditation at this stage. Ibid., p. 84.

428 Ibid., p. 86.

429 Geshe Gedün Lodrö describes six dimensions of the effort at this stage. They are (1) intentness toward the meditation object, (2) continuous application, (3) steady effort, (4) effort based in continuous application, (5) effort undisturbed by hardships, and (6) effort that is not satisfied with what has been accomplished so far. Ibid., pp. 88–89.

430 Tsong kha pa (2001–4), vol. 3, p. 75.

431 The sūtric tradition describes the outcome of concentration in terms of "serviceability" of the mind. For example, "Thus, the aim of attaining a concentration in which your mind is non-discursively stabilized on a single object without distraction is to have mental serviceability" (Tsong kha pa [2001–4], vol. 3, p. 22).

432 For an additional discussion of the nine stages in the mahāmudrā tradition see Gyatso (1982), p. 157–69.

433 Special insight ripens into awakened wisdom over time. The respective technical terms for these are *shes rab* and *ye shes*.

434 Drikung Kyabgon Chetsang Rinpoche (1999), p. 47.

435 *Bhāvanākrama* II: 1. In general, special-insight practice pertains to developing an understanding of emptiness. In particular, there are different degrees of understanding emptiness. For example, Tashi Namgyel sets forth three levels of understanding in a highly condensed root-text definition of special insight, the first two levels of which apply to the ordinary understanding of emptiness and the last one to the extraordinary level of understanding emptiness:

> 1. An entity of the mind cannot be recognized.
> 2. Unobstructed [events], in clarity.
> 3. The knowledge of which you become aware-in-and-by-itself, peacefully. It is the cause of [the enlightenment] experience without cause. This is special insight. (TN, root text, p. 668)

436 For a discussion of these terms see Stcherbatsky (1962), pp. 1–46.

437 For a detailed discussion of the effects of conceptualization see Lamrimpa (1999), pp. 31–46. According to Lamrimpa, conceptualization functions to fuse the actual perceptual object with ideas and concepts about the object. Such "false superimposition" (p. 41) of concepts upon a perceived object obscures pure, "nonconceptual awareness" of it.

438 Gampopa (1971), p. 204. For a discussion of the forms of knowledge, see Stcherbatsky (1962), 1:59–78.

439 Gampopa (1971), p. 202.

440 Ibid., p. 203.

441 Tashi Namgyel continues with the following passage from the *Dharmasaṃgītisūtra:*

The arhat petitions the Bodhisattva with his all-powerful intelligence, "Are *dharmas* anything that is produced or made to be?" [The bodhisattva answers,] "*Dharmas* do not stay in sense objects nor tend to stay anywhere else. If this were so, dharmas would not depend on the mind. Thus, they are mind-only, the same mind that tries to grasp, attain, or subdue them. Set up the mind in samādhi or after-samādhi and come to realize this." (TN, p. 335)

442 Tashi Namgyel relies heavily on the *Lankavatarasūtra* for his exposition of the doctrine of mind-only. See Suzuki (1932).

443 "If you think, you will find what you experience directly to be Mind. Due to bewilderment, an object in space and time is seen as an Appearance because Mind arises in such a way." Gampopa goes on to cite a passage from the *Lanka* as his "scriptural authority." See Gampopa (1981), p. 208. The later mahāmudrā commentators follow Gampopa's exposition of the doctrine of mind-only quite closely, even though the emptiness meditations themselves tend to be recast in Prāsaṅgika terms, because the Prāsaṅgika approach negates the Mind-only assumption that consciousness is real. For example, Lamrimpa ([1999], p. 27) says, "Based upon the authority of the great pandit Asaṅga, you would conclude that such consciousness does exist, but based upon the authority of Candrakirti, you would refute it."

444 Lamrimpa (1999), pp. 61–63.

445 Ibid., p. 66.

446 Lodrö (1998), p. 187.

447 For a discussion of the two kinds of emptiness, see Sopa and Hopkins (1976), pp. xxiv–xxv.

448 "When one says that the mind does not exist, we mean that the mind does not exist as a material thing with a form, limits and characteristics which can be defined by the senses. This does not mean that the mind does not exist at all." Bokar Rinpoche (1993), p. 120.

449 The material for each of these four stages can be found in the following: (1) TN, pp. 339–41; (2) TN, pp. 341–46; (3) TN, pp. 346–56; and (4) TN, pp. 356–63. These four sections pertain only to emptiness of the person. The material on the emptiness of phenomena is discussed after that in a condensed form; see TN, pp. 363–77.

450 An example of an erroneous view is that of Hva shan. This view is set forth and refuted by Kamalaśīla (1971) in his famous *Bhāvanākrama*.

451 For a good definition of the five skandhas, as well as a classic meditation upon them, see Buddhaghosa (1976), 2:479–546.

452 According to Geshe Gedün Lodrö ([1998], p. 163), the practitioner who has achieved either the eighth or the ninth stage of calming/staying practice can conduct a samādhi meditation on emptiness.

453 For an excellent discussion of the incomplete methods of the kuśali practitioners and the pandits, see TN, pp. 125–28. According to the commentator, the kuśali practice is "only samādhi meditation." They falsely think that meditation alone is sufficient. As a result, they try to bring about the cessation of all notions and cognitions to the point where they can no longer gain special insight. The pandits, on the other hand, correctly depend on the oral readings so as to understand the view,

but fail to meditate, so they understand the view merely intellectually. Complete understanding must utilize both examination meditation and samādhi meditation.

454 Jampel Pawo omits the preliminary examination meditation and goes right into the samādhi meditation.

455 See Sopa and Hopkins (1976), pp. 51–145, for a complete account of the tenets of each of the main Buddhist philosophical schools.

456 Cited from the *Dharmasaṃgītisūtra.*

457 For a thorough discussion of the terms *entity (ngo bo), nature (rang bzhin),* and *aspects (rnam pa),* see TN, pp. 404–18. Here these terms are defined according to their contextual usage. The reader might also take note of the verb *ngo bzung,* which means "to recognize." Literally, however, the verb means to "grasp an entity," that is, to correctly grasp the real-entity or real nature of the mind, namely emptiness.

458 Buddhaghosa (1976), p. 680.

459 The six realms are the hell worlds, the world of hungry ghosts, the animal world, the human world, the world of the gods, and the world of the titans. The three times are the past, the present, and the future.

460 Kamalaśila (1971), 3:1.

461 Ibid.

462 The word *kaśyapa* is equivalent to *öd srungs* in Tibetan, which means "light-guarded," here an epithet for emptiness.

463 Quoted from the *Mahāratnakuṭasūtra.*

464 H.H. the Dalai Lama ([2000], pp. 146–48) discusses the difference between nonaffirming- and affirming-negation strategies to establish the realization of emptiness. See also Lamrimpa's ([1999], pp. 77–78, 127–28) discussion of simple *(med dgag)* and complex *(ma yin dgag)* negations.

465 From the *Rathakūṭapariprcchā Sūtra.*

466 "However, since the self does not exist objectively from its own side, there is no alternative but to conclude that the self exists purely by conceptual designation" (Lodro [1998], p. 83).

467 The term *rang bzhin,* like *ngo bo,* is very difficult to define. As both terms are very similar in meaning, and synonymous in certain contexts, scholars have had considerable difficulty distinguishing them. This is because not enough attention has been paid to the exact context in which the terms are used. Tashi Namgyel devotes an entire section of his commentary to delineating the contextual use of these words (TN, pp. 404–18). Also, consider the appendix to Suzuki's translation of the *Laṅkāvatārasūtra* (see Suzuki [1932], appendix, pp. 1–7), where he comments on the seemingly contradictory and confusing use of these terms. Tashi Namgyel offers a way of standardizing their use.

468 This is a passage quoted from the *Sūtra That Teaches Great Compassion (Mahākaruṇā-nirdeśaūstra).*

469 This is a passage quoted from the *The Gathered Secret (Saṃcayagāthā Sūtra).*

470 "In the *Great Commentary to the Kālacakra* it says,

> Now, what is awareness? Awareness is said to be,
> Noncognition, awareness-itself, that is, the emptiness of all aspects.
> Although unchanging, awareness is without representation, stainless, and has a
> real nature, which is bliss.
> Awareness is essentially cause and effect.
> Cause and effect are mixed into one, like something consumed by a fire."
> (TN, p. 412)

471 This statement needs to be qualified. Remember that cognitions are transformable mental factors. They can be positive or negative depending on the context. Therefore only false cognitions are eradicated.

472 The latter section refers to the "samādhi meditation on emptiness of phenomena." The three parts of the "samādhi meditation"—setting up, bringing forth special insight, and the benefit—are collapsed into a single subsection of the commentary.

473 This is explained in a final section, entitled "Explaining the Representation in Meditation Stages" (TN, p. 371).

474 Thrangu (2004), p. 133.

475 Lamrimpa (1999), p. 94.

476 *Gzhugs brnyen* is equivalent to the Sanskrit *pratibimbakam*. This reflective process is discussed in Kamaśīla (1971), 3:1–3.

477 Cf. TN, pp. 377–87, to JP, f. 66a–70b.

478 For a discussion of the two truths, see Sopa and Hopkins (1976), p. xxviii.

479 This phrase is found in most of the texts; cf. TN, p. 377; JP, f. 65b.

480 Although each author focuses upon some shift in temporality, different stages are emphasized. For example, Pema Karpo and Jampel Pawo stress the initial phase of arising, while Tashi Namgyel writes two sections, one each, on the awareness of the unit (arising, staying, and ceasing) and the awareness of the arising and passing away, but says relatively little about the initial phase of arising. Other authors collapse the first two stages into a single phase.

481 *rnam rtog* = "all types of mental events." These are further subdivided into *snang ba* and *rtog pa,* that is, perceptions and cognitions. The use of the intensifier *rnam* is intended to mark all the mental events as opposed to specific classes of events.

482 Tashi Namgyel is not unaware of the initial phase of arising, as he uses the same phrase "happens to arise or has arisen" (TN, p. 377).

483 The root text reads, *snang ba tsam.* The commentary reads, *snang ba sna tshogs. Mere perception* and *various perceptions* are synonyms, if seen from the perspective of emptiness of phenomena.

484 For a detailed description of the meditation on the arising and passing away, see Buddhaghosa (1976), 2:734–44.

485 "Both elements, mind and mind-as-arising, are the same entity *(ngo bo gcid)* in an ultimate sense, although in a relative sense they appear to be different."

A new important term has been introduced by Tashi Namgyel to depict the realization of the same entity:

> The meaning of *the same entity*
> in this [set of exercises] is as follows:

...having put in order [the thing] in the foregoing exercises, the exercises now in
question must take both staying and moving—the emptiness, whose real nature
has no recognizable entity,
and the movement in this state—respectively.
[These are] one taste *[ro gcig]*, though they
appear to be different *[tha dad]*. (TN, p. 387)

Tashi Namgyel's term *same entity* is analogous to Jampel Pawo's term *simultaneous*.
Both suggest the sameness of seeming difference, like water and waves.

486 One reason that the realization is so convincing is that it pertains to the immediacy
of experience. The temporal experience of mental formations is such that there is
awareness of events at the exact moment that they arise, though they pass away very
quickly. Jampel Pawo introduces another phrase, also to become very important in
later excercises. It is "from the beginning" *(gdod nas)*. When the skill of recognition
is perfected, the practitioner actually attains the same special insight at the very
moment a mental formation actually begins to arise. The mental continuum is experienced as a continuous generation of the same certainty.

487 Intellectual understanding *(go ba)* from the examination meditation leads to experience *(nyam len)* of the samādhi meditation, which in turn leads to understanding
(rtogs pa) during the skill meditation.

488 Buddhaghosa (1976), 2:748–65.

489 Both Tashi Namgyel and Jampel Pawo rely on standard Mahāyāna sources, for example, *Bhāvanākrama*.

490 Cf. TN, p. 386, to JP, f. 68b.

491 "Whosoever understands that if the mind 'exists,' all phenomena must 'exist'; if it
does 'not exist,' all phenomena are destroyed."

> *sems yod gyur chos kun yod rigs te/*
> *sems med pa las chos shig su yis rtogs.* (Śabari, quoted in JP, f. 72a)

The contrast here is between the two mistaken extreme views of existence and
nonexistence.

492 Chokyi Nyima Rinpoche (1989), p. 148: "The four extremes are: existence and nonexistence, both and neither. The eight constructs are: arising and ceasing, being sin-
gular and plural, coming and going, and being the same or being different."

493 Here, we see how important terms such as *elaboration* alter their meaning with the
context, or stage of practice. In the mind-isolation exercise, *elaboration* referred to
thinking processes. Here *elaboration* refers to a more fundamental process: temporal
unfolding, irrespective of the content of experience.

494 Jampel Pawo begins his commentary with a review of the technical term *dmigs pa*, "to
represent." In concentration, the same term was used to signify the passage from the
emanating to the absorbed condition of the seed. When the mind stayed in its unag-
gregated form, no object of awareness could be represented. In special-insight practice the term was used again to signify the discovery of nonentityness of the mind after
an exhaustive search. In both previous cases the term *representing* suggests the construction of the respective objects of awareness into a thing or an entity. Now again
the term has the same meaning, though used in a new context. In representing time,

time also becomes a thing or an entity. When the practitioner does not represent time, he or she dissolves temporal distinctions.

495 Quoted from the *Enumeration of the Amassed Triple Gem:*

> *de ltar sems yong su 'tshol te/ ci 'das pa'm/ ma 'ongs pa'm/ da ltar byung ba zhig gam/ de la 'das pa'i sems gang yin pa ni zad pa'i/ ma ongs pa gang yin pa ni ma skye pa'i/ da ltar byund ba ni gnas pa med doi/ zhes dang/ sems ni kun tu mi dangs so/ gang mi dmigs pa te ni 'das pa ma yin no/ ma 'ongs pa ma yin no/ da ltar byung pa ma yin no/ gang 'das pa ma yin/ ma 'ong pa ma yin/ da ltar byung pa ma yin pa de ni dus gsum la yang dag par 'das po'i.*

496 *Rang gi blos btags pa tsam du* = "mere construct." The main authors agree in their use of this term, cf. PK, f. 10b; JP, f. 71a; and TN, pp. 388–90. The Prāsaṅgika influence is evident.

497 There are three ordinary emptinesses—emptiness of the person, emptiness of phenomena, and emptiness of time. The practitioner has now realized the latter, and so achieves "final purification."

498 See H.H. the Dalai Lama and Berzin (1997), p. 71–93. The Mahāyāna distinction between gross and subtle emptiness is similar to the mahāmudrā distinction between ordinary and extraordinary practices (e.g., PK, f. 12a).

499 Because the yoga of unelaboration points back to the previous meditations on emptiness and points forward to an entirely new set of special insights, it is a transitional exercise. Therefore some authors, notably Wangchug Dorjé, collapse the distinction between the skill and unelaboration meditations. By collapsing the meditation into a single unit of practice, the author is able to preserve the continuity with the previous, ordinary understanding of emptiness. Other authors collapse the distinction between the unelaboration and the subsequent extraordinary meditations. In so doing they emphasize the radically new experiences that come forth upon the eradication of seeming temporal unfolding, that is, subsequent to the nondissolution experience. Tashi Namgyel and Jampel Pawo emphasize both the continuity and the discontinuity with the previous ordinary special-insight meditations.

500 *De stong pa nyid sgom pa mang bas gnas gang gang gang du sems 'phros shing* [emptiness stays everywhere the mind is elaborated] (JP, f. 76a), quoted from *The Precious Jewel of the Cloud Meditation-Stages ('Phags pa dkon mchog sprin sgom rim du 'drangs pa].* B. Alan Wallace ([2001], p. 112) says, "Examining the unborn nature of awareness is the meditative practice of turning the attention in upon itself to observe the observer....The practice of observing the observer delves into the unborn nature of awareness itself, dismantling the dichotomy between inside and outside." Later (p. 116) he adds, "The experience of unborn awareness entails a spacious dissolution into a great expanse with no object, without obstruction and without intentionality."

501 JK, 5:287. The Tibetan version of Śabari's passage reads: *mi dmigs dus gsum ma skyes 'gag pa med/ de nyid gzhan du 'gyur ba med pa ni/ rang bzhin bde ba chen po'i gnas lugs yin.*

502 *Dialectical negation* is the negation of two opposing views in favor of another position. *Direct negation* is the negation of one or more views without advocating another position.

503 See Buddhaghosa (1976), 2:748–60, regarding the Theravada dissolution experience.

504 For English studies of the Madhyamakan dialectic, the reader is referred to Murti (1955), Streng (1967), and Sopa and Hopkins (1976).

505 *Yin lugs* is equivalent to *gshis lugs*, but not equivalent to *gnas lugs*. The "way of being" and the "way the realized mind stays" describe successive refinements of the natural mind.

506 *nyer zhi zhir bstan* = "become almost calm again and again." The addition of the qualifier *nyer*, "almost," is intended to prevent the extreme view of dissolution *('gag pa)*.

507 For a discussion of the doctrine of dependent origination, see Conze (1967), pp. 156–58. Note that Conze translates the term as "conditioned co-production." Although this translation captures the interdependent aspect of the term, it misses the related meaning, namely that all phenomena are interconnected. For a more updated discussion of the interrelationship between dependent arising and emptiness, see Napper (1989).

508 The key to establishing the Middle Path is the eradication of the extreme views of the reality and irreality of seeming temporal unfolding. The root texts and commentaries illustrate the eradication of temporality through a number of technical terms. First are the terms that negate any of the three units of temporal experience:

> *Without arising, without staying, without ceasing* (TN, root text, p. 666)
> *Without arising and passing away* (*skye 'gag med;* JP, f. 70b, 71b; TN, p. 389)
> *Without immediately occurring time* (*glo bur med;* TN, p. 389)

In addition to negating the individual modes of temporal experience, there are phrases that negate time in a more general manner:

> *Really passing beyond the three times* (JP, f. 70b)
> *Being without the past, without the present, and without the future* (JP, f. 70b)
> *Not changing into something else* (*de nyid gzhan du 'gyur ba med;* JP, f. 69b)

There are also terms that are designed to negate the extreme view of the irreality of time.

509 "Various types of ideation naturally arise, and they are self-arisen and self-ceasing. They naturally vanish" (Karma Chagmé ([2000], p. 100).

510 Tashi Namgyel defines *unelaboration yoga* as follows:

> Because the way the realized mind stays, like space, is without elaboration of the three (arising, staying, ceasing), without eternalism or nihilism, without coming and going, and so on, it is called "unelaboration." (TN, p. 707)

Tashi Namgyel captures both the positive and the negative assertions in a single definition of *unelaboration*. "Like space" is a positive assertion, while "without elaboration of the three...etc.," is a negative assertion.

511 The phrase "without hope and fear" seems to be a direct refutation of the Theravada position. The dissolution experience in Theravada Buddhism is described in terms of "terror," "danger," and "desire for deliverance." See Buddhaghosa (1976), 2:755–65.

512 *Lhun gyis grub pa'i rig 'dzin.* See Duff (1999–2003).

513 Cf. PK, f. 11b.

514 For Jampel Pawo's version of the protecting instructions, see JP, f. 74b–75a.

515 Pema Karpo's root instructions on the one and many suggest a protecting exercise. Again they are given in dialectical form:

Examine whether the mind exists as one or exists as many.

If it is one, how can it be one when the so-called mind seems to arise as various?

If it is many, how can all these become the same entity or the equanimity in emptiness?

When you are free from such extremes, it is called mahāmudrā, or not completely staying. (PK, f. 11b)

The root instructions remind the practitioner to protect equanimity. The yoga of unelaboration is the first approximation of equanimity, called one-taste yoga.

Jampel Pawo explains the root instructions as a "song method." In such instructions, the lama directly empowers the practitioner with the appropriate knowledge. For example, the lama would give direct instructions so that the practitioner not be mistaken while he or she is in the unelaboration samādhi. When the direct method is not available, the commentator suggests a "sūtra method." The practitioner is told to review the initial meditations on emptiness and then repeat the meditations for the "searching mind."

516 JP, f. 77a–77b:

Those spoken of previously and called the experience of the ordinary staying/calm and special-insight practice comprise the ordinary meditative path of the three vehicles because staying/calm and special-insight practice are certainly necessary to generate the enlightenment in each of the three vehicles, respectively. So that the practitioner does not make any mistake during the special-insight practices of the three vehicles, to correctly understand these, he or she needs to have both the selflessness of the person and the selflessness of phenomena.

517 "We must not leave our Mahamudra practice simply focused on the conventional nature of mind as mere arising and engaging. We must supplement it with meditation on the deepest nature of mind, and then meditate on the inseparability of the conventional and deepest levels of the nature of mind" (Dalai Lama and Berzin [1997], p. 77).

518 The related practices are discussed at great length in JK, 5:542–46. Though constituting a distinct body of practice, the extraordinary practices of the mahāmudrā bear a complicated relationship to the tantric visualization and energy yogas, on the one hand, and the ordinary staying/calm and special-insight practices, on the other.

519 "Then you arrive at the alaya, an unwavering state of consciousness, where consciousness remains without fluctuating, and without following after objects" (Dalai Lama [2000], p. 178).

520 See Dalai Lama and Berzin (1997), p. 6, for a discussion of the coarse and subtle emptinesses.

521 Ibid., p. 67.

522 Karma Chagmé (2000), p. 178.

523 Dalai Lama and Berzin (1997), p. 62.

524 Napper (1989).

525 "When the time comes that you can perceive simultaneously the appearance of things without this causing their voidness to be obscured to your mind, and their voidness without your mind ceasing to make their appearance dawn, you have directly manifested the excellent pathway mind that perceives every single, integrated point of voidness and

dependent arising to be synonymous." This definition of one-taste yoga comes from Dalai Lama and Berzin (1997), p. 101.

526 Jamgön Kongtrül (1992), p. 64.

527 Dalai Lama and Berzin (1997), p. 61.

528 "Therefore since you know bliss and emptiness…one taste" is a quote from the root text (PK, f. 12a).

529 Quoting the *Hevajra Tantra*.

530 What makes one-taste yoga so very different from the yoga of unelaboration is the "reappearance of seeming appearance." Jampel Pawo uses the now-familiar form "appearance-only," which is qualified in two ways: only *(tsam)* and not made to happen *(sgrub med)*. He also uses the terms *appearance* and *emptiness*, but further qualifies his position by saying that they are the same, a pair, or "one taste" (JP, f. 77b–78a).

531 "In fact, its voidness and appearance establish each other. Consequently, voidness dawns to us in the sense of dependent arising and dependent arising dawns in the sense of voidness" (Dalai Lama and Berzin [1997], p. 159).

532 See TN, pp. 441–60, for a discussion of how mistakes become wisdom during samādhi.

533 This is a quotation from Milarepa. Cf. JP, f. 78b, to TN, p. 448, for variations on this same passage.

534 Welcoming phenomena in mahāmudrā is in direct contrast to the disgust with these same phenomena in the Theravada system, at the same stage of practice. See *Visuddhimagga*, 2:753–58.

535 Chokyi Nyima Rinpoche (1989), p. 34.

536 "In the past, for transmission, it was sufficient for the master and disciple to simply rest their minds together in the composure of innate wakefulness…The student would recognize the nature of his own mind through one of these instructions. However, we are not at that stage presently, and therefore must depend upon words and explanations" (Ibid., p. 35).

537 Tashi Namgyel uses the term *dgos pa*, which means "a necessity or need." See Duff (1999–2003).

538 *Real-entity (rang bzhin)* is here translated as "natural condition" to fit the context.

539 *Enlightenment* means two things. First, it means "liberation from negative emotional states and false conceptualization." Second, it means "the manifestation of awakened wisdom." Thus there are two terms for enlightenment: *thar ba* = liberation; *ye shes* = awakened wisdom.

540 See Karme Chagmé's ([2000], pp. 245–49) discussion of the stages of one taste. See also Jamgön Kongtrül (1992), pp. 64, 68; and Tsele Natsok Rangdrol (1989), pp. 42ff. Karma Chagmé (pp. 250–52) adds that the subtle habit of reinstating dualistic appearance is not completely eradicated after mastery of one-taste yoga.

541 These various degrees of awakened wisdom as illustrated by the sun metaphors are from an oral commentary by Drikung Kyabgon Chetsang Rinpoche (1999), pp. 94–95.

542 During this final rearrangement, awakened wisdom comes forth. Knowledge is no longer dependent on any mental content or any mental processes.

543 *gnyug ma* = *bcos med*. "In this context, 'intrinsic state' should be understood to mean the natural condition of the fundamental ground that is not corrupted by thought activity" (Eighth Situpa Tenpa'i Nyinchay [1995], p. 84).

544 "Don't corrupt practice with your own fabrications of resting in clarity, resting in emptiness, or resting in unification, with deliberate attempts to stop thinking or hold your attention on the subject, or with, in short, any deliberate, contrived meditation…there is no idea fabricated by the mind that can qualify as meditation" (Ibid., pp. 82, 84).

545 "The difference between the one taste and nonmeditation has to do with whether or not subtle dualistic appearances have been purified and whether or not you exert the effort of mindfulness" (Karma Chagmé [2000], p. 252).

546 "Omniscience is the full consummation, or perfection, of the mind's ability to perceive objects. It is omniscient in the sense that it can know each and every thing without being obstructed by differences of time and space"(Dalai Lama [2001], p. 30).

547 See Dhargyey (1974), pp. 204–6, for a discussion of the buddha bodies.

548 From the *King's Songs* of Saraha, verse 34. See Guenther (1969), pp. 183–86.

549 Jamgön Kongtrül (1992), p. 45.

550 From Gampopa's *Explanation of the Sole Path*, in JK, 5:542–46.

551 *Skyong ba*. Lhalungpa translates this term as "consolidation" of the extraordinary meditation experience (Takpo Tashi Namgyel [1986]). *Consolidation* implies having to do something to fix the realization. I have translated the passage as "protecting" because protecting implies a way of seeing rather than a way of doing something.

552 *Samādhi* = *nyam bzhag; postsamādhi* = *rje thob*. The former term refers to the actual meditation state. As the practitioner progresses farther along the path, meditation experiences are more unlike ordinary experience. Thus these states strongly affect experience after coming out of the formal meditation state. This is called the postsamādhi state. The practitioner should make an extra effort to maintain the special insight during the postsamādhi state and not get caught up in seeing the world in an ordinary way.

553 This is set forth in two subsections: "(b) Generally, the Way to Protect Using Mindfulness, Intelligence, and Concern; (c) Specifically, Illustrating the Importance of Mindfulness" (TN, pp. 480–95).

554 "With effortless, mindful awareness one should meditate. To the extent that one can remain in this state, to that extent one becomes inseparable from the precious guru and non-dual with the Dharmakaya wisdom of all the buddhas" (Gyaltsen [1986], p. 79).

555 Lhalungpa translates these as "active and spontaneous mindfulness" (Takpo Tashi Namgyel [1986], p. 258).

556 According to H.H. the Dalai Lama (2001), "ultimate bodhicitta is transcendental and free from all elaborations" and is "achieved through constant and respectful familiarity with the yoga of calm abiding meditation and special insight over a long period of time" (p. 81).

557 According to Pagmodrupa and Jigten Sumgön, originators of the Five-Parts Mahāmudrā school, not-taking-to-mind anything was the highest of all the mahāmudrā instructions to be passed down the generations. See Gyaltsen and Rogers (1986), p. 82.

558 Guenther and Kawamura (1975), p. 28.

559 The previous term, *yid*, is now qualified: *gnyug ma'i yid*, "natural mind." The commentator still wants to use the term *yid* because he wants to preserve the relative dimension

of truth. So that the reader will not confuse the relative activity of the natural mind with the false activity of the ordinary mind, the author has qualified the term.

560 Tib., *'du shes;* Skt., *saṃskaras.*

561 Wangchuk Dorje ([1978], p. 151) calls this initial, unstable moment of recognition of awakened wisdom a "flash experience."

562 See Rechung, *Clear-Wisdom Mahamudra,* in JK, 5:326–32.

563 "Therefore, primordial clear light mind arises simultaneously with each moment of experience, with an everlasting, constant nature. On the path, through various methods, we cause that clear light mind to arise as a blissful awareness simultaneously with each moment" (Dalai Lama and Berzin [1997], p. 195).

564 The root text reads, *mig lam nas mdor bas chog pa* (TN, root text, p. 6); the commentary reads, *mig lam nas mdor tsam du bskyang bar chog pa* (TN, p. 529).

565 "This yoga is called supreme non-representation because, when the yogin has reached this stage, all forms of representation disappear" (Tucci [1986], p. 482, translating from Kamalaśila's *Bhāvanākrama I*).

566 The term is given as *rang babs* when used during the preliminary mind isolations (PK, f. 3b), and as *rang bzhin* when used in nonmeditation yoga (TN, p. 514).

567 The source appears to be Saraha's *King's Songs,* vv. 29–30. See Guenther (1969), pp. 169–76.

568 Gampopa has his own condensed version of these practices. They are cited in TN, p. 511.

569 Künga Rinchen of the Five-Parts Mahāmudrā school, however, defines *freshness* as "the state beginning after the cessation of a conceptual thought and lasting until the arising of another conceptual thought." See Gyaltsen and Rogers (1986), p. 86. Karma Chagmé (2000) defines *freshness* as follows: "'Fresh consciousness' means that this state of consciousness is unmixed with any fabrications or artificial contrivances of the conventional mind. It is free from conceptual elaboration....The term 'fresh' when modifying consciousness or appearances doesn't mean 'new.' Rather it indicates primordial purity. Even if gold is buried in the ground, its nature remains primordially pure.... So too, fresh consciousness, our own innate nature, may be obscured, but it cannot be stained" (pp. 247–48). Tashi Namgyel defines *freshness* less in terms of the relative presence or absence of thought content than in terms of the absence of reactivity to thought. See Gyaltsen and Rogers (1986), p. 86.

570 Künga Rinchen defines *nonartificial* as "without making any changes" once the clear-light/awareness mind is set up as the object of continuous mindfulness. See Gyaltsen and Rogers, (1986), p. 86. Chokyi Nyima Rinpoche (1989) defines it as "not trying to alter, change, correct, or fabricate anything; just simply letting it remain as it is" (p. 187).

571 See TN, pp. 512–14, for a discussion of the other protecting instructions. These include instructions by Maitripa, Nāgārjuna, Gampopa, and Khedrub Je.

572 Cf. TN, pp. 515–27, for a detailed discussion of the distilled essence of nonmeditation protecting instructions.

573 Berzin (n.d.), p. 603.

574 *dang po'i sems.* "The mind moves in the general direction of, or turns toward, whatever arises, but it does not fix the event, does not take-to-mind the event" (TN, p. 533).

575 Karma Chagmé (2000), pp. 254–59.

576 *Basis enlightenment* has been described elsewhere as "the vision of extinction into

reality-itself" because "Experiences are extinguished, the material body is extinguished, the grasping of the sense faculties is extinguished, the assemblage of deluded thoughts is extinguished, all philosophical tenets and elusive appearances are extinguished, and then your contaminated body disappears and you become a *buddha*.... It is called *the extinction into reality itself*, but it is not nonexistence as in the case of nihilism.... Rather, inexpressible primordial wisdom of knowledge and excellent qualities become manifest" (Karma Chagmé [2000], pp. 174–75).

577 Rechung, in JK, 5:326–332.

578 Ibid., 5:509.

579 Ibid., 5:510.

580 "Without the light of wisdom, the latent potential of the disturbing emotions cannot be thoroughly destroyed" (Dalai Lama [2001], p. 82).

581 Eighth Situpa and the Third Karmapa (1995), p. 52.

582 This explanation is given by Kalu Rinpoche (1997), p. 29.

583 Tsele Natsok Rangdrol (1989), p. 64.

584 Kalu Rinpoche (1997), p. 67.

585 For a description of the special abilities that come with enlightenment, see Eighth Situpa and the Third Karmapa (1995), pp. 120–25.

586 Literally, "sphere of activity." The passage refers to the fact that awakened wisdom has no specific locus or sphere, unlike seeming individual consciousness, which seems packaged and located in time and space.

587 The sections on cutting off mistakes are found in TN, pp. 551–62, and JP, f. 85a–85b.

588 The order in which the commentators present this differs, as illustrated here:

Jampel Pawo:	Tashi Namgyel:
Natural condition	Natural condition
Sealing	Path
Remedy	Remedy
Path	Sealing

This book follows Jampel Pawo's model. The reason for the difference in order is unclear.

589 The four paths are one-pointedness, unelaboration, one taste, and nonmeditation.

590 See TN, pp. 562–86; JP, f. 85a; and PK, f. 14a.

591 The psychic powers are as follows: supernormal strength, invisibility, levitation, materialization, knowledge of the moment of death and rebirth, ability to see across long distances, ability to hear over long distances, ability to read minds, knowledge of the future, and knowledge of past lives.

592 Wangchuk Dorje (1978), pp. 138–39.

593 Pema Karpo (1970).

594 Buddhaghosa (1976), 1:144–84.

595 See TN, pp. 586–90; JP, f. 84b–85b; and PK, f. 14a.

596 See Dhargyey (1974), p. 49.

597 See TN, pp. 330–49.

598 *Path walking* is often translated as "enhancement" because these practices serve to enhance the realization. See Tsele Natsok Rangdrol (1989), p. 57; Wangchuk Dorje (1978), p. 115; Chokyi Nyima Rinpoche (1989), pp. 215–29.

599 Chokyi Nyima Rinpoche (1989), pp. 215–29.

600 Wangchuk Dorje (1978), p. 115.
601 Atiśa (1983), p. 57.
602 *sgang dril = snyan gyi shog dril.*
603 Title of text illegible on block print.
604 The reference to son-and-mother consciousness refers to how seemingly individually packaged consciousness (son) and the ground-consciousness or dharmakāya (mother) merge during mahāmudrā enlightenment and also at the time of subtle death. For a discussion of this, see Jamgön Kongtrül (1992), pp. 65, 75; and Gyatso (1982), p. 95.
605 Ibid.

GLOSSARY

absorbed seed	bsdu ba'i thig le
absorbing visualization	bsdu ba'i dmigs pa
action	bya ba
admiration	mos pa
admiration-respect	mos gus pa
advanced preliminaries	khyad par sngon 'gro
aggregated	'dus byas
all phenomena as emanations of the mind	thams cad sems kyi rnam 'phrol
always there	ma skyes
always there [from mind-persepctive]	skye med
appearance as it really is	yang dag par snang
appearance like a mirage	sgyu ma lta bu
appearance only	snang tsam
arisen	shar ba
arisen or have arisen	shar ram 'char
arisen-only	shar tsam
arising and passing away	skye 'gag
arising conditions	rkyen chags
arising, staying, ceasing [of mental events]	byung, gnas, song
artificial construction	bcos ma
as if it were a real object	don ltar
at the very moment it arises	skye ba'i skad cig
attribute	mtshan ma
awakened mind	byang chub kyi sems
awakened wisdom	ye shes
awakened wisdom body	ye shes chos sku

awareness	rig pa
awareness itself each and every moment	so sor rang rig
awareness of awareness itself	rang rig pa'i dran pa
awareness-in-and-by-itself	rang gyis rang rig
awareness-itself	rang rig pa
balancing the mind	mnyam par 'jog pa
basis [ground]	gzhi
becoming assured [of the insight]	'phrug tshul
becoming calm	zhi ba
beginner	las dang po pa
being-done-with	zad pa; zin byed pa
belief	yid ches ba
benefit	phan yon; yon tan
beyond notions	blo 'das
beyond stages [of meditation]	sa med
biased samadhi	phyogs re ba; phyogs ris ba
bliss	bde ba
bodhisattva	byang chub sems pa
body isolation	lus dben
body points	lus gnad
brahman's thread	bram ze skud pa
breath	rlung
breath meditation	rlung can
brightness of mind	dwangs
buddha	sang rgyas
building the vessel	snod kyi dag pa
calming the mind	zhi bar byed ba
calming/staying concentration	zhi gnas
carefree	lhod de
categorizing	rtsis gdab
cause	rgyu
cause and effect of karma	las 'bras
causing faith to arise	dad pa'i 'don pa
central energy channel	dbu ma

certain knowledge	nges shes
certain truth	nges don
certainty	nges pa
cessation	'gag pa
child viewing the temple	bu chang lha khang blta
clarity	gsal ba
clarity—intense or vivid	gsal ngar
cleansing	sbyang ba
clear light mind	od gsal
closely established mindfulness	dran pa nyer bzhag
coarse [level]	rags
cognition	rtog pa
color	kha dtog
coming and going movement	'ong ba dang 'gro ba
compassion	'snying rje
complete purification	rnam par dag pa
complete staying	rnam par gnas pa
completely going off track	ye shor
completely purified	rnam bynag
concentration	sems bzhung
concentration with support	rten can
concentration without support	mtshan med; rten med
conceptual grasping	blo yis 'dzin pa
conceptualization associated with perception	snang cha
concern	bag yod pa
concomitant	lhan ne; do mar
condensed style of instruction	bsdu ba
condensed unit of practice	thun bsdu's tshe
condition	rkyen
confession	gshags pa
conflictual emotions	nyon mong
contemplation	bsam gtan
continuous	lhug pa
continuous [staying]	rgyun du

continuous nonmeditation	sgom khor yug
continuous staying	gnas ba'i rgyun
continuously directing the mind	rgyun du 'jog pa
conventional truth	drang don
counting the breath	grangs ba
crossing over	la bzla ba
cutting off the root	rtsa bcod
cutting off doubt	sgro 'dogs bcod
cutting off meditation	bcod pa
cycle of breath	dbugs pa
dependent origination	brten 'brel
desire	'dod pa
devotional mind	smon pa'i sems pa
devotional prayer	smom lam
dharma	chos
dharma body	chos sku
diamond recitation	rdo rje'i bzlas ba
difficulties	dka ngal
diligence	brtson 'grus
direct experience	nyams len
directing the mind	sems gtod
directly	mgon du
disciplining the mind	dul bar byed ba
disrespect	ma gus pa
dissolution experience	'gog pa; 'gags pa
dissolving visualization	shin ba'i dmigs pa
distraction	gyeng pa
doing something to meditate	sgom byed
doorway	'jug sgo
dorje sem pa meditation	rdo rje sems pa'i sgom bzlas nyid
doubt	the tshoms
dullness [laxity]	bying ba
each and every moment	so sor rtog pa
earnest application	nan tan

easing up	glod pa
effort	'bad pa
effortless	rtsol med
elaboration of thought	spros pa'i rtog pa
elephant pricked by thorns	glang po che la tsher ma btab pa
emanating seed	'char ba'i thig le
emanation body	sprul sku
emanation of nothing	med sprul
empowerment	byin gyis brlabs
emptiness	stong ba
emptiness of phenomena	chos stong ba
emptiness of the person	bdag nyid stong ba
energy channels	rtsa
energy currents	rlung
enjoyment body	longs spyod sku
enlightened attitude [bodhicitta]	byang chub sems
enlightened attitude which desires	'dod pa'i bynag chub sems
enlightened attitude which perseveres	gnyer ba'i byang chub sems
entity [self-existent thing]	ngo bo
equanimity	btang snyoms
equipose	mnyam bzhag
erroneous view	'khrul lugs
error	nor ba
essential practices	dngos gzhi
ethical behavior	tshul khrims
event [mental]; to occur, happen	'byung ba
event that emanates or shines luminously	'char ba
event-perspective	chos
everyday life events	spyod yul
examination-meditation	dpyad sgom
exhalation	kyen rgyu
expanded commentary	khrid yig
expanse	gu yangs

explanatory commentary	'grel ba
extraordinary	thun mong ma yin pa
extraordinary preliminaries	thun mong ma yin pa'i sngon 'gro
faith [trust]	dad pa
faith which desires direct experience	mngon 'dod dad pa
faith which is belief	yid shes kyi dad pa
faith which purifies	dang pa'i dad pa
faithful recognition	dad pa la ngo shes pa
faulty [flawed]	skyon
fear	dogs pa
final liberation	thar ba
finding the view	lta ba rnyed pa
five elements	'byung ba lnga
five main energy channels	rlung lnga
five mental factors making the object certain	yul nges lnga
five signs of dwelling	'jug rtags lnga
five signs of purification	dag rtags lnga
flightiness	rgod pa
following the breath's movement	rjes su 'gro ba
form	gzugs
four immeasurables	tshad med bzhi
four influences	dbang bzhi
four means to set up the mind	bzhag thabs bzhi
four opponent powers	stobs bzhi
four ways of missing it	shor sa bzhi
freely offering	mchod pa
fresh [free of conceptualization]	gnyug ma
freshly	so mar
from the undistracted perspective of the extraordinary mind	ma yengs pa'i ngang nas
fruition [of enlightenment]	'bras bu
fundamental flaws	nor sa

gaze	lta stangs
generating faith	dad pa bskyed pa
generating visualization	dmigs skye
generation stage	bskyed rim
giving	sbyin pa
giving and taking practice	gtong len
go astray	'chor ba
going astray	gol sa
grasping appearances as seemingly external	phyi rol snang ba'i 'dzin pa
grasping preciousness	gces pa bzhung
grasping things as real	'thas par gyur ba
great abandonment [relative truth]	spangs ba chen po
great bliss	bde chen
great penetration of the always there mind	skye med zang thal chen po
great perfection yoga	dzog chen
great seed	thig le chen po
great understanding [ultimate truth]	rtogs pa chen po
guru yoga	bla ma'i rnal 'byor
hearing	thos pa
hold [apprehend] the intended meditation object	'dzin pa
holy being	skyes bu dam pa
ignorance	mi shes
illusory-like clear appearances	snang gsal bzhip pa
immediately occuring [momentary]	glo bur
immovable	mi gyo ba
immovable body	lus mi gyo ba
impermanence	mi rtag
in a single instant	dus skad cig
indistinguishable [nondual]	dphye med
influence	dbang po
inhalation	thur sel

innate mind [buddha-nature]	gnyug ma'i yid
inspiration	kun slong
insubstantial meditation objects	dngos med
intellectual understanding	go ba
intelligence [vigilance]	shes bzhin
intended object	dmigs pa'i yul
intensify	sgrims pa
interconnected	rten 'brel
interpreted truth	drang don
interest	'dun pa
inward focus	nang du
joy	dga
karma [actions that ripen over time]	las
kindness	drin
knowledge of the ordinary	tha mal gyi shes ba
lack of faith	ma dad pa
lama [spiritual guide]	bla ma
left alone	rang sa
letting it settle into itself	rang babs bzhag
liberation [from the roots of suffering]	grol ba
like looking in a mirror	me long la bltas nas shes pa
like space [description of the mind]	nam mkha' lta bu
limit of the examination	dpyad pa'i mthar
listening	nyan pa
locus of activity	spyod yul
longing	yid la gdung ba skyes ba
mahāmudrā	phyag rgya chen po
making a connection	'brel 'jog tsam gyis
making calm	zhi bar bya ba
mandala offering	mchod pa'i mandala
means to set up the mind	bzhag thabs
meditating one-pointedly	rtse gcig tu byed pa

meditation	sgom ba
meditation on non-duality	snyom 'jug
meditation stages	sgom rim
meeting and destroying post-samādhi practice	phad 'joms
mental continuum	rgyun
mental events	rnam rtog
mental factor	sems 'byung
mere attributes	mtshan ma tsam
mere construct	btags pa tsam bu
mere hearing	thos tsam
mere self recognition	rang ngo shes
merit	bsod nams
middle path	lam dbu ma
mind and body points	lus gnad dang sems gnad
mind arisen as various [sense appearances]	sems ni sna tshogs rnams su shar
mind as a non-entity	ngo bo nyid med
mind as the intended meditation object	yid dmigs pa
mind isolation	yid dben
mind-itself	rang gi sems
mind-only	sems tsam
mind-perspective	chos can
mindfulness	dran pa
mindfulness of the simultaneous mind	yang dag pa'i dran pa'i zung 'jug gi dran pa
mindfulness that is inconceivable	blo bral lam blo 'das kyi dran pa
mindfulness that recognizes emptiness	stong nyid ngo shes kyi dran pa
mindfulness that takes things as real	'a thas dran pa
mindfulness with erroneous conceptualization	dran rtog
mindfulness without [artificial activity]	dran med

mindfulness—four types	dran pa bzhi po
mindfulness-awareness	dran rig
missing it	shor sa
misunderstanding the truth	mi rtogs pa
moment by moment arising	thol skye
momentary	glo bur
momentary arising	thol ba
motivating force	kun slong; kun nas slong ba
movement and stillness meditation	gnas dang 'gyu
moving	'gyu ba
mundane object of perception	ma dag pa
nakedly	gcer bu; gcer gyis
nihilism and eternalism	rtag pa dang chad pa
nine states of the mind staying	sems gnas dgu
no self-existent nature	rang bzhin med
non dual	gnyis med
non-aggregated appearances	'dus ma byas
non-artificial	ma bcos pa
non-constructed	ma bcos pa
non-dissolution experience	ma zin pa; gags med pa; ma 'gag pa
non-entityness [no-thingness]	ngo bo nyid med
non-existent	yin par med
non-representation meditation	dmigs med
nonconceptual stillness	mi rtog
nonmeditation	las med
not abandon or take up [coarse-level mental activity]	spang blang med
not analysing	mi dpyad
not anticipating	mi sems
not artificially constructed	bcos med
not chasing after post-samādhi experience	phyi snyag
not constructed	ma bcos
not meditating	mi sgom
not prevent or make happen	dgag sgrub med

not reacting to whatever has arisen	gang shar bzom med
not recalling	mi mno
not recognized	mi ngo bzhung
not reflecting	mi bsam
not take to mind anything particular	yid la ma byed pa
nothing but inactivity	byas med tsam
notions	blo
obscuration	sgrib pa
obstacles	'gog pa; gegs pa
obstacles to spiritual development	bar chad
omniscience	thams cad mkhyen pa
one taste	ro snyoms
one-pointedness	rtse gcig
opponent powers	ldog pa'i stobs
oral advice	man ngag
oral reading	lung
ordinary consciousness	rnam shes
ordinary mind	tha mal
ordinary preliminaries	thun mong yin pa'i sngon 'gro
ordinary protecting practice	sgrub rkyen
outline style of instruction	sa bcad
pair [nondual simultaneous mind]	zung 'zug
partial staying	gnas cha
passions	'khu phrig
path	lam
path awareness	lam rig
path-walking practices [post-enlightenment]	lam 'khyer
perceiving	snang ba
perfection stage	rdzogs rim
perspective	ngang
pervade [saturate]	khyab
pervading itself [saturation]	khyab bdag
placing the mind	sems 'jog pa

play of the always there mind	rol du
pliancy	shin sbyangs
point [to keep track of]	gnad
pointing out	ngo sprod pa
post-samādhi state	rjes thob
power	stobs
power of mindfulness	dran pa'i stobs
practical manual	khri
practice	sbyor ba
practice modules	thun
prayer	gsol ba 'debs pa
precious	gnyes
precious opportunity	dal 'byor
precious seed	snying po'i thig le
preliminary practice	sngon 'gro
pride	nga rgyal
pride about meditation gains	rlom pa
produced-en-masse	lhun gyis grub
propensities	bag chags
proper action	las rung
protecting instructions	skyong ba
purified	dag pa
put in order the mental continuum	rgyun gtan la dbab pa
putting in order	gtan la phebs; gtan la phab ba
rare chance	skal ba
real entity [real thing]	rang ngo
real mindfulness	yang dag pa'i dran pa
real nature [of the mind]	rang bzhin
really staying [from the extraordinary mind-perspective]	ye nas gnas pa
rearrangement [of mental continuum]	sgrig pa
reasoning	gzhig
recitation	bzlas ba

recognize	ngo shes pa
recognize in and of itself	rang ngo shes ba
reflected image	snang brnyan
reflecting	bsam pa
refuge object	skyabs yul
regret	rnam par sun pa
remedy [antidote]	gnyen po
removing flaws	skyon sel
renunciation	nges 'byung
representation	dmigs pa
resetting the mind	slan te 'jog pa
respect	gus pa
respect with speech	ngag gus
respect with the body	lus gus
respect with the mind	yid gus
restraint	sdom pa
reverse samādhi	bzlog pa'i sgom pa
ripen [develop over time]	smin ba
roaming [of subtle-level mind to sense impressions]	'pho ba; phyan ba
roaming of mind to sense objects	sems yul la 'phyan ba
root text	rtsa
samādhi	ting nge 'dzin
samādhi-meditation	'jog sgom
same taste	ro snyoms
saṃsāra	'khor ba
sealing [emptiness]	rtsol ba 'debs
search	tshol ba
searching everywhere	sems kun tu 'tshol ba
searching mind	sems 'tshol
searching thoroughly	yong su tshol ba
secret path	gsangs lam
seed	thig le
seed meditation	thig le
seed syllable	yig 'bru

seeming appearance	spang gyi 'dug pa
seeming clarity	gsal bzhin
self aware each and every moment	so sor rang rig
self-cherishing	bdag gces 'dzin pa
self-contentedly	rang gar
self-purified	rang dag
self staying [of the awakened mind]	rang gnas
self-calm	rang zhi
self-clarity	rang gsal
self-contentedly	rang thang
self-existent nature	rang mtshan
self-existing entity or thing	bdag nyid
self-grasping	bdag 'dzin
self-liberated	rang grol
self-purified	rang dag
self-skill	rang rtsal
sense door	'char sgo
sense object	yul don
sense organ	dbang po
sense perceiver	dbang shes
sensory stimulation	reg pa
service	rim gro
set up or establish	'jog pa
setting the mind closely	nye bar 'jog pa
settling into itself	rang babs; rnal du phebs
settling the mind	sems 'jog
seven-limbed prayer	yan lag bdun
signs	rtags
silence [cutting off speech]	smra bcad
simple undistraction	ma yengs tsam
simultaneous	lhan cig skyes sbyor
simultaneous from the event-perspective—thoughts	rtog pa'i lhan skye

simultaneous from the event-perspective—perception	snang pa'i lhan skyes
simultaneous from the mind-perspective	sems nyid lhan skyes
single concept	rtog gcig
six antidotes	gnyen drug
six defilements	dri ma drug
six perfections	phar phyin drug
six sense systems	tshog drug
skill	rtsal
skill of representing	dmigs pa'i rtsal
skillful means	thabs
skillful non-means	thabs med
slowly	cham me
slowly [unhurried]	'hol le
space yoga	nam mkha'i rnal 'byor
special insight	lhag mthong
special instructions to set up enlightenment	khyad par
speech isolation	ngag bden
spiritual advice	gdams pa
spiritual community	dge 'dun
spontaneous presence	lhun gyis grub
spritual friend	dge bshes
stages of practice	rim pa
stages of the path	lam rim
stay [on intended meditation object]	gnas ba
steady concentration	brtan po
stopping the mind [from coarse-level elaboration]	sems med
store consciousness	kun gzhi
straw rope	sog phon thag pa
subsidiary energy channels	yan lag gi rlung
substance	dngos bo
subtle [level]	phra ba

subtle attributes	mtshan ma phra mo
subtle cognition [mind-moments]	'phra ba'i rtog pa
subtle dullness [laxity]	bying ba's phra mo
suffering	sdug bsngal
sufferings of saṃsāra	'khor ba'i nyes dmigs
support	bstan
supporting representation	dmigs rten
supreme bliss	bde steng
supreme clarity	gsal steng
take to mind [mentally engage] the intended object	yid la byed pa
take up and abandon	blang dor
taking refuge	skyabs 'gro ba
taming the mind	'dul byi sems
thinking about the past [memory]	'das pa
thinking about present experience	da lta
thinking about the future [anticipation]	ma 'ongs pa
thoroughly calming the mind	nye bar zhi bar byed ba
three isolations	dben gsum
three jewels	dkon mchog gsum
three times [past, present, and future]	dus gsum
three wisdom bodies	sku 'sum
to build up mental content	bcos pa
to cut off	bcod pa
to equalize	snyoms pa
to know	shes ba
to prevent or make something happen	dgagsgrub
transitional period from samādhi to waking	rjes thob
true characteristics	mtshan don
truth	don
ultimate truth	don dam
unborn from the beginning	gdad nas skye med

unborn mind [from event perspective]	skye med
unceasing signs	ma zin gyi rtags
unconcern	bag pheb
undefiled	dri med; ma bslad
understanding	rtogs pa
undistracted	ma yengs pa
unique qualities	mtshan nyid
unobstructed	ma 'gag pa
unobstructed flow	rgyun mi chad
unwavering faith	dad pa mi 'gyur ba
various appearances	sna tshogs du snang
various sense impressions	sna tshogs
vase breathing	bum ba can
vibrancy	shig ge ba
view	lta ba
viewed with equanimity	mnyam pa zhog
viewing the mind as if it were an entity or thing	sems ngo bo lta
virtue	dge ba
virtue practice	dge sbyor
virtuous behaviors	dge ba's las
virtuous object of perception	dag pa
visualization meditation	sgom dmigs
vow	dam tsig
waver	tshom tshom
way [to practice]	tshul
way of placing the mind	'dug tshul
way the realized mind appears	snag lugs; snang tshul
way the realized mind happens by itself	'dug tsul
way the realized mind stays	gnas lugs
weight [of past actions]	mthu; lci
whatever happens to arise or to have arisen	shar ba 'am 'char do bcug nas

whatever has arisen in the mind	gang shar
wisdom	shes rab
wish-granting gem	yid bzhin gyi norbu
without independent existence	rang skyu thub ba med par
without making something happen	sgrub med
without obstruction	'gags med
wrong view	blta log
yoga of nonmeditation	sgom med kyi rnal 'byor
yoga of one taste	ro gcig gi rnal 'byor
yoga of unelaboration	spros bral gyi rnal 'byor bsgom pa

BIBLIOGRAPHY

TIBETAN WORKS

Bkra shis rnam rgyal, Dwags po Paṇ chen. 1974. *Nges don phyag rgya chen po'i sgom rim gsal bar byed pa'i legs bsad zla ba'i od zer.* Delhi: Blockprint from La stod rTshib ri par ma by Karma chos 'phel.

———. *Phyag rgya chen po'i khrid yig chen mo gnyug ma'i de nyid gsal ba.* In 'Jam mgon Kong sprul (1971) 5:651–702.

Chos kyi 'byung gnas, Eighth Situ. *Phyag chen lnga ldan gyi khrid yig.* In 'Jam mgon Kong sprul (1971) 6:430–41.

Dbang phyug rdo rje (Karmapa IX). *Phyag rgya chen po lhan cig skyes sbyor gyi khrid kyi spyi sdom rtsa tshig.* In 'Jam mgon Kong sprul (1971) 6:62–69.

———. *Phyag rgya chen po lhan cig skye sbyor gyi khrid yig zin bris snying po gsal ba'i sgron me bdud rtsi 'i nying khu chos sku mdzub tshugs su ngo sprod pa.* In 'Jam mgon Kong sprul (1971) 6:70–104.

———. *Sgrub brgyud karmakam tshang pa'i phyag rgya chen lhan cig skye sbyor gyi sngon 'gro bzhi sbyor sogs kyi ngag 'don 'phags lam bgrod pa'i shing rta.* In 'Jam mgon Kong sprul (1971) 6:105–22.

'Jam dpal dpa' bo. 1969. *Phyag rgya chen po lhan cig skyes sbyor dngos gzhi'i khrid yig cung zad spros pa sems kyi rdo rje'i nges gnas gsal bar byed pa.* Chemre, India: Blockprint of the He mi rGod Tshang Monastery.

'Jam mgon Kong sprul Blo gros mtha' yas. 1971. *Gdams ngag mdzod: [A Treasury of Instructions and Techniques for Spiritual Realisation].* New Delhi: N. Lungtok and N. Gyaltsan.

Khro phu Lo tsa ba Byams pa dpal. *Khro phu bka' brgyud las byung ba'i phyag rgya chen po lnga ldan gyi khrid yig.* In 'Jam mgon Kong sprul (1971) 6:530–32.

Kun dga' bstan 'dzin. 1974. *Phyag rgya chen po lhan cig skyes sbyor gyi sngon 'gro'i khrid yig zab rgyas chos kyi rgya mtsho chen po nas snying po ye shes kyi nor bu 'dren par byed pa'i gru chen.* Palampur, India: Blockprint from Byar Skyid phug blockprint of the Tibetan Craft Community.

Marpa. *Mnga' bdag mar pa lo tsa bas dpal sa ra ha las gsan pa'i phyags rgya chen po yid la mi byed pa snying po don gyi gdams ngag yi ge bzhi pa'i don rdo rje'i mgur du bzhengs pa.* In 'Jam mgon Kong sprul (1971) 5:63–66.

Mi bskyod Dorjé. *Dpal karma pa chen po la brten pa'i thun bzhi'i bla ma'i rnal byor dmigs khrid dang bcas pa.* In 'Jam mgon Kong sprul (1971) 6:269–83.

Mtshur ston lugs pa. *Phyag rgya chen po tshig bsdus pa.* In 'Jam mgon Kong sprul (1971) 5: 524–27.

Nadapada (Nāropa). *Phyag rgya chen po'i tshig bsdus pa.* In 'Jam mgon Kong sprul (1971) 5:47–48.

Padma dKar po. 1970. *Bsre pho'i khrid yig [A Practical Manual of Energy Yoga].* Solukhumbu: Trakar Monastery.

———. *Chos rje brug pa'i lugs kyi phyag rgya chen po lhan cig skyes sbyor gyi khrid yig.* In 'Jam mgon Kong sprul (1971) 7:19–33.

———. *Phyag chen gyi zin bris bzhugs.* [Practice Guidelines on Mhāmudrā]. n.p.

———. *Phyag chen lhan cig skyes sbyor gyi khrid yig.* In 'Jam mgon Kong sprul (1971) 6:1–16.

———. *Ro snyoms skor drug gi nyams len sgong du dril ba ('Brug lugs ro snyoms sgang dril).* In 'Jam mgon Kong sprul (1971) 6:81–88.

Rang byung rdo rje (Third Karmapa). 1970. *Nges don phyag rgya chen po'i smon lam.* n.p.

———. *Phyag rgya chen po lhan cig skyes sbyor gyi khrid yig.* In 'Jam mgon Kong sprul (1971) 6:1–16.

Ras chung, Rdo rje grags. *Bde mchog snyan brgyud kyi 'og sgo bde ba chen po gzhan lus phyag reya ma bsten pa'i gdams pa ye shes gsal ba'i sgrun me.* In 'Jam mgon Kong sprul (1971) 5:326–32.

Śabari. *Do ha mdzod ces bya phyag rgya chen po man ngag (Snying po don gyi man ngag).* In 'Jam mgon Kong sprul (1971) 5:28–33.

Sgam po pa. *Rje sgam po pa's phyag rgya chen po lam gcig chod.* In 'Jam mgon Kong sprul (1971) 5:67–69.

Stag lung thang pa Bkra shis dpal. *Phyag rgya chen po lhan cig skyes sbyor gyi khrid yig gzhung chung rdo rje'i tshig rkang yid bzhin gyi nor bu.* In 'Jam mgon Kong sprul (1971) 6:511–29.

Suzuki, D.T. 1962. *Catalogue and Index of the Tibetan Tripiṭaka.* Tokyo: Suzuki Research Foundation.

Tilopa. 1962. *Dohākośa [Treasury of Songs].* Tibetan Tripitaka 3132–33, f. 150b–157b. Ed. D. T. Suzuki. Tokyo: Tibetan Tripitaka Research Foundation.

———. *Gangāma.* In 'Jam mgon Kong sprul (1971) 5:33–36.

SANSKRIT AND PALI WORKS

Asaṅga. 1973. *Śrāvakabhūmi [Grounds of Hearers].* P. 5537, vol. 110. Tibetan Sanskrit Works Series. Vol. 14. Ed. Karunesha Shukla. Patna, India: Jayaswal Research Institute.

———. 1950. *Abhidharmasamuccaya [Summary of Manifest Knowledge].* P. 5550. Visva-Bharati Series. No. 12. Ed. Pralhad Pradhan. Santiniketan: Visva-Bharati (Santiniketan Press).

Kamalaśila. 1971. *Bhāvanākrama [Stages of Meditation]. First Bhāvanākrama.* Ed. G. Tucci. *Minor Buddhist Texts, II,* Serie Orientale Roma IX, 2. Rome: IS.M.E.O., 1958. *Third Bhāvanākrama,* G. Tucci, ed. *Minor Buddhist Texts, III,* Serie Orientale Roma XLIII. Rome: IS.M.E.O.

Maitreya. 1971. *Madhyāntavibhaṅgaśāstra [Differentiation of the Middle and the Extremes].* Ed. Ramchandra Paneya. Delhi: Motilal Banarsidass.

———. 1970. *Mahāyānasūtrālaṃkāra [Ornament for the Mahāyāna Sutras]. Buddhist Sanskrit Texts.* No. 13. Ed. Sitansusekhar Bagchi. Darbhanga, India: Mithila Institute. See translation below under Maitreyanātha.

Patañjali. 1914. *The Yoga-System of Patañjali.* Trans. James Houghton Woods. Delhi: Motilal Banarsidass.

Soma Thera, trans. 1967. *Satipaṭṭhānā Sutta and Commentary [The Way of Mindfulness].* Kandy, Ceylon: Buddhist Publication Society.

Vasubandhu. 1975. *Abhidharmakośakārikā [Treasury of Manifest Knowledge].* Ed. P. Pradhan. Patna, India: Jayaswal Research Institute.

ENGLISH WORKS

Akishige, Y., ed. 1970. *Psychological Studies on Zen.* Tokyo: Zen Institute of Komazawa University.

Alexander, Franz and Thomas M. French. 1946. *Psychoanalytic Psychotherapy.* New York: Ronald Press.

Atiśa. 1983. *A Lamp for the Path and Commentary.* Trans. Richard Sherburne, S.J. London: George Allen and Unwin.

Bahr, Donald M., et al. 1974. *Piman Shamanism and Staying Sickness.* Tucson: Univ. of Arizona Press.

Barlow, David H., ed. 1993. *Clinical Handbook of Psychological Disorders: A Step-by-Step Treatment Manual.* 2nd ed. New York: Guilford.

Berzin, Alexander. 2000. *Relating to a Spiritual Teacher: Building a Healthy Relationship.* Ithaca, NY: Snow Lion.

———. n.d. *Śamatha and Vipaśyanā.* Dharamsala: Library of Tibetan Works and Archives.

Beyer, Stephan. 1973. *The Cult of Tārā: Magic and Ritual in Tibet.* Berkeley: Univ. of California Press.

———. 1974. *The Buddhist Experience: Sources and Interpretations.* Ed. Frederick J. Streng. Encino, CA: Dickenson.

Bharati, Aghananda. 1965. *The Tantric Tradition.* New York: Doubleday & Co.

Bhattacharyya, Benoytosh. 1964. *An Introduction to Buddhist Esoterism.* Varanasi, India: Chowkhamba Sanskrit Series Office.

Bokar Rinpoche. 1993. *Meditation Advice to Beginners.* Ed. Jennifer Pessereau. Trans. Christiane Buchet. San Francisco: Clear Point Press.

Buddhaghosa, Bhadantācariya. 1976. *The Path of Purification: Visuddhimagga.* Trans. Bhikkhu Ñānamoli, 2 vols. Berkeley: Shambhala, 1976. [New edition: Seattle: BPS Pariyatti Editions, 1999.]

Chang, Garma C. C., trans. 1962. *The Hundred Thousand Songs of Milarepa.* New Hyde Park, NY: University Books.

———. 1963. *Teachings of Tibetan Yoga.* New Hyde Park, NY: University Books.

Chattopadhyaya, Alaka. 1967. *Atisa and Tibet.* Calcutta, India: R. Maitra at R. D. Press.

Chokyi Nyima Rinpoche. 1989. *The Union of Mahamudra and Dzogchen.* Hong Kong: Ranjung Yeshe.

Conze, Edward. 1967. *Buddhist Thought in India.* Ann Arbor: Univ. of Michigan Press.

Cozort, Daniel. 1986. *Highest Yoga Tantra.* Ithaca, NY: Snow Lion.

Dalai Lama, H.H. the. 2001. *Stages of Meditation.* Trans. Geshe Lobsang Jordhen et al. Ithaca, NY: Snow Lion.

———. 2000. *Dzogchen: The Heart Essence of the Great Perfection.* Ed. Patrick Gaffney. Trans. Geshe Thupten Jinpa and Richard Barron. Ithaca, NY: Snow Lion.

Dalai Lama, H.H. the, and Alexander Berzin. 1997. *The Gelug/Kagyü Tradition of Mahamudra.* Ithaca, NY: Snow Lion.

Dalai Lama, H.H. the, Tsong ka pa, and Jeffrey Hopkins. 1981. *Deity Yoga in Action and Performance Tantra.* Ithaca, NY: Snow Lion.

Das, Sarat Chandra. 1973. *A Tibetan-English Dictionary.* Eds. Graham Sandberg and A. William Heyde. Delhi: Motilal Barnarsidass.

Dasgupta, S. B. 1969. *Obscure Religious Cults.* 3rd ed. Calcutta: Firma K. L. Mukhopadhyay.

———. 1950. *An Introduction to Tantric Buddhism.* Calcutta: Univ. of Calcutta.

Dayal, Har. 1970. *The Bodhisattva Doctrine in Sanskrit Literature.* Delhi, India: Motilal Barnarsidass.

Dhargyey, Geshey Ngawang. 1974. *Tibetan Tradition of Mental Development.* Dharamsala: Library of Tibetan Works and Archives.

Dowman, Keith. 1985. *Masters of Mahāmudrā: Songs and Histories of the Eighty-Four Buddhist Siddhas.* Albany: State Univ. of New York Press.

Drikung Kyabgön Chetsang Rinpoche. 1999. *The Practice of Mahamudra.* Ithaca, NY: Snow Lion.

Duff, Lotsawa Tony. 1999–2003. *The Illuminator Tibetan-English Dictionary.* Fully Edited New Electronic Edition. Lotsawa Tony Duff and the Pema Karpo Translation Committee.

Eighth Situpa Tenpa'i Nyinchay. 1995. *Mahumudra Teachings of the Supreme Siddhas.* Introduction by Thrangu Rinpoche. Trans. Lama Sherab Dorje. Ithaca, NY: Snow Lion.

Eliade, Mircea. 1969. *Yoga: Immortality and Freedom.* Trans. Willard R. Trask. Bollingen Series LVI. Princeton NJ: Princeton Univ. Press.

Evans-Wentz, W. Y., ed. 1935. *Tibetan Yoga and Secret Doctrines.* Trans. Lama Dawa Samdup. New York: Oxford Univ. Press.

———. 1928. *Tibet's Great Yogi Milarepa.* New York: Oxford Univ. Press.

Frake, Charles O. 1964. "A Structural Description of Subanum 'Religious Behavior.'" *Explorations in Cultural Anthropology: Essays in Honor of George Peter Murdock.* Ed. Ward H. Goodenough. New York: McGraw-Hill.

[Gampopa] sGam po pa. 1971. *The Jewel Ornament of Liberation.* Trans. and ann. Herbert V. Guenther. Boulder: Prajna Press.

Goldstein, Joseph. 1976. *The Experience of Insight: A Natural Unfolding.* Santa Cruz, CA: Unity Press.

'Gos Lo-tsā-ba Gzhon-nu-dpal. 1949–53. *The Blue Annals.* Trans. George N. Roerich. Calcutta: Royal Asiatic Society of Bengal.

Guenther, Herbert V. 1963. *The Life and Teaching of Naropa.* Oxford: Clarendon Press.

———. 1969. *The Royal Song of Saraha: A Study in the History of Buddhist Thought.* Seattle: University of Washington Press.

———. 1974. *Philosophy and Psychology of the Abhidharma.* Berkeley: Shambhala.

———. 1975. "Mahamudra: The Method of Self-Acualization." *The Tibet Journal* 1.1:5–20.

———. 1992. *Meditation Differently: Phenomenological-Psychological Aspects of Tibetan Buddhist (Mahamudra and sNying-thig) Practices from Original Tibetan Sources.* Delhi: Motilal Barnarsidass.

Guenther, Herbert V. and Leslie S. Kawamura. 1975. *Mind in Buddhist Psychology: A Translation of Ye Shes rgyal mTshan's The Necklace of Clear Understanding.* Berkeley: Dharma Publishing.

Gyaltsen, Khenpo Könchog. 1986. *Prayer Flags: The Life and Spiritual Teachings of Jigten Sumgon.* Ithaca, NY: Snow Lion.

Gyaltsen, Khenpo Könchog and Katherine Rogers. 1986. *The Garland of Mahamudra Practices: A Translation of Kunga Richen's Clarifying the Jewel Rosary of the Profound Fivefold Path.* Ithaca, NY: Snow Lion.

Gyaltsen, Khenpo Könchog and Victoria Huckenpahler. 1990. *The Great Kagyü Masters.* Ithaca, NY: Snow Lion.

Gyamtso Rinpoche, Khenpo Tsultrim. 1986. *Progressive Stages of Meditation on Emptiness.* Trans. Shenpen Hookham. Oxford: Lonchen Foundation.

Gyatso, Geshe Kelsang. 1982. *Clear Light of Bliss.* London: Tharpa Publications.

Hopkins, Jeffrey. 1983. *Meditation on Emptiness.* Boston: Wisdom Publications.

James, William. 1950. *The Principles of Psychology.* New York: Dover Publications.

Jamgon Kongtrul. 1977. *The Torch of Certainty.* Trans. Judith Hanson. Berkeley: Shambhala.

————. 1992. *Cloudless Sky: The Mahamudra Path of the Tibetan Buddhist Kagyu School.* Boston: Shambhala.

————. 1994. *Jamgön Kongtrül's Retreat Manual.* Trans. Ngawang Zangpo. Ithaca, NY: Snow Lion.

————. 1996. *Creation and Completion.* Trans. Sarah Harding. Boston: Wisdom Publications [rev. ed. with commentary by Thrangu Rinpoche, 2002].

Jaschke, H. A. 1972. *A Tibetan-English Dictionary.* London: Routledge and Kegan Paul Ltd.

Kagyu Thubten Chöling. 1999. *Karmapa: The Sacred Prophecy.* Eds. Willa Baker et al. Wappinger Falls, NY: Kagyu Thubten Chöling Publications Committee.

Kalu Rinpoche. 1997. *Luminous Mind: The Way of the Buddha.* Trans. Maria Montenegro. Boston: Wisdom Publications.

Karma Chagmé. 2000. *Naked Awareness: Practical Instructions on the Union of Mahamudra and Dzogchen.* Eds. Lindy Steele and B. Alan Wallace. Trans. B. Alan Wallace. Ithaca, NY: Snow Lion.

————. 1998. *A Spacious Path to Freedom: Practical Instruction on the Union of Mahamudra and Atiyoga.* Ithaca, NY: Snow Lion.

Lambert, Michael J. 1992. "Psychotherapy Outcome Research: Implications for Integrative and Eclectic Models." *Handbook of Psychotherapy Integration.* Eds. John C. Norcross and Marvin R. Goldfried. New York: Basic.

Lamrimpa, Gen. 1992. *Śamatha Meditation.* Trans. B. Alan Wallace. Ed. Hart Sprager. Ithaca, NY: Snow Lion.

————. 1999. *Realizing Emptiness: Madhyamaka Insight Meditation.* Trans. B. Alan Wallace. Ithaca, NY: Snow Lion.

Lancaster, Lewis, ed. 1977. *Prajñāpāramitā and Related Systems.* Berkeley: Berkeley Buddhist Studies Series.

Lati Rinbochay and Elizabeth Napper. 1980. *Mind in Tibetan Buddhism.* Ithaca, NY: Snow Lion.

Lati Rinbochay, Denma Locho Rinbochay, Leah Zahler, and Jeffrey Hopkins. 1983. *Meditative States in Tibetan Buddhism: The Concentrations and Formless Absorptions.* London: Wisdom Publications.

Lobsang Gyatso. 1992. *The Harmony of Emptiness and Dependent Arising: A Commentary to Tsongkhpa's The Essence of Eloquent Speech Praise to the Buddha for Teaching Profound Dependent-Arising.* Dharamsala: Library of Tibetan Works and Archives.

Lodrö, Geshe Gedün. 1998. *Calm Abiding and Special Insight: Achieving Spiritual Transformation Through Meditation.* Trans. Jeffrey Hopkins. Ithaca, NY: Snow Lion.

Luborsky, L. and Paul Crits-Christoph. *Understanding Transference: The Core Conflictual Relationship Theme Method.* Washington, D.C.: American Psychological Association.

Maitreya. 2000. *Buddha Nature: The Mahayana Uttaratantra Shastra.* Trans. Rosemary Fuchs. Ithaca, NY: Snow Lion.

Maitreyanātha/Āryāsaṅga. 2004. *The Universal Vehicle Discourse Literature (Mahāyānasūtrālaṃkāra), Together with its Commentary (Bhāsya) by Vasubandhu.* Trans. from Sanskrit, Tibetan, and Chinese by L. Jamspal et al. Editor-in-Chief Robert A. F. Thurman. New York: American Institute of Buddhist Studies.

Murti, T. R.V. 1955. *The Central Philosophy of Buddhism: A Study of the Madhyamika System.* London: George Allen and Unwin.

Nagao, Gadjin M. 1979. "From Madhyamaka to Yogācāra: An Analysis of MMK, XXIV.18 and MV, I.1–2." *Journal of the International Association of Buddhist Studies* 2.1:29–43.

Nalanda Translation Committee under the direction of Chögyam Trungpa. 1999. *The Rain of Wisdom: The Essence of the Ocean of True Meaning.* Boston: Shambhala.

Napper, Elizabeth. 1989. *Dependent Arising and Emptiness.* Boston: Wisdom Publications.

Norbu, Chogyal Namkai. 1996. *Dzogchen: The Self-Perfected State.* Ed. Adriano Clemente. Trans. John Shane. Ithaca, NY: Snow Lion.

Nyanamoli Thera, trans. 1969. *The Patimokkha (227 Fundamental Rules of a Bhikku).* Bangkok: King Maha Makuta's Academy.

Nyanaponika Thera. 1969. *The Heart of Buddhist Meditation: A Handbook of Mental Training Based on the Buddha's Way of Mindfulness.* New York: Citadel Press.

Padma Karpo Ngawang Norbu. 1991. *The Practice of Co-Emergent Mahamudra: Essence of the Mahamudra.* Trans. Ven. Anzan Hoshin Sensei. Ottawa: Great Matter Publications.

Panchen Lama, First. 1976. *The Great Seal of Voidness: The Root Text for the Gelug/Kagyü Tradition of Mahamudra.* Dharamsala: Library of Tibetan Works and Archives.

Pettit, John W. 1999. *Mipham's Beacon of Certainty: Illuminating the View of Dzogchen, the Great Perfection.* Boston: Wisdom Publications.

Prebish, Charles S. 1975. *Buddhist Monastic Discipline; The Sanskrit Prātimokṣa Sūtras of the Mahāsāmghikas and Mūlasarvāstivadins.* University Park: Pennsylvania State Univ. Press.

Rieff, Philip. 1959. *Freud: The Mind of the Moralist.* New York: Doubleday.

Schmid, Toni. 1958. *The Eighty-Five Siddhas.* Sven Hedin, Leader of the Sino-Swedish Expedition. Pub. 42. Stockholm: Statens Etnografiska Museum.

Shantideva. 1982. *A Guide to the Bodhisattva Way of Life.* Trans. Stephen Batchelor. Dharamsala: Library of Tibetan Works and Archives.

————. 1970. *Bodhicaryāvatāra [Entering the Path of Enlightenment]*. Trans. Marion L. Matics. London: Macmillan & Co.

Shenge, Malati J. 1967. "Śrīsahajasiddhi." *Indo-Iranian Journal* 10:24–49.

————. 1964. *Advayasiddhi*. Series 8. Baroda: M. S. Oriental Series.

Snellgrove, David. 1959. *The Hevajra Tantra: A Critical Study*. London: Oxford Univ. Press.

Sopa, Geshe Lhundup and Jeffrey Hopkins. 1976. *Practice and Theory of Tibetan Buddhism*. New York: Grove Press.

Stcherbatsky, Th. 1962. *Buddhist Logic*. New York: Dover Publications.

Streng, Frederick J. 1967. *Emptiness: A Study in Religious Meaning*. New York: Abingdon Press.

Suzuki, Daisetz Teitaro. 1932. *The Lankavatara Sutra: A Mahayana Text*. London: Routledge & Kegan Paul Ltd.

Taranatha. 1970. *History of Buddhism in India*. Ed. Debiprasad Chattopadhyaya Lama Chimpa. Trans. Alaka Chattopadhyaya. Simla: Indian Institute of Advanced Study.

Tashi Namgyal, Takpo. 1986. *Mahāmudrā [the Moonlight]: The Quintessence of Mind and Meditation*. Trans. and ann. Lobsang P. Lhalungpa. Boston: Shambhala [new ed., Boston: Wisdom Publications, 2006].

Thinley, Karma. 1980. *The History of the Sixteen Karmapas of Tibet*. Boulder, CO: Prajna Press.

Thrangu Rinpoche, Khenchen. 1993. *The Practice of Tranquility and Insight: A Guide to Tibetan Buddhist Meditation*. Trans. Peter Roberts. Ithaca, NY: Snow Lion.

————. 2004. *Essentials of Mahamudra: Looking Directly at the Mind*. Boston: Wisdom Publications.

Toulmin, Stephen. 1972. *Human Understanding. Vol. 1: The Collective Use and Evolution of Concepts*. Princeton, NJ: Princeton Univ. Press.

Tripathi, Chhoe Lal. 1972. *The Problem of Knowledge in Yogacara Buddhism*. Varanasi, India: Bharat-Bharati.

Trungpa, Chögyam. 1976. *The Myth of Freedom and a Way of Meditation*. Boston: Shambhala.

————. 1980. *The Rain of Wisdom: The Essence of the Ocean of True Meaning*. Trans. Nalana Translation Committee. Boston: Shambhala.

Tsele Natsok Rangdrol. 1989. *Lamp of Mahamudra*. Trans. Erik Pema Kunsang. Boston: Shambhala.

Tsong kha pa. 2001–4. *The Great Treatise on the Stages of the Path to Enlightenment*. 3 vols. Lamrim Chenmo Translation Committee. Editor-in-Chief Joshua W. C. Cutler. Ed. Guy Newland. Ithaca, NY: Snow Lion.

Tucci, Giuseppe. 1986. *Minor Buddhist Texts: First Bhāvanākrama of Kamalasila*. Vols. 1–2. Delhi: Motilal Barnarsidass.

Wach, Joachim. 1951. *Types of Religious Experience: Christian and Non-Christian.* Chicago: Univ. of Chicago Press.

Wallace, B. Alan. 2001. *Buddhism with an Attitude: The Tibetan Seven-Point Mind-Training.* Ed. Lynn Quirolo. Ithaca, NY: Snow Lion.

[Wangchug Dorjé] dBaṅ Phyug rDo rJe (IXth Gyalwa Karmapa). 1974. *Foundational Practices: Excerpts from "The Chariot for Travelling the Supreme Path."* Trans. Ingrid M. McLeod. Vancouver: Kagyu Kunchab Choling.

Wangchuk Dorje, Ninth Karmapa. 1978. *The Mahāmudrā: Eliminating the Darkness of Ignorance.* Ed. and trans. Alexander Berzin. Dharamsala: Library of Tibetan Works and Archives.

Wangyal, Geshe. 1973. *The Door of Liberation: Essential Teachings of the Tibetan Buddhist Tradition.* New York: Maurice Girodias [rev. ed., Boston: Wisdom Publications, 1995].

Wayman, Alex. 1977. *Yoga of the Guhyasamajatantra: The Arcane Lore of Forty Verses.* Delhi: Motilal Barnarsidass.

Wilbur, Kenneth, Jack Engler, and Daniel Brown. 1987. *Transformations of Consciousness.* Boston: Shambhala.

Willis, Janice D. 1995. *Enlightened Beings: Life Stories from the Ganden Oral Tradition.* Boston: Wisdom Publications.

———. 1972. *The Diamond Light: An Introduction to Tibetan Buddhist Meditations.* New York: Simon & Schuster.

Wylie, Turrell. 1959. "A Standard System of Tibetan Transcription." *Harvard Journal of Asiatic Studies* 22, pp. 261–67.

Yeshe, Lama Thubten. 1998. *The Bliss of Inner Fire: Heart Practice of the Six Yogas of Naropa.* Boston: Wisdom Publications.

INDEX

About Wisdom

WISDOM PUBLICATIONS, a nonprofit publisher, is dedicated to making available authentic works relating to Buddhism for the benefit of all. We publish books by ancient and modern masters in all traditions of Buddhism, translations of important texts, and original scholarship. Additionally, we offer books that explore East-West themes unfolding as traditional Buddhism encounters our modern culture in all its aspects. Our titles are published with the appreciation of Buddhism as a living philosophy, and with the special commitment to preserve and transmit important works from Buddhism's many traditions.

To learn more about Wisdom, or to browse books online, visit our website at www.wisdompubs.org.

You may request a copy of our catalog online or by writing to this address:

Wisdom Publications
199 Elm Street
Somerville, Massachusetts 02144 USA
Telephone: 617-776-7416
Fax: 617-776-7841
Email: info@wisdompubs.org
www.wisdompubs.org

THE WISDOM TRUST

As a nonprofit publisher, Wisdom is dedicated to the publication of Dharma books for the benefit of all sentient beings and dependent upon the kindness and generosity of sponsors in order to do so. If you would like to make a donation to Wisdom, you may do so through our website or our Somerville office. If you would like to help sponsor the publication of a book, please write or email us at the address above.

Thank you.

Wisdom Publications is a nonprofit, charitable 501(c)(3) organization and a part of the Foundation for the Preservation of the Mahayana Tradition (FPMT).

Mahāmudrā

The Moonlight—Quintessence of
Mind and Meditation
Dakpo Tashi Namgyal
Translated by Lobsang P. Lhalungpa
Foreword by The Dalai Lama
532 pp, ISBN 0-86171-299-4, $34.95

A new edition of Tashi Namgyal's exhaustive work
Features a new foreword by the Dalai Lama, plus production values befitting a work of this stature.

A Song for the King

Saraha on Mahāmudrā Meditation
Khenchen Thrangu Rinpoche
Edited and root text translated by Michele Martin
192 pp, ISBN 0-86171-503-9, $14.95

"The teachings by contemporary master Khenchen
Thrangu Rinpoche, so smoothly translated here, help
the reader to savor the richness and contemplative
instructions of Saraha's verses. An eloquent, welcome
contribution."—Kurtis R. Schaeffer, author of
Dreaming the Great Brahmin

Essentials of Mahāmudrā

Looking Directly at the Mind
Khenchen Thrangu Rinpoche
288 pp, ISBN 0-86171-371-0, $16.95

This introduction, a commentary on Tashi Namgyal's
Mahāmudrā, is unmatched in its directness.

"Makes the practice of mahāmudrā easily accessible to
Westerners' everyday lives. A wonderful way of bringing us to the path."—*Mandala*